The Carmina Burana: Songs from Benediktbeuern

A Full and Faithful Translation with Critical Annotations

by

Tariq Marshall

ISBN-10: 1463728654
ISBN-13: 978-1463728656

DEDICATIO

Dedico hoc totum opus Susannae Artifici et Franco Carusonio, sine quorum auxilio, et spiritali et aerario, interpretatio haec numquam perfecta esset, atque Magistro Franco Beznero, sine quo haud cognovissem Carmina Burana; nam antequam factus sum eius discipulus in Universitate Californiensi apud Berkeley haud scivi Carmina Burana esse. Maximas gratias vobis omnibus ago.

Scripsi hoc Angelopoli in die vicesimo tertio mensis Iulii anno MMXI. Perfeci meum opus totum eodem die in hora prima ante meridiem.

TARICUS MARSALLUS

TRANSLATOR'S NOTE

In this first complete English translation of the *Carmina Burana*, or Songs from Benediktbeuern—the name of the monastery in Bavaria where the 13th-century manuscript was discovered in 1803—I sought to translate as faithfully as possible the Latin and Middle High German into English that is florid, but never at the expense of the source languages. At times words have been added to the English—either for sense or euphony—that appear not in the Latin or Middle High German, but never in such a way that the source language is distorted or fades away against the splendor of the English. It is for this reason that that I eschewed any inclination to retain the original rhyme scheme in any of the poems, for though such translations lead unto pulchritudinous English verse, they are invariably to the detriment of the source language, whose original tenor is often lost; nevertheless rhyming sequences occasionally debouch in my translation, though not intentionally and at no language's expense. Because of the age of the text, which was putatively completed or compiled in the mid-13th century and not rediscovered until the first decade of the 19th century, slight changes to the corrupted or senseless sequences of text were necessary and are indicated with *italics* along with any other additions made to the text, such as the titles to each of the poems in the corpus, whose addition I believed would be a fine show of deference to these wondrous *innominata poemata*, a sort of poetic christening after more than eight centuries of namelessness.

The *Carmina Burana* is truly a seminal work of the Middle Ages, as it exposes an often unseen facet of the medieval ethos through the eyes (and quills) of a vast variety of minds: from Philip the Chancellor (1160-1236), a French theologian and lyric poet, to Peter of Blois (1135-1211), a French poet and diplomat, to Walter of Châtillon (12th ct.), a French writer and theologian, to Walther von der Vogelweide (1170-1230), a celebrated Middle High German minnesinger, to Hugo Primas or Orléans (ca. 1090-ca. 1160), a scholar from the University of Paris, to Otloh of St. Emmeram (1010-1072), a Benedictine monk from Regensburg, to Marbodius of Rennes (1035-1123), the Bishop of Rennes in Brittany, to a plenitude of anonymous others, this unique corpus captures the views of authors from various paths of life over the span of three centuries. Religious hypocrisy, courtly love, jingoism, homosexuality, hope and lack thereof, eschatology, rape, remission of sins, Jesus' birth and passion and resurrection, unwed pregnancy, students' struggle with their passions under the weight of mortifying church doctrines, a debate between anthropomorphic water and wine, a Gamblers' High Mass, odes to fallen kings and saints, and panegyrics to Crusaders and hungry poets are among the pantheon of topics that comprise this unique collection of songs.

Table of Contents

The Moral
and
Satirical Songs

[De avaritia]

I. *Manus Sacra* (ca. 1170)

Manus ferens munera
pium facit impium;
nummus iungit federa,
nummus dat consilium;
nummus lenit aspera,
nummus sedat prelium.
nummus in prelatis
est pro iure satis;
nummo locum datis
vos, qui iudicatis.

Nummus ubi loquitur,
fit iuris confusio;
pauper retro pellitur,
quem defendit ratio,
sed dives attrahitur
pretiosus pretio.
hunc iudex adorat,
facit, quod implorat;
pro quo nummus orat,
explet, quod laborat.

Nummus ubi predicat,
labitur iustitia,
et causam, que claudicat,
rectam facit curia,
pauperem diiudicat
veniens pecunia.
sic diiudicatur,
a quo nichil datur;
iure sic privatur,
si nil offeratur.

Sunt potentum digiti
trahentes pecuniam;
tali preda prediti
non dant gratis gratiam,
sed licet illiciti
censum censent veniam.

[On Avarice]

1. *The Hallowed Hand* (ca. 1170)

The hand bearing gifts
makes pious an impious man.
Money forges alliances,
Money gives counsel;
Money softens what is harsh,
Money settles what is strifeful.
Money set in prelates' hands
is sufficient legal ground.
Ye, who adjudicate on matters of law,
grant money a seat of rank and power.

Where Money has say,
civil rights are confounded:
the pauper, on whose side is the law,
is cast to the back and dismissed,
whilst the rich man, treasured for his wealth,
is drawn to the court to be heard.[1]
The arbiter adores the latter man,
and what he beseeches, the arbiter performs.
Money pleads the case on his behalf
and brings to completion what he strives to achieve.

Where Money preaches,
justice slips and falls:
the court upholds
a limping case.
The arrival of pelf decides
the fate of the indigent man.
Thus judged is he
who gives not;
thus stripped of justice
is he, who offers naught.

The fingers of powerful men
are drawing in hoards of cash.
Endowed with such spoils,
they do not offer favor for free.
But, although forbidden, they deem
complaisance a source of wealth.

clericis non morum
cura, sed nummorum,
quorum nescit chorum
chorus angelorum.

«Date, vobis dabitur:
talis est auctoritas»
danti pie loquitur
impiorum pietas;
sed adverse premitur
pauperum adversitas.
quo vult, ducit frena,
cuius bursa plena;
sancta dat crumena,
sancta fit amena.

Hec est causa curie,
quam daturus perficit;
defectu pecunie
causa Codri deficit.
tale fedus hodie
defedat et inficit
nostros ablativos,
qui absorbent vivos,
moti per dativos
movent genitivos.

II. *Nuntium e Dea* (ca. 1170)

«Responde, qui tanta cupis!»
modo Copia dicat.
«Pone modum! que vis dono.»
«Volo plena sit arca.»
«Plena sit!»
«Adde duas!»
«Addo.»
«Si quattuor essent, Sufficerent.»
«Sic semper agis: cum plurima dono,
Plus queris, nec plenus eris, donec morieris.»

III. *Epulae Diaboli* (ca. 1170)
Gualterius de Castillione (ca. 1135 - ca. 1179)

The clerics' concern is not
of character, but of net worth;
this group of men is not known
to the chorus of angels above.[2]

"Give! It shall be given you!"
So the Holy Scripture avers.
Piously to the giver speaks
the piety of the impious throng.
But adversely to adversity
are the poor, their enemies, exposed.
Whithersoever he wishes,
he, whose purse is full, leads the reins.
The purse administers the sacraments;
rendering bliss, it becomes sacred.

This is the lawsuit at the court
that he with open wallet wins:
for want of money
Codrus[3] loses his case.
Such a compact today
sullies and befouls
our ablatives
that swallow men alive;
set in motion through the dative,
they arouse our genitive.[4]

2. *Message from a Goddess* (ca. 1170)

The goddess Abundance now says to me:
"Answer me, O desirer of so much!
Set a bound! I shall grant what you wish."
"I want a full coffer."
"Let it be full!"
"Add two more to that!"
"So granted."
"If there were four, the number would suffice."
Such is your habit: when I give so very much, you still seek more,
nor will you ever be sated, until dead in the ground you are."

3. *The Devil's Feast* (ca. 1170)
by Walter of Châtillon (ca. 1135-1179)

Ecce torpet probitas,
virtus sepelitur;
fit iam parca largitas,
parcitas largitur;
verum dicit falsitas,
veritas mentitur.

Refl.   Omnes iura ledunt
et ad res illicitas
licite recedunt.

Regnat avaritia,
regnant et avari;
mente quivis anxia
nititur ditari,
cum sit summa gloria
censu gloriari.

Refl.   Omnes iura ledunt
et ad prava quelibet
impie recedunt.

Multum habet oneris
do das dedi dare;
verbum hoc pre ceteris
norunt ignorare
divites, quos poteris
mari comparare.

Refl.   Omnes iura ledunt
et in rerum numeris
numeros excedunt.

Cunctis est equaliter
insita cupido;
perit fides turpiter,
nullus fidus fido,
nec Iunoni Iupiter
nec Enee Dido.

Refl.   Omnes iura ledunt
et ad mala devia
licite recedunt.

Behold! Probity lies dumb;
virtue is inhumed.
Generosity is now scarce;
parsimony abounds.
Falsity speaks truth;
truth tells lies.

Refr.   All flout the law
         and lawfully retire
         to illicit affairs.

Avarice holds sway,
and the avaricious rule.
Anyone of solicitous mind
strives to enrich himself,
since it is the highest glory
to pride oneself on his wealth.

Refr.   All flout the law
         and anyone who desires retires
         impiously to endeavors perverse.

A great burden he bears:
"I give, you give, I have given, to give."
This word before all others
rich men know to ignore—
men, whom you could compare
to the insatiable sea.

Refr.   All flout the law
         and surpass in possessions
         the numbers themselves.

Greed is sown equally in all men;
fidelity perishes in shame;
no one is faithful
to another loyal soul:
neither is Jupiter to Juno
nor Dido to Aeneas.

Refr.   All flout the law
         and lawfully withdraw
         to desolate coverts of turpitude.

Si recte discernere
velis, non est vita,
quod sic vivit temere
gens hec imperita;
non est enim vivere,
si quis vivit ita.

Refl.   Omnes iura ledunt
         et fidem in opere
         quolibet excedunt.

IV. *Vespere Exiti*

Amaris stupens casibus
vox exultationis
organa in salicibus
suspendit Babylonis;
captiva est confusionis,
involuta doloribus
Sion cantica leta sonis
permutavit flebilibus.

Propter scelus perfidie,
quo mundus inquinatur,
fluctuantis ecclesie
sic status naufragatur.
gratia prostat et scortatur
foro venalis curie;
iuris libertas ancillatur
obsecundans pecunie.

Hypocrisis, fraus pullulat
et menda falsitatis,
que titulum detitulat
vere simplicitatis.
frigescit ignis caritatis,
fides a cunctis exulat,
aculeus cupiditatis
quos mordet atque stimulat.

V. *Adventus Secundus* (ca. 1150)

Flete Flenda

If thou wishest to discern correctly,
know that it is not life
that this ignorant race
so indiscreetly lives;
for it is not life,
if anyone lives so.

Refr.   All flout the law
         and depart from faith
         in any business they undertake.

4. *On the Eve of Perdition*

Struck senseless by bitter misfortunes,[5]
the voice of jubilation
has hung its instruments
on the willows of Babylon;[6]
a prisoner of disorder,
enveloped in grief,
Zion has exchanged
joyous songs for tearful tones.

Because of the crime of perfidy,
whereby the world is befouled,
the state of the undulating church
is thus left wrecked upon the shores.
Grace is prostituted and put up for sale
in the marketplace of the venal court.
Licentiousness attends upon
and obeys almighty pelf.

Hypocrisy, fraud,
and the blemish of falsehood
debouch and rob of its honor
probity's noble title.
The fire of charity grows cold;[7]
faith lives in exile from all men.
The sting of cupidity
bites and incites them.

5. *The Second Coming* (ca. 1150)

Beweep the things that must be wept.

perhorrete perhorrenda
lugete lugenda
pavete pavenda
dolete dolenda!

Etates Currunt
anni labuntur
vitium remanet
peccata crescunt
tyranni statuuntur.

Virtus Cessat
ecclesia calcatur
clerus ambit
Mammon regnat
simonia dominatur.

Pontifices Errant
reges turbantur
proceres turbant
sacraria sordent
leges violantur.

Abbas Inflatur
possessa vastat
prebendam minuit
contio declamitat
fessa astat.

Militibus Gaudet
laude inescatur
monachos horret
mundalia colit
fraude insidiatur.

Subiecti Dissiliunt
stulti gaudent
gnari merent
contemptus attollitur
inulti audent.

Ordo Languet
pudicitia sordescit

Be affrighted of what must be feared.
Bewail what must be mourned.
Dread what one must dread.
Lament what must be moaned.

The ages are running fast;
the years are gliding by.
Vice remains,
sins in number grow,
and tyrants are on the rise.

Virtue ceases;
the church is trodden underfoot.
The cleric obtains his ministries by fraud.
Mammon[8] holds sway;
simony dominates.

The bishops are astray,
the kings are confused,
the princes are the cause,
the sacristies lie befouled,
and the laws are transgressed.

The abbot is distended,
devastates everything he owns,
and diminishes his prebend;
the convent blusters—
powerless, it stands by.

The riders are his pride,
by praise he is lured,
to him anathema are monks,
worldly things he adores,
and with guile he lies in wait.

Subjects overleap fealty's bounds;
dunderheads rejoice;
the learned grieve;
the scorned are elevated;
the unpunished become bold.

Order is languid;
shamefacedness is imbrued;

pietas refugit
doctrina rarescit
sophia hebescit.

Insons Plectitur
pupillus artatur
humilis teritur
viduata premitur
pusillus spoliatur.

Ingenuus Servit
servus honoratur
parasitus tonat
scurra imperitat
protervus domniatur.

Elluo Prestat
periurus ditatur
raptor viget
fallax excellit
Epicurus decoratur.

Delicie Enervant
fastus turget
inimicitie exercentur
tumor furit
astus urget.

Blandimenta Suadent
mine adduntur
rabies sevit
usura tractatur
rapine aguntur.

Idcirco Cedimur
pesti incidimus
detrimentum patimur
grave languescimus
mesti imus.

Aër Tabet
languores adaugentur
incendia consumunt

piety flees;
erudition dwindles;
wisdom grows dim.

The innocent man is punished;
the orphan is straitened;
the poor man is trodden underfoot;
the widow is oppressed;
the little child is robbed.

The freeborn man becomes a slave;
the bondman is esteemed;
the parasite thunders;
the coxcomb[9] gives commands;
the wanton man holds dominion.

The wastrel excels;
the perjurer grows rich;
the bandit flourishes;
the swindler triumphs;
the epicurean is honored by all.

Voluptuousness enervates all;
arrogance gasconades;
enmity circulates;
commotion raves;
cunning presses hard.

Flattery exhorts;
threats then follow;
fury riots;
usury is wielded;
rapine is rife.

For these reasons we are struck down,
into pestilence we fall,
loss do we suffer,
grave maladies do we endure,
and in a vacuum of sorrow we waft and wade.

The air is vanishing,
the sicknesses are waxing,
the flames are devouring,

mucro sevit
timores habentur.

Aurum Fallit
censores falluntur
pravi presunt
iusti desunt
meliores rapiuntur.

Giraldus Prefuit
mores ornavit
deflendus ruit
ovile orbavit
dolores cumulavit.

Omnipotens Audi
penis tollatur
hostis fugiat
paradisus pateat
amenis foveatur.

VI. *Umbrae in Caligine*

Florebat olim studium,
nunc vertitur in tedium;
iam scire diu viguit,
sed ludere prevaluit.
iam pueris astutia
contingit ante tempora,
qui per malivolentiam
excludunt sapientiam.
sed retro actis seculis
vix licuit discipulis
tandem nonagenarium
quiescere post studium.
at nunc decennes pueri
decusso iugo liberi
se nunc magistros iactitant,
ceci cecos precipitant,
implumes aves volitant,
brunelli chordas incitant,
boves in aula salitant,
stive precones militant.

the dagger is raging,
and fears are fanning out.

Gold deceives,
the judges are chicaned,
the vicious take the lead,
the just are all gone,
and better men are carried off.

Gerald[10] was once our chieftain;
his way of life was an ornament of every virtue.
A loss to be lamented, he passed away,
orphaned his flock,
and by his quietus piled high our sorrows.

O Omnipotent One, hear my prayer:
let him be lifted from all our anguish,
let the fiend be put to flight,
let paradise stand open to him,
and let him be warmed by supreme delight.

6. *Shadows In the Gloom*

Study once flourished;
now to weariness it has turned.
Long ago knowledge thrived,
but frivolity has prevailed.
Guile now seizes
boys before their time,
who in malevolence
shut wisdom out.
But long ago in centuries past
students were scarcely allowed
a long-awaited rest
after studies spanning ninety days.
But now ten-year-old boys,
free from the yoke now cast aside,[11]
freely boast that they are teachers.
The blind goad the blind,[12]
birds without plumes take to flight,
and Burnelluses[13] strike the strings.
Oxen dance in the palace halls;
heralds of the plough serve as knights.

in taberna Gregorius
iam disputat inglorius;
severitas Ieronymi
partem causatur obuli;
Augustinus de segete,
Benedictus de vegete
sunt colloquentes clanculo
et ad macellum sedulo.
Mariam gravat sessio,
nec Marthe placet actio;
iam Lie venter sterilis,
Rachel lippescit oculis.
Catonis iam rigiditas
convertitur ad ganeas,
et castitas Lucretie
turpi servit lascivie.
quod prior etas respuit,
iam nunc latius claruit;
iam calidum in frigidum
et humidum in aridum,
virtus migrat in vitium,
opus transit in otium;
nunc cuncte res a debita
exorbitantur semita.
vir prudens hoc consideret,
cor mundet et exoneret,
ne frustra dicat «Domine!»
in ultimo examine;
quem iudex tunc arguerit,
appellare non poterit.

VII. *Folia Virtutis*

Postquam nobilitas servilia cepit amare,
Cepit nobilitas cum servis degenerare.

Nobilitas, quam non probitas regit atque tuetur,
Lapsa iacet nullique placet, quia nulla videtur.

Nobilitas hominis mens est, deitatis imago.
Nobilitas hominis virtutum clara propago.
Nobilitas hominis mentem frenare furentem.
Nobilitas hominis humilem relevare iacentem.

In the tavern Gregory the Great,[14]
respected little now, holds a disputation.
The ascetic Jerome[15] now
litigates for a penny's share.
Augustine[16] discusses seedlings,
Benedict[17] casks of wine,
when they parley at the meat market
in secret and with business in mind.
Sitting is nettlesome to Mary,
and action pleases Martha not.[18]
In our day Leah's womb is sterile,
and Rachel becomes bleary-eyed.[19]
Nowadays abstemious Cato[20]
directs his course to the eateries,
and the chastity of Lucretia[21]
is a slave to vile lasciviousness.
What the previous age repudiated
ours so widely now has esteemed.
Hot now turns to cold
and wet to dry.
Virtue migrates into vice
and work into idle sloth.
Now all things deviate
from the path of right.
The wise man should be mindful of this,
his heart he should exonerate and cleanse,
lest in vain he say, "Lord!"[22]
on the final judgment day:
for the judge will then show him
what he could not in life name.

7. Leaves of Virtue

After the nobility elected to love servile things,
it began to degenerate together with slaves.

The nobility, whom integrity does not rule nor guard,
after its fall, lies dead and pleases none, for it is noble no more.

The nobility of man is his soul and his likeness to God.
The nobility of man is the illustrious offspring of his virtues.[23]
The nobility of man is the bridling of a raging mind.
The nobility of man if lifting the humble from the ground.

Nobilitas hominis nature iura tenere.
Nobilitas hominis nisi turpia nulla timere.

Nobilis est ille, quem virtus nobilitavit;
Degener est ille, quem virtus nulla beavit.

VIII. *Gratiae Venum* (ca. 1170)
Gualterius de Castillione (ca. 1135 - ca. 1179)

Licet eger cum egrotis
et ignotus cum ignotis
fungar tamen vice cotis,
ius usurpans sacerdotis.
flete, Sion filie!
presides ecclesie
imitantur hodie
Christum a remotis.

Si privata degens vita
vel sacerdos vel levita
sibi dari vult petita,
hac incedit via trita:
previa fit pactio
Simonis auspicio,
cui succedit datio:
sic fit Giezita.

Iacet ordo clericalis
in respectu laicalis,
sponsa Christi fit mercalis,
generosa generalis;
veneunt altaria,
venit eucharistia,
cum sit nugatoria
gratia venalis.

Donum Dei non donatur,
nisi gratis conferatur;
quod qui vendit vel mercatur,
lepra Syri vulneratur.
quem sic ambit ambitus,
idolorum servitus,
templo sancti Spiritus

The nobility of man is upholding nature's laws.
The nobility of man is fearing nothing except turpitude.

Noble is he whom virtue has ennobled.
Degenerate is he whom no virtue has blessed.

8. *The Sale of Grace* (ca. 1170)
by Walter of Châtillon (ca. 1135 - ca. 1179)

Although myself a sick man among the sick
and a nameless soul among unknowns,
I shall nevertheless perform the duty of a whetstone,[24]
and arrogate the bishop's sovereign right.
Weep, daughters of Zion![25]
The heads of the Church
today are imitating Christ
a world away from all.

If, living without an exalted station,
the priest or the deacon wishes
the things he seeks be given him,
he proceeds along this beaten path:
a pact beforehand is made
in the spirit of Simon Magus,[26]
whereupon gifts follow:
he thus becomes a follower of Gehazi.[27]

The clerical order lies dead
before the eyes of the laity.
The bride of Christ[28] becomes
a purchasable good,
the noble woman
a miserable whore.
Altars are sold along with the Eucharist,
though grace sold has no true value.

The gift of God is not given
unless it is conferred for free;
he who sells or trades it,
is smitten with a Syrian's leprosy.[29]
He around whom ambition revolves—
service to idols, that is to say—
unifies himself not in any way

non compaginatur.

Si quis tenet hunc tenorem,
frustra dicit se pastorem
nec se regit ut rectorem,
renum mersus in ardorem.
hec est enim alia
sanguisuge filia,
quam venalis curia
duxit in uxorem.

In diebus iuventutis
timent annos senectutis,
ne fortuna destitutis
desit eis splendor cutis.
et dum querunt medium,
vergunt in contrarium;
fallit enim vitium
specie virtutis.

Ut iam loquar inamenum:
sanctum chrisma datur venum,
iuvenantur corda senum
nec refrenant motus renum.
senes et decrepiti
quasi modo geniti
nectaris illiciti
hauriunt venenum.

Ergo nemo vivit purus,
castitatis perit murus,
commendatur Epicurus
nec spectatur moriturus.
grata sunt convivia;
auro vel pecunia
cuncta facit pervia
pontifex futurus.

IX. *Caupones Fidei*

Iudas gehennam meruit,
quod Christum semel vendidit;
vos autem michi dicite:

with the temple of the Holy Spirit.[30]

If anyone maintains this course,
in vain does he call himself a shepherd,
nor does he govern himself as a leader,
having plunged into the heat of the loins.
She truly is the second
daughter of that leech,[31]
whom the venal court
its wife has made.

In the days of youth they fear
the years of senectitude,[32]
and the day flesh's splendor
will leave them destitute of wealth.
And whilst they seek a middle course,
they turn to the other extreme,
for vice chicanes
under virtue's guise.

Now I shall speak on something abominable:
the sacred anointing is put up for sale,
the hearts of old men act with youthful indiscretion,
and they give full vent to the motions of the loins.
The old and decrepit,
as if they were just now born,
quaff the poison
of a forbidden nectar.

Therefore no one lives free from sin:
the wall of chastity perishes,
the epicurean is praised,
and no one is mindful
of his eventual demise.
Welcome are the banquets,
and for gold or money
the future bishop unbolts all doors.

9. *Hawkers of Faith*

Judas earned his place in hell,
because he sold Christ but once.
But tell me now:

qui septies cotidie
corpus vendunt dominicum,
quod superat supplicium?

Perpendite subtiliter:
cum vendant missam viliter
et peccent in alterutrum
sumendo plus vel modicum,
quod anhelant ad munera,
finis est avaritia.

Petrus damnato Simone
gravi sub anathemate
docuit, ut fidelibus
non esset locus amplius
in donis spiritalibus
emptis a venditoribus.

Multi nunc damnant Simonem
Magum magis quam demonem,
heredes autem Simonis
suis fovent blanditiis.
Simon nondum est mortuus,
si vivit in heredibus.

Quamvis cogente Abraham
Ephron sumens pecuniam
agrum sepulcro vendidit,
Ephran vocari meruit;
nunc Ephranitas dicere
multos potestis simile.

X. *Tirones Magi*

Ecce sonat in aperto
vox clamantis in deserto:
nos desertum, nos deserti,
nos de pena sumus certi.
nullus fere vitam querit,
et sic omne vivens perit.
omnes quidem sumus rei,
nullus imitator Dei,
nullus vult portare crucem,

what punishment awaits
those, who seven times a day
sell the body of the Lord?

Carefully consider this:
although they sell the mass cheaply
and sin against one another
by taking more or but a little,
because they pant at the sight of gifts,
it is all avarice in the end.

Peter condemned Simon
and sharply anathematized him,
whereby he taught that the pious,
apropos of spiritual gifts,
should have no future community
with the hucksters of such wares.

Many now condemn Simon Magus
more emphatically than they do the Devil;
still the heirs of Simon caress them
with the allurements they dangle about.[33]
Simon is not yet dead,
if he lives through his heirs.

Since Ephron accepted money,
albeit at Abraham's behest,
when he sold a field as a site for a tomb,
he deserved to be called Ephran;
In a similar wise, you can now
call many Ephranites.[34]

10. *The Sorcerer's Apprentices*

Behold, in the open sounds the voice
of one shouting in the desert waste:[35]
we are the desert, we are the deserted,
we are certain of our punishment.
Scarcely does anyone obtain the jewel of life,
and thus every living thing fades away.
We all assuredly share blame for this:
no one is in the discipleship of Christ,[36]
no one wishes to carry the cross,[37]

nullus Christum sequi ducem.
quis est verax, quis est bonus,
vel quis Dei portat onus?
ut in uno claudam plura:
mors extendit sua iura.
iam mors regnat in prelatis:
nolunt sanctum dare gratis,
quod promittunt sub ingressu,
sancte mentis in excessu;
postquam sedent iam securi,
contradicunt sancto iuri.
rose fiunt saliunca,
domus Dei fit spelunca.
sunt latrones, non latores,
legis Dei destructores.
Simon sedens inter eos
dat magnates esse reos.
Simon prefert malos bonis,
Simon totus est in donis,
Simon regnat apud Austrum,
Simon frangit omne claustrum.
cum non datur, Simon stridet,
sed si detur, Simon ridet;
Simon aufert, Simon donat,
hunc expellit, hunc coronat,
hunc circumdat gravi peste,
illum nuptiali veste;
illi donat diadema,
qui nunc erat anathema.
iam se Simon non abscondit,
res permiscet et confundit.
iste Simon confundatur,
cui tantum posse datur!
Simon Petrus hunc elusit
et ab alto iusum trusit;
dum superbit motus penna,
datus fuit in gehenna.
quisquis eum imitatur,
cum eodem puniatur
et sepultus in infernum
penas luat in eternum! Amen.

XI. Versus de Nummo

no one follows His lead.
Who is veracious, who is good,
and who carries the onus of God?
To sum up many ideas in one phrase:
death exercises its own laws.
Already death reigns in the prelates' circle.[38]
They wish not to give something sacred for free,
which they vow to do in the beginning
in the specious projection of a pious soul.
After they are settled, now free from care,
they contradict the sacrosanct law.
Roses become nards;[39]
the home of God becomes a cave.
They are thieves, not donors,
destroyers of God's law;
Simon sits among them
and transforms great men into fiends.
Simon prefers iniquitous men to good,
Simon thinks of nothing other than gifts,
Simon rules in the South[40]
and breaks every bastion in twain.
When something is not given, Simon screams;
but if it be granted, Simon smiles with glee.
Simon takes; Simon gives.
This one he banishes; that man he crowns.
This lad he envelopes in an illness grave;
that fellow he in a nuptial vest enfolds.
A diadem he sets on that man's head,
who hitherto has been excommunicated.
In our time Simon does not hide himself or his ways,
but muddles and confounds every affair.
Let this Simon be brought to ruin,
to whom such power is given!
Peter eluded this Simon's grasp
and thrust him down from his lofty seat.
Whilst he stood proud on tumult's wing
sent was he to hell's domain.
May whoever imitates this con
be chastised with the same,
interred in hell's flames,
and suffer punishments for all eternity! Amen.

11. Ode to Mammon

In terra summus   rex est hoc tempore Nummus.
Nummum mirantur   reges et ei famulantur.
Nummo venalis   favet ordo pontificalis.
Nummus in abbatum   cameris retinet dominatum.
Nummum nigrorum   veneratur turba priorum.
Nummus magnorum   fit iudex conciliorum.
Nummus bella gerit,   nec si vult, pax sibi deerit.
Nummus agit lites,   quia vult deponere dites.
Erigit ad plenum   de stercore Nummus egenum.
Omnia Nummus emit   venditque, dat et data demit.
Nummus adulatur,   Nummus post blanda minatur.
Nummus mentitur,   Nummus verax reperitur.
Nummus periuros   miseros facit et perituros.
Nummus avarorum   deus est et spes cupidorum.
Nummus in errorem   mulierum ducit amorem.
Nummus venales   dominas facit imperiales.
Nummus raptores   facit ipsos nobiliores.
Nummus habet plures   quam celum sidera fures.
Si Nummus placitat,   cito cuncta pericula vitat.
Si Nummus vicit,   dominus cum iudice dicit:
«Nummus ludebat,   agnum niveum capiebat.»
Nummus, rex magnus,   dixit: «Niger est meus agnus».
Nummus fautores   habet astantes seniores.
Si Nummus loquitur,   pauper tacet; hoc bene scitur.
Nummus merores   reprimit relevatque labores.
Nummus corda necat   sapientum, lumina cecat.
Nummus, ut est certum,   stultum docet esse disertum.
Nummus habet medicos,   fictos acquirit amicos.
In Nummi mensa   sunt splendida fercula densa.
Nummus laudatos   pisces comedit piperatos.
Francorum vinum   Nummus bibit atque marinum.
Nummus famosas   vestes gerit et pretiosas.
Nummo splendorem   dant vestes exteriorem.
Nummus eos gestat   lapides, quos India prestat.
Nummus dulce putat,   quod eum gens tota salutat.
Nummus et invadit   et que vult oppida tradit.
Nummus adoratur,   quia virtutes operatur:
Hic egros sanat,   secat, urit et aspera planat,
Vile facit carum,   quod dulce est, reddit amarum
Et facit audire   surdum claudumque salire.
De Nummo quedam   maiora prioribus edam:
Vidi cantantem   Nummum, missam celebrantem;
Nummus cantabat,   Nummus responsa parabat;

On earth the loftiest ruler in this age is Mammon.
Kings marvel at and wait upon Mammon.
The venal pontifical order is devoted to Mammon.
In the chambers of the abbots Mammon holds command.
The throng of black priors[41] venerates Mammon.
Mammon is made the arbiter of great councils.
Mammon leads wars, and, if It so wishes, peace will not fail.
Mammon drives lawsuits because It wishes to beggar the rich.
Mammon raises a pauper from dung to abundance.
Mammon buys and sells all; It gives and takes back all gifts.
Mammon fawns, then flatters, then threatens.
Mammon lies, but Mammon is still seen as truthful.
Mammon makes perjurers of abject and imperiled men.
Mammon is the god of the avaricious and the gluttons' hope.
Mammon draws women's love into error.
Mammon makes doxies of queens.
Mammon makes brigands of the high nobles themselves.
Mammon has more thieves than the firmament has stars.
If Mammon pleases both parties, swiftly it avoids all trials.
If Mammon prevails, the lord of the manor and the judge say:
"Mammon was only japing, for the lamb It caught was white."
Mammon, the great king, then says, "Black is my lamb."[42]
Mammon has as promoters upright older men.
If Mammon speaks, the pauper hushes; 'tis a fact well known.
Mammon curbs sorrows and lightens toils.
Mammon slays the hearts of the wise and blinds their eyes.
Mammon, 'tis certain!, teaches eloquence to fools.
Mammon locates doctors and secures invented friends.
On Mammon's table is a dense crowd of exquisite foods.
Mammon dines on succulent, peppered fish.
Mammon quaffs the wines of the Franks and those overseas.
Mammon wears haute fashions and expensive clothes.
The apparel affords Mammon a splendid shell.
Mammon wears those stones that India preserves.
Mammon thinks it delightful that every nation salutes It.
Mammon both invades and surrenders the towns It wishes.
Mammon is hallowed because of the wonders It works.
It heals the sick, operates, cauterizes, and levels uneven health.
It makes costly the cheap and bitter the sweet.
It enables the deaf to hear and the lame to leap.
I shall tell of a work of Mammon greater than any told before:
I watched Mammon lead a High Mass and the flock celebrate.
Mammon sang; Mammon provided the response.

Vidi, quod flebat,   dum sermonem faciebat,
Et subridebat,   populum quia decipiebat.
Nullus honoratur   sine Nummo, nullus amatur.
Quem genus infamat,   Nummus: «Probus est homo!» clamat.
Ecce patet cuique,   quod Nummus regnat ubique.
Sed quia consumi   poterit cito gloria Nummi,
Ex hac esse schola   non vult Sapientia sola.

XII. *Uvae Detractionis*

Procurans odium   effectu proprio
vix detrahentium   gaudet intentio.
nexus est cordium   ipsa detractio:
sic per contrarium   ab hoste nescio
fit hic provisio;
in hoc amantium   felix condicio.

Insultus talium   prodesse sentio,
tollendi tedium   fulsit occasio;
suspendunt gaudium   pravo consilio,
sed desiderium   auget dilatio:
tali remedio
de spinis hostium   uvas vindemio.

XIII. *Meditationes de Invidia*

Invidus invidia comburitur intus et extra.

Invidus alterius rebus macrescit opimis.
Invidia Siculi non invenere tyranni
Maius tormentum. qui non moderabitur ire,
Infectum volet esse, dolor quod suaserit aut mens.
                    Horatius, *Epistulae* 1.2.57-60

Invidiosus ego, non invidus esse laboro.

Iustius invidia nichil est, que protinus ipsos
Corripit auctores excruciatque suos.

Invidiam nimio cultu vitare memento.
                    Disticha Catonis 2.13.1

XIV. *Oda ad Fortunam*

I saw It drop tears, whilst Its sermon It gave,
and saw It cast a secret smile, because It had them chicaned.
Without Mammon no one is honored, and no one is loved.
When all defame one, Mammon shouts "He's a just soul!"
Behold, it is ostensible to all that Mammon rules the world.
But because the glory of Mammon can be swiftly consumed,
wisdom alone wishes not to be of this school.

12. *The Grapes of Slander*

The aim of slanderers, to engender dislike,
scarcely rejoices in its own effect.
Slander itself is the binder of hearts:
so in a reversal of his intent
an enemy inadvertently becomes an aide.
Therein it proves to be the lovers' happy state.

I know that the insults of such men are of use,
for an opportunity to do away with weariness has shined.[43]
They thwart joy with malicious intent,
but cunctation only compounds desire.
With such a remedy I gather grapes
from my enemies' thorns.

13. *Meditations on Envy*

"The jealous man is burned by envy, within and without."

"The jealous man grows lean on another's prosperity.
Envy—not once did the Sicilian tyrants invent a greater torment.
He who will not his ire control will wish undone
what his pain or temper advised."

Horace, *Epistles* 1.2.57-60

"Envied, not envious, do I strive to be."

"Nothing is more just than envy, which forthwith
arrests its own authors and tortures them."

"Remember to eschew jealousy with excessive care."

Distichs of Cato 2.3.1

14. *Ode to Fortune*

O varium Fortune lubricum,
dans dubium tribunal iudicum,
non modicum paras huic premium,
quem colere tua vult gratia
et petere rote sublimia,
dans dubia tamen, prepostere
de stercore pauperem erigens,
de rhetore consulem eligens.

Edificat Fortuna, diruit;
nunc abdicat, quos prius coluit;
quos noluit, iterum vendicat
hec opera sibi contraria,
dans munera nimis labilia;
mobilia sunt Sortis federa,
que debiles ditans nobilitat
et nobiles premens debilitat.

Quid Dario regnasse profuit?
Pompeïo quid Roma tribuit?
Succubuit uterque gladio.
eligere media tutius
quam petere rote sublimius
et gravius a summo ruere:
fit gravior lapsus a prosperis
et durior ab ipsis asperis.

Subsidio Fortune labilis
cum prelio Troia tunc nobilis,
nunc flebilis ruit incendio?
quis sanguinis Romani gratiam,
quis nominis Greci facundiam,
quis gloriam fregit Carthaginis?
Sors lubrica, que dedit, abstulit;
hec unica que fovit, perculit.

Nil gratius Fortune gratia,
nil dulcius est inter dulcia
quam gloria, si staret longius.
sed labitur ut olus marcidum
et sequitur agrum nunc floridum,
quem aridum cras cernes. igitur
improprium non edo canticum:

O fickle, slippery state of Fortune!
Capricious is the tribune of judges you appoint.
To him you furnish no small reward,
whom your favor desires to coddle,
and whom it wishes to see scale the heights of your wheel.
Uncertain though are your gifts, when in a reversal of hierarchy
you raise a pauper from the dung
and elect a consul from the orators' throng.[44]

Fortuna builds; Fortuna destroys.
Now she renounces those, whom she cherished before,
and claims in turn those, whom she cast away in scorn.
This wayward skivvy[45] contradicts herself
and allots gifts that readily flee the recipient's grasp.
Faithless are the pacts made with Chance;
she enriches and ennobles the poor;
she strikes down the nobles and pauperizes them all.

Of what use was it to Darius[46] that he once was king?
What did his reign in Rome bestow upon Pompey the Great?[47]
Both succumbed to the sword.
Choosing the middle is safer than seeking
the summit of the wheel, for more painful
is the plunge from its lofty peak:
a graver and harsher fall from prosperity
is made than one from tribulations low to the ground.

Did not mighty Troy, then renowned,
now bewept, fall in battle to ashes and flame
with slippery Fortune's aid?[48]
Who was it that shattered
Roman blood's high esteem,
the eloquence of the Hellenes, and Carthage's palmy days?
Mercurial Chance took back what she gave!
It is she alone who cherishes and destroys.

Nothing is more welcome than Fortuna's favor;
nothing is sweeter among all things sweet
than glory that lasts a very long while.
But it falls from grace, like addled greens,
and takes after the field that, blooming now,
will tomorrow present a withered state of decay.
Therefore I do not indite an unseemly song at all.

o varium Fortune lubricum.

XV. *Hortulanus Constans*

Celum, non animum
mutat stabilitas,
firmans id optimum,
quod mentis firmitas
vovet - cum animi
tamen iudicio;
nam si turpissimi
voti consilio
vis scelus imprimi
facto nefario,
debet hec perimi
facta promissio.

Non erat stabilis
gradus, qui cecidit,
pes eius labilis
domus, que occidit.
hinc tu considera,
quid agi censceas,
dum res est libera;
sic sta, ne iaceas;
prius delibera,
quod factum subeas,
ne die postera
sero peniteas.

Facti dimidium
habet, qui ceperit,
ceptum negotium
si non omiserit,
non tantum deditus
circa principia,
nedum sollicitus
pro finis gloria;
nam rerum exitus
librat industria,
subit introitus
preceps incuria.

O so fickle is the state of Fortune's slippery slopes.

15. *The Constant Gardener*

The clime, not the mind,
does constancy change;[49]
it guarantees the very best
that a steadfast heart can pledge—
with the rational judgment
of the sensibility nevertheless.
For if thou by the design
of a most immoral vow
shouldst wish to imprint the stamp
of turpitude through an evil deed,
this promise made
must be forthwith annulled.

Unstable was
the step that fell;
gliding was the foundation
of the house that gave way.[50]
Hence bethink thyself
what in thy opinion should be done,
so long as the matter is open still.
Thus stand up, lest thou lie dead.[51]
Determine which business
thou wouldst negotiate first,
lest too late thou rue
the following day.

Half of the deed has he accomplished,
who has the enterprise begun,[52]
provided he does not abort
the undertaking he began
and be enthusiastic only
about the beginning,
but less passionate
for the glorious end.
For industry determines
the denouement of things,
and temerity and carelessness
approach only their starting point.

Coronat militem
finis, non prelium;
dat hoc ancipitem
metam, is bravium;
iste quod tribuit,
dictat stabilitas;
istud quod metuit,
inducit levitas;
nam palmam annuit
mentis integritas,
quam dari respuit
vaga mobilitas.

Mutat cum Proteo
figuram levitas,
assumit ideo
formas incognitas;
vultum constantia
conservans intimum,
alpha principia
et o novissimum
flectens fit media,
dans finem optimum,
mutans in varia
celum, non animum.

XVI. *Circum Rotam Fortunae*

Fortune plango vulnera
stillantibus ocellis,
quod sua michi munera
subtrahit rebellis.
verum est, quod legitur
fronte capillata,
sed plerumque sequitur
Occasio calvata.

In Fortune solio
sederam elatus,
prosperitatis vario
flore coronatus;
quicquid enim florui
felix et beatus,

The end of the battle crowns
the warrior, not the battle itself;
in this way he makes his prize
an uncertain goal.
Constancy dictates
what he devotes to the cause,
and fickleness establishes
what he fears.
For the integrity of the heart
grants victory's palm,
whose very conferral
wayward inconstancy spurns.

Like Proteus[53] caprice
mutates its shape
and thus assumes
unknown forms.
Constancy maintains
its essential face,
bends an alpha inception
to an omega conclusion,
achieves the very best
consummation,
and variously changes
but the clime, not the mind.

16. *Round Fortune's Wheel*

I do lament Fortuna's wounds,
my little eyes with tears suffused,
because she in rebellious strife
withholds from me her gifts.
True it is, as the books do tell,
that long tresses are draped o'er Opportunity's brow,
but almost always she passes by
with a bald occiput grasped by none.[54]

Exalted sat I
on Fortuna's throne,
crowned with prosperity's
fickle blooms;
I abounded in everything,
felicitous and blessed;

nunc a summo corrui
gloria privatus.

Fortune rota volvitur:
descendo minoratus;
alter in altum tollitur;
nimis exaltatus
rex sedet in vertice -
caveat ruinam!
nam sub axe legimus
Hecubam reginam.

XVII. *Magnum Opus Orffi*

O Fortuna, velut luna
statu variabilis,
semper crescis aut decrescis;
vita detestabilis
nunc obdurat et tunc curat
ludo mentis aciem,
egestatem, potestatem
dissolvit ut glaciem.

Sors immanis et inanis,
rota tu volubilis,
status malus, vana salus
semper dissolubilis,
obumbrata et velata
michi quoque niteris;
nunc per ludum dorsum nudum
fero tui sceleris.

Sors salutis et virtutis
michi nunc contraria,
est affectus et defectus
semper in angaria.
hac in hora sine mora
corde pulsum tangite;
quod per sortem sternit fortem,
mecum omnes plangite!

XVIII. *Meditationes de Fortuna*

now from the pinnacle
have I fallen, of glory bereft.

Fortune's wheel now turns:
diminished, I descend,
whilst another to the top is raised;
elevated too high,
the king is seated at the peak—
but he should beware of the fall!
For we read that even Queen Hecuba[55]
came beneath the wheel.

17. *Orff's Masterwork*[56]

O Fortuna, variable in phase
like the moon,
always you wax or wane:
detestable is your life's way!
Now she palsies, then in sport she spurs[57]
the acuity of the mind;
penury, power,
she dissolves like ice.

Luck, fearsome and vain,
you are a spinning wheel,
an injurious state, a treacherous salvation,
always ready to dissolve;
shadowed and veiled,
you strive after me, too;
by the sport of your turpitude
my back is now nude.

The lot of prosperity and of might
is now contrary to me.
My desire and my failure
are forever vassals to thee.
In this hour without delay
bestir this stroke of the string:
since Fortune through lot prostrates the strong,
be this my and your dirgeful song!

18. *Meditations on Fortune*

O Fortuna levis! cui vis das munera que vis,
Et cui vis que vis auferet hora brevis.

Passibus ambiguis Fortuna volubilis errat
Et manet in nullo certa tenaxque loco;
Sed modo leta manet, modo vultus sumit acerbos,
Et tantum constans in levitate manet.

Ovidius, Tristia 5, 8, 15-18

Dat Fortuna bonum, sed non durabile donum;
Attollit pronum, faciens de rege colonum.

Quos vult Sors ditat, quos non vult, sub pede tritat.

Qui petit alta nimis, retro lapsus ponitur imis.

XVIIIa. *Circus*

Regnabo; regno;   regnavi; sum sine regno.

XIX. *Magnanimitas Sapientium* (ca. 1170)
Gualterius de Castillione (ca. 1135 - ca. 1179)

Fas et nefas ambulant
pene passu pari;
prodigus non redimit
vitium avari;
virtus temperantia
quadam singulari
debet medium
ad utrumque vitium
caute contemplari.

Si legisse memoras
ethicam Catonis,
in qua scriptum legitur:
«ambula cum bonis»,
cum ad dandi gloriam
animum disponis,
supra cetera
primum hoc considera,
quis sit dignus donis.

"O fickle Fortune! To anyone you please you give the gifts
you wish, then a brief hour will take everything from him!"

"With dithery steps, volatile Fortune wanders about
and sits certain and fixed in no locale.
But sometimes she is happy, and sometimes she assumes
a repellant face—only in her frivolity does her constancy dwell."

Ovid, *Lamentations*, 5.8.15-18

"Fortune gives a good, though transient, gift.
She elevates a downcast man, and makes a farmer of a king."

"Lot enriches whom she will; the rest she grinds beneath her heel."

"Who seeks extreme heights, falls back and is set in the deep."

18a. *The Circle*

I will rule; I do rule; I did rule; I am without rule.

19. *Magnanimity of the Wise* (ca. 1170)
by Walter of Châtillon (ca.1135 - ca. 1179)

Good and Evil walk abreast
with almost the same steps;
the prodigal does not redeem
the vice of the avaricious man.
Virtue must consider cautiously,
with a temperance nonpareil,
the middle[58]
between two
opposing poles of vice.

If thou rememberest thy reading
of the Ethics of Cato
in which the line
"walk with good men" is read,[59]
then, when thou resolvest
upon the glory of giving,[60]
above the rest
perpend this first:
who is worthy of thy gifts.

Vultu licet hilari,
verbo licet blando
sis equalis omnibus;
unum tamen mando:
si vis recte gloriam
promereri dando,
primum videas
granum inter paleas,
cui des et quando.

Dare non ut convenit
non est a virtute,
bonum est secundum quid,
sed non absolute;
digne dare poteris
et mereri tute
famam muneris,
si me prius noveris
intus et in cute.

Si prudenter triticum
paleis emundas,
famam emis munere;
sed caveto, dum das,
largitatis oleum
male non effundas.
in te glorior:
cum sim Codro Codrior,
omnibus habundas.

XX. *Meditationes Virtutis*

Est modus in verbis, duo sunt contraria verba:
«Do das» et «teneo» contendunt lite superba.
Per «do das» largi conantur semper amari,
Set «teneo tenui» miseri potiuntur avari.

Sicut in omne quod est mensuram ponere prodest,
Sic sine mensura non stabit regia cura.

Virtus est medium vitiorum utrimque reductum,
Et mala sunt vicina bonis; errore sub illo

Admittedly thou shouldst
with a friendly expression and a kind word
greet all in the same way;
nevertheless I consign this one pearl:
if thou wishest to earn rightly
glory through giving,
thou shouldst first discern
the grain among the chaff:
when and to whom thou shouldst give.[61]

Inappropriate giving
is not the fruit of virtue.
It is a relative good,
not an absolute.
Thou canst give properly
and earn unobjectionable renown
for thy generosity,
if thou first attainest
a knowledge of me inside and out.[62]

If thou prudently winnowest out
the wheat from the straw,
thou purchasest glory through thy gift.
But be vigilant, whilst thou givest,
against spilling the oil of largess.
I pride myself in thee:[63]
though I am more Codrus
than Codrus himself,[64]
thou art abundant to all.[65]

20. *Meditations on Virtue*

"Every word has its own scope;[66] two words are antitheses:
'I give, you give' and 'I possess' contend in a conceited strife.
By 'I give, you give' generous men assay always to be loved.
But 'I possess, I possessed' miserable niggards own."

"Just as it is beneficial in all affairs to set a measure,
so too the sovereignty of a king will not last without one."

"Virtue is the middle path of vice, removed from either extreme,
and bad stands well-nigh good; due to this fallacy dread,

virtus pro vitio crimina sepe tulit.

> Horatius, *Epistulae* 1.18.9
> Ovidius, *Remedia Amoris* 323-24

Dum stultus vitat vitia, in contraria currit;
Fallit enim vitium specie virtutis et umbra.

> Horatius, *Satirae* 1.2.24
> Juvenalis, *Satirae* 14.109

XXI. *Peccati Vicarii*
Philippus Cancellarius (ca. 1170 - 1236)

Veritas veritatum,
via, vita, veritas,
per veritatis semitas
eliminans peccatum!
te verbum incarnatum
clamant fides, spes, caritas,
tu prime pacis statum
reformas post reatum,
tu post carnis delicias
das gratias, ut facias
beatum.
o quam mira potentia,
quam regia vox principis,
cum egrotanti precipis:
«surge, tolle grabatum!»

Omnia sub peccato
clausit Ade meritum;
dum pronior in vetitum
non paruit mandato,
de statu tam beato
nos dedit in interitum;
de morsu venenato
fel inhesit palato
per hoc culpe dispendium
in vitium nascentium
translato.
mortis amare poculum
in seculum transfunditur,
nil cui dulce bibitur
de vase vitiato.

virtue has often borne calumny in vice's stead."[67]

Horace, *Epistles* 1.18.9

Ovid, *The Cure for Love* 323-24

"When the fool tries to avoid a folly, into its opposite he runs;
for vice deceives under virtue's pretense and silhouette.[68]

Horace, *Satires* 1.2.24

Juvenal, *Satires* 14.109

21. *Vicars of Sin*
by Philip the Chancellor (ca. 1170 – ca. 1236)

O Truth of truths,[69]
path, life, truth,[70]
through the tracks of truth,
you eradicate all sin!
Faith, hope, and charity shout[71]
that you are the incarnate word.
You restore after the Fall of Man
the state of primordial peace.
After carnal lust you grant
the sweet gifts of grace,
so that you may reforge a blessed state.
O how wondrous a power,
how regal the lord's voice,
when you enjoin the sick
to "arise, take up thy bed!"[72]

The fault of Adam circumscribed
all things within the radius of sin;
when he, too disposed to the forbidden,
did not obey God's command,
from our so blissful state
he brought us to our ruin;
from the envenomed bite[73]
gall cleaved to his palate
which, as the cost of his blemish,
was translated into
all his progeny's vice.
The draught of bitter death
is transfused into our age;[74]
nothing sweet is drunk to it
from such a corrupted glass.

Spiritus veritatis,
spiritus consilii
modo penam supplicii
non reddit pro peccatis,
ut timor castitatis,
quo revertentur filii,
castiget in prelatis
fermentum vetustatis.
sed quando sponsus veniet,
inveniet, quid faciet
ingratis.
non huic penam abstulit,
cui distulit, sed animam
nunc impinguat ad victimam
adeps iniquitatis.

Tarditas prelatorum
iudicem exasperat;
sed his qui solus reserat
medullas animorum,
a fructibus eorum
novit eos et tolerat,
quos extra viam morum
fert impetus errorum.
sed «ecce» clamat «venio
cum gladio fiagitio
malorum!»
et cum purgabit aream,
tunc paleam abiciet:
sic erit, quando veniet
ille Sanctus Sanctorum.

Cecidit in preclaris
hominum funiculus;
sed nostre mentis oculus
per vias huius maris
ad vie singularis
metam contendit sedulus.
sed luxus secularis
per ministros altaris
nunc solis vacat opibus
patentibus hiatibus
avaris.

The spirit of truth,
the spirit of right counsel,
does not yet render the penalty
of divine punishment for sins,
so that the reverence for purity,
whereby sons are returned to the path direct,
may first attempt to mend
the olden mischief of the prelature's men.
But when the Bridegroom comes,[75]
He will ascertain what to do
with ingrates who have squandered
the chance to evils undo.
He has not commuted their sentences,
but only delayed, yet the grease of their iniquities
now fattens their souls for the final offering.[76]

The tardiness of the prelates
exasperates the Judge,
but He alone reveals
the marrow of their souls,
knows them by their fruits,[77]
and observes those whom
the impulse for folly
leads outside the path of right.
But "Behold," He exclaims,
"I come with sword in answer
to the ignominies of wicked men."
And when He purges
the threshing floor
He shall then cast out the chaff.[78]
Thus it shall be, when that Saint of saints comes.

The lot of mankind fell with clarity,[79]
 and the eye of our souls
through the paths of this sea
sedulously strove for the goal
of this singular way.[80]
But secular splendor
among the altar's knaves
now devotes itself only
to might and wealth
that stand open
to avaricious whims.

sic per prelatos mammone
mors anime concipitur,
dum cunctis male vivitur
ad formam exemplaris.

XXII. *Hortus Animae*
Philippus Cancellarius (ca. 1170 - 1236)

Homo, quo vigeas vide!
Dei fidei adhereas,
in spe gaudeas,
et in fide intus ardeas,
foris luceas,
turturis retorqueas
os ad ascellas.
docens ita
verbo, vita
oris vomere
de cordibus fidelium
evellas lolium,
lilium insere rose,
ut alium per hoc corripere
speciose valeas.
virtuti, saluti omnium studeas,
noxias delicias detesteris,
opera considera,
que si non feceris, damnaberis.
hac in via milita gratie
et premia cogita patrie,
et sic tuum cor
in perpetuum gaudebit.

XXIII. *Sacerdos Benignus*

Vide, qui nosti litteras
et bene doces vivere,
quid sit doctrina littere,
de quo et ad quid referas.
diligenter considera,
si sis doctor, quid doceas,
et quod doces, hoc teneas,
ne tua perdant opera
ETERNA CHRISTI MUNERA.

Thus on account of the prelates
the death of the soul by Mammon is conceived,
whilst all live in deviance
from the example's frame.

22. *Garden of the Soul*
by Philip the Chancellor (ca. 1170-1236)

Man, see through Whom thou art strong!
Thou shouldst adhere to thy faith in God,
thou shouldst in hope take joy,
and in thy faith glow deep within;
outside thou shouldst shine,
and thou shouldst twist back to its shoulders
the beak of the turtledove.[81]
Teaching thus by thy word and way of life,
thou shouldst with the plough of thy mouth
eradicate the darnel
from the hearts of faithful men.
Plant thou a lily of chastity between each rose of love,
so that thereby thou mayest in splendor discharge
the duty of fraternal correction.[82]
Strive thou after virtue and the salvation of all,
and hold thou in abomination harmful delights.
Consider thou good works:
if thou performest none, thou shalt be damned.
On this path of grace perform thy service
with valiant mien, and think always on
the celestial fatherland's rewards;
and thus thy heart forever will be
the sacred home of mirth.

23. *The Good Priest*

Consider thou, lettered man
and teacher of right living,
what the writing's instruction is,
and about what and for what purpose thou lecturest.
Consider thou attentively,
if thou a teacher desirest to be,
what thou shouldst teach,
and that thou upholdest thy teachings, lest thy works lose
THE ETERNAL GIFTS OF CHRIST.

Vide, qui colis studium
pro Dei ministerio,
ne abutaris studio
suspirans ad dispendium
lucri, nec te participes
coniuge vite vitio;
namque multos invenio,
qui sunt huius participes,
ECCLESIARUM PRINCIPES.

Vide, qui debes sumere
religionis gloriam
summi per Dei gratiam,
ne te possit decipere
nec trudat in interitum
Philisteus improvide
– namque prodent te Dalide –
ut non amittas meritum,
DEUS, TUORUM MILITUM.

XXIV. *Fugiatis Vanitatem!*

Iste mundus   furibundus   falsa prestat gaudia,
Quia fluunt   et decurrunt   ceu campi lilia.
Laus mundana,   vita vana   vera tollit premia,
Nam impellit   et submergit   animas in tartara.
Lex carnalis   et mortalis   valde transitoria
Fugit, transit   velut umbra,   que non est corporea.
Quod videmus   vel tenemus   in presenti patria,
Dimittemus   et perdemus   quasi quercus folia.
Fugiamus,   contemnamus   huius vite dulcia,
Ne perdamus   in futuro   pretiosa munera!
Conteramus,   confringamus   carnis desideria,
Ut cum iustis   et electis   in celesti gloria
Gratulari   mereamur   per eterna secula!
Amen.

XXV. *Proverbia*

Vivere sub meta   lex precipit atque propheta.

Est velut unda maris   vox, gloria, laus popularis.

See to it, thou, who appliest himself
to study in the service of God,
that thou dost not thy studies misuse,
nor sigh over a profit's loss,
nor associate thyself with vice,
the constant companion of life;
for I behold many, who are
partakers of this vicious strain:
THE PRINCES OF THE CHURCH.

See to it, thou, who shouldst assume
the glory of religion through the grace
of the highest God,
that a Philistine[83] is not able
to chicane nor drive thee,
in a moment of unwariness, to ruin—
for then the Delilahs[84] will betray thee!
Do not let fall the recompense,
O GOD, OF THY WARRIOR KNIGHTS!

24. *Away With Vanity*!

This raging world furnishes false delights,
since they fade and set like the lilies of the field.[85]
Secular glory and a life of vanity defraud mankind of true rewards,
for they drive into and submerge souls in the infernal depths.
The carnal, mortal, most transient law[86] takes to flight
and passes away like a disembodied silhouette.[87]
What we in the fatherland of this present life see and hold,
we shall renounce and lose, as the oak does its leaves.[88]
We should eschew, we should contemn the vain pleasures of this life,
lest we in the hereafter lose the truly precious gifts.
Let us trample and let us dash the desires of the flesh,[89]
so that with the just and chosen in heaven's glory
we may forever be entitled to manifest our joy.
Amen.

25. *Aphorisms*

"The law and prophets bid us to live within measure."[90]

"Like a wave of the sea are the voice, glory, and laud of man."

Omina sunt hominum tenui pendentia filo.
Ovidius, Ex Ponto 4.3.35

Qui differt penas,   peccandi laxat habenas.

Nil fieri stulte   credit, qui peccat inulte.

Discit enim citius meminitque libentius illud,
Quod quis deridet, quam quod probat et veneratur.
Horatius, Epistulae 2.2.262-3

De correctione hominum

XXVI. *Petitum Cancellarii*
Philippus Cancellarius (ca. 1170 - 1236)

Ad cor tuum revertere,
condicionis misere
homo! cur spernis vivere?
cur dedicas te vitiis?
cur indulges malitiis?
cur excessus non corrigis
nec gressus tuos dirigis
in semitis iustitie,
sed contra te cotidie
iram Dei exasperas?
in te succidi metue
radices ficus fatue,
cum fructus nullos atteras!

O condicio misera!
considera, quam aspera
sit hec vita, mors altera,
que sic immutat statum!
cur non purgas reatum
sine mora, cum sit hora
tibi mortis incognita!
et in vita
caritas, que non proficit,
prorsus aret et deficit
nec efficit beatum.

"The fortunes of men hang on a slender thread."

Ovid, *Letters from the Black Sea* 4.3.35

"Who delays the penalty, lets loose the reins of sin."

"Unpunished sinners foolishly trust that no retribution comes."

"He learns more quickly and sooner recalls what another derides
than that which someone esteems and reveres."

Horace, *Epistles*, 2.2.262-3

On the Correction of Men

26. *The Chancellor's Plea*
by Philip the Chancellor (ca. 1170 – 1236)

Turn back unto thy heart,[91]
man of wretched state![92]
Mankind! Why dost thou disdain life,[93]
why dost thou dedicate thyself to vice,
why dost thou indulge in sin?
Why dost thou not set right thy blunders,
why directest thou not thy steps[94]
along the paths of righteousness,[95]
but rather against thyself provokest thou
the wrath of God everyday?
Have fear that the roots on thee
of the foolish fig tree will be cut away,
since thou yieldest no fruit![96]

O wretched condition!
Consider how harsh this life—
a second death—is
because it so inexorably metamorphoses!
Why dost thou not purge
thyself of guilt without delay,
since the hour of death
is not known to thee?
And in life love that benefits none[97]
withereth utterly, dieth away,
and leadeth unto no beatitude.

Si vocatus ad nuptias
advenias
sine veste nuptiali,
a curia regali
expelleris,
et obviam si veneris
sponso lampade vacua,
es quasi virgo fatua.

Ergo vide, ne dormias,
sed vigilans aperias
Domino, cum pulsaverit!
beatus, quem invenerit
vigilantem, cum venerit!

XXVII. *Beati*
Philippus Cancellarius (ca. 1170 - 1236)

Bonum est confidere
in dominorum Domino,
bonum est spem ponere
in spei nostre termino.
qui de regum potentia,
non de Dei clementia
spem concipis,
te decipis
et excipis
ab aula summi principis.
quid in opum aggere
exaggeras peccatum?
in Deo cogitatum
tuum iacta,
prius acta
studeas corrigere,
in labore manuum
et sudore vultuum
pane tuo vescere!

Carnis ab ergastulo
liber eat spiritus,
ne peccati vinculo
vinciatur
et trahatur

If, invited to the wedding,
thou shouldst arrive
without a nuptial vest,[98]
ejected wilt thou be
from the royal court;[99]
and if thou comest to meet the Bridegroom[100]
with an empty lamp in hand,
thou art like a foolish virgin.[101]

Therefore see to it that thou dost not sleep,
but that thou, in wakefulness,
openest to the Lord, when He knocketh.
Blessed is he, whom He findeth
awake when He cometh!

27. *The Blessed*
by Philip the Chancellor (ca. 1170 -1236)

Good it is to confide
in the Lord of Lords;[102]
good it is to place hope
in our hope's aim.
Thou who conceivest a hope
for the power of kings
and not the mercy of God,
deceivest
and withdrawest
thyself from the palace
of the highest lord.
Wherefore heapest up thou sin
in a mound of pelf?
Cast thy worrisome thoughts
in God before thou strivest
to atone for thy prior acts:
by the labor of thy hands
and the sweat of thy face
thou shouldst consume thy bread![103]

Let the spirit go free
from the penitentiary
of the flesh,
lest it be bound
by the fetters of sin

ad inferni gemitus,
ubi locus flentium,
ubi stridor dentium,
ubi pena gehennali
affliguntur omnes mali
in die novissimo,
in die gravissimo,
quando iudex venerit,
ut trituret aream
et exstirpet vineam,
que fructum non fecerit.
sic granum a palea
separabit,
congregabit
triticum in horrea.

O beati
mundo corde,
quos peccati
tersa sorde
vitium non inquinat,
scelus non examinat,
nec arguunt peccata,
qui Domini mandata
custodiunt
et sitiunt!
beati qui esuriunt
et confidunt in Domino
nec cogitant de crastino!
beati qui non implicant
se curis temporalibus,
qui talentum multiplicant
et verbum Dei predicant
omissis secularibus!

XXVIII. *Index Otlohi*
Otloh Ratisbonensis (ca. 1010 - ca. 1070)

Laudat rite Deum,   qui vere diligit illum.
Lumbos precingit,   qui carnis vota restringit.
Maxime querendum,   quod semper erit retinendum.
Nil peccant oculi,   si mens velit his dominari.
Ne tardare velis,   si quem convertere possis.

and haled into the moans of hell,
the home of the tearful
and the screeching of teeth,[104]
where all wicked men,
by the inferno's vengeance,
are dashed on the final day—
on the most grave of days—
when the Judge cometh
to thresh the threshing floor
and to extirpate the vine
that hath produced no fruit.
Thus the grain from the chaff
He will separate
and the wheat in granaries
He will store.[105]

Blessed are
the pure of heart,[106]
whom vice doth not befoul—
since the sordidness
of sin has been wiped away—
whom crime does not assay,
nor do sins denounce,
who heed
and thirst
for the mandates of God![107]
Blessed are they who hunger for
and confide in God[108]
and who think not on the morrow![109]
Blessed are they who don't entangle
themselves in temporal solicitudes,
who multiply the talent,[110]
and preach the word of God,
having dismissed all secular concerns!

28. *Otloh's List*
by Otloh of St. Emmeram (ca. 1010 – ca. 1070)

Rightly doth he praise God, who truly cherisheth him.
He girdeth his loins, who restraineth the desires of the flesh.
He must especially seek to gain what he can always keep.
The eyes sin not, if the heart be willing to dominate them.
Delay thou not, if the opportunity to convert one should arise.

Nisus stultorum   par semper erit sociorum.
Omne, quod est iustum,   merito dici valet unum.
Os, quod mentitur,   animam iugulare probatur.
O quantis curis   mens indiget omnibus horis!
Peccans cottidie   studeat se mox reparare.

De conversione hominum

XXIX. *Pericla Libidinis*
Petrus Blesensis (ca. 1135 – ca. 1204)

In lacu miserie
et luto luxurie
volveris, inutile
tempus perdens, Panphile!
cur offensas numinum
aut derisum hominum
non metuis,
dum destruis
corpus, rem et animam?
salva saltem ultimam
vite portiunculam,
offerens celestibus
pro iuvente floribus
senectutis stipulam!

Forsan ludo Veneris
ultra vires ureris,
ut amoris tedium
tibi sit remedium.
sed si te medullitus
exsiccatum penitus
exhaurias,
ut febrias,
nichil tamen proficis,
dum ad tempus deficis;
nam insurget artius
Hydra multiplicior,
et post casum fortior
surget Terre filius.

Ut stes pede stabili
sine casu facili,

Fools' efforts will always be the same as the striving of allies.
Everything just can deservedly be called an indivisible whole.
It hath been shewn that a mouth that lieth slayeth the soul.[112]
O how many concerns the heart doth spin hour after hour!
Who sins should strive everyday to renew himself anon.

On the Conversion of Men

29. *Perils of Lust*
by Peter of Blois (ca. 1135 – ca.1204)

In the pit of misery
and the mire of debauchery[113]
thou rollest and whirlest,
fecklessly wasting time, O Pamphilus![114]
Why fearest thou not
the wrath of God
or the derision of men,
whilst thou destroyest
thy body, fortune, and soul?
Save at least the last small portion of thy life,
to offer the celestials
a haulm of senectitude
in place of the lost flowers
of thy spent youth!

Perchance through the sport of Venus
thou art inflamed beyond thy strength,
such that an aversion to the pleasures
of love is thy only remedy.
But if thou shouldst exhaust thyself
to thy very core,
desiccated deep within,
to the point that thou burnest with fever,
nevertheless thou accomplishest nothing,
when thou withdrawest
but for the moment.
For a more manifold Hydra will arise[115]
with greater vigor, and after each fall,
the son of Earth will stand stronger than before.[116]

Stand thou fast on a steady foot
without coming to a fall for a trifle;

cave precipitium,
devitando vitium.
sed si te vexaverit
aut si comprehenderit
Egyptia,
mox pallia
fugitivus desere,
nec lucteris temere;
nam resistens vincitur
in hoc belli genere,
et qui novit cedere,
fugiendo fugitur.

XXX. *Reventus a Iuventute* (ca. 1170)
Petrus Blesensis (ca. 1135 - ca. 1204)

Dum iuventus floruit,
licuit   et libuit
facere, quod placuit,
iuxta voluntatem
currere,   peragere
carnis voluptatem.

Amodo sic agere,
vivere   tam libere,
talem vitam ducere
viri vetat etas,
perimit   et eximit
leges assuetas.

Etas illa monuit,
docuit,   consuluit,
sic et etas annuit:
«nichil est exclusum!»
omnia   cum venia
contulit ad usum.

Volo resipiscere,
linquere,   corrigere,
quod commisi temere;
deinceps intendam
seriis,   pro vitiis
virtutes rependam.

beware of disaster, by avoiding vice.
But if that Egyptian seductress[117]
tormenteth or detaineth thee,
quickly run away, forsake the veils,
and trammel not thyself
recklessly in a struggle;
for he who resisteth
in this type of war
is subdued,
and he, who knoweth
how to withdraw,
escapeth by fleeing.

30. *The Return from Youth* (ca. 1170)
by Peter of Blois (ca. 1135 – ca. 1204)

When his flower
of youth was in bloom,
it was possible and agreeable
for a lad to do what he pleased,
to run according to his own will,
and to indulge in the pleasures of the flesh.

Henceforth acting thus,
living so unfettered and free,
and leading such a life
the age of manhood forbids;[118]
it eradicates and annuls
a boy's wonted laws.

That stage in life served
as remembrancer, tutor, and counselor wise;[119]
likewise it favored the maxim:
"Nothing is forbidden!"
With indulgence it brought together
all things for its enjoyment and use.

I wish to return unto my senses,
to abandon and set right
what I in temerity committed.
Henceforth I will turn to serious affairs
and expiate my past mischief
through virtuous works.

XXXI. *Mea Pueritia Perdita* (ca. 1170/80)
Petrus Blesensis (ca. 1135 - ca. 1204)

Vite perdite me legi subdideram,
minus licite dum fregi, quod voveram;
sed ad vite vesperam
corrigendum legi,
quicquid ante perperam
puerilis egi.

Rerum exitus dum quero discutere,
falsum penitus a vero discernere,
falso fallor opere,
bravium si spero
me virtutum metere,
vitia dum sero.

Non sum duplici perplexus itinere,
nec addidici reflexus a venere,
nec fraudavi temere
coniugis amplexus;
Dalidam dans, temere
ut fraudetur sexus!

Famem siliqua porcorum non abstulit,
que ad lubrica errorum me contulit.
sed scriptura consulit,
viam intrem morum,
que prelarga protulit
pabula donorum.

Dum considero, quid Dine contigerit,
finem confero rapine quis fuerit;
scio: vix evaserit
mens corrupta fine,
diu quam contraxerit,
maculam sentine.

Preter meritum me neci non dedero,
si ad vomitum, quem ieci, rediero,
nec a verbo aspero
liberum me feci,
servus si serviero

31. *My Wasted Youth* (ca. 1170/80)
by Peter of Blois (ca. 1135 – ca. 1204)

I had subordinated myself to the law of profligate life,
when I sinfully broke my vow.
But on the eve of my life,
I have chosen to set right
whatever mistakes
I made as a boy.

Whilst I assay to examine the end of things
and to divorce completely falsehood from truth,
I am deceived by a false labor,
if I hope to reap the laurel of victory
for my virtuous deeds,
whilst I sow the seeds of vice.

The forked path did not tempt me,[120]
venery I did not learn to shun,
and yet in my levity I did not steal
the embraces of a spouse,
but withheld them from Delilah,[121]
lest my sex in a tender way be duped!

The husks of sows[122] did not take away the hunger
that brought me unto the slippery seasons
of my follies and blunders.
But Holy Scripture advised me
to enter upon the path of virtue,
which offered a bounty of foods as gifts.

When I reflect on what befell Dinah[123]
and consider what end that rape assumed,
I then know that a corrupt heart
scarcely escapes its doom,
so long as it has contracted
the stain of its labors' swill.

I will not have given myself to a death
contrary to my desert, if I return
to the vomit[124] I have expelled,
nor will I have freed myself
from a harsh verdict[125]

vitiorum feci.

Vie veteris immuto vestigia,
ire Veneris refuto per devia:
via namque regia
curritur in tuto;
si quis cedit alia,
semper est in luto.

Beli solium, Sinonis astutiam,
confer Tullium, Zenonis prudentiam:
nil conferre sentiam,
his abutens bonis,
ni fugiendo fugiam
Dalidam Samsonis.

Ergo veniam de rei miseria
ut inveniam de Dei clementia:
hec et his similia
quod peregi, rei
sola parcens gratia
miserere mei!

XXXII. *De Passione*

Cur homo torquetur?   ne fastus ei dominetur.
Cur homo torquetur?   ut ei meritum cumuletur.
Cur homo torquetur?   ut Christus glorificetur.
Cur homo torquetur?   ut penis culpa pietur.
Cur homo torquetur?   ut dupliciter crucietur.

Gratia sola Dei,   quos vult, facit alta mereri.

De ammonitione prelatorum

XXXIII. *Consilium ad Sacerdotem*
Petrus Blesensis (ca. 1135 - ca. 1204)

Non te lusisse pudeat,
sed ludum non incidere
et que lusisti temere,
ad vite frugem vertere.
magistra morum doceat

if as a slave I serve the dregs of vice.

So I alter the tracks of the old path
and refuse to traverse love's devious trails,
for the king's road
is in safety coursed.
If anyone withdraws from it,
forever steeped in mire is he.

Combine Belus' sway[126] with Sinon's craft,[127]
and Cicero's eloquence with Zeno's sagacity:[128]
I, exploiting these goods to their fullest, know
that nothing would be of use,
if I should not escape Samson's Delilah
by the swiftest of flight.[129]

Therefore to light upon a pardon
from the affliction of a guilty man
from the merciful hand of God, I pray:
O Matchless, Sparing Grace of God,
for these and similar sins I have committed,
take pity on my plight!

32. *On Suffering*

Why must man suffer? So that pride may not rule him.
Why must man suffer? So that he may gather his deserts.
Why must man suffer? So that Christ may be exalted.
Why must man suffer? So that through pain sin may be atoned.
Why must man suffer? So that he doubly may be racked.[130]

God's grace alone makes those he chooses earn their heights.

On Admonishing Prelates

33. *Advice to a Priest*
by Peter of Blois (ca. 1135 – ca. 1204)

You should not be ashamed of your past disports,[131]
but you should be mortified at your failure to desist
from your old games and aimless, reckless ways
and your refusal to turn to the fruit of life.
The schoolmistress of ethics, Reason,

te ratio,
ut dignus pontificio,
divini dono numinis,
ad laudem Christi nominis
fungaris sacerdotio.

Sis pius, iustus, sobrius,
prudens, pudicus, humilis,
in lege Dei docilis,
et ne sis arbor sterilis;
tuo te regas aptius
officio,
expulso procul vitio
munderis labe criminis,
ut mundus munde Virginis
ministres in altario.

Pius protector pauperum
omni petenti tribue,
malos potenter argue
manusque sacras ablue
a sordidorum munerum
contagio,
nullus te palpet premio,
quesita gratis gratia
largire beneficia,
sed dignis beneficio.

Non des ministris scelerum
non tua, sed ecclesie,
sub pietatis specie;
non abutaris impie
commisso tibi pauperum
suffragio,
nil a te ferat histrio,
et tibi non allicias
infames amicitias
de Christi patrimonio.

Ministros immunditie
a te repellas longius:
bonorum vitam fortius
pravus depravat socius

should teach you that to be deemed worthy
of the bishopric, a gift from the power divine,
you should administer
the episcopal office
to the glory of Christ's name.

You should be pious, just, sensible,
prudent, modest, humble,[132]
versed in God's law,
and not be a fruitless tree;[133]
you should govern yourself
more duly than your office,
and having banished vice to far-off realms,
you should cleanse yourself of blighting reproach,[134]
so that you, free from sin,
may serve the altar of the Virgin pure.

As benevolent protector of the poor,
give unto all who seek your charity;
with a forceful voice censure the wicked
and wash your sacred hands
of the contagion of sordid gifts.
None should flatter you
with lucre of any kind.
Without charge you should lavish
the benefits you have freely received,
but only to those who a benefice deserve.

You should not give, under kindness' guise,
to the attendants of sin that which is not yours,
but belongs to the church.
You should not pitilessly misuse
the paupers' farthing entrusted to you;
from you the entertainer
should carry nothing away,
nor should you attract,
with the patrimony of Christ,
to yourself friendships of ill repute.

You should keep very far from you
the ministers of impurity and filth:
an ally perverse boldly depraves
the lives and ways of good men

et afficit infamie
dispendio;
sic trahitur presumptio
a convictu similium,
prelati vita vilium
vilescit contubernio.

Caute dispone domui,
pauca, sed vera loquere,
verba confirmes opere,
quia non decet temere
os sacerdotis pollui
mendacio;
prudentium consilio
te frui non displiceat,
nec te sinistre moveat
salubris exhortatio.

Teneris, ut abstineas
ab omni mala specie,
sub freno temperantie
magistra pudicitie,
sobrietate, floreas,
ne vario
vagoque desiderio
declines ad illecebras,
sed cece mentis tenebras
purga virtutis radio.

XXXIV. *Casus Sion*
Philippus Cancellarius (ca. 1170 - 1236)

Deduc, Sion, uberrimas
velut torrentem lacrimas!
nam qui pro tuis patribus
nati sunt tibi filii,
quorum dedisti manibus
tui sceptrum imperii,
fures et furum socii
turbato rerum ordine
abutuntur regimine
pastoralis officii.

and inflicts the loss of their good names;[135]
so much is the presumption of similar minds
drawn from their jointly quartered lives;
thus the life of the prelate
becomes worthless when
he lives and messes with vile men.

Prudently arrange your home,[136]
speak you briefly but true words;
strengthen your words through acts akin,
for it befits not a bishop's mouth
to be defiled carelessly
with mendacity's help.
It should not displease you to enjoy
the counsel of sagacious men,
nor should an expedient exhortation
put you in an wicked mood.

You are required to abstain
from every semblance of evil;[137]
under the rein of temperance,
chastity's noble tutoress,
may you soberly bloom,
lest you fall into allurements
by way of variable and vagrant whims,
but rout the darkness
of a blind heart
with virtue's ever refulgent ray.

34. *The Fall of Zion*
by Philip the Chancellor (ca. 1170 – 1236)

Let run, Zion, like a torrent,
a most copious stream of tears![138]
For, in place of your fathers,
the sons born to you,[139]
in whose hands you have set
the scepter of supreme command,
are thieves and their confederates.[140]
The order of things now disturbed,
these brigands are abusing
the pastorate's rule.

Ad corpus infirmitas
capitis descendit,
singulosque gravitas
artus apprehendit,
refrigescit karitas,
nec iam se extendit
ad amorem proximi;
nam videmus opprimi
pupilum a potente,
nec est qui salvum faciat
vel qui iustum eripiat
ab impio premente.

Vide, Deus ultionum,
vide, videns omnia,
quod spelunca vispillonum
facta est Ecclesia,
quod in templum Salomonis
venit princeps Babylonis
et excelsum sibi thronum
posuit in medio!
sed arrepto gladio
scelus hoc ulciscere!
veni, iudex gentium,
cathedras vendentium
columbas evertere!

XXXV. *Fides Comparativa*

Magnus maior maximus,
parvus minor minimus:
gradus istos repperi,
per quos gradus comperi
augeri et conteri
gradus status hominis,
prout datur dignitas,
dignitatum quantitas
quantitasque nominis.

Magni parvus extiti,
parvi magnus meriti,
parveque sunt gratie
diviti contrarie:

The sickness of the head
to the body descends;[141]
heaviness seizes
every single limb;
love grows cold,[142]
nor does it now reach out to a neighbor.
For we see an orphan being crushed
by a powerful man,
and there is no one
who would protect him
or rescue the just
from the wicked oppressor.[143]

Behold, God of vengeance,
behold, You, Who behold all:
the Church has become
a robbers' den;[144]
into the Temple of Solomon
the king of Babylon has come
and set his high throne in its midst
before the eyes of all![145]
Unsheathe Your sword
and this sacrilege avenge!
Come, Judge of men,
and overturn the seats
of men selling doves![146]

35. *Comparative Faith*

Great, greater, greatest,
small, smaller, smallest:
I have learned those degrees;[147]
I have discovered that through them
the steps of man's state
are elevated and sunk,
according to the rank conferred,
the sum of offices he holds,
and the ponderosity of his name.

I am a dwarf of origin great,
I am a giant of little worth,
receipt of small gifts
befits a rich man not:

cui plus datur hodie,
magis est obnoxius,
quique minus habuit
et minus attribuit,
minus reddit gratius.

Viri fratres presules,
rationis consules,
me non imitemini!
ne sic operemini
super gregem Domini,
pervigil sit animus,
sit lumen in manibus,
presit custos renibus
magnus maior maximus!

XXXVI. *Pastor Bonus Gregis*

Nulli beneficium
iuste penitudinis
amputatur,
nulli maius vitium
quam ingratitudinis
imputatur.
ergo, presul confitens,
esto vere penitens,
quia nil confessio
lavat, cui contritio
denegatur.

Si confessus fueris
ore, fit confessio
ad salutem,
corde si contereris;
animi contritio
dat virtutem,
ut salutem habeas;
ut virtutem teneas,
relictis prioribus
tuam orna moribus
iuventutem.

Virtute, non sanguine

he, to whom more is given today,
is more beholden than who says nay;[148]
but anyone who has received less
and bestowed less as well,
renders far less graciously.

O noble brothers,[149] presiders,
highest magistrates of reason,
do not imitate my ways![150]
do not perform your works thus
for the flock of the Lord;
let your heart be watchful,
let there be light in your hands,[151]
let Him as keeper rule your loins—
He, the great, the greater, the greatest!

36. *The Good Shepherd of the Flock*

The benefaction
of right repentance
is pruned from none;
nothing greater than
ingratitude's fault
is credited to anyone.
So then, bishop, if thou art confessing,
be thou truly penitent,
because a confession
that lacks contrition
washes nothing away.

If thou shouldst confess in words,
the confession thy salvation becomes,
if in it thou shouldst
employ thy heart.
Contrition of the heart
endows virtue upon thee,
so that thou mayest deliverance enjoy;
so that thou mayest virtue possess,
abandon thou thy quondam ways
and decorate thy youth
with manners refined.

It befits thee to rely upon virtue

decet niti;
sub honorum culmine
corde miti
foveas innoxium;
reprime flagitium
superbi et impii;
supremi iudicii
memor iuste iudica,
predicans non claudica.

Tuum sit contemnere
contemnentes
et fovere munere
nil habentes.
relevato debiles
et exaltes bumiles.
in te sit humilitas,
cui mixta sit gravitas,
ut lene corripias
et serene lenias.

Cui magis committitur,
ab eo plus exigitur.
quid Domino retribuis
pro tot, que tibi tribuit,
quod lac et lanam eruis
gregis, cuius constituit
te pastorem?
sed cave ne, cum venerit,
te districte tunc conterat
ut raptorem!
districtus iudex aderit;
nunc sustinens considerat
peccatorem.

Cum subiectis ne pereas,
exempla prava timeas
in subiectos transfundere;
nam quanto gradus altior
cum graviori pondere,
tanto labenti gravior
lapsus datur.
ne desperes, si criminis

and not the ancestry of thy blood.
Beneath the pillar of
thy ecclesiastical majesty thou shouldst
nurture the innocent with a gentle heart.
Keep thou in check the opprobrium
of arrogance and iniquity.
Mindful of the law supreme,
judge thou justly and waver not,
when thou dost preach!

Let contempt of scorners
be thy domain
and support with gifts those
who have nothing to their name.
Lift thou up the weak
and exalt the poor;
let there exist in thee humility
and with it let dignity be mixed,
so that thou mayest chide gently
and clearly soothe.

To whom more is entrusted,
more is exacted from him.
How repayest thou the Lord
for the many things He bestowed upon thee,
when thou demandest milk
and wool from the flock,
whose shepherd He commissioned thee to be?
Rather be thou on thy guard
lest, when He comes, He crush thee
then severely as if thou art a thief!
As a stringent Judge will He appear;
though enduring thee now,
He reckons thee a man of sin.

Lest thou perish with thy subjects,
thou shouldst fear the transfusion
of thy perverse models into them.
For a more grievous fall is imposed
when thou plungest from thy heights
as a higher step plummets
with a deadlier weight.
Despair thou not,

in latens precipitium
pes labatur,
nam iuste penitudinis
nemini beneficium
amputatur.

XXXVII. *Discrimines in Claustro* (ca. 1187/88)

In Gedeonis area
vellus aret extentum,
et demolitur tinea
regale vestimentum,
superhabundat palea,
que sepelit frumentum,
et loquitur iumentum,
nec redit bos ad horrea,
sed sequitur carpentum.

Exit rumor discriminis
de Grandimontis cella,
que tam sancte dulcedinis
late fundebat mella;
preposteratur ordinis
plantatio novella,
dum movet in se bella,
bases in summo culminis
ponens, non capitella.

Quod sanctum sacerdotium,
quod unctio regalis
se curvet ad imperium
et vocem subiugalis,
humanum est mysterium
et furor laicalis.
favor tamen venalis,
qui non intrant per ostium,
fovet eos sub alis.

Clausa quondam religio
vel otium secretum
nunc subiacet opprobrio
per vulgus indiscretum,
quod tali tirocinio

if thy foot should slip
into the lurking precipice of sin,
for the benefaction
of right repentance
is pruned from none.

37. *Cloistered Crises* (ca. 1187/88)

On Gideon's[152] threshing floor
the outstretched wool grows dry,
and the moth consumes[153]
the king's robe;
chaff, which overwhelms
the grain, superabounds,
and the beast of burden talks;[154]
the ox returns not to the barn,
but follows behind the cart.

The rumor of a crisis emanates
from the cloister of Grandmont,[155]
whence earlier streamed far and wide
the honey of such sweet holiness.
The setting of the new order[156]
is inverted and placed atop the head,
when it stirs up internecine wars
and sets the bases, not the capitals,
atop its pillars' heights.

That the holy priesthood,
that the anointed King[157]
bend themselves to the dominion
and voice of a burdened beast
is a mortal mystery[158]
and the madness of the laity.[159]
Favor, though, mind you, is for sale:
them, who enter not through the door,[160]
it takes and warms beneath its wings.

The once so cloistered convent,[161]
a remote seat of tranquility,
now is subject to opprobrium
by the indiscretions of the rabble,
which was not accustomed

non erat assuetum;
et, quod format, decretum
non legis patrocinio
nec litteris est fretum.

Sub brevi doctus tempore
stultus dum incappatur,
pleno prophetat pectore,
ructans interpretatur
et disputat cum rhetore,
qui tacet et miratur,
quod vir iustus tollatur
et assumptus de stercore
sententias loquatur.

Ve, ve, qui regis filiam
das in manu lenonis!
ve, qui profanas gloriam
tante devotionis,
qui cellam pigmentariam
et opus Salomonis
fraude rapis predonis,
si certius inspiciam
ad rem condicionis!

XXXVIII. *Sapientia Otlohi*
Otloh Ratisbonensis (ca. 1010 - ca. 1070)

Doctrine verba paucis   prosunt sine factis.
Eloquium sanctum   pretiosum fit super aurum.
Expers doctrine   tenebras patietur ubique.
Est quasi vas vacuum,   cui cura deest animarum.

XXXIX. *Reges Avaritiae* (ca. 1120)

In huius mundi patria
regnat idolatria;
ubique sunt venalia
dona spiritalia.
custodes sunt raptores
atque lupi pastores,
principes et reges
subverterunt leges.

to an apprenticeship of that sort.
The decree that this rabble fashions
is not under the protection of law
nor does it rely on letters of any kind.

As soon as the dolt is in the capuchin enrobed,
now erudite after but one lesson brief,
he prophesies with full breast;
belching, he expounds and contends
in words with the rhetorician,
who stands silent and marvels
that the just man is eradicated
and one picked up from dung[162]
voices in lectures his thoughts.[163]

Woe, woe to thee, who passest the daughter
of the king into the hands of the pimp![164]
Woe to thee who profanest the glory
of piety so great, who dost plunder
the chamber of spices and the Temple of Solomon
with the skullduggery of a thief—
such thou dost and such thou art,
if I look more intently
upon the case's facts.

38. *Otloh's Wisdom*
by Otloh of St. Emmeram (ca. 1010 – ca. 1070)

Without deeds the words of the doctrine avail few.
Holy words are more precious than gold.
One destitute of knowledge will suffer darkness everywhere.
He is like an empty vessel, who has no concern for souls.

39. *Kings of Greed* (ca. 1120)

In the fatherland of this world
idolatry as sovereign reigns.[165]
Everywhere are spiritual gifts
put up for sale.
The guardians are thieves
and the shepherds are wolves;
princes and kings
have subverted the laws.

hac incerta domo
insanit omnis homo.
sed ista cum vento
transibunt in momento.

Lia placet lipposa,
sed Rachel flet formosa,
que diu manens sterilis
ob immanitatem sceleris
generat anicilla;
nam Raab ancilla
navem mundi mersit,
discordia dispersit
mortis seminaria,
et mundi luminaria
luminant obscure;
pauci vivunt secure.

Doctores apostolici
et iudices katholici
quidam colunt Albinum
et diligunt Rufinum,
cessant iudicare
et student devorare
gregem sibi commissum;
hi cadunt in abyssum.
si cecus ducit cecum,
in fossam cadit secum.
hi tales subsannantur
et infra castra cremantur.

Episcopi cornuti
conticuere muti,
ad predam sunt parati
et indecenter coronati;
pro virga ferunt lanceam,
pro infula galeam,
clipeum pro stola
- hec mortis erit mola -,
loricam pro alba
- hec occasio calva -,
pellem pro humerali
pro ritu seculari.

In this uncertain home,
all mankind is insane;
but all these things will in but a moment[166]
pass away with the wind.

Blear-eyed Leah is pleasing,
but beautiful Rachel weeps,
who, long remaining infertile,
because of the enormity of evil,
only as an old woman gives birth.[167]
For Rahab, but a harlot,
sunk mankind's ship;[168]
discord scattered
the seeds of death,
and the light-givers of the world
radiate a gloomy glow;
few in safety live.

Certain apostolic teachers
and the arbiters of Christendom
venerate Saint Albinus
and love Saint Rufinus,[169]
cease to execute justice for
and strive to devour
the flock commended to them.
They fall into the abyss.
If the blind leads the blind,
they fall together into the pit.[170]
Men such as these are mocked
and burned inside the camp.[171]

The bishops with their horned caps
became still and mute;
they lie in wait for booty
and wear unseemly crowns.[172]
Instead of a staff they carry a spear;
instead of a miter they wear a helm;
a shield they bear instead of a stole—
this becomes the millstone of death[173]—
a corselet instead of an alb—
this side of Opportunity is bald[174]—
a pelt in place of an amice:
all in keeping with the secular rite.

Sicut fortes incedunt
et a Deo discedunt,
ut leones feroces
et ut aquile veloces,
ut apri frendentes
exacuere dentes,
linguas ut serpentes
pugnare non valentes,
mundo consentientes
et tempus redimentes,
quia dies sunt mali,
iure imperiali.

Principes et abbates
ceterique vates,
ceteri doctores
iura deposuerunt,
canones ac decreta.
sicut scripsit propheta,
Deum exacerbaverunt
et Sanctum Israel blasphemaverunt.

Monachi sunt nigri
et in regula sunt pigri,
bene cucullati
et male coronati.
quidam sunt cani
et sensibus profani.
quidam sunt fratres
et verentur ut patres.
dicuntur Norpertini
et non Augustini.
in cano vestimento
novo gaudent invento.

XXXIXa. *Post Carnem*

In huius mundi domo
miser qui vivis homo,
quod cinis es, memento:
transibis in momento.
post carnem cinis eris
atque morte teneris.

Like warriors they stride
and depart from God.
Like ferocious lions
and like swift hawks,[175]
like gnashing boars
they whet their tusks;
tongues like serpents have they,[176]
who cannot fight at all;
they are all secularly disposed,
and they buy up time,
since evil are the days[177]
according to imperial law.[178]

The abbots and the princes
and the rest of the bishops
and the remainder of teachers
have dethroned the law,
the canons, and the decree.[179]
Just as the prophet wrote:
they have provoked God's wrath[180]
and blasphemed the Sacred One of Israel.[181]

Yonder are the black monks:[182]
indolent in following the rule are they,
well-hooded and poorly-crowned.
Other monks are dressed in white[183]
and are profane in their thoughts.
Some of them are only brothers
and yet they revere themselves as padres.
They call themselves Norbertines,
not Augustinians.
In their white habits,
they rejoice in having
invented something new.

39a. *After the Flesh*

O mankind, who as a beggar livest
in the domicile of this world,
remember that thou art ash
and shalt perish in brief time.
After the flesh, ash wilt thou be
as well as confined to death's domain.

cinis et origo.
sit tibi formido,
cum spiritus cadit
et ad Dominum vadit,
qui eum dedit.
miser, qui hoc non credit.

Vanitatum vanitas
et omnia vanitas!
est animalis homo
in huius mundi domo.
cuncta, que sub sole,
assimilantur mole,
nam omnia volvuntur,
quedam dissolvuntur,
quedam ad vitam crescunt
et omnia decrescunt.
sed spiritalis homo
Dei regnat in domo.

XXXIXb. *Ad Pedem Altaris*

Cum vadis ad altare
missam celebrare,
te debes preparare,
vetus expurgare
de corde fermentum;
sic offer sacramentum:
invoca Christum,
psalmum dicas istum:
«Iudica»
teque ipsum preiudica,
israel et Iuda
cordis mala denuda.

XL. *Plura Proverbia*

Quicquid habes meriti, preventrix gratia donat;
Nil Deus in nobis preter sua dona coronat.

Agricolis fessis   cum venerit ultima messis,
Semina dant fructum,   detergunt gaudia luctum.

Ash is also thy origin.
A terror it should be to thee,
when the pneuma stagnates
and returns to the Lord,
Who first gave it thee.
A wretch is he who this truth doth not believe.

The vanity of vanities,[184]
nothing but vanity
is the animal nature of man[185]
in the house of this world.
All things that lie under the sun[186]
are to a millwheel akin,
for all things in circles whirl about:
some things are at the stage of dissolution
whilst other things are coming to life,
but all things eventually cease to be alive.
But the spiritual man stands
sovereign in the house of God.

39b. *At the Foot of the Altar*

When thou proceedest
to the altar, to celebrate mass,
thou shouldst prepare thyself
to purge the leaven[187]
from thy heart.
Offer thou the holy mysteries thus:
invoke thou Christ
and sing thou this psalm:
"'Judge me, O Lord,'[188]
and, Israel and Judah,[189] preempt
thy judgment, and expose betimes
the obliquities of thy heart!"

40. *More Proverbs*

Whatever merit thou hast, grace in anticipation thee gives.
God crowns us with nothing except His own gifts.

When the final harvest has come for the weary farmers,[190]
the seeds yield fruit and mirth wipes away grief.[191]

Os habet immite,   qui non fert gaudia vite.

XLI. *Exitium Romae* (ca. 1171/75)
Gualterius de Castillione (ca. 1135 - ca. 1179)

Propter Sion non tacebo,
sed ruinas Rome flebo,
quousque iustitia
rursus nobis oriatur
et ut lampas accendatur
iustus in ecclesia.

Sedet vilis et in luto
princeps facta sub tributo;
quod solebam dicere:
Romam esse derelictam,
desolatam et afflictam,
expertus sum opere.

Vidi, vidi caput mundi,
instar maris et profundi
vorax guttur Siculi.
ibi mundi bithalassus,
ibi sorbet aurum Crassus
et argentum seculi.

Ibi latrat Scylla rapax
et Charybdis auri capax
potius quam navium;
ibi cursus galearum
et conflictus piratarum,
id est cardinalium.

Syrtes insunt huic profundo
et Sirenes, toti mundo
minantes naufragium.
os humanum foris patet,
in occulto cordis latet
deforme demonium.

Habes iuxta rationem
bithalassum per Franconem;
quod ne credas frivolum:

He has an inexorable face, who bears not the joy of life.

41. *The Fall of Rome* (ca. 1171/75)
by Walter of Châtillon (ca. 1135 – ca. 1179)

For Zion's sake I shall not hold my peace,[192]
but I shall weep o'er the Fall of Rome
until justice rises again for our sake,
and the righteous man
like a blazing torch
shines in the Church.[193]

Vile and in muck sits[194]
the Prince under tribute placed;[195]
what I was wont to say before—
that Rome was completely forsaken,
desolated,[196] and cast down—
I have learned from experience today.

I saw, I beheld the capital
of the world as the sea
and the Sicilian deep's voracious maw;
there are the two seas of the world,
there Crassus[197] sucks in
the gold and silver of our age.

There roar rapacious Scylla and Charybidis,[198]
who has more capacity for gold than ships;
there are the coursings
of the bootleggers' ships
and the battles of the pirates—
that is, the cardinals.

The Syrtes[199] belong to this sea
as do the Sirens[200] who menace
all the world with shipwrecks.
Outside they show a human form,
but in the chamber of their hearts
lurks an unsightly demon.

You should consider with reason's aid
the double ocean that runs through Franco,[201]
think not of it as trivial:

ibi duplex mare fervet,
a quo non est qui reservet
sibi valens obolum.

Ibi fluctus colliduntur,
ibi panni submerguntur,
byssus, ostrum, purpure;
ibi mundus deglutitur,
immo totus sepelitur
in Franconis gutture.

Franco nulli miseretur,
nullum sexum reveretur,
nulli parcit sanguini.
omnes illi dona ferunt;
illuc enim ascenderunt
tribus, tribus Domini.

Canes Scylle possunt dici
veritatis inimici,
advocati Curie,
qui latrando falsa fingunt,
mergunt simul et confringunt
carinam pecunie.

Iste probat se legistam,
ille vero decretistam,
inducens Gelasium;
ad probandum questionem
hic intendit actionem
regundorum finium.

Nunc rem sermo prosequatur:
hic Charybdis debacchatur,
id est cancellaria,
ubi nemo gratus gratis
neque datur absque datis
Gratiani gratia.

Plumbum, quod hic informatur,
super aurum dominatur
et massam argenteam;
equitatis phantasia

there boils a double sea,
from which no one can save
but one farthing for himself.

There the billows of the deep collide,
there tattered fabrics are submerged:
linen, scarlet, and purple cloths.
There the world is swallowed whole—
nay, completely entombed
in Franco's maw.

Franco has compassion for none;
he reverences neither man nor lass,
nor spares he any rank or class.
All bring gifts to this man,
for thither the tribes ascended,
the tribes of the Lord.[202]

The hounds of Scylla[203]
can be called the fiends of truth,
the counselors at the court,
who bark and fashion falsities
and simultaneously overwhelm
and shatter a money-laden boat.

This one purports to be a jurist,
but that one a decretist claims to be,
citing the authority of Gelasius;[204]
to try the subject of inquiry,
this other one invokes the action
for definition of boundaries.[205]

Now let a satire attend this affair:
Here rages in abandon Charybdis,
that is, the papal secretariat,
where no one is welcome for free
nor is the favor of Gratian
granted without gifts.

Lead, which here is given form,
reigns sovereign above
gold and silver's weight;
the phantom of equity

sedet teste Zacharia
super bullam plumbeam.

Qui sunt Syrtes vel Sirenes?
qui sermone blando lenes
attrahunt byzantium;
spem pretendunt lenitatis,
sed procella parcitatis
supinant marsupium.

Dulci cantu blandiuntur
ut Sirenes, et loquuntur
primo quedam dulcia:
«Frare, ben je te cognosco,
certe nichil a te posco,
nam tu es de Francia.

Terra vestra bene cepit
et benigne nos excepit
in portu concilii.
nostri estis, nostri! cuius?
sacrosancte sedis huius
speciales filii.

Nos peccata relaxamus
et laxatos collocamus
sedibus ethereis.
nos habemus Petri leges
ad ligandos omnes reges
in manicis ferreis.»

Ita dicunt cardinales,
ita solent di carnales
in primis allicere.
sic instillant fel draconis,
et in fine lectionis
cogunt bursam vomere.

Cardinales, ut predixi,
novo iure Crucifixi
vendunt patrimonium.
Petrus foris, intus Nero,
intus lupi, foris vero

sits above the leaden bulla[206]
with Zacharias as witness.[207]

Who are the Syrtes and the Sirens?
Those who with flattering words
gently draw in Byzantine coins of gold.[208]
They extend the hope of climatic lenity,
but with a hurricane of parsimony
they hurl the purse on its back.

With a dulcet song they wheedle
like Sirens and issue at first
some verbal sweetnesses:
"Brother, I mean you well;
be assured that I ask nothing of you,
for you come from France.

"Your country has well embraced[209]
and kindly received us
in a council's haven.[210]
You are ours, ours! Whose?
Favorite children
of this very sacred throne.

"We forgive sins
and place the absolved
in ethereal realms.[211]
We have the laws of Saint Peter
to bind fast all kings
in fetters of iron."[212]

These are the cardinals' words;
in this way the carnal gods[213]
are especially wont to entice all.
Thus they instill dragon's gall
and at the end of the lection
squeeze the purse with a plow.

The cardinals, as I have said,
sell the patrimony of Him,
Who in a new way is crucified again.
Saint Peter on the outset, Nero deep within,
they are wolves inside, but appear

sicut agni ovium.

Tales regunt Petri navem,
tales habent eius clavem,
ligandi potentiam.
hi nos docent, sed indocti,
hi nos docent, et nox nocti
indicat scientiam.

In galea sedet una
mundi lues inportuna,
camelos deglutiens.
involuta canopeo
cuncta vorat sicut leo
rapiens et rugiens.

Hic piratis principatur,
Spurius qui nuncupatur,
sedens in insidiis,
ventre grosso, lata cute,
grande monstrum nec virtute
redemptum a vitiis.

Maris huius non est dea
Thetis, mater Achillea,
de qua sepe legimus,
immo mater sterlingorum,
sancta soror loculorum,
quam nos Bursam dicimus.

Hec dum pregnat, ductor ratis
epulatur cum piratis
et amicos reperit;
nam si Bursa detumescit,
surgunt venti, mare crescit,
et carina deperit.

Tunc occurrunt cautes rati,
donec omnes sint privati
tam nummis quam vestibus.
tunc securus fit viator,
quia nudus, et cantator
it coram latronibus.

as the sheep's lambs.[214]

Men of this sort control Peter's ship;
men of this sort possess his key:
the power to bind.
These men teach us, but are untaught;
these men teach us, and night imparts
knowledge to night.[215]

In a unique robbery vessel sits
the grievous pestilence of the world,
devouring camels.[216]
Enveloped in a mosquito net,[217]
it devours all in the manner
of a rapacious, roaring lion.

This is the captain of the pirates,
Spurius by name,[218] lying in wait
with a well-padded paunch
of mammoth girth[219]—
an immane monster unransomed
from vice's clutch by virtue's helm.

Thetis, the mother of Achilles,
Thetis, about whom we often read,
is not the goddess of this sea;
nay, here rules the mother of sterling,
the sacred sister of pockets,
whom we call the Purse.

When she is pregnant,
the shipman feasts with pirates
and finds in them his friends,
but if the Purse ceases to swell,
winds surge, the lofty waves rise,
and perishes the ship.[220]

Then the ship crashes into the crags
until all have been deprived
of their money and their clothes.
Then the wayfarer becomes carefree,
because he is naked, and then sings
in the face of thieves.[221]

Qui sunt cautes? ianitores,
per quos, licet seviores
tigribus et beluis,
intrat saccus ere plenus,
pauper autem et egenus
tollitur a ianuis.

Quod si verum placet scribi,
duo tantum portus ibi,
due tantum insule,
ad quas licet applicari
et iacturam reparari
confracte navicule.

Petrus enim Papiensis,
qui electus est Meldensis,
portus recte dicitur.
nam cum mare fluctus tollit,
ipse solus mare mollit,
et ad ipsum fugitur.

Est et ibi maior portus,
fetus ager, florens ortus,
pietatis balsamum:
Alexander ille meus,
meus, inquam, cui det Deus
paradisi thalamum.

Ille fovet litteratos,
cunctos malis incurvatos,
si posset, erigeret.
verus esset cultor Dei,
nisi latus Elisei
Giezi corrumperet.

Sed ne rursus in hoc mari
me contingat naufragari,
dictis finem faciam,
quia, dum securus eo,
ne submergar, ori meo
posui custodiam.

XLII. Carmen rebelle

Who are the crags? The doorkeepers[222]
past whom—though they are more
savage than tigers and feral beasts—
the purse fraught with cash enters the Curia;
the penurious, needy man, howbeit,
is removed from the doors.

But if it pleases that the truth be written,
know that there are but two havens there,
only two islands
where one may set anchor
and repair the damage
to a broken skiff.

Namely Pietro da Pavia,[223]
the bishop-elect of Meaux,
is deservedly called a port.
For when the sea raises its waves,
he alone mollifies the thalassic unrest,
 and one then flees to him.

And yet a greater haven is there,
a fertile field, a blooming garden,
the balsam of mansuetude:
my dear Alexander,[224] yes, my dear,
I say, to whom God should vouchsafe
the bridal chamber of paradise.

He cherishes men of letters;
he would uplift, if he could, all,
who are weighted with the burden of sin.
He would be a true servant of God,
unless even here a Gehazi
should stab Elisha in the back.[225]

But lest it again fall upon my lot
to be wrecked upon this sea,
I shall bring my verse to a close,
because lest I be submerged,
whilst I row free from care,
I have set a watcher on my mouth.

42. The Rebellious Song

Gualterius de Castillione (ca. 1135 - ca. 1179)

Utar contra vitia   carmine rebelli.
mel proponunt alii,   fel supponunt melli,
pectus subest ferreum   deaurate pelli
et leonis spolium   induunt aselli.

Disputat cum animo   facies rebellis,
mel ab ore profluit,   mens est plena fellis;
non est totum melleum,   quod est instar mellis,
facies est alia   pectoris quam pellis.

Vitium in opere,   virtus est in ore,
tegunt picem animi   niveo colore,
membra dolent singula   capitis dolore
et radici consonat   ramus in sapore.

Roma mundi caput est,   sed nil capit mundum,
quod pendet a capite,   totum est immundum;
trahit enim vitium   primum in secundum,
et de fundo redolet,   quod est iuxta fundum.

Roma capit singulos   et res singulorum,
Romanorum curia   non est nisi forum.
ibi sunt venalia   iura senatorum,
et solvit contraria   copia nummorum.

In hoc consistorio   si quis causam regat
suam vel alterius,   hoc inprimis legat:
nisi det pecuniam,   Roma totum negat;
qui plus dat pecunie,   melius allegat.

Romani capitulum   habent in decretis,
ut petentes audiant   manibus repletis.
dabis, aut non dabitur,   petunt, quando petis,
qua mensura seminas,   et eadem metis.

Munus et petitio   currunt passu pari,
opereris munere,   si vis operari;
Tullium ne timeas,   si velit causari:
Nummus eloquentia   gaudet singolari.

Nummis in hac curia   non est qui non vacet;

by Walter of Châtillon (ca. 1135 – ca. 1179)

I shall wield against vice a rebellious song.
Others set forth honey, hiding beneath it gall;
an iron heart lies beneath a gilded hide;
asses' colts don the skin of lions.

The rebel's exterior contends with his soul:
honey flows from his lips, but his heart is full of gall.
It is not entirely honey, what its likeness assumes.
The heart's aspect is different from the sight of the skin.

Vicious in deeds, virtuous in words, they cover
the pitch of their souls with the color of snow.
Because of the head's sickness each of the limbs also grieves,
and the bough in flavor is consonant with the root.[226]

Rome is the head of the world, but contains nothing pure;
what hangs from this head is wholly impure,
for the first vice leads unto the second
and what sits beside the dregs reeks of them, too.

Rome collars one after the other and all each man owns.
The Curia of Rome is naught but a marketplace.
There the senators' decrees are up for sale,
and a wealth of coins decides the suits.

If anyone before this ecclesiastical council should win a suit,
either for himself or another, he would read the following first:
unless he gives money, Rome denies all;
who gives more money, more successfully suborns.

The Romans have in their decrees a paragraph that mandates
that they hearken to claimants who come with full hands.
Give, else nil be given thee;[227] they seek, whilst you sue.[228]
The measure with which you sow, you will also reap.[229]

A gift and a petition run in step; produce a gift,
if you desire to accomplish anything.
You should not fear Cicero, if he wish to plead your case:
Money delights in its unique, Tullian eloquence.

In this Curia there is not one whose mind does not for money vie.

crux placet, rotunditas   et albedo placet;
et cum totum placeat   et Romanos placet,
ubi nummus loquitur,   et lex omnis tacet.

Si quo grandi munere   bene pascas manum,
frustra quis obiceret   vel Iustinianum
vel Sanctorum canones,   quia tamquam vanum
transeunt has paleas   et imbursant granum.

Solam avaritiam   Rome nevit Parca:
parcit danti munera,   parco non est parca,
nummus est pro numine   et pro Marco marca,
et est minus celebris   ara quam sit arca.

Cum ad papam veneris,   habe pro constanti:
non est locus pauperi,   soli favet danti,
vel si munus prestitum   non sit aliquanti,
respondet: «hec tibia   non est michi tanti.»

Papa, si rem tangimus,   nomen habet a re:
quicquid habent alii,   solus vult papare,
vel si verbum gallicum   vis apocopare,
«paies! paies!»   dist li mot, si vis impetrare.

Porta querit, chartula   querit, bulla querit,
papa querit, etiam   cardinalis querit,
omnes querunt, et si des -   si quid uni deerit,
totum mare salsum est,   tota causa perit.

Das istis, das aliis,   addis dona datis,
et cum satis dederis,   querunt ultra satis;
o vos burse turgide,   Romam veniatis:
Rome viget physica   bursis constipatis.

Predantur marsupium   singuli paulatim,
magna, maior, maxima   preda fit gradatim.
quid irem per singula?   colligam summatim:
omnes bursam strangulant,   et exspirat statim.

Bursa tamen Tityi   iecur imitatur:
fugit res, ut redeat,   perit, ut nascatur.
et hoc pacto loculum   Roma depredatur,
ut, cum totum dederit,   totus impleatur.

Pleasing is the cross, the rotunda, and its marble whiteness.
And since it so greatly pleases, the Romans are pleased
wheresoever money has say and all the law stands silent.

If with some lavish gift you feed a hand well,
in vain does another invoke Justinian[230]
or the canons of the Saints, because as trifles
the judges ignore this chaff and sack the grain.[231]

The Parca[232] in Rome is acquainted only with greed;
she spares the giver of gifts, but is not sparing of the poor.
Money is as godhood, the mark[233] is as Saint Mark,[234]
and the altar is less honored than the Almighty coffer.

When you come to the Pope, hold the following as a constant:
a pauper has no place there; he favors only those who give.
And when a gift of considerable value is not displayed,
His Eminence says, "This shawm is of little value to me."[235]

The Pope, if we examine his substance, secures his name
from his function: whatever others possess, he alone wishes
to consume, or you wish to apocopate a word of the Gauls:
"Paies! Paies!"[236] he says, if you wish to obtain by request.

The door seeks to gain, as do the document and the papal bull.
The Pope and even the cardinals—all there—seek to gain,
and if you should give, if but one thing is wanting,
the entire sea is oversalted, and the whole case is lost.

You give to these, you give to others, and you add gifts to those given;
and when you have given enough, they look beyond sufficiency.
O swelling purses, come ye to Rome:
natural philosophy thrives here when purses are in crowds.

Little by little they plunder each man's purse;
great, greater, greatest, the loot gradually becomes.
Why do I recount each one? I shall draw them all in sum:
All throttle the purse, and at once it gives up the ghost.

Nevertheless the purse in death copies after Tityos' liver:[237]
Its substance vanishes, only to return; it dies only to be reborn.
In this way Roma plunders the coffer so that, when it has given
all that it holds, the casket may again be completely filled.

Redeunt a curia   capite cornuto;
ima tenet Iupiter,   celum habet Pluto,
et accedit dignitas   animali bruto
tamquam gemma stercori   vel pictura luto.

Divites divitibus   dant, ut sumant ibi,
et occurrunt munera   relative sibi.
lex est ista celebris,   quam fecerunt scribi:
«Si tu michi dederis,   ego dabo tibi.»

XLIII. *Roma Languens* (ca. 1160 ?)

Roma, tue mentis oblita sanitate
desipis, cum resipis cordis tarditate.
lampas caret oleo, male sed mercatur,
sponsus ut cum venerit, salus obumbratur,
pietas nec audit superne civitatis,
foris dum inclamitat vox calamitatis.

O sedes apostolica,
que vix latet, katholica,
convertere! convertere!
iam mundus languet opere.

Perit lex,manet fex, bibit grex
virus hoc letale;
pastor cedit, lupus redit, morsu ledit
permale.

Claudicat ecclesia patribus orbata,
sternitur iustitia capite truncata.
princeps tenebrarum se sentit gloriari
orbis fluxa, miseri student quem sectari.

Ludit ad interitum rerum coniectura
quodam vili scemate, docet ut natura.
basem rei publice, sortem senatorum
machina corrodit presentium malorum,
de qua, † sed diviguit, stirpe solidatur,
cuius et propagine solium letatur.

O decus exaltabile,
saluti collaudabile

They return from the curia with horns on their heads.[238]
Jupiter rules the underworld; Pluto holds the sky. [239]
Rank and dignity befall an irrational beast,
as a jewel comes to dung and a painting to muck.

Rich give unto rich, that they may lay hold of something there;
the gifts avail themselves and thus one another.
That is the celebrated law, which they caused to be written thus:
"if you give unto me, I will give unto thee."

43. *Languishing Rome* (ca. 1160 ?)

O Rome, since you have lost a healthy mind and savor
of a foolish heart, like a dolt you are deporting yourself.
The lamp has no oil and oil's purchase is impossible,
and when the groom comes, your salvation will be eclipsed;
and the good Lord of the city on high will hear it not,
when outside the voice of the hapless cries aloud for aid.

O apostolic seat, which,
being universal, cannot be concealed,
convert, convert!
Already is the world tired of good works.[240]

The law vanishes, the dregs remain,
and the flock drinks this deadly poison.[241]
The shepherd withdraws,[242] the wolf returns; [243]
its bite causes very bad wounds.

The Church is lame, deprived of its fathers.
Justice, decapitated, is thrown to the ground.
The prince of darkness[244] feels his renown waxing
as the world decays, and caitiffs are eager to follow him.

The machine of the world frolics towards destruction
by way of a certain vile pattern, as nature instructs.
The foundation of the state, the status of the princes,[245]
the machine of present ills gnaws to bits and pieces.
But if the state solidifies itself again in the root from which
it drew its might, its throne too will rejoice in its new sprays.

O praiseworthy adornment,
commendable for its salvation,[246]

complectere! complectere!
iam languet mundus opere.

Sed cum sis plena vis, cedat lis,
vitia premantur,
orbe leto, tristi spreto iure freto
pellantur!

Aruit spes estuans diuturnitate,
secula iam pereunt imbecillitate,
ordo principatus est mente discrepata
volvitur † in serie mundo non piata.
falso quoque veritas convincitur augurio,
nec altus est in Israel fidem dans centurio.

XLIV. *Evangelium secundum Marcas*

Initium sancti evangelii secundum marcas argenti:
In illo tempore: dixit papa Romanis: «Cum venerit filius hominis ad sedem
maiestatis nostre, primum dicite: ‹Amice, ad quid venisti?› At ille si
perseveraverit pulsans nil dans vobis, eicite eum in tenebras exteriores.»
Factum est autem, ut quidam pauper clericus veniret ad curiam domini
pape, et exclamavit dicens: «Miseremini mei saltem vos, hostiarii pape,
quia manus paupertatis tetigit me. Ego vero egenus et pauper sum, ideo
peto, ut subveniatis calamitati et miserie mee.» Illi autem audientes
indignati sunt valde et dixerunt: «Amice, paupertas tua tecum sit in
perditione. Vade retro, satanas, quia non sapis ea, que sapiunt nummi.
Amen, amen, dico tibi: non intrabis in gaudium domini tui, donec dederis
novissimum quadrantem.» Pauper vero abiit et vendidit pallium et tunicam
et universa que habuit et dedit cardinalibus et hostiariis et camerariis. At
illi dixerunt: «Et hoc quid est inter tantos?» Et eiecerunt eum ante fores, et
egressus foras flevit amare et non habens consolationem. Postea venit ad
curiam quidam clericus dives, incrassatus, impinguatus, dilatatus, qui
propter seditionem fecerat homicidium. Hic primo dedit hostiario, secundo
camerario, tertio cardinalibus. At illi arbitrati sunt inter eos, quod essent
plus accepturi. Audiens autem dominus papa cardinales et ministros
plurima dona a clerico accepisse, infirmatus est usque ad mortem. Dives
vero misit sibi electuarium aureum et argenteum, et statim sanatus est.
Tunc dominus papa ad se vocavit cardinales et ministros et dixit eis:
«Fratres, videte, ne aliquis vos seducat inanibus verbis. Exemplum enim do
vobis, ut, quemadmodum ego capio, ita et vos capiatis.»

embrace, embrace! Already
is the world tired of good works.

But since you are full of puissance,
let the lawsuit settle itself, let all vices be crushed,
let them be banished from the face of the earth, which rejoices now
in the rejection of sorrows and in the law in which it can trust!

Fervid hope has thirsted for far too long;
anemic and feeble, the ages now draw to a close.
The order of princes is of discordant minds;
it rolls in a line made pure without lustration of any kind.
The truth is quelled by a mendacious prophecy,
and no captain who avows his faith was raised in Israel.[247]

44. *The Gospel According to Marks*

The beginning of the Holy Gospel according to Marks of Silver:
In that time the Pope to the Romans said: "When the son of man cometh
to the seat of our majesty, say ye first to him: 'Friend, why hast thou
come?' But if he continueth to knock and give naught to ye, eject him into
the outdoor gloom." And it so happened that a poor cleric came to the
Curia of the lord Pope and exclaimed: "At least take ye pity on me,
ostiaries of the Pope, because the hand of poverty hath touched me. I am
but needy and indigent, and so I ask that ye come to my aid in my calamity
and wretched state." But as they listened, they grew indignant and said:
"Friend, let thy poverty be with thee in perdition. Go hence, Satan, for thou
thinkest not on what money doth. Amen, amen, I say to thee—thou shalt
not come into the joy of thy lord, until thou renderest thy very last mite."
So he left, sold his cloak and tunic and all he owned, and gave his earnings
to the cardinals, ostiaries, and chamberlains. But they said to him: "What
is this thing among such great men?" And they threw him to the front of
the doors. He went out, wept bitterly, and had no consolation. Afterwards
to the Curia came a rich cleric—fattened with income, plumped up by a
sinecure, enlarged by his holdings—who in a riot had committed homicide.
He gave first to the ostiary, then to the chamberlain, and then to the
cardinals. But they thought among themselves they would receive more.
But when the lord Pope heard that the cardinals and attendants had
received a hoard of gifts from the cleric, he became deathly ill. But the rich
cleric gave him an electuary of gold and silver, and forthwith he was cured.
Then the lord Pope called the cardinals and ministers before his eminence
and said: "See to it, brothers, that no one seduces ye with empty words. A
model I offer ye, so that, as I grab, you will also seize."[248]

XLV. *Mos Vetus* (ca. 1180)

Roma, tenens morem   nondum satiata priorem
Donas donanti,   parcis tibi participanti;
Sed miser immunis   censetur, eum quia punis.
«Accipe» «sume» «cape»   tria sunt gratissima pape;
«Nil do» «nil presto»   nequeunt succurrere mesto.
Non est Romanis   cure legatus inanis.
Si dederis marcas   et eis impleveris arcas,
Pena solveris,   quacumque ligatus haberis.
Ergo non nosco,   quamvis cognoscere posco,
In quo papalis   res distet et imperialis:
Rex capit argentum,   marcarum milia centum;
Et facit illud idem   paparum curia pridem.
Rex capit audenter,   sed domnus papa latenter.
Ergo pari pena   rapientes sic aliena
Condemnabuntur,   quia Simonis acta secuntur.

Curia Romana   non curat ovem sine lana.

Roma manus rodit,   quos rodere non valet, odit.

De cruce signatis

XLVI. *Ad Victoriam!* (ante 1149)

Fides cum Ydolatria
pugnavit, teste gratia,
agresti vultu turbida,
mundi non querit tegmina,
sed forti fidens pectore,
dives una cum paupere.

Propheta teste misera
tu Babylonis filia,
beatus est, qui parvulos
petre collidit tuos.
prisci das penas sceleris
Chaldea nunc metropolis.

Iohannes super bestiam
sedere vidit feminam
ornatam, ut est meretrix,

45. *The Old Way* (ca. 1180)

Rome, not yet sated, thou maintainest thy old way:
thou givest back unto thy giver and sparest him, who shareth with thee.
But the giftless beggar is damned, since thou punishest him.[249]
"Receive" "take" "seize" are the Pope's three favorite words.
"I give naught" "I present nil"—such words cannot help a dejected soul.
An empty-handed envoy is of no concern to the Romans.
If thou givest mark after mark and fillest their safes,
thou wilt be loosed from the debt that binds thee.
Therefore I know not, although I desire to know,
wherein the distinction between pope's and emperor's rule lies:
the king seizes silver—one hundred thousand marks!
He seizes it exactly as the Curia of Popes has long done.
The king boldly plunders; the lord Pope stealthily purloins.
Thus, they in pillaging what is not theirs shall be condemned
to the same agony, for they emulate Simon's deeds.

The Curia in Rome cares not for a flock without wool.

Rome gnaws at hands; it hates those men it cannot consume.

On the Crusaders

46. *To Victory!* (before 1149)

Faith fought with idolatry,
whilst grace witnessed all;
with fierce, stormy aspect,
it seeks not the armor of the world,
but trusts in its intrepid heart[250]—
a single, rich warrior against an indigent foe.

According to the prophet's testimony,
wretched daughter of Babylon,
blessed be he who smites
thy young kith on the rock.[251]
For thy earlier crimes payest thou now,
Chaldean Metropolis, the penalty.[252]

John saw sitting
atop the beast
a woman dressed as a whore,

in forma Babylonis.
sed tempus adest calicis
ad feces usque sceleris.

Princeps vocatur principum,
qui colla premit gentium,
costam scandat tetragoni
sedentis ut eterni,
sub Herculis memoria
vexilla ponens rosea.

Navis in artemonem
quem Deus ponet hominem,
velum triangulatum
cuius regat pulcherrimum?
hoc militum tripudio
letetur Pacis Visio!

Confusionis civitas
decepit te, Gentilitas,
inniteris harundini
cladem lature manui;
revertere, revertere,
factoris opus respice!

Qui colunt cacodemones,
non fiunt illis similes,
qui fibris non utuntur,
dum illis insculpuntur,
nec vox inest nec ratio
nec locus in arbitrio?

Beati sunt mucrones,
quos portant Christi milites
suffulti crucis tegmine,
sub cuius gaudent robore,
quorum felix atrocitas
constringit te, Gentilitas.

De viis atque sepibus
et mundi voluptatibus
compellimur intrare,
nunc nuper epulare

who personified Babylon.[253]
But the time is now at hand to empty
the chalice of sin all the way to the dregs.[254]

The prince of princes he is called,
who breaks the infidels' necks;[255]
he will land on the coast of the tetragon,
which sits enthroned in a seemingly eternal reign,[256]
and plant on the monument
of Hercules[257] rose-red banners.

Will God position this man
as the headsail of His ship,
to captain His most beautiful
three-cornered sail?[258]
The Vision of Peace[259] rejoices
in the jubilation of the riders!

The City of Bedlam[260]
has bewitched thee, O Heathendom:
thou art buttressing thyself on a reed
that will bring harm unto thy hand.[261]
Turn back, turn back!
Consider the Creator's work![262]

Do they who worship cacodemons
not become similar unto those
who cannot use their sinews,
although they by sinews were cut,
and have neither a voice, nor reason,
nor choice over where they stand?[263]

Blessed are the falchions[264]
wielded by the riders of Christ,
sustained by the cross' shield,
beneath whose strength they rejoice.
Their happy harshness forces
thee down, O Heathendom!

From the highways and hedges
and away from the pleasures of the world
we are compelled to enter.
Now, now feast ye,

gustu sepe medullitus;
quam suavis sit Dominus.

Nam panis filiorum
fit cibus catulorum
sub mensa pii Domini
de verbis evangelii;
gaude, Syrophenissa!
iam venit tua filia.

Forum est Ierosolymis
in campo libertatis,
quod Rex regum instituit.
mercator prudens aderit;
qui vitam velit emere,
festinet illuc currere!

Non tamen ita properet,
quin coniugi provideat
de rebus necessariis
una cum parvis liberis;
quod quidem nisi faciat,
ignoro quid proficiat.

Sepulcrum gloriosum
prophetis declaratum
impugnatur a canibus,
quibus sanctum non dabimus,
nec porcis margarite
mittuntur deridende.

Ad multas mansiones
in domo patris stabiles
nummi trahit conventio;
nec gravet operatio:
pondus diei preterit,
merces perennis aderit.

Novissimus fit primus
et primus fit novissimus;
dispar quidem vocatio,
sed par remuneratio,
dum cunctis laborantibus

and always savor in your heart
how sweet the Lord is![265]

For the bread of the children
is becoming the kibbles of whelps
beneath the table of the good Lord,
according to the gospel's words.
Rejoice, O Syrophenician dame!
Thy daughter now comes![266]

The forum in Jerusalem
is situated in liberty's field,
a forum established by the King of kings.
A clever merchant will be there;
he, who would like to purchase life,
should thither run in haste![267]

He still should not hasten so,
but first make provision for
his wife and little children's
daily bread and drink.
Surely if he defaults on this,
I know not then what he gains.

The tomb declared
glorious by the prophets[268]
is assailed by dogs,
to whom we shall give nothing sacred;
nor will pearls be cast before swine,
so that they may them deride.[269]

Unto many everlasting mansions
in the home of the Father[270]
leads the agreement on pay,[271]
nor does the labor incommode:
the fardel of the day passes away,
and an eternal reward stands by.

Last becomes first,
and first becomes last.
Disparate surely is the hour
of the call, but equal is the pay,
since the denarius of eternal life

vite datur denarius.

Non hic mutatur sedes,
non corrumpuntur edes,
non maior hic minori,
non pauper ditiori,
non obstat alter alteri,
nec locus est opprobrii.

XLVII. *Crucifixio Secunda* (ca. 1187/89)

Crucifigat omnes
Domini crux altera,
nova Christi vulnera!
arbor salutifera
perditur; sepulcrum
gens evertit extera
violente;   plena gente
sola sedet civitas;
agni fedus   rapit hedus;
plorat dotes perditas
sponsa Sion; immolatur
Ananias; incurvatur
cornu David; flagellatur
mundus;
ab iniustis abdicatur,
per quem iuste iudicatur
mundus.

O quam dignos luctus!
exulat rex omnium,
baculus fidelium
sustinet opprobrium
gentis infidelis;
cedit parti gentium
pars totalis;   iam regalis
in luto et latere
elaborat   tellus, plorat
Moysen fatiscere.
homo, Dei miserere!
fili, patris ius tuere!
in incerto certum quere,
ducis

is given to all who toil away.

Here one's dwelling is not changed,
here the homes are not razed,
here the greater man assails not the lesser,
nor does the pauper the wealthy man attack;
in sum, no man opposes the other,
and here opprobrium hath no place.[272]

47. *The Second Crucifixion* (ca. 1187/89)

Let the second cross of the Lord,[273]
the fresh, new wounds of Christ,
inflict upon all the agony He endured![274]
The healing tree is lost;[275]
with raw violence a foreign race
devastates the tomb;
the once populous city now sits alone;[276]
a ram breaks the covenant of the lamb;[277]
Zion the bride weeps
over the wedding gifts lost;[278]
Ananias is slain;[279]
David's horn is bowed;[280]
the sinless are lashed;
denounced by the wicked
is He, by Whom
the world
will rightly be judged.

O how seemly are our sorrows!
The King of all men lives in exile
amongst strange men;
the staff of the faithful[281] sustains
the ignominy of the infidels.
The side of universal right[282]
gives way to heathendom.
Now the land of kings[283] labors
in mud and brick[284] and weeps
as it marks that Moses is sick.[285]
O mankind, have pity for God!
O son, defend thy sire's law![286]
Seek thou something certain
in uncertain times:

ducum dona promerere
et lucrare lucem vere
lucis!

Quisquis es signatus
fidei charactere,
fidem factis assere,
rugientes contere
catulos leonum,
miserans intuere
corde tristi   damnum Christi!
longus Cedar incola,
surge, vide,   ne de fide
reproberis frivola!
suda martyr in agone
spe mercedis et corone!
derelicta Babylone
pugna
pro celesti regione,
aqua vite! te compone
pugna!

XLVIIa. *Mores Humani*

Curritur ad vocem
nummi vel ad sonitum;
hec est vox ad placitum.
omnes ultra debitum,
ut exempla docent,
nitimur in vetitum.
disce morem   et errorem,
fac et tu similiter!
hac in vita   nichil vita,
vive sic, non aliter!
cleri vivas ad mensuram,
qui pro censu dat censuram.
quando iacis in capturam
rete,
messem vides iam maturam;
et tu saltem per usuram
mete!

Si quis in hoc artem

earning the guerdon
of the campaign Leader of leaders,
and winning the Light of true light![287]

Whoever hath been stamped
with the mark of faith,[288]
assert thy fealty through thy works,
crush the roaring
offspring of lions,[289]
and look with compassion
and a heavy heart at Christ's distress!
Longtime inhabitant of Cedar,[290]
rise, observe, lest thou
be condemned for frivolous faith!
Strive thou, martyr, in combat
in anticipation of the reward and crown.
Abandon thou Babylon[291]
and fight for the celestial realm,
the water of life![292]
Gear up for war
and enter the fight!

47a. *Human Ways*

One runneth to the call
of money or to its din;
for it is the voice that pleaseth.
We all strive beyond our duty,
as the popular models teach,
for things that are forbidden.[293]
Learn their custom and folly,
and follow a similar vein![294]
Shun nothing in this life—
live thus, not otherwise!
Live by the principle of the cleric,
who metes out a judgment that fits
the size of the bribe.
When thou castest thy net for a haul,[295]
thou seest that already the harvest is ripe;[296]
reap thou too at least
through usury's employ!

If anyone in this host

populo non noverit,
per quam mundus vixerit,
omnia cum viderit,
eligat hanc partem
aut nichil decreverit:
quod vis, aude   dolo, fraude,
mos gerendus Thaidi.
mundo gere   morem, vere
nil vitandum credidi.
legi nichil sit astrictum,
iuri nichil sit addictum!
sanciatur hoc edictum
tibi.
ubi virtus est delietum,
Deo nichil est relictum
ibi.

XLVIII. *Ortus Dei*

Quod spiritu   David precinuit,
nunc exposuit
nobis Deus,   et sic innotuit.
Sarracenus   sepulcrum polluit,
quo recubuit,
qui pro nobis   crucifixus fuit.
quantum nobis   in hoc condoluit,
quantum nobis   propitius fuit,
dum sic voluit
mortem pati   cruce, nec meruit!

Refl.   Exsurgat Deus!

Et dissipet   hostes, quos habuit,
postquam prebuit
Sarracenis   locum, quo iacuit,
quia nobis   propitius fuit,
dum sic voluit
mortem pati   cruce, nec meruit!
duo ligna   diu non habuit
Sarreptina,   quibus ut caruit,
semper doluit
et dolebit,   dum rehabuerit.

knoweth not the art,[297]
for which all mankind hath lived,[298]
he should, when he hath seen all this,
choose this portion,[299] else
he hath nothing discerned.
Dare what thou wilt with tricks and fraud,
and let Thais[300] have her way;.
Comply with the ways of the world.
Nothing is to be avoided—
truly is this my credo of life.
Let nothing be obliged to the law;
let nothing be to justice devoted!
Let this edict be dedicated
unto thee.
Where virtue is a crime,
there is nothing left to God.

48. *The Rise of God*

What David in the Holy Spirit
prophesied in song,[301]
now God has shown to us,
and it has thus become known:
The Saracen[302] defiled the tomb, wherein He lay,
Who for us had been nailed to the cross.
How greatly did He suffer for us!
How gracious was He unto us,
when He willed to suffer thus a death
on the cross, which He did not earn!

Refr.   May God rise![303]

And may He dispel[303] the fiends, whom He gained,
after He ceded to the Saracens the site, where He lay,
for He was gracious unto us, when He willed
to suffer thus death on the cross,
which He did not deserve!
Not long did the widow of Zarephath[304]
possess two logs; when she lost them,
she was happy no more,
and she will grieve until
she has them again in her charge.

Refl.   Exsurgat Deus!

Sunamitis   clamat pro filio,
qui occubuit,
nec Giezi   sanare potuit;
Heliseus   nisi met venerit,
non surrexerit,
et os ori   recte coniunxerit.
Heliseus   nisi nunc venerit,
ni peccata   compassus tulerit,
non habuerit
ecclesia   crucem, qua caruit.

Refl.   Exsurgat Deus!

Et adiuvet   in hoc exercitu
quos signaverit
signo crucis,   qua nos redemerit!
iam venie   tempus advenerit,
quo potuerit
se salvare,   qui crucem ceperit.
nunc videat   quisque, quid fecerit,
quibus et quot   Deum offenderit!
quod si viderit
et se signet,   his solutus erit.

Refl.   Exsurgat Deus!

Exsurrexit!   et nos assurgere
ei propere
iam tenemur   atque succurrere.
Ierusalem   voluit perdere,
ut hoc opere
sic possemus   culpas diluere.
nam si vellet,   hostes destruere
absque nobis   et terram solvere
posset propere,
cum sibi nil   possit resistere.

Refl.   Exsurgat Deus!

XLVIIIa. *Miles Diei* (ca. 1170)
Otto von Botenlauben (*Kraus Lieder Dichter* 41.13)

Refr.   May God rise!

The Shunammite woman[305]
shouts for her fallen son,
whom Gehazi[306] could not heal.
Unless Elisha comes
and presses his mouth to his,
the child will not rise.
If Elisha comes not now,
if he does not in compassion
take away our sins, the Church will not have
the cross, which it has long been without.[307]

Refr.   May God rise!

And may He succor in this affliction
those whom He has stamped with the seal
of the cross, whereon He redeemed us!
Now the time of mercy has come,
when he can save himself,
who has wrongly taken the cross.
Now let each one see, what he has done,
by what kind of and how many transgressions
he has offended God! But if he sees them
and signs himself, he will be absolved of all.

Refr.   May God rise!

He has risen! Now we
are bound to raise ourselves
and in haste rush to His aid!
He willed intently Jerusalem's loss
so that through this meritorious deed
we could thus wash our sins away.
For if He willed, He could dispatch
the fiend forthwith and free His holy land
without our aid, since nothing
can His might withstand.[308]

Refr.   May God rise!

48a. *The Knight of Day* (ca. 1170)
by Otto von Botenlauben (*The Kraus Songwriters* 41.13)

Horstu, uriunt, den wahter an der cinne,
wes sin sanch ueriach?
wir mûzen uns schaiden nu, lieber man.
also schiet din lip nu jungest hinnen,
do der tach ûf brach
unde uns diu naht so fluhtechlichen tran.
naht git senfte, we tût tach.
Owe, herce lieb, in mach
din nu uerbergen niht.
uns nimit diu freude gar daz grawe lieht.
stand ûf, riter!

XLIX. *Templum Christi* (ca. 1170)

Tonat evangelica   clara vox in mundo:
«qui dormis in pulvere,   surge de profondo
luce sua Dominus   te illuminabit
et a malis omnibus   animam salvabit.

Memor esto, iuvenis,   tui creatoris.
crux Christi te moneat   omnibus in horis.
cape mente, cogita   corde de futuris,
quod ad radicem arboris   sit posita securis.

Senes et decrepiti,   vobis est oblata
vera penitentia   cruce Christi data.
dies vestra desiit   et est inclinata,
nam ad umbram vergitur   fine desperata.

Ecce cum fiducia   venit regnum Dei.
illud primum querite   vos, qui estis rei.
carnem crucifigite   famulantes ei
et in psalmis dicite: ‹miserere mei!›

O peccatrix anima,   si vis dealbari
et ab omni crimine   penitus mundari,
te in cruce Domini   oportet gloriari
et in ipso penitus   ab hoste liberari.

Iacob scale summitas   altera calcatur,
in qua Christi passio   nobis reseratur.
Tyrus alta desinit,   in se reprobatur;
in Iudea Domini   mons uber adoratur.

Hearest thou, O gallant, the sentry on the battlement?
Hearest thou, what his song proclaimed?
We must now sunder, beloved man,
just as thou only recently didst hence depart,
when the day broke and the night
like a fugitive hastened away from us.
Night offers weal; day renders woe.
Alas, my dearest, I can now
no longer thee veil.
The gloaming robs us of our joy.
O my rider, now arise!

49. *The Temple of Christ* (ca. 1170)

The clear voice of the Gospel thunders in the world:
"Thou who sleepest in dust, rise from the deep!
The Lord shall illuminate thee with his light[309]
and shall save thy soul from all iniquities.

"Be mindful, O youth, of thy Creator.[310]
May the cross of Christ remind thee in all hours.
Capture in thy mind, think in thy heart about what is to come,
that the ax hath been set at the tree's root.[311]

"Enfeebled old men, true penitence hath been
offered also to ye, offered in the cross of Christ.
Your day is ended and has declined, for it turns
to the shadow without hope of arresting its demise.

"Behold the kingdom of God with assurance is come.
Seek that first, ye, who are burdened with guilt.
Crucify your flesh, ye, who are varlets thereto,[312]
and sing with the psalmists 'Have mercy on me!'

"O sinful soul, if thou wishest to be whitewashed
and purged fully of all thy crimes,
thou must glory thyself in the cross of the Lord
and in it be liberated utterly from the fiend.

"Scaled is the highest rung of the other Jacob's ladder,[313]
through which the passion of the Christ is unclosed to us.
Proud Tyre meets its end, condemned by its own guilt,[314]
whilst, in Judea, the rich mount of the Lord is adored.

O fidelis anima,   clama de profundis,
de terrenis fugito   rebus et immundis.
cruce Christi naviga   velis in secundis,
ne te ventus turbinis   suffocet in undis.

Cum per ignem venerit   nos iudicaturus
homo Dei filius,   nulli parcens, durus,
eius omnis crucifer   erit tunc securus,
gratulans cum angelis,   candidus et purus.

In die iudicii   cum sol obscuratur
et lumen fidelibus   crucis Christi datur,
tunc in peccatoribus   hostis dominatur;
sed ab hoste crucifer   tunc omnis liberatur.

Ergo Christi milites   fugite beati
huius mundi gloriam   cruce iam signati,
in qua Christus moriens   mortem superavit
atque suo sanguine   peccata nostra lavit.

Quid erit, cum stabimus   ante tribunal Christi?
pandens sua vulnera dicet: ‹;quid fecisti?
pro te crucem subii;   quare non subisti
hanc loco penitentie?   vade, iam peristi!›

Ergo fetens Lazarus   ducatur in exemplum
digne penitentibus,   ut sint eius templum,
in quo virtus habitat   sue passionis;
hanc impleat et muniat   ipse suis donis!»

L. *Calamitas Gravis* (1188)

Heu, voce flebili   cogor enarrare
facinus, quod accidit   nuper ultra mare,
quando Saladino con-   cessum est vastare
terram, quam dignatus est   Christus sic amare.

Exeunte Iunio   anno post milleno
centum et octoginta   iunctis cum septeno,
quo respexit Dominus   mundum sorde pleno
erigens de pulvere,   pauperem a ceno,

Malus comes Tripolis,   mentem ferens ream,

"O faithful spirit, shout from the depths;[315]
flee from terrestrial and impure affaires!
Navigate on Christ's cross with propitious sails,
lest a gale suffocates thee on the waves.

"When in fire our Judge cometh, the Man
and Son of God—sparing none, stolid—
then will every man, who weareth the cross of Christ,
be secure, with angels rejoice, candid and pure.

"On the day of judgment, when the sun is darkened[316]
and the light of Christ's cross is given unto the faithful,
then the fiend rules over sinners, but every cross-bearer
then is freed from his grasp.

"Therefore, blessed riders of Christ, eschew
the glory of this world, since you already are signed
with the cross, on which the dying Christ overcame death
and with his blood washed away our sins.[317]

"What shall be, when we stand before the tribunal of Christ?
Baring His wounds, He will say, 'What hast thou achieved?
For thee I shouldered the cross; why didst thou not use
this cross as penitence? Begone! Now thou art doomed!'

"Therefore by all who wish to do their penance rightly,
mephitic Lazarus should be followed as a model[318]
that they be His temple, in which the power of His sufferance dwells.[319]
Let Him fill and fortify it with His gifts of grace!"

50. *A Misfortune Grave* (1188)

Alas, with tearful voice I am compelled to relate a crime,
which occurred recently on the far side of the sea,
when Saladin[320] was allowed to desolate the land,
which Christ deemed so very worthy of His love.

At the end of June, one thousand one hundred
eighty-seven years after that year, in which the Lord
beheld the world steeped in squalor
and raised the pauper from dust and ordure,

The wicked count[322] of Tripoli, harboring

magna cum tyrannide   tenens Tabariam,
Turcos suis fraudibus   ducit in Iudeam
atque primum occupat   totam Galileam.

Saladinus convocat   barbaros per gyrum,
habitantes Phrygiam,   Pontum usque Tyrum,
Agarenos populos,   Arabem et Syrum,
ab Egypti finibus   usque in Epirum.

Veniunt Hircomili,   et Trogodite,
Mauri atque Getuli,   Barbari et Scythe,
filii Moab, Amon   et Ismahelite,
atque cum his omnibus   sunt Amalechite.

Turcos ac Massagetas   precipit adesse,
Bactri atque Sarmates   nolunt hinc abesse,
currunt Quadi, Vandili,   Medi atque Perse,
undique conveniunt   gentes sic diverse.

Terram intrant inclitam,   cuncta devastantes,
capiunt Christicolas,   senes et infantes,
et ut fere pessime   sanguinem amantes
iugulant puerulos,   dividunt pregnantes.

Saladino igitur   terram sic ingresso
rex atque Templarii   currunt ex adverso,
totis obstant nisibus   barbaro perverso,
cupientes populo   subvenire presso.

Turchi pugnant acriter   iacula mittentes,
Christianos vulnerant,   cedunt resistentes,
et ut male bestie   dentibus frementes
territant sonipedes   tubis perstrepentes.

Nostri se dum sentiunt   ita pregravatos
et a malis gentibus   undique vallatos,
stringunt suis manibus   enses deauratos
atque truncant fortiter   barbaros armatos.

Plus quam decem milia   erant Christiani,
sed pro uno quolibet   ter centum pagani;
sic pugnando comminus   Bactri et Hircani,
vix ex nostris aliqui   evaserunt sani.

a criminal mind and ruling Tiberias with great tyranny,
leads into Judea the Turks[323] by his own deceit,
and occupies first all of Galilee.

Saladin summons to assembly the barbarians, who inhabit Phrygia,
the coast of the Black Sea and all the way down to Tyre,
the people descended from Hagar,[324] the Arabs and Syrians,
from the bounds of Egypt all the way unto Epirus.

Coming are the Hircomili[325] and the Troglodytes,
the Moors and the Gaetulians, the Barbarians and the Scythians,
the sons of Moab, Ammon, and the Ishmaelites,
and with all these the Amalekites.

He bids the Turks and Massageteans be present,
the Bactrians and Sarmatians are unwilling to be hence,
the Quadi, the Vandals, the Medes, and the Persians hie hither—
from all sides heathens so diverse swarm into one.

They enter an illustrious land and devastate all;
they capture Christians, old and young,
and like wild, sanguine beasts they strangle
little children and split open pregnant wombs.[326]

Therefore, since Saladin hath entered thus, the king[327]
and the Templar Knights[328] rush against him and oppose amain
the perverse barbarian through their desire to come
to the succor of the oppressed people.

The Turks fight fiercely, wound Christians
with their arrow shots, slay all who put up a resistance,
and, like wild beasts that gnash their teeth,[329] terrify
the horses with their trumpets' blare.

Our men see that they are thus hard pressed
and surrounded on all sides by wicked pagans;
they draw with their hands their gilt swords
and heroically maim the armed barbarians.

There were more than ten thousand Christians,
but three hundred pagans for each one; when they fought
hand-to-hand with the Bactrians and Hyrcanians,
scarcely did any of ours escape unscathed.

Rex cum cruce capitur,   alii truncantur,
Templarii ter centum   capti decollantur,
quorum nulla corpora   sepulture dantur,
sed a Christo anime   celo coronantur.

Nostre postquam acies   ita sunt confracte,
currunt crudelissime   gentes illa parte,
urbem Acrim capiunt   absque ullo Marte
atque omnes alias   manu, simul arte.

Surim solam liberat   nautica marinus,
marchio clarissimus,   vere palatinus,
cuius vires approbat   Grecus et Latinus,
timet quoque plurimum   ferox Saladinus,

Latro ille pessimus,   terre devastator,
per quam suis pedibus   transiit Salvator,
natus qui ex virgine   omnium creator
in presepi ponitur   celi fabricator.

Inde siccis pedibus   maria calcavit
et ex quinque panibus   multos satiavit,
quem Iohannes predicans   digito monstravit,
et Iordanus sentiens   post retrogradavit.

Cruci demum fixus est   Deus homo natus,
aquam atque sanguinem   sparsit eius latus,
quo ac tali pretio   mundus est salvatus,
qui per primum hominem   fuerat damnatus.

Heu, terra inclita,   terra vere bona,
sola digna perfrui   florida corona,
terra, cui dederat   Deus tanta dona,
heu, quantum impia te   nunc cingit zona!

Heu, heu, Domine,   gloria iustorum,
angelorum bonitas,   salus peccatorum:
ecce canes comedunt   panes filiorum,
velut aqua funditur   sanguis nunc sanctorum.

Flete, omnes populi,   flete, et non parum,
graves luctus facite   planctum et amarum,
flumina effundite   multa lacrimarum;

The king is captured and with him the cross, all are mangled,
three hundred captive Templar knights are beheaded,
none of whose bodies are a burial granted,
but their souls are crowned by Christ in heaven.

After our armies have been thus destroyed,
the cruelest heathens swarm o'er all the land,
capture the city of Acre[330] without a fight
and the rest of the cities by force as well as craft.

Only Tyre is liberated by the commander
of the Mediterranean fleet, the most illustrious marquis,[331]
a true paladin,[332] of whose strength Greek and Latin alike approve
and which even the fierce Saladin deeply fears.

Saladin, that worst of brigands, that devastator of the land,
through which the Savior by foot did tread,
Who, as Creator of all things, was born of a virgin,
and, the Architect of heaven, was placed in a crib.[333]

Thence with dry feet did He walk o'er the seas
and sate many with but five loaves of bread,
He, Whom John[334] in his prophecy with his finger pointed out,
for Whom the river Jordan, after it touched Him, did recede.

Finally, God, born as man, was nailed to the cross,
and His flank did shoot a stream of water and blood,[335]
through Him and at such a price was the world saved,
which had been damned and devastated by the first man.

Alas, illustrious land, a land truly good,
which alone deserves a crown of blooms,
O land, to which God gave gifts so great,
alas, how blasphemous a belt girds thee now!

Alas, alas, Lord, Glory of upright souls,
Nobility of angels, Salvation of sinners,
behold! Dogs consume the bread of Thy sons,[336]
and the blood of saints is now like water spilled.

Weep, all nations, weep, and not but a little,
grieve deeply in your souls and raise a bitter lamentation,
effuse many streams of tears;

sic ruinam plangite   urbium sanctarum!

Flete amarissime,   omnes auditores,
magni atque minimi,   fratres et sorores!
mutate in melius   vitam atque mores;
nam de celo prospicit   Deus peccatores.

Dat flagella impiis,   punit delinquentes,
et per tempus corrigit   stulta presumentes,
humiles glorificat,   deicit potentes,
recipit ut filios   digne penitentes.

Sic iratus Dominus   quondam Israheli,
iudicans ex nubibus   et de alto celi,
archam testamenti accensus igne zeli
tradidisse legitur   populo crudeli.

Sed et quamvis viribus   hec putabant acta,
sunt compulsi plangere   statim sua facta,
coegerunt reddere   minera cum arca
nam illorum viscera   tabe putrefacta.

Convertamur igitur   et peniteamus,
mala, que commisimus,   fletu deleamus
atque Deo munera   digne offeramus,
ut placatus lacrimis   donet, quod rogamus!

LI. *Lacrimae Gaeae*

Debacchatur mundus pomo,
quod comedit primus homo.
demonstratur nobis tomo,
quod privamur nostra domo.

Refl.   Prohdolor!
         Moyses et Aaron,
         rex David et Salomon,
         Ierusalem et Gion,
         mundus plorat et Sion.

Ecce tempus, tempus mestum,
propter plebem fit infestum;
patet enim manifestum,

thus rue ye the blight of the sacred cities.

Weep most bitterly, all ye listeners,
great and small, brothers and sisters!
Transmute for the better your lives and ways,
for God looks down upon sinners from heaven.

He lashes the Godless, punishes transgressors,
and at the right time corrects presumptuous fools;
He glorifies the humble, precipitates the puissant,[337] and takes up
as His children those who performed their penance with all propriety.

In this way, we read, God once in wrath towards Israel,
adjudicating from the clouds and the height of heaven,
burning with a zealous fire, passed down the Ark
of the Covenant unto the hands of an inhumane folk.

And yet—although they thought this was accomplished
by their own strength, they were forthwith compelled to lament their deeds;
they forced the Israelites to yield the Ark and pay tribute to them,
since their viscera were putrefied from corruption.[338]

Therefore let us convert ourselves and repent;
the sins we have committed let us erase with tears;
and let us offer gifts unto God, as is seemly, so that He,
appeased by our tears, will vouchsafe us our prayers!

51. *Gaea's Tears*

The world blusters because of the apple,
which the first man consumed.
In the Holy Book it is shown to us
that we are deprived of our home.[339]

Refr.   Woe and alas!
           Moses and Aaron,
           King David and Solomon,
           Jerusalem and Gihon,[340]
           the world weeps and Zion, too.

Behold our times, a woeful time;
because of the people it has become a dangerous time,
for it is so very ostensible that

quod plebs temptat inhonestum.

Refl.   Prohdolor!
         Moyses et Aaron,
         rex David et Salomon,
         Ierusalem et Gion,
         mundus plorat et Sion.

Alteratur creatura,
fit nevosa, pro, natura.
quid superbit limatura,
de qua summis nulla cura?

Refl.   Prohdolor!
         Moyses et Aaron,
         rex David et Salomon,
         Ierusalem et Gion,
         mundus plorat et Sion.

Homo reus captivatur,
dum hic vagus exulatur;
non de iure gratulatur,
dum hic brevis moriatur.

Refl.   Prohdolor!
         Moyses et Aaron,
         rex David et Salomon,
         Ierusalem et Gion,
         mundus plorat et Sion.

LIa. *Fortitudo in Sede Sancto* (ca. 1168/69)

Imperator rex Grecorum,
minas spernens paganorum,
auro sumpto thesaurorum
parat sumptus armatorum.

Refl.   Ayos
         o theos athanathos,
         ysma sather yschyros!
         miserere kyrios,
         salva tuos famulos!

the people are observing an evil way.

> *Refr.*   Woe and alas!
> Moses and Aaron,
> King David and Solomon,
> Jerusalem and Gihon,
> the world weeps and Zion, too.

Creation changes for the worse:
it becomes faulty as to its nature.
Why are filings orgulous, when
the lords above care nothing for them?[341]

> Refr.   Woe and alas!
> Moses and Aaron,
> King David and Solomon,
> Jerusalem and Gihon,
> the world weeps and Zion, too.

The guilty man is taken captive,[342]
so long as he wanders here in exile;
he does not rejoice as a matter of law,
since he dies after but a brief stay on earth.

> Refr.   Woe and alas!
> Moses and Aaron,
> King David and Salomon,
> Jerusalem and Gihon,
> the world weeps and Zion, too.

51a. *Valiance in the Holy Realm* (ca. 1168/69)

The basileus, the king of the Greeks,[343]
spurns the threats of heathendom;
having fetched gold from his treasuries,
he raises an army to conquer them.

> Refr.   O Holy,
> Immortal God,
> have pity for us,
> O Savior Strong!
> Lord, deliver thy servants![344]

Almaricus miles fortis,
rex communis nostre sortis,
in Egypto fractis portis
Turcos stravit dire mortis.

Refl.   Ayos
         o theos athanathos,
         ysma sather yschyros!
         miserere kyrios,
         salva tuos famulos!

Omnis ergo Christianus
ad Egyptum tendat manus!
semper ibi degat sanus,
destruatur rex paganus!

Refl.   Ayos
         o theos athanathos,
         ysma sather yschyros!
         miserere kyrios,
         salva tuos famulos!

LII. *Dies Iubalaei* (ca. 1130)

Nomen a solemnibus   trahit Solemniacum;
solemnizent igitur   omnes preter monachum,
qui sibi virilia   resecavit, Serracum;
illum hinc excipimus   quasi demoniacum;
ipse solus lugeat   reus apud Eacum!

Exultemus et cantemus   canticum victorie,
et clamemus quas debemus   laudes regi glorie,
qui salvavit urbem David   a paganis hodie!

Refl.   Festum agitur,
         dies recolitur,
         in qua Dagon frangitur,
         et Amalec vincitur,
         natus Agar pellitur,
         Ierusalem eripitur
         et Christianis redditur;
         diem colamus igitur!

The valiant rider Amalric,[345]
the king of our shared lot,
broke through the gates of Egypt
and cast down the Turks, who met a terrible end.

Refr.   O Holy,
          Immortal God,
          have pity for us,
          O Savior Strong!
          Lord, deliver thy servants!

Every Christian therefore should
stretch out his hands to Egypt's realms!
Unscathed should he there ever be,
but destroyed the heathen king should be!

Refr.   O Holy,
          Immortal God,
          have pity for us,
          O Savior Strong!
          Lord, deliver thy servants!

52. *A Day of Jubilee* (ca. 1130)

From feasts and fests Solignac[346] derives its name.
Therefore all should be festively overjoyed, except the monk
Serracus,[347] who unmanned himself. That is why we regard him
as one by the devil possessed. He alone, guilt-ridden,
should grieve in the home of Aeacus, hell's judge![348]

Let us exult and let us sing a victorious song
and let us shout due praises to our King of glory,[349]
who saved today from the heathens David's city!

Refr.   A festival is held.
          Celebrated is the day,
          on which Dagon[350] is dashed,
          Amalek[351] is subdued,
          the son of Hagar[352] is banished,
          Jerusalem is rescued
          and to the Christians returned.
          Let us therefore celebrate the day!

Hec urbs nobilissima   prima regem habuit,
in hac urbe maxima   Domino complacuit,
in hac propter hominem   crucifigi voluit,
hic super apostolos   Spiritus intonuit.

Urbs insignis,   ad quam ignis   venit annis singulis,
quo monstratur,   quod amatur   omnibus in seculis,
honoranda,   frequentanda   regibus et populis!

Refl.   Festum agitur,
         dies recolitur,
         in qua Dagon frangitur,
         et Amalec vincitur,
         natus Agar pellitur,
         Ierusalem eripitur
         et Christianis redditur;
         diem colamus igitur!

Urbs sacrata celitus,   adamata superis,
legis tabernaculum,   templum arche federis,
hospitale pauperum   et asylum miseris!
non timebis aliquod,   dum in ea manseris.

Tanta lucis claritate   superatur sol et luna,
tanta vicit sanctitate   omnes urbes hec urbs una;
non elegit frustra locum   Gebuseus Areuna.

Refl.   Festum agitur,
         dies recolitur,
         in qua Dagon frangitur,
         et Amalec vincitur,
         natus Agar pellitur,
         Ierusalem eripitur
         et Christianis redditur;
         diem colamus igitur!

LIII. *Finis Schismatis* (1177)

Anno Christi   incarnationis,
anno nostre   reparationis
millesimo centesimo
septuagesimo septimo
rex eterne glorie

This most noble city was the first to have a king.[353]
In this greatest of cities the Lord was pleased.
And in this city was he for mankind willing to be crucified.
And here above the apostles the Holy Spirit thundered.[354]

This remarkable city to which fire comes every single year,[355]
whereby it is shown that it is loved in every age,
is honored and thronged by kings and the people!

Refr.   A festival is held.
         Celebrated is the day,
         on which Dagon is dashed,
         Amalek is subdued,
         the son of Hagar is banished,
         Jerusalem is rescued
         and to the Christians returned.
         Let us therefore celebrate the day!

A city, hallowed by heaven and beloved by beings divine,
tabernacle of the law, temple of the Ark of the Covenant,
shelter of paupers and sanctuary for hapless souls!
Thou shalt fear nothing whilst thou dost in it dwell!

By a light of such splendor the sun and moon are overcome;
by holiness so great this one city conquers all other realms.
Not in vain did Arunah the Jebusite choose a threshing site.[356]

Refr.   A festival is held.
         Celebrated is the day,
         on which Dagon is dashed,
         Amalek is subdued,
         the son of Hagar is banished,
         Jerusalem is rescued
         and to the Christians returned.
         Let us therefore celebrate the day!

53. *The Schism's End* (1177)

In the year of Christ's incarnation,
in the year of our salvation—
one thousand one hundred
seventy-seven—
the King of eternal glory,[357]

dono sue gratie
tenebrosam nebulam
scismatis fugavit
quassamque naviculam
Simonis salvavit.

Hoc chaos obduxerat
orbem, immo infecerat
annis quater quinis
scismatum pruinis;
scintilla caritatis alserat
facta iam cinis.

Hoc decus concordie
sanxit flos Saxonie,
noster felix pontifex
Wichmannus, omnis pacis artifex,
mira gratia,
per quem talia
fiunt consilia,
que hunc errorem
valent reducere sic ad pacis honorem.

Victor imperatoris
ensis, cum mucrone Petri prisci moris
unitate dimicans, feliciter maioris
vim resecat erroris.

Gaude, mater   Roma triumphalis!
ecce, nauta   iam universalis
de profundo maris hieme remige integro portum pacis adiit,
dum pietatis dexteram tetigit.

Felix acumen huius mentis,
qui cum tribus elementis
†aliis ac dirimit litem pacis ligamentis!

Nunc Sion letetur gens,
quia Dominus exsurgens
miserans cor lenit;
tempus enim venit.

Huius anni magnalia

by the gift of his grace,
dispelled the dark cloud
of the Schism[358]
and saved Simon's
weather-beaten skiff.[359]

This chaos had overwhelmed the world—
nay, it had completely infected it—
for twenty years[360] with the rime of schisms.
The spark of charity had grown cold[361]
and had already been
turned to ash.

The flower of Saxony rendered
sacred this glorious concord,
our blessed Bishop Wichmann,[362]
the architect of all this peace,
a man of miraculous grace,
through whom such resolutions
are passed that are thus
able to reduce this folly
unto the beauty of peace.

The victorious sword of the emperor,
which, in conjunction with Peter's sword,
fights in the unity of the old way,[363]
successfully stops the greater blunder's violence.[364]

Rejoice, triumphant mother Rome! Behold! Now comes
the helmsman of the world's church[365] from the depth of the sea
with an intact crew, in spite of the storm, and he has approached
the haven of peace, because he grasped piety's right hand.

Blessed is the acumen of his mind
who with three principles and other
bands of peace cuts through this strife.[366]

Now the people of Zion should rejoice
because the rising Lord in compassion
has softened His heart,
for the time has come.[367]

The mighty works of this year

sunt iubilei gaudia;
exstirpantur zizania,
flavet seges triticea,
et palee de area
ventantur foras horrea.

Hoc decus concordie
canat vox ecclesie!
hec nova tripudia
requirat casta Sion filia!

LIIIa. *Venator Prudens* (ca. 1177/79)

Passeres illos, qui transmigrant supra montes,
Alexander tertius sagax et fidelis archivenator illaqueavit,

Vulpes, que demoliuntur vineas, captivavit,
anguem stravit,
qui disseminavit
discolum virus, quod infrigidavit
igniculum fidei, quique cecavit.

LIV. *Festus Demoniorum*

Omne genus demoniorum
cecorum, claudorum sive confusorum,
attendite iussum meorum
et vocationem verborum.

Omnis creatura phantasmatum,
que corroboratis principatum
serpentis tortuosi, venenosi,
qui traxit per superbiam
stellarum partem tertiam,
Gordan, Ingordin et Ingordan:
per sigillum Salomonis
et per magos Pharaonis
omnes vos coniuro
omnes exorcizo
per tres magos Caspar,
Melchior et Balthasar,
per regem David,
qui Saul sedavit,

are as the joys of the year of jubilee.[368]
The darnel is eradicated;
gold is the field of wheat.
And the chaff is winnowed
on the threshing floor outside the barns.

The voice of the church sings
of this glorious concord!
Zion, the chaste daughter, should
seek again these new festive joys!

53a. *The Prudent Hunter* (ca. 1177/79)

Those sparrows that fly above the mountains
Alexander III[369] our wise and faithful lead hunter ensnared.

He captured the fox that destroyed the vines;
he cast down the snake
that a bitter poison spread wide,
which cooled the little fire of faith:
the snake that blinded us all.

54. *The Demons' Ball*

Demons of every stock—
be ye blind, lame, or mad—
hearken to the bidding
and the summons of my words!

Every nature of ye wicked ghosts,
who strengthen the tortuous,
poisonous serpent's sway,
who in arrogance drew
a third part of the stars,
Gordan, Ingordin, and Ingordan:[370]
by the Seal of Solomon[371]
and Pharaoh's magicians
I conjure ye all,
I exorcise all ye
by the three magi, Caspar,
Melchior, and Balthasar,[372]
by King David,
who pacified Saul,[373]

cum iubilavit,
vosque fugavit.

Vos attestor, vos contestor
per mandatum Domini,
ne zeletis, quem soletis
vos vexare, homini,
ut compareatis
et post discedatis
et cum desperatis
chaos incolatis.

Attestor, contestor
per timendum, per tremendum
diem iudicii, eterni supplicii,
diem miserie, perennis tristitie,
qui ducturus est vos in infernum,
salvaturus est nos in eternum.

Per nomen mirabile atque ineffabile
Dei tetragrammaton,
ut expaveatis et perhorreatis,
vos exorcizo, Larve,
Fauni, Manes, Nymphe,
Sirene, Adryades,
Satyri, Incubi, Penates,
ut cito abeatis,
chaos incolatis,
ne vas corrumpatis
christianitatis.

Tu nos, Deus, conservare ab hostibus digneris!

LV. *Quid Diabolus Dixit*

Amara tanta tyri   pastos sycalos sycaliri
Ellivoli scarras   polili posylique lyvarras.

HIC FINIUNTUR CARMINA MORALIA ET SATIRICA.

when he made music
and routed ye all.

I invoke and call ye to witness
by the mandate of the Lord:
be ye not zealous for the man
whom ye are wont to annoy,
but appear ye
and thereafter depart
and dwell in chaos
with shades void of hope.

I invoke, I call to witness
by the terrible, by the dreadful
day of judgment, of eternal punishment,
a day of misery, of perennial gloom,
that will usher ye into hell,
but will us forever preserve.

By the miraculous and ineffable
Tetragrammaton of God[374]—
to inspire fear and dread in ye!—
I exorcise ye, lemures,
fauns, manes, nymphs,
sirens, dryads,
satyrs, incubi, penates,[375]
that ye may swiftly depart,
that ye may in chaos loom,
lest ye defile and corrupt
the vessel of christendom.[376]

O God, in Thy goodness, save us from these demons!

55. *What The Devil Said*

Amara tanta tyri pastos sycalos sycaliri
Ellivoli scarra polili posylique lyvarras.[377]

HERE END THE MORAL AND SATIRICAL SONGS.

The Love Songs

Incipiunt jubilii

LVI. *Ortus Veris*

Ianus annum circinat,
ver estatem nuntiat
calcat Phebus ungula,
dum in Taurum flectitur,
Arietis repagula.

Refl.   Amor cuncta superat,
        Amor dura terebrat.

Procul sint omnia tristia!
dulcia gaudia
sollemnizent Veneris gymnasia!
decet iocundari,
quos militare contigit
Dioneo lari.

Refl.   Amor cuncta superat,
        Amor dura terebrat.

Dum alumnus Palladis
Cytheree scolam
introissem, inter multas
bene cultas
vidi unam solam
facie Tyndaridi
ac Veneri secundam,
plenam elegantie
et magis pudibundam.

Refl.   Amor cuncta superat,
        Amor dura terebrat.

Differentem omnibus
amo differenter.
novus ignis in me furit
et adurit
indeficienter.
nulla magis nobilis,
habilis,

The songs of jubilation commence.

56. *The Dawn of Spring*

Janus rounds the year,
spring heralds the summer,
Phoebus treads with his hoof
upon the bolts of Aries' pen,
whilst he turns into the Bull.[1]

Refr.   Love conquers all;[2]
         love bores through the hard.

May all sorrows be far, far away!
May sweet joys celebrate
the communities of love!
Seemly it is now for those to rejoice,
who perform their service
in Dione's court.[3]

Refr.   Love conquers all;
         love bores through the hard.

When I, a student of Pallas,[4]
had entered Cytherea's school,
I saw among many very lovely maids
one who in visage was second
only to Helen
and Venus divine,
a maiden full of elegance
and more modest
than the rest.

Refr.   Love conquers all;
         love bores through the hard.

I love in a different way
a girl who is different from all.
A new fire in me rages
and burns me
without end.
No girl is more noble,
no girl is more fine,

pulchra vel amabilis,
nulla minus mobilis,
instabilis,
infronita reperitur
vel fide mutabilis.
eius letum vivere
est meum delectari.
diligi si merear,
hoc meum est beari.

Refl.   Vincit Amor omnia,
            regit Amor omnia.

Parce, puer, puero!
fave, Venus, tenero,
ignem movens,
ignem fovens,
ne mori sit, quod vixero,
nec sit ut Daphnes Phebo,
cui me ipsum dedo!
olim tiro Palladis
nunc tuo iuri cedo.

Refl.   Vincit Amor omnia,
            regit Amor omnia.

LVII. *Carmen Phrisonis*

«Bruma, veris emula,
sua iam repagula
dolet demoliri;
demandat Februario,
ne se a solis radio
sinat deliniri.

Omnis nexus elementorum
legem blandam sentit amorum.
sed Hymeneus eorum
iugalem ordinat torum,
votis allubescens deorum
piorum.

Sed Aquilonis

no girl is more beautiful
or more worthy of love than mine;
a less fickle lass
you will not find,
nor one less inconstant, less cheeky,
or less unfaithful than mine.
Her happy life is my delight.
If I be but worthy of her love,
truly blessed will I regard myself.

Refr.   Love conquers all;
           love bores through the hard.

Have mercy, boyish god,[5] upon a lad!
Be kind, Venus, to a tender youth,
in whom you kindle the fire
and nurture its heat,
lest it be death that I live
and as Daphne was to Apollo[6]
be to me she, to whom I have given my soul!
Once Athena's pupil,
I now yield unto your sway!

Refr.   Love conquers all;
           love bores through the hard.

57. *Phrison's Song*

"Winter, the rival of spring,
now deeply grieves
over the destruction of her bars.
She bids February not to let itself
be melted away
by the rays of the sun.

"Every nexus of the elements
feels the alluring law of love.
And Hymenaeus[7] arranges
their marital union
and pleases the laws
of the benignant gods.

"But the wrath of the North Wind,

ira predonis
elementis officit,
ne pariant; nec tamen in hoc proficit.
sed Hymeneus obicit
eius se turbini;
in hoc enim numini
deserviunt Dione.

Felicibus stipendiis
Dione freta gaudiis
gaudet suos extollere.
qui se suo iugo libere
non denegant submittere,
quam felici vivere
vult eos pro munere!

Optat Thetis
auram quietis,
ut celo caput exerat
suosque fructus proferat.
Ceres quoque secus undam cursitat
et tristia sollicitat
inferorum numina
pro surrepta Proserpina.

Elementa supera
coeunt et infera.
hinc illis vocabula
sunt attributa mascula;
illis vero feminina
congrue sunt deputata nomina,
quia rerum semina
concipiunt ut femina.

Sol, quia regnat in Piscibus
celestibus,
dat copiam plenariam
piscationi,
reddens formam turbide Iunoni.»

Ista Phrison decantabat
iuxta regis filiam,
egram que se simulabat,

a brigand, opposes the elements,
lest they produce any scion at all;
still it does not succeed in this assay.
Hymenaeus launches himself
against the Wind's hurricane.
Then with their parturition
the elements zealously serve Dione.

"Dione, buttressed by joys,
rejoices in decking her votaries
with beatifying rewards.
As a favor, she wishes exceedingly
happy lives for them,
who do not refuse to submit
 to her yoke of their own accord.

"Thetis[8] wishes for a quiet,
gentle breeze, so that she may
raise high her head unto the sky
and bring forth her wondrous fruits.
Ceres also runs along the waves of the sea
and solicits the underworld's lugubrious gods
for Proserpine who was purloined
from her and the upper world.[9]

"The elements above and below unite.[10]
Hence masculine names
were to the former assigned,
and feminine names suitably
were to the latter allotted,
because they assimilate
the seeds of things
as women do.

"The sun, because it reigns in Pisces' house,[11]
gives to the fisherman
a bounteous haul
and returns beauty
to stormy Juno."[12]

These words sang Phrison[13]
beside the daughter of the king,
who pretended she was ill,

dum perrexit per viam
desponsari, sed hec gnanus
notans sponso retulit.
mox truncatur ut profanus.
tandem sponso detulit.

LVIII. *Chorea Avium*

Iam ver oritur.
veris flore variata
tellus redimitur.
excitat in gaudium
cor concentus avium
voce relativa
Iovem salutantium.
in his philomena
Tereum reiterat
et iam fatum antiquatum
querule retractat.
sed dum fatis obicit
Itym perditum,
merula choraulica
carmina coaptat.

Istis insultantibus
casibus fatalibus
in choree speciem
res reciprocatur.
his autem conciliis
noster adest Iupiter
cum sua Iunone,
Cupido cum Dione,
post hos Argus stellifer
et Narcissus floriger
Orphëusque plectriger,
Faunus quoque corniger.

Inter hec sollemnia
communia
alterno motu laterum
lascive iactant corpora
collata
nunc occurrens,

when she proceeded on her journey
to be affianced, but the dwarf noted everything
and reported them to the bridegroom.
Anon he was decapitated as a slanderous knave.
Thereupon she at last truckled to the groom.

58. *The Dance of the Birds*

Spring now dawns.
The painted earth is redeemed
by the flowers of the spring.
The heart in joy awakens
the concerts of the birds,
and each salutes Jove with its own song.
Beneath them the nightingale
repeats the name Tereus
and now treats again
with a plaintive warble
her loss in olden times.[14]
Whilst she relates
the loss of Itys to the fates,
the blackbird as her aulete
plays to her songs.

While these songs curse
the fateful misfortunes that she met,
the world sways to and fro
in the semblance of a dance.
But our Jupiter is present
at these conventions
with Hera his wife,
as well as Cupid and Dione,
and after these starry Argus
and flowery Narcissus
and Orpheus with lyre in hand
and the horned god Pan.[15]

At these universal festivities,
swaying left and right,
the feathered dancers playfully
and in concert cast their bodies
hither and thither,
now converging,

nunc procurrens
contio pennata:

Mergus aquaticus,
aquila munificus,
bubo noctivagus,
cygnus flumineus,
phenix unica,
perdix lethargica,
hirundo domestica,
columba turtisona,
upupa galigera,
anser sagax,
vultur edax,
psittacus gelboicus,
miluus gyrovagus,
alaudula garrula,
ciconia rostrisona.

His et consimilibus
paria sunt gaudia;
demulcet enim omnia
hec consors consonantia.

Tempus est letitie.
nostro tempore
vernant flores
in pratis virentibus,
et suis rebus
decus auget Phebus
in nostris finibus.

LIX. *In Umbra Tiliae*

Ecce, chorus virginum,
tempore vernali,
dum solis incendium
radios equali
moderatur ordine,
nubilo semoto
fronde pausa tilie
Cypridis in voto!

now diverging—
the following winged throng:

The loon,
the noble eagle,
the night-wandering owl,
the swan of the river,
the phoenix living alone,
the lethargic partridge,
the swallow of the home,
the cooing turtle dove,
the helmeted hoopoe,
the wise goose,
the gluttonous vulture,
the colorful parrot,
the encircling kite,
the chattering little lark,
and the beak-clacking stork.

The joys are commensurate
with these birds and their congeners,
for this polyphonic harmony
lightens everything.

The time is one of joy.
In this our time,
flowers bloom
in meadows green.
Phoebus increases the splendor
of his world
within our bounds.

59. *In the Shadow of the Linden*

Behold, a band of maidens!
In the time of spring,
when the fire of the sun
disposes its rays in equal lengths,
muddled am I in my retreat,[16]
when the linden's foliage
is my journey's pause,
because for Cypris I do long![17]

Refl.   Cypridis in voto
          fronde pausa tilie,
          Cypridis in voto!

In hac valle florida
floreus flagratus,
inter septa lilia
locus purpuratus.
dum garritus merule
dulciter alludit,
philomena carnmine
dulcia concludit.

Refl.   Cypridis in voto
          fronde pausa tilie,
          Cypridis in voto!

Acies virginea
redimita flore –
quis enarret talia!
quantoque decore
prenitent ad liquidum
Veneris occulta!
Dido necis meritum
proferat inulta.

Refl.   Cypridis in voto
          fronde pausa tilie,
          Cypridis in voto!

Per florenta nemorum
me fortuna vexit.
arcum Cupidineum
vernula retexit.
quam inter Veneream
diligo cohortem,
langueo, dum videam
libiti consortem.

Refl.   Cypridis in voto
          fronde pausa tilie,
          Cypridis in voto.

Refr.   For Cypris I do long
when the linden's foliage is my journey's pause—
O for Cypris I do long!

In this blooming vale,
within a lilied hedge,
is a flowering, fragrant
place in purple clad.
When the merle's treble
sweetly rings,
the nightingale in song
rounds off the melody.

Refr.   For Cypris I do long
when the linden's foliage is my journey's pause—
O for Cypris I do long!

An army of maidens
bedecked with blooms—
who could relate such sights
and explain with what allure
the coverts of Venus
unmistakably shine?!
Dido[18] should present her suicide to a court,
for every judge would acquit her of her crime!

Refr.   For Cypris I do long
when the linden's foliage is my journey's pause—
O for Cypris I do long!

Over a carpet of flowers in the woods
the goddess Fortuna carried me.
Cupid's bow did a serving maid reveal,
whom among Venus' cohort I love so:
I languish with lust,
until I see
the helpmeet
of my pleasure.

Refr.   For Cypris I do long
when the linden's foliage is my journey's pause—
O for Cypris I do long!

Questio per singulas
oritur: honesta
potiorque dignitas
casta vel incesta?
Flora, consors Phyllidis,
est sententiata:
«caste non est similis
turpiter amata.»

Refl.   Cypridis in voto
         fronde pausa tilie,
         Cypridis in voto!

Iuno, Pallas, Dione,
Cytherea dura
affirmant interprete
Flore verbi iura:
«flagrabit felicius
nectare mellito
castam amans potius
quam in ‹infinito›.»

Refl.   Cypridis in voto
         fronde pausa tilie,
         Cypridis in voto!

Iura grata refero
puellarum ludis.
Vigeant in prospero
pudice futuris!
actibus emeritas
nulla salutaris,
contingat iocunditas
† spes adulta caris!

Refl.   Cypridis in voto
         fronde pausa tilie,
         Cypridis in voto!

LX. *Conclave Amoris* (ca. 1100 ?)

Captus amore gravi
me parem rebar avi

A question for every girl arises:
who is more handsome
and of greater worth,
the chaste maiden or the lewd wench?
Flora, Phyllis' playmate,[19]
rendered the verdict:
"In no way similar to the chaste virgin
is the shamefully beloved wench."

   Refr.   For Cypris I do long
          when the linden's foliage is my journey's pause—
          O for Cypris I do long!

Juno, Pallas, Dione,
and relentless Cytherea
endorse the arbitrament
that the jurist Flora pronounced:
"In the eyes of a chaste lass
he will more happily glow
in nectar honey-sweet
than in a wench without bounds."

   Refr.   For Cypris I do long
          when the linden's foliage is my journey's pause—
          O for Cypris I do long!

The welcome rules do I relate
for the games of maidens:
May chaste lasses in prosperity
thrive in all their future affairs!
Let no salutary delight befall
the lots of women burnt out
by their lascivious pursuits:[20]
let their hope and grace be consumed![21]

   Refr.   For Cypris I do long
          when the linden's foliage is my journey's pause—
          O for Cypris I do long!

60. *The Cage of Love* (ca. 1100 ?)

Held captive by a grievous love
I considered myself the equal of a bird

fede revincte lari,
que procul ethra videt
nec modulando silet.

[Inde perire libet] et
psallere, virgo, pridem,
non semper hec ibidem,
quam scrutabundus amor
notarat et amaror.

[Hinc ortus ille clamor]
est bilis amarissima,
qualem gignit Sardonia.
in incentivo Veneris
eiusque miri generis
militiam proponere,
non posse votum solvere.

Hec, ecce, virgo inclita,
tibi notabis edita:
Amor instillat, quare
te, virgo, salutare
velim; sed onus grave
videris acerbare,
dum affligis immeritum,
grave ferens imperium,
vilipendens obloquium,
me minans in interitum,
fidem promittens alteri,
contradicendo Cypridi.

Ecce querimonia,
quam genuit amor;
me misit in suspiria
Venereus favor.
Cuncta sprevi virginum
ego tripudia,
te volens michi iungere.
modo diludia
quesivique gratiam;
sed iam alterius
captas benivolentiam;
quo nil deterius

that is bound to a loathsome cage:
he views the aether only from far away
and yet does not cease to sing.

Pleasing it is for me to depart thence
and to sing as I did long ago.
But she stays not always in the same place:
my probing love observes her
and bitterness afflicts me.

That shout, which has sprung hence,
is bile of the most bitter sort,
likened to what the crowfoot[22] yields.
Alas, because of the temptations
of Venus and her wondrous scion
to dedicate myself to her troop,
I am unable to fulfill my oath!

Behold, O illustrious maiden,
and mark well these my words:
Love instills in me my reason
for wishing to greet you, lass,
but you seem to aggravate
my heavy burden, when
you cudgel my guiltless soul,
bear my biddings as impositions,
vilipend my objections,
drive me straight to ruin,
pledge your fidelity to another,
in contradiction of Cypris.

Behold the complaint,
which love begot:
an inclination for Venus
sent me deep into sighs.
All the dances
with other maidens
did I shun,
because I wanted to join you to me;
I sought only tranquility
and thy grace, but now you
grab at another's devotion:
anything baser than this

queo fari.
nec solari
me curat Glycerium;
me fastidit
et allidit,
estimans inglorium.
Bella gero
cum se vero
Cypridis ob meritum.

Dum mens unam te recolit
famaque nefas comperit,
pupilla fletum protulit;
iam expedit,
ut vera loquamur.
Amaveram pre ceteris
te, sed amici veteris
es iam oblita; superis
vel inferis
ream te criminamur?

Dolor, fletus,
ire, metus
tremebundis artubus
simul incubuere.
Pre dolore
verso more
canticum conticuit;
nil restat nisi flere.

Sorte dira
pendet lyra,
spreta luget. Atropos
filum cessavit nere.
Me mergis hic,
cum sis illic;
nutando sic
non stabis hic.

Sed lubrica   contagia
te gaudes insectari;
prostibulum patibulo
iam meruit piari.

I cannot possibly name.
Glycerium[23] has no care
for my consolation;
she disdains
and smites me, too,
and considers me a fameless cur.
Wars I carry on with her,
surely at the fault
of Cypris.

When my heart thinks on you alone,
and your reputation discloses misdeeds,
my eyes well up with tears.
Now it is most expedient
for us to speak the truth.
I had loved you before all others,
but you have now forgotten
your loving friend of old;
by the gods above or below do we
accuse your soul of a felony?

Pain, tears, wrath,
and dread have in unison
weighed upon my trembling,
quivering limbs!
Under the force of pain,
I have changed my ways;
my song has fallen unto silent days.
Nothing remains except to weep.

A horrible fate,
the lyre now hangs;
spurned, it grieves.
Atropos has ceased to spin the thread.[24]
You drown me here,
when you are over there.
Wavering and tottering thus,
you will not be permanently here.

But you rejoice in your pursuit
of slippery contact and touch.
The whore has now earned
the gibbet as her punishment.

en, oro te per superos:
tibi ames obnoxios;
reclude secretarios,
quos nil iuvat amari!

Si lethargum vite
insectabor lite,
† hanc colis rite,
† et ego te
in soliloquiorum
carmine canebam,
te unam sapiebam,
idque iustum rebar;
sed nichil audis horum.

Michi te subdideras
et amore iunxeras
fallentis vite semitas,
et te ita subverteras,
ut redimam me vivere
presumptuosa temere
amores vi transponeres,
ut cor meum contereres.

Usque quo te perferam,
quam premit emulatio?
Ut quid agis perperam,
o dira simulatio?

Ex fraudibus alternis
et ignominia
cur emula superbis,
bifrons, ingloria?
cum federa discerpis,
o preceps nimia,
te funditus evertis
ceu Bachanaria.

Si balbi more veritus
nil ausim fari penitus,
† obnixeram emeritus,
quem captat hic interitus.

Behold! I pray thee by the gods above:
Love those who are obedient to you,
shut off the passage for your furtive men,
whom being loved does not delight!

If I bring legal proceedings
against an unconscious man,
you conduct a trial that exhausts
every aspect of the law.
And yet I sang of you
in a lyric of soliloquies.
I was acquainted with no one
but you, which I considered right.
But you want to hear nothing of these.

You had devoted yourself to me
and in love had bound together
the paths of a life of lies,[25]
and have so perverted yourself that I
purchase back my life.
You would, presumptuous girl,
thoughtlessly and unlawfully give your love to another,
to triturate my heart.

How long am I to suffer you,
whom jealousy heavily weighs down?
Why act you so perversely,
O horrible forger of pretense?

O jealous, two-faced, dishonorable
wench, why are you proud
of your interchanging deceits
and all of your ignominious ways?
When you breach a pact,
O inordinately precipitous girl,
you totally upheave yourself
like a raving bacchante.[26]

If I timidly, like a stammering fool,
should not dare to say anything at all,
I would have resisted like a discharged troop,
whom here his destiny overtakes.

O Cypris alma, conspice
tue clientem opere
penamque nobis exime,
quam patimur indebite!
tu lamiam interripe
eiusque rixas opprime!

LXa. *Amor Secretus*

Cupido mentem gyrat
telumque minans vibrat,
Favonius aspirat
nectar, quo Venus inflat
medullitus; id teneris
pergratum est in feminis,
quas alit affabilitas
atque cordis simplicitas.

Semel, opto, basia
michi quod offerat,
quam sorte de infantia
Natura venustat.
post hanc nulla complacet,
quam sic assumpserim,
cum potius amabiles
te propter spreverim.

Iam odorus noster torus
demoratur; inscia
es optata, sed vocata
non occurris, intima.

Gaude, proles regia,
que vite privilegia
gestas! ecce Venerea
collegia
per te floruerunt.

Si iam detur optio,
tuo quod utar osculo
et membris in crepuscolo
sub otio,
aspera non erunt.

O nourishing Cypris, observe
the retainer of your work,
and take away from us
the punishment
we suffer without desert.
Reave the lamia[27] and quell her strife!

60a. *Secret Love*

Cupid whirls and reels about the heart
and menacingly brandishes his dart;
the West Wind breathes upon the nectar,
with which Venus fills men deep within.
This most pleasant state we seek
is in delicate women,
whom kindness and simplicity
of the heart sustain.

I wish that at least once
she would offer me her kisses,
she, whom Nature by lot
made lovely from infancy.
If I had made her thus my own,
I would take pleasure in no other girl,
since I would rather spurn
amiable lasses for the sake of you.

Now our fragrant bed tarries in anticipation.
Unbeknownst to you, you are much desired by me,
but, when I call you, you don't appear,
my most intimate darling dear.

Rejoice, royal issue,
who wield the privileges
of life! Behold!
Venus' communities
have flourished through you!

If the liberty to choose were granted me now,
to enjoy your kisses and tender limbs
in leisure of the twilight,
there would exist
in life nothing harsh.

matutini sideris
iubar preis, et lilium
rosaque periere.
micat ebur dentium
per labium, ut Sirium
credat quis enitere.

Si Menalus   fatidicus
virginibus
michi det omne fari,
Etna, mons occiduus,
Ponto ferat minas prius,
quam desinat, virgo, tuus
honor laudari.

Amores ergo fidibus
canendi sunt his rudibus,
cibentur ut his fructibus:
stipendium erit Venus.

Furores quando lenit
Venus, que corda ferit,
incitamentum Veneris
fastidium est ceteris.
quod laudis michi titulum
clarumque det obsequium!

Intemerata virginum,
serena respice
et generosa supplicis
iam vota perfice!

LXI. *Pomum Eius Oculi*

Siquem Pieridum ditavit contio,
nulli Teïorum aptetur otio
par Phebi cithare
sum in verno nectare.
cui pre cunctis virginum obedio,
† vita me potest alere vel mortis tedio.
† sed decus hoc intimum
mavult potissimum.

You precede the beam of the morning star,
and the lily and rose fade beside your beauty's sun.
The ivory of your teeth
gleams through your lips,
such that one would believe
Sirius is shining forth from them.

If oracular Maenalus[28]
should give me the sight
to vaticinate every maiden's fate,
such would be my prophecy:
"Mount Etna will sink into and suffer
the menaces of the sea, before your honor,
maiden, will cease to be praised."

Love should be sung
to my unpolished lyre,
that it may by these fruits be fed:
love will be my reward.

When Venus, who strikes hearts,
satisfies a furious desire,
a renewed sting of Venus
is annoying to other men.
But this should bring glory to me
and enable splendid indulgence!

O thou inviolate of maidens,
look upon me with friendly eyne,
and fulfill now the wishes
of thy suppliant!

61. *The Apple of His Eye*

If a chorus of Muses has enriched some man,
he should not adapt himself to the idle Anacreontics.[29]
I am akin to Phoebus' harp
amid the fragrance of spring.
She, whom I obey before all other maids,
can infuse me with life or the weariness of death.
But the latter, her most intimate virtue,
she prefers above all the rest.

Terminum vidit brume desolatio;
gaudent funditus in florum exordio,
qui norunt Cypridem,
plaudentes eidem.
nunquam tanti cordis fui, pro Iupiter!
de spe Venerea, opinor; iugiter
me vita fertilis
alit et spes habilis.

Me risu linea
regit virginea;
nunc ergo tinea
meroris pellitur,
dolor avellitur,
tremor percellitur.
cui tanta claritas
ac mira caritas,
fecunda largitas
semper et undique
arrident utique,
hanc opto denique.

Ne miretur ducis tante
quis sublimitatem,
que me verbi vi prestante
doctum reddit plus quam ante,
stillans largitatem!

O decora super ora
belli Absalonis
et non talis, ut mortalis
sis conditionis!
michi soli, virgo, noli
esse refragata!
queso finem, ut reclinem
a re desperata.

Tuum prestolor nuntium:
dele merorem conscium,
mundani decus iubaris,
o verecunda Tyndaris!

Apollo mire vinctus est

The desolation of winter found an end;
most energetically rejoice in the exordium
of the blooms do they, who are acquainted
with Cypris and render plaudits to her.
Never was I of higher spirits, O Father Jupiter!
The hope for love's bliss dominates my thoughts;
fruitful life and nimble hope
continually invigorate me.

She, a portrait of a maiden,
rules me with her laugh.
So now the moth of grief
is into exile shooed,
the pain is rent away,
and the shivering is dashed.
She, upon whom great celebrity
and remarkable kindness
and prolific beneficence
always and everywhere
are smiling without fail,
is in fine the one I desire.

Let no one marvel at the sublimity
of a conductress such as she,
who by the extraordinary power of her words
leaves me more learned than before,
when she her rich gifts exudes!

O thou beauty surpassing that
of handsome Absalom[30]
and not of such a nature
that gives the impression
that thou art of mortal form![31]
Me alone, maiden, do not thou repulse!
I beg for acquittal, that I may rest
from a desperate struggle.

I wait for thy message: end thou my grief,
of which thou art very aware,
thou glorious light that illuminates the world,
thou virginal, maidenly Helen of Troy!

Apollo was wondrously bound,

Peneide respecta;
sic meus amor tinctus est
re veteri deiecta.
magnetem verum iterat
virgo mire perfecta,
attractu crebro superat
me gratia directa.
miranda de Priamide
rememorantur gesta,
qui militavit floride;
sed squalent mea festa.

Florenti desolatio
non esset conturbatio;
sed mea plus tremit ratio,
† quam Dionea sit dilatio.
quid facio?

Gratia, solacia
donato menti languide,
mea dos, amorum flos,
morigerata vivide!
amantum lis, te, quicquid vis,
da laudi bene placide!
nil tibi par, electe lar
letitie fervide.

Te visa primitus
exarsi penitus;
proinde gemitus
durat perenniter.
tu deme leniter
illatum duriter!
† hec est dira sors,
nec durior est mors.
num mee vite sors
stat ritu prospero?
quam soli confero,
repugnat tenero!

Huic me corde flagrante
nosco intricatum,
cuius nutu me versante

when nymphal Daphne he beheld.
In this way was my love tinged,
after I cast aside the things of eld.
This wondrously exquisite maiden
is a genuine magnet: by its perpetual
attraction the grace that beams
from her totally overcomes me.
Called to my mind now are all
the awesome deeds of Priam's son,[32]
who gloriously performed his military service:
my banquets, howbeit, lie neglected and cold.

Pauperism would not
confound my blooming luck,
but my reason is in greater fear
of how long love's union will be delayed.
What am I to do?

Grace, bring solace to a sick mind,
my treasure, my flower of love
of vivacious disposition!
O lovers' matter of dispute,
whatever its essence be,
devote thy pleasure to my praise!
Nothing is thy equal,
O lofty home of glowing mirth.

When I first saw thee,
I burned deep within;
thence a perennial sigh began.
Take away with gentle hand
what was with cruelty
on me imposed!
A terrible fate this is;
not even is death more harsh!
Does the lot of my life not adhere
to some prosperous ritual or rite?
She, whom I liken to the sun,
resists her young admirer!

I know that I, glowing within,
am with her intertwined.
If she is willing to change

et ad votum conspirante
me fero beatum.

Aptiorem, dulciorem
nollem reperire,
quam elegi, mee legi
si dat subvenire.
plus amarem, plus optarem
sui verbi dona,
quam si mundi † vi iocundi
fungerer corona.

Sed primum exaltandus est
risus clarificatus,
a quo Iovis secundus est,
michi significatus.
effectum si non invenit,
ut me velit amare,
pie rogo, quod convenit:
me queat tolerare.

Sed si nos, Discordia,
tuo more disponis,
mutabo iam primordia
mee professionis.

Ergo, nitidior sidere,
respice, si me vis vivere!
nam flores constat emergere;
tuo me solatum federe
da ludere!

LXII. *Mirum Inducens Somno*

Dum Diane vitrea
sero lampas oritur
et a fratris rosea
luce dum succenditur,
dulcis aura zephyri
spirans omnes etheri
nubes tollit; sic emollit
vis chordarum pectora
et immutat cor, quod nutat

my situation and accord with my wish,
I find myself in a state of bliss.

I cannot imagine finding a better,
more wonderful girl than she, whom I chose,
if she agrees to submit to my law.
More so did I love,
more so did I desire
the sweet gifts of her word
as if I by the force of law would possess
the crown of a joyous world.

First to be praised
is her radiant smile,
which heralded unto me that
it is second in rank after Jove.[33]
If it does not so happen that she
is ready to give her love to me,
then I kindly ask that she agree
at the very least to be able to tolerate me.

But if you, Discord, seek to rule
our relationship in accord
with your divisive art,
at the outset I shall then my pledge withdraw.

Therefore you, who shine more brightly
than a star, look upon me, if you wish me life!
For it is certain that the flowers are emerging.
Solaced by your bond of love,
give me leave to make sport!

62. *Hypnogogic Wonder*

When in the evening
Diana's glassy lamp doth arise[34]
and when she is succeeded
by her brother's rosy light,[35]
the balmy breath of the zephyr sweet
scatters from the ether all the clouds.
In this way the power of the strings
softens hearts and morphs
the faltering mind so that

ad amoris pignora.

Letum iubar Hesperi
gratiorem dat humorem
roris soporiferi
mortalium generi.

O quam felix est antidotum soporis,
quod curarum tempestates sedat et doloris!
dum surrepit clausis oculorum poris,
ipsum gaudio equiperat dulcedini amoris.

Morphëus in mentem
trahit impellentem
ventum lenem segetes maturas,
murmura rivorum per harenas puras,
circulares ambitus molendinorum,
qui furantur somno lumen oculorum.

Post blanda Veneris commercia
lassatur cerebri substantia.
hinc caligant mira novitate
oculi nantes in palpebrarum rate.
hei, quam felix transitus amoris ad soporem,
sed suavior regressus ad amorem!

Ex alvo leta fumus evaporat,
qui capitis tres cellulas irrorat;
hic infumat oculos
ad soporem pendulos
et palpebras sua fumositate
replet, ne visus exspatietur late.
unde ligant oculos virtutes animales,
que sunt magis vise ministeriales.

Fronde sub arboris amena,
dum querens canit philomena,
suave est quiescere,
suavius ludere
in gramine cum virgine speciosa.
si variarum odor herbarum
spiraverit, si dederit torum rosa,
dulciter soporis alimonia

it becomes capable of love's securities.

The happy beam of the evening star
sends to the mortal race
the more agreeable moisture
of hypnogogic dew.

O how blissful is the antidote of sleep,
which calms the tempests of solicitudes and grief!
When it creeps into the closed passages of the eyne,
it equals in joy the very sweetness of love.

Morpheus[36] draws into the mind
the gentle wind that drives in crops ripe,
the murmur of rivers
through stark beds of sand,
the circular gestures of millwheels,
which all steal in sleep the light of the eyes.

After the pleasure of the commerce of love
the substance of the brain is of vigor deprived.
Hence in marvelous novelty do eyes
swimming in the raft of the lids grow dull.
Alas, how happy is the passage from love into sleep,
but more sweeter is the return to love!

From the happy womb of love fumes the steam
and bedews the three chambers of the head;[37]
here it fogs the eyes that are
staggering into sleep
and fills the lids with its moisture,
lest the sight roam far off.
In this way the bodily powers[38] bind the eyes,
powers more often deemed subservient.

Under the pleasant foliage of a tree[39]
as the nightingale warbles her plaint,
sweet it is to rest, and sweeter it is to play
in the grass with a comely lass.
If various herbs emit their perfumes,
if roses frame a bed,
then takes one, flaccid
after the works of love

post Veneris defessa commercia
captatur, dum lassis instillatur.

O in quantis
animus amantis
variatur vacillantis!
ut vaga ratis per equora,
dum caret ancora,
fluctuat inter spem metumque dubia
sic Veneris militia.

LXIII. *Casus Amorabundus et Herculeus*
Petrus Blesensis (ca. 1135 - ca. 1204)

Olim sudor Herculis,
monstra late conterens,
pestes orbis auferens,
claris longe titulis
enituit;
sed tandem defloruit
fama prius celebris,
cecis clausa tenebris,
Ioles illecebris
Alcide captivato.

Refl.   Amor fame meritum
         deflorat,
         amans tempus perditum
         non plorat,
         sed temere diffluere sub Venere
         laborat.

 Hydra damno capitum
facta locupletior,
omni peste sevior,
reddere sollicitum
non potuit,
quem puella domuit.
iugo cessit Veneris
vir, qui maior superis
celum tulit humeris
Atlante fatigato.

the sweet nourishment of sleep,
which into wearied minds drips.

O in how many
does the mind
of the vacillating lover sway!
Just as a skiff wandering o'er the sea
without an anchor wavers unsteadily
between hope and dread,
so does life in Aphrodite's service.

63. *The Amorous Herculean Fall*
by Peter of Blois (ca. 1135 – 1204)

Whilom the sweat of Hercules
subdued monsters everywhere,
rid the world of pestilence,
and shined brightly far and wide
in the luster of titles of honor;
but at last his fame, once celebrated,
was mewed up in dark gloom,
when Alcides
was ensnared
by the allurements of Iole.[40]

Refr.   Love deflowers
         the value of fame,
         nor does the lover rue
         the loss of time,
         but recklessly does he strive to be dissolved
         under Venus' thumb.

The Hydra,[41] made richer
by the loss of a head and fiercer
than every pest known to man,
could not dismay the hero,
whom a maiden did break.
He truckled to Venus' yoke,
a man, who, greater
than the gods above,
shouldered the mighty heavens
when Atlas was fatigued.

Refl.   Amor fame meritum
         deflorat,
         amans tempus perditum
         non plorat,
         sed temere diffluere sub Venere
         laborat.

Caco tristis halitus
et flammarum vomitus
vel fuga Nesso duplici
non profuit;
Geryon Hesperius
ianitorque Stygius,
uterque forma triplici
non terruit,
quem captivum tenuit
risu puella simplici.

Refl.   Amor fame meritum
         deflorat,
         amans tempus perditum
         non plorat,
         sed temere diffluere sub Venere
         laborat.

Jugo cessit tenero,
somno qui letifero
horti custodem divitis
implicuit,
frontis Acheloie
cornu dedit Copie,
apro, leone domitis
enituit,
Thraces equos imbuit
cruenti cede hospitis.

Refl.   Amor fame meritum
         deflorat,
         amans tempus perditum
         non plorat,
         sed temere diffluere sub Venere
         laborat.

Refr.   Love deflowers
        the value of fame,
        nor does the lover rue
        the loss of time,
        but recklessly does he strive to be dissolved
        under Venus' thumb.

A harsh puff of breath and spew
of flames were to Cacus of no avail,
nor did flight assist Nessus,
who assumed two forms.
Hesperian Geryon
and the gate-hound of Styx[42]—
both of triple form—
affrighted not the man,
whom a girl held captive
with a guileless laugh.

Refr.   Love deflowers
        the value of fame,
        nor does the lover rue
        the loss of time,
        but recklessly does he strive to be dissolved
        under Venus' thumb.

To the tender yoke he yielded,
who enveloped the sentry
of the rich garden
in fatal slumber
and gave to the goddess of Abundance
the horn from Achelous' brow,
who distinguished himself
through the conquest of the boar and lion
and filled the mares of Thrace
with the corpse of a sanguinary host.[43]

Refr.   Love deflowers
        the value of fame,
        nor does the lover rue
        the loss of time,
        but recklessly does he strive to be dissolved
        under Venus' thumb.

Antei Libyci
luctam sustinuit,
casus sophistici
fraudes cohibuit,
cadere dum vetuit;
sed qui sic explicuit
lucte nodosos nexus,
vincitur et vincitur,
dum labitur
magna Iovis soboles
ad Ioles amplexus.

    Refl.   Amor fame meritum
            deflorat,
            amans tempus perditum
            non plorat,
            sed temere diffluere sub Venere
            laborat.

Tantis floruerat
laborum titulis,
quem blandis carcerat
puella vinculis.
et dum lambit osculis,
nectar huic labellulis
Venereum propinat;
vir solutus otiis
Venereis
laborum memoriam
et gloriam inclinat.

    Refl.   Amor fame meritum
            deflorat,
            amans tempus perditum
            non plorat,
            sed temere diffluere sub Venere
            laborat.

Sed Alcide fortior
aggredior
pugnam contra Venerem.
ut superem hanc, fugio;
in hoc enim prelio

He sustained a match
with Antaeus of Libya[44]
and foiled the tricks
of a sophistic fall[45]
by precluding his opponent's
every plunge.
But he who thus disengaged
the perilous clasps of the fight,
was conquered and fettered
when he, the scion of mighty Jove,
slipped into the embraces of Iole.

Refr.   Love deflowers
         the value of fame,
         nor does the lover rue
         the loss of time,
         but recklessly does he strive to be dissolved
         under Venus' thumb.

By the great titles conferred
on his labors flowered he,
whom a girl immures
with bewitching bonds.
And whilst she lathers him with kisses,
the nectar of Venus her lips distill
waters his ever amorous soul.
The man who has abandoned himself
to the leisures of Aphrodite
thinks no longer on his labors
or their consequent glory.

Refr.   Love deflowers
         the value of fame,
         nor does the lover rue
         the loss of time,
         but recklessly does he strive to be dissolved
         under Venus' thumb.

But I, stronger than Alcides,
undertake a battle
against Lady Cythera.
So that I may conquer her, I flee.
For in this type of war

fugiendo fortius
et melius pugnatur,
sicque Venus vincitur:
dum fugitur, fugatur.

Refl.   Amor fame meritum
deflorat,
amans tempus perditum
non plorat,
sed temere diffluere sub Venere
laborat.

Dulces nodos Veneris
et carceris
blandi seras resero,
de cetero ad alia
dum traducor studia.
o Lycori, valeas
et voveas, quod vovi:
ab amore spiritum
sollicitum removi.

Refl.   Amor fame meritum
deflorat,
amans tempus perditum
non plorat,   ·
sed temere diffluere sub Venere
laborat.

LXIV. De XII virtutibus Herculis
Ausonius (ca. 310 – ca. 395)

Prima Cleonei tolerata erumna leonis.
Proxima Lerneam ferro et face contudit hydram.
Mox Erymantheum vis tertia perculit aprum.
Eripedis quarto tulit aurea cornua cervi.
Stymphalidas pepulit volucres discrimine quinto.
Threiciam sexto spoliavit Amazona balteo.
Septima in Augeis stabulis impensa laboris.
Octava expulso numeratur adoria tauro.
In Diomedeis victoria nona quadrigis.
Geryone extincto decimam dat Hiberia palmam.
Undecimo mala Hesperidum districta triumpho.

a soldier more valiantly and effectively
fights by fleeing away.
And in this way Venus is subdued:
when he flees, she is put to flight.

Refr.   Love deflowers
           the value of fame,
           nor does the lover rue
           the loss of time,
           but recklessly does he strive to be dissolved
           under Venus' thumb.

The sweet bonds of Venus I unlock
and the bars of her alluring prison I break,
when from the rest I spirit me away
and devote my mind to other things.
O Lycoris,[46] may you be strong
and vow to me what I have vowed:
I have removed a soul,
harrowed by love,
from its affliction's source.

Refr.   Love deflowers
           the value of fame,
           nor does the lover rue
           the loss of time,
           but recklessly does he strive to be dissolved
           under Venus' thumb.

64. On the Twelve Virtuous Labors of Hercules[47]
by Ausonius (ca. 310 - ca. 395)

The first toil he sustained was the defeat of the Nemean lion.[48]
For his second he dashed the Lernaean Hydra with firebrand and sword.
For his third feat of strength he slew the Erymanthian boar.
Fourth, he won the golden antlers of the swift-footed stag.
His fifth distinction marked the death of the Stymphalian birds.
For his sixth he stole the Thracian Amazon Queen's belt.
His seventh labor applied to his toils in the Augean stalls.
The expelled Cretan Bull won him an eighth reward of valor.
His ninth victory was over Diomedes' carriage and four.
Spain confers upon him his tenth victory palm for Geryon's doom.
For the eleventh triumph he plucked the apples of the Hesperides.

Cerberus extremi suprema est meta laboris.

LXV. *Symphonia Rhythmoides*

Quocumque more motu volvuntur tempora,
eadem fretus eucrasi pulso tympana.

Seu Philogeus in imis moretur,
aut Euricteus solito vernali semine rubens notetur,
vel dum coruscus Acteon estivo lumine repletur,
sive Lampas radians autumni copia ditetur:
ab uno semper numine michi salus debetur.

Brevi spectata Basythea immisit,
quod expectata tempore tanto Euryale tandem subrisit.
sola Euphrosyne strictrici emula fautrix michi sit,
cui Dione nudula per quandam dulciter arrisit!
nam allotheta cecinit hoc carmen, quod promisit.

Cypris barbata gaudeat occultu
iam renovata maturo tumultu!
virgo dudum femine
habitum mentita,
nec fallit in virgine
Veneris perita.
nomine pudico palliat
Venereum libamen,
provida, ne palam ebulliat
experte rei famen.
devirginata tamen
non horruit, cum iteravit nature luctamen.

Fautor sis, Paris, Veneris agonis!
Venus, fruaris amplexibus Adonis!
myrtum libans Indicam
fanis Citheronis
testem ponam pedicam
mee conditionis.
Delio liberior immobili
non superor cohorte.
spes lassam rem impulit, dum nobili
fruar tori consorte.
nec admittetur forte;

But Cerberus was the final goal of his last, most arduous task.

65. *A Rhythmic Symphony*

In whatever way the times are set in motion, I, supported
by the same happy temperament,[49] strike the tambourine.

Whether Philogeus[50] tarries in the lowest realms
or Erythreus[51] with wonted vernal seeds marks itself with a red glow,
or flashing Acteon[52] is filled with estival light,
or radiant Lampas[53] is enriched with the abundance of autumn:
always from one godhead[54] is salvation owed to me.

Basythea,[55] but briefly glimpsed, incited Euryale,[56] for whom
I have so long waited, to smile upon me at last. May Euphrosyne[57] alone,
who can take on any shackling witch, be to me favorably disposed,
a patroness at whom naked Dione, through a certain lady, sweetly smiled!
Another typesetter sang this song, as pledged.[58]

May bearded Cypris[59] rejoice in stealth,
after she has gathered new energies
for the ripe insurrection of sexuality!
Long ago the young lass, giving lies to her names,
assumed the nature of a woman, but it lies not hidden
in a maiden, if she has experienced love.
With a chaste name she cloaks
her libation of Venus' tonic,
careful not to allow the tidings
of her experience to openly bubble out.
Nevertheless the deflowered maiden was ruffled not,
when she repeated the struggle of her nature.[60]

Be, O Paris, my great patron
in Venus' contest in the public games!
Venus, you should enjoy Adonis' embraces at last![61]
Offering the Indian myrtle-berry,
I shall set on the shrines of Cithaeron[62]
the foot fetter as a witness to my new condition.[63]
Freer than Apollo, I am not surmounted
by the throng of immobile gods.
Hope stimulates a flaccid thing,
until I enjoy the noble companion of my bed.
No "perchance" should be admitted,

nam intra seram militavi virginalis porte.

Pallerem,   nisi me   veteri   miranda decore
virgo probaret;
marcerem,   nisi spe   Veneri   fuscata timore
me stimularet.

Inclita   res ita   cognita,   perdita   dat michi fata;
namque rogavi,
Cui pia   basia,   dulcia,   suavia,   congeminata
multiplicavi.

Hac bibo pocula vite,
hoc decus est michi mite,
que satis est michi culta,
obvia secula multa.

Sat modo mature
sum confessus eam;
† claudit opus dure,
dum complector eam.

Gratia letitie
iure cupita,
moribus et facie
tam redimita,
flosculo presignis,
dote leporis,
Foveat me signis
dulcis amoris!

Hoc memor corde serva,
quod te mea Minerva
nunc prudens, nunc proterva
multiformis hactenus   declarat harmonia:
prosa, versu, satira   psallens et rhythmachia
te per orbem intonat   scolaris symphonia.

Siquis versat, quod verso,
amans et e converso
corde nichil diverso
petat, optet, supplicet,   ut duret amor meus,
ego vicem replicans   non ero fraudis reus,

for behind the bar of the virginal gate have I fought.

I would grow pale, if the maiden, wondrous
in her familiar beauty, did not of me approve.
I would wither, if she did not stir me to love's pleasure
through her anticipation hidden behind a specious fear.

A glorious affair I have come to know thus:
her loss would be my death, for I have invited her again,
she, to whom I had given in countless numbers
loving, sweet, reciprocal kisses.

Through her I drink the goblets of life,
and this is a fruitful glory to me.
She alone is enough for me,
if I may worship her for every eon and age.

Now I have praised her well
with seasoned art.
Vigorously does the labor close,
when I her in my arms enfold.

May she, who is justly desired
for her graceful felicity,
who has been crowned with manners
and a wondrous physiognomy,
who is distinguished by her florid speech
and a dowry of wit and charm,
nurture me with the tokens
of sweet, sweet love!

Infix this deep within thy heart, that my poetry,[64]
now lettered, now wanton and pert,[65]
glorifies thee in a harmony of many forms:
singing in prose, verse, and a mix of both[66]
and in rhythmic stanzas, a scholastic symphony
rings thy name throughout all the world.

If anyone meditates on the matters I treat,
anyone who loves and is loved, may he,
with the selfsame heart, sue, wish, and pray that my love last.
I, in turn, not a perpetrator of fraud, shall requite this service,
so that through the confidence of such a pact,

ut tali freto federe   sit annus iubileus!

LXVI. *Axis Quattuor Equi Solis*

Acteon, Lampos,   Erythreus et Philogeus:
Istis nominibus   poterit spectare peritus
Quemque diem tantum   tempus retinere quaternum.
Acteon primum   Greci dicunt rubicundum:
Nam sol purpureum   iam mane novo tenet ortum.
Post graditur Lampos, est qui cognomine fulgens:
Nam tunc splendorem   sentimus sole micantem.
Ardens Erythreus   sequitur, sic iure vocatus:
Est nam quisque dies medius   fervore repletus.
Post hos extremus   procedit tunc Philogeus,
Dictus amans terram,   quod vespere tendit ad illam:
Nam vult occasum   terris inducere certum.

LXVII. *Virgo Suprema* (ca. 1170)
Petrus Blesensis (ca. 1135 - ca. 1204)

A globo veteri
cum rerum faciem
traxissent superi
mundique seriem
prudens explicuit
et texuit Natura,
iam preconceperat,
quod fuerat factura.

Que causas machine
mundane suscitans,
de nostra virgine
iam dudum cogitans
Plus hanc excoluit,
plus prebuit honoris,
dans privilegium
et pretium laboris.

In hac pre ceteris
totius operis
Nature lucet opera.
tot munera
nulli favoris contulit,

this may be the year of jubilee!^67

66. The Four Steeds of The Chariot of the Sun

Acteon, Lampas, Erythreus, and Philogeus:
the adept can gather from these names
that every day contains only four spaces of time.
The first, Acteon, the Greeks nominate "The Red,"
for the sun, when morning breaks, then holds a purple rise.
After him comes Lampos, whose name means "The Bright,"
for we see then the splendor that flashes from the sun's eye.
Fiery Erythreus follows, who for this reason is rightly named:
the middle course of each day is fraught with heat.
The last of these, Philogeus then proceeds, hight "The Lover of Earth,"
because in the evening he bends his course to her,
for he wants to draw o'er the lands a sure setting and an end.

67. A Maiden Supreme (ca 1170)
by Peter of Blois (ca. 1135 – ca. 1204)

When the lords of the empyrean
drew from the old mass
a distinct shape for all things therein,
and Nature in her sagacity
evolved and weaved
the ordered chain of the world,
since she had already conceived in advance
what she would create.

When she set in motion
the causation of the world's machine,
she had long before factored our maiden
into her ultimate plan:
she fashioned her more finely,
furnished her with beauty and charm,
and bestowed on her manufacture
the privilege and price of great labor.

In her more than all other works
does the industry of Nature shine.
So many gifts
of favor did she
bestow on none before,

sed extulit
hanc ultra cetera.

Et, que puellulis
avara singulis
solet partiri singula:
huic sedula
impendit copiosius
et plenius
forme munuscula.

Nature studio
longe venustata,
contendit lilio
rugis non crispata
frons nivea.
simplices siderea
luce micant ocelli.

Omnes amantium
trahit in se visus,
spondens remedium
verecunda risus
lascivia.
arcus supercilia
discriminant gemelli.

Ab utriusque luminis confinio
moderati libraminis iudicio
naris eminentia
producitur venuste
quadam temperantia:
nec nimis erigitur
nec premitur iniuste.

Allicit verbis dulcibus et osculis,
castigate tumentibus labellulis,
roseo nectareus
odor infusus ori.
pariter eburneus
sedet ordo dentium
par nivium candori.

but she exalted the maiden
above all other things.

And she, who is wont
to covetously allot
to each girl only assets discrete,
sedulously applied to my dame
the gifts of beauty in greater abundance
and thoroughness
than the world had ever seen.

Made lovely in the most charming way
by Nature's zealous strain,
her snow-white brow,
by no wrinkle distorted,
rivals the flower lily.
Her ingenuous, starry eyne
blaze with a refulgent light.

She draws all the glances of suitors
unto her glorious, angelic sight,
because she promises a remedy:
her bashful,
yet wanton, laugh.
Twin arches separate
her lovely eyebrows.

From the border of both eyes,
at the discretion of a balanced symmetry,
the hillocks of her nose are drawn forth
with a certain temperance
in their projection:
neither excessively raised
nor unjustly oppressed are they.

With sweet words and kisses
she entices and with her mildly
tumescent little lips;
around her rosy mouth rests
the fragrance of nectar.
Evenly sit an ebony succession of teeth
that glow brightly in snowy whiteness.

Certant nivi, micant lene
pectus, mentum, colla, gene;
sed, ne candore nimio
evanescant in pallorem,
precastigat hunc candorem
rosam maritans lilio
prudentior   Natura,
ut ex his fiat aptior
et gratior mixtura.

Rapit michi me Coronis,
privilegiata donis
et Gratiarum flosculis.
nam Natura, dulcioris
alimenta dans erroris,
dum in stuporem populis
hanc omnibus ostendit,
in risu blando retia
Veneria tetendit.

LXVIII. *Ver: Fabula Brevis*

Saturni sidus lividum   Mercurio micante
fugatur ab Apolline   Risum Iovis nudante;
redit ab exilio   ver coma rutilante.

Cantu nemus avium
lascivia canentium
suave delinitur,
fronde redimitur;
vernant spine floribus
micantibus, signantibus
Venerem, quia spina
pungit, flos blanditur.

Mater Venus subditis amori
dulcia stipendia copia
largiri delectatur uberiori.

Dulcis aura Zephyri
spirans ab occidente
Iovis favet sideri
alacriori mente,

Her breast, her chin, her neck, her cheeks
vie with the snow and softly gleam,
but, lest they vanish in a pallor
through their exaggerated whiteness,
wiser Nature restrains this whiteness in advance
by wedding the rose to the lily,
so that from this union may be born
a mixture more suitable
and more pleasant in form.

Myself from me Coronis[68] steals,
favored with the Graces' florets and gifts.
For Nature, who fuels a sweeter lunacy,
exhibited this girl
to the astonishment
of all the world,
and unharnessed
with her enticing laugh
all of Venus' fetching nets.[69]

68. *Spring: A Brief Tale*

When Mercury shines, Saturn's livid star[70]
is routed by Apollo, who uncovered the smile of Jove.[71]
With glowing red hair[72] spring from exile returns.

A delightful grove of singing birds
is encircled with a sportive song
and with a garland of foliage crowned;
the thorns are green
with tremulous blooms
and betoken Venus,
since the thorn pricks
and the flower allures.

Mother Venus is delighted to lavish
upon the subjects of love
sweet stipends in most plentiful abundance.

The breeze of the sweet Zephyr
blowing in from the west
favors the star of Jupiter;
more active in spirit,

Aquilonem carceri
Eolo nolente
deputans; sic ceteri
glaciales spiritus diffugiunt repente.
redit calor etheri,
dum caligo nubium rarescit Sole Taurum tenente.

Sic beati spes, halitus fiagrans oris tenelli,
dum acclinat basium,
scindit nubem omnium
curarum; sed avelli
nescit, ni congressio sit arcani medica duelli.

Felix hora huius duelli,
cui contingit nectar adunare melli!
quam felix unio,
cuius suavitatis poculo
sopiuntur sensus et ocelli!

LXIX. *Amor Brumalis*

Estas in exilium
iam peregrinatur,
leto nemus avium
cantu viduatur,
pallet viror frondium,
campus defloratur.
exaruit, quod floruit,
quia felicem statum
nemoris vis frigoris
sinistra denudavit
et ethera silentio
turbavit, exilio
dum aves relegavit.

Sed amorem, qui calorem
nutrit, nulla vis frigoris valet attenuare,
sed ea riformare
studet, que corruperat brume torpor. amare
crucior, morior
vulnere, quo glorior.
eia, si me sanare
uno vellet osculo,

it condemns the North Wind
to the inertia of a prison
against Aeolus' will.[73]
Thus the rest of the icy winds in great haste fly asunder.
Warmth returns to the ether, since the gloom of the clouds
diminishes when the sun reigns in Taurus' house.[74]

Thus the anticipation of happiness,
the fragrant breath from her tender little mouth,
when she plants a kiss on me, cleaves the clouds of all my cares;
but she knows not how to tear herself away,
if the clash of the secret war be not resolved.

Happy is the hour of this war, upon whose lot
the mixing of nectar and honey falls!
How blessed a union,
by whose draught of sweetness
the senses and eyes are lulled to sleep!

69. *Winter Love*

Now the summer
journeys into exile;
the woods are bereft
of the joyous song of birds;
the verdure of the leaves
grows faint and pale;
and deflowered are the fields.
What once flourished has dried away,
because the sinister power of frost
has denuded the woods' blessed state
and disrupted with silence
the ethereal vault,
when it has banished every bird.

But no force of cold can enfeeble love,
which nourishes the heat,
for love strives to remold the things
that the torpor of winter had marred.
Bitter agonies do I suffer:
from the wound in which I glory
I am moribund. Woe and alas!
If only she would heal me with but one kiss,

que cor felici iaculo
gaudet vulnerare!

Lasciva, blandi risus,
omnes in se trahit visus.
labia Veneria tumentia
– sed castigate – dant errorem
leniorem, dum dulcorem
instillant, favum mellis, osculando,
ut me mortalem negem aliquando.
leta frons tam nivea,
lux oculorum aurea,
cesaries subrubea,
manus vincentes lilia
me trahunt in suspiria.
rideo, cum video
cuncta tam elegantia,
tam regia, tam suavia, tam dulcia.

LXX. *Commercium Amorum*

Estatis florigero tempore
sub umbrosa residens arbore,
avibus canentibus in nemore,
sibilante serotino frigore,
mee Thisbes adoptato fruebar eloquio,
colloquens de Veneris blandissimo commercio.

Eius vultus, forma, cultus
pre puellis, ut sol stellis,
sic prelucet. o inducet
hanc nostra ratio,
ut dignetur suo
nos beare consortio?

Nil ergo restat satius,
quam cecam mentis flammam
denudare diffusius.
audaces fortuna iuvat penitus.
his ergo sit introitus:

«Ignem cecum sub pectore
longo depasco tempore,

she who rejoices in wounding
with a happy bolt my heart!

Her frisky nature, her coaxing smiles
draw all glances unto her sight.
The lips of Venus, swelling—
but not in unpleasant excess—
cause all too idle wanderings,
when she with kisses sweetness instills,
like sweet virgin honey, so that I may at last deny
that I am a mere mortal in any wise.
Her pleasant, ever snowy brow,
the golden light of her eyes,
her shimmering red hair,
her hands surpassing lilies
haul me into sighs.
I smile, when I behold her sight:
all so elegant, so regal, so lovely, so sweet.

70. *A Lovers' Exchange*

In the flowerful time of summer,
I reposed beneath a shady tree—
as the birds were singing in the wood
and the cool evening wind was rustling—
and enjoyed the fine words of my Thisbe[75]
and a discussion about the most blissful union of love.

Her face, her form, her refinement
outshine all other maidenly sights,
as the sun surpasses the stars.
O, will our discourse bring her
to deem us worthy of the blessing
of her loving company?

Therefore nothing better remains,
but to reveal the hidden fire
of my soul in greater detail.
Fortune succors the bold in full.[76]
Let this be the inception of my flames:

"Long have I fed off a fire
concealed deep beneath my breast,[77]

qui vires miro robore
toto diffundit corpore.
quem tu sola, percipere
si vis, potes extinguere,
. . meum semivivere
felici ligans federe.»

«Amoris spes est dubia,
aut verax aut contraria.
amanti necessaria
virtutis est constantia.
pre ceteris virtutibus est patientia
amoris famulantia.
Sed et ignem, qui discurrit per precordia,
fax extinguat alia!
Noster amor non furtiva, non fragilia
amplexatur gaudia.»

«Ignis, quo crucior,
immo quo glorior,
ignis est invisibilis.
si non extinguitur,
a qua succenditur,
manet inextinguibilis.
est ergo tuo munere
me mori vel me vivere.»

«Quid refert pro re pendula
vite pati pericula?
est pater,   est mater,
est frater,   qui quater
die me pro te corripiunt,
et vetulas   per cellulas
et iuvenes per speculas
deputantes nos custodiunt;
argumque centioculum
plus tremo quam patibulum.
est ergo dignum
virum benignum
vitare signum,
unde malignum
murmur cursitat per populum.»

a fire that with miraculous force
diffuses its powers all through my frame.
Only you alone can extinguish it,
if you care to perceive it at all,
and bind my half-dead self to you
by a compact sublime."

"Dubious is the hope for love:
it's either a reality or a fiction.
Constancy of virtue
is a lover's necessity.
Before all other virtues
is patience love's valet.
But the fire, too, which rushes through
all the body's alleys and gates,
is extinguished by yet another flambeau!
My love does not embrace furtive, flighty joys."

"The fire that afflicts me,
nay, of which I boast,
is a fire unseen by the eye.
If it be not extinguished
by its maiden kindler,
forever will it abide.
It is thus in your hands
whether I die or live."

"Of what use is it to me to suffer
life's perils for such a pendulous affair?
There is the father, the mother,
the brother, who four times a day
scold me on your account
and observe us by dispatching
old women to all the little rooms
and to all the watchtowers blokes.
I quake more at hundred-eyed Argus
than at the gallows of forked frame.
Therefore it is just and meet
that a man of kind disposition
shun every token
whence a malignant murmur
courses through the people."

«Times in vanum!
tam est arcanum,
quod nec Vulcanum
curo cum sophisticis catenis.
Stilbontis more
Letheo rore
Argum sopore
premam, oculis clausis centenis.»

«In trutina mentis dubia
fluctuant contraria
lascivus amor et pudicitia.
† sed eligo, quod video:
collum iugo prebeo,
ad iugum tamen suave transeo.»

«Non bene dixeris
iugum secretum Veneris,
quo nil liberius,
nil dulcius,   nil melius.
O quam dulcia
sunt hec gaudia!
Veneris furta sunt pia.
ergo propera
ad hec munera!
carent laude dona sera.»

«Dulcissime!
totam subdo tibi me.»

LXXI. *Fraus Amoris*

Axe Phebus aureo
celsiora lustrat
et nitore roseo
radios illustrat.

Venustata Cybele
facie florente
florem nato Semele
dat Phebo favente.

Aurarum suavium

"You fear in vain!
The whole issue is so mysterious
that I fear not even Vulcan
with his slender steel nets.[78]
As guileful Stilbon[79] once performed,
I will overwhelm Argus with sleep
by the persuasion of Lethe's hypnogogic dew
and shut out the light of his hundred eyes."

"On the wavering balance of my soul,
two opposites oscillate to and fro:
lascivious love and modest restraint.
But I choose what I see:
I offer my neck to the yoke,
but into a sweet yoke I pass."

"'Tis wrong that you name
the mystery of love a 'yoke,'
for nothing is freer than it,
nothing sweeter, nothing better.
O how sweet are these delights!
Pious are the tricks
and crafts of love!
Therefore hie to these gifts!
Belated presents
earn no praise!"

At last exclaims my darling girl,[80]
"Sweetest of men, I submit all of me to thee!"

71. *Love's Deceit*

With his golden chariot
Phoebus travels round
the upper air and lights up
his rays in a rosy gleam.

Lovely Cybele,[81]
of a visage blossoming,
gives a flower to Semele's son[82]
with the blessing of Apollo.

By the delightful grace

gratia iuvante
sonat nemus avium
voce modulante.

Philomena querule
Terea retractat,
dum canendo merule
carmina coaptat.

Iam Dionea leta chorea
sedulo resonat cantibus horum,
iamque Dione iocis, agone
relevat, cruciat corda suorum.

Me quoque subtrahit   illa sopori
invigilareque   cogit amori.
Tela Cupidinis   aurea gesto,
igne cremantia   corda molesto.

Quod michi datur, expaveo,
quodque negatur, hoc aveo
mente severa.

Que michi cedit, hanc caveo;
que non obedit, huic faveo
sumque re vera
infelix, seu peream
seu relever per eam.

Que cupit, hanc fugio,
que fugit, hanc cupio;
plus renuo debitum,
plus feror in vetitum;
plus licet illibitum,
plus libet illicitum.

O metuenda
Dione decreta!
o fugienda
venena secreta,
fraude verenda
doloque repleta,
docta furoris

of the breezes sweet
the forest of birds rings
with melodious songs.

The nightingale indulges
in tuneful plaints over Tereus' deed
whilst she accords her song
with the treble of the merle.

Now Dione's happy roundelay
thunders eagerly with their songs.
And now Dione lightens her votaries' hearts
with jest and sport— and harrows them as well.

She subtracts me also from slumber
and compels me to bestow pains upon love.
Cupid's golden arrows I bear;
his fire annoys burning hearts.

What is vouchsafed to me I fear;
what is denied me I crave
with a soul in gloom steeped.

Whatever maiden yields to me, against her I guard myself;
and whosoever rejects my suit
I befriend and I am indeed
unhappy whether I perish
or through her am relieved.

I flee her, who is desirous;
she, whom I desire, flees me.
The more I oppose my duty,
the more I am led into the taboo.
The more the cheerless is licensed,
the more pleasing the forbidden becomes.

O ye decrees of Dione,
that must be held in dread!
O ye secret, seductive drugs
that must by all be fled!
Fearsome for her treachery
and full of deceit is she;
schooled in the heat

in estu punire,
quos dat amoris
amara subire,
plena livoris
urentis et ire!

Hinc michi metus abundat,
hinc ora fletus inundat,
hinc michi pallor in ore
est, quia fallor amore.

LXXII. *Petrus Superator*
Petrus Blesensis (ca. 1135 - ca. 1204)

Grates ago Veneri,
que prosperi
michi risus numine
de virgine
mea gratum et optatum
contulit tropheum.

Dudum militaveram,
nec poteram
hoc frui stipendio;
nunc sentio
me beari, serenari
vultum Dioneum.

Visu, colloquio,
contactu, basio
frui virgo dederat;
sed aberat
linea posterior
et melior amori.
quam nisi transiero,
de cetero
sunt, que dantur alia,
materia furori.

Ad metam propero.
sed fletu tenero
mea me sollicitat,
dum dubitat

of lunatic rage to martyr those,
whom she prompts to subject
themselves to love's bitterness,
she is replete
with scorching malice and ire!

Hence I wade in dread;
hence tears flood my face.
Hence a pallor draws itself over my mouth,
because I am by love deceived.

72. *Peter the Conqueror*
by Peter of Blois (ca. 1135 – ca. 1204)

Thanks I give to Venus,
who by the power
of her favorable smile upon me
vouchsafed me a thankworthy
and desired victory
over my girl.

Long had I soldiered in her troop
and was yet unable
to enjoy her pay;
now I sense that I
am being blessed
and Dione's face is brightening.

The enjoyment of her visage,
her conversation,
her touch, and her kiss
the maiden had granted.
Yet the last
and highest step
of my love[83] failed.
If I do not cross this goal line,
all the other concessions
are but tinder for my raving desire.

I hasten to the finish line,
but with tender tears
my maiden upsets me,
because the young lass

solvere virguncula
repagula pudoris.
flentis bibo lacrimas
dulcissimas;
sic me plus inebrio,
plus haurio fervoris.

Delibuta lacrimis
oscula plus sapiunt,
blandimentis intimis
mentem plus alliciunt.
ergo magis capior,
et acrior vis flamme recalescit.
sed dolor Coronidis
se tumidis
exerit singultibus
nec precibus mitescit.

Preces addo precibus
basiaque basiis;
fletus illa fletibus,
iurgia conviciis,
meque cernit oculo
nunc emulo, nunc quasi supplicanti;
nam nunc lite dimicat,
nunc supplicat;
dumque prece blandior,
fit surdior
precanti.

Vim nimis audax infero.
hec ungue sevit aspero,
comas vellit, vim repellit strenua,
sese plicat et intricat genua,
ne ianua pudoris resolvatur.

Sed tandem ultra milito,
triumphum do proposito.
per amplexus firmo nexus, brachia
eius ligo, pressa figo basia;
sic regia Diones reseratur.

Res utrique placuit,

hesitates to loosen
her pudency's latch.
When she weeps,
I drink the sweetest drops of brine.
The more I thus fill myself,
the more passion I imbibe.

The more her tear-anointed kisses
savor of brackish dew,
the more they allure the mind
with intimate delights.
Therefore the more I am enthralled,
the more fiercely the force of the flame warms.
But the pain of Coronis reveals itself
with tumid fits of teary rattles and croaks[84]
and by solemn prayers
is not subdued.

Prayers upon prayers I heap,
and kisses to kisses I add;
tears in a sea of brine she gushes
and quarrels with insults she compounds.
And she marks my every move
with an eye that's now jealous
and now almost suppliant.
For now she vies against me in a suit,
and now entreatingly she pleads her case;
and when I comply with her plea,
more deaf than one in prayer she turns.

Too boldly I exert my lustful will.
With razor-sharp nails she assumes a fitful rage,
she plucks my hair and vigorously repulses my forceful advance;
she coils herself up and clasps her knees,
lest the door to her chastity be unsealed.

But at last I let loose all engines of war
and set upon my scheme a triumphant crown.
Through an embrace, I strengthen my clasp;
I bind her arms and plant heavy kisses on her flesh.
In this way is Dione's royal court unlocked.

The affair pleased us both,

et me minus arguit
mitior amasia, dans basia mellita.
et subridens tremulis
semiclausis oculis,
veluti sub anxio suspirio sopita.

LXXIII. *Flamma Vernalis*

Clausus Cronos et serato
carcere ver exit,
risu Iovis reserato
faciem detexit

Coma celum rutilante
Cynthius emundat
et terrena mediante
aere fecundat.

Purpurato   flore prato
ver tenet primatum,
ex argenti   renitenti
specie renatum.

Iam odora   Rheam Flora
chlamyde vestivit,
que ridenti   et florenti
specie lascivit.

Vernant veris ad amena
thyma, rose, lilia.
His alludit philomena,
merops et luscinia.

Satyros hoc excitat
et Dryadum choreas,
redivivis incitat
hoc ignibus Napeas.

Hoc Cupido concitus,
hoc amor innovatur,
hoc ego sollicitus,
hoc michi me furatur.

and my darling of gentler nature
already chided me less violently
and gave kisses of honey to me;
and she smiled a little with quivering, half-closed lids,
as if she, with an anxious sigh, were lulled to rest.

73. *Vernal Flame*

Cronus is confined and Spring
sprouts out from the bolted prison,
burst open by the smile of Jove.
She uncovered her face:

With his fiery red strands
the Cynthian[85] cleanses the sky
and, as the air floats between,
fertilizes the earth.

A meadow of purple flowers,
the spring holds first rank,
born anew from the glistening
face of winter's silver hoar.

Already has fragrant Flora
dressed Rhea[86] in a stately cloak,
and the latter frolics
with a smiling, flowering mien.

In the mildness of spring flourish
the thyme, roses, and lilies.
The swallow, bee-eater, and nightingale[87]
with these flowers frolic and cavort.

This spectacle excites the satyrs
and the Dryads'[88] roundelays,
and, with newly-kindled fires,
rouses the nymphs of the vales.

Cupid is stirred by this, too,
and the game of love is renewed;
harrowed, though, by this am I,
as it purloins myself from me.

Ignem alo tacitum,
amo, nec ad placitum,
ut qui contra libitum
cupio prohibitum.
votis Venus meritum
rite facit irritum,
trudit in interitum,
quem rebar emeritum.

Si quis amans per amare mereri   posset amari,
posset Amor michi velle mederi   dando beari.
Quot faciles   michi cerno medelas   posse parari,
tot steriles   ibi perdo querelas   absque levari.

Imminet exitus   igne vigente,
morte medullitus   ossa tenente.
Quod caro predicat   hec macilenta
hoc sibi vendicat   usque perempta.

Dum mala sentio,   summa malorum,
pectora saucia,   plena furorum,
pellere semina   nitor amorum.

Ast Venus artibus   usa nefandis,
dum bene palliat   aspera blandis,
unguibus attrahit   omnia pandis.

Parce dato pia,   Cypris, agone,
et quia vincimur,   arma repone,
et quibus es Venus,   esto Dione!

LXXIV. *Veris Animi*

Letabundus rediit
avium concentus,
ver iocundum prodiit;
gaudeat iuventus,
nova ferens gaudia!
modo vernant omnia;
Phebus serenatur;
redolens temperiem
novo flore faciem
Flora renovatur.

I nurse a hidden flame, I love,
though against my decided intent;
I lust after the forbidden,
though against my wish.
What I've earned, through uttered vows
with due religious rites, Venus invalidates,
and thrusts straight into ruin me, whom I thought
had long been discharged from her service.

If any lover through loving could deserve to be loved again,
then Cupid could be blessed by giving, if he would fain cure.
So many fruitless complaints I discard without any relief
as I see easy remedies that could be provided for my grief.

The end hangs o'er my head with a vigorous fury;
death is gripping my skeleton deep within.
My emaciated flesh bears witness to this;
irrecoverably dissolved, it assumes this claim.

When I sense sufferings, the extremest of them—
mortally wounded hearts filled with lunatic whims—
I endeavor to rout the seeds of love.

But Venus employs her damnable arts:
whilst she cloaks the harsh with seductive charms,
she lures all unto herself with retracted claws.

Mercy, benign Cypris, I concede defeat,
and because we are conquered, lay down your arms,
and to all, for whom you are Venus, be also Dione![89]

74. *The Pride of Spring*

The joyous concert of birds
has returned, and delightful
spring has debouched.
All youths should rejoice,
and with them bring new delights!
Now all things grow green;
Phoebus' clear light breaks;
smelling of temperateness,
Flora restores her visage
with colorful, new blooms.

Risu Iovis pellitur
torpor hiemalis,
altius extollitur
cursus estivalis
solis, beneficio
recipit teporem.
sic ad instar temporis
nostri Venus pectoris
reficit ardorem.

Estum vitant Dryades
colle sub umbroso;
prodeunt Oreades
cetu glorioso;
Satyrorum contio
psallit cum tripudio
Tempe per amena;
his alludens concinit,
cum iocundi meminit
veris, philomena.

Estas ab exilio
redit exoptata,
picto ridet gremio
tellus purpurata.
miti cum susurrio
suo domicilio
gryllus delectatur.
hoc canoro, iubilo,
multiformi sibilo
nemus gloriatur.

Applaudamus igitur
rerum novitati!
felix, qui diligitur
voti compos grati,
dono letus Veneris,
cuius ara teneris
floribus odorat.
miser e contrario,
qui sublato bravio
sine spe laborat.

By Jove's smile the torpor
of winter is driven away;
higher and higher climbs
the summer on its course
with the aid of the sun;
gentle warmth takes back the world.
Going by the time of year,
Venus rekindles
the fire of our hearts.

The Dryads avoid the heat
beneath a shady hill;
the Oreads[90] come forth
in a glorious train;
a gathering of Satyrs
sing to a dance
through the pleasant Vale of Tempe.[91]
Sporting with them sings the nightingale,
as she recalls
the delights of spring.

The summer from exile returns,
longed for ever so much;
the purple earth smiles
upon her painted lap.
With a gentle murmur
the cricket takes delight
in his wondrous home.
Of this melodious song
and this manifold hum
the enlivened forest is proud.

Let us therefore applaud
the reformation of the world!
Happy is he who is loved
and whose heart's desire is fulfilled,[92]
who is beatified by the gift of Venus,
and whose altar is perfumed
with delicate blooms.
On the contrary is he miserable,
who, cheated of his reward,
drudges without any hope at all.

LXXV. *Gaudia Iuventutis*

Omittamus studia,
dulce est desipere,
et carpamus dulcia
iuventutis tenere!
res est apra senectuti
seriis intendere.

Refl.   Velox etas preterit
        studio detenta,
        lascivire suggerit
        tenera iuventa.

Ver etatis labitur,
hiems nostra properat,
vita damnum patitur,
cura carnem macerat.
sanguis aret, hebet pectus,
minuuntur gaudia,
nos deterret iam senectus
morborum familia.

Refl.   Velox etas preterit
        studio detenta,
        lascivire suggerit
        tenera iuventa.

Imitemur superos!
digna est sententia,
et amoris teneros
iam venantur retia.
voto nostro serviamus!
mos est iste numinum.
ad plateas descendamus
et choreas virginum!

Refl.   Velox etas preterit
        studio detenta,
        lascivire suggerit
        tenera iuventa.

Ibi, que fit facilis,

75. *The Joys of Youth*

Let us neglect our studies—
sweet it is to act as sots—
and harvest the sweetnesses
of our tender youth!
It befits only the old to turn
their attention to earnest affairs.

Refr.   Swiftly does the time fly by,
when by study it's detained,
and the tender age of youth
prompts the heart to play.

The spring of life glides away,
and winter hastens along;
our vitality forfeits itself,
and anxiety macerates the form.
The blood dries up, the heart
grows dull, delights are abated,
and senectitude now arrests us
with a household of ills.

Refr.   Swiftly does the time fly by,
when by study it's detained,
and the tender age of youth
prompts the heart to play.

Let us imitate the gods above!
A worthy determination is it,
as even now nets chase
after tender, enamored lads.
Let us serve our desires!
Such is the way of the gods.
Let us descend on the streets
and the dances of virgins!

Refr.   Swiftly does the time fly by,
when by study it's detained,
and the tender age of youth
prompts the heart to play.

There the opportunity to observe

est videndi copia,
ibi fulget mobilis
membrorum lascivia.
dum puelle se movendo
gestibus lasciviunt,
asto videns, et videndo
me michi subripiunt.

Refl.   Velox etas preterit
         studio detenta,
         lascivire suggerit
         tenera iuventa.

LXXVI. *Nox Veneris Sacrae*

Dum caupona verterem   vino debachatus,
secus templum Veneris   eram hospitatus.
solus ibam, prospere   vestibus ornatus,
plenum ferens loculum   ad sinistrum latus.

Almi templi ianua   servabatur plene;
ingredi non poteram,   ut optavi bene.
intus erat sonitus   dulcis cantilene;
estimabam, plurime   quod essent Sirene.

Cum custode ianue   parum requievi;
erat virgo nobilis,   pulchra, statu brevi.
secum dans colloquia   in sermone levi
tandem desiderium   intrandi explevi.

In ingressu ianue   sedens invitatus
ab hac pulchra virgine   sum interrogatus:
«unde es, o iuvenis,   hucce applicatus?»
cui dixi: «domina,   vestri comitatus.»

«Que est causa, dicito,   huc tui adventus?
qualis ad hec litora   appulit te ventus?
duxit te necessitas   et tua iuventus?»
dixi: «necessario   venio detentus.

Intus et exterius   asto vulneratus
a sagitta Veneris;   ex quo fui natus,
telum fero pectore   nondum medicatus.

the dancers favorably manifests.[93]
There shine the playful
motions of their limbs.[94]
Whilst the maidens gyrate, sport,
frolic, and frisk, I stand by and watch,
and, as I espy their capers,
they steal myself from me.

> *Refr.*   Swiftly does the time fly by,
>   when by study it's detained,
>   and the tender age of youth
>   prompts the heart to play.

76. *Night of the Sacred Venus*

When I turned away from the tavern where I had smashed myself
with wine, I saw that next to the Temple of Venus I had caroused
and lodged. Alone I advanced, prosperous as I was,
bedecked in fine clothes, carrying a full purse on my left.

The door of the propitious temple was well-sentineled;
I could not enter, as I wished well to do.
Inside rang the sound of a sweet song;
and I thought it was a Sirens' throng.

I rested a short while with the guard of the door:
a noble lass was she, beautiful and in stature small.
With her I conversed in soft, playful words
and at last fulfilled my desire to enter the fane.

Upon passing through the door, I was invited to sit[95]
by this beautiful girl and then was asked: "Whence are you,
O youth, directed to this place?" And to her I said,
"Mistress, I was accompanied here by one of your coterie."[96]

"Tell me, what is the reason behind your arrival here?
What sort of wind has driven you to these shores?
Did necessity and your young manhood lead you here?"
Quoth I, "I necessarily came, held back from this place.

"Before you I stand wounded inside and out
by Venus' harsh, captive bolt; since the day of my birth
I have carried a missile in my breast and have not yet healed.

cursu veni tacito,   quo sim liberatus.

Incessanter rogo te,   virgo tu beata,
ut hec verba Veneri   nunties legata.»
ipsa, mota precibus,   fortiter rogata,
nuntiavit Veneri   verba destinata:

«Secretorum omnium   salus o divina,
que es dulcis prepotens   amoris regina,
egrum quendam iuvenem   tua medicina
procurare studeas,   obsecro, festina!»

Iussu sacre Veneris   ductus in conclavi,
cernens eius speciem   fortiter expavi.
flexis tandem genibus   ipsam salutavi,
«salve,» dicens, «inclita   Venus, quam optavi!»

«Quis es,» inquit, «iuvenis,   qui tam bene faris?
quid venisti, dicito!   quomodo vocaris?
es tu forte iuvenis   ille dictus Paris?
ista de quo retulit,   cur sic infirmaris?»

«Venus clementissima,   felix creatura,
cerno, quod preterita   noscis et futura.
ipse sum miserrimus,   res iam peritura,
quem sanare poteris   tua levi cura.»

«Bene»,» inquit, «veneris,   noster o dilecte
iuvenis! Aptissime   sodes nostre secte.
si tu das denarios   monete electe,
dabitur consilium   salutis perfecte.»

«Ecce,» dixi, «loculus   extat nummis plenus.
totum quippe tribuam   tibi, sacra Venus.
si tu das consilium,   ut sat sim serenus,
tuum in perpetuum   venerabor genus.»

Ambo iunctis manibus   ivimus mature,
ubi stabant plurime   belle creature.
omnes erant similes,   unius nature
et unius habitus   atque vestiture.

Nobis propinquantibus   omnes surrexere.

Come have I on a silent march, so that I may be liberated.

"Incessantly I ask you, you splendid lass, to relay
as my envoy these my words to Lady Venus."
She, moved by my prayers and vigorously solicited,
heralded these words to Venus, as she was elected to do:

"O divine salvation and keeper of all secrets,
who are the plenipotentiary queen of sweet love,
strive, I pray, to attend to a certain sick youth
with the speedy power of your medicine!"

At her bidding I was led into the chamber of sacred Venus.
When I caught sight of her beauty, I shuddered violently.
At last on bent knees, I greeted her: "Hello," said I,
"illustrious Venus, for whom I have intensely yearned."

"Who are you, young man," said she, "who speaks such beautiful words?
Speak! Why have you come and how are you called?
Are you perchance that famous youth hight Paris?[97]
Why are you, of whom my lady has me informed, so infirm?"

"Most merciful Venus, blessed creation, I see
that you are acquainted with both the past and the future.
I am a most abject man, and soon my life will end.
But you can restore me with your soothing care."

"Welcome, our beloved young man!" said she,
"most suitable addition to our sect, if you please.
If you render coins of exquisite mintage,
counsel shall be given for your perfect healing."

"Behold," said I, "here stands forth a purse full of coins.
By all means, sacred Venus, I shall bestow it all upon you.
If you help me to become sufficiently blithe,
forever will I bow before you and kiss your feet."[98]

With speed we both went hand in hand to where
there stood a massive throng of damsels fair.
All were similar in every way: of one nature,
of the same semblance and dress.

They all rose at the goddess' and my approach.

quas ut salutavimus,   responsum dedere:
«bene vos veneritis!   velitis sedere!»
Venus inquit: «aliud   volumus explere.»

Innuens his omnibus   iubet ire cito.
pariter remansimus   in loco munito
solis quiescentibus;   strato redimito
plura pertractavimus   sermone polito.

Exuit se vestibus   genitrix Amoris,
carnes ut ostenderet   nivei decoris.
sternens eam lectulo   fere decem horis
mitigavi rabiem   febrici doloris.

Postmodum transivimus   ire balneatum
in hortanum balneum   Iovi consecratum.
huius aqua balnei me   sensi purgatum
omnibus languoribus   beneque piatum.

Ultra modum debilis,   balneo afflictus,
fame validissima   steteram astrictus.
versus contra Venerem   «quasi derelictus,»
dixi «vellem edere,   siquis inest victus!»

Perdices et anseres   ducte sunt coquine,
plura volatilia,   grues et galline;
pro placentis ductus est   modius farine.
preparatis omnibus   pransus sum festine.

Tribus, reor, mensibus   secum sum moratus,
plenum ferens loculum   fui vir ornatus;
recedens a Venere   sum nunc allevatus
nummis atque vestibus;   sum sic pauperatus.

Terreat vos, iuvenes,   istud quod auditis!
dum sagittam Veneris   penes vos sentitis,
mei este memores!   vos, quocumque itis,
liberi poteritis   esse, si velitis.

LXXVII. *Flos Gloriosus Amoris*

Si linguis angelicis   loquar et humanis,
non valeret exprimi   palma, nec in annis,

When we greeted them, they rendered this response:
"Welcome! Please sit down with us!" Then said Venus,
"We purpose to perform something else."

She gave them all a sign and bid them to go in haste.
Together we stayed there, and alone we reposed
after we had locked the chamber's door.[99] On a garlanded
couch, we discussed a great many things in polished words.

The mother of Cupid then unclothed herself,
to display her glorious, snow-white form.
I spread her out upon the couch and for almost ten hours
soothed the fury of my throbbing fever.

Thereafter we went for a bath
in a garden pool sacred to Jove.
I felt that I was purged, by the water of this pool,
of all languor and fully absolved.

Exhausted beyond measure, enfeebled by the bath,
I stood there bound by a most powerful hunger.
I turned to Venus and said, "Like a beggar I would
like something to eat, if there be any food in the house."

Partridges and geese were brought to the kitchen,
and an assortment of poultry, cranes, and chickens.
For baking cakes, a peck of cornmeal was brought forth.
When all was ready, I, with greedy haste, ate the meal.

I tarried with her for three months, I believe;
carrying a full purse, I was a man furnished well.
Departing from Venus, I am now lightened of coinage
and of clothes; and in this way was I made a pauper.

That which you've heard should frighten you, lads!
When you sense the arrow of Venus overpowering you,
be mindful of me and my tale! Whithersoever you wend,
you can be unshackled and free, if you, wanderer, but intend.

77. Love's Glorious Blossom

If I should speak in both angel and human tongues,[100]
the victory could not be expressed, in any years to come,

per quam recte preferor   cunctis Christianis,
tamen invidentibus   emulis profanis.

Pange, lingua, igitur   causas et causatum!
nomen tamen domine   serva palliatum,
ut non sit in populo   illud divulgatum,
quod secretum gentibus   extat et celatum.

In virgulto florido   stabam et ameno,
vertens hec in pectore: «quid facturus ero?
dubito, quod semina   in harena sero;
mundi florem diligens   ecce iam despero.

Si despero, merito   nullus admiretur;
nam per quandam vetulam   rosa prohibetur,
ut non amet aliquem   atque non ametur.
quam Pluto subripere,   flagito, dignetur!»

Cumque meo animo   verterem predicta,
optans, anum raperet   fulminis sagitta,
ecce, retrospiciens   sata post relicta,
audias, quid viderim,   dum morarer ita:

Vidi florem floridum,   vidi florum florem,
vidi rosam Madii   cunctis pulchriorem,
vidi stellam splendidam,   cunctis clariorem,
per quam ego degeram   lapsus in amorem.

Cum vidissem itaque,   quod semper optavi,
tunc ineffabiliter   mecum exultavi,
surgensque velociter   ad hanc properavi,
hisque retro poplite   flexo salutavi:

«Ave, formosissima,   gemma pretiosa,
ave, decus virginum,   virgo gloriosa,
ave, lumen luminum,   ave, mundi rosa,
Blanziflour et Helena,   Venus generosa!»

Tunc respondit inquiens   stella matutina:
«ille, qui terrestria   regit et divina,
dans in herba violas   et rosas in spina,
tibi salus, gloria   sit et medicina!»

by which I am rightly raised above all Christian folk,
despite blasphemous rivals' envious, high dudgeon.

Sing therefore, O tongue of mine, the causes and the effect!
Nevertheless keep disguised the mistress' name,
lest it be spread among the people and nations
what is from the pagans kept secret and concealed.

In a flowery, pleasant bush I stood, whirling
these thoughts in my breast: "What should I do?
I hesitate to plant seeds in the sand.[101]
Loving the flower of all the world, lo!, I now am in despair.

"If I despair, no one need really wonder why;
for by an old crone my rose is kept from me,
such that she loves no one and is loved by none.
May Pluto deign to steal her away, I do fiercely pray!"

And while in my heart I spun the aforesaid things,
I wished that a bolt of lightning would strike the old hag;
lo! I looked back upon the fields of grain that I had left behind,
and now hearken to what I saw, as I tarried on yonder height:

I saw a blooming flower, I beheld the flower of flowers,
I looked upon the little rose of May, more beautiful than
all the others and a splendid star, brighter than all the rest,
through which I slipped and into love passed.

And when I beheld what I had desired all my life,
in my heart I then sprang up in supremely ineffable joy,[102]
and rising swiftly I hastened to this noble dame[103]
and greeted her in turn on bended knee with these words:[104]

"Hail, most beautiful, precious jewel,[105]
hail, glory of maidens, glorious virgin,
hail, light of lights, hail, rose of the world,
O Blanscheflur[106] and Helen, O eminent Venus!

Then the morning star answered and said:
"He, who rules the terrestrial and supernal realms,
who between the grasses lets grow violets and roses
amidst thorns, let him be thy salvation, glory, and cure!"

Cui dixi: «dulcissima!   cor michi fatetur,
quod meus fert animus,   ut per te salvetur.
nam a quodam didici,   sicut perhibetur,
quod ille, qui percutit,   melius medetur.»

«Mea sic ledentia   iam fuisse tela
dicis? nego; sed tamen   posita querela
vulnus atque vulneris   causas nunc revela,
ut te sanem postmodum   gracili medela!»

«Vulnera cur detegam,   que sunt manifesta?
estas quinta periit,   properat en sexta,
quod te in tripudio   quadam die festa
vidi; cunctis speculum   eras et fenestra.

Cum vidissem itaque,   cepi tunc mirari,
dicens: «ecce mulier   digna venerari!
hec excedit virgines   cunctas absque pari,
hec est clara facie,   hec est vultus clari!»

Visus tuus splendidus   erat et amenus,
tamquam aer lucidus   nitens et serenus;
unde dixi sepius: «Deus, Deus meus!
estne illa Helena   vel est dea Venus?»

Aurea mirifice   coma dependebat,
tamquam massa nivea   gula candescebat,
pectus erat gracile;   cunctis innuebat,
quod super aromata   cuncta redolebat.

In iocunda facie   stelle radiabant,
eboris materiam   dentes vendicabant,
plus, quam dicam, speciem   membra geminabant:
quidni, si hec omnium   mentem alligabant?

Forma tua fulgida   tunc me catenavit,
michi mentem, animum   et cor immutavit.
tibi loqui spiritus   ilico speravit;
posse spem veruntamen   numquam roboravit.

Ergo meus animus   recte vulneratur.
ecce, vita graviter   michi novercatur.
quis umquam, quis aliquo   tantum molestatur,

To her I said, "Sweetest lady! My heart confesses to me,
that my soul is compelled to be saved through thee!
For I learned from a certain man, as it is presented
in the tomes, that he heals it best, who caused the wound."

"Thou statest it was my missiles that so caused thy wounds?
That I deny, but with the accusation laid aside,
unveil thou now the wound and its causes, so that I may
afterwards heal thee by means of a simple cure!"

"Why should I expose the wounds, which are already manifest?
The fifth summer has passed, and now the sixth is rushing by
that I first saw thee at a holiday dance;
thou wert the mirror and window to all!

"When I first caught sight of thee, I was then in wonder
taken up and said: 'Here is a maiden worthy of my praise!
A maiden without equal, she surpasses all the rest.
She is of clear complexion; she is of refulgent face!'

"The sight of thee was splendid and agreeable to my eyne,
as the luminous air shines brilliantly and clear.
Whereupon I continued my speech: 'God, my God!
Is she the illustrious Helen or the Venus sublime?'

"Wonderfully hanged her tresses of gold;
white as a mound of snow shimmered her throat;
slender and tender was her breast; she hinted to all
that she smelled sweeter than all aromatic perfumes.[107]

"On her lovely visage the stars brightly beamed;
and her teeth could lay claim on ivory's theme!
Her limbs doubled in beauty more than I can possibly word.
What wonder is it if these assets enthrall all men's hearts?

"Thy blazing pulchritude then manacled all of me
and metamorphosed my mind, soul, and heart—all three.
My heart instantly hoped to share speech with thee,
but the faculty ne'er strengthened my hope's lee.

"Therefore it is rightly alleged that my spirit carries wounds.
Behold how life treats me with vehement contumely.
When and where is one tribulated more than he,

quam qui sperat aliquid   et spe defraudatur?

Telum semper pectore   clausum portitavi,
milies et milies   inde suspiravi,
dicens: «rerum conditor,   quid in te peccavi?
omnium amantium   pondera portavi.

Fugit a me bibere,   cibus et dormire,
medicinam nequeo   malis invenire.
Christe, non me desinas   taliter perire,
sed dignare misero   digne subvenire!»

Has et plures numero   pertuli iacturas,
nec ullum solacium   munit meas curas,
ni quod sepe sepius   per noctes obscuras
per imaginarias   tecum sum figuras.

Rosa, videns igitur,   quam sim vulneratus,
quot et quantos tulerim   per te cruciatus,
dicens «placet!» itaque   fac, ut sim sanatus,
per te sim incolumis   et vivificatus!

Quod quidem si feceris,   in te gloriabor,
tamquam cedrus Libani   florens exaltabor.
sed si, quod non vereor,   in te defraudabor,
patiar naufragium vel periclitabor.»

Inquit rosa fulgida: «multa subportasti,
nec ignota penitus   michi revelasti.
sed que pro te tulerim,   numquam somniasti;
plura sunt, que sustuli,   quam que recitasti.

Sed omitto penitus   recitationem,
volens talem sumere   satisfactionem,
que prestabit gaudium   et sanationem
et medelam conferet   melle dulciorem.

Dicas ergo, iuvenis,   quod in mente geris!
an argentum postulas,   per quod tu diteris,
pretioso lapide   an quod tu orneris?
nam si esse poterit,   dabo, quicquid queris.»

«Non est id, quod postulo,   lapis nec argentum,

who hopes for something and then is cheated of his dream?

"Always have I carried a missile shut up in my breast,[108]
whereupon I have many thousand times sighed, saying:
'Founder of all things, how have I sinned against You?'[109]
I have carried the weights of all paramours in the world.

"'Drink, food, and sleep all flee my sight,
nor can I discover any medicine for this plight.
Christ, do not leave me to die in this way,
but deign most kindly to assist a hapless man!'

"These losses have I suffered and many more beyond count,
nor does any solace strengthen me in my concerns,
unless time after time in the darkness of night
I am with thee in the tableaus of my dreams.

"Rose, seeing now how I have been wounded by thee,
how many and great are the torments I've borne
through thee, say 'It is decided' and render me
healed, whole, and revivified through thee!

"Assuredly, if thou this dost, I shall glory in thee.
Like Lebanon's cedar, I in bloom shall rise to great heights.[110]
But if I am wrong about thee, which I do not fear I am,
I shall suffer a shipwreck or be exposed to risk."

Quoth the glowing rose, "Many sorrows hast thou shouldered,
nor hast thou revealed things to me completely unknown.
But what I have suffered for thee, thou hast in thy dreams ne'er seen.
I have borne more sufferings than thou didst recite.

"But I neglect the full and complete list,
wanting more to express an apology to thee
that will bring about joy and healing
and confer a cure sweeter than honey on thee.

"Express then, youth, what thou bearest in thy core!
Dost thou demand silver, to enrich thyself,
or to be with a precious stone adorned?
For if it be possible, I shall give whatever thou dost seek."

"My desire inclines not toward stones and argent,

immo prebens omnibus   maius nutrimentum,
dans impossibilibus   facilem eventum
et quod mestis gaudium   donat luculentum.»

«Quicquid velis, talia   nequeo prescire;
tuis tamen precibus   opto consentire.
ergo, quicquid habeo,   sedulus inquire,
sumens, si, quod appetis,   potes invenire!»

Quid plus? collo virginis   brachia iactavi,
mille dedi basia,   mille reportavi,
atque sepe sepius   dicens affirmavi:
«certe, certe istud est   id, quod anhelavi!»

Quis ignorat, amodo   cuncta que secuntur?
dolor et suspiria   procul repelluntur,
paradisi gaudia   nobis inducuntur,
cuncteque delicie   simul apponuntur.

Hic amplexus gaudium   est centuplicatum,
hic mecum et domine   pullulat optatum,
hic amantum bravium   est a me portatum,
hic est meum igitur   nomen exaltatum.

Quisquis amat, itaque   mei recordetur
nec diffidat illico,   licet amaretur!
illi nempe aliqua   dies ostendetur,
qua penarum gloriam   post adipiscetur.

Ex amaris equidem   grata generantur,
non sine laboribus   maxima parantur,
dulce mel qui appetunt,   sepe stimulantur;
sperent ergo melius,   qui plus amarantur!

LXXVIII. *Virgo Amabilis*

Anni novi rediit novitas,
hiemis cedit asperitas,
breves dies prolongantur,
elementa temperantur
subintrante Ianuario.
mens estu languet vario
propter puellam, quam diligo.

but chases after something that furnishes greater support,
that vouchsafes the impossible a pleasant outcome,
and grants the disconsolate the splendor of joy."

"Whatever thou cravest, I cannot foreknow.
But thy orisons I do wish very much to fulfill.
Therefore zealously seek thou after what I possess,
taking up, if thou canst discover it, whatever thou dost wish."

What more? I cast my arms around the maiden's neck,
gave her a thousand kisses and obtained a thousand more,
and repeatedly asseverated to her these words:
"No doubt, no doubt, that is for what I did thirst!"

Who knows not henceforth all that follows?[111]
Pain and grievous sighs are driven far away,
the joys of paradise are drawn over us,
and all manner of dishes are served up at once.

Here the joy of an embrace is wondrously centupled.
Here sprouts the wish of me and my mistress.
Here the guerdon of lovers was borne by me.
Here therefore was my name exalted highly.[112]

Thus should every lover bethink himself of me
and not at once lose faith, even if bitterness is his lot![113]
Some day will assuredly be shown to him, whereon
he at last will acquire the glory for all his travails.

Verily from bitter things are pleasant ones born.
Not without labors are the greatest things forged:
those who strive after sweet honey are often stung;
let them then hope for better, who are embittered the more!

78. *A Loveworthy Maid*

The novelty of a new year has returned;
the harshness of winter now withdraws.
Short days are now lengthened,
the elements temper themselves,
as January now upon them steals.
My soul is weak from a variable heat
because of the girl I love.

Prudens est multumque formosa,
pulchrior lilio vel rosa;
gracili coartatur statura,
prestantior omni creatura;
placet plus Francie regina.
michi mors est iam vicina,
nisi sanet me flos de spina.

Venus me telo vulneravit
aureo, quod cor penetravit,
Cupido faces instillavit,
Amor amorem inspiravit
iuvencule, pro qua volo mori.
non iungar cariori,
licet accrescat dolor dolori.

Illius captus sum amore,
cuius flos adhuc est in flore.
dulcis fit labor in hoc labore,
osculum si sumat os ab ore.
non tactu sanabor labiorum,
nisi cor unum fiat duorum
et idem velle. vale, flos florum!

LXXIX. *Defectum Tentamentum*

Estivali sub fervore,
quando cuncta sunt in flore,
totus eram in ardore.
sub olive me decore,
estu fessum et sudore,
detinebat mora.

Erat arbor hec in prato
quovis flore picturato,
herba, fonte, situ grato,
sed et umbra, flatu dato.
stilo non pinxisset Plato
loca gratiora.

Subest fons vivacis vene,
adest cantus philomene
Naiadumque cantilene.

Smart is she and very shapely, too,
more beautiful than a lily or rose;
confined by a slender build is she,
more extraordinary than every creation I've seen:
she pleases me more than the Queen of France.
But death will soon befall me, unless
I am healed by her, the flower on the sloe.

Venus wounded me with a golden dart,
which pierced through my heart;
Cupid instilled his torched in me,
and Love inspired love for a young
maiden, for whom I am willing to die.
Let me be joined to no one dearer,
even if pain should be annexed to dole.

Held captive am I by my love for her,
whose flower is hitherto in fresh bloom.
Sweet becomes the toil in this labor,
if my mouth take up a kiss from hers.
Not by the touch of her lips will I be cured,
unless one heart be made from two and be of one will.[114]
O flower of all flowers, in this prevail!

79. A Failed Attempt

Beneath the heat of summer,
when all things are in bloom,
I was completely aflame.
Beneath a splendid olive tree
detained was I by pause, wearied
from the heat inside me and without.[115]

This tree stood in a meadow
that was embroidered with blooms,
grass, a fountain, and a delightful locale,
but also given shade and a gentle breeze.
Plato with his style could not have limned
a more pleasant and more lovely site.

Hidden beneath is a spring of living water,
and the treble of the nightingale is at hand;
present, too, are the songs of the Naiads:[116]

paradisus hic est pene;
non sunt loca, scio plene,
his iocundiora.

Hic dum placet delectari
delectatque iocundari
et ab estu relevari,
cerno forma singolari
pastorellam sine pari
colligentem mora.

In amorem vise cedo;
fecit Venus hoc, ut credo.
«ades!» inquam, «non sum predo,
nichil tollo, nichil ledo.
me meaque tibi dedo,
pulchrior quam Flora!»

Que respondit verbo brevi:
«ludos viri non assuevi.
sunt parentes michi sevi;
mater longioris evi
irascetur pro re levi.
parce nunc in hora!»

LXXX. *Renovatio Terrae*

Estivali gaudio
tellus renovatur,
militandi studio
Venus excitatur.
gaudet chorus iuvenum,
dum turba frequens avium
garritu modulatur.

Refl.   Quanta sunt gaudia
         amanti et amato,
         sine fellis macula
         dilecte sociato!
         iam revernant omnia
         nobis delectabilia,
         hiems eradicatur.

it is almost an earthbound paradise there.
There are no climes of which I'm fully aware
that are more delightful than those which my eyes did bear.

While here it pleases me to be charmed
and charms me into taking delight
and finding relief from the heat,
I see a shepherd girl without equal
and of singular form,
collecting mulberries sweet.

I fall in love at the sight of her;
Venus effected this, I believe.
"Come over here," I said, "a bandit am not I.
I won't take from you, nor wound you in any wise.
Myself and mine I give to you,
who Flora's bloom outshine!"[117]

Succinctly did she respond:
"Unaccustomed am I to men's games of love;
my parents are not of savage line.
My mother, who is advanced in years,
will be furious over this trivial affair!
On the hour now desist!"

80. *Earth's Rebirth*

In estival joy
is the earth renewed.
By the zeal of service to love
is Venus aroused.
A band of young lads takes delight,
whilst a populous throng of avians
twitters and chirps.

Refr.   How great are the joys,
when one loves and is loved,
when without the stain of gall
a lad is joined to a beloved girl!
Now spring forth again
all our delights and bliss:
eradicated is the winter's chill.

Ornantur prata floribus
varii coloris,
quorum delectatio
causa fit amoris.
gaudet chorus iuvenum,
dum turba frequens avium
garritu modulatur.

Refl.   Quanta sunt gaudia
amanti et amato,
sine fellis macula
dilecte sociato!
iam revernant omnia
nobis delectabilia,
hiems eradicatur.

In calore vivido
nunc reformantur omnia,
hiemali tedio
que viluere languida.
tellus ferens gramina
decoratur floribus,
et vestiuntur nemora
frondosis arboribus.

Refl.   Quanta sunt gaudia
amanti et amato,
sine fellis macula
dilecte sociato!
iam revernant omnia
nobis delectabilia,
hiems eradicatur.

Amorum officiis
hec arrident tempora,
geminatis sociis
restaurantur federa.
festa colit Veneris
puellaris curia,
propinat Amor teneris
amaris miscens dulcia.

Refl.   Quanta sunt gaudia

The meadows are adorned
with flowers of various hues,
the delightfulness of which
becomes an occasion for love's suits.
A chorus of young lads takes delight,
whilst a populous throng of avians
twitters and chirps.

Refr.   How great are the joys,
when one loves and is loved,
when without the stain of gall
a lad is joined to a beloved girl!
Now spring forth again
all our delights and bliss:
eradicated is the winter's chill.

In this animated heat
all things are now renewed,
which in the tedium of winter
were listless and laid low.
The earth yields sweet grasses
and is with flowers bejeweled,
and the woods are accoutered
with the livery of leafy trees.

Refr.   How great are the joys,
when one loves and is loved,
when without the stain of gall
a lad is joined to a beloved girl!
Now spring forth again
all our delights and bliss:
eradicated is the winter's chill.

These times smile upon
the ceremonies of love;
lovers' pacts are reforged
by partnered pairs.
The court of maidens celebrates
Venus' festive days,
whilst Love waters tender hearts
and mixes draughts bittersweet.

Refr.   How great are the joys,

amanti et amato,
sine fellis macula
dilecte sociato!
iam revernant omnia
nobis delectabilia,
hiems eradicatur.

LXXXI. *Saltate Ad Planctum Solis*

Solis iubar nituit,
nuntians in mundum,
quod nobis emicuit
tempus letabundum.
ver, quod nunc apparuit,
dans solum fecundum,
salutari meruit
per carmen iocundum.

Refl.   Ergo nostra contio
         psallat cum tripudio
         dulci melodia!

Fugiente penitus
hiemis algore
spirat ether tacitus
estu gratiore.
discendente celitus
salutari rore
fecundatur funditus
tellus ex humore.

Refl.   Ergo nostra contio
         psallat cum tripudio
          melodia!

Sol extinctus fuerat,
modo renitescit;
frigus invaluerat,
sed modo tepescit;
nix, que nos obruerat,
ex estu liquescit;
qui prius aruerat,
campus revirescit.

when one loves and is loved,
when without the stain of gall
a lad is joined to a beloved girl!
Now spring forth again
all our delights and bliss:
eradicated is the winter's chill.

81. *Dance to the Beat of the Sun*

The sun's beam glistens,
promulgating unto the world
that the time of mirth now
has broken forth for us.
The spring, which has now appeared,
blessing with fertility the earth,
has earned a salutation
through a joyous song.

Refr.   With a measured stamp then
           our flock should sing
           to an ever sweet and joyous strain!

As the cold of winter
puts all its essence to flight,
the still air above breathes
a more warming sigh.[118]
From heaven descend
salutary drops of dew,
and the earth is fertilized
by the moisture it endows.

Refr.   With a measured stamp then
           our flock should sing
           to an ever sweet and joyous strain!

The sun that had been extinguished
now to brilliancy returns.
An icy chill had prevailed,
but now the clime grows warm.
The snow that had inhumed us
now deliquesces from the heat.
The field that had been dry before
now bursts into color again.

Refl.   Ergo nostra contio
         psallat cum tripudio
         dulci melodia!

Philomena stridula
voce modulatur;
floridum alaudula
tempus salutatur.
anus, licet vetula,
mire petulatur;
lascivit iuvencula,
cum sic recreatur.

Refl.   Ergo nostra contio
         psallat cum tripudio
         dulci melodia!

LXXXII. *Disputatio Thymi et Lapathii*

Frigus hinc est horridum,
tempus adest floridum.
veris ab instantia
tellus iam fit gravida;
in partum inde solvitur,
dum florere cernitur.

Refl.   O o o a i a e !
         amor † insolabile!
         clerus scit diligere
         virginem plus milite!

Sol tellurem recreat,
ne fetus eius pereat;
ab aeris temperantia
rerum fit materia,
unde muitiplicia
generantur semina.

Refl.   O o o a i a e !
         amor † insolabile!
         clerus scit diligere
         virginem plus milite!

Refr.   With a measured stamp then
our flock should sing
to an ever sweet and joyous strain!

The nightingale warbles
in the highest tones;
the little lark greets
this time of the flowers;
the old woman, though advanced in years,
is astonishingly engaging in mischievous affairs,
when the frolicsome young lass
thus returns to cheer again.

Refr.   With a measured stamp then
our flock should sing
to an ever sweet and joyous strain!

82. *Thyme and Sorrel's Disputation*

The horrific cold is far away;
the time of the flowers is at bay.[119]
From the presence of spring
the earth now bears young
and unseals herself for birth,
as blooming jewels are discerned.

Refr.   O o o a i a e![120]
O my dearest, there is no balm!
The cleric knows how to love
a maiden better than a knight!

The sun recreates the earth,
lest her offspring die away.
From the temperateness
of the air, the essence
of all things is made,
whence various seeds are born.

Refr.   O o o a i a e!
O my dearest, there is no balm!
The cleric knows how to love
a maiden better than a knight!

Mons vestitur floribus
et sonat a volucribus;
in silvis aves concinunt
dulciterque garriunt;
nec philomena desinit,
iacturam suam meminit.

Refl.   O o o a i a e !
amor † insolabile!
clerus scit diligere
virginem plus milite!

Ridet terre facies
colores per multiplices.
nunc audite, virgines:
non amant recte milites!
miles caret viribus
nature et virtutibus!

Refl.   O o o a i a e !
amor † insolabile!
clerus scit diligere
virginem plus milite!

Thymus et lapathium
inierunt hoc consilium:
«propter formam milites
nobis sunt amabiles.»
«de quibus stulta ratio,
suspensa est solatio.»

Refl.   O o o a i a e !
amor † insolabile!
clerus scit diligere
virginem plus milite!

«Sed in cordibus milites
depingunt nostras facies,
cum serico in palliis,
colore et in clipeis.»
«quid prosunt nobis talia,
cum forma perit propria?

The mountain is robed in flowers
and rings with the treble of birds.
In the woods these singers in harmony
chirp and in sweet innocence prate.
Nor does the nightingale cease
to remember her bereft state.

Refr.   O o o a i a e!
        O my dearest, there is no balm!
        The cleric knows how to love
        a maiden better than a knight!

Terra's visage smiles
through a myriad of colors bright.[121]
Now hearken, ye maidens:
Chevaliers do not rightly love!
The knight has no natural strength
nor excellence of any type!

Refr.   O o o a i a e!
        O my dearest, there is no balm!
        The cleric knows how to love
        a maiden better than a soldier!

Thyme and Sorrel[122] together
engaged in the following deliberation:
"Because of their appearance
knights are loveable to us."
"Their imbecilic reason
wavers in giving solace."

Refr.   O o o a i a e!
        O my dearest, there is no balm!
        The cleric knows how to love
        a maiden better than a knight!

"But knights on their hearts
paint our comely faces,
with silk on their mantles
and colors on their shields."
"What use are such things to us,
when our physical beauty perishes?"

Refl.   O o o a i a e !
       amor † insolabile!
       clerus scit diligere
       virginem plus milite!

Clerici in frigore
observant nos in semine,
pannorum in velamine,
deinde et in pyxide.»
mox de omni clerico
Amoris fit conclusio.

Refl.   O o o a i a e !
       amor † insolabile!
       clerus scit diligere
       virginem plus milite!

LXXXIII. *Petrus et Virgo Sua*
Petrus Blesensis (ca. 1135 - ca. 1204)

Sevit aure spiritus, et arborum
come fluunt penitus vi frigorum;
silent cantus nemorum.
nunc torpescit vere solo
fervens amor pecorum;
semper amans sequi nolo
novas vices temporum
bestiali more.

Refl.   Quam dulcia stipendia
       et gaudia felicia
       sunt hec hore nostre Flore!

Nec de longo conqueror obsequio:
nobili remuneror stipendio,
leto letor premio.
dum salutat me loquaci
Flora supercilio,
mente satis non capaci
gaudia concipio,
glorior labore.

Refl.   Quam dulcia stipendia

Refr.   O o o a i a e!
O my dearest, there is no balm!
The cleric knows how to love
a maiden better than a knight!

"The clerics pay attention to us
when they provide us with spelt,
with cloths we can wear as robes,
and finally with a small toiletry box."
Anon Love's peroration on every cleric
is rendered: he deserves to be loved.[123]

Refr.   O o o a i a e!
O my dearest, there is no balm!
The cleric knows how to love
a maiden better than a knight!

83. *Peter and His Maid*
by Peter of Blois (ca. 1135 – ca. 1204)

Violently blow the winds, and completely disappear
the tresses of the trees from the force of the hoar.
Silent are all the sweet sylvan songs;
now benumbed is the animals' lust
that boils only in the spring.
Ever a lover, I want not to follow
these new changes of the year
like a ductile ox.

Refr.   How sweet are these stipends
and how blissful are these delights:
these hours spent with our lovely Flora!

I repine not about the long service at all:
I am remunerated with excellent pay.
I take joy in my happy reward.
When Flora greets me
with her eloquent eyebrow,
joys I take up in my heart
that has not for so many room enough,
and then glory in my labor.

Refr.   How sweet are these stipends

et gaudia felicia
sunt hec hore nostre Flore!

Michi sors obsequitur non aspera:
dum secreta luditur in camera,
favet Venus prospera.
nudam fovet Floram lectus:
caro candet tenera,
virginale lucet pectus,
parum surgunt ubera
modico tumore.

Refl.   Quam dulcia stipendia
         et gaudia felicia
         sunt hec hore nostre Flore!

Hominem transgredior et superum
sublimari glorior ad numerum,
sinum tractans tenerum
cursu vago dum beata
manus it et uberum
regionem pervagata
descendit ad uterum
tactu leviore.

Refl.   Quam dulcia stipendia
         et gaudia felicia
         sunt hec hore nostre Flore!

A tenello tenera pectusculo
distenduntur latera pro modulo;
caro carens scrupulo
levem tactum non offendit.
gracilis sub cingulo
umbilicum preextendit
paululum ventriculo
tumescentiore.

Refl.   Quam dulcia stipendia
         et gaudia felicia
         sunt hec hore nostre Flore!

Vota blando stimulat lenimine

and how blissful are these delights:
these hours spent with our lovely Flora!

A fate not at all harsh yields to my will:
whilst in a secret chamber the game of love is played,
Venus is kind and propitious to me.
The bed warms Flora, who lies there nude:
Her tender flesh glows,
her virginal torso shines,
her breasts rise not too high,
modest even in their swelling.

Refr.   How sweet are these stipends
and how blissful are these delights:
these hours spent with our lovely Flora!

I transcend the mortality of man
and glory in my elevation
to the number of the gods,
when I hold in hand her tender bosom
and my blessed hand moves on a vagrant course
and, having wandered through
the districts of her breasts,
descends to her stomach
with a gentler caress.

Refr.   How sweet are these stipends
and how blissful are these delights:
these hours spent with our lovely Flora!

From her tender little breasts her soft flanks tauten
in such elegant proportions.
Her flawless body does not give way
to a gentle touch.
Slender about the waistline,
she projects her navel but a little
from her lightly vaulted belly.

Refr.   How sweet are these stipends
and how blissful are these delights:
these hours spent with our lovely Flora!

Her rosy chalice's curls

pubes, que vix pullulat
in virgine tenui lanugine.
crus vestitum moderata
tenerum pinguedine
levigatur occultata
nervorum compagine,
radians candore.

Refl.   Quam dulcia stipendia
         et gaudia felicia
         sunt hec hore nostre Flore!

O si forte Iupiter hanc videat,
timeo, ne pariter incaleat
et ad fraudes redeat:
si vel Danes pluens *antrum*
imbre dulci mulceat,
vel Europes intret taurum,
vel Ledeo candeat
rursus in olore.

Refl.   Quam dulcia stipendia
         et gaudia felicia
         sunt hec hore nostre Flore!

LXXXIV. *Duellum Petri*
Petrus Blesensis (ca. 1135 - ca. 1204)

Dum prius inculta
coleret virgulta
estas iam adulta,
hieme sepulta,
vidi viridi
Phyllidem sub tilia,
vidi Phyllidi
quevis arridentia.
invideo, dum video.
sic capi cogit sedulus
me laqueo virgineo
cordis venator oculus
visa captus virgine.

Refl.   Ha morior!

arouse thirsty cravings for
the alluring elixir that they adorn;[124]
such tresses scarcely sprout forth
in a tender maiden's down.[125]
Her delicate legs, enrobed in a tempered layer of flesh,
with whiteness glowing, are brightened to incandescence
by the hidden junction of her nerves.[126]

Refr.   How sweet are these stipends
          and how blissful are these delights:
          these hours spent with our lovely Flora!

O, if Jupiter should by chance catch sight of this girl,
I fear that he would glow with the same passion I do
and revert back to his olden tricks:[127]
either he, as a light rain,[128]
would bewitch Danaë's cave with sweet dew,
or assume the semblance of Europa's bull,
or blaze inside Leda again
in the guise of a swan.[129]

Refr.   How sweet are these stipends
          and how blissful are these delights:
          these hours spent with our lovely Flora!

84. *Peter's War*
by Peter of Blois (ca. 1135 – ca. 1204)

When the summer, now ripened
by winter's sepulture,
was cultivating
the once bleak shrubs,
I beheld Phyllis
beneath a linden green
and saw everything
smile upon her.
Jealous was I, as I watched these sights.
My eye, a keen hunter of the heart,
captivated by her sight,
thus drives me into the snare
of the virgin's noose.

Refr.   O heavens, I am dying!

sed quavis dulcedine
mors dulcior.
sic amanti vivitur,
dum sic amans moritur.

Fronte explicata
exiit in prata,
ceu Dione nata,
Veneris legata.
videns, invidens
huc spe duce rapior.
ridens residens
residenti blandior.
sed tremula virguncula
frondis in modum tremule,
ut primula discipula
nondum subducta ferule,
tremit ad blanditias.

Refl.   Ha morior!
         sed *propter delicias*
         mors dulcior.
         sic amanti vivitur,
         dum sic amans moritur.

Respondendi metus
trahit hanc ad fletus.
sed raptura letus
Amor indiscretus
meam in eam,
ut pudoris tangere
queam lineam,
 manum mittit propere.
dum propero, vim infero
posti minante machina;
nec supero, nam aspero
defendens ungue limina
obserat introitus.

Refl.   Ha morior!
         sed hec michi penitus
         mors dulcior.
         sic amanti vivitur,

But with this sweetness
a sweeter death it is.
For the lover it spells life
when he so lovingly dies.

With a cheerful mien[130]
she went off into the meadows,
like a daughter of Dione,
like an emissary of Venus.
As I watched her, I was jealous,
and, with hope as my conductress,
hurried to her seat.
I sat down with a smile
and fondled her as she did rest.
But the timid little lass quivered at my caress
like the tremulous leaves of a tree
and behaved like a beginning schoolgirl,
who had not yet from the rod been spared.

Refr.   O heavens, I am dying!
But with these delights[131]
a sweeter death it is.
For the lover it spells life
when he so lovingly dies.

The fear of responding to me[132]
hauled this girl into tears.
But indiscreet Love,
happy in its plundering,
sent in my hand with haste
towards the girl,
so I could touch
the brink of her shame.
I rushed in and launched an assault,
with a menacing siege engine,
upon her barricaded door.
But overcome her I did not, for with sharp fingernails
she defended the thresholds and barred the entry points.

Refr.   O heavens, I am dying!
But this to me is wholly
a sweeter demise.
For the lover it spells life

dum sic amans moritur.

Tantalus admotum
non amitto potum!
sed ne tamen totum
frustret illa votum,
suo denuo
iungens collo brachium
ruo, diruo
tricaturas crurium.
ut virginem devirginem,
me toti totum insero;
ut cardinem determinem
duellum istud refero:
sic in castris milito.

Refl.   Ha morior!
         sed *cum placito*
         mors dulcior.
         sic amanti vivitur,
         dum sic amans moritur.

LXXXV. *Iuliana Dulcis* (ca. 1150)

Veris dulcis in tempore
florenti stat sub arbore
Iuliana cum sorore.
         Dulcis amor!

Refl.   Qui te caret hoc tempore,
         fit vilior.

Ecce florescunt arbores,
lascive canunt volucres;
inde tepescunt virgines.
         Dulcis amor!

Refl.   Qui te caret hoc tempore,
         fit vilior.

Ecce florescunt lilia,
et virginum dant agmina
summo deorum carmina.

when he so lovingly dies.

Not as Tantalus will I let
the incoming drink slip away![133]
But lest that girl still foil
my entire desire and urge
I advance again,
wrap my arms around her neck,
and tear asunder the twisted bulwark of her legs.
To deflower the virgin,
I implant all of myself in her.
To enclose this frontier within my boundary line,[134]
I register this valiant duel in verse and rhyme:[135]
and so in this camp I perform
my service to the uniform.

Refr.   O heavens, I am dying!
         But with this pleasantry[136]
         a sweeter death it is.
         For the lover it spells life
         when he so lovingly dies.

85. *Sweet Juliana* (ca. 1150)

In the time of sweet spring,
beneath a flowering tree,
stands Juliana and her sister.
         Sweet love!

Refr.   Who is without thee in this season
         becomes less worthful for his treason.

Behold the verdure of the trees!
The birds are frolicking in song.
And for this reason all the virgins grow warm.
         Sweet love!

Refr.   Who is without thee in this season
         becomes less worthful for his treason.

Lo! The lilies are blooming bright,
and trains of maidens are raising songs
to the highest of the gods.[137]

Dulcis amor!

Refl.   Qui te caret hoc tempore,
            fit vilior.

Si tenerem, quam cupio,
in nemore sub folio,
oscularer cum gaudio.
            Dulcis amor!

Refl.   Qui te caret hoc tempore,
            fit vilior.

LXXXVI. *Carmen Perversi*

Non contrecto,
quam affecto;
ex directo
ad te specto
et annecto
nec deflecto
cilia.

Refl.   Experire, filia, virilia:
            semper sunt senilia labilia,
            sola iuvenilia stabilia.
            hec sunt utensilia agilia,
            facilia, gracilia,
            fragilia, humilia,
            mobilia, docilia,
            habilia, *sessilia*,
            et si qua sunt similia.

Post fervorem
celi rorem,
post virorem
album florem,
post candorem
dant odorem
lilia.

Refl.   Experire, filia, virilia:
            semper sunt senilia labilia,

Sweet love!

Refr.   Who is without thee in this season
becomes less worthful for his treason.

If I were holding her, for whom I pine,
in the woods beneath a canopy sublime,
I would kiss her with great joy!
Sweet love!

Refr.   Who is without thee in this season
becomes less worthful for his treason.

86. *A Pervert's Song*

I touch not the girl,
whom I pursue.
I look at you
directly
and on you fix my gaze
and ne'er do I
deflect my eyes.

Refr.   Try, pretty child, my manly gear:
Ever floppy is the equipment of old men;
only youths' gadgets are able to stand.
These tools are nimble, dexterous,
slender, tender,
unassuming, moveable,
quick to learn, expert,
fit for sitting upon,[138]
and whatever suchlike occurs to you.[139]

After the raging heat
falls heaven's dew;
after green leaves
follow white blossoms;
after the white luster
the lilies emit
sweet perfumes.

Refr.   Try, pretty child, my manly gear:
Ever floppy is the equipment of old men;

sola iuvenilia stabilia.
hec sunt utensilia agilia,
facilia, gracilia,
fragilia, humilia,
mobilia, docilia,
habilia, *sessilia*,
et si qua sunt similia.

LXXXVII. *Oda ad Amorem*

Amor tenet omnia,
mutat cordis intima,
querit Amor devia.
Amor melle dulcior,
felle fit amarior.
Amor cecus, † caret pudicitia;
frigidus et calidus et tepidus,
Amor audax, pavidus,
est fidus atque perfidus.

Tempus est idoneum,
querat Amor socium:
nunc garritus avium.
Amor regit iuvenes,
Amor capit virgines.
ve senectus!   tibi sunt incommoda.
va t'an oy! iuvencula Theoclea
tenet me gratissima;
tu pestis, dico, pessima.

† Frigidus *nec* calidus
numquam tibi socius!
dormit dolens sepius
in natura frigidus;
nichil tibi vilius.
Venus tenet   iuvenes in gaudio;
sana sic coniunctio,
quam diligo, tuo fit imperio.
quid melius sit, nescio.

Amor volat undique;
captus est libidine.
iuvenes iuvencule

only youths' gadgets are able to stand.
These tools are nimble, dexterous,
slender, tender,
unassuming, moveable,
quick to learn, expert,
fit for sitting upon,
and whatever suchlike occurs to you.

87. *Ode to Cupid*

Cupid rules all things;
Cupid transforms the inmost depths of the heart;
Cupid seeks pathless retreats;
Cupid is sweeter than honey
and more bitter than gall becomes.
Cupid the blind lacks shamefaced restraint.[140]
Cold and hot and tepid,
Cupid is daring and yet full of fear;
loyal is he and treacherous all the same.

The time of year is suited to him,
and Cupid seeks a compatriot:
now the twitter of the birds.
Cupid sways young lads,
Cupid captures virgins' hearts.
Alas, senectitude, detriments are your lot![141]
Avaunt![142] Most charming Theoclea
now binds me fast.[143]
A very foul pestilence you are, I say.

One who is cold and not hot
should never be a friend to you![144]
He sleeps more often because he's in pain
and is frigid in sexual affairs.[145]
Nothing is more useless to you.[146]
Venus keeps young lads in perennial bliss.
Thus a healthy union (O how I cherish it!)
is forged by your command.
I know of nothing better than this.

Cupid flies everywhere,
captivated by sensual desire.
Lads and lasses come together,

que secuntur mentio;
si que sine socio,
illa vero   caret omni gloria;
tenet noctis infima sub intima
cardinis custodia.
sic fit res amarissima.

Amor simplex, callidus;
rufus Amor, pallidus;
truculens in omnibus,
Amor est placabilis,
constans et instabilis.
Amor artis   regitur imperio.
ludit Amor lectulo iam clanculo
noctis in silentio:
fit captus Amor laqueo.

LXXXVIII. *Cecilia*

Amor habet superos:
Iovem amat Iuno;
motus premens efferos
imperat Neptuno;
Pluto tenens inferos
mitis est hoc uno.

Refl.   Amoris solamine
         virgino cum virgine;
         aro non in semine,
         pecco sine crimine.

Amor trahit teneros
molliori nexu,
rigidos et asperos
duro frangit flexu;
capitur rhinoceros
virginis amplexu.

Refl.   Amoris solamine
         virgino cum virgine;
         aro non in semine,
         pecco sine crimine.

events that rightly follow his model.
If a maiden has no friend,
she has indeed no glory at all.
She holds the darkest things of night
beneath the most secret prison of her core.[147]
In this way a most bitter affair is forged.

Cupid is guileless; Cupid has craft;
Cupid is red; Cupid is colorless;
Fierce in all things,
Cupid is easily appeased;
constant and fickle always is he.
Cupid is ruled by the power of his art.
Cupid plays his game in bed;
now in secret, in the still of the night:
Cupid is in a noose ensnared.

88. Cecilia

Cupid rules the gods above:
Juno loves the mighty Jupiter;
Cupid dominates Neptune when
he suppresses the violent winds;[148]
Pluto, the tyrant of the underworld,
is tempered only by this god.

Refr.   Through Cupid's solace
        I play the virgin with a lass.[149]
        I plough without a seed;
        I sin without misdeed.

Cupid drags tender lads
with a rather soft braid,
but the rigid and austere
he softens with a harsh twist.
A unicorn is captured
by a maiden's hug.[150]

Refr.   Through Cupid's solace
        I play the virgin with a lass.
        I plough without a seed;
        I sin without misdeed.

Virginis egregie
ignibus calesco
et eius cotidie
in amore cresco;
sol est in meridie,
nec ego tepesco.

Refl.   Amoris solamine
         virgino cum virgine;
         aro non in semine,
         pecco sine crimine.

Gratus super omnia
ludus est puelle,
et eius precordia
omni carent felle;
sunt, que prestat, basia
dulciora melle.

Refl.   Amoris solamine
         virgino cum virgine;
         aro non in semine,
         pecco sine crimine.

Ludo cum Cecilia;
nichil timeatis!
sum quasi custodia
fragilis etatis,
ne marcescant lilia
sue castitatis.

Refl.   Amoris solamine
         virgino cum virgine;
         aro non in semine,
         pecco sine crimine.

Flos est; florem frangere
non est res secura.
uvam sino crescere,
donec sit matura;
spes me facit vivere
letum re ventura.

I am inflamed with passion
for a surpassing lass,
and everyday I grow
in my love for her.
The sun sits in the seat of noon,
and still my flames do not cool.[151]

Refr.   Through Cupid's solace
            I play the virgin with a lass.
            I plough without a seed;
            I sin without misdeed.

Exceedingly delightful
is the playfulness
of the girl[152]
and her heart is free of all gall.
The kisses she gives
are sweeter than honey.

Refr.   Through Cupid's solace
            I play the virgin with a lass.
            I plough without a seed;
            I sin without misdeed.

I am frisking with Cecilia;
nothing should ye fear!
I am like a guardian
of her fragile age,
lest the lilies
of her chastity decay.

Refr.   Through Cupid's solace
            I play the virgin with a lass.
            I plough without a seed;
            I sin without misdeed.

A flower she is; and violating a flower
is not a secure affair.
I allow the grape to grow,
until it is ripe and mature.
Hope keeps me alive,
happy in the event on the rise.

Refl.   Amoris solamine
         virgino cum virgine;
         aro non in semine,
         pecco sine crimine.

Virgo cum virginibus
horreo corruptas,
et cum meretricibus
simul odi nuptas;
nam in istis talibus
turpis est voluptas.

Refl.   Amoris solamine
         virgino cum virgine;
         aro non in semine,
         pecco sine crimine.

Quicquid agant ceteri,
virgo, sic agamus,
ut, quem decet fieri,
ludum faciamus;
ambo sumus teneri;
tenere ludamus!

Refl.   Amoris solamine
         virgino cum virgine;
         aro non in semine,
         pecco sine crimine.

Volo tantum ludere,
id est: contemplari,
presens loqui, tangere,
tandem osculari;
quintum, quod est agere,
noli suspicari!

Refl.   Amoris solamine
         virgino cum virgine;
         aro non in semine,
         pecco sine crimine.

LXXXVIIIa. *Nati Sub Eadem Longinquitate Caeli* (ca. 1130)

Refr.   Through Cupid's solace
I play the virgin with a lass.
I plough without a seed;
I sin without misdeed.

A virgin among virgins,
I shy away from spoiled dames;
and together with the harlots
I despise married girls;
for among such lasses as these
sensual pleasure is vile and base.

Refr.   Through Cupid's solace
I play the virgin with a lass.
I plough without a seed;
I sin without misdeed.

Whatever the rest may do,
maiden, let us do, too,
so that we may play a game
that is fitting to be made;
we both are tender youths;
let us tenderly cavort!

Refr.   Through Cupid's solace
I play the virgin with a lass.
I plough without a seed;
I sin without misdeed.

I wish only to disport, that is, to gaze
into your eyes, discourse face-to-face,
touch your flaxen hair, and finally
plant kisses on your lips;
the fifth thing there is to do,
do not deem, my dear, suspect!

Refr.   Through Cupid's solace
I play the virgin with a lass.
I plough without a seed;
I sin without misdeed.

88a. *Born Beneath the Same Reach of Sky* (ca. 1130)

Iove cum Mercurio   Geminos tenente
et a Libra Venere   Martem espellente
virgo nostra nascitur,   Tauro tunc latente.

Natus ego pariter   sub eisdem signis
pari par coniunctus sum   legibus benignis:
paribus est ignibus   par accensus ignis.

Solus solam diligo,   sic me sola solum,
nec est, cui liceat   immiscere dolum;
non in vanum variant   signa nostra polum.

Obicit «ab alio»   forsitan «amatur,»
ut, quod «solus» dixerim,   ita refellatur;
sed ut dictum maneat,   sic determinatur.

LXXXIX. *Duo Boni Pastores* (ca. 1100/1150)

«Nos duo boni
sub aere tetro.
sint tibi toni
sub celeri metro!
tempore solis
stant pecora retro.»

Herba tenella
flore coronatur,
rosa novella
rubore notatur;
nigra puella
veste † coronatur.

Tunica lata
succincta balteo,
circumligata
frons filo rubeo;
stat inclinata
sub alto pilleo.

Labor mutavit
puelle faciem
et alteravit
eiusdem speciem,

When Jove and Mercury stood in the house of the Twins
and celestial Venus drove Mars off the Libra's scale,
our maiden was born—then the Bull was in hiding.[153]

Together with her was I born underneath the same signs;
I was joined to my equal by fate's ever propitious laws.
Through the same stars like fires were given light.

I alone love only her; thus she alone loves only me.
There is no one who may mingle with this any deceit.
Not in vain do our signs change the firmament's design.

Objection: "By another man"—perhaps—"is she loved,"
such that my assertion "alone" is disproved.
But as my words do stand, it is thus ruled.

89. *Two Good Shepherds* (ca. 1100/1150)

"We are two good lads[154]
under a hideous mist.
Set thy tones
to a swift meter![155]
In the time of the sun
the sheep retreat."[156]

The tender little grass
is crowned with blooms.
The young rose
is marked with red.
And a girl is decked
with a robe of black.[157]

Her expansive tunic
is upheld by a belt.
A red band is wrapped
around her head.
Beneath a lofty cap
she stands in a stoop.

Hardship has changed
the face of the girl
and has fully altered
her mien;

decoloravit
eam per maciern.

Ducit puella
gregem parvulum,
et cum capella
caprum vetulum
et cum asella
ligat vitulum.

Polus obscura
nube tegitur.
virgo matura
mox egreditur,
voce secura
nos alloquitur:

«Ecce † pastores
temerarii,
gregis pastores
conducticii,
fabulatores
vaniloquii!

Abominantur
opus manuum,
lucra sectantur,
amant otium,
nec meditantur
curam ovium.

Prodiga pastus
est turba pullorum:
copia lactis
non ordine morum
rebus attractis
stat ut vile forum.

Nec res succedunt
nec locus in tuto:
vellera cadunt
de spinis in luto,
palam accedunt

through its macerations[158]
trial has discolored her face.

The girl guides
a very small flock:
a she-goat
and a little old buck,
and to a she-ass
she binds a calf.

The empyrean is covered
by a lowery cloud;
anon the maiden
speedily marches up.
She speaks to us in
an insouciant tone:

"Behold the reckless
shepherds yonder,
the hired hands
of the herd,[159]
the fabulists
of idle talk!

"They detest
labor of the hands,
follow after profits,
love leisure dearly,
and think not on
the sheep's care.

"The throng of calves
is prodigal of its food:
for its abundance of milk,
not its moral degree,
with goods gathered together,
it stands as a cheap marketplace.

"Nothing prospers; no place is safe:
their wool falls into muck
ruffled by thorns.
Without disguise,
approach the wolves

lupi cane muto.»

Aspero verbo
tractans de pratica,
valde superbo
vultu phrenetica,
ore acerbo
cessavit rustica.

«Vellem, ut scires
pastorum carmina!
dum viri vires
non habes femina,
numquam aspires
ad viri culmina!

Est tua cura
labor femine:
sic *solum* cura
opus femine
virgo, mensura
filum stamine!

Gere, puella,
morem pecori:
languet asella,
stupent teneri,
iungit capella
latus lateri.

Parvula fides
† sociis otium;
garrula rides
magisterium,
subdola strides
contra pretium.

 Sumus pastores
nos egregii,
procuratores
gregis regii,
solicantores
soliloquii.»

because the watchdog is dumb."[160]

After she with harsh words
treated of the active life—
fanatically and with
an exceedingly arrogant air—
the churlish lass ended her rant
with a bitter countenance.

"I would that you knew
the shepherds' songs!
Since you, woman, have not
the energies of man,
never should you breathe
upon the pillars of them!

"Your purview is
the feminine craft:
attend only[161]
to the work of a wench
and measure, lass,
the thread in a web!

"Conduct yourself, girl,
as the sheep and goats:
When the she-ass is sick,
the tender foals are struck aghast;
the sheep flock
side-by-side.

"The faintheartedness[162] of your kind
is but a diversion to lads such as us.
With blather you ridicule
the lecturer's position and rank.
From behind[163] you screech
against something invaluable.

"Eminent shepherds
are we, keepers
of the royal herd,
We alone are
the singers
of the soliloquy!"

XC. *Scholaris et Pastor Muliebris*

Exiit diluculo
rustica puella
cum grege, cum baculo,
cum lana novella.

Sunt in grege parvulo
ovis et asella,
vitula cum vitulo,
caper et capella.

Conspexit in cespite
scolarem sedere:
«quid tu facis, domine?
veni mecum ludere!»

XCI. De sacerdotibus

Sacerdotes, mementote:
nichil maius sacerdote,
qui, ditatus sacra dote,
ruga caret omnis note.

Mementote tot et tanti,
quid ingratum sit Tonanti,
ad virtutem nos hortanti,
cum sic ait: «este sancti!

Sanctus ego; sancti sitis,
conformari si velitis
michi, qui sum vera vitis,
qui sum pius, qui sum mitis!»

Obedite summo vati,
sacerdotes consecrati!
ad hoc estis ordinati,
sacris aris mancipati.

Corpus Christi vos tractatis.
quod si digne faciatis,
non expertes castitatis,
ore, corde Deo gratis,

90. *The Scholar and the Shepherdess*

At daybreak came forth
a country lass with a flock,
carrying a staff,
together with virgin wool.

There were in the little herd
a sheep and a small she-ass,
a cow-calf and young bull,
a buck and a she-goat.

Sitting in a grassy field,
a student she then espied.
"What are you doing, mister?
Come with me and play!"

91. On Priests

Priests, be mindful of this:
Nothing is greater than a priest,
who enriched with a sacred dowry,
lacks the wrinkle of all disgrace.

Remember from the teachings many and great,
what is disagreeable to the Thunderer above,
Who is to virtue urging us on,
when He says: "Be holy![164]

"I am sacred; you thirst for something pure,
if you desire to be fashioned after Me,
Who am the True Vine,[165] Who am pious,
and Who am kindly disposed!"

Obey the Greatest Teacher,
O consecrated priests!
Be ordained according to this,
O subjects to the sacred altars!

You wield the body of Christ.
But if you should rightly do it—
ye, who are not destitute of purity—
by offering freely a mouth and heart to God,

cum electis et beatis
in conspectu maiestatis
regnaturos vos sciatis!

O quam fortis armatura,
qua vestitur vestra cura;
sed si forte contra iura
faciatis, ruitura!

Nota vobis est scriptura:
«cum offertis Deo tura,
si mens vestra non sit pura,
non sunt illi placitura.»

Miserorum contemptores
si vos estis contra mores
vel altaris mercatores,
fures estis, non pastores.

O sacerdos hic, responde,
cuius manus sunt immunde,
qui frequenter et iocunde
cum uxore dormis, unde
mane surgens missam dicis,
corpus Christi benedicis,
post amplexus meretricis,
minus quam tu peccatricis!

Scire velim causam, quare
sacrosanctum ad altare
statim venis immolare,
dignus virgis vapulare.

Vapulare virgis dignus,
dum amoris tantum pignus
corvus tractas et non cygnus,
iam non heres, sed privignus.

Dignus morte, dignus penis
ad altare Christi venis
cum fetore, cum obscenis,
osculando fictis genis.

with chosen, blessed beings,
in the sight of majesty,
know that you would rule!

O how strong is the armor,[166]
with which your pastorate is clothed;
but if by chance you commit deeds against the laws,
from you it will straightway fall!

The words of the Scripture are known to you:
"When you offer frankincense to God,
if your spirit be not pure,
its oblation will not please Him at all."[167]

If you be despisers of the wretched,
contrary to the ecclesiastical order's ways,
or merchants on high altars,
then not shepherds, but thieves, are ye.

O thou priest, respond here and now,
whose hands are besmirched
and who often and with pleasure sleep with a wench:
how hast thou the nerve, when thou wakest
in the morn, to read the mass
and consecrate the body of the Christ,
after receiving the embraces of a whore,
who herself is less sinful than thou thyself art?!

Would I knew the reason
why thou forthwith to the altar comest,
to bring thither a sacrosanct offering,
thou, who deservest to be cudgeled with sticks.

Worthy of a flogging with switches thou art,
when thou takest in hand so lofty a pledge of Godly love,
though thou art a crow and certainly not a swan,
no longer an heir, but a merely stepson.

Deserving death, deserving punishments,
thou comest to the altar of Christ
with a stench and offensive thoughts,
giving kisses to invented cheeks.[168]

Plenus sorde, plenus mendis
ad auctorem manus tendis,
quem contemnis, quem offendis,
meretricem dum ascendis.

Castitatis non imbute,
sed immundus corde, cute
animarum pro salute
missam cantas, o pollute!

Quali corde quo vel ore
corpus Christi cum cruore
tractas, surgens de fetore,
dignus plagis et tortore?

Quali vultu, quali fronte,
non compulsus, immo sponte,
ore, corde, lingua sonte
de tam sacro bibis fonte?

Miror ego, miror plane,
quod sub illo latet pane
corpus Christi, quod profane
manus tractant ille mane.

Miror, nisi tu mireris,
quod a terra non sorberis,
dum, quod sepe prohiberis,
iterare non vereris.

Forte putas manus mundas,
cum frequenter fundis undas?
quas frequenter quamvis fundas,
tam fetentes non emundas.

Lava manus, aquas funde:
quamvis clare, quamvis munde,
quamvis fuse sint abunde,
numquam purgant eas unde.

Purgamentum vis audire?
si reatum vis finire,
mox divine cessant ire,

Full of filth, full of blunders,
thou stretchest thy hands to the Creator Supreme,
whom thou contemnest, whom thou offendest,
when thou mountest a whore.

Not with the spirit of charity imbued,
but sullied in thy heart and on thy skin,
thou singest the mass for the salvation of souls,
o thou maculated ass!

With what kind of heart or what kind of mouth
dost thou handle the body of Christ with gory hands,
thou, who risest from noisome foulness,
who art worthy of buffets and a hangman?

With what countenance, with what brow—
not compelled, nay, of thy own free will—
with what mouth, what heart, what criminal tongue
dost thou drink from so sacred a font?

I wonder, I marvel completely
that under that bread hides
the body of Christ that those hands
profane in the morning do touch.

I marvel, if thou shouldst not marvel at all,
that thou art not swallowed by the earth's maw,
since thou art not afraid to repeat
what thou art repeatedly forbidden to do.

Perchance thou thinkest that thy hands are clean,
since thou dost frequently decant holy waters?
Though very often thou mayest them pour,
thou dost not cleanse such mephitic hands.

Wash thou thy hands; pour thou the waters:
though they are clear, though they are clean,
though they aboundingly have been teemed,
never do they purge thy hands.

Thou wishest to hear of a means of purification?
If thou desirest to end thy impeached state,
anon the divine wrath ceases,

nec te potest impedire.

Si cor scissum, cor contritum
habes, neque iuxta ritum
lectum petis infrunitum,
numquam erit requisitum.

Sed reatum cum deploras
et adire mox laboras,
quod plorandum esse noras,
Deum magis inhonoras.

Nichil valet hic ploratus,
nec dimissus est reatus,
sed est magis augmentatus,
Deus magis irritatus.

XCII. De Phyllide et Flora

Anni parte florida,   celo puriore,
picto terre gremio   vario colore,
dum fugaret sidera   nuntius Aurore,
liquit somnus oculos   Phyllidis et Flore.

Placuit virginibus   ire spatiatum,
nam soporem reicit   pectus sauciatum;
equis ergo passibus   exeunt in pratum,
ut et locus faciat   ludum esse gratum.

Eunt ambe virgines   et ambe regine,
Phyllis coma libera,   Flore compto crine.
non sunt forme virginum,   sed forme divine,
et respondent facies   luci matutine.

Nec stirpe nec facie   nec ornatu viles
et annos et animos   habent iuveniles;
sed sunt parum impares   et parum hostiles,
nam huic placet clericus   et huic placet miles.

Non eis distantia   corporis aut oris,
omnia communia   sunt intus et foris,
sunt unius habitus   et unius moris;
sola differentia   modus est amoris.

and nothing can thee impede.

If a rent heart thou hast, if a pounded heart thou bearest,
and, together with religious observance,
thou beseechest a serious expiation chosen just for thee,
never will it have been sought in vain.

But thou speciously ruest thy criminal ways
and strivest to undergo at a later time
what thou hast known must be repented anon—
more gravely then thou dishonorest God.

This kind of lamentation hath no effect,
nor hath thy guiltiness been dismissed,
but it hath been augmented the more,
and God hath been further incensed.

92. The Song of Phyllis and Flora

In the year's time of the blooms, when the welkin was especially clear,
when the lap of the earth was painted with a plethora of hues,
when Aurora's herald[169] put the stars to flight,
sleep abandoned the eyes of Phyllis and Flora.

It pleased the maidens to promenade,
for their wounded hearts repudiated sleep;
so side-by-side they proceeded into the meadow,
so that the setting would make their game delightful.

Both maidens, both queens, they thither advanced,
Flora with her free-flowing hair, Phyllis' tied back.
They were not of maidenly form, but of form divine,
and their visages were akin to the morning light.

Not mean in stock nor complexion nor dress,
they had both the years and spirits of youths;
but betwixt the twain was a small inequality and enmity,
for one loved a cleric and the other a knight.

Not distant at all in body or face,
sharing all qualities within and without,
they were of one nature and one way of life;
the only difference was their mode of love.

Susurrabat modicum   ventus tempestivus,
locus erat viridi   gramine festivus,
et in ipso gramine   defluebat rivus
vivus atque garrulo   murmure lascivus.

Ad augmentum decoris   et caloris minus
fuit secus rivulum   spatiosa pinus,
venustata folio,   late pandens sinus,
nec intrare poterat   calor peregrinus.

Consedere virgines;   herba sedem dedit.
Phyllis iuxta rivulum,   Flora longe sedit.
et dum sedet utraque,   dum in sese redit,
amor corda vulnerat   et utramque ledit.

Amor est interius   latens et occultus
et corde certissimos   elicit singultus;
pallor genas inficit,   alternantur vultus,
sed in verecundia   furor est sepultus.

Phyilis in suspirio   Floram deprehendit,
et hanc de consimili   Flora reprehendit;
altera sic alteri   mutuo rependit;
tandem morbum detegit   et vulnus ostendit.

Ille sermo mutuus   multum habet more,
et est quidem series   tota de amore;
amor est in animis,   amor est in ore.
tandem Phyllis incipit   et arridet Flore.

«Miles», inquit, «inclite,   mea cura, Paris!
ubi modo militas   et ubi moraris?
o vita militie,   vita singularis,
sola digna gaudio   Dionei laris!»

Dum puella militem   recolit amicum,
Flora ridens oculos   iacit in obliquum
et in risu loquitur   verbum inimicum:
«amas,» inquit, «poteras   dicere: mendicum.

Sed quid Alcibiades   facit, mea cura,
res creata dignior   omni creatura,
quem beavit omnibus   gratiis Natura?

The seasonable wind whispered but a little,
the festive locale sported verdant grass,
and through that very grass a rivulet flowed,
animated and petulant, with a garrulous splash.

To the growth of the beauty and diminution of the heat,
there was a mighty pine along the running stream.
Beautified by a leafy mantle, it spread its boughs wide,[170]
and no heat from without could enter its foreign realm.

There the maidens rested; the grass furnished them a seat.
Phyllis sat beside the brook; Flora sat further away.
And whilst both reposed, and each occupied herself,
love wounded their hearts and injured them both.

Love, lurking and concealed deep within their breasts,
elicited from their hearts unequivocal sighs wetted with tears;
wanness marked their cheeks; their expressions shifted about,
but in bashfulness did they suppress their feeling of fury.

Phyllis caught Flora in a deep sigh,
but Flora accused her of the same crime.
They bandied charges back and forth, until they
finally uncovered the malady and revealed the wound.

These reciprocal words extended a great length,
and surely became a whole treatise on the theme of love.
Full of love were both their hearts and their mouths.
So Phyllis began and laughed at Flora:

"O illustrious knight," said she, "my darling, Paris![171]
Where art thou serving, and where tarriest?
O thou singular life of the valiant rider,
alone thou meritest the joy of Dione's court!"

Whilst the girl reflected on her knightly friend,
Flora, laughing, cast her eyes askance,
and with a smile voiced these hostile words:
"Thou couldst also have said, 'I love a beggar.'

"But how fares Alcibiades,[172] my darling love,
a being more refined than all other creatures,
whom Nature hath blessed with all her graces?

o sola felicia   clericorum iura!»

Floram Phyllis arguit   de sermone duro
et sermone loquitur   Floram commoturo;
nam «ecce virgunculam»   inquit «corde puro,
cuius pectus nobile   servit Epicuro!

Surge, surge, misera,   de furore fedo!
solum esse clericum   Epicurum credo;
nichil elegantie   clerico concedo,
cuius implet latera   moles et pinguedo.

A castris Cupidinis   cor habet remotum,
qui somnum desiderat   et cibum et potum.
o puella nobilis,   omnibus est notum,
quod est longe militis   ab hoc voto votum.

Solis necessariis   miles est contentus,
somno, cibo, potui   non vivit intentus;
amor illi prohibet,   ne sit somnolentus,
cibus, potus militis   amor et iuventus.

Quis amicos copulet   nostros loro pari?
lex, natura sineret   illos copulari?
meus novit ludere,   tuus epulari;
meo semper proprium   dare, tuo dari.»

Haurit Flora sanguinem   vultu verecundo
et apparet pulchrior   in risu secundo,
et tandem eloquio   reserat facundo,
quod corde conceperat   artibus fecundo.

«Satis», inquit, «libere,   Phyllis, es locuta,
multum es eloquio   velox et acuta,
sed non efficaciter   verum prosecuta,
ut per te prevaleat   lilio cicuta.

Dixisti de clerico,   quod indulget sibi,
servum somni nominas   et potus et cibi.
sic solet ab invido   probitas describi;
ecce, parum patere,   respondebo tibi.

Tot et tanta, fateor,   sunt amici mei,

O blessed are only the powers of the clerics!"

Phyllis scolded Flora for her harsh remark
and spoke to her in words that would stir her ire:
For she said, "Behold the little maid, pure of heart,
whose noble breast is a slave to Epicurus' flock!

"Rise, rise, wretched girl, from thy foul infatuation!
I believe that the cleric is nothing but a bon vivant!
No tasteful propriety do I concede to the cleric,
whose flanks are filled with shapeless bulk and fat.

"Far from Cupid's camp his heart doth dwell,
whose desires lean towards sleep, food, and swills.
O eminent girl, it is known to all, that the knight's
desires are quite far from the cleric's pangs.

"The knight is content with only the necessities;
he lives not intent on sleep, vittles, and draughts.
Love forbids him from feeling somnolent,
and love and youth are his pabulum and his drink.

"Who would tie our friends with the same line?
Would the law, would Nature allow them to be bound?
Mine knows how to frolic and jest, and thine to feast.
'Tis the mark of mine ever to give, but thine only to receive."

Flora's face drew blood in shame, but appeared prettier
in the jest that followed, when she at last revealed,
in eloquent words, what she had conceived
in her soul that in great learning abounded:

"Quite impertinently didst thou speak," quoth she,
"and very swift and cunning art thou in speech,
but thou didst not effectively present the truth,
such that through thee hemlock over a lily prevails.

"Thou spakest that the cleric indulges himself
and named him a slave to sleep, drink, and food.
Thus by an envier is probity wont to be described.
Now then, have a little patience: I shall to thee rejoin.

So many and great things, I confess, my friend holds,

quod numquam incogitat   aliene rei.
celle mellis, olei,   Cereris, Lyei,
aurum, gemme, pocula   famulantur ei.

In tam dulci copia   vite clericalis,
quod non potest aliqua   pingi voce talis,
volat et duplicibus   Amor plaudit alis,
Amor indeficiens,   Amor immortalis.

Sentit tela Veneris   et Amoris ictus,
non est tamen clericus   macer aut afflictus,
quippe nulla gaudii   parte derelictus;
cui respondet animus   domine non fictus.

Macer est et pallidus   tuus preelectus,
pauper et vix pallio   sine pelle tectus,
non sunt artus validi   nec robustum pectus;
nam cum causa deficit,   deest et effectus.

Turpis est pauperies   imminens amanti.
quid prestare poterit   miles postulanti?
sed dat multa clericus   et ex abundanti;
tante sunt divitie   redditusque tanti.»

Flore Phyllis obicit: «multum es perita
in utrisque studiis   et utraque vita,
satis probabiliter   et pulchre mentita;
sed hec altercatio   non quiescet ita.

Cum orbem letificat   hora lucis feste,
tunc apparet clericus   satis inhoneste,
in tonsura capitis   et in atra veste
portans testimonium   voluptatis meste.

Non est ullus adeo   fatuus aut cecus,
cui non appareat   militare decus.
tuus est in otio   quasi brutum pecus;
meum terit galea,   meum portat equus.

Meus armis dissipat   inimicas sedes,
et si forte prelium   solus init pedes,
dum tenet Bucephalam   suus Ganymedes,
ille me commemorat   inter ipsas cedes.

that he never thinks on another's worldly goods.
Cellars of honey, olive oil, cereals, and wines,
and gold, gems, and goblets all wait upon his eyes.

"In that ever so sweet abundance of the cleric's life,
such that cannot be painted by any voice, even sublime,[173]
Cupid flies and claps with both his wings,
Cupid Everlasting, Cupid Immortal.

He feels the darts of Venus and Cupid's blows,
but still the cleric is not meager or afflicted at all,
for he is not forsaken by any share in the pleasure.
To him the unfeigned passion of his mistress responds."

"Lean and pale is thy chosen lad—a pauper is he,
clad with a threadbare mantle devoid of any felt;
his limbs are not strong nor his breast robust,
for where the cause fails there is no effect.

"Foul is the penury that overhangs thy lover's head.
What could a knight proffer a girl when she asks?
But the cleric grants many things from a limitless supply:
so great are his riches; so great are his receipts."

Phyllis objected to Flora: "Very shrewd art thou
in both classes' pursuits and ways of life;
very laudably and beautifully didst thou lie,
but this altercation is not settled thereby.

"When the hour of the festal light gladdens the world,
then the cleric appears in a most unsightly costume
with his tonsure on his head and in a black habit,
carrying the proof of his woeful inclination.

"There is not anyone so fatuous and blind,
that the glorious sight of the knight would not pierce his eyes.
Thine resembles in his leisure an irrational beast;
with mine is the helm occupied; mine is carried by a steed.

"Mine with his weapons demolishes enemy castles,
and if by chance he enters a footfight alone,
when his Ganymede holds the steed Bucephala,[174]
he thinks on me even amidst that very red carnage.

Redit fusis hostibus   et pugna confecta
et me sepe respicit   galea reiecta.
ex his et ex aliis   ratione recta
est vita militie   michi preelecta.»

Novit iram Phyllidis   et pectus anhelum
et remittit multiplex   illi Flora telum.
«frustra», dixit, «loqueris   os ponens in celum,
et per acum niteris   figere camelum.

Mel pro felle deseris   et pro falso verum,
que probas militiam   reprobando clerum.
facit amor militem   strenuum et ferum?
non! immo pauperies   et defectus rerum.

Pulchra Phyllis, utinam   sapienter ames
nec veris sententiis   amplius reclames!
tuum domat militem   et sitis et fames,
quibus mortis petitur   et inferni trames.

Multum est calamitas   militis attrita,
sors illius dura est   et in arto sita,
cuius est in pendulo   dubioque vita,
ut habere valeat   vite requisita.

Non dicas opprobrium,   si cognoscas morem,
vestem nigram clerici,   comam breviorem:
habet ista clericus   ad summum honorem,
ut sese significet   omnibus maiorem.

Universa clerico   constat esse prona,
et signum imperii   portat in corona.
imperat militibus   et largitur dona:
famulante maior est   imperans persona.

Otiosum clericum   semper esse iuras:
viles spernit operas,   fateor, et duras;
sed cum eius animus   evolat ad curas,
celi vias dividit   et rerum naturas.

Meus est in purpura,   tuus in lorica;
tuus est in prelio,   meus in lectica,
ubi gesta principum   relegit antiqua,

"When the enemy is routed and the fighting is done,
he returns, casts off his helm, and oft his attention to me turns.
For these and other reasons it is right
that the life of the knight does my praise indite."

Flora marked Phyllis' ire and puffing chest and sent
a fusillade of bullets back her way: "In vain," she said,
"dost thou speak with thy mouth to the sky,
and thou strivest to thread a camel through a needle's eye.[175]

"Honey for gall dost thou desert and for falsehood truth,[176]
when thou judgest the knight by censuring the cleric.
Doth love make a knight restive and savage?
Nay, rather his poverty and want of goods.

"Beautiful Phyllis, if only thou didst wisely love
and not exclaim anymore against my truthful assertions.
Both thirst and hunger subdue thy knight, whereby
the crossway of death and the underworld is sought.

"Very depressing is thy knight's wretched state:
his lot is adverse and is set in dire straits,
and his life is cast in suspension and doubt,
so that he may hold but life's basic essentials.

"If thou knewest their significance, thou wouldst not call
ignominious the cleric's black robe and shorn scalp:
the cleric wears these as a show of his consummate majesty,
to demonstrate that he is greater than all others.

"It is well established that all things bow themselves to him
and that in his crown of hair the sign of his supremacy he wears.
He rules o'er the knights and bestows gifts upon them.[177]
He, who commands, is greater than he, who serves.

"Thou dost decree that the cleric is always at leisure:
servile and strenuous toils I confess he spurns,
but when his spirit flies forth to his official duties,
he divides the paths of heaven and the natures of the world.

"Mine is clothed in garment of purple, thine in a cuirass;
thine fights in battle; mine sits on a travelling sedan,
whereupon he is engrossed in the deeds of the princes of eld

scribit, querit, cogitat   totum de amica.

Quid Dione valeat   et amoris deus,
primus novit clericus   et instruxit meus;
factus est per clericum   miles Cythereus.
his est et huiusmodi   tuus sermo reus.»

Liquit Flora pariter   vocem et certamen
et sibi Cupidinis   exigit examen.
Phyllis primum obstrepit,   acquiescit tamen,
et probato iudice   redeunt per gramen.

Totum in Cupidine   certamen est situm;
suum dicunt iudicem   verum et peritum,
quia vite noverit   utriusque ritum;
et iam sese preparant,   ut eant auditum.

Pari forma virgines   et pari pudore,
pari voto militant   et pari colore:
Phyllis veste candida,   Flora bicolore;
mulus vector Phyllidis   erat, equus Flore.

Mulus quidem Phyllidis   mulus erat unus,
quem creavit, aluit,   domuit Neptunus.
hunc post apri rabiem,   post Adonis funus
misit pro solacio   Cytheree munus.

Pulchre matri Phyllidis   et probe regine
illum tandem prebuit   Venus Hiberine,
eo quod indulserat   opere divine;
ecce Phyllis possidet   illum leto fine.

Faciebat nimium   virginis persone:
pulcher erat, habilis   et stature bone,
qualem esse decuit,   quem a regione
tam longinqua miserat   Nereus Dione.

Qui de superpositis   et de freno querunt,
quod totum argenteum   dentes muli terunt,
sciant, quod hec omnia   talia fuerunt,
qualia Neptunium   munus decuerunt.

Non decore caruit   illa Phyllis hora,

and all he writes, seeks, and thinks revolves around his girl.

"Of what Dione and the god of love are capable
the first cleric knew and my cleric has taught.
Through the cleric the knight became a Cytherean rider.
By these and other reasons thy sermon is impeached."

Flora ended her speech and at the same time the dispute
and demanded that an examination be administered by Cupid.
Phyllis first raised objections, but then acquiesced,
and, when they agreed on the judge, they returned to the grass.

The entire case lay in Cupid's hands.
They called their judge veracious and adept,
because he was versed in the ways of both lives.
They then prepared for their journey to hear his verdict.

Maidens of congruent comeliness and shame,
both fought with the same intent and cast of diction.
Phyllis sported a white dress, Flora a two-colored one;
Phyllis was conveyed by a mule and Flora a horse.

Phyllis' mule was truly one of a kind, a mule
whom Neptune had created, raised, and tamed.
After the boar's wrath and Adonis' obsequies,
he sent him as a gift to Venus as a solace for her loss.[178]

Finally, Venus offered him to the beautiful mother
of Phyllis and virtuous queen of Spain, whereupon
she devoted herself to the works of the goddess.
Then, in a happy end, Phyllis took possession of him.

The beast suited the virgin most excellently:
it was beautiful, nimble, and of magnificent physique;
these qualities befit such an animal, whom to Dione
Nereus[179] had dispatched from a region so far away.

Whoever asks now about the blanket, saddle, and bit—
as for the latter, the mule's teeth wore away all its silver—
should know that all these items were of such a sort
that befit a gift from Neptune, a god.

So at that hour Phyllis was not without splendor,

sed multum apparuit   dives et decora;
et non minus habuit   utriusque Flora,
nam equi predivitis   freno domat ora.

Equus ille, domitus   Pegaseis loris,
multum pulchritudinis   habet et valoris,
pictus artificio   varii coloris;
nam mixtus nigredini   color est oloris.

Forme fuit habilis,   etatis primeve,
et respexit paululum   tumide, non seve;
cervix fuit ardua,   coma sparsa leve,
auris parva, prominens   pectus, caput breve.

Dorso pando iacuit   virgini sessure
spina, que non senserat   aliquid pressure.
pede cavo, tibia   recta, largo crure,
totum fuit sonipes   studium Nature.

Equo superposita   faciebat sella;
ebur enim medium   clausit auri cella,
et, cum essent quattuor   selle capitella,
venustavit singulum   gemma quasi stella.

Multa de preteritis   rebus et ignotis
erant mirabilibus   ibi sculpta notis;
nuptie Mercurii   superis admotis,
fedus, matrimonium,   plenitudo dotis.

Nullus ibi locus est   vacuus aut planus;
habet plus, quam capiat   animus humanus.
solus illa sculpserat,   que spectans Vulcanus
vix hoc suas credidit   potuisse manus.

Pretermisso clipeo   Mulciber Achillis
laboravit phaleras   et indulsit illis;
ferraturam pedibus   et frenum maxillis
et habenas addidit   de sponse capillis.

Sellam texit purpura   subinsuta bysso,
quam Minerva, reliquo   studio dimisso,
acantho texuerat   et flore narcisso
et per tenas margine   fimbriavit scisso.

but appeared more wealthy and decorous;
nor was Flora wanting either of these twain,
since she steered a richly-bridled steed with her reins.

That illustrious horse was trained on Pegasus' very straps,
possessed a wealth of beauty and grandeur,
and his body was a tableau of contrasting hues,
for on it was mixed the color of a swan with black.

He was of seemly form and in the first epoch of life
and glanced a trifle timidly, but never savagely glared.
His neck was lofty, his mane lightly dispersed,
his ears small, his chest prominent, and stocky his head.

Under his curved back, as a seat for the young lass,
lay his spine, which sensed not any pressure from above.
With his hollow hooves, even bones, and massive thighs,
the steed was the handiwork of all of Nature's diligence.

The saddle atop the steed beseemed him so very much:
the middle was of ebony enclosed in a ring of gold,
and, although the saddle had four pommels in all,
a gem adorned each one of them that glistened like a star.

Many histories passed and things unknown
were into that saddle most wonderfully carved:
the wedding of Mercury[180] attended by all the gods,
the compact, the ceremony, and the great dowry divine.

No place thereupon was empty or without relief;
it held more images than the human mind could store;
Vulcan alone had sculpted them; at the sight of the product
he could not believe it was the work of his own hands.

He had laid the shield of Achilles[181] aside and worked
on the saddle's bosses, dedicating himself to them entirely.
He forged shoes for the hooves, a bit for the jaws,
and added to the reins the tresses of his spouse.[182]

He spread o'er the saddle a purple manta underlaid
with byssus,[183] which Minerva, neglecting her other labors,
had woven from acanthus leaves and narcissus petals[184]
and on all sides had trimmed with a fringed border.

Volant equis pariter   due domicelle;
vultus verecundi sunt   et gene tenelle.
sic emergunt lilia,   sic rose novelle,
sic decurrunt pariter   due celo stelle.

Ad Amoris destinant   ire paradisum.
dulcis ira commovet   utriusque visum;
Phyllis Flore, Phyllidi   Flora movet risum.
fert Phyllis accipitrem   manu, Flora nisum.

Parvo tractu temporis   nemus est inventum.
ad ingressum nemoris   murmurat fluentum,
ventus inde redolet   myrrham et pigmentum,
audiuntur tympana   cithareque centum.

Quicquid potest hominum   comprehendi mente,
totum ibi virgines   audiunt repente:
vocum differente   sunt illic invente,
sonat diatessaron,   sonat diapente.

Sonant et mirabili   plaudunt harmonia
tympanum, psalterium,   lyra, symphonia,
sonant ibi phiale   voce valde pia,
et buxus multiplici   cantum prodit via.

Sonant omnes avium   lingue voce plena:
vox auditur merule   dulcis et amena,
corydalus, graculus   atque philomena,
que non cessat conqueri   de transacta pena.

Instrumento musico,   vocibus canoris,
tunc diversi specie   contemplata floris,
tunc odoris gratia   redundante foris
coniectatur teneri   thalamus Amoris.

Virgines introeunt   modico timore
et eundo propius   crescunt in amore.
sonat queque volucrum   proprio rumore,
accenduntur animi   vario clamore.

Immortalis fieret   ibi manens homo.
arbor ibi quelibet   suo gaudet pomo,
vie myrrha, cinnamo   flagrant et amomo;

Together the two mistresses flew on their steeds:
their faces were coquettish; tender were their cheeks.
Thus emerge lilies; thus new roses debouch;
thus two stars race together on their heavenly trail.

They intended to ride to Cupid's Eden.
A sweet thrill changed the glances of both.
Phyllis raised Flora's laugh and Flora raised hers;
Phyllis carried in her hand a falcon, Flora a sparrowhawk.

After a brief interval, the sacred grove was found.
At the entrance of the wood murmured a brook,
the wind blowing thence smelled of myrrh and herbs,
and one hundred drums and harps were heard.

Whatever can be grasped by the senses of man,
there it all suddenly assailed the maidens' ears.
There they learned the invention of polyphonic movements:
the forest sounded the fourth and then rang out the fifth.

The drum, the psaltery, the lyre, and the hurdy-gurdy
all resounded and clapped in miraculous harmony;
thuribles jangled with ever so pious voices,
and the boxwood flute produced a multimodal song.

All the voices of the birds rang with treble full:
discerned were the sweet, melodious warbles
of the merle, crested lark, jackdaw, and nightingale,
who never ceases to bewail her olden dole.

The musical instruments, the dulcet twitters,
then the majestic sight of various flowers,
then the overflowing grace of their outdoor perfumes—
all this augured the presence of boyish Cupid's inner room.

The maidens entered with a moderate share of fear,
and the closer they came to him, the more their love grew.
Each of the birds chirped its own unique notes and by
this polyphonic strain the maidens' hearts were inflamed.

Any mortal man there would surely immortal become.
Every tree there delighted in its plenitude of fruits;
the paths were perfumed with myrrh, cinnamon, and balsam.

coniectari poterat   dominus ex domo.

Vident choros iuvenum   et domicellarum,
singulorum corpora   corpora stellarum.
capiuntur subito   corda puellarum
in tanto miraculo   rerum novellarum.

Sistunt equos pariter   et descendunt, pene
oblite propositi   sono cantilene.
sed auditur iterum   cantus philomene,
et statim virginee   recalescunt vene.

Circa silve medium   locus est occultus,
ubi viget maxime   suus deo cultus:
Fauni, Nymphe, Satyri,   comitatus multus
tympanizant, concinunt   ante dei vultus.

Portant vina manibus   et coronas florum;
Bacchus Nymphas instruit   et choros Faunorum.
servant pedum ordinem   et instrumentorum;
sed Silenus titubat   nec psallit in chorum.

Somno vergit senior   asino prevectus
et in risus copiam   solvit dei pectus.
clamat «vina!» remanet   clamor imperfectus:
viam vocis impedit   vinum et senectus.

Inter hec aspicitur   Cytheree natus:
vultus est sidereus,   vertex est pennatus,
arcum leva possidet   et sagittas latus;
satis potest conici   potens et elatus.

Sceptro puer nititur   floribus perplexo,
stillat odor nectaris   de capillo pexo.
tres assistunt Gratie   digito connexo
et amoris calicem   tenent genu flexo.

Appropinquant virgines   et adorant tute
deum venerabili   cinctum iuventute;
gloriantur numinis   in tanta virtute.
quas deus considerans   prevenit salute.

Causam vie postulat;   aperitur causa,

The proprietor could be surmised from the home.

They saw bands of tender lads and lasses;
the body of each beamed like a star.
The hearts of the maidens were suddenly enraptured
by the great miracle of the novelty of all.

They placed their equines together and from them alighted;
amid the tune of the dance they almost forgot the purport of their visit.
The threnodies of the nightingale were heard again,
and forthwith their virgin veins grew warm.

In the midst of the wood lay a secluded place,
where the cult of the god was in most lively bloom.
Fauns, nymphs, satyrs—a massive cortege—
sang to crashing timbrels before the face of the god.

They carried wine in their hands and chaplets of flowers.
Bacchus instructed the nymphs and choruses of fauns.
They paid attention to the beat of their feet and instruments.
But Silenus[185] tottered and reeled and disrupted the song.

Being older, he sank into sleep, carried forth on an ass,[186]
and elicited from the god's heart laughter immense.
"Wine!" he shouted, and yet the shout remained incomplete:
His tonic and senectitude congested his words' streets.

Amidst these festivities the son of Cytherea was seen.
Starry was his visage; alary was his crown.
In his left hand he held a bow and arrows on his hip.
He could be regarded as exceedingly mighty and tall.

The boy rested upon a scepter entangled in blooms;
from his combed hair dripped the fragrance of nectar.
The Three Graces, with fingers entwined, formed his convoy,
and held the chalice of love on bended knees.

The maidens cautiously approached and prayed
to the god, who was girt in a cast of youth august.
They gloried in the mighty powers of the deity;
looking upon them, the god came forth with a greeting.

He asked the cause of their journey; they made the reason clear.

et laudatur utraque   tantum pondus ausa.
ad utramque loquitur: «modo parum pausa,
donec res iudicio   reseretur clausa!»

Deus erat; virgines   norunt deum esse:
retractari singula   non fuit necesse.
equos suos deserunt   et quiescunt fesse.
Amor suis imperat,   iudicent expresse.

Amor habet iudices,   Amor habet iura:
sunt Amoris iudices   Usus et Natura;
istis tota data est   curie censura,
quoniam preterita   sciunt et futura.

Eunt et iustitie   ventilant vigorem,
ventilatum retrahunt   curie rigorem:
secundum scientiam   et secundum morem
ad amorem clericum   dicunt aptiorem.

Comprobavit curia   dictionem iuris
et teneri voluit   etiam futuris.
parum ergo precavent   rebus nocituris,
que sequuntur militem   et fatentur pluris.

XCIII. *Insula Virginalis*

Hortum habet insula   virgo virginalem.
hunc ingressus virginem   unam in sodalem
spe robustus † virginis   elegi principalem.

Letus ergo socia   elegantis forme
– nil huic laudis defuit,   nil affuit enorme –
cum hac feci geminum   cor meum uniforme.

Est amore dulcius   rerum in natura
nichil et amarius   conditione dura:
dolus et invidia   amoris sunt scissura.

XCIIIa. *Capere Unicornem*

Cum Fortuna voluit   me vivere beatum,
forma, bonis moribus   fecit bene gratum
et in altis sedibus   sedere laureatum.

Both were commended for having ventured so great a toil.
He then addressed the two: "Now a moment's pause
until this tortuous issue is by a ruling unwound."

He was the god; the maidens knew it was so.
It was not necessary that each point be examined anew.
They left their horses behind and, wearied, sought repose.
Cupid bid his entourage to render a clear arbitrament.

Cupid had judges; Cupid had laws.
Custom and Nature were Cupid's arbiters.
The court's entire decision was dependent on them,
since these chancellors knew both past and future affairs.

They went to work and fanned the force of justice.
They cashiered the once-wielded severity of the court:
in accordance with jurisprudence and consuetudinary law,
they decreed that the cleric's love is the seemlier.

The court assented to the ruling of the magistrates
and even decided to be bound by it in future disputes.
All too little then do maidens seek to avert injurious affairs,
who pursue the knight and maintain that he is of a higher class.

93. *The Virgin Island*

There is a virgin isle that has a virginal garden.
I entered it and chose for myself, inflamed
by the prospect of a maid, one to be my boon companion.

Happy therefore was I in my confederate of elegant form,
who was not deficient in praise nor rich in anything enorm,
and with her I combined my ingenuous heart.

Nothing in the nature of things is sweeter than love
and nothing is more bitter than its harsh condition:
artifice and jealousy mark the rending of love.

93a. *To Capture a Unicorn*

When Fortuna decided to bless my life,[187] she made me,
because of my form and good ways, one held in high regard[188]
and an occupant of lofty seats with a laurel wreath atop my crown.

Modo flos preteriit   mee iuventutis,
in se trahit omnia   tempus senectutis;
inde sum in gratia   novissime salutis.

Rhinoceros virginibus   se solet exhibere;
sed cuius est virginitas   intemerata vere,
suo potest gremio   hunc sola retinere.

Igitur que iuveni   virgo sociatur
et me senem spreverit,   iure defraudatur,
ut ab hac rhinoceros   se capi patiatur. –

In tritura virginum   debetur seniori
pro mercede palea,   frumentum iuniori;
inde senex aream   relinque successori.

XCIV. *Milites Veneris*

Congaudentes ludite,
choros simul ducite!
iuvenes sunt lepidi,
senes sunt decrepiti!

Refl.   Audi, bela mia,
        mille modos Veneris!
        da (hi!) zevaleria!

Militemus Veneri,
nos qui sumus teneri!
Veneris tentoria
res est amatoria!

Refl.   Audi, bela mia,
        mille modos Veneris!
        da (hi!) zevaleria!

Iuvenes amabiles,
igni comparabiles;
senes sunt horribiles,
frigori consimiles!

Refl.   Audi, bela mia,
        mille modos Veneris!

But now the flower of my youth has passed,
and old age draws all calamities unto itself.
Thus I am in the service of my final salvation.

The unicorn is wont to show itself to maids.[189]
But only a lass whose virginity is truly undefiled
can hold this beast in her very lap.

Therefore a maiden who associates with a lad
and has spurned my ancient self is rightly cozened,
so that the unicorn may allow itself to be captured by her.

On the threshing floor of maidens the chaff is due
to an older man as his reward and to the younger grain.
Therefore, old man, leave to a successor the threshing floor!

94. *Venus' Knights*

Be merry and enjoy yourselves
and all together dance!
Young lads are charming;
old fools are decrepit!

Refr.   Hearken, my beautiful lass,
            to a thousand modes of love
            from (ay!) the Cytherean knighthood![190]

Let us ride in Venus' service,
we, who are young!
The tent of Venus is
a matter of love!

Refr.   Hearken, my beautiful lass,
            to a thousand modes of love
            from (ay!) the Cytherean knighthood!

The lads are worthy of love!
They are comparable to fire!
The old men are a horror;
they are similar to ice!

Refr.   Hearken, my beautiful lass,
            to a thousand modes of love

da (hi!) zevaleria!

XCV. *Cinaedus Non Sum!*

Cur suspectum   me tenet domina?
cur tam torva   sunt in me lumina?
testor celum   celique numina:
que veretur,   non novi crimina!

Refl.   Tort a vers mei ma dama!

Celum prius   candebit messibus,
feret aer   ulmos cum vitibus,
dabit mare   feras venantibus,
quam Sodome   me iungam civibus!

Refl.   Tort a vers mei ma dama!

Licet multa   tyrannus spondeat
et me gravis   paupertas urgeat,
non sum tamen,   cui plus placeat
id, quod prosit,   quam quod conveniat.

Refl.   Tort a vers mei ma dama!

Naturali   contentus Venere
non didici   pati, sed agere.
malo mundus   et pauper vivere
quam pollutus   dives existere.

Refl.   Tort a vers mei ma dama!

Pura semper   ab hac infamia
nostra fuit   minor Britannia.
ha peream,   quam per me patria
sordis huius   sumat initia!

Refl.   Tort a vers mei ma dama!

XCVI. *Ad Sequendum Virgines!*

Iuvenes amoriferi,
virgines amplexamini!

from (ay!) the Cytherean knighthood!

95. *I Am Not a Catamite!*

Why does my mistress hold me in suspicion?
Why do her eyes glare at me so wildly?
I swear by heaven and the supernal gods
that of the offenses she fears I have no guilty knowledge!

Refr.   My mistress is wrong, as far as I'm concerned![191]

The firmament will glow white with harvest fields,
the air will carry vine-covered elms,
and the sea will give beasts to huntsmen
before I would join the denizens of Sodom![192]

 Refr.   My mistress is wrong, as far as I'm concerned!

Even if a tyrant promised me many gifts
and oppressive poverty pressed me to go,
I still am not one who finds more pleasure
in advantage than in propriety's will.

Refr.   My mistress is wrong, as far as I'm concerned!

Content with natural sexual union,
I have not learned passive play, but only the active part.
I would rather live inviolate and poor
than lead life, defiled and rich.

Refr.   My mistress is wrong, as far as I'm concerned!

Free from this infamy
our England always was.
I would rather die than see through me
my fatherland take up the beginnings of this filth!

Refr.   My mistress is wrong, as far as I'm concerned!

96. *To The Suit of Maidens!*

Beloved young lads,
embrace the virgins.

ludos incitat
avium con centus.

Refl.   O vireat,
         o floreat,
         o gaudeat
         in tempore iuventus!

Domicelli, surgite!
domicellas querite!
ludos incitat
avium concentus.

Refl.   O vireat,
         o floreat,
         o gaudeat
         in tempore iuventus!

Cum ipsam intueor. . .

XCVII. *Apollonius Princeps Tyri*

«O Antioche,
cur decipis me
atque quasi servum reicis me?
quid agam? quid faciam?
dolo lugeo, fleo.
luctus est doloris,
fletus mali moris.
pereo!

Heu me miserum,
passum naufragium!
Astragis suscipior ad hospitium.
video, doceo
lyram, manu tango, amo.
amor est flos floris,
lyra est decoris.
gaudeo!

Post tristitiam fient gaudia,
post gaudium erit tristitia»:
sunt vera proverbia,

A concert of birds
arouses these games!

Refr.   Let it green,
let it blossom,
let it rejoice:
youth in this time of spring!

Young masters, rise ye!
Seek young mistresses!
A concert of birds
arouses these games!

Refr.   Let it green,
let it blossom,
let it rejoice:
youth in this time of spring!

When I look upon her....

97. *Apollonius, Tyrian Prince*[193]

"O Antiochus, why chicane you me
and spurn me as if I were a slave?
What should I do? What should I fashion?
Because of your deceit
I mourn, I weep.
The grief rises from my pain,
the tears from your malice.
O, I am perishing!

"Ay, wretched me,
alas, my shipwrecked self!
Into Astrages' hospitality am I received.
I see her, I teach her the lyre,
I touch her, I love her.
My love is the flower of flowers,
the lyre is one of glory.
Happy I am!

"After the sorrow joys will follow;
after joy there will be dole."
These apothegms hold true

que fatentur talia.
dicta veritatis,
dicta claritatis
amantur.

Ab Astrage lecto suscipior
et in maris fluctibus relinquor.
Tharsia nascitur; mater deicitur
pulchra cum merore;
Tharsia cum flore
nutritur.

Frugibus fames hinc tollitur.
Strangolio, Dyniasiadi committitur
flos floris. doleo!»

Liocardadis hic moritur,
ex ere species monstratur.
traditur invidia
flos amoris Tharsia
servo.
naute eam liberant,
servum quoque fugant
gladio.

Apollonii nata venditur
et a Lenone emitur.
pretium proponitur:
sexaginta nummos.
cottidie pretium hec redemit,
virgo tamen mansit
precibus.

Apollonius natam querens querentem
Dyniasiadem videt et flentem.
sepulcrum monstratur,
mors ut videatur
nate.
«quid non flent mei oculi?
Tharsia num vivit
filia?»

Puppes litori approximantur.

that confess such plights.
Words of truth,
words of clarity
are treasured quite.

"I am taken up by Astrages' bed
and forsaken by her on the waves of the sea.
Tharsia is born,
but her beautiful mother
is cast down with grief!
Tharsia is suckled by a flower.

"With grains the hunger is allayed.
To Stranguilio and Dyniasias the flower of flowers
is commended. O, I grieve in pain!"

In this place Ligoridis dies;
here a statue of bronze is displayed.
Out of jealousy
one hands over Tharsia,
the flower of love, to a slave.
Sailors free her
and with swords
put the slave to flight.

The daughter of Apollonius is sold
and purchased by Leno.
A price is proposed:
sixty coins.
Everyday she obtained the price,
but still remained a virgin
by dint of her prayers.

As Apollonius searches for his daughter,
he sees Dyniasias bewailing and weeping.
A sepulcher is shown,
such that it seems
that his daughter is dead.
"Why do my eyes not shed tears?
Is Tharsia my daughter
still alive?"

Ships are approaching the shore.

vera inveniuntur
† Tharsiam lyrantem coram Tyrio.
hec prius despicitur,
postea cognoscitur.
post multa opposita
nata fuit reddita
patri.

Voce celesti Iohannis in insula
Astrages regi fit cognita.
Astrages cognoscitur,
Tharsia maritatur
Arfaxo.
leno destruitur,
Strangolius deicitur
omnibus.

XCVIII. *Nuptiae Aeneae*

Troie post excidium
dux Eneas Latium
errans fato sequitur;
sed errat feliciter,
dum in regno taliter
Didonis excipitur:
si hospes felicior,
hospita vix largior
aliqua percipitur.

Troas actos per maria
Dido suscepit Tyria,
passisque tot naufragia
larga pandit hospitia,
et Eneam intuita,
supplex, miratur, quod ita
leta nitescat facies,
larga, crispata sit cesaries.
mox ad sororem properat
eique clausam mentem reserat:

«Anna, lux mea, dux
iste quis sit, ambigo;
quis honor, quis color

The truth is discovered that Tharsia is
playing the lyre before the Tyrian Prince.
At first disdained,
she is afterwards agnized.
After myriad adversities,
the daughter to her father
was restored.

Through a heavenly voice, on the island of John,[194]
the king espies his beloved Astrages again.
Astrages is recognized;
Tharsia is wed
to her savior Arfaxus the prince.
Leno is annihilated,
and slain by the mob
is the faithless Stranguilio.

98. *The Marriage of Aeneas*[195]

After the destruction of Troy
the leader Aeneas sought
Latium on his fated odyssey.
But he wandered with blessings,
since he thus found a reception
in the realm of Queen Dido:
perhaps there is a guest more hapful than he,
but still a more munificent hostess than she
can scarcely be perceived.

Tyrian Dido took in the Trojans,
who were driven across the sea,
and to men who had suffered so many wrecks
she extended generous hospitalities.
And when she beheld Aeneas,
she was stunned that the face
of a suppliant so mirthfully shined
and marveled o'er his bounty of auburn curls.[196]
Anon she hastened to her sister
and revealed her hidden thoughts to her:

"Anna, my light, who that leader is
keeps me in suspense.
What nobility, what color

vultu, vix intelligo.
at reor, vereor
hunc nostra conubia
poscere; id vere
portendunt insomnia.

Ecce quam forti pectore,
Amoris quasi facie!
heu, sors hunc que per bibula
Scylle traxit pericula!

Si Sychei coniugis mei
hymenei pacti rei
non detraherem, non cogerem, non lederem,
huic uni me forsan subdere
possem culpe; me prius perdere
velit Iupiter turpiter,
fulmine de culmine
deiectam Carthaginis,
quam regina se nouis
Dido committat dominis.»

Anna refert: «Absiste,
mi soror, nec resiste
amori blando: si iste
iungetur tibi suisque
extollet te virtutibus,
Carthago crescet opibus.»

His accensa Phenissa
in furores Elissa
venandi sub imagine,
effuso nimbi turbine,
antro cum duce latuit
eique se supposuit.

Propositionibus
tribus dux expositis
syllogizat; motibus
fallit hec oppositis;
sed quamvis cogentibus
argumentis utitur,
tamen eis brevibus

rests on his face,
I scarcely understand.
But I trow—I fear—
that this man asks us for our hand.
Truly my dreams portend this event.

"Behold how valiant is his breast,
how his aspect resembles Cupid's very own.
Alas, what lot hauled him
through Scylla's engulfing perils!

"If I were not dishonoring the sealed bond
of marriage to Sychaeus my groom,
if I were not coercing him, if I were not infringing his rights,
then to this one temptation I could perhaps submit.
But may Jupiter slay me ignominiously
by casting his bolt my way,
upon my ejection
from Carthage's lofty throne,
before Queen Dido subjects
herself to new lords."

Anna rejoined:
"Cease this, my sister,
and resist not alluring love!
If that man be joined to thee
and elevate thee with his heroic feats,
Carthage's might will surely grow."

By these words Phoenician Elissa[197]
was fired into an amorous fury:
beneath the mask of a hunt
and the effusion of a whirling cloud,
she hid in a cave with the prince
and made herself his own.

The prince voiced three propositions
and a conclusion by syllogism was reached.
With opposite motives
she tried to vie with him:
although she employed
compelling arguments,
she in brief time was nevertheless

tantum horis fallitur.

Et sic amborum in coniugio
leta resplenduit etherea regio;
nam ad amoris gaudia
rident, clarescunt omma.

XCIX. *Mors Reginae Sidoniae*

Superbi Paridis   leve iudicium,
Helene species   amata nimium
fit casus Troïe   deponens Ilium.

Hinc dolens Eneas   querit diffugium,
ascendit dubios   labores navium,
venit Carthaginem,   Didonis solium.

Hunc regno suscipit   Dido Sidonia,
et plus quam decuit   amore saucia
moras non patitur   iungi connubia.

O Amor improbe,   sic vincis omnia,
sic tuis viribus   redduntur mollia,
et morti proxima   sunt tua gaudia!

Eneas igitur   egre corripitur
et in Italiam   ire precipitur.
quod amans audiens   Dido concutitur:

«Enea domine,   quid est, quod audio?
Didonem miseram   dabis exitio?
quam dura premia   pro beneficio!

Nudum exceperam,   egentem omnium;
deos offenderat   nostrum conubium.
quid agam, nescio;   mors est consilium.

Anna, quid audio,   soror dulcissima?
iam volant carbasa   ora finitima.
abrumpe miseram   lucem asperrima!»

† Dido nobilis   spreta relinquitur
atque Lavinie   thalamus queritur,

greatly disappointed by them.

And so when both were joined,
the ethereal territory in happiness gleamed.
For upon the joys of love
all things smile and beam.

99. *The Death of A Sidonian Queen*

The frivolous judgment of orgulous Paris[198]
and Helen's all too admired mien
became the fall of Troy, the toppler of Ilium's heights.

Thence woeful Aeneas took to scattered flight,
boarded the perilous toils of an oceanic odyssey,
and came at last to Carthage, the seat of Dido's majesty.

Dido of Sidon received him in her realm,
and beyond obligation, smitten by love,
she suffered no cunctation in the nuptial rite.

O nefarious Cupid, you so conquer all things,
thus by your powers effeminacies are rendered,
and on the threshold of death your delights stand!

Aeneas therefore was severely reproved
and bidden to set his course for Italy's shores.
Love-struck Dido, hearing of this, was deeply alarmed:

"Lord Aeneas, what is this that I hear?
You wish to send wretched Dido to death?
How cruel is the reward for the kindness I showed you!

"I took you in naked, destitute of all,
but the gods have taken umbrage at our union!
What I should do, I know not. Death shall be my counsel.

"Anna, most beloved sister, what do I hear?
Already fly the sails away on the nearby strand.
Shatter this wretched light by a most bitter death!"

Noble Dido was forsaken in scorn,
and the bridechamber of Lavinia was sought;

et Anna propere   pro maga mittitur.

«O ensis perfidi,   fortiter ilia
mea pertransiens   deme suspiria!»
amantes miseri,   timete talia!

XCIXa. *Error Paridis*

Armat amor Paridem; vult Tyndaridem, rapit illam;
Res patet; hostis adest; pugnatur; menia cedunt.

XCIXb. *Causa Mortis*

Prebuit Eneas et causam mortis et ensem;
Illa sua Dido concidit usa manu.

C. *Questus Didonis*

O decus, o Libye regnum, Carthaginis urbem!
O lacerandas fratris opes, o Punica regna!

O duces Phrygios,
o dulces advenas,
quos tanto tempore
dispersos equore
iam hiems septima
iactaverat ob odium Iunonis,
Scyllea rabies,
Cyclopum sanies,
Celeno pessima
traduxerat ad solium Didonis!

Qui me crudelibus
exercent odiis,
arentis Libye
post casum Phrygie
quos regno naufragos
exceperam! me miseram! quid feci,
que meis emulis,
ignotis populis
et genti barbare,
Sidonios ac Tyrios subieci!

Anna, to fetch a sorceress, was quickly sent off.

"O perfidious sword, take away my sighs
in your brave passage through my core!"
O wretched lovers, be fearful of these blights!

99a. *The Folly of Paris*

Love arms Paris: Helen he desires and rapes. The deed lies open;
the enemy moves in; a fight ensues; the walls cave in.

99b. *Death's Cause*

Aeneas supplied a reason for death and the sword.
Illustrious Dido fell lifeless by her own hand's work.

100. *Dido's Lament*

"O Glory, O Sovereignty of Libya, O Carthaginian State!
O fraternal treasures riven by fate,[199] woe, thou Punic Realm!

"O Phrygian leaders,[200]
O sweet new arrivals,
whom then for so long,
because of Juno's wrath,
the seventh winter had tossed
and scattered o'er the sea,
whom Scylla's fury, the Cyclops' slaver,
and most vicious Celaeno[201]
had dragged to the soil
of Dido the Queen!

"They plague me now
with cruel offences,
I, who had received
these ruined men
in the realm of arid Libya
after Troy's collapse!
Ay, wretched me!
What have I done, who have submitted
my Sidonians and Tyrians to my foes,
to unknown peoples and to a barbarian race?!

Achi dolant!
achi dolant!
iam volant carbasa!
iam nulla spes Didonis!
ve Tyriis colonis!
plangite, Sidonii,
quod in ore gladii deperii
per amorem Phrygii predonis!

Eneas, hospes Phrygius,
Iarbas, hostis Tyrius,
multo me temptant crimine,
sed vario discrimine.
nam sitientis Libye
regina spreta linquitur,
et thalamos Lavinie
Troianus hospes sequitur!
quid agam misera?
Dido regnat altera!
hai, vixi nimium!
mors agat cetera!

Deserta siti regio
me gravi cingit prelio,
fratris me terret feritas
et Numadum crudelitas.
insultant hoc proverbio:
«Dido se fecit Helenam:
regina nostra gremio
Troianum fovit advenam!»
gravis conditio,
furiosa ratio,
si mala perferam
pro beneficio!

Anna, vides, que sit fides
deceptoris perfidi?
fraude ficta me relicta
regna ftigit Punica!
nil sorori nisi mori,
soror, restat, unica.

Sevit Scylla, nec tranquilla

"Alas, may they suffer!
Woe, may they grieve!
The sails already fly in the wind!
Already Dido hath no hope!
Woe to the Tyrian settlers!
Lament, O Sidonians, I that have perished
on the hilt of the sword out of my love
for a Phrygian plunderer!

"Aeneas, Phrygian guest,
and Iarbas, Tyre's fiend,
bring many evils upon me,
but in different ways,
for now thirsty Libya's Queen
is spurned and abandoned,
and Lavinia's bridechamber
our Trojan guest pursues!
What is my wretched self to do?
Another Dido[202] will be his queen!
Alas, I have lived for far too long!
Now may death take care of what remains!

"This land, a thirsting desert,
surrounds me with heavy wars,
my brother's truculence and the cruelty of the Numidians
together terrorize my soul.
They revile me with these words:
'Dido has made herself a Helen:
our queen warmed in her lap
a transient from Troy!'
Insufferable condition,
furious irrationality
that I should suffer ills
for charitable deeds!

"Anna, do you see what the trustworthiness
of this perfidious deceiver is?
Under well-contrived subterfuge,
after abandoning me, he flees this Punic realm!
Sole sister, all that remains now
for your sister is death!

"Scylla roars, nor set they sail

se proimttunt equora;
solvit ratem tempestatem
nec exhorret Phrygius.
dulcis soror, ut quid moror,
aut quid cessat gladius?

Fulget sidus Orionis,
sevit hiems Aquilonis,
Scylla regnat equore.
tempestatis tempore,
Palinure, non secure
classem solvis litore!

Solvit ratem dux Troianus;
solvat ensem nostra manus
in iacturam sanguinis!
Vale, flos Carthaginis!
hec, Enea, fer trophea,
causa tanti criminis!

O dulcis anima,
vite spes unica!
Phlegethontis, Acherontis
latebras ac tenebras
mox adeas horroris,
nec Pyrois te circulus moretur!

Eneam sequere,
nec desere
suaves illecebras
amoris,
nec dulces nodos Veneris
perdideris,
sed nostri conscia
sis nuntia
doloris!

CI. *Lacrimae Hecubae*

Pergama flere volo,   fato Danais data solo,
Solo capta dolo,   capta redacta solo.

Ex Helicone sona,   que prima tenes Helicona,

upon a tranquil sea!
The Phrygian releases his ships,
but fears not the gales.
Sweet sister, why do I delay,
or why does my falchion sit so idle?

"The star of Orion blazes,
the blasts of the North Wind rage,
and Scylla reigns o'er all the deep.
In tempestuous climes, Palinurus,[203]
you unsafely release your fleet
from the shore!

"The Trojan prince cuts the hawser.
Our hand then should unsheathe the sword
and let flow the blood!
Farewell, flower of Carthage!
Bear, Aeneas, this as a trophy that thou art
the cause of so great an offence!

"O sweet soul, sole hope of life!
Anon may thou see
Phlegethon's and Acheron's[204]
shadow kingdom of horrors,
and may the circle of fire-hoofed Pyrois[205]
not detain thee in any way!

"Follow after Aeneas,
and do not cease
to ensnare him
with the sweet
allurements of love,
nor lose thou the sweet fetters
of the consummation thereof,
but, privy to my grief,
be to him my messenger!"

101. *Hecuba's Tears*

I want to weep for Troy, which fell to the Greeks only by the will of fate,
that was captured only by deceit and razed to the ground.

Sing from Helicon, you who rule o'er Helicon's heights,[206]

Et metra me dona   promere posse bona!

Est Paris absque pare;   querit, videt, audet amare,
Audet temptare   furta, pericla, mare.

Vadit et accedit,   clam tollit clamque recedit;
Nauta solo cedit,   fit fuga, predo redit.

Tuta libido maris   dat tura libidinis aris,
Civibus ignaris,   quod parat arma Paris.

Post cursus Helene   currunt Larissa, Mycene,
Mille rates plene fortibus absque sene.

Exsuperare ratus viduatorem viduatus
Federe nudatus   federat ense latus.

Greco ductori   prohibet dolor esse timori
Pro consorte tori   vivere sive mori.

Pergama dia secus   figit tentoria Grecus,
Impetitur mechus   et fabricatur equus.

Plena male prolis   parit hostem machina molis,
Destruiturque dolis   tam populosa polis.

Tradunt cuncta neci,   predeque cupidine ceci
Obfirmant Greci   pectora clausa preci.

Hinc ardent edes,   hinc detruncat Diomedes
Per varias cedes   brachia, crura, pedes.

Multatur cede   predo Paris a Diomede,
Seque sue tede   reddit alumna Lede.

Femina digna mori   redamatur amore priori,
Reddita victori   deliciisque tori.

Seva, quid evadis?   non tradita cetera tradis!
Cur rea tu cladis   non quoque clade cadis?

Si fueris lota, si vita   sequens bona tota,
Non eris ignota,   non eris absque nota.

and give me the ability to bring forth sweet, mellifluous verse!

Paris is nonpareil; he seeks, he sees, he dares to love.
He boldly hazards larcenies, their concomitant perils, and the sea.

He rushes and advances; secretly he plunders and withdraws.
The sailor sets sail, takes flight, and a robber returns home.

The man's lechery in safety offers frankincense to the altars of lust;
but the citizens know not that Paris has started a war.

On Helen's trail, from Larissa and Mycenae, race a thousand ships
replete with valiant soldiers and not even one senescent man.

The cuckolded lord is intent on vanquishing his wife's thief;
robbed of his nuptial pact, he allies his hip with his sword.

Pain forbids the Greek leader to entertain any fears
of living or dying for the consort of his bed.

The Greek pitches tents in front of Olympian Troy;
the adulterer is attacked, and a horse is framed.

Pregnant with a wicked seed, the massive engine births a fiend,
and, through chicaneries, a densely-populated city is destroyed.

The Greeks deliver all unto death and, blind with a lust
for booty, harden their breasts already closed to prayers.

On this side the houses burn, and with various strokes
Diomedes[207] lops off arms, legs, and feet.

Paris the plunderer is by Diomedes punished with death,
but Leda's daughter returns to her nuptial torch.[208]

This woman, who deserves death, is loved anew with the love of before
and returned to the victor and the delights of the bed.

O hellcat, why go you free? Unbetrayed, you betray all the rest!
Why do you, the culprit of the fall, fall not also dead?

Even if you are laved, if your whole life after this is free of ill,
you will still not be vulgar nor without the mark of disgrace.

Passa modo Paridem,   Paridem modo, Thesea pridem,
Es factura fidem,   ne redeas in idem?

Rumor de veteri   faciet ventura timeri;
Cras poterunt fieri   turpia sicut heri.

Femina victa mero   quod inhereat ebria vero,
Nec fieri spero   nec fideiussor ero.

Expleta cede   superadditur Hecuba prede,
Tractatur fede,   cogitur ire pede.

In faciem Dorum,   crinem laniata decorum,
Subsequitur lorum   per theatrale forum.

Vivit, at invita,   quia vivit paupere vita,
et planctus inita vociferatur ita:

«Iuno, quid est, quod agis? post tante funera stragis
Totne putas plagis   addere posse magis?

Ergo reoccides   hos, quos occidit Atrides?
Ergo reoccides,   quos obiisse vides?

Nullum iam reperis,   nullum, nec sic misereris,
Immo persequeris   reliquias cineris!

Nemo rebellatur,   et Iuno belligeratur,
Bellaque sectatur   sanguine mucro satur!

Me, me, Iuno, feri!   feriendo potes misereri!
Fac obitu celeri   corpus anile teri!

Usque modo flevi   casus, incommoda levi;
Quod superest evi,   corripe fine brevi!

Perstitit ira dei   dare cetera perniciei;
Miror, quod sit ei   mentio nulla mei.

Nemo mei meminit;   gladius, qui cetera finit,
Mecum fedus init,   me superesse sinit.

Concutit ossa metus,   fit spiritus irrequietus,

Only just bent to Paris' will, only just, and Theseus' long ago,
would you agree to avoid a relapse into the same vice again?

The tale of old shall cause the future to be feared:
the same iniquities of yesterday can befall the world tomorrow.

That a drunken woman, subdued by wine, will stick to truth
I neither anticipate will happen nor will I the surety be.

The slaughter wrought, Hecuba is superadded to the loot;
cruelly handled is she and compelled to go on foot.

Before the eyes of the Greeks, her glorious tresses rent,
she follows on a rein through the forum that becomes her stage.

She lives, but unwillingly, because it is a penurious life.
She begins to wail and lays down her plaint in these words:

"Juno, what are you perpetrating now? After the obsequies
for so great a heap, do you think you can add to so many injuries?

"Will you then slay these again, whom Atrides has killed?
Will you then fell again those you see dead upon the ground?

"You find now no one, no one!, nor feel you any pity at all,
but rather persecute the remnants of the piteous ash!

"No one is revolting, and yet Juno still fights,
and her sword, sated with blood, pursues more war.

"Me, me, Juno, smite! You can show compassion by slaying me.
With a swift exit let my old body be ground to decimated meat!

"Hitherto I have only bewept these misfortunes and concealed
the injuries. What life remains, snatch up for a swift end!

"The rage of the god has persisted in sending all unto death;
I marvel that he has made no mention of me.

"No one remembers me; the falchion that finished the others,
has entered into a pact with me: it lets me to survive unwillingly.

"Dread rattles my bones, and restless my spirit becomes,

Dum renovat fletus   denuo cura vetus.

Urbs retro sublimis   et abundans rebus opimis
Una fit e minimis,   adnichilata nimis.

Urbs celebris dudum,   dum terminat alea ludum,
Ecce solum nudum,   pastus erit pecudum!

Ve tibi, Troia, peris!   iam non michi Troia videris,
Iamiam bobus eris   pascua, lustra feris.

Urbs fortunata,   si posses vincere fata,
Vel possent fata   segnius esse rata!

Regna beata satis,   urbs prime nobilitatis,
Dives honoratis   dantibus atque datis!

Regna beata satis,   donec nocuere beatis
Preda voluptatis   et male fausta ratis!

Urbs bona, piena bono,   foris, intus, cive, colono,
Predita patrono,   preditus ille throno!

Plena potentatu,   celeberrima, digna relatu,
Felicissima tu   principe, cive, statu!

Curia personis,   urbs civibus, arva colonis,
Terra suis donis,   horrea plena bonis!

Si commendemus,   que commendare solemus:
Cultus supremus   rus, ager, unda, nemus.

Potum vineta,   pastum dabat area leta,
Merces moneta   navigiumque freta.»

Urbs vetus et clara,   bona valde, tam bona, rara,
Tam bona, tam cara   fit pecualis hara.

Dives ab antiquo,   dum fato fertur iniquo,
Deperit in modico,   fit nichil ex aliquo.

Causa rei talis   meretrix fuit exitialis,
Femina fatalis,   femina feta malis.

whilst my old solicitude conjures up new tears.

"The once-exalted city that abounded in capital treasures
becomes one of the smallest and is reduced to absolute nil.

"This once-populous city, until the die ended the game, behold!
is now bare soil and will be soon but fodder for the cattle!

"Woe, Troy, fallen are you! Already you seem not Troy to me.
Now you will be a bovine pasture and the haunt of wild beasts.

"O happy city, if you could conquer fate,
or if fates could be more slowly fulfilled!

"O most blessed kingdom, city of the highest nobility,
 rich in distinguished givers and gifts!

"O most prosperous kingdom, until the spoil of pleasure
and an inauspicious ship injured your beatitude!

"O noble city, full of good, both outside and in, endowed
with denizens, farmers, and a patron gifted with a throne!

"O realm full of might, most illustrious, and worthy of report,
and most blessed in your prince, citizenry, and circumstance.

"The court was rich in varlets, the city in burghers,
the fields in farmers, the earth in her own gifts, and the silos in wares.

"If I should mention what I am wont to commend:
supreme agriculture, fields, farms, water, and woods.

"Drinks, vineyards, and food did the joyous countryside give;
goods, gold pieces, and ships the great ocean deigned to yield."

The old, renowned city, so very prosperous, so good,
so rare, so fortunate, so dear, becomes a cattle stall.

Rich from time immemorial, until it was brought to a sinister fate;
before long it perished and became nothing from pith.

A destructive harlot was the cause of such an affair—
a femme fatale, a woman so very rich in ills.

CII. *Victoria Principis Troiani*

Fervet amore Paris,   Troianis immolat aris,
Fratribus ignaris   scinditur unda maris.

Temptat Tyndaridem,   favet illa, relinquit Atridem,
Prompta sequi Paridem,   passa perire fidem.

Equora raptor arat,   tenet, affectu quod amarat,
Se res declarat,   Grecia bella parat.

Contra Dardanidem   res provocat ista Tytidem,
Incitat Eacidem   Pallas ad illud idem.

Argos nudatur,   classis coit, unda minatur,
Hostia mactatur,   aura quieta datur.

Passa freti strepitus   Phrygium rapit ancora litus,
Obstruit introitus   Hector ad arma citus.

Ilios arma gerit,   Helenam sua Grecia querit,
Fraus aditus aperit,   hostis ab hoste perit.

Sub Danaum pube,   telorum territa nube,
Infremit urbs Hecube,   flant resonantque tube.

Miles ad arma fremit,   vite fraus Hectora demit,
Urbem pugna premit,   Troia sub hoste tremit.

Ars nisi ditaret   Danaos numenque iuvaret,
Murus adhuc staret,   qui modo rege caret.

Queritur ars, fit equus,   latet intra viscera Grecus,
Fit Priamus cecus,   ducitur intro pecus.

Flendo Sinon orat,   Ithacus fallendo laborat,
Urbem flamma vorat,   machina claustra forat.

Credula fallaci,   flamme subiecta voraci,
Passa dolos Ithaci   Troia fit esca faci.

Ars urbem tradit,   urbs in discrimina vadit,
Ignis edax radit   Pergama, Troia cadit.

102. *The Trojan Prince's Victory*

Paris burns with love; he lays votives upon the altars of Troy.
Unbeknownst to his brothers, the waves of the sea are cut.

He tempts Tyndareus' daughter; she favors him, and leaves Atrides.[209]
Ready to follow Paris, she lets her faith pass away.

The thief plows the sea and holds with ignoble desire what his lust
had eyed. The affair declares itself, and Greece wages war.

This event sets Diomedes against Paris, Dardan's fruit;
Pallas rouses Aeacus' issue[210] to the very same animus.

Argos is exposed, its fleet assembles, the ocean's swell is threatening,
a victim[211] is immolated, and a gentle wind blows.

The anchor suffers the roar of the sea and seizes the Phrygian coast.
An arm-wielding Hector[212] obstructs the entry points.

Ilion takes up arms; Helen is sought by her Grecian home.
Deceit unseals the gates, and enemy by enemy is undone.

Under the crew of the Danaans and a terrifying cloud of spears
Hecuba's city roars, and war's trumpets resound and blare.

Soldiers snort at their weapons, and deceit steals Hector's life.
The fight overwhelms the city; Troy trembles beneath its foe.

If craft were not enriching the Greeks and a divinity were not
at their side, the wall would still stand, which now lacks a king.

Art is sought, a horse is made, inside its bowels lurk the Greeks;
Priam grows blind, and the animal is led inside.

Sinon begs through tears, Odysseus toils in the feint,
flames consume the city, and the machine pierces the fort.

Credulous Troy, subjected to a treacherous, voracious blaze,
submitted to the Odysseus' intrigues, becomes the torch's food.

A ruse hands over the city, the city rushes into doom,
a ravenous fire sweeps Pergama, and Troy woefully falls.

Urbis opes lacere   flammis alimenta dedere,
Igni cessere   menia, claustra, sere.

Argis exosa   iacet Ilios, ante iocosa,
Inclita, formosa,   nunc rubus, ante rosa.

Igni sublatus   fugit, omnia ferre paratus,
Firma classe ratus   te Cytherea, satus.

Tellus fatalis   peritur navalibus alis,
Obviat ira salis   peste, furore, malis.

Pestem concepit   mare, fluctus surgere cepit,
Puppibus obrepit   spuma, procella strepit.

Flat Notus insanus,   insurgit turbo profanus,
Navita Troianus   utitur arte manus.

Huc quasi delira   pelagi succenditur ira,
Stat prope mors dira,   stat procul inde lyra.

Rebus sublatis,   currentibus ordine fatis,
Regnis optatis   utitur arte ratis.

Pacem vestigat,   sed eum lis dira fatigat
Et furor instigat   et nova pugna ligat.

Pugna predatur,   furit in Turnum, dominatur,
Viscera scrutatur   sanguine mucro satur.

Cepta luens sceleris   te victum, Turne, fateris,
Obrutus ense peris,   preda cibusque feris.

Enee cedit   victoria, pugna recedit,
Pugne succedit   gloria, paxque redit.

Sub vinclo fidei   post inclita facta trophei
Regia nupsit ei   virgo favore dei.

CIII. *Eia Amor Me Urit!*

Eia dolor! nunc me solor velut olor
albus neci proximus.

The treasures of the mangled city gave nourishment to the flames;
the walls, the locks, the bolts all truckled to the blaze.

Ilion, an anathema to Argives, lies in ruin—a city once merry,
celebrated, handsome—now a bramble bush, before a rose.

He was lifted from the fire and escaped, prepared to endure all ills,
trusting in his steady fleet, your issue Aeneas, O Cytherea.

The destined country is sought on naval wings; the wrath
of the sea thwarts them with death, madness, and suffering.

The ocean hatches up banes; the waves begin to rise
to great heights, foam raids the decks, and a gale howls.

The raving south wind blasts, an unholy cyclone forms,
and the Trojan sailor parlays the skill of his hands.

The wrath of the deep then erupts as if in a delirium;
a dreadful death awaits nearby; the lyre stands far away.

All possessions are lost, as the fates run in proper form,
he employs his seafaring skills in pursuit of the desired realm.

He seeks out peace, but a terrible strife wearies his soul;
madness incites it, and a new war him surrounds.

In battle he plunders, against Turnus[213] he rages and prevails;
his blood-soaked sword then explores Turnus' entrails.

Atoning for your iniquities, you confess, Turnus, your defeat.
Overwhelmed by steel you die, now booty and food for beasts.

The victory goes to Aeneas, and the battle then retreats.
Glory follows after it, and peace to the Italian realm returns.

Under a bond of trust and after his glorious deed of victory,
Aeneas wed the king's daughter[214] with the blessing of god.

103. *Alack, Love Is Burning Me!*

Alack, the pain!
I am now consoled

abiectus lugeo,
despectus pereo,
exclusus langueo.

Urit Venus corde tenus, quam nec Rhenus
nec Euphrates maximus
valet estinguere.
me sola solvere
potest vel perdere.

Cur, livens Invidia,
nocte nata Stygia,
lingua balbens impia,
mea turbas gaudia,
vecte claudens pervia
michi quondam ostia,
uni unam negans, brunam florulam,
nec pallentem nec habentem maculam,
casti floris, celi roris emulam,
vas auratum, aromatum virgulam?

Virgo, par Tyndaridi,
tuo fave Paridi!
rosa prati floridi,
nil repugnes Cypridi,
luctus plena turbidi
morsu dentis invidi
Venus urit, Amor furit, solitum,
rapit sibi servum tibi deditum.
tibi cedo, flexus dedo poplitum.

Parce supplici!
more medici
sana crematum,
laxa reatum,
solve ligatum
catena duplici!

Cantus rhythmici
iocis refici
Musa letatur;
rauca precatur,
sue reddatur

like the white swan close to death.
Downcast, I grieve; disdained, I die;
disowned, I waste away.

A love burns me down to the core
which neither the Rhine
nor the mightiest Euphrates can douse.
It alone can deliver
or all of me destroy.

Why, O leaden Envy, child of the Stygian night,
do you confound my delights,
babbling with a dastardly tongue,
closing with a bolt the doors that were once open to me,
denying one brown little flower to one tender lad,
a flower that pales not
nor possesses even a mark,
a rival of the chaste blossom
and heaven's dew, a golden vessel,
and a fragrant little bouquet?

O maiden, Helen's equal, favor thy Paris!
O rose of a flowering meadow, resist not the Cyprian!,[215]
full of turbid grief as thou art
from the bite of a jealous maw.
Venus burns and Cupid raves, in their usual way,
and takes possession of
thy servant devoted to thee.
To thee I yield, to thee I give
the bendings of my knees.

Spare a supplicant!
As doctor,
heal my burns,
mitigate my guilt,
release a man bound
by duplicate chains!

The Muse rejoices
in refreshing herself
with the jokes of a rhythmic song.
Hoarse, she beseeches
that the poet be restored

vates Eurydici!

Rerum decus!
corde mechus
in te, cecus
tui solis radio,
vultu lucifluo
succensus estuo,
nil dispar mortuo.

Finem velis
dare telis!
tunc in celis
Iovis fungar solio,
Platone doctior,
Samsone fortior,
Augusto ditior!

Virgo, par Tyndaridi,
tuo fave Paridi!
rosa prati floridi,
nil repugnes Cypridi,
luctus plena turbidi
morsu dentis invidi
Venus urit, Amor furit, solitum,
rapit sibi servum tibi deditum.
tibi cedo, flexus dedo poplitum.

Terso vulnere
tuo munere
vita recrescat,
flamma quiescat,
que nos inescat
effreni Venere!

Docta ludere
iuncto federe
vulnus emunda,
virgo iocunda,
non me venunda
sub mortis pondere!

Vis amoris intus, foris me furoris

to his beloved Eurydice's form!

O glory of the world!
An adulterer at heart,
blinded by the ray of thy sun
and beaming face,
I burn with fever for thee,
singed deep within,
not at all unlike a dying man.

Cease to cast
thy missiles at me!
Then in the heavens
I shall wield the sway of Jove,
I, more lettered than Plato,
stronger than Samson,
and richer than Augustus!

O maiden, Helen's equal, favor thy Paris!
O rose of a flowering meadow, resist not the Cyprian!,[215]
full of turbid grief as thou art
from the bite of a jealous maw!
Venus burns and Cupid raves, in their usual way,
and takes possession of
thy servant devoted to thee.
To thee I yield, to thee I give
the bendings of my knees.

When the wound is cleansed
through thy aid
my life would begin anew,
the fires would rest,
which inveigle us now
to be unbridled in lust!

Versed in the game of love,
seal with me a pact
and purify this my wound,
and, O jocular lass,
put me not up for sale
under the weight of death.

The power of love molests me inside and out

sui vexat stimulis.
o Venus aurea!
immitis es dea;
nam face flammea
me peruris. quidnam furis? cur me duris
sauciasti iaculis?
igne demolior;
mors michi melior
quam vita longior!

Incessanter ardeo
nexu vinctus igneo.
toto nisu studeo,
ut haustu Venereo
eius bibam puteo,
nec tamen prevaleo.
me Corinna Iove digna nexuit,
suis frenis et habenis domuit.
que me vinxit et constrinxit artius,
laxet parum vim flammarum citius!

Lesa timpora,
tusa pectora
usta dehiscunt,
quassa tremiscunt
sub tua Venere.

Ut quid urgeor?
ut quid torqueor?
subveni oranti,
parce precanti,
diu ploranti
sub tuo carcere!

CIV. *Venus Crudelis*

Egre fero, quod egroto;
nam ex toto meo voto
Venus obviat,
dum me sauciat,
nec concedit, dum me ledit,
meam michi cedere.
moriar in Venere!

with the stings of its insanity.
O golden-tressed Venus!
An ungentle goddess are you!
For with a firebrand you scorch me!
Why do you rage?
Why have you wounded
me with rough bolts?
I am undone by fire.
Death seems better to me than a longer life!

Without end I burn, bound with a flaming cord.
With all my effort I strive to drink from her well
a draught of love, and yet I don't prevail.
Corinna, worthy of Jove,
has fettered me with her bridle
and tamed me with her reins.
She who bound me and laced me
into narrower restraints,
should quickly relax the heat
of the flames even but a little.

My wounded head,
my bruised chest
burst open inflamed,
and, shattered, tremble
in their longing for thee.

Why am I beset?
Why am I wrenched?
Come to the aid of a suppliant,
spare one who sends thee prayers,
who for so long has wept
inside thy prison of despair!

104. *Venus the Cruel*

Wearily do I bear the fact that I am ill!
For Venus completely thwarts my wishes,
whilst she wounds me,
and she forbids,
whilst she afflicts me,
my girl's submission to me.
In Venus may I die!

Nuper senex iuvenesco,
desenesco nec compesco
motus animi.
nam cum proximi
me castigant, plus instigant
et me cogunt furere.
moriar in Venere!

Uror igne consumptivo;
iam non vivo. recidivo
morbo crucior,
vivens morior.
plus leditur, qui premitur
invitus sub onere.
moriar in Venere!

Amor noster senuit,
dum re peramata renovata
Veneris scintillula
nove novellula
michi me subripuit.
in hac flamma morior,
dum iocunde saucior.
honestate criminis
culpa deculpatur,
et furori virginis
forma suffragatur.

Utinam hanc sarcinam
Flora mecum sentiat,
michi servo serviat!
nam summum est solacium
cuiuslibet doloris,
ut sibi iungat alium
participem laboris.

Bis pungitur, qui nititur
repugnare stimulo.
ergo iuste patior et crucior
milies ac pluries
mortis sub articulo.
parce, Venus, parce!
noster ignis estuat

Recently my old self grew young again,
my old years faded away, and I did not curb
the stir of emotions brewing inside of me.
For when my brothers castigate me,
they but goad me the more
and drive me into a fit of mad love!
In Venus may I die!

I am burned by a consumptive fire;
already I am not alive.
I am tortured by a recurring disease;
whilst I live, I am dying.
He is injured the more, who is unwillingly
pressed beneath a load.
In Venus may I die!

My love grew old with decay,
until that little spark of Venus—
revived as a new flicker from a fresh flame
by an exceedingly beloved being—
purloined myself from me.
In this fire I die, as I
am delightfully singed.
My fault is carved away
by the beauty of the crime,
as her loveliness supports
my searing passion for the maiden.

I would that Flora would feel
the burden together with me
and be a servant to me, her slave!
For it is the greatest palliative
for every type of pain
that allies itself with
a companion in suffering.

Twice is he stung, who strives
to resist the sting.
Thus I rightly suffer and am tortured
a thousand times and many more
up to death's brink.
Spare me, Venus, spare!
Our fire rages violently

principis in arce.

CIVa. *Paululum Consilium*

Non honor est, sed onus species lesura ferentes;
Si qua voles apte nubere, nube pari!
Ovidius, Heroides 9.31-32

CV. *Amor Maestus*

Dum curata vegetarem
soporique membra darem
et langueret animalis,
prevaleret naturalis
virtutis dominium,
en Cupido pharetratus,
crinali, torque spoliatus,
manu multa tactis alis,
mesto vultu, numquam talis,
visus est per somnium.

Quem ut vidi perturbatum
habituque disturbatum,
membra stupor ingens pressit.
qui paulatim ut recessit
a membris organicis,
causam quero mesti vultus
et sic deformati cultus,
cur sint ale contrectate
nec, ut decet, ordinate,
causam et itineris.

Amor, quondam vultu suavis,
nunc merore gravi gravis,
ut me vidit percunctari
responsumque prestolari,
reddit causam singulis:

«Vertitur in luctum   organum Amoris,
canticum subductum   absinthio doloris,
vigor priscus abiit,   evanuit iam virtus.
Me vis deseruit,   periere Cupidinis arcus!

in the citadel of a king!

104a. *A Little Advice*

Not an honor, but an onus, is a beauty that injures its bearers!
If thou, a girl, wishest to be married happily, wed a man equal to thee!

Ovid, *The Heroines* 9.31-32

105. *Cupid Forlorn*

Whilst I was nourishing the things in my care
and yielding my limbs to sleep,
and my spirit's sway was growing faint
as the lordship of my bodily power
was intensifying its might,[216]
behold! in a dream
Cupid appeared to me with his quiver,
despoiled of his hair-band and necklace,
with terribly disheveled wings,
and a sorrowful visage I had never seen.

As I gazed upon his confounded state
and his accoutrement so disarrayed,
a great numbness overwhelmed my limbs.
As it withdrew little by little
from my body and its organs,
I inquired of the cause of his lugubrious face
and his so unkempt, disfigured semblance,
why his wings were ragged and not
smoothly disposed, as is meet,
and the reason for his coming to me.

When Cupid, once sweet in visage,
now burdened with heavy grief,
saw me questioning him
and awaiting a response,
he laid down the reason, point-by-point:

"To sorrow Cupid's instrument turns, his song
is stolen by the wormwood of grief, his former vigor
has withdrawn, and now his energy has vanished away.
Power has forsaken me; the bows of Cupid have perished!

Artes amatorie   iam non instruuntur
a Nasone tradite,   passim pervertuntur;
nam siquis istis utitur   more modernorum,
Turpiter abutitur   hac assuetudine morum.

Naso, meis artibus   feliciter instructus
mundique voluptatibus   et regulis subductus,
ab errore studuit   mundum revocare;
Qui sibi notus erat,   docuit sapienter amare.

Veneris mysteria   iam non occultantur
cistis, sed exposita   coram presentantur.
proh dolor, non dedecet   palam commisceri?
Precipue Cytherea iubet   sua sacra taceri!

Amoris ob infamiam   moderni gloriantur,
sine re iactantiam a   nxii venantur,
iactantes sacra Veneris   corporibus non tactis.
Eheu, nocturnis   titulos imponimus actis!

Res arcana Veneris,   virtutibus habenda
optimisque meritis   et moribus emenda,
prostat in prostibulo,   redigitur in pactum;
Tanta meum populo   ius est ad damna redactum!»

CVI. *Vincula Veneris*

Veneris vincula
vinctus sustineo.
pereant iacula,
quibus sic pereo!
fixus sum aureo,
figitur plumbeo
florens virguncula,
unde scintillula
salit, de stipula
qua totus ardeo.

Flora, iam noveris,
quod sim sollicitus!
tui spes muneris
michi fit exitus.
nam tibi deditus

"The art of love is no longer taught as Ovid
once transmitted, but now is all in all perverted.
For if anyone use it in the manner of today,
he, inured to such behavior, shamefully abuses it.

"Ovid, happily versed in my arts and held aloof
from the pleasures and consuetudes of this world,
labored to recall the world from its folly, and showed
one who knew himself how wisely to love.

"The mysteries of Venus today are not concealed
in sacred chests, but laid forth and presented to all.
Alas, is it seemly to be coupled in the public's eyne?
Cytherea principally bids her rites to be suppressed.

"Of Cupid's infamy our contemporaries boast;
anxiously they pursue unempirical ostentation,
vaunting Venus' sacraments with bodies untouched;
alas, we impose heroic titles on their nocturnal acts!

"Venus' secret, which should be held only through virtuous deeds
and gained through paramount services and exemplary conduct,
is now set out for sale in a brothel and reduced to a pact;
my law has become the people's great detriment!"

106. *Venus' Bonds*

Bound, I sustain
Venus' shackles.
May her darts vanish,
by which I thus perish!
A golden shaft is lodged in my breast,
while one of lead is fixed[217]
in the heart of a blooming lass,
from whom a little spark leaps,
as if from a tindery haulm,
which sets all of my aflame.

Flora, now you will know
that I am in distress.
The hope for your gift
spells the end of my life.
For I have been devoted to you

michi sum perditus.
mollis in asperis,
cecus plus ceteris
ad iubar sideris
tui sum territus.

Venus amplectitur
nigros et niveos;
sepe traducitur
preter idoneos.
mores nunc aureos,
nunc habet ferreos.
amans dum fallitur,
amor subvertitur;
merito dicitur
metamorphoseos.

Amor mutabilis
marcidus areat!
verax et habilis
floreus maneat!
amans sic palleat,
voto dum studeat:
plus est amabilis.
ergo sit similis
animi vigilis:
hoc signum teneat!

CVII. *Cruciationes Amoris*

Dira vi amoris teror
et Venereo axe feror,
igni ferventi suffocatus;
deme pia cruciatus!

Ignis vivi tu scintilla,
discurrens cordis ad vexilla,
igni incumbens non pauxillo
conclusi mentis te sigillo.

Meret cor, quod gaudebat
die, quo te cognoscebat
singularem et pudicam,

and have ruined myself.
Too tender for rough times
and blinder than all others,
I am terrified by the glare
of your starry eyes.

Venus embraces
both black and white lads
and is often taken as wife
by less than suitable mates.
Now her conduct is golden;
now her behavior is iron.
When a lover is chicaned,
love is turned upside down.
Rightly is love called
a metamorphosis.

May mercurial love
dry up and wilt!
May veracious and seemly love
blossom and thrive!
The lover should thus grow pale
when he with yearning strives:
all the more worthy of love is he.
Therefore let him be similar
to an ever watchful mind:
may he possess this token sublime!

107. *The Tortures of Love*

By Cupid's fearsome power I am brayed;
I am carried along, broken on Venus' wheel,
and suffocated by the searing blaze!
Be gracious and end my pain!

You, the spark of a living flame,
run through me to the banners of my heart;
lying upon a massive fire,
I have closed you in the seal of my heart.

Now the heart grieves that once rejoiced
on the day it recognized you,
nonpareil and chaste,

te adoptabat in amicam.

Profero pectoris singultus
et mestitie tumultus,
nam amoris tui vigor
urget me, et illi ligor.

Virginale lilium,
tuum presta subsidium!
missus in exilium
querit a te consilium.

Nescit, quid agat; moritur,
amore tui vehitur,
telo necatur Veneris,
sibi ni subveneris.

Iure Veneris orbata,
castitas redintegrata,
vultu decenti perornata,
veste sophie decorata:

Tibi soli psallo; noli
despicere. . . . .
per me, precor, velis coli,
lucens ut stella poli!

CVIII. *Scholaris Libidinosus*
Petrus Blesensis (ca. 1135 - ca. 1204)

Vacillantis trutine
libramine
mens suspensa fluctuat
et estuat
in tumultus anxios,
dum se vertit
et bipertit
motus in contrarios.

Refl.   O langueo!
         causam languoris video
         nec caveo,
         vivens et prudens pereo.

and made you my girl.

I bring forth the sighs of my breast
and the confusion of my sorrow,
for the force of my love for you
bears down on me and to it I am bound.

O virginal lily,
furnish your aid!
One sent into exile
seeks counsel from you.

He knows not at all what to do; he is dying.
Out of love for you he is broken on the wheel;[218]
by Venus' missile he is slain,
unless you come to his aid.

You are outside Venus' jurisdiction,
your chastity has been restored,
you are with a seemly face adorned,
and you are draped with wisdom's dress.

To you alone I sing,
do not despise your former mate;
Let yourself, I pray, be adored by me,
you, who shine as heaven's star!

108. *The Lusting Scholar*
by Peter of Blois (ca. 1135 – ca. 1204)

In the oscillation
of its swaying scale,
my suspended heart wavers
to and fro, into and out of
tremulous solicitude,
whilst it turns
and divides in two
in its opposing motions.

Refr.   O, I am wasting away!
I see the cause of it,
but take no heed:
living and knowing, I die.

Me vacare studio
vult Ratio.
sed dum Amor alteram
vult operam,
in diversa rapior,
Ratione
cum Dione
dimicante crucior.

Refl.   O langueo!
          causam languoris video
          nec caveo,
          vivens et prudens pereo.

Sicut in arbore
frons tremula, navicula
levis in equore,
dum caret ancore
subsidio, contrario
flatu concussa fluitat:
sic agitat,
sic turbine sollicitat
me dubio
hinc Amor, inde Ratio.

Refl.   O langueo!
          causam languoris video
          nec caveo,
          vivens et prudens pereo.

Sub libra pondero,
quid melius, et dubius
mecum delibero.
nunc menti refero
delicias Venerias:
que mea michi Florula
det oscula,
qui risus, que labellula,
que facies,
frons, naris aut cesaries.

Refl.   O langueo!
          causam languoris video

Reason wishes that
I be void of zeal.
But since Cupid
desires another task,
I am drawn in two directions:
because Reason vies
with Dione,
I am racked with dole.

    Refr.   O, I am wasting away!
             I see the cause of it,
             but take no heed:
             living and knowing, I die.

Like a trembling leaf sitting in a tree,
or a frivolous little skiff
o'er the expanse of the sea
that, because it lacks an anchor's aid,
is shaken by adverse winds
as it helplessly floats:
just so I am disquieted
and by a manifold storm vexed,
with Cupid on one side
and Reason opposite him.

    Refr.   O, I am wasting away!
             I see the cause of it,
             but take no heed:
             living and knowing, I die.

Upon the scale I weigh
what is better and, still irresolute,
deliberate with myself.
I hold before my eyes
the pleasures of love:
the sweet kisses
my Florula gives me,
her smile, her lips,
her visage, her forehead,
her nose, and her hair.

    Refr.   O, I am wasting away!
             I see the cause of it,

nec caveo,
vivens et prudens pereo.

His invitat
et irritat
Amor me blanditiis.
sed aliis
Ratio sollicitat
et excitat
me studiis.

Refl.   O langueo!
causam languoris video
nec caveo,
vivens et prudens pereo.

Nam solari
me scolari
cogitat exilio.
sed, Ratio,
procul abi! vinceris
sub Veneris
imperio.

Refl.   O langueo!
causam languoris video
nec caveo,
vivens et prudens pereo.

CIX. *Puella Infida*

Multiformi succendente
Veneris scintilla
vagor mente discurrente me mergente
curarum seva Scylla.
nam ad velle meum,
quod speravi melius,
votum Dioneum
cedit in contrarium.

Refl.   Sic sic amans rapior
pendulus in varium.

but take no heed:
living and knowing, I die.

Cupid feasts on these
and inflames me
with his allurements.
But Reason lures
and stirs me
to other pursuits.

Refr.   O, I am wasting away!
         I see the cause of it,
         but take no heed:
         living and knowing, I die.

Cupid drives me
from scholarly exile
unto the pleasing
comforts of love.
But you, Reason,
go far away!
You are conquered
under Venus' sway!

Refr.   O, I am wasting away!
         I see the cause of it,
         but take no heed:
         living and knowing, I die.

109. *A Faithless Girl*

Since a multiform spark of Venus ignites me,
I wander with a dissipated heart,
and the merciless Scylla of my solicitudes
sucks me into the deep.
For as far as my intentions are concerned,
Dione's desire,
which I hoped would be better,
opposes every purpose of mine.

Refr.   So I love, and so I am dragged
         unstably to and fro.

Delium flagrantem,
procantem, anhelantem
Daphne respuit, rennuit,
puduit amplexari.
michi refragari
nititur, que petitur;
subvertitur spes mea,
quia Cytherea,
lese pacis rea,
cedit in contrarium.

Refl.   Sic sic amans rapior
         pendulus in varium.

Quid insudo Veneri?
quid parco verbis, verberi?
que michi sic est oneri,
iam subridet alteri.
morior, morior, morior!
iam illum vult audire,
iam discit lascivire,
iam parat consentire.
morior, morior, morior!
in qua flecti glorior,
ad me non reflectitur.
cur Venus istud patitur,
quod ea, que diligitur,
cedit in contrarium?

Refl.   Sic sic amans rapior
         pendulus in varium.

CX. *Illecebratus Amore*

Quis furor est in amore!
corde, simul ore
cogor innovari;
cordis agente dolore
fluctuantis more
videor mutari
Veneris ad nutum,
corque prius tutum,
curis non imbutum

When Apollo glowed,
asked for her hand,
and gasped at her sight, Daphne refused him,
repulsed him, and found shame in his embrace.
She endeavors to resist me,
she, whom I pursue.
My hopes are subverted,
because Cytherea,
the culprit of my marred peace,
thwarts my every move.

Refr.   So I love, and so I am dragged
         unstably to and fro.

Why should I sweat over Venus?
Why should I spare invectives and the lash?
She, who encumbers me thus,
now smiles upon another lad.
I die! I die! I die!
Already she wants to listen to him;
already she learns the role of libertine;
already she is about to consent to him.
I die! I die! I die!
She towards whom I am proud to gravitate
reciprocates to me no love.
Why does Venus allow
a maiden who is loved
to be contrary to me?

Refr.   So I love, and so I am dragged
         unstably to and fro.

110. *Enticed by Love*

What madness there is in love!
She compels me to become
another in heart and in words.
The pain of my heart takes the helm,
and I seem to be changing
into a ductile wave, subject
to Venus' nod and whim,
and I sense that my heart,
once secure nor imbrued with cares,

sentio Veneris officio turbari.

Ad Dryades ego veni,
iamque visu lem
cepi speculari
quasque decoris ameni;
sed unam inveni
pulchram absque pari.
subito procellam
volvor in novellam,
cepitque puellam
oculus cordis hanc preambulus venari.

CXI. *Dura Longinquitas a Puella Formosa*

O comes amoris, dolor,
cuius mala male solor,
an habes remedium?
dolor urget me, nec mirum,
quem a predilecta dirum,
en, vocat exilium,
cuius laus est singularis,
pro qua non curasset Paris
Helene consortium.

Sed quid queror me remotum
illi esse, que devotum
me fastidit hominem,
cuius nomen tam verendum,
quod nec michi presumendum
est, ut eam nominem?
ob quam causam mei mali
me frequenter vultu tali
respicit, quo neminem.

Ergo solus solam amo,
cuius captus sum ab hamo,
nec vicem reciprocat.
quam enutrit vallis quedam,
quam ut paradisum credam,
in qua pius collocat
hanc creator creaturam,
vultu claram, mente puram,

is being agitated under Venus' will.

I came to the Dryads and then with a kind face
began to observe that each is of pleasant grace.
But I found one who was beautiful beyond compare.
Suddenly I rolled
into a new storm,
and then my eye,
the tracking hound
of my heart,
began to trace
the trail of this girl.

111. *Harsh Distance from a Comely Girl*

O pain, companion of love,
whose agonies I fail to assuage—
or perhaps you have a remedy?—
grief, not wonderment, presses upon me,
whom, lo!, dreadful exile calls
away from a most beloved girl,
whose praise is nonpareil,
in whose place Paris would not
have taken Helen as wife.

But why do I complain
that I am from her removed,
who loathes me, her faithful varlet?
She, whose name is so reverenced
that I must not presume
to give voice to such sacred tones?
For this transgression of mine
she frequently glares at me with such a mien
that effectively reduces me to absolute nothing.

Therefore I alone love only her,
by whose hook I am ensnared;
nor does she reciprocate in turn.
A certain valley sustains her,
a valley I believe to be Paradise,
in which the Gracious Creator
situates this lovely creature—
bright in visage, pure in spirit,

quam cor meum invocat.

Gaude, vallis insignita,
vallis rosis redimita,
vallis, flos convallium,
inter valles vallis una,
quam collaudat sol et luna,
dulcis cantus avium!
te collaudat philomena,
vallis dulcis et amena,
mestis dans solicium!

CXII. *Eripe Me, O Virgo!*

Dudum voveram
recta sapere,
Amor, operam
tuam fugere -
et quod spreveram,
sector temere,
vivo perperam;
sed promiseram
resipere.

Languet iterum
morbo veteri
pectus tenerum,
vacans Veneri.
pudet liberum
servum fieri,
iugum asperum
cogit miserum
me conqueri.

Sed iam postulo,
quod sis facilis,
virgo seculo
tam amabilis,
solis oculo
comparabilis,
que pro speculo
servis populo
spectabilis!

whom my heart calls by name.

Rejoice, O glorious valley,
valley of roses wreathed round,
valley, flower of valleys,
singular valley among valleys,
celebrated by the sun and moon
and the sweet songs of the birds!
The nightingale praises thee,
sweet and pleasant vale
that gives solace to the dejected!

112. *Rescue Me, O Lass!*

Long ago had I vowed
to be rational in my ways
and, Cupid, to shun
your amorous works,
and what I had spurned
I now recklessly pursue
and lead a life of perversity.
But I had promised
to savor of reason.

My tender heart
languishes again
with its old disease:
devoting itself to Venus.
It shames a free man
to become a slave.
The harsh yoke
compels me to bemoan
my wretched state.

But now I ask
that you yield,
O maiden so beloved
by all the world,
comparable to
the glowing eye of the sun,
who, visible to all,
serve mankind
as its mirror!

CXIIa. *Ustus a Virgine*

Div mich singen tůt,
getorste ih si nennen!
trurech ist min můt.
owi, vrowe, wenne
wildu mir wesen gvot?
ih reche dir mine hende;
du brennest mih ane glůt!
svoze, die ungenade wende!

CXIII. *Ad Gaudia!*

Transit nix et glacies
spirante Favonio,
terre nitet ficies
ortu florum vario;
et michi materies
amor est, quem sentio,
          ad gaudia!

Refl.   Temporis nos ammonet
         lascivia.

Agnosco vestigia
rursus flamme veteris;
planctus et suspiria
nove signa Veneris,
† a, quae manent tristia
amantes pre ceteris
          ad gaudia!

Refl.   Temporis nos ammonet
         lascivia.

Illa, pro qua gravior
mens amorem patitur,
iusto plus asperior,
nec michi compatitur.
amans, et non mentior,
nec vivit nec moritur.
          ad gaudia!

112a. *Burned by a Maiden*

Her, who inspires my song,
I must only venture to praise.
My spirit is sad.
Alas, lady, when will you
be kind to me?
I stretch out my hands to you
and you burn me, even without fire.
O my love, cease your dismissive ways!

113. *To Joys!*

Snow and ice melt away
as Favonius[219] comes to life;
the face of the earth shines
in the dawn of various blooms.
The love I feel
is my fuel.
            To joys!

Refr.   The jollity of the time
            urges us on.

I recognize again
the traces of an old flame:
the laments and sighs,
the tokens of a new love.
Ah, what sorrows await lovers
more than all other men!
            To joys!

Refr.   The jollity of the time
            urges us on.

She, for whom my heart, heavier than
it is wont to be, suffers the pain of love,
is harsher than is meet and just,
nor has she any compassion for me.
The lover—and I do not lie—
is neither alive nor dead.
            To joys!

Refl.   Temporis nos ammonet
         lascivia.

Hic amor, hic odium;
quid eligam, nescio.
sic feror in dubium;
sed cum hanc respicio,
me furatur inscium,
et prorsus deficio
         ad gaudia!

Refl.   Temporis nos ammonet
         lascivia.

Non est finis precibus,
quamvis cantu finiam:
superis faventibus
adhuc illi serviam,
unde letis plausibus
optata percipiam!
         ad gaudia!

Refl.   Temporis nos ammonet
         lascivia.

CXIIIa. *Querela Virginalis*
Dietmar von Eist (*Des Minnesangs Frühling* 32.1)

«Vvaz ist fur daz senen gůt,   daz wip nah lieben manne hat?
wie gerne daz min herçe erchande, wan daz iz so bedwungen stat!»
also reit ein vrowe schone.
«an ein ende ih des wol chome,
wan div hůte;
selten sin vergezzen wirt   in minem můte.»

CXIV. *In Limine Mortis*

Tempus accedit floridum,
hiems discedit temere;
omne, quod fuit aridum,
germen suum vult gignere.
quamdiu modo vixeris,
semper letare, iuvenis,   quia nescis, cum deperis!

Refr.   The jollity of the time
          urges us on.

On this side is love, on that side hate:
I know not which I should choose.
In this way I am driven into doubt.
But when I look upon her,
she robs me of all awareness
and my senses fully withdraw from me.
          To joys!

Refr.   The jollity of the time
          urges us on.

This is not the end of my pleas,
although I am concluding my song:
with the gods smiling upon my designs,
I shall serve this maiden still,
whereby under the joyous din of plaudits
I shall receive the things for which I yearn!
          To joys!

Refr.   The jollity of the time
          urges us on.

113a. *A Maiden's Complaint*
by Dietmar von Aist (*The Spring of the Courtly Lovesong* 32.1)

"What helps against the yearning that a woman has
for a beloved man? How fain would my heart find it out,
since it is so very by it overwhelmed."
So uttered a beautiful maid.
"I would probably know the solution, if the watchdogs
were not there. But he will never be forgotten in my heart."

114. *On the Threshold of Death*

The time of the flowers has approached;
now the winter precipitously retreats.
Everything that once was dry
now wishes to sprout and fruit its seed.
So long as you are still alive, rejoice always, lad,
since you know not when you will be dead!

Prata iam rident omnia,
est dulce flores carpere;
sed nox donat his somnia,
qui semper vellent ludere.
ve, ve, miser quid faciam?
Venus, michi subvenias!   tuam iam colo gratiam.

Plangit cor meum misere,
quia caret solacio;
si velles, hoc cognoscere
bene posses, ut sentio.
o tu virgo pulcherrima,
si non audis me miserum,   michi mors est asperrima!

Dulcis appares omnibus,
sed es michi dulcissima;
tu pre cunctis virginibus
incedis ut castissima.
† o tu mitis considera!
† nam pro te gemitus passus sum et suspiria.

CXIVa. *Festus Dies Amoris*

Der al der werlt ein meister si,
der geb der lieben gûten tach,
von der ih wol getrostet pin.
si hat mir al min ungemach
mit ir gûte gar benomen.
unstæte hat si mir erwert;   ih pin sin an ir genade chomen.

CXV. *S.N.N.!*[220]

Nobilis, mei   miserere, precor!
tua facies   ensis est, quo necor,
nam medullitus   amat meum te cor:
        subveni!

Refl.   Amor improbus   omnia superat.
        subveni!

Come sperulas   tue eliciunt,
cordi sedulas   flammas adiciunt;
hebet animus,   vires deficiunt:

All the meadows now with gaiety laugh,
and the pleasure of picking flowers returns.
But the night casts dreams o'er those
who wish always to frolic and play.
Alas, alas, what am wretched I to do?
Venus, come to my aid! I now worship your grace!

My heart beats with a lugubrious tattoo,
because it solace lacks.
If you were willing, you could
well recognize that; this I surely know.
O you most seraphic maid, if you
do not give ear to my woe, a harshest death will visit me!

Sweet you appear to all others' eyes,
but you are the sweetest in mine;
You before all other maidens
as the most chaste stride.
O gentle one, give thought to this,
since over you I have heaved groans and sighs!

114a. *Love's Holiday*

He who rules over all the world, should give
a happy day to love, which has solaced me so well.
Through its sweet kindness
it has freed me from all grief.
It has protected me from inconstancy,
and thus her favor I have attained.

115. *S.O.S.!*

Noble lass, take pity on me, I pray!
Your face is a sword, by which I am slain,
for my heart loves you to its very core:
            send me your aid!

Refr.   Ruthless Cupid conquers all!
            Send to me your aid!

Your tresses summon up my tears
and fan unremitting flames through my heart;
my spirit is dull, and my strength withdraws:

subveni!

Refl.   Amor improbus   omnia superat.
subveni!

Odor roseus   spirat a labiis;
speciosior   pre cunctis finis,
melle dulcior,   pulchrior liliis,
subveni!

Refl.   Amor improbus   omnia superat.
subveni!

Decor prevalet   candori etheris.
ad pretorium   presentor Veneris.
ecce pereo,   si non subveneris!
subveni!

Refl.   Amor improbus   omnia superat.
subveni!

CXVa. *Species Periculosa*

Edile vrowe min,
gnade mane ih dich!
din wunnechlicher schin
vil gar verderbet mich.
sůze, erchenne dich!
din lip der ist mir ze wunnechlich.

Refl.   Nach im ist mir not;
sůze vrowe, gnade, alde ih pin tot!

CXVI. *Tumultus Animalis*

Sic mea fata canendo solor,
ut nece proxima facit olor.
blandus heret meo corde dolor,
roseus effugit ore color.
cura crescente,
labore vigente,
vigore labente
miser morior;

send me your aid!

Refr.   Ruthless Cupid conquers all!
         Send to me your aid!

A rosy fragrance rises from your lips;
you are more beauteous than all other girls,
sweeter than honey, prettier than lilies.
         Send me your aid!

Refr.   Ruthless Cupid conquers all!
         Send to me your aid!

Your beauty outshines the splendor of heaven.
I am presented to Venus the commandress' tent.
Behold, I will die, if you help me not!
         Send me your aid!

Refr.   Ruthless Cupid conquers all!
         Send to me your aid!

115a. *Dangerous Beauty*

My noble lady, I beg of thee,
show thou mercy unto me!
Thy enchanting semblance
drives me straight into the ground.
O my sweetness, be kind to me!
I cannot resist thy alluring form!

Refr.   All my efforts belong to thee!
         Lovely girl, have pity, lest I die away!

116. *Spiritual Turmoil*

I assuage my fate with a song,
as does a swan on the brink of death.
A seductive grief sits fast in my heart,
and from my face flees all the red.
My solicitude waxes,
my anguish thrives;
my vigor wanes,
an abject man I die.

tam male pectora multat amor.
a morior, a morior, a morior,
dum, quod amem, cogor et non amor!

Felicitate Iovem supero,
si me dignetur, quam desidero,
si sua labra semel novero;
una cum illa si dormiero,
mortem subire,
placenter obire
vitamque finire
statim potero,
tanta si gaudia non rupero.
a potero, a potero, a potero,
prima si gaudia concepero!

CXVII. *Non Iste Sum!*

Lingua mendax et dolosa,
lingua procax, venenosa,
lingua digna detruncari
et in igne concremari,
que me dicit deceptorem
et non fidum amatorem,
quam amabam, dimisisse
et ad alteram transisse!

Sciat deus, sciant dei:
non sum reus huius rei!
sciant dei, sciat deus:
huius rei non sum reus!

Unde iuro Musas novem,
quod et maius est, per Iovem,
qui pro Dane sumpsit auri,
in Europa formam tauri;
iuro Phebum, iuro Martem,
qui amoris sciant artem;
iuro quoque te, Cupido,
arcum cuius reformido;
arcum iuro cum sagittis,
quas frequenter in me mittis:
sine fraude, sine dolo

So ruthlessly does love punish my breast!
Alas, I'm dying, alack, I die, woe to me, I pass,
when I am coerced to love and yet am not loved back!

I shall conquer Jupiter with my felicity,
if she, whom I desire, deems me worthy;
if I acquaint myself but once with her lips,
if I sleep with her but one night,
I could at once
submit to death,
with pleasure die,
and end my life,
if I do not annul such great joys!
Yes, I could, yea, I could, aye, I could,
if of these principal delights I lay hold!

117. *I'm Not He!*

The mendacious, deceitful tongue,
venomous and bold,
deserves to be lopped
and consumed in a fire,
because it claims that I am a fraud
and a faithless paramour,
and maintains that I have forsaken my girl
and shifted my gaze to another lass!

May God know, may the gods perceive,
that I am not the perpetrator of this crime!
May the gods know, may God perceive,
that I am innocent of this wicked deed!

Hence I swear by the Muses nine
and, better yet, by Jove in the sky,
who donned the guise of gold for Danaë
and the form of a bull before Europa's eyes.
I swear by Phoebus, I swear by Mars,
who both are versed in the art of love;
by you as well, Cupid, I swear,
of whose bow I shake with fear.
I swear by the bow and all its bolts,
which frequently you launch at me:
without artifice and without deceit,

fedus hoc servare volo!

Volo fedus observare!
et ad hec dicemus, quare:
inter choros puellarum
nichil vidi tam preclarum.
Inter quas appares ita
ut in auro margarita.
humeri, pectus et venter
sunt formata tam decenter;

Frons et gula, labra, mentum
dant amoris alimentum;
crines eius adamavi,
quoniam fuere flavi.

Ergo dum nox erit dies,
et dum labor erit quies,
et dum aqua erit ignis,
et dum silva sine lignis,
et dum mare sine velis,
et dum Parthus sine telis,
cara michi semper eris:
nisi fallar, non falleris!

CXVIII. *O Exeam!*

Doleo, quod nimium
patior exilium.
pereat hoc studium,
si m'en iré,
si non reddit gaudium,
cui tant abé!

Tua pulchra facies
me fey planser milies;
pectus habet glacies.
a remender
statim vivus fierem
per un baser!

Prohdolor, quid faciam?
ut quid novi Franciam?

I wish to preserve this covenant sweet!

I wish to hold fast to this bond,
and on top of this I shall sing why:
among the bands of maidens
I saw nothing so remarkable.
Among them you come in sight
like a pearl in a setting of gold.
Your shoulders, breast, and body beyond
are so gracefully formed.

Her brow and throat, her lips
and chin, fuel the fires of love.
Her tresses I so deeply adored
for they emitted rays of gold.

Therefore until night is day,
until toil becomes rest,
until water is as fire,
and until the forest lacks trees,
until the sea is without sails,
until the Parthian[221] wants for missiles,
always will you be treasured by me.
If I be not chicaned, you will be not deceived!

118. *O Let Me Leave!*

I grieve that in exile
I suffer too much!
May this study fade away!
I must begone,
if she grants me not the joy,
for which I yearn desperately!

Thy beautiful semblance
inspires a thousand tears;
a sheet of ice rules thy breast,
as far as conveying comfort goes.
Quickly would I spring to life
through but one sweet kiss!

Alack, alas! What should I do?
Why must I acquaint myself with France?

perdo amicitiam
de la gentil?
miser corde fugiam
de cest pays?

Cum venray in mon pays,
altri drud i avra bris.
† podyra mi lassa dis.
me miserum!
suffero par sue amor
supplicium.

Dies, nox et omnia
michi sunt contraria.
virginum colloquia
me fay planszer.
† oy suvenz suspirer plu
me fay temer.

O sodales, ludite!
vos qui scitis, dicite;
michi mesto parcite:
grand ey dolur!
attamen consulite
per vostre honur!

Amia, pro vostre honur
doleo, suspir et plur;
par tut semplant ey dolur
grande d'amer.
fugio nunc; socii,
laissiez m'aler!

CXIX. *Excitatus ad Amorem*

Dulce solum   natalis patrie,
domus ioci,   thalamus gratie,
vos relinquam   aut cras aut hodie,
periturus   amoris rabie.

Vale tellus,   valete socii,
quos benigno   favore colui,
et me dulcis   consortem studii

Am I losing the friendship
of a lovely lass?
A wretch at heart,
am I to flee this land?

When I wend to my homeland,
she will probably have taken another lad.
She says only, "Leave me ever in peace!"
Ay, unlucky me!
Through her love I suffer
the agony of death!

Day, night, and in general all
conspire against poor me!
Maidenly prattle
makes me cry;
often I hear her sigh,
which but sets my fears high.

O cronies mine, yourselves enjoy;
you who know yourselves, speak ye;
but spare this lad, hapless in peace:
I experience great pain!
But consult me
for your honor's sake!

O lady mine, for thy honor's sake
I suffer, I sigh, and I weep.
Throughout my body I bear great dole,
which originates from bitter love.
Now I flee; o comrades mine,
let me leave, *laissez-moi partir*!

119. *Awakened to Love*

The sweet soil of my native land,
the home of jest, the chamber of grace,
I shall leave you either tomorrow or today,
moribund from the madness of love.

Farewell, sweet land; comrades, adieu,
whom I with such kind favor tilled,
and grieve for me, the consort

deplangite,   qui vobis perii!

Igne novo   Veneris saucia
mens, que prius   non novit talia,
nunc fatetur   vera proverbia:
«ubi amor,   ibi miseria.»

Quot sunt apes   in Hyble vallibus,
quot vestitur   Dodona frondibus
et quot natant   pisces equoribus,
tot abundat   amor doloribus.

CXIXa. *Temperantia*

Semper ad omne quod est   mensuram ponere prodest,
Sic sine mensura   non stabit regia cura.

CXX. *Factastne Meretrix?*

Rumor letalis me crebro vulnerat
meisque malis dolores aggerat.
me male multat vox tui criminis,
que iam resultat in mundi terminis.
invida Fama tibi novercatur;
cautius ama, ne comperiatur!
quod agis, age tenebris
procul a fame palpebris!
letatur amor latebris
cum dulcibus illecebris
et murmure iocoso.

Nulla notavit te turpis fabula,
dum nos ligavit amoris copula.
sed frigescente nostro cupidine
sordes repente funebri crimine.
Fama letata novis hymeneis
irrevocata ruit in plateis.
patet lupanar omnium
pudoris, en, palatium,
nam virginale lilium
marcet a tactu vilium
commercio probroso.

of your sweet studies, who perished for you!

By a new fire of love my heart is singed,
which formerly knew not of such things,
but now confesses these apothegms:
"Where there is love, misery lurks there."

As many bees as there are in Hybla's vales,
as many leaves that adorn Dodona's grove,[222]
and as many fish swim in the seas—
in so many sorrows does love abound.

119a. *Temperance*

Always does it avail to observe a measure in all things;
thus without measure regal power will not perdure.

120. *Has She Become A Whore?*

A fatal rumor repeatedly wounds me
and heaps sorrows upon my maladies.
Talk of your indiscretion heavily aggrieves me,
gossip that now reverberates
in the farthest corners of the world.
The jealous goddess Fama treats you with harshness;
love cautiously, lest the tryst be unveiled!
Whatever you do, in darkness do it far from Fama's ken!
Love makes merry in hidden retreats
with sweet charms and lures
and bantering whispers.

No shameful tale has branded you,
when the knot of love has bound us two.
But our passion has begun to chill,
and you are sullied with a fatal charge.
Fama, who delights in new nuptial affairs,
cannot be recalled and rushes through the streets.
The bordello now lies open to all,
what once was a palace of decency,
for the virginal lily shrivels,
when it in shameful commerce
is touched by sordid folks.

Nunc plango florem etatis tenere,
nitidiorem Veneris sidere,
tunc columbinam mentis dulcedinem
nunc serpentinam amaritudinem.
verbo rogantes removes hostili,
munera dantes foves in cubili.
illos abire precipis,
a quibus nichil accipis;
cecos claudosque recipis,
viros illustres decipis
cum melle venenoso.

CXXa. *Cupido Omnibus Dominatur*

Vincit Amor quemque,   sed numquam vincitur ipse.

CXXI. *Mea Femina Nova*

Tange, sodes, citharam   manu letiore,
et cantemus pariter   voce clariore!
factus ab amasia   viduus priore
caleo nunc alia   multo meliore.
clavus clavo retunditur,
amor amore pellitur,
iam nunc prior contemnitur,
quia nova diligitur;
igitur leto iure psallitur.

Prior trux et arrogans,   humilis secunda;
prior effrons, impudens,   nova verecunda;
prior patet omnibus   meretrix immunda,
hec me solum diligit   mente pudibunda;
prior pecuniosior,
rapacior, versutior,
hec nova curialior,
formosior, nobilior,
letior. . . . . potior.

Hec, quam modo diligo,   cunctis est amanda,
nulla de nostratibus   ei comparanda.
communiter omnibus   esset collaudanda –
sed tractari refugit; in hoc est damnanda!
mittam eam in ambulis

Now I weep over the flower of a tender age
that shined more brightly than Venus' star,
then the dovelike sweetness of her whole being
that now smacks of the bitterness of a snake.
You repulse those, who ask with hostile words,
and in your bed you pamper those who bring you gifts.
You direct those to leave,
from whom you nothing receive.
The blind and lame you take in,
and you cheat illustrious men
with an envenomed honey.

120a. *Cupid Rules All*

Cupid conquers every man, but never is himself subdued.

121. *My New Dame*

Strum, fellow, the cithern with a merrier hand,
and let us sing together with a treble more clear!
Divorced from my former paramour,
I burn now for another, much better lass!
A nail is obtunded by a second;
love is expelled by another love.
Already now is my bygone lover scorned,
because a new maiden is now adored;
therefore with happy right my song is played and rung.

The first was fierce and orgulous; the second knows humility.
The last was shameless and impudent, the new girl venerably shy.
The former was a filthy whore whose legs lay open to all;
the present girl loves only me and is of a chaste mind.
The quondam lass was more a social climber,
more rapacious, more wily in her designs;
the girl who is now mine is more mannerly,
more finely crafted, more noble, more jovial,
and more preferable in every regard.

This maiden whom I cherish now is worthy of the love of all;
no lady among our countrywomen is even comparable to her.
She would be unanimously lauded by all, but she
shuns my touch, and for this deserves a reprimand!
I shall send her to the riding rings,

et castigabo virgulis
et tangam eam stimulis,
ut facio iuvenculis;
vinculis vinciam, si consulis.

«Non erit, ut arbitror, opus hic tanta vi;
nam cum secum luderem nuper in conclavi,
dixit: "tractas teneram tactu nimis gravi!
tolle, vel suavius utere suavi!"»
exierat de balneo;
nunc operit, quo gaudeo.
non ferreo, sed carneo
calcanda est calcaneo.
ideo valeas, quam valeo!

CXXIa. *Inventio Dei*

Non est crimen amor, quia, si scelus esset amare,
Nollet amore Deus etiam divina ligare.

CXXII. *Nenia ad Regem*

Expirante primitivo
probitatis fomite
laus expirat, adoptivo
carens laudis capite.
splendor vite singularis,
flos marcescens militaris
vergit in interitum,
dum humane iubar sortis,
rex virtutum, dire mortis
fatis solvit debitum.

Cuius morte Mors regale
decus privat apice,
qua virtutis integrale
robur mutat Anglice,
qua lux orbis tanta luce,
Normannorum tanto duce
destituta deperit,
nubes tristis denigratum,
suo clima desolatum
sole nostrum operit.

I shall flog her with little wands,
and I shall smite her with spurs,
as I do with untamed stallions,
and I shall fasten her to a tether, if you counsel me so.

In my opinion, it will not be a labor of such force here,
for when I frolicked with her in her chamber recently,
she said, "You handle a tender maiden far too roughly;
desist, or with more mansuetude employ a soft caress!"
She went straightway out of the bath
and then covered that in which I take delight.
With a spur not of iron, but of flesh
she must be goaded into my hands.
And so my desire goes, "May you fare better than I!"

121a. *The Invention of God*

Love is not a crime, for, if loving were a sin,
God would not also bind divinities through it.

122. *Dirge to a King*[223]

When the primal tinder
of probity expires,
glory expires, too,
since it lacks its adoptive head.
The splendor of an exemplary life,
the flower of knighthood
droops and to ruin turns,
when the light of humanity,
the king of virtues, pays its dues
to the fate of fearsome death.

Through his death Mors deprives
the royal emblem of its head,
and by it the untouched strength
of English virtue degenerates and dims;
the light of the world dies off,
destitute of such a beacon—
of so great a Norman leader.
A blackened cloud of sorrow
then shadows our clime,
forsaken by its sun.

Plange regem, Anglia
nuda patrocinio,
fulcimento Gallia,
virtus domicilio,
probitas preconio,
preside militia,
opum abundantia
hoc casu dativo,
duces amicitia,
pauper vocativo!

Luge, funde gemitus,
gemina suspiria,
tanti regis obitus
redimens solacia,
miles, querimonia,
cuius lapsu deditus
militum exercitus
flebili iacture
tanti ducis gemitus
Mortis solvit iure!

O Mors ceca, cecitatis
nos premens articulo,
omnis ausa probitatis
derogare titulo,
prelatorum speculo
orbem privans, largitatis
totius igniculo,

O noverca vite, mori
digna, laudis invida,
proh! preclarum perfida
manu regem acriori
peste rapis morbida!

CXXIIa. *Gaudia Fragilia*
Marbod Redonensis (ca. 1035 - 1123)

Vite presentis   si comparo gaudia ventis,
Cum neutrum duret,   nemo reprendere curet!

CXXIII. *Naenia Waltheri*

Weep for your king, England!
You are bare of your defense!
Gaul, you, too, have lost your brace.
Virtue, your home has evanesced.
Integrity, your herald will not be touched again.
Knightage, your leader has ridden off.
Prosperity, your dative case[224]
has been given to a heavenly throng.
Princes, you have lost a friend;
paupers, your vocative was summoned off![225]

Lament, heave groans,
redouble your sighs,
purchasing, o rider, via plaints
consolation for the death
of such a paramount king,
by whose passing the host
of knights, ever loyal to him,
by right of Mors pay heavy sighs
to the rueful loss
of so capital a captain.

O blind Mors, who depress us
with your articles of blindness,
you ventured to derogate
the noble title of all excellence,
and deprived the world
of a model for all dignitaries,
and of the spark of every beneficence.

O cruel stepmother of life,
worthy of death, jealous of praise,
O alas! with a perfidious hand
you snatch away a remarkable king
with a fierce and deadly strain!

122a. *Fragile Joys*
by Marbodius of Rennes (ca. 1035-1123)

If I compare the joys of this life to the winds,
no one should rebuke me, since neither ever lasts.

123. *Walter's Threnody*

Gualterius de Castillione (ca. 1135 - ca. 1179)

Versa est in luctum
cithara Waltheri,
non quia se ductum
extra gregem cleri
vel eiectum doleat
vel abiecti lugeat
vilitatem morbi,
sed quia considerat,
quod finis accelerat
improvisus orbi.

Refl.   Libet intueri
iudices ecclesie,
quorum status hodie
peior est quam heri.

Umbra cum videmus
valles operiri,
proximo debemus
noctem experiri;
sed cum montes videris
et colles cum ceteris
rebus obscurari,
nec fallis nec falleris,
si mundo tunc asseris
noctem dominari.

Refl.   Libet intueri
iudices ecclesie,
quorum status hodie
peior est quam heri.

Per convalles nota
laicos exleges,
notos turpi nota
principes et reges,
quos pari iudicio
luxus et ambitio
quasi nox obscurat,
quos celestis ultio
bisacuto gladio

by Walter of Châtillon (ca. 1135 – ca. 1179)

Walter's cithern has turned to woe,[226]
not because it laments
that he as an outcast
must leave behind
the clerical fellowship
or because it rues the vileness
of his abject disease,
but because it ponders
that quickly and unexpectedly
the world is rushing to its end.

    Refr.   One needs only to observe
           the leaders of the Church,
           who are more depraved today
           than were their yestern ways.

When we see shadows
covering our vales,
we must take into account
the swift incursion of the night.
But when you see the mountains
and the hills and all the remaining things
descending into the depths of darkness,
then you deceive neither yourself nor another,
if then you assert that the night
is assuming dominion over the world.

    Refr.   One needs only to observe
           the leaders of the Church,
           who are more depraved today
           than were their yestern ways.

Mark throughout the valleys
the lawless members of the laity,
the princes and kings stamped
with the stigma of infamy,
whom, with impartial judgment,
lechery and ambition
blacken like the night,
whom divine vengeance
with a twice-sharpened sword

perdere maturat.

Refl.   Libet intueri
        iudices ecclesie,
        quorum status hodie
        peior est quam heri.

Restat, ut per montes
figurate notes
scripturarum fontes,
Christi sacerdotes;
colles dicti mystice,
eo quod in vertice
Sion constituti
mundo sunt pro speculo,
si legis oraculo
vellent non abuti.

Refl.   Libet intueri
        iudices ecclesie,
        quorum status hodie
        peior est quam heri.

Iubent nostri colles
dari cunctis fenum
et preferri molles
sanctitati senum;
fit hereditarium
Dei sanctuarium,
et ad Christi dotes
preponuntur hodie
expertes scientie
presulum nepotes.

Refl.   Si rem bene notes,
        succedunt in vitium
        et in beneficium
        terreni nepotes.

Veniat in brevi,
Iesu, bene Deus,
finis huius evi
annus iubileus!

hastens to completely destroy.

Refr.   One needs only to observe
        the leaders of the Church,
        who are more depraved today
        than were their yestern ways.

It remains for you to represent
figuratively through the mountains
the springs of Scriptural understanding.
The priests of Christ
are allegorically hight hills,
because they, situated
on the peak of Zion, serve
the world as its mirror,
if they desire not to abuse
the oracle of God's law.

Refr.   One needs only to observe
        the leaders of the Church,
        who are more depraved today
        than were their yestern ways.

Our hills command
that hay be given to all
and that spoiled youths be preferred
to the moral purity of the old.
The sanctuary of God
becomes hereditable,
and over the dowries of Christ today
they are appointed the command—
void of knowledge of any sort,
the nephews of the bishops.

Refr.   If you carefully observe the affair,
        then you see that their earthen relatives
        are their successors in profligacy
        and in sinecure.

O Jesus, O good God,
let the year of jubilation
in brief time come,
the herald of this era's end.

moriar, ne videam
Antichristi frameam,
cuius precessores
iam non sani dogmatis
stant in Monte Chrismatis
censuum censores!

Refl.   Si rem bene notes,
         succedunt in vitium
         et in beneficium
         terreni nepotes.

CXXIIIa. *Nuntium e Vate*

Ludit in humanis divina potentia rebus,
Et certam presens vix habet hora fidem.
                Ovidius, *Ex Ponto*, 4.3.49-50

CXXIV. *Lacrimae pro Philippo*

Dum Philippus moritur
Palatini gladio.
virtus mox conteritur
scelerosi vitio.

Dulcis mos obtegitur
a doli diluvio.
hëu, quo progreditur
fidei transgressio!

Lex amara legitur,
dum caret principio,
mel in fel convertitur,
nulla viget ratio.

CXXV. *Te Paeniteat!*
Otloh Ratisbonensis (ca. 1010 - ca. 1070)

Ante Dei vultum   nil pravi constat inultum.
Felices oculi,   qui cernunt gaudia celi!
Grande scelus grandi   studio debet superari.

CXXVI. *Tumor Peccati*

Let me die, lest I see
the Antichrist's blade,
whose harbingers of false doctrine
now stand atop
the Mountain of Anointing,[227]
as overseers of wealth!

Refr.   If you carefully observe the affair,
then you see that their earthen relatives
are their successors in profligacy
and in sinecure.

123a. *Message from A Bard*

Divine power plays its games in human affairs; and hardly
does the present hour hold a definite promise of the next.
Ovid, *Letters from the Black Sea* 4.3.49-50

124. *Tears for Philip*[228]

When Philip died
by the sword of the count palatine,
virtue was thereupon annihilated
by this iniquitous misdeed.

Amiable manner was interred
under the flood of deceit;
alas, how far and wide
the breach of faith did proceed!

A bitter law was read aloud,
when the law lacked an author;
honey was converted to gall,
and reason did not survive.

125. *Repent!*
by Otloh of St. Emmeram (ca. 1010 – ca. 1070)

Before the face of God no shameful act stands unpunished.
Blessed are the eyes that espy the joys of heaven!
A great crime must be overtopped with a great endeavor.

126. *The Swell of Sin*

Huc usque, me miseram!
rem bene celaveram
et amavi callide.

Res mea tandem patuit,
nam venter intumuit,
partus instat gravide.

Hinc mater me verberat,
hinc pater improperat,
ambo tractant aspere.

Sola domi sedeo,
egredi non audeo
nec inpalam ludere.

Cum foris egredior,
a cunctis inspicior,
quasi monstrum fuerim.

Cum vident hunc uterum,
alter pulsar alterum,
silent, dum transierim.

Semper pulsant cubito,
me designant digito,
ac si mirum fecerim.

Nutibus me indicant,
dignam rogo iudicant,
quod semel peccaverim.

Quid percurram singula?
ego sum in fabula
et in ore omnium.

Ex eo vim patior,
iam dolore morior,
semper sum in lacrimis.

Hoc dolorem cumulat,
quod amicus exulat
propter illud paululum.

Unlucky am I! Hitherto had I
concealed the affair so well,
and shrewdly did I love.

My affair at last is exposed,
for my belly has swelled up with life,
and a strenuous parturition now draws nigh.

For this my mother lashes me,
for this my father scolds me:
both treat me with harshness.

I sit alone at home;
I dare not venture outdoors,
nor openly with others play.

When I do step outside,
I am looked upon by all,
as if I a monster am.

When they see this paunch,
they nudge one another;
then silently they wait, until I pass.

They always poke with their elbows
and with a finger point me out,
as if I had performed a marvel.

They indicate me with nods,
they deem me worthy of the stake,
because I committed a single sin.

Why should I list every detail?
I am the focal point of gossip
and sit on the tongues of all.

This heavily aggrieves me:
already am I dying from pain,
and always am I in tears.

This overloads my grief,
that my lover is in exile
because of this trifling sin.

Ob patris sevitiam
recessit in Franciam
a finibus ultimis.

Sum in tristitia
de eius absentia
in doloris cumulum.

CXXVII. *Esto Aliquid Praeter Monachum!*

Deus pater, adiuva,
quia mors est proxima!
festina succurrere!
iam me vult invadere!

Dona, pater, spatium,
da michi consilium!
faciam me monachum,
si concedis crastinum.

«O mi dilectissime,
quid iam cupis agere?
secus tibi consule,
noli me relinquere!»

Tua, frater, pietas
movet michi lacrimas,
qui eris ut orphanus,
postquam ero monachus.

«Ergo mane paululum
saltim per hoc triduum!
forsan hoc periculum
non erit mortiferum.»

Tanta est angustia,
que percurrit viscera,
quod est michi dubia
vita quoque crastina.

«Monachorum regula
non est tibi cognita?
ieiunant cottidie,

Because of my father's wild fury,
my swain has withdrawn to France
from these farthest bounds.

I am in sorrow
over his absence
and in a heap of dole.

127. *Be Anything But A Monk!*

Father God, help me,
for death is drawing near!
Post in haste Your aid!
Already it wants to assail me!

Give me, Father, reprieve,
give to me Your advice!
I shall make myself a monk,
if You vouchsafe me the morrow!

"O my most beloved brother,
what do you wish now to do?
Think it over otherwise,
and forsake me not!"

Your love, brother,
moves me to tears,
for you will be orphaned,
after I become a monk.

"Therefore tarry but a moment,
at least for the next three days!
Perhaps this impending peril
will bring upon you no death."

So great is the distress
that pervades my innards,
that I am doubtful as to whether
I tomorrow will still be alive.

"Know you not then
the rule of monks?
Everyday they fast

vigilant assidue.»

Qui pro Deo vigilant,
coronari postulant;
qui pro Deo esurit,
satiari exigit.

«Dura donant pabula,
fabas ac legumina,
post tale convivium
potum aque modicum.»

Quid prosunt convivia
quidve Dionysia,
dum impleta dapibus
caro datur vermibus?

«Vel parentum gemitus
moveat te penitus,
qui te plangunt monachum
veluti iam mortuum!»

Qui parentes diligit
atque Deum negligit,
reus inde fuerit,
quando iudex venerit.

«Numquam magis videris,
quem tu tantum diligis:
illum Parme clericum
Guidonem pulcherrimum.»

† Hunc numquam relinquerem,
nisi mori crederem;
sed cum mors est dubia,
postponamus omnia.

«O ars dialectica,
numquam esses cognita,
que tot facis clericos
exules ac miseros!»

Hëu michi misero!

and constantly keep awake."

Who keeps watch for God,
desires to be crowned.
Who hungers for God,
rightly satiety procures.

"Harsh foods do they serve:
beans and vegetables,
after which banquet follows
a middling sip of water."

Of what avail are festive feasts,
or carousels brimming with wine,
when the body, stuffed with food,
is given as slop to the worms?

"At least the sighs of your parents
should move you deep within,
who weep that you are a monk,
almost as if you are dead!"

Who loves his parents
and yet neglects God,
will thence be a guilty soul,
when the Arbiter doth come.

"Never will you see him again,
whom you so dearly love:
that cleric from Parma,
most beautiful Guido."

Him I would never leave behind,
if I did not believe that I shall die.
But since death comes at a time unknown,
let us postpone everything and all.

"O art of disputation, ne'er
would you have been known,
who turn so many clerics
into exiles and urchins!"

Alas my wretched state!

quid agam, iam nescio.
longo in exilio
sum sine consilio.

Parce, frater, fletibus!
forsitan fit melius.
iam mutatur animus:
nondum ero monachus.

CXXVIII. *Navigator Errans*

Remigabat naufragus
olim sine portu;
verrebatur pelagus
Aquilonis ortu.
dum navis ab equore
diu quassaretur,
non fuit in litore,
qui compateretur.

Tandem duo pueri
portum innuere
fatigato pauperi
vitam reddidere.
iuvenum discretio
signat ei portum;
cedit huic compendio,
quicquid est distortum.

CXXIX. *Clericus Instar Job*

Exul ego clericus   ad laborem natus
tribulor multotiens   paupertati datus.

Litterarum studiis   vellem insudare,
nisi quod inopia   cogit me cessare.

Ille meus tenuis   nimis est amictus;
sepe frigus patior   calore relictus.

Interesse laudibus   non possum divinis,
nec misse nec vespere,   dum cantetur finis.

What I should do, I know not.
In lengthy banishment
I am without any counsel!

Spare, brother, your tears!
Perhaps it is better this way.
Already my heart has changed:
a monk I will no longer be.

128. *The Lost Navigator*

A shipwrecked sailor once rowed
and a haven could not find.
The sea was driven along
by the rise of the North Wind.
Whilst the ship for so long
was being battered by the sea,
no one was on the shore,
who had any compassion at all.

At last two boys signaled
the location of a harbor to him
and restored to life
the exhausted wretch.
The youths' shrewdness
showed him the way to the port;
whatever is distorted
yields to this direct path.

129. *The Cleric of Job*

I, a cleric far from home, was to ill luck born;[229]
I am harrowed beyond count, extradited to pauperdom.

I would labor over the pursuit of erudition,
if poverty did not compel me to stop.

This my mantle is too thin;
bereft of warmth, I often suffer the cold.

I cannot take part in the lauds, Mass,
nor Vespers, until the singing ends.

Decus N.   dum sitis insigne,
postulo suffragia   de vobis iam digne.

Ergo mentem capite   similem Martini:
vestibus induite   corpus peregrini,

Ut vos Deus transferat   ad regna polorum!
ibi dona conferat   vobis beatorum.

CXXX. *Cantus Cycni*

Olim lacus colueram,
olim pulcher exstiteram,
dum cygnus ego fueram.
miser! miser!

Refl.   Modo niger
          et ustus fortiter!

Eram nive candidior,
quavis ave formosior;
modo sum corvo nigrior.
miser! miser!

Refl.   Modo niger
          et ustus fortiter!

Me rogus urit fortiter,
gyrat, regyrat garcifer;
propinat me nunc dapifer.
miser! miser!

Refl.   Modo niger
          et ustus fortiter!

Mallem in aquis vivere,
nudo semper sub aere,
quam in hoc mergi pipere.
miser! miser!

Refl.   Modo niger
          et ustus fortiter!

Since ye are the noted jewel of the city N.,
I now entreat with all reverence your aid.

Therefore assume Saint Martin's disposition,
and bedeck with vesture this foreigner's frame,

So that God may raise you to His heavenly realms.
There may He confer upon you the meed of the saints.

130. *The Swan Song*

Once did I inhabit the lakes,
once was I a beautiful sight,
when I was a swan of white.
Wretched me! Wretched me!

Refr.   Now black am I
           and thoroughly burned!

I was whiter than the snow
and more comely than any bird.
Now I am blacker than the crow.
Wretched me! Wretched me!

Refr.   Now black am I
           and thoroughly burned!

A fire scorched me irreparably to the core;
fore and aft the scullion hovered round my hull.
The table servant then rushed to me.
Wretched me! Wretched me!

Refr.   Now black am I
           and thoroughly burned!

I would rather live in the waters,
always beneath a bare vault of sky,
than in this pepper sauce be drowned.
Wretched me! Wretched me!

Refr.   Now black am I
           and thoroughly burned!

Nunc in scutella iaceo
et volitare nequeo;
dentes Prendente video –
miser! miser!

Refl.   Modo niger
         et ustus fortiter!

CXXXI. *Ubi Est Caritas?*
Philippus Cancellarius (ca. 1170 - 1236)

Dic, Christi veritas,
dic, cara raritas,
dic, rara Caritas:
ubi nunc habitas?
aut in Valle Visionis?
aut in throno Pharaonis?
aut in alto cum Nerone?
aut in antro cum Theone?
vel in fiscella scirpea
cum Moyse plorante?
vel in domo Romulea
cum Bulla fulminante?

Respondit Caritas:
«homo, quid dubitas?
quid me sollicitas?
non sum, quo mussitas,
nec in euro nec in austro,
nec in foro nec in claustro,
nec in bysso vel cuculla,
nec in bello nec in bulla:
de Iericho sum veniens,
ploro cum sauciato,
quem duplex Levi transiens
non astitit grabato.»

O vox prophetica,
o Nathan, predica:
culpa Davitica
patet non modica!
dicit Nathan: «non clamabo»,
«neque» David «planctum dabo»,

Now on a salver dead I lie,
and never again can I fly.
Gnashing teeth are my last sight.
Wretched me! Wretched me!

Refr.   Now black am I
           and thoroughly burned!

131. *Where Is Love?*
by Philip the Chancellor (ca. 1170 – ca. 1236)

Speak, truth of Christ,
speak, priceless treasure,
speak, love so rare,
where do you now dwell?
In the Valley of Vision?[230]
or on Pharaoh's throne?
or on the ruling seat beside Nero?
or in a cave with Theon?[231]
or in a small basket of rushes
with the wailing baby Moses?[232]
or in the home of Romulus
with a flashing Bulla?[233]

Love responds:
"Mankind, why art thou in doubt?
Why dost thou pester me?
I am not where you keep silent,
neither in the East nor in the South,
nor in the forum nor in the cloister,
nor in fine linen nor in the habits of monks,
nor in battle nor in the papal bull.
I come from the city of Jericho,
and I weep with the wounded man,
whom two Levites passing
did not assist with a bed."[234]

O prophetic voice,
O Nathan,[235] loudly declare:
the crime of David[236]
is clearly not slight at all!
Nathan speaks: "I shall not shout,
nor make David the object of lament,"

cum sit Christi rupta vestis,
contra Christum Christus testis.
ve, ve vobis, hypocrite,
qui culicem colatis!
que Cesaris sunt, reddite,
ut Christo serviatis!

CXXXIa. *Curia Iniustitiae*
Philippus Cancellarius (ca. 1170 - 1236)

Bulla fulminante
sub iudice tonante,
reo appellante,
sententia gravante
Veritas supprimitur,
distrahitur et venditur
Iustitia prostante;
itur et recurritur
ad Curiam, nec ante
quid consequitur,
quam exuitur quadrante.

Pape ianitores
Cerbero surdiores.
in spe vana plores,
nam etiamsi fores
Orphëus, quem audiit
Pluto deus Tartareus,
non ideo perores,
malleus argenteus
ni feriat ad fores,
ubi Protëus
variat mille colores.

Si queris prebendas,
vitam frustra commendas;
mores non pretendas,
ne iudicem offendas!
frustra tuis litteris
inniteris; moraberis
per plurimas kalendas –
tandem exspectaveris
a ceteris ferendas,

because the robe of Christ is rent
and one anointed is a witness against the Christ![237]
Woe, woe to you, hypocrites,
who strain at a gnat![238]
Render to Caesar what is his,[239]
so that you may serve the Christ!

131a. *The Court of Injustice*
by Philip the Chancellor (ca. 1170 – ca. 1236)

When the bulla shines bright,
as a judge thunders his decree,
when the accused appeals,
because a false verdict weighs upon him,
then the truth is suppressed,
pulled asunder, and sold,
because justice prostitutes itself.
One comes and goes
to the Curia, but not before
he reaches his goal of ridding
himself of his very last quarter.

The doorkeepers of the Pope
are more unlistening than Cerberus.
You would wail in misguided hope,
for, even if you should bore through
as Orpheus once did, to whom
the Tartarean god Pluto gave his ear,
you would not persuade those within,
unless a hammer of silver
should strike at the doors,
where Proteus[240] changes
into a thousand shades.

If on a quest for prebends you are,
in vain you evidence your way of life;
do not allege your decency as your cause,
lest you give umbrage to the judge!
In vain do you invoke
your learning and letters:
you will be stalled for many months;
finally you will wait for a future date
that others will receive instead,

paris ponderis
pretio nisi contendas.

Iupiter, dum orat
Danen, frustra laborat;
sed eam deflorat,
auro dum se colorat:
auro nil potentius,
nil gratius, nec Tullius
facundius perorat.
sed hos urit acrius,
quos amplius   honorat;
nichil iustius,
calidum Crassus dum vorat!

CXXXII. *Voces Vernales*

Iam vernali tempore
terra viret germine,
sol novo cum iubare.
frondent nemora,
candent lilia,
florent omnia.

Est celi serenitas,
aeris suavitas,
ventorum tranquillitas;
est temperies
clara et dies,
cantant volucres:

Merulus cincitat,
acredula rupillulat,
turdus truculat
et sturnus pusitat,
turtur gemitat,
palumbes plausitat,
perdix cicabat,
anser craccitat,
cignus drensat,
pavo paululat,
gallina gacillat,
ciconia clocturat,

unless you stake a wager in the race
with a bribe of equal weight.

So long as Jupiter pleads for Danaë,
his toil is in vain.
But he still deflowers her,
when he dons a golden rain:
nothing is mightier than gold,
nothing is more welcome—
not even more cogent is Cicero himself.
But it more fiercely burns those,
whom it more amply adorns.
Nothing is more just than that,
since Crassus devours it hot.

132. *Voices of Spring*

Already in this time of spring
the earth is green with fresh shoots,
and the sun with a new light glows.
The woods put forth myriad leaves,
the lilies radiate a plethora of hues,
and all things else are in bloom.

The empyrean is clear,
the air is sweet,
and the zephyrs calmly blow.
Temperateness abounds,
and refulgent is the day,
and all together the birds sing.

The blackbird warbles,
the throstle chimes,
the fieldfare sobs,
the starling babbles,
the turtle dove sighs,
the wood pigeon coos,
the partridge chatters,
the goose gabbles,
the swan sounds a shrill ring,
the peacock shrieks,
the hen cackles,
the stork clacks,

pica concinnat,
hirundo et trisphat,
apes bombilat,
merops sincidulat.

Bubo bubilat
et guculus guculat,
passer sonstitiat
et corvus croccitat,
vultur pulpat,
accipiter pipat,
carrus titubat,
cornix garrulat,
aquila clangit,
milvus lipit,
anas tetrinnit,
graculus fringit,
vespertilio et stridit,
butio et butit,
grus et grurit,
cicada fretendit.

Onager mugilat,
et tigris raceat,
cervus docitat,
et verres quirritat,
leo rugit,
pardus ferit,
panther caurit,
elephans barrit,
linx et frennit,
aper frendit,
aries braterat,
ovis atque balat,
taurus mugit,
equus et hinnit.

Lepus vagit,
et vulpis gannit,
ursus uncat,
et lupus ululat,
canis latrat,
catulus glutinat,

the magpie mocks,
the swallow twitters,
the bees hum,
and the bee-eater knocks.

The horned owl hoots,
the cuckoo toots,
the sparrow chirps,
the raven caws,
the vulture screeches,
the hawk peeps,
the barn owl snores,
the crow blathers,
the eagle calls out,
the kite whistles in,
the duck quacks,
the jackdaw crows,
the bat beeps,
the bittern strums,
the crane trills,
the cicada saws.

The wild ass brays,
the tiger grumbles,
the stag bells,
the pig grunts,
the lion roars,
the leopard purrs,
the panther snarls,
the elephant trumpets,
the lynx spits,
the wild boar gnashes,
the ram lows,
the sheep bleats,
the bull bellows,
and the horse whinnies.

The hare squalls,
the fox yelps,
the bear growls,
the wolf howls,
the dog barks,
the puppy whimpers,

rana coaxat,
anguis sibilat,
grillus grillat,
sorex desticat,
mus et minnit,
mustela drindrit,
sus et grunnit,
asinus et rudit.

He sunt voces volucrum
necnon quadrupedum,
quarum modulamina
vincit phenix unica.

Iam horrifer Aquilo
suavi cedit Zephiro,
sole in estifero
degente domicilio.
dulcisona resonat harundo.
floride cum floridis
florent vites pampinis.
odorifera
surgunt gramina,
gaudet agricola.

Nunc dracones fluminum
scatent emanantium;
imber saluberrimus
irrigat terram funditus;
cataractas reserat Olimpus.
redolent aromata,
cum cinnamomo balsama.
virent viola,
rosa et ambrosia.
coeunt animalia.

CXXXIII. Nomina avium

Hic volucres celi   referam sermone fideli:
Accipiter, nisus,   capus atque ciconia, picus,
Pica, merops meropis,   larus atque loaficus, ibis,
Ardea vel turtur   seu bubo, monedula, vultur.
His assint aquile,   pitrisculus herodiusque.

the frog croaks,
the serpent hisses,
the grasshopper chirps,
the shrew squeaks,
the mouse screaks,
the weasel whines,
the sow snorts,
and the donkey heehaws.

These are the voices of the birds
and of the quadrupeds as well.
But the melodies of all of these
the matchless phoenix overpowers.

Now the frightful North Wind
yields to the gentle western breeze,
when our terrene home basks
in the sultry summer sun.
The sweet sounding reed whispers.
The vines in full bloom
now stand wrapped in tendrils;
the fragrant grasses,
enlivened, rise tall,
and the farmer rejoices.

The snakes of the leaping rivers
now spring forth and abound.
A most salubrious rain
completely soaks the earth;
Olympus its floodgates unseals.
Cinnamon and balsam
exude their perfumes.
The violet, rose, and sage
all fragrantly bloom.
The animals form amorous leagues.

133. The Names of the Birds

In this song I shall faithfully relate the birds of the sky:
the hawk, the sparrow-hawk, the capon and the stork, the woodpecker,
the magpie, the bee-eater, the buzzard and the harrier, the ibis, the heron
and turtle dove, also the horned owl, the jackdaw, and the vulture.
With these should consort the eagle, the wren, and the peregrine falcon.

Natura pariles   hic state columba, palumbes,
Corvus edax, cornix,   upupe, ficedula, perdix,
Noctua, fringellus   seu nycticorax, amarellus,
Milvus et inde parix,   onocrotalus, anser et orix,
Cygnus, olor, sturnus,   mergus turdelaque, turdus,
Quasquila cum merula,   phasianus et ortygometra,
Grus vel pellicanus,   pavo vel anas, alietus,
Aurificeps, cupude,   sepicecula cruriculeque.
Graculus haut deerit,   furfarius hic residebit,
Sparalus, attage,   mullis vaga cum struthione,
Sic cuculus, fulica,   sic psitacus atque cicada.
Te, vespertilio   vel hirundo, non reticebo.
Tu michi dulcisonam   cape, mirle celer, philomenam!
Laudula nulla tuum   fugiatve cicendula raptum!
Hic et lusciniam   cum luciliis cape parvam!
Nullus te passer   fugiat, licet hunc tegat asser!
Versu stare nequit   carduelis, quique recedit.

CXXXIV. De nominibus ferarum

Nomina paucarum   sunt hic socianda ferarum.
Sed leo sit primus,   qui cunctarum basiléus.
Hunc panthera, tigris   comitentur cum leopardis.
Rhinoceros sevus   comprenditur atque camelus.
Hinc etiam validos   elephantes iungo vel uros.
Bubalus, alces, pardus   velox nimiumque dromedus,
Ursus, aper, cervus   avide sumuntur in esus,
Hinnulus et caprea,   capricornus, simia, spinga,
Lynx, lupus atque lepus,   vulpes, vulpecula, melus,
Martarus et mygale,   luter, castor tebelusque,
Mus, mustela, sorex,   glis gliris hyenaque cimex.
Copulo spiriolum;   reliquorum do tibi nullum.

CXXXV. *Bruma Superata*

Cedit, hiems, tua durities;
frigor abit, rigor et glacies
brumalis et feritas, rabies,
torpor et improba segnities,
pallor et ira, dolor, macies.

Veris adest elegans acies,
clara nitet sine nube dies,

Stand you here, wood pigeon and dove, perfect matches in your natures;
you, gluttonous raven, crow, hoopoe, fig-pecker, partridge,
owl, finch, night raven, yellowhammer,
kite, and on the other side assemble ye, chickadee, bittern, goose, and jay,
swan, whooper swan, starling, loon, throstle, fieldfare,
quail and merle, pheasant and landrail,
crane and pelican, peacock and duck, golden eagle,
kingfisher, red-breasted robin, wagtail, and warbler.
The jackdaw should not be away; let here reside the hornero,
black grouse and hazel hen, wild goose and ostrich,
likewise the cuckoo, the coot, the parrot, and the cricket.
You, bat and also swallow, I shall not conceal.
You, swift blackbird, catch for me the dulcet nightingale!
Let no lark or kestrel escape your abducting force!
Here seize also the little thrush nightingale and the wagtail!
Let no sparrow elude you, though a copse may cover him.
But the goldfinch cannot stand in verse and flies off then.

134. On the Names of Beasts

The names of a few beasts are to be associated in this song.
But let the lion be first, who is the king of all.
The panther, tiger, and leopards should accompany him.
The fierce rhinoceros and the camel are captured.
I join to these, too, robust elephants and aurochs;
the bison, the elk, the panther, the all too fast dromedary,
the bear, the boar, the stag are eagerly taken up as food,
along with the young mule and roe, the ibex, the ape, the vervet,
the lynx, the wolf and the hare, the fox, the vixen, the badger,
the marten, the ermine, the otter, the beaver and the sable,
the mouse, the weasel, the shrew, the dormouse, the hyena, and the bug;
I add to these the squirrel— of the remaining beasts I offer thee none.

135. *Winter's Defeat*

Winter, your severity concedes defeat.
Withdraw do the chill, rigor, and ice,
the truculence of winter and its fury,
numbness and inordinate sluggishness,
wanness and ire, pain and meagerness.

The vibrant radiance of spring has broken.
The clear day shines without a cloud.

nocte micant Pliadum facies;
grata datur modo temperies,
temporis optima mollities.

Est pura mundi superficies,
gramine redolent planities,
induitur foliis abies,
picta canit volucrum series,
prata virent, iuvenum requies.

Nunc, Amor aureus, advenies,
indomitos tibi subicies.
tendo manus; michi quid facies?
quam dederas, rogo, concilies,
et dabitur saliens aries!

CXXXVa.
Walther von der Vogelweide (ca. 1170 - ca. 1230)

Der starche winder hat uns uerlan,
div sumerçit ist schone getan;
walt vnde heide sih ih nu an,
lovp vnde blůmen, chle wolgetan;
dauon mag uns frovde nimmer zergan.

CXXXVI. *Aprilis Renovatus*

Omnia sol temperat purus et subtilis,
nova mundo reserat facies Aprilis;
ad amorem properat animus herilis,
et iocundis imperat deus puerilis.

Rerum tanta novitas in sollemni vere
et veris auctoritas iubet nos gaudere.
vices prebet solitas; et in tuto vere
fides est et probitas tuum retinere.

Ama me fideliter! fidem meam nota:
de corde totaliter et ex mente tota
sum presentialiter absens in remota.
quisquis amat aliter, volvitur in rota.

CXXXVIa. *Eius Virgo Perfecta*

Through the night the cluster of Pleiades gleams.[241]
Now a pleasant warmth is conceded
and the most wonderful tenderness of this time.

Undefiled is surface of the world,
the plains are redolent of fresh grass,
the silver fir dresses itself in leaves,
a painted train of birds joyously sings,
and the meadows bloom, the respite of youths.

Now, golden Cupid, you will come
and bow to you the untamed lot.
I extend my hand—what will you do for me?
I pray that you incline to me the girl, whom you had granted me,
and I will sacrifice a feisty ram to thee.

135a. *Joy Without End*
by Walter von der Vogelweide (ca. 1170-1230)

The powerful winter has left us behind,
and lovely is the summertime;
now I eye the woods and moors,
leaves and flowers, and a pretty clover;
thence I want our joy never to melt away.

136. *April Renewed*

The sun tempers all things, spotless and keen,
the face of April uncloses new things to the scene;
the master's heart hastens to love,
and the puerile god rules over the blithe.

So great is the renewal of the world in the festivals of the spring,
and the vernal might bids us to rejoice and take delight.
It offers wonted interchanges, and in this truly safe haven
it is the mark of fidelity and probity to retain your dear friend.

Love me faithfully! Mark my loyalty:
with all my heart and soul I am utterly crazy for you,
even when I am away. Whoever loves in a different wise
merits a breaking on the wheel.

136a. *The Maiden of His Ideal*

Solde ih noch den tach geleben, daç ih wunschen solde
nah der, div mir frovde geben nach, ob si noh wolde!
min herçe můz nah ir streben; mohtih si han holde,
so wolde ih in wunne sweben, swere ih nimmer dolde.

CXXXVII. *Reventus Veris*

Ver redit optatum cum gaudio,
flore decoratum purpureo.
aves edunt cantus   quam dulciter!
revirescit nemus,
campus est amenus totaliter.

Iuvenes, ut flores accipiant
et se per odores reficiant,
virgines assumant   alacriter
et eant in prata
floribus ornata communiter!

CXXXVIIa. *Maius Mirus*

Springerwir den reigen nu, vrowe min!
vrovn uns gegen den meigen! uns chumet sin schin.
der winder der heiden   tet senediv not;
der ist nu çergangen,
si ist wunnechlich bevangen von blůmen rot.

CXXXVIII. *Sub Sole Estivali*

Veris leta facies mundo propitiatur,
hiemalis acies victa iam fugatur.
in vestitu vario Flora principatur,
nemorum dulcisono que cantu celebratur.

Flore fusus gremio Phebus novo more
risum dat, huic vario iam stipate flore.
Zephyrus nectareo spirans it odore.
certatim pro bravio curramus in amore!

Litteratos convocat decus virginale;
laicorum execrat pectus bestiale.
cunctos amor incitat, numen generale;
Venus se communicat, per iubar estivale.

I should live to see the day that I can conjure up a girl,
who would grant me joys, if she but chose.
My heart moons over her. I would possess her affection,
I would in ecstasy swim, I would have no more grief to suffer.

137. *The Return of Spring*

The much desiderated spring with jubilance returns,
wondrously spangled with purple blooms.
How sweetly the birds proclaim their songs!
The woods grow green again, and the fields
evoke delight, as far as the eye can espy.

So that they may pick flowers and refresh themselves
with their perfumes, lads should in elated alacrity
take up young maidens and together wend
through the grasslands
painted with blooms!

137a. *Wondrous May*

We now want to dance a roundelay, my lady fair,
and delight in the May, for it comes to reveal itself.
The winter that harrowed the moor,
with unsatisfied desire, now has passed.
But it now dons a delightful brocade of bright red flowers.

138. *Beneath the Summer Sun*

The blissful face of spring is propitious to the world;
the battle line of winter now is routed in defeat.
In a multicolored gown Flora now holds sway
and is celebrated in song by the sweet music of the woods.

Phoebus, draped on Flora's lap, smiles at her in a new wise,
as jewels in bloom now environ her in a dazzling palette of hues.
Zephyrus in his course exhales the essence of nectar everywhere.
In contest let us run for the reward in love!

The graceful maidens convoke cultured lads of erudition,
and the laity's bestial mind execrates them to hell.
Cupid stirs all to action, the universal divinity.
All have a share in Venus under the summer's beam.

Citharizat cantico dulcis philomena;
flore rident vario prata iam serena;
turba salit avium silve per amena;
chorus promit virginum iam gaudia millena.

CXXXVIIIa. *Corona Maii*

In liehter varwe stat der walt,
der vogele schal nu donet,
div wunne ist worden manichvalt;
des meien tugende chronet
senide liebe; wer were alt,
da sih div çit so schonet?
her meie, iv ist der bris geçalt!
der winder si gehonet!

CXXXIX. *Secutores Cupidinis Domini*

Tempus transit horridum, frigus hiemale,
redit, quod est placidum, tempus estivale.
quod cum Amor exigit sibi principale,
qui Amorem diligit, dicat ei vale!

Mutatis temporibus tellus parit flores,
pro diversis floribus variat colores.
variis coloribus prata dant odores,
philomena cantibus suscitat amores.

Quisquis amat, gaudeat tempus se videre,
in quo sua debeat gaudia tenere!
et cum Amor floreat, qui iubet gaudere,
iam non sit, qui audeat inter nos lugere!

Unam quidem postulo tantum michi dari,
cuius quidem osculo potest mors vitari.
huic amoris vinculo cupio ligari;
dulce est, hoc iaculo velle vulnerari.

Si post vulnus risero, dulcis est lesura;
si post risum flevero – talis est natura;
sed cum etas venerit senectutis dura,
lugeat, quod fecero, pro pena futura.

The sweet nightingale harps her tender song.
In a colored array of blossoms, the cheerful meadows now laugh.
A flock of birds bounds through the pleasant haunts of the woods.
Now a dance of maidens summons up a thousand joys.

138a. *The Crown of May*

In a bright array of colors the woodlands tower high,
the voices of the birds again lift trebles to the sky,
pleasure and bliss have become now manifold;
the virtue of May crowns love's longing of old.
Who would feel like aged pawns,
since a season so beautiful dawns?
Lordly May, upon you is the guerdon conferred!
May the winter be reviled and to exile spurred!

139. *Followers of Lord Cupid*

The frightful time of year passes, winter's gripping chill,
and the time of summer, ever pleasing, now returns to our hills.
Since Cupid lays his claim upon this capital time,
he, who cherishes Cupid, should to him his welcome chime!

The climate has changed and the earth yields blooms,
and to her flowered tableau she applies various hues.
So diverse in their colors, the meadows emit perfumes,
and the nightingale in song stirs up the suits of love.

Whoever loves should rejoice at the mere vision of this time,
in which he is obligated to maintain his joy!
And when Cupid triumphs who bids all us to take mirth,
he should not now be present, who dares to grieve among us!

Forsooth I ask only that one girl be given to me,
by whose tender kiss death can assuredly be escaped.
By this fetter of love I wish to be bound;
sweet it is to be wounded willingly by this shaft.

If I smile after the blow is dealt, then sweet is the consequent pain;
if I weep after I smile, then such is nature's way.
But when the harsh age of senectitude comes,
may it lament what I have done vis-à-vis the coming sentence.

Sed quod eam diligo, mira res videtur;
onus est, quo alligor, et vix sustinetur.
unum de me iudico, quod verum habetur:
morior, quam eligo nisi michi detur.

CXXXIXa. *Vigoratus Vere*

Zergangen ist der winder chalt,
der mih so sere můte,
gelovbet stat der grůne walt;
des frovet sih min gemůte.
nieman chan nu werden alt!
vrovde han ih manichualt
von eines wibes gůte.

CXL. *Virtutes Veris*

Terra iam pandit gremium   vernali lenitate,
quod gelu triste clauserat   brumali feritate.
dulci venit strepitu   Favonius cum vere,
sevum spirans Boreas   nos cessat commovere.
tam grata rerum novitas   quem patitur silere?

Nunc ergo canunt volucres,   nunc cantum promunt iuvenes,
modo ferro durior   est, quem non mollit Venus,
et saxo frigidior,   qui non est igne plenus.
pellantur nubes animi,   dum aer est serenus!

Ecce iam vernant omnia   fructu redivivo,
pulso per temperiem   tam frigore nocivo.
tellus feta sui par-   tus grande decus, flores
gignit odoriferos   nec non multos colores.
Catonis visis talibus   immutarentur mores!

Fronde nemus induitur,   iam canit philomena,
cum variis coloribus   iam prata sunt amena.
spatiari dulce est   per loca nemorosa,
dulcius est carpere   iam lilium cum rosa,
dulcissimum est ludere   cum virgine formosa!

Verum, cum mente talia   recensens oblectamina,
sentio, quod anxia   fiunt mea precordia:
si friget, in qua ardeo,   nec michi vult calere,

But because I love her, a marvelous affair is seems.
A burden is my shackle, and scarcely is it sustained.
One thing about me I conclude holds truth:
I die, if she I choose is not given to me.

139a. *Invigorated by Spring*

Gone is the cold winter
that bore down on me.
In verdure stands the wood,
which fills my heart with joy.
In this time no one at all can feel old!
I hold manifold joys
from a lovely dame!

140. *Vernal Powers*

In vernal tenderness the earth now opens her lap,
which the harsh frost with fierce storms had sealed.
With a sweet rustle come the zephyr and the spring;
the North Wind ceases to smite us with cruel blasts.
Whom does this so welcome novelty of all allow rest?

Thus the birds now sing; now youths unsheathe their songs;
now harder than iron is he whom Venus does not make soft,
and colder than stone is he who is not full of fire.
Away with the clouds of the soul, whilst the air is so serene!

Behold, all things stand green, and fruitfulness is revived,
since the injurious cold's banishment by the temperate clime.
The fertile earth births the sublime glory of her womb:
fragrant flowers and a myriad of resplendent hues.
Such sights would change Cato's stoic ways!

The forest is dressed in leaves; now the nightingale sings;
with a panoply of colors now pleasant are the heaths.
Sweet it is to saunter through the coverts of the woods;
sweeter it is to pick now a lily and a rose;
sweetest it is to frolic with a prepossessing girl!

But, when I recount these delights in my soul,
I feel my heart with tense anxiety grow.
If frigid she be, for whom I burn, and unwilling to warm to me,

quid tunc cantus volucrum   michi queunt valere,
quid tunc veris presentia?   iam hiems erit vere!

CXLa. *Festus in Prato*

Nu suln wir alle frovde han,
die zit mit sange wol began!
wir sehen blûmen stan,
div heide ist wunnechclich getan.
tanzen, reien, springerwir   mit frovde vnde ovch mit schalle!
daz zimet gûten chinden als iz sol; nu schinſen mit dem balle!
min vrowe ist ganzer tugende vol;   ih wiez, wiez iv geualle.

CXLI. *Puella Rigida*

Florent omnes arbores,
dulce canunt volucres;
revirescunt frutices,
congaudete, iuvenes!

Meror abit squalidus,
Amor adit calidus!
superat velocius,
qui non amat ocius.

Virgo tu pulcherrima,
cum non sis acerrima,
verba das asperrima,
sicut sis deterrima.

Viribus infirmior
ab Amore ferior,
vulnera experior;
si non sanas, morior.

«Quid tu captas, iuvenis?
queris, que non invenis.
Mecum queris ludere –
nulli me coniungere,
cum Phenice complice
vitam volo ducere.»

Sed Amor durus est,

how then can the birdsong and the presence of spring
be in force? Truly it will then be a winter to me!

140a. *Fest on the Heath*

Now let us all indulge in mirth;
honor the season with songs!
We espy the flowers' rise; the heath is wonderfully adorned!
Let us dance and leap in a roundel gay
and with sublime elation carols lay.
This delights fine youths, as it should; now to a game of ball!
My lady is full of sheer virtues! I know this pleases you all!

141. *A Rigid Girl*

All the trees now blossom bright;
birds chirp sweet songs in delight.
The shrubs at last grow green again,
so let us rejoice, all young men!

The gloom of sorrow now departs,
the warmth of love now builds its marts!
More swiftly does it overcome
who does not sooner its lyre strum!

O thou most beautiful lassie,
though thou art not the most severe,
thou givest me words most sassy,
as if thou be of murkiest mere.

All too feeble in my powers,
I am struck by Cupid's glowers,
myriad wounds now suffer I,
Curest me not, and I shall die.

"At what do you grab, youthful mind?
You seek what you will never find!
"You seek to play with me in fun—
but I would bind myself with none;
the phoenix as my ally one,
I want to lead my life undone."

But Cupid is harsh,

ferus est, fortis est.
qui nos vincit iuvenes,
vincat et iuvenculas
ultra modum rigidas!

«Video dictis his,
quid tu vis, quid tu sis,
quod amare bene scis;
et amari valeo,
et iam intus ardeo.»

CXLIa. *Incipium Novum*

Div heide   grûnet vnde der walt.
stolçe meide,   wesent palt!
die volgele singent manichualt,
zergangen ist der winder chalt.

CXLII. *Vulpecula Sola*

Tempus adest floridum,   surgunt namque flores
vernales; mox in omnibus   immutantur mores.
hoc, quod frigus leserat,   reparant calores;
cernimus hoc fieri   per multos colores.

Stant prata plena floribus,   in quibus nos ludamus!
virgines cum clericis   simul procedamus,
per amorem Veneris   ludum faciamus,
ceteris virginibus   ut hoc referamus!

«O dilecta domina,   cur sic alienaris?
an nescis, o carissima,   quod sic adamaris?
si tu esses Helena,   vellem esse Paris!
tamen potest fieri   noster amor talis.»

CXLIIa. *Forte Virgo Nacta*

Ih solde eines morgenes gan eine wise breite;
do sah ih eine maget stan, div grûzte mih bereite.
si sprah: «liebe, war wend ir? durfent ir geleite?
gegen den fûzen neig ih ir, gnade ih ir des seite.

CXLIII. *Iussus Veneris*

Cupid is fierce, Cupid is strong.
He, who subdues us men,
should also conquer maidens,
who are stern beyond measure!

"From thy words I realize now
what thou wilt, what thou art,
that thou art well capable of loving, too,
but I am capable of being loved,
and already hotly glow within."

141a. *A New Beginning*

Verdant are the forest and the moor,
O majestic maidens, be not coy!
The birds are whistling arrays of songs,
and gone is the winter cold.

142. *A Lone Vixen*

The flowering season is at hand, for now rise the vernal blooms;
and soon transformed are the manners in all!
This, which the frost once had marred, the warmth now repairs.
We see this happening everywhere by the panoply of hues!

Stand now the meadows full of gems, where we may cavort!
Let us, virgins and students, together advance
and play through our love for Lady Venus
and then to the other maidens this report!

"O beloved mistress, why do you thus distance yourself?
Or know you not, O dearest lass, that you are so truly loved?
If you were Helen, I would I were Paris!
Such can our love still become!"

142a. *A Maiden Met By Chance*

One morning did I wend over a grassland wide.
There saw I a maiden stand, who greeted me in a friendly voice.
"Whither go you, lover?" said she. "May I accompany you?"
Down to her feet I bowed myself and thanked her for her offer.

143. *Venus' Bidding*

Ecce gratum et optatum
ver reducit gaudia:
purpuratum floret pratum,
sol serenat omnia.
iam iam cedant tristia!
estas redit, nunc recedit
hiemis sevitia.

Iam liquescit et decrescit
grando, nix et cetera;
bruma fugit, et iam sugit
veris tellus ubera.
illi mens est misera,
qui nec vivit nec lascivit
sub estatis dextera!

Gloriantur et letantur
in melle dulcedinis,
qui conantur, ut utantur
premio Cupidinis.
simus iussu Cypridis
gloriantes et letantes
pares esse Paridis!

CXLIIIa. *Foedus Virginis*
Reinmar von Hagenau (*Des Minnesangs Frühling* 203.10)

«Ze niwen vrovden stat min mǔt
 hohe,» sprah ein schone wip.
«ein ritter minen willen tǔt;
der hat geliebet mir den lip.
ich wil im iemmer holder sin
danne deheinem mage min;
ih erzeige ime wibes triwe schin.»

CXLIV. *Prata Viridia*

Iam iam virent prata,   iam iam virgines
iocundantur, terre   ridet facies.
estas nunc apparuit,
ornatusque florum   lete claruit.

Nemus revirescit,   frondent frutices,

Behold the welcome and long-desired spring
restores to us our joys:
in purple dyes the meadow blooms;
the sun brightens all.
Now, now, let sorrows be far away!
The summer returns, and now withdraws
the wrath of the winter.

Now melt away and disappear
hail, snow, and the rest.
Winter flees, and now drinks the earth
from the breasts of spring.
Wretched is his heart
who comes not to life nor gambols about
under summer's sway!

They glory and find delight
in honey sweetness,
who endeavor to make use
of Cupid's reward.
Let us, as Cypris commands,
proud and blithe,
be the equals of Paris!

143a. *The Damsel's Pact*
by Reinmar von Hagenau (*The Spring of the Courtly Lovesong* 203.10)

"I live in proud anticipation
of a new joy,"
spake a comely lass.
"A knight fulfills my every wish.
Forever I will love him more
than any of my kith and kin.
I will show to him the sheen of uxorious fealty."

144. *Green Meadows*

Now, now the meadows are green; now, now the maidens
disport themselves; and smiles now the face of the earth.
The summer has now appeared,
and gaily shines its dress of blooms.

Green again is the wood, and leaves the bushes bear;

hiems seva cessit;   leti iuvenes,
congaudete floribus!
Amor allicit vos iam virginibus.

Ergo militemus   simul Veneri
tristia vitemus   nosque teneri!
visus et colloquia,
spes amorque trahant   nos ad gaudia!

CXLIVa. *Aspectus Gratus*

Ich han gesehen, daz mir in dem herçen sanfte tuot:
des grůnen lovbes pin ich worden wolgemůt;
div heide wunnechlichen stat;
mir ist liep, daz si also uil der schonen blůmen hat.

CXLV. *Terra Musaque*

Musa venit carmine;
dulci modulamine
pariter cantemus!
ecce virent omnia: prata, rus et nemus.

Mane garrit laudila,
lupilulat acredula;
iubente natura
philomena queritur   antiqua de iactura.

Hirundo iam finsat,
cygnus dulce trinxat
memorando fata,
cuculat et cuculus   per nemora vernata.

Pulchre cantant volucres;
terre nitet facies
vario colore
et in partum solvitur   redolens odore.

Late pandit tilia
frondes, ramos, folia;
thymus est sub ea
viridi cum gramine,   in quo fit chorea.

savage winter has withdrawn;
merry lads, rejoice at these flowers!
Cupid now beckons you to the virgins.

Therefore let us serve together in Venus' troop
and, tender as we are, avoid all melancholy things:
Let visitations and talks and hope
and love lead us unto bliss!

144a. *A Pleasant Sight*

I have seen something that pleasantly strikes me in my heart:
the fresh green foliage puts me in a happy mood,
the fields present a wonderful sight—
I rejoice that there bloom so very many flowers.

145. *Terra and The Muse*

The Muse comes with a song;
in a sweet melody let us together sing!
Behold! All things are green:
the meadow, field, and grove.

In the morning lilts the lark,
and also caws the crow;
at nature's bidding the nightingale
repines about her olden loss.

The swallow now chirrups,
the swan a sweet treble sings,
heralding his ineluctable fate,
and the cuckoo "koo-koos" through the blossomed woods.

Beautifully sing the birds.
The face of Terra shines
with a plethora of hues,
and in birth emits her progeny of perfumes.

Far and wide spreads the linden
its twigs, boughs, and leaves.
Under it sits the thyme and the grass green,
whereupon a dance is stamped to a beat.

Patet et in gramine
iocundo rivus murmure;
locus est festivus.
ventus cum temperie   susurrat tempestivus.

CXLVa. *Utinam!*

Uvere div werlt alle min
von deme mere unze an den Rin,
des wolt ih mih darben,
daz chunichin von Engellant   lege an minem arme!

CXLVI. *Virgo Caelestis*

Tellus flore vario vestitur
et veris presentia sentitur,
philomena dulciter   modulans auditur;
sic hiemis sevitia finitur.

Rubent gene, coma disgregata
fronte cedit parum inclinata;
tota ridet facies;   felix et beata,
que tantis est virtutibus ornata!

Gracilis sub cingulo de more
ista vincit balsamum odore;
felix, qui cum virgine   fruitur sopore!
hic deis adequabitur honore.

Distant supercilia decenti
et equali spatio ridenti.
os invitat osculum   simile poscenti;
subvenias, mi domina, cadenti!

Vulneratus nequeo sanari,
nulla vite poterit spes dari,
nisi me pre ceteris   velis consolari,
que cuncta vincis forma singolari!

CXLVIa. *Mitte Ei Fidem Meam!*

Nahtegel, sing einen don mit sinne
miner hohgemûten chuniginne!

Right through the grass runs
a river with a joyous roar;
truly festive is the place.
The wind of spring softly susurrates.

145a. *If Only!*

If all this world were truly mine
from the wide sea to the Rhine,
I would relinquish it all without alarms,
if the Queen of England would lie in my arms.

146. *A Heavenly Maid*

The earth is decked in various blooms
and spring's enlivening presence is perceived.
The nightingale is heard modulating her sweet song;
thus the fury of winter is gone.

Ruddy cheeks and parted hair that frames
a lightly-inclined brow, and a smile across
the entire face—happy and blessed is she,
who is adorned with such virtues innate!

Slender is she about the waist in a seemly way,
and her scent overpowers the aroma of the balsam.
Happy is he, who enjoys sweet rest with this maiden fair!
Such a distinction makes him the equal of the gods.

When she laughs, her brows part a graceful
and equidistant space. Her mouth invites a kiss
from him who pleads for such kisses, too.
I am falling, milady; prithee come to my aid!

Wounded, I cannot be healed,
no hope of survival can be given me,
unless you be willing to console me before all others,
you, who conquer all with your nonpareil beauty.

146a. *Send Her My Surety!*

Nightingale, sing a daedal song
for my cheerful queen!

chunde ir, daz min steter můt   vnde min herçe brinne
nah irm sůzen libe vnde nah ir minne!

CXLVII. *Dimidium Prioris Sui*

Si de more cum honore
lete viverem
nec meroris nec doloris
librum legerem,
salutarem gramina,
me novarem, mundo darem
nova carmina.

Tamen cano, sed de vano
statu Veneris,
cuius Paris et scolaris
sum cum ceteris
qui noverunt varia
decantare, veri dare
sua gaudia.

Cutis aret, quia caret
leto pectore;
curans curo; de futuro
timens tempore
nequeo cum talibus
accubare vel durare
sub rivalibus.

CXLVIIa. *Vir Cordis Elati*
Reinmar von Hagenau (*Des Minnesangs Frühling* 203.10)

Sage, daz ih dirs iemmer lone:
hast du den uil lieben man gesehen?
ist iz war, lebet er so schone,
als si sagent vnde ih dih hore iehen?
«vrowe, ih sah in: er ist vro;
sin herçe stat, ob ir gebietet, iemmer ho.»

CXLVIII. *Prex Auxilii Venerei*

Floret tellus floribus,
variis coloribus,

Tell her my unwavering sentiment and my heart
burn for her sweet body and love!

147. *Half of His Former He*

If I could lead a happy life,
honorable and decorous,
and read not the book
of sorrow or of pain,
I would salute the grasses,
renew myself, and give the world
a new train of songs.

Still I sing, but about
Venus' delusive state,
to which I, a Paris
and a bookish boy,
with the rest belong,
who know how to craft various songs
and to sing to the spring its joys.

My skin is parched because it lacks
a happy and a bonny breast.
Anxious, I have many cares;
of the future I am in fear;
with such people I cannot sit,
nor under such rivals
can I perdure.

147a. *The Man of Heart High*
by Reinmar von Hagenau (*The Spring of the Courtly Lovesong* 203.10)

"Pray tell—and I will always give you thanks:
Have you seen the much beloved man?
Is it really true that he leads so admirable a life
as the people say and as I from your mouth hear?"
"Mistress, I have him seen, and joyful is he;
his heart, if you command, will always be high."

148. *Prayer for Venus' Aid*

The earth with blossoms is bejeweled
and of so many dazzling colors and hues,

floret et cum gramine.

Faveant amoribus
iuvenes cum moribus
vario solamine!

Venus assit omnibus
ad eam clamantibus,
assit cum Cupidine!

Assit iam iuvenibus
iuvamen poscentibus,
ut prosint his domine!

Venus, que est et erat,
tela sua proferat
in amantes puellas!

Que amantes munerat,
iuvenes non conterat
nec pulchras domicellas!

CXLVIIIa. *Venus Nos Excludit!*

Nu sin stolz vnde hovisch,
nu sin stolz vnde houisch,
nu sin houisch vnde stolz!

Venus schivzet iren bolz,
Uenus schivzet irn bolz,
Uenus schivzet irn bolz!

CXLIX. *Quis Me Nunc Amabit?*

Floret silva nobilis
floribus et foliis.
ubi est antiquus
meus amicus?
hinc equitavit!
eia! quis me amabit?

Refl.   Floret silva undique;
         nah mime gesellen ist mir we!

and greenly, too, springs the grass.

Let us lads look after
our sweethearts dear
with decorum and multifoliate aid!

May Venus help all
who for her aid call,
may she succor together with Cupid!

May she now be among lads
who her assistance entreat,
that their mistresses be kind to them!

May Venus, who always is and was,
steer her missiles
at loving maidens!

She, who gifts upon lovers bestows,
should not annihilate young men
nor destroy the damsels fair!

148a. *Venus Shuts Us Out!*

Now let us be courtly and proud,
now let us be refined and unbowed,
now let us be polite and high-browed.

Venus shuts her bolts!
Venus shuts her bolts!
Venus shuts her bolts!

149. *Who Will Love Me Now?*

The noble forest blooms—
flowers and leaves sit all around.
Where is now
my olden friend?
He has ridden off!
Alas! Who will love me now?

Refr.   The forest blossoms everywhere;
no, my friends, I feel only woe!

Grůnet der walt allenthalben.
wa ist min geselle also lange?
der ist geriten hinnen.
owi! wer sol mich minnen?

CL. *Turba Felix*

Redivivo vernat flore
tellus, que tam diu marcuit,
et vernali sol calore
pulso brume statu claruit.
iam philomena dulciter
dulcisonis concentibus   delectat cor suaviter.

Estas nunc tenella vestit
fronde nuditatem arborum.
puellaris turba gestit
florem contemplari nemorum.
hanc sequatur cum gaudio
iam iuvenum militia,   dulcis et leta contio!

Ergo leti aspirantes
dulcem rerum ad temperiem
iocundemur, gratulantes
Veneream ad blanditiem
et aurea Cupidinis
ad iacula! sit animus   velox ad cultum virginis!

CLa. *Sine Corona Rex*
Heinrich von Morungen (*Des Minnesangs Frühling* 142.19)

Ich pin cheiser ane chrone
vnde ane lant: daz meine ih an dem mům;
ern gestůnt mir nie so schone.
wol ir liebe, div mir sanfte tům!
daz machet mir ein vrowe gům.
ih wil ir dienen iemmer mer; ih engesah nie wip so wol gemům.

CLI. *Margarita in Auro*

Virent prata   hiemata
tersa rabie,
florum data   mundo grata

Green again stands the wondrous holt.
Where is now my longtime friend?
He has ridden far from here.
Alas! Who will love me now?

150. *The Happy Throng*

The flowers are revived and earth blooms gay,
which for so long was feeble with decay,
and the sun in the heat of spring shines bright
after the expulsion of winter's blight.
Now the nightingale sweetly delights
our hearts with ever dulcet symphonies.

Now the tide of spring engulfs
the arboreal bareness with tender leaves.
A band of maidens now exults
in beholding the dazzling, sylvan blooms.
Let now march behind a laddish troop in joy—
the sum of this: a sweet and happy throng!

Therefore let us all mirthfully aspire
to the pleasant temper of the world
and let us all assume delight,
giving thanks to Venus' charms
and to Cupid's golden shafts!
Let the heart be swift in the care of virgins!

150a. *A King Uncrowned*
By Heinrich von Morungen (*The Spring of the Courtly Lovesong* 142.19)

I am a king without a crown
or land: so feel I in my heart.
Never did my mood take such cheer.
Happy be her love, which is so good to me!
All this is the working of a noble dame, whom I will
for all eternity serve. Ne'er saw I a lass of such magnanimity!

151. *The Pearl in the Gold*

The grasslands stand animate and green,
since the winter's fury has been wiped away.
The gifts of flowers to the world

rident facie.

solis radio
nitent, albent,   rubent, candent,
veris, ritus iura pandent
ortu vario.

Aves dulci melodia
sonant garrule,
omni via   voce pia
volant sedule,
et in nemore
frondes, flores   et odores
sunt; ardescunt iuniores
hoc in tempore.

Congregatur,   augmentatur
cetus iuvenum,
adunatur,   colletatur
chorus virginum;
et sub tilia
ad choreas   Venereas
salit mater, inter eas
sua filia.

Restat una,   quam fortuna
dante veneror,
clarens luna   opportuna,
ob quam vulneror
dans suspiria.
preelecta,   simplex, recta
cordi meo est invecta
mutans tristia.

Quam dum cerno,   de superno
puto vigere.
cuncta sperno,   donec sterno
solam Venere.
hanc desidero
ulnis plecti   et subnecti,
loco leto   in secreto
si contigero.

smile with a pleasant mien.

Wakened by the rays of the sun,
they shine, shimmer, and glow red and white,
and by their multicolored rising
attest to the rightful dominion of spring.

The garrulous birds pour forth
a mellifluous melody sweet.
On every path, with gentle voice,
they busily flitter to and fro;
leaves, flowers, and fragrances
in the forest abound;
in this time inflamed
with passion are the youths.

The horde of young lads gathers
and in numbers is ever increased;
and the circle of maidens
unites and dances to a united beat.
And beneath the linden
in Venus' roundelays
leaps the mother and her daughter
in the same festive ring.

One girl rests, whom I revere—
Fortune gave her to me!—
a shining, auspicious moon,
on whose account I am wounded
and heave heavy sighs.
She, most choice, ingenuous, just,
is carried always in my heart,
and transmutes sorrow into joy.

When I set my eyes on her, I believe
I draw my power from a heavenly well.
I spurn all things, until I lay
her down alone on Venus' sheets.
Would that she were enwrapped
in my arms and beneath me tied
in a blissful, hidden place,
if luck does me betide!

CLIa. *Flores et Trifolia*
Walter von der Vogelweide (51.29.3)

So wol dir, meie, wie du scheidest
allez ane haz!
wie wol du die bovme cleidest
vnde die heide baz!
(div hat varue me).
«du bist churçer, ih pin langer!»
also stritent si uf dein anger,
blůmen vnde chle.

CLII. *Aestas Unica*

Estas non apparuit   preteritis temporibus,
que sic clara fuerit;   ornantur prata floribus.

Refl.   Aves nunc in silva canunt
et canendo dulce garriunt.

Iuno Iovem superat   amore maritali;
Mars a Vulcano capitur   rete artificiali.

Refl.   Aves nunc in silva canunt
et canendo dulce garriunt.

In exemplum Veneris   hec fabula proponitur;
Phebus Daphnem sequitur,   Europa tauro luditur.

Refl.   Aves nunc in silva canunt
et canendo dulce garriunt.

Amor querit iuvenes, ut ludant cum virginibus;
Venus despicit senes, qui impleti sunt doloribus.

Refl.   Aves nunc in silva canunt
et canendo dulce garriunt.

CLIIa. *Aestas Serena*

Ich gesach den sumer nie, daz er so schone duhte mich:
mit menigen blůmen wolgetan div heide hat gezieret sih.
sanges ist der walt so vol;

151a. *The Flowers and the Clovers*
by Walter von der Vogelweide (51.29.3)

Happy be you, May, since you now
peacefully dispose all things in several ways!
How beautifully you dress the trees
and ameliorate the moors
(which are more colorful still).
"You are shorter! I am longer!"
So squabble in this way
the flowers and clovers.

152. *A Singular Summer*

Never was there in the ages past a summer so very bright;
the meadows are bedizened with the jewels of blooms.

Refr.   The winged troubadours now sing in the woods,
and their song is sweet warbling and chirps.

Juno conquers Jove with conjugal love.
Mars is captured by Vulcan in a crafted, cunning net.

Refr.   The winged troubadours now sing in the woods,
and their song is sweet warbling and chirps.

As examples of Venus' bustles, these myths are proposed:
Apollo chases Daphne, Europa is tricked by the shape of a bull.

Refr.   The winged troubadours now sing in the woods,
and their song is sweet warbling and chirps.

Cupid seeks young lads for games of love with young maids.
Venus disdains old men, who are filled with aches and pains.

Refr.   The winged troubadours now sing in the woods,
and their song is sweet warbling and chirps.

152a. *A Summer Serene*

I never before saw a summer that seemed so beautiful to me.
With many fine blooms was the meadow adorned.
The woods are so full of song;

div zit div tût den chleinen volgelen wol.

CLIII. *Una Puella Mea*

Tempus transit gelidum, mundus renovatur,
verque redit floridum, forma rebus datur.
avis modulatur,
modulans letatur
lucidior et lenior
aer iam serenatur;
iam florea, iam frondea
silva comis densatur.

Ludunt super gramina virgines decore,
quarum nova carmina dulci sonant ore.
annuunt favore
volucres canore,
favet et odore
tellus picta flore.
cor igitur et cingitur
et tangitur   amore,
virginibus et avibus
strepentibus sonore.

Tendit modo retia puer pharetratus;
cui deorum curia prebet famulatus,
cuius dominatus
nimium est latus,
per hunc triumphatus
sum et sauciatus:
pugnaveram et fueram
in primis reluctatus,
sed iterum per puerum
sum Veneri prostratus.

Unam, huius vulnere saucius, amavi,
quam sub firmo federe michi copulavi.
fidem, quam iuravi,
numquam violavi;
rei tam suavi
totum me dicavi.
quam dulcia sunt basia
puelle!   iam gustavi:

this season is a boon for little birds.

153. *My One Girl*

Passes now the season of hoar; renewed now is the world;
returns the spring of flowers; beauty blazes in all things.
A bird now twitters a song,
whose notes uplift his soul.
The empyrean, clearer and gentler now,
already sets itself alight;
the forest, already blooming, already covered with leaves,
is thickened with a foliar crown.

Beautiful damsels now cavort over the fresh, green grass;
new pastorales brightly ring from their pleasing lips.
The musical birds nod in goodwill,
and the earth, embroidered with blooms,
shows favor to the maidens
with her sweet perfumes.
The heart thus is wreathed
and struck with love,
when the maidens and the birds raise
such jubilant tones.

Now the quivered boy god stretches out his nets,
to whom the Olympian court offers its service
and whose dominion
it extends so very wide;
this god has triumphed over me
and dealt me many blows:
against him had I fought
and in the beginning I had resisted him,
but again through this boy
I was to Venus bowed.

Injured by his bolt, I loved but one lass,
whom, through a solid pact, I had coupled to myself.
The fidelity I swore
never violate did I;
I devoted my whole self
to so delightful an enterprise.
How sweet are the kisses of the girl;
already I have savored them!

nec cinnamum et balsamum
esset tam dulce favi!

CLIIIa. *Cruciatio Reservando*

Vrowe, ih pin dir undertan des la mich geniezen!
ih diene dir, so ih beste chan; des wil dih verdriezen.
nu wil du mine sinne
mit dime gewalte sliezen.
nu woldih diner minne
vil sůze wunne niezen.
vil reine wip, din schoner lip
wil mih ze sere schiezen!
uz dime gebot ih nimmer chume,
obz alle wibe hiezen!

CLIV. *Gradus Amoris*

Est Amor alatus   puer et levis, est pharetratus.
Etas amentem   probat et ratione carentem;
Vulnificus pharetra   signatur, mobilis ala;
Nudus formatur,   quia nil est, quo teneatur.
Insipiens, fugitans,   temeraria tela cruentans
Mittit pentagonas   nervo stridente sagittas,
Quod sunt quinque modi,   quibus associamur amori:
Visus; colloquium;   tactus; compar labiorum
Nectaris alterni   permixtio, commoda fini;
In lecto quintum   tacite Venus exprimit actum.

CLV. *Alta Cupido*

Quam pulchra nitet facie,
que cordis trahit intima!
hec est, de cuius specie
omnis amans dat plurima
cum fletibus suspiria.
hec processit de regia
prole. multa
dat hec et aufert gaudia.

Hec est, que caret macula
totaliter. venenea
traiecit Amor iacula

Neither cinnamon nor balsam
could be so honeysweet as they!

153a. *Torture by Reservation*

Mistress, I am a tributary to you!
Let me enjoy something as my due!
I serve you, lady, as best I can, but it seems only a vexation to you.
Now you wish to entomb my passions through your cruel decree.
But I would like now to feast
on the many sweet pleasures of your love.
O lady so perfect and so fine,
your gorgeous body desires to shoot me until I die!
At your bidding I never come,
though all other ladies invite the labor's sum!

154. *The Steps of Love*

Cupid is a frivolous lad, winged and with arrows equipped!
His puerile age demonstrates his lack of reason and sense.
His quiver betokens his buffets, his wings his inconstancy.
He is depicted as nude, because he is held by nothing at all.
Unwise is he and fickle, too; he stains red his reckless bolts.
He sends off from his whistling string his arrows of five points,
because there are five modes by which we in love are joined:
sight, dialogue, touch, the even mixing of the reciprocal nectar
of the lips—the stepwise preparation for the ultimate goal:
in bed the fifth transaction Venus tacitly expresses.

155. *Deep Longing*

How brightly shines the beautiful face of her,
who tugs at the inmost strings of my heart!
She is a lady, for whose pulchritude
every lover heaves myriad sighs
through a deluge of hot tears.
She descends from a royal line.
Many blissful delights
she gives and takes away.

She is a lass, who is flawless
in every way. For this reason
Cupid cast his poisoned shafts

ob hoc in mei viscera
cordis. quapropter langueo,
quod promere erubeo.
sic estuo,
eius igne exardeo.

Sitio, quod igniferos
dolores fero, sedule
si non exoro superos:
Altitonum cum Hercule
et Iunonem cum Pallade
et Helenam cum Venere,
non prospere
hanc me continget vincere.

CLVa. *Pulcherrima Omnium*

Si ist schoener den urowe Dido was,
si ist schoener denne vrowe Helena,
si ist schoener denne vrowe Pallas,
si ist schoener denne vrowe Ecuba;
si ist minnechlicher denne vrowe Isabel
unde urolicher denne Gaudile;
mines hercen chle
ist tugunde richer denne Baldine.

CLVI. De vere

Salve, ver optatum,
amantibus gratum,
gaudiorum fax, multorum
florum incrementum!
multitudo florum
et color colorum,
salvetote et estote
iocorum augmentum!
dulcis avium concentus
sonat; gaudeat iuventus!
hiems seva transiit,   nam lenis spirat ventus.

Tellus purpurata
floribus, et prata
revirescunt, umbre crescunt,

straight into my heart's caverns.
On this account I pine away,
for what I am ashamed to say.
Thus I boil deep within,
and in her fire I burn.

I thirst, for I bear
fiery griefs; if I do not
with diligence the gods entreat—
The Thunderer and Hercules,
Juno and Athena,
Helen and Cytherea—
then surmounting her will not
favorably fall upon my lot.

155a. *Most Beautiful of All*

She is comelier than Queen Dido was;
she is more beautiful than Mistress Helena;
she is more attractive than Lady Minerva;
she is more handsome than Madam Hecuba;
she is dearer than Regal Isabel
and more mirthful than Gaudile;
the clover of my heart
is a virtue richer than Baldine.[242]

156. La Primavera

Greetings, desiderated spring,
ever welcome guest to lovers,
flambeau of joys,
augmentation of many flowers!
Myriad of blossoms,
lord of colors,
be you well and be
our amusements' increase!
A sweet orchestra of birds rings its notes;
may the youth take up sweet, sweet mirth!
Winter's blasts have passed away, for a gentle wind blows.

The earth is mantled
with purple jewels,
the meadows are all green-hued,

nemus redimitur.
lascivit natura
omnis creatura
leto vultu, claro cultu
Amor investitur.
Venus subditos titillat,
dum nature nectar stillat;
sic ardor Venereus   amantibus scintillat.

O quam felix hora,
in qua tam decora
sumpsit vitam sic politam,
amenam, iocundam!
o quam crines flavi!
in ea nil pravi
scio fore, in amore
nescio secundam.
frons nimirum coronata,
supercilia nigrata
et ad Iris formulam   in fine recurvata.

Nivei candoris,
rosei ruboris
sunt maxille; inter mille
par non est inventa.
labia rotunda
atque rubicunda,
albi dentes sunt nitentes;
in sermone lenta.
longe manus, longum latus,
guttur et totus ornatus
est cum diligentia   divina compilatus.

Ardoris scintilla
devolans ab illa,
quam pre totis amo notis,
cor meum ignivit,
quod cor fit favilla.
Veneris ancilla
si non curat, ardor durat,
moritur, qui vivit.
ergo fac, benigna Phyllis,
ut iocunder in tranquillis,

the shadows wax, and the forest is wreathed.
Nature is full of lust for life,
and a joyous mien
every creature dights.
In bright apparel Cupid is clothed.
Venus tickles her subjects,
as nature's nectar drips down.
Thus her passion in lovers glows.

O what a happy hour,
when so wondrous a lass
assumed a life so very refined,
delightful, and merry!
O how golden is her hair!
I know that nothing vulgar
would ever rest on her!
In lovingness I know she is second to none.
Her forehead truly wears a crown,
and black are her lofty brows
that, as Iris', are at the ends upcurved.

Snow white and rosy red are her cheeks;
among a thousand
her equal is not found.
Her lips are round
and the deepest red,
her teeth are niveous
and dazzlingly flash;
reserved is she in speech.
Her hands are slender, her hips are high,
her throat and entire semblance were crafted
by the assiduity of the gods divine.

A spark of passion flies down from her,
whom I love more than all girls known;
it has set my heart aflame,
which will turn to ash,
if this maid of Venus
does not tend to it:
for the heat will endure,
then will he die, who is yet alive.
Therefore allow me, good Phyllis,
to delight myself in placidity and peace,

dum os ori iungitur   et pectora mamillis!

CLVII. *Virgo et Ovis*

Lucis orto sidere
exit virgo propere
facie vernali,
oves iussa regere
baculo pastorali.

Sol effundens radium
dat calorem nimium.
virgo speciosa
solem vitat noxium
sub arbore frondosa.

Dum procedo paululum,
lingue solvo vinculum:
«salve, rege digna!
audi, queso, servulum,
esto michi benigna!»

«Cur salutas virginem,
que non novit hominem,
ex quo fuit nata?
sciat Deus! neminem
inveni per hec prata.»

Forte lupus aderat,
quem fames expulerat
gutturis avari.
ove rapta properat,
cupiens saturari.

Dum puella cerneret,
quod sic ovem perderet,
pleno clamat ore:
«siquis ovem redderet,
me gaudeat uxore!»

Mox ut vocem audio,
denudato gladio
lupus immolatur,

when mouth to mouth and breast to breasts are joined!

157. *The Maiden and the Sheep*

When the star of light dawned,
a virgin emerged in haste
of a sublimely vernal face,
and, as bidden, shepherded the sheep
with a pastoral staff.

The sun poured forth its rays
and yielded a surfeit of heat.
The ever so beautiful maiden
shunned the singeing beams
beneath a leafy tree.

When I debouched but a little,
I unsealed the bond of my tongue:
"Hello, maiden worthy of a king!
Hearken, I pray, to thy knave,
and be gracious unto me!"

"Why greet you thus a maiden young,
who has known no men
from the day of her birth?
By Jove, I have never found anyone
roaming through these fields!"

By chance a wolf came along,
whom his greedy maw's hunger
had driven to the woolen throng.
It snatched a sheep and hied away,
desiring to cloy itself with its meat.

When the maiden observed
that she had thus lost the sheep,
she a full mouth loudly teemed:
"If anyone returns this sheep,
may he rejoice in me as his wife!"

As soon as I heard her voice,
I unsheathed my sword
and slew the wolf,

ovis ab exitio
redempta reportatur.

CLVIII. *Scelus Iuxta Nemorem*

Vere dulci mediante,
non in Maio, paulo ante,
luce solis radiante,
virgo vultu elegante
fronde stabat sub vernante
canens cum cicuta.

Illuc veni fato dante.
nympha non est forme tante,
equipollens eius plante!
que me viso festinante
grege fugit cum balante,
metu dissoluta.

Clamans tendit ad ovile.
hanc sequendo precor:
«sile! nichil timeas hostile!»
preces spernit, et monile,
quod ostendi, tenet vile
virgo, sic locuta:

«Munus vestrum», inquit, «nolo,
quia pleni estis dolo!»
etsi se defendit colo,
comprehensam ieci solo;
clarior non est sub polo
vilibus induta!

Satis illi fuit grave,
michi gratum et suave.
«quid fecisti», inquit, «prave!
ve ve tibi! tamen ave!
ne reveles ulli cave,
ut sim domi tuta!

Si senserit meus pater
vel Martinus maior frater,
erit michi dies ater;

and carried back the sheep
rescued from doom.

158. *Crime Beside a Grove*

In the sweet half-point of spring,
not in May, but an inch before,
when the sun was glowing bright,
a virgin of elegant mien stood
beneath a fresh, green leaf
and made music on her flute.

Thither I came by dint of fate.
No nymph ever possessed such a form,
nor could match the grace of her sole!
When she saw me coming in haste,
she fled with her bleating flock,
beside herself with fear.

Shouting, she made for the sheepfold;
pursuing her, I prayed: "Be still!
You need fear nothing inimical!"
She spurned my orisons,
and the necklace I showed her
she reviled in these words:

"Thy gift," quoth she, "I do not want,
because thou art with treachery fraught!"
Albeit she defended herself with her staff,
I seized and threw her to the ground.
A fairer body beneath a shabby dress
was never beneath the heavens shewn!

It was considerably grievous for her,
but pleasurable and sweet for me.
"What hast thou done?" she cried. "Wicked soul,
woe, woe to thee! And nevertheless God save thee!
Take care to reveal this to none,
lest harm or ill befall me at home!

"If my father suspects this misdeed
or my older brother Martin,
a black day will it be for me;

vel si sciret mea mater,
cum sit angue peior quater,
virgis sum tributa!»

CLIX. *Repetitio Est Mater Memoriae I*

Hoc poema est verbatim omnino idem ac poema LXXXV Codicis Burani.

CLX. *Era Doloris*

Dum estas inchoatur
ameno tempore
Phebusque dominatur
depulso frigore,
unius in amore
puelle vulneror,
multimodo dolore
per quem et atteror.

CLXI. *Terra Florata*

Ab estatis foribus
nos Amor salutat,
humus picta floribus
faciem commutat.
flores amoriferi
iam arrident tempori;
perit absque Venere
flos etatis tenere.

Omnium principium
dies est vernalis,
vere mundus celebrat
diem sui natalis.
omnes huius temporis
dies festi Veneris.
regna Iovis omnia
hec agant sollemnia!

CLXIa. *Aestatis Iuventus*

Div werlt frovt sih uber al
gegen der sumerzite:

or if my mother should learn of it,
since she is four times nastier than a snake,
I would be given to the switch!"

159. *Repetition Is The Mother of Memory I*

This poem is, word-for-word, the same as poem 85 of the Codex Buranus.

160. *Lady Pain*

When summer begins
in the time of pleasantry,
and Phoebus holds sway
after the freeze's expulsion,
the love for one maid
wounds me deeply
and causes manifold pain,
by which I am exhausted.

161. *Flowered Earth*

From summer's threshold
Cupid greets us; and earth,
now bloom-spangled,
transmutes her visage.
Flowers, love's awakeners,
now smile upon the season.
Without Venus the blossom
of tender youth fades.

The beginning of all things
is the day of the spring,
when the world celebrates
the day of her birth.
All the days of this season
are the festivals of Venus.
May all the realms of Jove above
observe these celebrations!

161a. *Summer's Prime*

All the world rejoices
at summer's prime:

aller slahte uogel schal
horet man nu wite,
dar zů blůmen vnde chle
hat div heide vil als ê,
grvone stat der schone walt;
des suln wir nu wesen balt!

CLXII. *Corona Litterosa*

O consocii,
quid vobis videtur?
quid negotii
nobis adoptetur?
leta Venus ad nos   iam ingredietur,
illam chorus Dryadum sequetur.

O vos socii,
tempus est iocundum,
dies otii
redeunt in mundum;
ergo congaudete,   cetum letabundum
tempus salutantes † iocundum.

Venus abdicans
cognatum Neptunum
venit applicans
Bachum oportunum,
quem dea pre cunctis   amplexatur unum,
quia tristem spernit et ieiunum.

His numinibus
volo famulari!
ius est omnibus,
qui volunt beari;
que dant eccellenti   populo scolari,
ut amet et faciat amari.

Ergo litteris
cetus hic imbutus
signa Veneris
militet secutus!
exturbetur autem   laicus ut brutus!
nam ad artem surdus est et mutus.

one now hears far and wide
choirs of birds raising hymns;
there, too, have the meadows
more flowers and clovers than ever;
and green stands the beauteous holt;
therefore let us all take heart!

162. *The Lettered Circle*

O comrades mine,
how seems it to you?[243]
Which business
should we undertake?
Joyous Venus will come to our home soon,
and a chorus of Dryads will be her retinue.

O compatriots mine,
the time is full of wonder;
the days of leisure at last
are returning to the world;
therefore make you merry and greet
the happy throng and the lovely age!

Venus, renouncing
Neptune, her kin,
comes and grafts herself
to Bacchus, who suits her whims;
the goddess embraces him before all others,
for he shuns the sourpuss and the teetotaler.

These divinities I desire to serve!
It is the duty of all,
who wish to be blessed!
They gift the noble, scholarly throng
so that members may love
and cause themselves to be loved.

Thus may this lettered circle
pursue and serve
under Venus' banners!
But let the layman be driven away
like a dumb beast! For he
is a deaf-mute to the art!

CLXIIa. *Indefatigabilis In Amore*

Svoziv vrowe min,
la mih des geniezen:
du bist min ovgenschin.
Venus wil mih schiezen!
nu la mih, chuniginne, diner minne niezen!
ia nemag mih nimmer din uerdriezen.

CLXIII. *Gravia Suspiria*

Longa spes et dubia
permixta timore
solvit in suspiria
mentem cum dolore,
que iam dudum anxia
mansit in amore.
nec tamen mestum   pello dolorem.

Heu, cure prolixitas
procurata parum
et loci diversitas
duxerunt in rarum,
quod pre cunctis caritas
cordis habet carum!
omnis largus   odit avarum.

In hoc loro stringitur
nodus absque nodo,
nec ullus recipitur
modus in hoc modo;
sed, qui numquam solvitur,
plus constringit modo.
lodircundeia!   lodircundeia!

Hanc amo pre ceteris,
quam non vincit rosa;
nec proferre poteris
cantibus nec prosa,
nec voce nec litteris,
quam sit speciosa.
flos in amore   spirat odore.

162a. *Tireless In Love*

My mistress sweet,
let me have advantage of it,
for you are the light of my eyes.
Venus aims her darts at me!
Now let me, queen, enjoy your love!
Forsooth I could never grow weary thereof!

163. *Heavy Sighs*

A protracted, uncertain hope,
thoroughly mixed with fear,
is the reason that my soul
with painful sighs cuts the air.
It has long remained
grievously lorn of love.
And still I oust not this rueful dolor.

Alas, a great space of curative time,
scarcely vouchsafed to my care,
and my sojourns abroad
were made very rare—
respite, which a heartfelt love
treasures more than all else!
All generous men a miser detest.

A knot without a knot
is firmly tied in this strap,
nor is any moderation
in this measure taken up,
but he, who never looses himself,
is only more tightly bound.
Lodircundeia! Lodircundeia![244]

I love this girl more than all others,
whom not even the roses surpass;
you could ne'er delineate with success,
in either mellifluous verse or prose,
or with a sweet voice or a cogent pen,
how beautiful this girl is.
The flowers, enamored of her, sigh a sweet perfume.

Inopino saucius
hesito stupore,
stulto carpor anxius
animi furore,
amens amans amplius
obligor amore.
nec tamen mestum   pello dolorem.

CLXIIIa. *Illecta in Laesuram*

Eine wunnechliche stat
het er mir bescheiden:
da die blůmen unde gras
stůden grůne baide,
dar chom ih, als er mih pat.
da geschah mir leide.
lodircundeie!   lodircundeie!

CLXIV. *Grammatica Cubiculi*

Ob amoris pressuram
medentis gero curam
amanti valituram.
cor estuat interius,
languet mens quondam pura,
affligor et exterius
propter nature iura.

«Si cupio sanari
aut vitam prolongari,
festinem gressu pari
ad Corinne presentiam,
de qua potest spes dari,
eius querendo gratiam:
sic quero reformari.

Hec dulcis in amore
est et plena decore;
rosa rubet rubore,
et lilium convallium
tota vincit odore;
favum mellis eximium
dulci propinat ore.

Smitten by an unexpected palsy,
I stand at a loss in an abyss of despair.
Apprehensive, I am enfeebled
by the foolish lunacy of my heart;
insensibly enamored, I am by love
trammeled up the more.
And still I oust not this rueful dolor.

163a. *Lured Into Harm*

A wondrous place
did he reveal to me:
where the flowers and grass
with fresh sap stood green.
Thither I came, as he had bidden.
And in that spot harm befell me.
Lodircundeie! Lodircundeie!

164. *Bedroom Grammar*

Against love's affliction
I administer an iatric nostrum
that will a lover effectively cure.
My heart boils deep within,
listless is my once undefiled mind,
and, on the outside, I am afflicted
because nature claims her rights.

"If I desiderate to be healed
or for my life to be prolonged,
I should hie at a steady pace
into Corinna's presence,
from whom I can draw hope,
and sue for her esteem:
thus to be restored I seek.

"She is sweet in love
and is full of grace;
her blush shames the rose,
and she wholly overwhelms
with her scent the lily of the vales.
From her sweet mouth she furnishes
extraordinary virgin honey sweet.

Non in visu defectus,
auditus nec abiectus;
eius ridet aspectus.
sed et istis iocundius:
locus sub veste tectus;
in hoc declinat melius
non obliquus, sed rectus.

Ubi si recubarem,
per partes declinarem,
casum pro casu darem;
nec presens nec preteritum
tempus considerarem,
sed ad laboris meritum
magis accelerarem!»

CLXIVa. *Servus Eius Amans*

Ih wolde gerne singen,
der werlde vrovde bringen,
mohte mir an ir gelingen,
der ih diene alle mine tage.
der minne wil mich twingen.
in mime herçen ich si trage;
noch lebe ih des gedingen.

CLXV. *Infirmus Amore*

Amor, telum es insignis Veneris.
voluntates mentis gyrans celeris,
amantum afflictio,
cordis fibras elicis et conteris.
vultu clarior sereno ceteris,
me tibi subicio:
defende, ne involvat me procella,
que versatur clauso cordis pessulo   in dulci puella!

Odor eius oris, fraglans lilium,
amoris initiat indicium:
exigenti osculum
nullum prebet homini fastidium.
frontis eius decens supercilium;
os renitet flosculum.

"Her visage is without a flaw;
the ring of her voice is praised;
her entire mien is one dazzling smile.
But there is something more delightful than these:
a place that is covered by her frock;
in this place better declines
not the bent case, but the straight.[245]

"If I could rest there, I would go
through the entire declension
and would every case explore;
neither present nor past tense
would I myself bethink,
but with greater velocity
hasten to the labor's reward!"

164a. *Her Loving Slave*

I would gladly sing,
and bring joy to the world,
if only I could have success with her,
whom I serve my every living day.
Her love wishes to overpower me.
In my heart I carry it;
for this hope I still live.

165. *Sick With Love*

Cupid, you are the weapon of extraordinary Venus.
You reel about the inclinations
of the reckless heart—the lovers' torment—
lure out the cardiac fibers, and then grind them into dust.
To you, who in the serenity of your visage
outshine every other soul, I bow:
protect me from the enveloping storm that whirls behind
the heart's hidden bolt in a sweet girl!

Her mouth's perfume, which is of lilies,
arouses the first symptom of infatuation:
for in the man, who exacts a kiss from her,
her breath causes no aversion at all.
Graceful are her forehead's brows,
like a tender floweret shines her mouth,

equalis illi nusquam reperitur;
felix est, qui osculis mellifluis   ipsius potitur!

Circumgyrantes canite concorditer!
pedem pedi committite hilariter,
congaudentes iubilo,
concrepando manuum cum plausibus!
solus solam veneror his laudibus,
terso mentis nubilo;
nam cum totalem video pudicam,
singolari gaudio tunc potior   optans in amicam.

CLXVa. *Quam Amabilissima*

Mir ist ein wip sere in min gemuote chomen,
uon der han ich gançer tugende vil vernomen;
des minnet si daz herçe min.
ir schoner lip hat mir vrovde vil gegeben.
solde ich nah dem wilien min div zit geleben,
daz ich ihr gelege bi,

CLXVI. *Miles Amoris*

Iam dudum Amoris militem
devotum me exhibui,
cuius nutu me precipitem
stulto commisi ausui,
amans in periculo
unam, que numquam   me pio respexit oculo.

Si adhuc cessarem penitus,
michi forte consulerem;
sed non fugat belli strepitus
nisi virum degenerem.
fiat, quod desidero!
vitam fortune   casibus securus offero.

Me sciat ipsa magnanimum,
maiorem meo corpore,
qui ramum scandens altissimum
fructum queram in arbore,
allegans: ingenio
non esse locum   in amante metus nescio!

and nowhere is her equal found;
blessed is he, who her honeyed kisses receives.

Wheel you round and round and a harmony raise high!
Match one foot to the other, merrily in time,
rejoicing all as one in a lively pastorale,
resounding together with the claps of hands!
I alone venerate only her with these praises,
when the clouds of my soul are dispelled;
for when I behold the totality of her chastity,
I occupy a singular joy and wish she were my girl!

165a. *As Lovely As Can Be*

With pain in my heart, to me came a maid,
of whose perfect virtue I have oft heard.
Therefore my heart loves her so.
Her beautiful body has given me manifold joys.
I could still, as is my wish, live for the time
when I may beside her lie!

166. *Soldier of Love*

Already for a long time had I shown
myself to be a devout soldier of Love,
at whose bidding I committed myself
to foolish, daring deeds headlong,
loving in the perilous battles but one,
who never on me cast a kind eye.

If I should now bring all to a close,
I would perchance be well-advised,
but the battle's din routs me not,
unless I were departing from manly pluck.
Let it be, as I will! Intrepid, I offer
my life to fortune's vicissitudes.

May she know that I magnanimous am
and mightier than my corporeal form,
that I am one who scales the loftiest bough
to pick from the tree its fruit, as I declare:
in a lover, who knows nothing of fear,
there is, woe!, no room for a daedal veer![246]

CLXVIa. *Dolor Sine Fine*
Reinmar von Hagenau (*Des Minnesangs Frühling* 185.28)

Solde auer ich mit sorgen iemmer leben,
swenne ander lute weren fro?
gvoten trost wil ih mir selbeme geben
vnde min gemůte tragen ho,
so von rehte ein selich man.
si sagent mir alle,   truren sta mir iemerlichen an.

CLXVII. *Virgo Matura*

Laboris remedium,
exulantis gaudium,
mitigat exilium
virginis memoria;
unicum solacium
eius michi gratia.

In absentem ardeo;
Venus enim aureo
nectit corda laqueo.
corporis distantia
merens tamen gaudeo
absentis presentia.

Nil proponens temere
diligebam tenere,
quam sciebam degere
sub etate tenera,
nil audens exigere
preter mentis federa.

Iam etas invaluit,
iam amor incaluit;
iam virgo maturuit,
iam tumescunt ubera;
iam frustra complacuit,
nisi fiant cetera.

Ergo iunctis mentibus
iungamur corporibus!
mellitis amplexibus

166a. *Grief Without End*
by Reinmar von Hagenau (*The Spring of the Courtly Lovesong* 185.28)

Must I forever experience grief,
whilst all other folks are merry?
I wish to afford myself good relief
and the highest spirits carry,
just as a truly fortunate swain!
They tell me all that rue and dole fit not at all my strain!

167. *The Ripe Maiden*

Labor's cure,
an outcast's joy—
the thought of my girl
mitigates my exiled fate.
My one true solace
is her grace.

I burn for her, who is absent from me,
for Venus binds my heart
with a golden noose.
When I am woeful about
my distance from her form,
I rejoice nevertheless
that she is present, when away.

Without a reckless design,
I loved her tenderly,
whom I knew was standing
in a tender stage of life; so I ventured
to demand naught except her soul's pact.

Now her age has prevailed;
now her passion has grown hot;
already has the maid matured:
already swell her breasts,
already has she loved in vain,
unless something further occurs.

Therefore, since our hearts are one,
let us join our bodies twain!
Let us enjoy honey-sweet embraces

fruamur cum gaudio!
flos pre cunctis floribus,
colluctemur serio!

Uvam dulcem premere,
mel de favo sugere:
quid hoc sit, exponere
tibi, virgo, cupio;
non verbo, sed opere
fiat expositio!

CLXVIIa. *Terra Sine Iuvenibus*

Swaz hie gat umbe,
daz sint alle megede;
die wellent an man
allen disen sumer gan!

CLXVIII. *Festus Dies Anniversarius*

Annualis mea
sospes sit et gaudeat!
arrideat,
cui se hec chorea
implicat, quam replico,
et precino:
pulchrior   et aptior   in mundo non est ea!

Fervens illa mea
ignis est, sed suavitas
et bonitas
renitent ex ea.
provocant me talia
ad gaudia,
tristorque cum suspiriis   sub lite Venerea.

Hospitalis mea,
candida et rubea,
amabilis.
Venus, amoris dea,
me tibi subicio,
auxilio
egens tuo; iam caleo   et pereo   in ea!

in an alliance with blissful joy!
Flower surpassing all other blooms,
let us now contend in earnest!

Pressing a sweet grape,
sucking honey from a comb:
I wish, virgin, to explain
what these are to you.
Not in words, but in deeds
let the demonstration be made!

167a. *Land of No Lads*

Those are all maidens,
who spin here in the dance,
lasses who wish to go
the whole summer without men!

168. *The Anniversary*

May my lady of one year
be happy and overjoyed!
May she smile, for to her
this chorus grafts itself,
which I now repeat
and make the precentor:
"No one in the world is more beautiful and endearing than she!"

This my girl is a blazing fire,
but sweetness and goodness
shine from her!
They call me forth
to such delights,
and I am sad and in sighs
under Venus' strife.

My hostess,
white and red,
how lovely is she!
Venus, goddess of love,
I subject myself to thee,
greatly in need of thy aid.
For now I burn and perish for her sake!

Collaudate meam,
pudicam, delectabilem,
amabilem!
amo ferventer eam.
per quam mestus vigeo
et gaudeo,
illam pre cunctis diligo   et veneror ut deam.

CLXVIIIa. *Vere Sine Amore*
Neidhart von Reuenthal (11.8)

Nu grvonet auer div heide,
mit grvoneme lovbe stat der walt;
der winder chalt
dwanch si sere beide.
div zit hat sich uerwandelot.
ein senediv not
mant mich an der gůten,   von der ih ungerne scheide.

CLXIX. *Procul ab Puella Mea*

Hebet sidus   leti visus
cordis nubilo,
tepet oris mei risus
carens iubilo;
iure mereo:
occultatur nam propinqua,
cordis vigor floret in qua;
totus hereo.

In Amoris hec chorea
cunctis prenitet,
cuius lumen a Phebea
luce renitet
et pro speculo
servit solo; illam colo,
eam volo nutu solo
in hoc seculo.

Tempus queror tam diurne
solitudinis,
quo furabar vi nocturne
aptitudinis

Praise my maiden, all of ye,
who is chaste, delectable,
worthy of love's lee!
I love her fervidly.
Through her I thrive,
when I am sad, and do rejoice:
I love her foremost and worship her as a being divine.

168a. *Loveless In Spring*
by Neidhart von Reuental (11.8)

Now the heath greens again;
with fresh leaves stands the holt:
the winter cold had dealt
violent buffets to both.
The season has transmuted itself.
The agony of yearning bethinks me of the good lass,
from whom myself I loathly divorce.

169. *Far Away from My Girl*

Dimly twinkle the stars of my happy eyne
because of the clouds in my soul;
lukewarm grows the smile of my face,
for I lack my jubilant song.
Rightly do I grieve: for concealed
is my intimate darling from me.
The verve of my heart beats in her,
and I with all fibers on her hang.

In Cupid's roundel
she outshines all;
her light shines back
from Phoebus' torch,
and serves the world as its glass sole.
I worship her and want to be
at her beck alone
for all my life to come.

In the day I repine
about my solitude's wide span,
when I by dint of opportunity
purloined in the night

oris basia,
a quo stillat cinnamomum
et rimatur cordis domum
dulcis cassia.

Tabet illa tamen, caret
spe solacii,
iuvenilis flos exaret.
tanti spatii
intercisio
annulletur, ut secura
adiunctivis prestet iura
hec divisio!

CLXIXa. *Desine Crudelis Esse!*
Walther von der Vogelweide (51.37.4)

Roter munt, wie du dich swachest!
la din lachen sin!
scheme dich, swenne du so lachest
nach deme schaden din!
dest niht wolgetan.
owi so verlorner stunde,
sol von minnechlichen munde
solich unminne ergan!

CLXX. *Apex Creationis*

Quelibet succenditur   vivens creatura
ad amoris gaudia;   meque traxit cura
insignite virginis,   in cuius figura
laboravit Deitas   et mater Natura.

Facies est nivea,   miranda decore,
os eius suffunditur   roseo rubore.
consurgenti cernitur   similis aurore,
irriganti climata   matutino rore.

Tota caret carie;   lampas oculorum
concertat carbunculo;   sicut flos est florum
rosa, supereminet   virginalem chorum.
. . . . scintillulas   excitat amorum.

kisses from her mouth,
whence cinnamon trickles
and sweet perfumes of the cassia
infiltrate the house of the heart.

Nevertheless she wastes away
and lacks any hope for solace;
her flower of youth is wilting.
This so long a recess
should be annulled,
so that this separation
may beget and bestow
unassailable possessory laws!

169a. *Cease to be Uncouth!*
by Walther von der Vogelweide (51.37.4)

Red mouth, O how you enfeeble yourself!
Let your laughter remain!
Shame on you, whenever you laugh
at my detriment and pain!
This is not a good thing at all.
Alas, it is so wasted an hour,
when from an enchanting mouth
such unkindness issues forth!

170. *The Peak of Creation*

Every living creature is inflamed by the joys of love;
the love for a striking lass took hold of my soul,
a maiden in whose manufacture
Divinity and Mother Nature greatly toiled.

Niveous is her face, miraculous is her form,
and her lips are infused with the red of the rose.
Her semblance is similar to the rising sun,
like a refreshing downpour of dew in the morn.

She is void of all decay; the lamps of her eyne zealously contend
with the dazzling cabochon. Like the flower of flowers,
the rose, she stands out in the maidenly throng
and ignites all the little sparklets of love.

CLXXa. *Virgines Venereae*

Min vrowe Uenus ist so gůt, si chan vrovde machen
den, swer iren willen tůt; der herçe můz lachen.
si hat vrowen in ir hůt, die lat si nit swachen.
swer gegen den hat hohen můt, der mach gerne wachen.

CLXXI. *Caminus Veneris*

De pollicito
mea mens elata
in proposito
vivit, animata
spei merito;
tamen dubito,
ne spes alterata
cedat subito.

Uni faveo,
uni, dico, stelle,
cuius roseo
basia cum melle
stillant oleo.
in hac rideo,
in ipsius velle
totus ardeo.

Amor nimius
incutit timorem,
timor anxius
suscitat ardorem
vehementius;
ita dubius
sentio dolorem
certo certius.

Totus Veneris
uror in camino;
donis Cereris,
satiatis vino
presto ceteris,
et cum superis
nectare divino

170a. *The Maids of Venus*

My Lady Venus is so kind; she can fill with true delight
those who fulfill her will: that their hearts smile bright.
She has maidens in her care, whom she lets not fall into disgrace.
Every man eagerly espies, who targets these maids with aims set high.

171. *Venus' Furnace*

By her promise
my spirit has
risen so very high
and lives for the prospect set,
fired by hope's reward.
Nevertheless I am uncertain
whether my hope will turn out to be
false and suddenly pass from me.

I am good to one maid,
to wit, one singular star,
whose kisses distill
the oil of the rose
and the honey of the comb.
In her eyes I smile;
I blaze and glow
in her will.

Love beyond measure
inspires great fear;
distressing fear
stirs up passion
hotter than before.
Wavering thus,
I feel much pain—
'tis something certain as can be.

In Venus' furnace
I am burned
to the core;
sated by Ceres' gifts,
I excel all the rest
who are filled with wine
and with the celestials

fruor frueris!

CLXXIa. *Era Mea, Trifolium Meum*

Vrowe, wesent vro!
trostent ivch der sumerzit!
div chumit iv also:
rosen, lilien si uns git.
vrowe, wesent vro!
wie tůt ir nu so,
daz ir so trurech sit?
der chle, der springet ho!

CLXXII. *Magi Amoris*

Lude, ludat, ludite!   iocantes nunc audite,
quos presentis gaudia   demulcent leta vite:
histrio tesseribus;
clericus amplexibus
deludat mulieres!

Amor est iam suavibus   canendus melodiis,
qui non tardet gravibus   detentus homiliis!
spondeat puellula
florens quasi rosula,
verbis devicta piis!

Dicat «ita!» facile,   nil deneget rogata,
non viri notitiam   rimetur prenotata!
faciat, quod petitur;
quod prece negligitur,
prestet virgo laudata!

CLXXIIa. *Tempus Aestivalis Veniat!*

Ich han eine senede not,   div tůt mir also we;
daz machet mir ein winder chalt   vnde ovch der wize sne.
chome mir div sumerzit,
so wolde ich prisen minen lip
umbe ein vil harte schoniz wip.

CLXXIII. *Poena Dulcissima*

enjoy nectar divine!²⁴⁷

171a. *Milady, My Clover*

Noble lady, be mirthful!
Trust in the summertime!
It comes for you as well:
roses, lilies it gives to you.
Be mirthful then, milady!
How is it possible
that now you are so sad?
The clover that shoots high into the air!

172. *Magicians of Love*

Play thou! All creatures should play! Play ye!
In your jesting now hearken, you, whom
the sweet joys of the present life caress:
as the showman with his dice cozens and dupes,
the student by his embraces should women delude!

Cupid must not be sung in sweet melodies;
he should tarry not in the detention of homilies grave!
The little lass, who flowers like a rose,
should pledge her tender hand,
softened by affectionate words!

Readily should she say, "Yes!" and not deny, when asked,
nor should the noted girl inquire of the swain's name!
She should do what is asked;
what is neglected in bidding or prayer
the much-lauded damsel should furnish yare!

172a. *May Summer Come*

I suffer the torment of yearning, which hurts me so.
It creates for me a cold winter and also white snow.
Summertime would come for me,
so I wanted to festoon my form
for the sake of a very beautiful girl.

173. *The Sweetest Pain*

Revirescit
et florescit
cor meum a gaudio.
ab hac peto
corde leto,
quam numquam deserui,
tota mente
ut repente
donet michi   gratiam, si merui.

Philomena
per amena
silve quando volitat
exultando
et cantando,
statim tui glorior.
miserere,
quia vere
in hac pena   dulcissima morior!

CLXXIIIa. *Aeternus Servus Suus*

Wol ir libe, div so schone
lebet, alsam div vrowe min!
si treit wol der eren chrone.
in ir dienest wil ich sin;
dest ein ende.
swer daz wende,
der enguuinne
hoher minne
nimmer me!

CLXXIV. *Veni Ad Me!*

Veni, veni, venias,
ne me mori facias!
hyria hyrie
nazaza trillirivos!

Pulchra tibi facies,
oculorum acies,
capiliorum series –
o quam clara species!

Greens again
and freshly blooms
my heart by dint of joy.
Of her, whom I
did never forsake,
I with a happy soul beg that she
swiftly and with all her heart
give me her grace,
if her grace I be worthy to receive.

When the nightingale
flutters through
the pleasant haunts of the wood
in triumph and in song,
I forthwith feel exalted,
all because of you.
Have pity, for truly
in this sweetest pain
I am approaching death's grim door!

173a. *Her Eternal Servant*

Happy be the inamorata, who leads
a life as perfect as my lovely dame's!
She wears forsooth a crown of glory.
In her service wish I to be—
that is final: no other possibility.
By him, who seeks
to change this will,
never should noble love
be swilled!

174. *Come to Me!*

Come, come, come to me,
lest you bear my death's blame!
Hyria, hyrie,
nazaza trillirivos![248]

Your beautiful visage,
the sheen of your eyes,
the plaiting of your tresses—
O how brilliant is your sight!

Rosa rubicundior,
lilio candidior,
omnibus formosior,
semper in te glorior!

CLXXIVa. *Veni Mox!*

Chume, chume, geselle min,
ih enbite harte din!
ih enbite harte din,
chum, chum, geselle min!

Sůzer roservarwer munt,
chum vnde mache mich gesunt!
chum vnde mache mich gesunt,
sůzer roservarwer munt!

CLXXV. *Cor Cineris*

Pre amoris tedio
vulneror remedio
cordis mei, telo;
patior naufragium   quassa rate, velo.

Aura spirans gratie,
† o puella, facie
rutilans decora,
me amantem respice   non tardanti mora!

Amoris transitio
me donat exitio,
cor cremat scintilla;
quam si non extinxeris,   cor erit favilla.

Vultus tuus urget me,
visus tuus ligat me
miserum frequenter,
amor tuus urit me   indeficienter.

Virgo tu dulcissima,
cum sis formosissima,
adhuc in hac cella
me egenum eripe   de ferventi procella!

Redder than the rose,
whiter than the lily,
comelier than all,
always are you my pride!

174a. *Come You Now!*

Come, come, helpmeet mine,
I wait for you so long!
I wait for you so long,
come, come, helpmeet mine!

Sweet, rose-colored mouth,
come and make me sound!
Come and make me sound,
sweet, rose-colored mouth!

175. *Heart of Ash*

Because Cupid hates me,
I am wounded by his shaft,
the sweet remedy of my heart.
I suffer a shipwreck; and battered are my sail and raft.

O gentle breeze of grace,
O maiden of handsome face
that beams a graceful glow of red: upon me, your admirer,
cast both your eyne without delay of any kind!

The infection of love
delivers me to death;
its spark is burning my heart;
if you do not extinguish it, my heart will turn to ash.

Your visage takes my breath away,
your glance binds me, a hapless swain,
over and over again—
your love burns me without end.

Since you, most beloved virgin,
are a most wondrously fashioned lass,
rescue me, a beggar in a chamber as yet,
from this raging typhoon!

CLXXVa. *Quod Est Optimum*

Taugen minne div ist gůt,
si chan geben hohen můt;
der sol man sih ulizen!
swer mit triwen der nit phliget,   deme sol man daz wizen!

CLXXVI. *Salubra Manus et Grata Vox*

Non est in medico semper, relevetur ut eger;
Interdum docta plus valet arte manus.
                    Ovidius, *Ex Ponto*, 1.3.17-18

Vim fidei menti   facundia dat sapienti,
Cum resonat plene   prolatio vocis amene.

CLXXVII. *Ibi Virgo Stetit*

Stetit puella
rufa tunica;
si quis eam tetigit,
tunica crepuit.
          eia!

Stetit puella
tamquam rosula:
facie splenduit
et os eius floruit.
          eia!

Stetit puella   bi einem bovme,
scripsit amorem   an eime lovbe.
dar chom Uenus also fram;
caritatem magnam,
hohe minne
bot si ir manne.

CLXXVIII. *Maior Quam Iuppiter*

Volo virum vivere   viriliter:
diligam, si diligar   equaliter;
sic amandum censeo,   non aliter.
hac in parte fortior   quam Iupiter

175a. *What Is Best*

Discreet love—this is good.
It can bestow high spirits.
One should cultivate it eagerly!
Any man, who is unreliable in love, deserves a sharp rebuke!

176. *A Healing Hand and a Pleasant Voice*

"It is not always through a doctor that a sick man is healed;
sometimes a hand is more powerful than a physician's art."
                    Ovid, *Letters from the Black Sea* 1.3.17

"Eloquence gives persuasiveness to the clever mind,
when the linguistic art of a pleasant voice resounds."

177. *There Stood A Maiden*

There stood a maiden
in a tunic of red;
if anyone touched it,
rustle it did.
        Eia!

There stood a maiden
like a little rose:
her visage glittered,
and her lips bloomed.
        Eia!

There stood a maiden beneath a tree;
she wrote her love upon a leaf.
Then Venus approached her at once;
Mighty adoration,
lofty, courtly love
she gave to her manly lord.

178. *Mightier than Father Zeus*

I wish to live manfully as a man.
I shall love, if I be loved the same.
To me, love should be so, not any other way.
On this point I am stronger than Jove—

nescio procari
commercio vulgari:
amaturus forsitan   volo prius amari.

Muliebris animi   superbiam
gravi supercilio   despiciam,
nec maiorem terminum   subiciam
neque bubus aratrum   preficiam.
displicet hic usus
in miseros diffusus;
malo plaudens ludere   quam plangere delusus.

Que cupit, ut placeat,   huic placeam;
ipsa prior faveat,   ut faveam.
non ludemus aliter   hanc aleam,
ne se granum reputet,   me paleam.
pari lege fori
deserviam amori,
ne prosternar impudens   femineo pudori.

Liber ego liberum   me iactito,
casto pene similis   Hippolyto,
nec me vincit mulier   tam subito.
que seducat, oculis   ac digito
dicat me placere
et diligat sincere;
hec michi protervitas   placet in muliere. –

Ecce michi displicet,   quod cecini,
et meo contrarius   sum carmini,
tue reus, domina,   dulcedini,
cuius elegantie   non memini.
quia sic erravi,
sum dignus pena gravi;
penitentem corripe,   si placet, in conclavi!

CLXXVIIIa. *Bene Venias, Aestas Serena!*

Ich wil den sumer gruzen,   so ih besten chan;
der winder hat mir hivre   leides vil getan.
des wil ich rûfen   in der vrowen ban:
«ich sih die heide   in grûner varwe stan!
dar suln wir alle gahen,

I know not to demand anything
from the common, unilateral trade:
first I want to be loved, then perhaps I will love the same.

Upon the arrogance of the female mind
I shall look down with brows raised high;
I shall not subject the superordinate to the hyponym
nor place the plow in charge of the oxen.
This custom, widespread among desperate men,
displeases my soul to no end.
I would rather disport with a clap than in derision rue.

The maid, who wishes to please me so, I would please in turn;
she should show her inclination first so that I may mine reveal.
We shall play this game in no other way,
lest she reckon me the chaff and herself the grain.
In accordance with equal market rights,
I shall serve only love, lest I in impudence
prostrate myself to womanly demureness.

A free lad, I boast of my liberty sweet,
almost as did Hippolytus the chaste;[249]
no woman so quickly subdues me,
who would lure me with glances and waves,
but should instead say that I please her
and then love me sincerely.
This pertness in a lady is very pleasing to me.

Behold! It displeases me what I have sung,
and I find myself in contradiction to my verse.
I have wronged your sweetness, mistress,
and your exquisiteness I did not bear in mind.
Because I have thus erred,
I deserve a punishment most severe;
flog this penitent, if you please, in your lovely bower!

178a. *Welcome, Summer Fair!*

I want to greet the summer, as best I can.
The winter of this year had treated me bad,
therefore I wish to exclaim under a lady's spell:
"I see the heath again sprouting up with green!
Thither we should all hasten

die sumerzit enphahen!
des tanzes ich beginnen sol,   wil ez iv niht versmahen!»

CLXXIX. *Caesus Amore*

Tempus est iocundum,   o virgines!
modo congaudete,   vos iuvenes!
    o! o!
    totus floreo!

Refl.   Iam amore virginali   totus ardeo;
        novus, novus amor   est, quo pereo!

Cantat philomena   sic dulciter,
et modulans auditur;   † intus caleo.
    o! o!
    totus floreo!

Refl.   Iam amore virginali   totus ardeo;
        novus, novus amor   est, quo pereo!

Flos est puellarum,   quam diligo,
et rosa rosarum,   qua caleo.
    o! o!
    totus floreo!

Refl.   Iam amore virginali   totus ardeo;
        novus, novus amor   est, quo pereo!

Tua me confortat   promissio,
tua me deportat   negatio.
    o! o!
    totus floreo!

Refl.   Iam amore virginali   totus ardeo;
        novus, novus amor   est, quo pereo!

Tua mecum ludit   virginitas,
tua me detrudit   simplicitas.
    o! o!
    totus floreo!

Refl.   Iam amore virginali   totus ardeo;

to welcome summer's age!
Let me begin the dance, if you be not loath to that!

179. *Slain by Love*

The time is delightful, O maidens fair!
Rejoice you now, young fellows and lads!
       Oh! Oh!
       I am fully in bloom!

Refr.   Now I burn all over in my love for a lass;
         it is a new, new love by which I'm slain!

The nightingale warbles so sweetly, and her scales
are drunk in by my ears; I am glowing deep within.
       Oh! Oh!
       I am fully in bloom!

Refr.   Now I burn all over in my love for a lass;
         it is a new, new love by which I'm slain!

She, whom I love, is the damsels' flower
and the rose of roses by whom I'm inflamed!
       Oh! Oh!
       I am fully in bloom!

Refr.   Now I burn all over in my love for a lass;
         it is a new, new love by which I'm slain!

Your troth, o darling, strengthens me;
your denial, lady, banishes my soul from me.
       Oh! Oh!
       I am fully in bloom!

Refr.   Now I burn all over in my love for a lass;
         it is a new, new love by which I'm slain!

Your maidenhood trifles with me;
your innocence drives me to despair.
       Oh! Oh!
       I am fully in bloom!

Refr.   Now I burn all over in my love for a lass;

novus, novus amor   est, quo pereo!

Sile, philomena,   pro tempore!
surge, cantilena,   de pectore!
        o! o!
        totus floreo!

Refl.   Iam amore virginali   totus ardeo;
        novus, novus amor   est, quo pereo!

Tempore brumali   vir patiens,
animo vernali   lasciviens,
        o! o!
        totus floreo!

Refl.   Iam amore virginali   totus ardeo;
        novus, novus amor   est, quo pereo!

Veni, domicella,   cum gaudio!
veni, veni, bella!   iam pereo!
        o! o!
        totus floreo!

Refl.   Iam amore virginali   totus ardeo;
        novus, novus amor   est, quo pereo!

CLXXIXa. *Epistula ad Virginem*

Einen brief ich sande
einer vrowen gůt,
div mich inme lande
beliben tůt.
stille ih ir enbot. ob sie in gelas,
dar an was
al mins herçen můt;
div reine ist wol behůt.

Refl.   Selich wip,
        vil sůziz wip,
        du gist wol hohen můt;
        schone ist div zit,
        bi dir swer lit,
        sanfte dem daz tůt.

it is a new, new love by which I'm slain!

Nightingale, be silent but for a while!
Rise, O ditty, from my breast!
    Oh! Oh!
    I am fully in bloom!

Refr.   Now I burn all over in my love for a lass;
    it is a new, new love by which I'm slain!

In the winter man suffers in self-control;
in the vernal mood he cannot himself restrain.
    Oh! Oh!
    I am fully in bloom!

Refr.   Now I burn all over in my love for a lass;
    it is a new, new love by which I'm slain!

Come, damsel fair, come with joy!
Come, come, beauty! I am almost dead!
    Oh! Oh!
    I am fully in bloom!

Refr.   Now I burn all over in my love for a lass;
    it is a new, new love by which I'm slain!

179a. *Letter to a Lass*

I sent a missive
to a noble dame,
who is the reason
I in this country remain.
Secretly I have notified her.
In case she has read the letter:
in it all my heart's yearning was written.
The perfect girl is under strict supervision.

Refr.   O lady, epitome of all bliss,
    O dame, quintessence of sweet,
    you well inspire a lofty mood!
    Wondrous is the time of year.
    Who lies next to you
    feels nothing but zest!

CLXXX. *Meam Epistulam Legisti?*

O mi dilectissima!
vultu serenissima
et mente legis sedula,
ut mea refert littera?

Refl.   Mandaliet! mandaliet!
            min geselle chovmet niet!

«Que est hec puellula,»
dixi, «tam precandida,
in cuius nitet facie
candor cum rubedine?»

Refl.   Mandaliet! mandaliet!
            min geselle chovmet niet!

Vultus tuus indicat,
quanta sit nobilitas,
que in tuo pectore
lac miscet cum sanguine.

Refl.   Mandaliet! mandaliet!
            min geselle chovmet niet!

«† Que est puellula
dulcis et suavissima?
eius amore caleo,
quod vivere vix valeo.»

Refl.   Mandaliet! mandaliet!
            min geselle chovmet niet!

Circa mea pectora
multa sunt suspiria
de tua pulchritudine,
que me ledunt misere.

Refl.   Mandaliet! mandaliet!
            min geselle chovmet niet!

Tui lucent oculi

180. *Have You Read My Letter?*

O my most beloved jewel!
Are you with most cheerful mien
and attentive heart reading
what my missive conveys?

Refr.   O canzonet! O canzonet!
            My squire does not come!

"Who is this little lass
so very fair," I said,
in whose face shines
pearl white and ruby red?"

Refr.   O canzonet! O canzonet!
            My squire does not come!

Your visage is proof
of your nobility high,
which mixes in your bosom
sweet milk with blood.

Refr.   O canzonet! O canzonet!
            My squire does not come!

Who is that sweet,
most lovely lass?
I smolder with love for her
so much that I can scarcely perdure."

Refr.   O canzonet! O canzonet!
            My squire does not come!

Around my heart
rise many sighs,
which your beauty fuels,
sighs that me so miserably wound.

Refr.   O canzonet! O canzonet!
            My squire does not come!

Your eyes blaze and stun

sicut solis radii,
sicut splendor fulguris,
qui lucem donat tenebris.

Refl.   Mandaliet! mandaliet!
         min geselle chovmet niet!

«Vellet Deus, vellent di,
quod mente proposui:
ut eius virginea
reserassem vincula!»

Refl.   Mandaliet! mandaliet!
         min geselle chovmet niet!

CLXXXa. *O Amator Mi*

Ich wil truren varen lan;
vf die heide sul wir gan,
vil liebe gespilen min!
da seh wir der blumen schin.

Refl.   Ich sage dir, ih sage dir,
         min geselle, chum mit mir!

Sůziv Minne, raine Min,
mache mir ein chrenzelin!
daz sol tragen ein stolzer man;
der wol wiben dienen chan!

Refl.   Ich sage dir, ih sage dir,
         min geselle, chum mit mir!

CLXXXI. *Revenias Ad Me!*

Quam Natura ceteris
mira preflorat arte,
querele cura veteris,
qua laude tuear te?

Refl.   Revertere, revertere
         iam, ut intueamur te!

like the rays of the sun
and a thunderbolt's white light
that illumes the black of night.

Refr.   O canzonet! O canzonet!
           My squire does not come!

May God and the gods fain grant
what I have proposed in my mind:
that I may unlock
her sweet virgin bonds!

Refr.   O canzonet! O canzonet!
           My squire does not come!

180a. *O Squire Mine*

I yearn to let the sorrow pass;
we should hasten to the moor,
o virgin playmate mine!
There let us the glint of blooms behold!

Refr.   To thee I say, to thee I say,
           come with me, O squire mine!

Sweetheart dear, darling pure,
weave for me a chaplet fine!
A garland should a proud man wear,
who can well serve mistresses fair!

Refr.   To thee I say, to thee I say,
           come with me, O squire mine!

181. *Return to Me!*

You, whom Nature with wondrous art
graces more than all the human lot,
who are the spring of my old lament,
with what praise earned can I see you again?

Refr.   Come you back, come back now,
           so that we may behold the lovely you!

Veneris! ad Venerem
instigor miro Marte;
si veneris, cur gemerem,
cura curatus Marthe?

Refl.   Revertere, revertere
         iam, ut intueamur te!

Ne mee blanditie
michi spem artes arte,
cum tue sint primitie
laudis in omni parte!

Refl.   Revertere, revertere
         iam, ut intueamur te!

Sed, respondens merito
laudis nunc per *me* parte,
velis, ut † null*o* verito
meam experiar te!

Refl.   Revertere, revertere
         iam, ut intueamur te!

CLXXXIa. *Pratum Fassum*

Der winder zeiget sine chraft
den blůmen vnde der weide;
zergannen ist ir grvoçiv chraft,
daz chlaget uns div heide.

Refl.   Vve tůt in rife vnde ovch der sne,
         da uon stat val der gruoůne chle.

Die uogele swigent gegen der zit;
si lebent in grozen sorgen,
durh daz der vrost in chelte git;
des ligent si verborgen.

Refl.   Vve tůt in rife vnde ovch der sne,
         da uon stat val der grůne chle.

CLXXXII. *Ama aut Eripe Meam Vitam!*

Come! For straight to Venus am I
being urged by Mars' awesome works;
If you came, why would I sigh,
healed as I am by Martha's care?[250]

Refr.   Come you back, come back now,
          so that we may behold the lovely you!

Throttle not with a grip tight
the hope for my sweet delight,
though every single side do crown
the first, first fruits of your renown!

Refr.   Come you back, come back now,
          so that we may behold the lovely you!

But, in repayment for the favor of the laud,
which you now have gained through me,
allow that I may know you only as mine
without having to fear another's suit!

Refr.   Come you back, come back now,
          so that we may behold the lovely you!

181a. *The Wearied Moor*

The winter reveals its power
to the flowers and the heath;
all their energy have they lost—
this to us repines the moor.

Refr.   Ail you do the rime and snow,
          whereby the green clover is pale!

The birds are silent in this season's face,
They live in great distress because
the hoarfrost freezes up their chords.
Therefore they lie hidden away.

Refr.   Ail you do the rime and snow,
          whereby the green clover is pale!

182. *Love or Take My Life!*

Sol solo in stellifero
stellas excedit radio;
sic unica, quam diligo,
michi placet et populo.

Refl.   Vos igitur, o socii,
nunc militetis Veneri!

Quecumque est, quam diligo,
quam super omnes eligo,
de qua frequenter cogito,
michi respondet merito.

Refl.   Vos igitur, o socii,
nunc militetis Veneri!

Aspectus eius liliis,
rosa genis est similis,
os dulce, latus gracile,
longitudinis modice.

Refl.   Vos igitur, o socii,
nunc militetis Veneri!

O si forem Mercurius
Philologie sedulus
et si sit in compedibus,
sibi iungerer clericus.

Refl.   Vos igitur, o socii,
nunc militetis Veneri!

Quid illud? possum dicere:
nosti quid velim petere,
festina moram rumpere,
fac mori vel fac vivere!

Refl.   Vos igitur, o socii,
nunc militetis Veneri!

CLXXXIIa. *Largitas Aestivalis*

Vns chumet ein lichte sumerzit:

The sun in the starry firmament
dims the vicinal lamps with its rays;
thus unique is the maiden of my eye,
who pleases both me and all the world.

Refr.   Therefore, you, compatriots mine,
          should now enlist in Venus' line!

Whoever she is, whom I love,
whom I prefer over all other girls,
and who is always in my thoughts,
she suits me according to my deserts.

Refr.   Therefore, you, compatriots mine,
          should now enlist in Venus' line!

The vision of her is the sight of lilies,
her cheeks are the roses' congeners,
sweet is her mouth, slender her flanks
which are of perfectly moderate length.

Refr.   Therefore, you, compatriots mine,
          should now enlist in Venus' line!

O! If I were winged Mercury,
I would, even if it must be in chains,
join myself to that lovely maid
as Philology's avid student.[251]

Refr.   Therefore, you, compatriots mine,
          should now enlist in Venus' line!

How come, you ask? I can explain:
You know what I intend to sue,
so swiftly rupture your hesitation,
and take my life or raise my soul![252]

Refr.   Therefore, you, compatriots mine,
          should now enlist in Venus' line!

182a. *Summer's Largess*

The refulgent summer is coming to us:

div heide in grůner varwe lit,
gras, blůmen, chle, lovp uns si git;
die wahsent alle widerstrit.

Refl.   Swer nah frovden weruen wil,
de habe můt vnde sinne vil!

CLXXXIII. *Ludus Cellae*

Si puer cum puellula
moraretur in cellula –

Refl.   Felix coniunctio
amore succrescente,   pari remedio
propulso procul tedio!

Fit ludus ineffabilis
membris † *con*sertis *h*abilis.

Refl.   Felix coniunctio
amore succrescente,   pari remedio
propulso procul tedio!

CLXXXIIIa. *Abi Secretim!*

Ich sich den morgensterne brehen.
nu, helt, la dich niht gerne sehen!
uil liebe, dest min rat.
swer tovgenlichen minnet,   wie tugentlich daz stat,
da frivnschaft hůte bat!

CLXXXIV. *Canticus Catinarum*

Virgo quedam nobilis,
div gie ze holçe vmbe rîs.
do si die burde do gebant,

Refl.   Heia, heia, wie si sanch!
cicha, cicha, wie si sanch!
vincula, vincula, vincula rumpebat.

Venit quidam iuvenis
pulcher et amabilis,

the moorland is clad in a doublet of green,
and gifts us with grass, flowers, clover, and leaf,
all of which grow in a vibrant, bucolic competition.

Refr. He, who wants to win delights,
should be of warm heart and very wise.

183. *Chamber Sport*

If it should happen that a lad
and lass in a chamber tarry—

Refr. O blissful union, when the passion
is growing and by the same cure
all loathing is driven far away!

An ineffable game commences
that is fit for limbs entwined!

Refr. O blissful union, when the passion
is growing and by the same cure
all loathing is driven far away!

183a. *Depart In Stealth!*

I see the morning star breaking.
Now, hero, don't purposely let yourself be seen!
O inamorato mine, that is my advice to you.
When one carries on a secret affair, how noble it is,
where the guardian is love!

184. *Chainsong*

A noble maiden
went into the forest to gather brush
and whilst she bound her sheaf,

Refr. Heia, heia, how she sang!
Cicha, cicha, how she rang!
The shackles, the shackles, the shackles she tore.

A young man came along,
handsome and fit for love,

der zetrant ir den bris.

Refl.   Heia, heia, wie si sanch!
         cicha, cicha, wie si sanch!
         vincula, vincula, vincula rumpebat.

Er uiench si bi der wizen hant,
er fůrt si in daz uogelsanch.

Refl.   Heia, heia, wie si sanch!
         cicha, cicha, wie si sanch!
         vincula, vincula, vincula rumpebat.

Venit † swe . . . Aquilo,
der warf si verre in einen loch,
er warf si verre in den walt.

Refl.   Heia, heia, wie si sanch!
         cicha, cicha, wie si sanch!
         vincula, vincula, vincula rumpebat.

CLXXXV. *Ignominia in Nemore*

Ich was ein chint so wolgetan,
virgo dum florebam,
do brist mich div werlt al,
omnibus placebam.

Refl.   Hoy et oe!
         maledicantur tilie
         iuxta viam posite!

Ia wolde ih an die wisen gan,
flores adunare,
do wolde mich ein ungetan
ibi deflorare.

Refl.   Hoy et oe!
         maledicantur tilie
         iuxta viam posite!

Er nam mich bi der wizen hant,
sed non indecenter,

who took away her honor.

Refr.   Heia, heia, how she sang!
Cicha, cicha, how she rang!
The shackles, the shackles, the shackles she tore.

He took her by her tender, white hand
and carried her off in the song of the birds.

Refr.   Heia, heia, how she sang!
Cicha, cicha, how she rang!
The shackles, the shackles, the shackles she tore.

The wild North Wind then came,
which carried her far away into a coppice,
which carried her far away into the woods.

Refr.   Heia, heia, how she sang!
Cicha, cicha, how she rang!
The shackles, the shackles, the shackles she tore.

185. *Dishonor In the Wood*

I was a beautiful child, when I
was in the flower of my virginity;
then my praise was sung everywhere;
I was pleasing to everyone's eyes.

Refr.   Alas and woe!
Cursed be the linden trees
that stand beside the road!

I wanted to wend across the meadow
to pick a fresh bouquet of blooms,
and there a villainous cad designed
to take away my flower.

Refr.   Alas and woe!
Cursed be the linden trees
that stand beside the road!

He took me by my soft white hand,
though not in an unseemly way,

er wist mich div wise lanch
valde fraudulenter.

Refl.   Hoy et oe!
        maledicantur tilie
        iuxta viam posite!

Er graif mir an daz wize gewant
valde indecenter,
er fůrte mih bi der hant
multum violenter.

Refl.   Hoy et oe!
        maledicantur tilie
        iuxta viam posite!

Er sprach: «vrowe, gewir baz!
nemus est remotum.»
dirre wech, der habe haz!
planxi et hoc totum.

Refl.   Hoy et oe!
        maledicantur tilie
        iuxta viam posite!

«Iz stat ein linde wolgetan
non procul a via,
da hab ich mine herphe lan,
tympanum cum lyra.»

Refl.   Hoy et oe!
        maledicantur tilie
        iuxta viam posite!

Do er zu der linden chom,
dixit «sedeamus»,
– div minne twanch sêre den man –
«ludum faciamus!»

Refl.   Hoy et oe!
        maledicantur tilie
        iuxta viam posite!

and conducted me across the moor,
with naught but fraud in mind.

Refr.   Alas and woe!
        Cursed be the linden trees
        that stand beside the road!

He clawed at my white garments
in a highly indecent way.
He hauled me off by my hand
with furiously brute force.

Refr.   Alas and woe!
        Cursed be the linden trees
        that stand beside the road!

"Lady, let's go on," said he,
"there is a secluded wood."
This path, it should be damned!
And all the while I cried.

Refr.   Alas and woe!
        Cursed be the linden trees
        that stand beside the road!

"By a linden imposing and fair,
not too from far the road,
there I left my harp behind,
my tambourine and fiddle."

Refr.   Alas and woe!
        Cursed be the linden trees
        that stand beside the road!

When he to the linden came,
"Let us sit down," he said—
desire pressed him very hard—
"let us make good sport!"

Refr.   Alas and woe!
        Cursed be the linden trees
        that stand beside the road!

Er graif mir an den wizen lip,
non absque timore,
er sprah: «ich mache dich ein wip,
dulcis es cum ore!»

Refl.   Hoy et oe!
         maledicantur tilie
         iuxta viam posite!

Er warf mir ûf daz hemdelin,
corpore detecta,
er rante mir in daz purgelin
cuspide erecta.

Refl.   Hoy et oe!
         maledicantur tilie
         iuxta viam posite!

Er nam den chocher unde den bogen,
bene venabatur!
der selbe hete mich betrogen.
«ludus compleatur!»

Refl.   Hoy et oe!
         maledicantur tilie
         iuxta viam posite!

CLXXXVI. *Flores, Flores!*

Suscipe, flos, florem,   quia flos designat amorem!
illo de flore   nimio sum captus amore;
Hunc florem, Flora   dulcissima, semper odora!
Nam velut aurora   fiet tua forma decora.
Florem, Flora, vide!   quem dum videas, michi ride!
Flori fare bene!   tua vox cantus philomene.
Oscula des flori!   rubeo flos convenit ori.

Flos in pictura   non est flos, immo figura;
Qui pingit florem,   non pingit floris odorem.

HIC FINIUNTUR CARMINA AMATORIA.

He palpated my white body,
though not without some fear,
"I will make a woman of you," quoth he,
"you're sweet and your mouth is, too!"

Refr.   Alas and woe!
           Cursed be the linden trees
           that stand beside the road!

He pulled up my kirtle
and exposed my naked form;
he breached my little castle
with an upraised spear.

Refr.   Alas and woe!
           Cursed be the linden trees
           that stand beside the road!

He took the quiver and the bow,
and he hunted with great skill!
But the same lad did me deceive,
so that his game could be fulfilled!

Refr.   Alas and woe!
           Cursed be the linden trees
           that stand beside the road!

186. *Flowers, Flowers!*

Take, O flower, a bloom, since it betokens love!
By love beyond measure this sweet flower seizes my very soul.
O sweetest Flora, always this wondrous blossom perfume!
For, radiating like Aurora, your beauty will ever be!
See the flower, Flora, and when you do, smile you on me, too!
Speak kindly to her; your voice is the song of the nightingale!
Kiss the flower! The flower befits your sweet, rosy mouth.

A flower in a portrait is not a flower—nay, it is a shade;
he, who paints a flower, its fragrance does not portray.

HERE END THE LOVE SONGS.

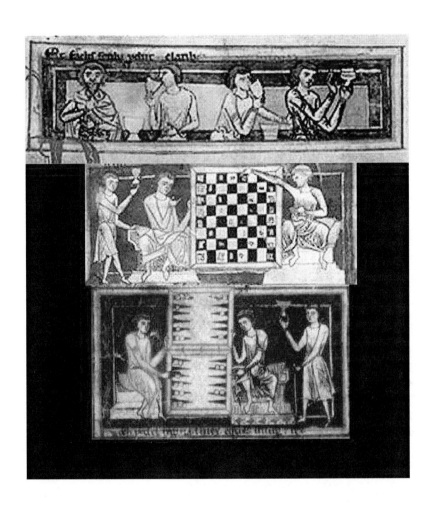

The Drinking Songs

NUNC INCIPIUNT CARMINA POTORIA.

CLXXXVII. *Curia Saecularis*

O curas hominum,
quos curat curia!
o quorum studia
non habent terminum!
talium si fidem
incurreret, desereret
Pylades Atridem;
alter enim Theseus
suum fastidit Thesea,
ubi regnat Proteus
et Fati ludit alea.

Ab aula principis,
si nichil habeas,
oportet abeas.
spem vanam concipis,
tenuis fortuna.
omnimoda ad commoda
omnium mens una:
a quo nil emungitur,
opus perdit et operam;
quod «habenti dabitur»,
tenent omnes ad litteram.

In levum vertitur
censure levitas.
fracta severitas
danti remittitur.
explicas decreta
ad libitum, si sonitum
dederit moneta.
plenis ere sacculis
rei pena diluitur.
locum dic a loculis,
unde locus si queritur.

Honorum titulis
carens ambitio
cum ficto gaudio

NOW BEGIN THE DRINKING SONGS.

187. *The Secular Court*

O the solicitudes of men
of whom the court takes care!
O ye, whose pursuits have no end!
If Pylades adopted
the fidelity of such men,
he would abandon Orestes,[1]
his ever faithful friend;
for Theseus would then contemn
the more beloved half of himself,[2]
where Proteus reigns
and the die of Fate plays its game.

From the palace of the prince,
if nothing you possess,
it behooves you to go far away.
An empty hope do you conceive
if paltry fortune be your lot.
To make a profit in every possible wise
they, of one mind, concur.
From whom nothing is gained,
he wastes his labor and pains,
because they follow to the letter
"it shall be given to him who has."[3]

Mild censure becomes pernicious to its speaker;
the flexion of a strict law
is awarded to a giver of pelf.
You interpret the decrees
at your own pleasure,
if money with a jingle
has sounded its presence.
With sacks full of money
the punishment of the transgressor is dissolved.
If asked whence the word "position" derives,
answer that it comes from pockets and safes.

Lacking the titles of office,
ambition with friendliness feigned
extends a kiss of love

pretendit singulis
osculum amoris;
sed eminet, cum obtinet
baculum pastoris.
quos mens intus clauserat,
mores ostentat libere;
quod occultum fuerat,
verbo prodit et opere.

Indignos allici
verbis alliciunt,
dolose capiunt
nummosos aulici;
sed hi, quos invadunt,
per retia subtilia
similes evadunt.
donum Sancti Spiritus
sic venit iam Simonibus.
conformatur penitus,
si danda fides canibus.

CLXXXVIII. *Dives et Amatus*

Diligitur, colitur,   quem sors illuminat ere;
Spernitur et premitur,   qui nulla videtur habere.

Si dives fueris,   multorum laude frueris;
At neglectus eris,   si copia nulla sit eris.

CLXXXIX. *Quando Romae...*
Philippus Cancellarius (ca. 1170 - 1236)

«Aristippe, quamvis sero,
tuo tamen tandem quero
frui consilio.
quid Rome faciam?
mentiri nescio.
potentum gratiam
dat adulatio.
si mordaci nitar vero,
Verri numquam carus ero.
meretur histrio
virtutis premium,

to every individual it meets.
But it stands out in eminence,
when it secures a shepherd's staff.
It freely manifests
the true character, which
the cunning mind had hidden deep within:
what once was hidden comes forth
through words and works.

Courtiers inveigle men with words
who don't deserve to be lured to them;
deceitfully do they seduce
all moneyed men.
These men upon whom they rush,
through fine nets try to flee.
The gift of the Holy Spirit
thus comes now
to Simon the Sorcerer's men.
Skillfully shaped it is,
if faith is to be offered to dogs.

188. *Rich and Loved*

Loved and worshipped is he, whom the lot of riches adorns;
scorned and oppressed is he, who seems to have naught at all.

If you are rich, the praise of many will you enjoy;
but neglected will you be, if no abundance of money is in your employ.

189. *When In Rome...*
Philip the Chancellor (ca. 1170-1236)

"Aristippus,[4] albeit late,
to enjoy thy counsel
I still should like.
What am I to do in Rome?
I am not an expert at lies.
Flattery earns one the favor
of powerful men.
If I should refer to an unpleasant truth,
dear shall I never be to the likes of Verres.[5]
An actor deserves
a reward for his pluck,

dum palpat vitium
dulci mendacio.»

«Diogenes, quid intendas,
– vis honores? vis prebendas? –
id prius explices.
presunt ecclesiis
hi, quibus displices,
nisi te vitiis
ipsorum implices.
carus eris, si commendas
in prelatis vite mendas.
culparum complices,
ministros sceleris
amant pre ceteris
sacri pontifices.»

«Nec potentum didici
vitiis applaudire
nec favorem querere
corde loquens duplici.
veritate simplici
semper uti soleo,
dari famam doleo
cuiquam preter merita
nec impinguo capita
peccatoris oleo.»

«Ergo procul exsules,
si mentiri dubitas!
simplex enim veritas
multos fecit exsules.
cole nostros presules
mollibus blanditiis
nec insultans vitiis
verbis hos exasperes,
horum si desideres
frui beneficiis.»

«Ergo, sicut consulis,
expedit, ut taceam
blandiensve placeam
mollibus auriculis

when he pays court to vice
with sweet untruth."

"Diogenes,[6] explain first and foremost
what it is you intend—
is it office you want
or prebends?
They rule the church—
these men, whom
you displease, unless
you join in their vices and faults.
Treasured you will be, if you praise
the stains in the lives of the prelates.
Our holy bishops love before all others
the accomplices in their crimes,
the abettors of their sins."

"I have neither learned how to applaud
the vices of powerful men
nor to speak with duplicitous heart[7]
to win the favor of them.
I am always accustomed
to employ the utmost simple truth;
I grieve that fame is given
to whomever beyond their own deserts
nor do I make fat with oil
the heads of any sinners."

"Therefore, you should be banished
far away hence, if you hesitate to lie!
In sooth the simple truth
has made exiles of many men!
Worship our patrons
with gentle blandishments!
And do not exasperate these men
with insults to their vice,
if you desiderate to enjoy
their favor and their aid."

"Therefore, according to your advice,
it is beneficial either to be silent
or with flatteries to please
the delicate little ears

potentium,
quibus me vis sic placere.
adulari vel tacere –
nichil ponis medium,
sicque, quasi faveam,
aliene subeam
culpe participium.»

«Culpe participio
ne formides pollui.
si potentum perfrui
vis favore, vitio
participes.
gaudent a convictu pari
suos sibi conformari
Giezi participes,
in promissis Protei
et sequaces Orphei
sacerdotum principes.»

«Vade retro, Satana,
tuas tolle fabulas!
quicquid enim consulas,
falsitatis organa,
voces adulantium, –
devoveo
nulliusque foveo
blandiendo vitium.
sed palponis nomen cavi,
cuius semper declinavi
fraudis artificium.»

«Ergo vivas modicus
et contentus modico;
nil est opus Cynico.
si vis esse Cynicus,
dicas vale curiis
et abeas
et nec te sic habeas,
ut applaudas vitiis.
cum perverso perverteris,
si potentum gratus queris
esse contuberniis.»

of powerful men whom you
want me in this way to please.
To adulate or to be silent—
you set nothing between the two,
and I should, as if I promote it,
become an accomplice
to another person's guilt."

"You should not be afraid to besmirch
yourself by sharing another's blame.
If you wish to enjoy thoroughly
the favor of puissant lords,
you should in vice take part.
When those in their coterie are fashioned
in their image, by sharing living quarters,
they—confederates of Gehazi, men like Proteus
in fidelity, and followers of Orpheus[8]—
rejoice in their success,
the princes of the priests."

"Go back, Satan, erase thy tales!
For whatever counsel
thou shouldst give—
organs of falsehood,
adulatory choirs' songs—
I wholly comminate;
nor do I encourage anyone's vice
through coaxing or gushing.
But I have always been on guard
against the reputation of a sycophant,
and his art of deceit I have always shunned."

"Then you should live
modestly and be content
with little, for the Cynic has no need.
If you desire to be a Cynic,
you should say farewell
to the courts and leave,
nor should you allow yourself
to give applause to misdeeds.
Among the corrupt, corrupted will you be,
if you seek to be the welcome houseguest
of men of plenipotentiary state."

CXC. *De Detractoribus*

Sunt detractores   inimicis deteriores.
Retro rodentes   et coram blanda loquentes
sunt magis infesti,   quoniam non sunt manifesti.

Lingua susurronis   est peior felle draconis.

CXCI. *Scholaris Errans*
Archipoeta (ca. 1161/67)

Estuans intrinsecus   ira vehementi
in amaritudine   loquor mee menti.
factus de materia   levis elementi
folio sum similis,   de quo ludunt venti.

Cum sit enim proprium   viro sapienti,
supra petram ponere   sedem fundamenti,
stultus ego comparor   fluvio labenti,
sub eodem aere   numquam permanenti.

Feror ego veluti   sine nauta navis,
ut per vias aeris   vaga fertur avis;
non me tenent vincula,   non me tenet clavis,
quero mei similes   et adiungor pravis.

Michi cordis gravitas   res videtur gravis,
iocus est amabilis   dulciorque favis.
quicquid Venus imperat,   labor est suavis,
que numquam in cordibus   habitat ignavis.

Via lata gradior   more iuventutis,
implico me vitiis   immemor virtutis,
voluptatis avidus   magis quam salutis,
mortuus in anima   curam gero cutis.

Presul discretissime,   veniam te precor,
morte bona morior,   dulci nece necor,
meum pectus sauciat   puellarum decor,
et quas tactu nequeo,   saltem corde mechor.

Res est arduissima   vincere naturam,
in aspectu virginis   mentem esse puram;

190. *On Detractors*

Worse than open enemies are detractors.
They, calumniating one behind his back and flattering in his sight,
are more inimical, because their perfidy is not manifest.

The tale-bearer's tongue is worse than the dragon's gall.

191. *The Wandering Student*
The Archpoet (ca. 1161/67)

Boiling deep inside with passionate ire,
I speak in bitterness to my heart.[9]
Forged from the essence of a light element,
I am similar to a leaf, with which the winds sport.

Since indeed it is characteristic of a wise man
to place the seat of his foundation upon a bedrock,
I, a fool, compare myself to a gliding stream,
above which the air never remains the same.

I am carried like a ship without a sailor,
like a wandering bird through the paths of the air;
no bonds detain me, nor does a latch: I seek out
people of my kind and align myself with venal chaps.

Gravity of the heart seems to me like a very heavy weight;
a joke is lovable and sweeter than honey.
Whatever Venus enjoins, the toil to me is sweet;
never in indolent hearts does the goddess dwell.

I walk along a broad path in the custom of a youth;
I, forgetting virtue, entangle myself in vice.
I am more eager for pleasure than salvation from sin;
dead in spirit, I much devotion to my flesh bear.

Wisest prince of the church, I pray for your mercy:
I am dying a beatific death; in a sweet wise am I being killed.
The beauty of maidens wounds my breast, and when I
cannot sleep with them, I go whoring at least in my thoughts.

To conquer one's nature is a most arduous task:
in the sight of a maiden, the mind is not pure at all.

iuvenes non possumus　legem sequi duram
leviumque corporum　non habere curam.

Quis in igne positus　igne non uratur?
quis Papie demorans　castus habeatur,
ubi Venus digito　iuvenes venatur,
oculis illaqueat,　facie predatur?

Si ponas Hippolytum　hodie Papie,
non erit Hippolytus　in sequenti die.
Veneris in thalamos　ducunt omnes vie,
non est in tot turribus　turris Alethie.

Secundo redarguor　etiam de ludo,
sed cum ludus corpore　me dimittit nudo,
frigidus exterius,　mentis estu sudo;
tunc versus et carmina　meliora cudo.

Teruo capitulo　memoro tabernam:
illam nullo tempore　sprevi neque spernam,
donec sanctos angelos　venientes cernam,
cantantes pro mortuis:　«Requiem eternam.»

Meum est propositum　in taberna mori,
ut sint vina proxima　morientis ori;
tunc cantabunt letius　angelorum chori:
«Sit Deus propitius　huic potatori.»

Poculis accenditur　animi lucerna,
cor imbutum nectare　volat ad superna.
michi sapit dulcius　vinum de taberna,
quam quod aqua miscuit　presulis pincerna.

Loca vitant publica　quidam poetarum
et secretas eligunt　sedes latebrarum,
student, instant, vigilant　nec laborant parum,
et vix tandem reddere　possunt opus clarum.

Ieiunant et abstinent　poetarum chori,
vitant rixas publicas　et tumultus fori,
et ut opus faciant,　quod non possit mori,
moriuntur studio　subditi labori.

We youths cannot follow an obdurate law
and must have a love for soft, beautiful bodies.

Who set in fire is not by it burned?
Who in Pavia[10] would not be considered chaste,
where Venus with her finger hunts youths,
ensnares them with her eyes, and robs them with her form?

If you should place Hippolytus[11] in Pavia today,
he will not be Hippolytus on the subsequent day.
All paths lead to Venus' bedchamber,
nor in so many towers is the Turret of Truth.

Secondly, I am also of gambling accused,
but when a game sends me home without any clothes,
I, though cold outside, sweat from the heat of my soul;
then I forge better verses and songs.

In the third chapter I make mention of the pub:
at no time have I spurned nor will I ever spurn it,
until I espy sacred angels coming en masse
and singing "Eternal Rest" for the departed dead.

My intention is to die in the tavern,
so that wines may be near my lips as I pass;
then choirs of angels will joyously sing:
"May God to this boozer be favorably inclined."

The lamp of my spirit is kindled by drafts;
my heart, filled with nectar, flies to heavenly heights.
The wine from the alehouse tastes sweeter to me
than what the bishop's butler mixes with water.

Certain poets avoid public places and select
secluded haunts as their retreats; they are eager,
importunate, never asleep, and always toiling away—
all to produce in the end no magnificent work.

The whole throng of poets fast and in abstinence live,
avoid political quarrel and the marketplace's bustle,
and, to produce a great work that will never fade away,
they die from their alacrity as slaves to their task.

Unicuique proprium   dat Natura munus:
ego numquam potui   scribere ieiunus,
me ieiunum vincere   posset puer unus.
sitim et ieiunium   odi tamquam funus.

Unicuique proprium   dat Natura donum:
ego versus faciens   bibo vinum bonum,
et quod habent purius   dolia cauponum;
vinum tale generat   copiam sermonum.

Tales versus facio,   quale vinum bibo,
nichil possum facere   nisi sumpto cibo;
nichil valent penitus,   que ieiunus scribo,
Nasonem post calices   carmine preibo.

Michi numquam spiritus   poetrie datur,
nisi prius fuerit   venter bene satur;
dum in arce cerebri   Bacchus dominatur,
in me Phebus irruit   et miranda fatur.

Ecce mee proditor   pravitatis fui,
de qua me redarguunt   servientes tui.
sed corum nullus est   accusator sui,
quamvis velint ludere   seculoque frui.

Iam nunc in presentia   presulis beati
secundum dominici   regulam mandati
mittat in me lapidem   neque parcat vati,
cuius non est animus   conscius peccati.

Sum locutus contra me,   quicquid de me novi,
et virus evomui,   quod tam diu fovi.
vita vetus displicet,   mores placent novi;
homo videt faciem,   sed cor patet Iovi.

Iam virtutes diligo,   vitiis irascor,
renovatus animo   spiritu renascor;
quasi modo genitus   novo lacte pascor,
ne sit meum amplius   vanitatis vas cor.

Electe Colonie,   parce penitenti,
fac misericordiam   veniam petenti,
et da penitentiam   culpam confitenti;

Nature vouchsafes every man a special gift:
I have never been able to write while parched;
a boy could outdo me in verse, if I am sober.
I detest thirst and hunger as I do death.

On each man Nature bestows a singular gift:
I, whilst composing verse, am quaffing good wine
that is even purer that what the casks of innkeepers contain.
Such wine generates a tremendous stream of words.

The character of my verses is the quality of my wine;
I can create nothing, unless I have had a bite of food.
My parlance, when I write sober, is not cogent at all;
when I sit behind brimming cups I precede Ovid in song.

The spirit of poesy is never granted to me,
unless my stomach has first been filled well;
when Bacchus rules in the citadel of my brain,
Phoebus rushes into it and heralds miraculous things.

Lo! I was the betrayer of my own perversity,
of which your knaves now accuse me.
But none of them is his own accuser,
though they wish to trifle and enjoy their age.

Then now in the presence of a wealthy bishop,
following the model of God's commandment,
he should cast stones at me and not spare the poet,
whose mind and soul are not conscious of any guilt.

I have accused myself of all my faults of which I'm aware,
I have expelled the poison, which I have nurtured for so long.
The old lifestyle is displeasing, but my new ways are not;
people only see the facade, but to Jove lies open the heart.

Now I value virtues and am nettled by vice;
with a renewed mindset, I am reborn in spirit.
As if cut from a new mold, I subsist on milk;
lest my heart be an ark of worldly vanity.

Chosen bishop of Köln, spare a penitent soul,
show compassion and mercy to a supplicant,
and offer penance to a confessor of his crimes.

feram, quicquid iusseris,   animo libenti.

Parcit enim subditis   leo, rex ferarum,
et est erga subditos   immemor irarum;
et vos idem facite,   principes terrarum:
quod caret dulcedine,   nimis est amarum.

CXCIa. *Pro Cibo Volens Facere Versum*

Cum sit fama multiplex   de te divulgata,
veritati consonent   omnia prolata;
colorare stultum est   bene colorata,
et non decet aliquem   serere iam sata.

Raptus ergo specie   fame decurrentis,
veni non immodicum   verba dare ventis;
sed ut rorem gratie   de profundo mentis,
precepit ut Dominus,   traham offerentis.

Vide, si complaceat   tibi me tenere:
in scribendis litteris   certus sum valere,
et si forsan accidat   opus imminere,
vices in dictamine   potero supplere.

Hoc si recusaveris,   audi, quod attendas:
paupertatis oneri   pie condescendas,
et ad penas hominis   huius depellendas
curam aliquatenus   muneris impendas.

Pater mi, sub brevi tam   multa comprehendi,
quia doctis decens est   modus hic loquendi,
et ut prorsus resecem   notam applaudendi,
non in verbo latius   placuit protendi.

CXCII. *Servo Bonis*

Si quis displiceat pravis, non sollicitetur;
Cum non sit pravus, nemo placere potest.

Opto placere bonis, pravis odiosus haberi;
Namque solent odio semper habere bonos.

I will willingly perform whatever you bid.

Even the lion, the king of beasts, spares his subjects,
and is unmindful of his rage against those very souls;
do you the same, princes of the lands:
what is void of sweetness is exceedingly bitter in taste.

191a. *Will Verse for Food*

Since your manifold fame has been spread far and wide,
all things brought forth should be consonant with truth;
foolish it is to color things that are already so well-hued,
nor does it befit anyone to plant what is already sown.

I, enraptured by the splendor of the renown that is running ahead of you,
have not come to cast words unrestrainedly at the winds,
but so that I—as the Lord has enjoined—may acquire
the dew of grace from the depth of a giving heart.

Consider whether it would please you to keep me in your court:
I am certain to provide capital service as a scrivener,
and, if perhaps a great poetic work should impend,
I could doubtlessly fill the shoes of your royal bard.

If you refuse this, hearken to what you should consider:
you should kindly condescend to one, burdened with poverty,
and bestow care to some degree on a gift to him,
to drive away the tribulations of this poor man.

My father, I have captured so much in so few words,
because this parlance beseems sagacious men,
and to completely deflect the reproach of applause,
I have decided not in further speeches to indulge.

192. *I Serve the Good*

If one should displease the vicious, he need not be distressed;
who is not perverse himself cannot win their favor.

I wish to please the good; I despise being esteemed by the bad;
for they are wont to view good folks with very hateful eyes.

CXCIII. De conflictu vini et aque
Petrus

Denudata veritate
succinctaque brevitate
ratione varia
dico, quod non copulari
debent, immo separari,
que sunt adversaria.

Cum in scypho reponuntur,
vinum aqua coniunguntur;
sed talis coniunctio
non est bona nec laudari
debet, immo nuncupari
melius confusio.

Vinum sentit aquam secum.
dolens inquit: «quis te mecum
ausus est coniungere?
exi! surge! vade foras!
non eodem loco moras
mecum debes facere.

Super terram debes teri
et cum terra commisceri,
ut in lutum transeas.
vilis et inverecunda
rimas queris, ut immunda
mundi loca subeas.

Mensa per te non ornatur,
nullus homo fabulatur
in tui presentia.
sed qui prius est iocundus,
ridens verboque facundus,
non rumpit silentia.

Cum quis de te forte potat,
si sit sanus, tunc egrotat,
conturbas precordia;
venter tonat, surgit ventus,
qui inclusus, non ademptus

193. On Water's Quarrel with Wine
by Peter

Under the constraint of naked truth
and in succinctness of the briefest sort,
I, with many reasons, do affirm
that two oppugnant things
must not ever be mixed,
but completely divorced.

When they are poured into a goblet,
water is mixed with wine;
but such a conjunction is not good
nor ought it receive any praise,
but is, in fact, better called
a confounding of things.

Wine feels water lying beside it.
Injured and in pain, it exclaims:
"Who has dared to couple you with me?
Out of my bed! Rise! Go off into the night!
Not in the same place should you
live together with me!

"Atop the marl you should be trodden
and should mingle yourself with the dirt,
so that you may cross over into muck.
Worthless and undignified,
you seek fissures, so that you may
penetrate the foul quarters of the earth.

"A table is not honored by you;
no one in your presence speaks.
But who was jocular before,
who laughed and whose speech
easily flowed, through you
no longer speaks a word.

"When one by chance partakes of you,
if he be healthy, he then grows ill;
you derange that poor man's bowels!
His stomach thunders, his winds surge,
which, if imprisoned and not paroled,

multa dat supplicia.

Quando venter est inflatus,
tunc diversos reddit flatus
ex utroque gutture,
et cum ita dispensatur
ventus, aer perturbatur
a corrupto munere.»

Aqua contra surgit ita:
«turpis iacet tua cita
cum magna miseria.
qui sunt tui potatores,
vitam perdunt atque mores
tendentes ad vitia.

Tu scis linguas impedire.
titubando solet ire
tua sumens basia;
verba recte non discernens,
centum putat esse cernens
duo luminaria.

Et qui tuus est amator?
homicida, fornicator,
Davus, Geta, Byrria!
tales tibi famulantur,
tales de te gloriantur
tabernali curia.

Propter tuam pravitatem
nullam habes libertatem,
domos tenes parvulas.
ego magna sum in mundo,
dissoluta me diffundo
per terre particulas.

Potum dono sitienti,
et salutem sum querenti
valde necessaria,
quia veho peregrinos
tam remotos quam vicinos
ad templi palatia.»

cause much torment and distress.

"When the belly is inflated,
then it trumpets various blasts
through both orifices afore and back,
and, when the wind thus settles,
the air is contaminated
by a rotten gift."

Water then against wine protests:
"Your life in ignominy lies low
together with great wretchedness.
Those, who are your imbibers,
ruin their lives, lose their manners,
and sink into deeds of vice.

"You know how to tangle tongues;
wont is he to stagger and reel,
who takes in your kisses.
He no longer knows what he says;
he thinks there are hundred lights,
when he sees but two.

"And who are your enthusiasts?
The murderer, the prostitute,
Davus, Geta, Byrria![12]
Such curs serve you,
such mongrels boast of you
in your court, which is but an inn.

"Because of your depravity,
you possess no freedom at all,
and you inhabit paltry homes.
A mighty station I hold in the world:
when I am unleashed, I pour
through every mite of land.

"I give refection to a thirsty soul,
and I am indispensable
to one seeking salvation,
because I transport pilgrims
from distant zones and vicinal frontiers
to the palace of temples, holy Jerusalem."

Vinum hec: «te plenam fraude
probas esse tali laude.
verum est, quod suscipis
naves. post hec intumescis;
dum franguntur, non quiescis
et sic eas decipis.

Qui non potest te potare
et te totam desiccare,
tendit ad pericula.
tibi credens sic declinat;
ita per te peregrinat
ad eterna secula.

Ego deus, et testatur
istud Naso; per me datur
cunctis sapientia.
cum non potant me magistri,
sensu carent, et ministri
non frequentant studia.

Non a falso potest verum
separare, ni qui merum
me potare nititur.
claudus currit, cecus videt,
eger surgit, deflens ridet,
per me mutus loquitur.

Per me senex iuvenescit,
per te ruit et senescit
iuvenum lascivia.
per me mundus reparatur,
per te nunquam generatur
filius vel filia.»

Aqua inquit: «tu es deus,
per quem iustus homo reus
malus, peior, pessimus.
verba facis semiplena
balbutire; cum lagena
sic fit sciens Didymus.

Execretur tale numen,

Wine retorts: "By your self-laudation
you demonstrate your deceitfulness.
It is true that you welcome ships;
but soon after you begin to swell.
Until they are shivered, you rest not,
and in this way you play a delusive host.

"He who cannot quaff your brine
nor dry up your vast stretch,
travels atop you unto doom.
Trusting you, he unsafely strays.
And so he wanders forever
through your watery ways.

"I am a god—Ovid attests to that![13]—
and through me wisdom
is infused in the hearts of all.
When teachers don't drink me,
they lack every spark of soul,
and no students ever throng their schools.

"One cannot separate truth from fraud
unless he endeavors to imbibe
my pure, unmixed spirit.
A lame man runs, a blind man sees,
a sick man rises; a woeful man smiles,
and a mute man speaks through me.

"Through me the dotard grows young;
through you tumbles and decays
the playfulness of young men.
Through me is the world reborn;
never through you is a son
or daughter conceived."

Water counters: "You are a god,
through whom a good man becomes
guilty, bad, worse, and the worst.
You inspire one to stammer out
words that are only half-full:
with a flask wise Didymus[14] becomes a babbling fool.

"Such a divinity should be cursed—

lima fraudis et acumen,
fons, origo criminis,
quod et bonis novercatur,
quod e terris se furatur
per adventum fluminis.

Ego loquor veritatem,
dono terris ubertatem,
per me vernant omnia.
cum non pluit, exarescunt
herbe, fruges et marcescunt
flores atque folia.

Mater tua tortuosa
numquam surgit fructuosa;
sed omnino sterilis,
sua coma denudata,
serpit humi desiccata,
vana fit et fragilis.

Fames terras comitatur
me cedente, perturbatur
deflens omnis populus;
pro me Christo Christianus,
tam Iudeus quam paganus
preces fundit sedulus.»

Vinum ait: «de te canis,
te collaudas verbis vanis,
alibi te vidimus.
universis cum sis nota
vilis et immunda tota,
credis, quod non novimus?

Tu fex rerum et sentina,
que descendunt de latrina,
suscipis, quod taceo.
sordes, feces et venena
multa rapis ut effrena,
que narrare nequeo.»

Aqua surgens se defendit
atque vinum reprehendit

a sharp file of skullduggery,
the font, the source of iniquity
that abuses even good men
and withdraws from all lands
when the rushing river comes.

"I am the voice of truth;
I give fertility to the earth;
through me all things spring:
when there is no rain,
the herbs and fruits dry up,
and flowers and leaves decay.

"Your tortuous mother
never rises with fruit,
but is wholly sterile
and denuded of her hair,
when parched, crawls on the soil,
and becomes pithless and brittle.

"Famine attends all the lands,
when I withdraw, and all people
wail and are fitfully discomposed.
The Christian petitions Christ for me;
the Jew and the heathen continuously
shed prayers in hope for my return."

Wine responds: "You sing your praise;
through rhetoric, you extol yourself,
but I see you in another light.
Since you are known in all places
as vile and wholly unclean, do you believe
that I don't know what you truly are?

"You, the brine and the sewer of things,
swallow what descends from the latrine;
I will say nothing of the rest.
Foulness, dregs, many poisons,
and things which I cannot name
you snatch up like an thief without rein."

Water rises, defends itself
and reprehends wine

de turpi colloquio:
«quis et qualis sit, non latet,
iste deus, immo patet
tali vaticinio.

Sermo tuus me non ledet,
tamen turpis male sedet
ore dei ratio.
ultra passus novem ferre
nolo virus nec sufferre,
sed a me proicio.»

Vinum ait: «exornata
verba sunt post terga data;
non excludis vitium.
multi ferre te viderunt
sordes, que non perierunt
per diei spatium!»

Audiens hec obstupescit
aqua, deflens obmutescit,
geminat suspiria.
vinum clamat: «quare taces?
patens est, quod victa iaces
rationis nescia.»

Ego Petrus disputator
huius cause terminator
omni dico populo:
quod hec miscens execretur
et a Christo separetur
in eterno seculo. Amen.

CXCIV. *Iunctiones Innaturalis*
Hugo Primas (ante 1160)

In cratere meo   Thetis est sociata Lyeo;
Est dea iuncta deo,   sed dea maior eo.
Nil valet hic vel ea,   nisi cum fuerint pharisea
Hec duo; propterea   sit deus absque dea.

Res tam diverse,   licet utraque sit bona per se,
Si sibi perverse   coeant, perdunt pariter se.

with a reviling rebuttal:
"The identity and nature of the god you are
is not hidden, but, nay, is manifest to all ears
from the prophecy you delivered.

"Your words harm me not,
but your vile argument sits
not well in the mouth of a god.
I will not endure filth
for more than nine paces,
but fling it away from myself."

Wine then says: "Florid words
were wasted on inattentive ears.
Still you drive not out your vice thereby.
Many have witnessed your carrying refuse
which remains in you
throughout all the day!"

Upon hearing this, water is stupefied
and loses its faculty of speech;
through its tears, it heaves heavy sighs.
Wine exclaims: "Why are you silent?
It is patent that you lie conquered
and know nothing of reasoned debate."

I am Peter the disputer
and terminator of this case,
and I declare to every race:
that mixing these is an execrable affair
and should be dissevered
from Christ for all eternity. Amen.

194. *Unnatural Unions*
by Hugo Primas (before 1160)

In my jug Thetis is joined with Lyaeus.[15]
The goddess is bound to the god, but she is greater than he.
Neither has power, unless the two divorce.[16]
Thus let the god be without the goddess.

If two different things come together in an unnatural way,
though each may be good by itself, they each other vitiate.

Non reminiscimini,   quod ad escas architriclini
In cyathis Domini   non est coniunx aqua vini?

CXCV. *Miranda Inebriantium Poculorum et Deciorum*

Si quis Deciorum   dives officio
gaudes in vagorum   esse consortio,
vina numquam spernas,
diligas tabernas.

Bacchi, qui est spiritus, infusio
gentes allicit bibendi studio;
curarumque tedium
solvit et dat gaudium.

Terminum nullum teneat nostra contio,
bibat funditus confisa Decio.
nam ferre scimus eum
Fortune clipeum.

Circa frequens studium sis sedula,
apta digitos, gens eris emula,
ad fraudem Decii
sub spe stipendii.

Qui perdit pallium,
scit esse Decium
Fortune nuntium
sibi non prospere,
dum ludit temere
gratis volens bibere.

Lusorum studia
sunt fraudis conscia;
perdentis tedia
sunt illi gaudium,
qui tenet pallium
per fraudis vitium.

Ne miretur homo, talis
quem tus es nudavit;
nam sors item cogit talis
dare penas factis malis

Remember ye not that at the banquets of the Toastmaster
water is not the consort of wine in the goblets of the Lord?

195. *The Wonders of Booze and Dice*

If you are one whose wealth rests in the service of dice
and you rejoice at being in the fellowship of vagabonds,
then you should never disdain wine,
and you should love the taverns.

The infusion of Bacchus, to wit, the spirit,
lures people to the study of drinking.
It dispels the irksomeness of solicitudes
and fills every breast with bliss.

Our community should observe no end and should drink
to the bottoms of the tankards with staunch trust in Decius.[17]
For we know that he carries
the shield of Fortune.

Be you with zeal concerned about constant study—
use your fingers well! You will be a vying people
in the deceitful game of dice
under the hope for profit.

Who loses his mantle
knows that Decius
heralds thereby
that Fortune is not favorable to him,
when he recklessly plays,
wanting to drink for free.

The gamesters' exertions
are not without deceit.
The anger of the loser
is a delight to him,
who has won his cloak
through the vice of fraud.

Such a man, whom the two-one[18]
has denuded, should not wonder why;
for just as Fortune compels him to make
amends to the dice, she has also allotted

Iovemque beavit.

Ut plus ludat,
quem sors nudat,
lucri spes hortatur;
sed dum testes
trahunt vestes
non auxiliatur.

In taberna
fraus eterna
semper est in ludo.
hanc qui amat,
sepe clamat
sedens dorso nudo:

«Ve tuis donis, Decie,
tibi fraus et insidie;
turbam facis lugentium,
paris stridorem dentium.

Lusorum enim studia
sunt fraudes et rapina,
que michi supplicia
merso dant in ruina.

Fortune bona primitus
voluntas est inversa,
in meque michi penitus
novercatur aversa.

In vase parapsidis
stat fronte capillata,
que nunc aures aspidis
habet, retro calvata.»

«Schuch!» clamat nudus in frigore,
cui gelu riget in pectore,
quem tremor angit in corpore:
– ut sedeat estatis tempore
sub arbore!

Per Decium

Jove success in his ill-begotten affairs.

Him, whom Fortune strips bare,
the hope for profit exhorts
to continue to play;
but if the witnesses rip
the clothes from his lich,
he receives no help at all.

In the tavern
eternal deceit
is always in play.
Who loves it
often exclaims
sitting with a naked back:

"Woe to your gifts, Decius,
you are full of fraud and perfidy!
You create a throng of rueful men;
you produce the grating of teeth.

"Indeed the pursuits of players
are chicanery and rapine,
which deal me a deathblow
submerged in ruin's tide.

"The earlier goodwill of Fortune
has been inverted; she has completely
turned away from me and treats me
harshly like an unfavored stepson.

"On a dessert dish she stands
with a proud head of hair;
she now has the ears of a viper
and a hairless occiput."

"Schuch," says the naked man in the cold,
in whose chest the chill frost congeals;
tremors throughout his body torment him
such that he wishes he were sitting beneath a tree,
bathed in the summer's lust.

By Decius the sentence

supplicium
suis datur cultoribus,
quos seviens
urget hiems
semper suis temporibus.

Sub digito
sollicito
latet fraus et deceptio;
hinc oritur,
dum luditur,
sepe litis dissensio.

Deceptoris est mos
velocis, ut tardos
et graves fraudet sors;
sint secum Decii,
sed furti conscii,
dum ludunt, socii.

Sub quorum studio
fraus et deceptio
regnant cum Decio;
non equis legibus
damna notavimus,
sed nexis retibus.

Corde si quis tam devoto
ludum imitatur,
huius rei testis Otto,
colum cuius regit Clotho,
quod sepe nudatur.

Causa ludi
sepe nudi
sunt mei consortes;
dum sic prestem,
super vestem
meam mittunt sortes.

Heu, pro ludo
sepe nudo
dat vestire saccus!

is handed down
to his reverencers,
whom cruel winter
harrows always
with its foul storms.

Beneath busy fingers
lurks fraud
and deceit.
Hence arise often,
during a game,
discord and disputes.

In the custom of a fast cheat,
Fortune chicanes players
with slow rolls and heavy hands;
but let comrades be aware,
during the game,
of the trickery of Decius the King of Games.

In their favorite occupation,
fraud and skullduggery
are co-rulers with King Dice;
not on the basis of fair laws
have we observed their penalties,
but in tightly-fastened nets.

If anyone practices the game
with all the devotion of his heart,
Otto, the witness of this undertaking,
whose life thread Clotho[19] holds in hand,
can testify to him that he often loses his clothes.

Because of the game
my comrades
are very often nude;
and when I vouch for them,
they cast lots
over my clothes.

Alas, a sack often serves
as clothing to one who is nude
on the game's account!

sed tum penas,
mortis venas
dat nescire Bacchus.

Tunc salutant peccarium
et laudant tabernarium,
excluditur denarius,
profertur sermo varius:

«Deu sal, misir bescher de vin!»
Tunc eum osculamur
Wir enachten niht uf den Rin,
sed Baccho famulamur.

Tunc rorant scyphi desuper
et canna pluit mustum,
et qui potaverit nuper,
bibat plus quam sit iustum.

Tunc postulantur tessere,
pro poculis iactatur,
nec de furore Boree
quisquam premeditatur.

CXCVI. *In Taberna*

In taberna quando sumus,
non curamus, quid sit humus,
sed ad ludum properamus,
cui semper insudamus.
quid agatur in taberna,
ubi nummus est pincerna,
hoc est opus, ut queratur,
sed quid loquar, audiatur.

Quidam ludunt, quidam bibunt,
quidam indiscrete vivunt.
sed in ludo qui morantur,
ex his quidam denudantur;
quidam ibi vestiuntur,
quidam saccis induuntur.
ibi nullus timet mortem,
sed pro Baccho mittunt sortem.

But then our patron Bacchus
lets us forget the pain
and the power of death.

Then they greet the mugs
and praise the host;
the denarius is excluded from here,
and on all sides these words resound:

"Greetings, monsieur, bring hither wine!"
Thereupon let us kiss its purple lips.
We don't deem us high atop the Rhine,
but we serve Bacchus, our patron saint.

Then the tumblers fall as dew from above;
the tankards rain upon us unfermented wine.
Who has only just drunk the elixir,
should imbibe it past his thirst.

Then they request the numbered cubes
and cast them for the next drink's round,
and not a soul wastes a thought
on the truculent Wind of the North.

196. *In the Tavern*

When we are in the tavern
we care about nothing mundane,
but we hasten to the game,
over which we always sweat.
What one does in the tavern,
where money is the butler,
it behooves one to discover himself,
but let what I say be heard.

Some men gamble, some men drink,
some live on discretion's brink!
But some of those who tarry
are denuded in the game:
some there come into clothes;
some are accoutered with sacks.
No one there has a fear of death,
but they draw lots for wine.

Primo pro nummata vini;
ex hac bibunt libertini.
semel bibunt pro captivis,
post hec bibunt ter pro vivis,
quater pro Christianis cunctis,
quinquies pro fidelibus defunctis,
sexies pro sororibus vanis,
septies pro militibus silvanis.

Octies pro fratribus perversis,
novies pro monachis dispersis,
decies pro navigantibus,
undecies pro discordantibus,
duodecies pro penitentibus,
tredecies pro iter agentibus.
tam pro papa quam pro rege
bibunt omnes sine lege.

Bibit hera, bibit herus,
bibit miles, bibit clerus,
bibit ille, bibit illa,
bibit servus cum ancilla,
bibit velox, bibit piger,
bibit albus, bibit niger,
bibit constans, bibit vagus,
bibit rudis, bibit magus,

Bibit pauper et egrotus,
bibit exul et ignotus,
bibit puer, bibit canus,
bibit presul et decanus,
bibit soror, bibit frater,
bibit anus, bibit mater,
bibit ista, bibit ille,
bibunt centum, bibunt mille.

Parum durant sex nummate,
† ubi ipsi immoderate
bibunt omnes sine meta,
quamvis bibant mente leta.
sic nos rodunt omnes gentes,
et sic erimus egentes.
qui nos rodunt, confundantur

First, they wassail to him who pays the bill,
then they all toast to whomever they will.
They drink once to the men in chains;
after this, thrice to all living remains;
four times to all Christian souls;
five times to all the faithful departed;
six times to the inglorious sisters;
seven times to the sylvan riders.

Eight times to the brothers perverse;
nine times to the monks dispersed;
ten times to the wayfarers of the sea;
eleven times to the squabblers of the world;
twelve times to all who bear repentant souls;
thirteen times to those who lie on the street.
Each drinks to the pope and to the king
as much it his own desire doth ring.

The mistress and the master together swill;
the rider and cleric around the wine mill;
that man drinks; that lady, too;
the slave together with the maid;
the swift man and he of a lazy trade;
the white man and the black man, too;
the steadfast man and he of inconstant hue;
and the rube and man of alchemical ado.

Drink the pauper and invalid as well;
the exile and he of foreign dell;
drink the boy and he at life's last beacon;
drinks the bishop, drinks the deacon;
drinks the sister, drinks the brother;
drinks the old woman, and drinks the mother;
that lassie drinks, and that fellow imbibes;
drink one hundred, drink a thousand tribes.

Six gold pieces go not very far,
when all drink without bridles
and without a goal line,
though with ever happy minds.
For this reason all the world slanders us,
and we shall be always penurious.
May our detractors be ruined and damned

et cum iustis non scribantur.

CXCVII. *Solium Bibitoris*

Dum domus lapidea
foro sita cernitur,
et † a fratris rosea
visus dum allicitur,
«dulcis» ferunt socii
«locus hic est hospitii.
Bacchus tollat, Venus molliat
vi bursarum pectora
et immutet et computet
vestes in pignora.

Molles cibos edere,
impinguari, dilatari
studeamus ex adipe,
alacriter bibere.»

Hei, quam felix est iam vita potatoris,
qui curarum tempestates sedat et meroris!
dum flavescit vinum in vitro subrubei coloris.

Bibuli lagenam
absorbent vino plenam,
vinum mixtum mellifluo odore,
claretum forte nectareo sapore.
scyphos crebros repetunt in sede maiestatis,
in qua iugum inops perdit sue paupertatis.

Omnes dicunt: «surgite, eamus!
venter exposcit, ut paululum edamus.
stomachus recusat potum diu carens cena,
et simplex erit gaudium, si cutis non sit plena.»

Ex domo strepunt gressu inequali;
nasturcio procumbunt plateali.
fratres nudi carent penula;
ad terram proni flectunt genua.
in luto strati dicunt: «orate!»
per posteriore dorsi vox auditur: «levate!
exaudite iam vestre sunt orationes,

and ne'er in the book of the just be scanned.

197. *The Boozer's Throne*

When one sees the house of stone in the marketplace's midst
and the eyes are inveigled by a brother's rosy light,
the comrades then say,
"Here stands a bar of pleasantry.
Bacchus should uplift our hearts,
Venus should lighten our spirits,
by her sachet's tender powers,
and thereafter transform
our raiment into securities
and accept them as currency.

"To eating tasty foods and being fattened
and amplified by their richest fare
let us devote our souls
and eagerly raise drinks to our lips!"

Ah! How happy is the life of the drunkard,
who slakes his storms of worries and grief,
when the auroral wine in the red glass breaks!

Boozers swallow flagons of wine,
wine infused with honeysweet perfumes,
and spiced wine that savors of nectar's dew.
They empty mug after mug on their majestic thrones,
whereupon the poor cast off
the yokes of pauperdom.

All then shout: "Onward, let us hence!
Our bellies bid us to enjoy a small meal!
The stomach, long lacking food, recuses all drinks,
and 'twill be but half a pleasure, if the paunch hath no fill."

With swayward steps, the winos roar out of the house,
and tumble flat onto the cress beside the road.
Naked are the cronies, for they have not their woolen coats.
Leaning towards the earth on bended knees
and lying in muck, they yell: "Let us pray!"
Behind their backs resounds a voice:
"Rise ye! Your obsecrations are already heard,

quia respexit Bacchus vestras compunctiones.»

CXCVIII. *Consilium Godefridi*
Godefridus Vincestriensis (ca. 1050 - 1107)

Mella, cibus dulcis, sunt sepe nocentia multis;
Divitie dulces pluribus, Alle, graves.

Esca quidem simplex sanum facit atque valentem,
Sed sanum multi destituere cibi.

CXCIX. *Merum*

Puri Bacchi meritum
licitat illicitum:
pocula festiva
non sunt consumptiva.
Bacchum colo
sine dolo,
quia volo,
quod os meum bibat.

Hac in plana tabula
mora detur sedula.
pares nostri, sortes,
pugnant sicut fortes;
nam per ludum
fero dudum
dorsum nudum
ut mei consortes.

Numquam erit habilis,
qui non sit instabilis
et corde iocundo
non sit vagus mundo
et recurrat
et transcurrat
et discurrat
in orbe rotundo.

Simon in Alsatiam
† visitare patriam
venit ad confratres

because Bacchus has your faithful compunction observed!"

198. *Gottfried's Counsel*
by Gottfried of Winchester (ca. 1050-1107)

Honey, a sweet fare, is oft injurious to many:
riches, though sweet, Allius, oppress many.

Simple food indeed makes one healthy and strong;
but many foods have ruined even men of sound minds.

199. *Unmixed Wine*

It is the fault of unmixed wine
that beckons me to the forbidden;
festival goblets
are not destructive.
I worship Bacchus
without deceit,
because I wish my mouth
to be furnished with drink.

Here at this flat table let
a bustling respite be permitted!
Our comrades, the dice,
valiantly strive in war!
Certainly because of it
I have long been
without a shirt on my back,
as have my gaming fellows and chaps.

He will never be a seemly lad,
who stays fixed to one place,
and fails to gallivant with a heart of mirth
all around the world—
both hastening hither
and speeding thither away
and crisscrossing
the globe every which way.

Simon came to Alsace
to visit his fatherland.
He came to his confreres

visitare pa*r*tes,
ubi vinum
et albinum
et rufinum
potant nostri fratres.

CC. *Hymnum ad Bacchum*

Bacche, bene venies   gratus et optatus,
per quem noster animus   fit letificatus.

Refl.   Istud vinum, bonum vinum,   vinum generosum,
         reddit virum curialem,   probum, animosum.

Bacchus forte superans   pectora virorum
in amorem concitat   animos eorum.

Refl.   Istud vinum, bonum vinum,   vinum generosum,
         reddit virum curialem,   probum, animosum.

Bacchus sepe visitans   mulierum genus
facit eas subditas   tibi, o tu Venus.

Refl.   Istud vinum, bonum vinum,   vinum generosum,
         reddit virum curialem,   probum, animosum.

Bacchus venas penetrans   calido liquore
facit eas igneas   Veneris ardore.

Refl.   Istud vinum, bonum vinum,   vinum generosum,
         reddit virum curialem,   probum, animosum.

Bacchus lenis leniens   curas et dolores
confert iocum, gaudia,   risus et amores.

Refl.   Istud vinum, bonum vinum,   vinum generosum,
         reddit virum curialem,   probum, animosum.

Bacchus mentem femine   solet hic lenire
cogit eam citius   viro consentire.

Refl.   Istud vinum, bonum vinum,   vinum generosum,
         reddit virum curialem,   probum, animosum.

to visit every part
where our brothers
drink wine,
both white
and red.

200. *Hymn to Bacchus*

Welcome, O pleasant, long-awaited Bacchus,
through whom our spirits become laden with joy!

Refr.   That wine, a good wine, a noble wine,
            makes a man courtly, virtuous, and brave!

Bacchus mightily overpowers the hearts of men
and awakens in them their lust for life!

Refr.   That wine, a good wine, a noble wine,
            makes a man courtly, virtuous, and brave!

Bacchus often seeks the female sex
and makes them subjects to you, O Venus.

Refr.   That wine, a good wine, a noble wine,
            makes a man courtly, virtuous, and brave!

Bacchus courses through veins with his hot liquor
and sets them aflame with the heat of love.

Refr.   That wine, a good wine, a noble wine,
            makes a man courtly, virtuous, and brave!

Gentle Bacchus softens our solicitudes and dole
and confers upon us banter, joy, laughter, and love.

Refr.   That wine, a good wine, a noble wine,
            makes a man courtly, virtuous, and brave!

Bacchus is wont to calm a woman's fitful mind
and drive her more swiftly into bending to man's will.

Refr.   That wine, a good wine, a noble wine,
            makes a man courtly, virtuous, and brave!

Bacchus illam facile   solet expugnare,
a qua prorsus coitum   nequit impetrare.

Refl.   Istud vinum, bonum vinum,   vinum generosum,
reddit virum curialem,   probum, animosum.

Bacchus numen faciens   hominem iocundum,
reddit eum pariter   doctum et facundum.

Refl.   Istud vinum, bonum vinum,   vinum generosum,
reddit virum curialem,   probum, animosum.

Bacche, deus inclite,   omnes hic astantes
leti sumus munera   tua prelibantes.

Refl.   Istud vinum, bonum vinum,   vinum generosum,
reddit virum curialem,   probum, animosum.

Omnes tibi canimus   maxima preconia,
te laudantes merito   tempora per omnia.

CCI. *Verba ad Vinum*

Tu das, Bacche, loqui, tu comprimis ora loquacis,
Ditas, deditas, tristia leta facis.
Concilias hostes, tu rumpis federa pacis,
Et qui nulla sciunt, omnia scire facis.
Multis clausa seris tibi panditur arca tenacis;
Tu das, ut detur, nil dare posse facis.
Das ceco visum, das claudo crura salacis:
Crederis esse deus, hec quia cuncta facis.

Ergo bibamus,   ne sitiamus,   vas repleamus.
Quisque suorum   posteriorum   sive priorum
Sit sine cura   morte futura   re peritura.

Pone merum et talos, pereat, qui crastina curat.
                              Appendix Vergiliana, Copa 37

Bacchus erat captus   vinclisque tenacibus aptus;
Noluit ergo deus   carceris esse reus.
Ast in conclavi   dirupit vincula sua vi
Et fractis foribus   prodiit e laribus.

Bacchus is accustomed to take by storm a girl with ease
from whom intercourse is not directly by request obtained.

Refr.   That wine, a good wine, a noble wine,
          makes a man courtly, virtuous, and brave!

Godly Bacchus beatifies every man
and renders him both sagacious and eloquent.

Refr.   That wine, a good wine, a noble wine,
          makes a man courtly, virtuous, and brave!

Bacchus, O illustrious god, all standing here
happily bring you as offerings your gifts.

Refr.   That wine, a good wine, a noble wine,
          makes a man courtly, virtuous, and brave!

We all sing to you the greatest hymns of praise,
lauding you, as you deserve, for all eternity.

201. *Words to the Wine*

"You, Bacchus, confer eloquence, curb the chatterbox's mouth,
you enrich, you make poor, and you turn sorrows to mirth.
You conciliate hostiles, you breach treaties of peace,
and to those, who know naught, you omniscience vouchsafe.
Sealed by many bolts, the skinflint's coffer opens itself to you.
You give, so that it may be given; you make giving impossible.
You grant vision to the blind and leaping limbs to the lame.
You are believed to be a god, because you do all these things."

"Therefore let us drink, lest we suffer thirst, and let us replenish
our goblets and cups! No one should worry about his ancestor or his scion,
since in death inevitable all estates will be lost."

"Set down wine and dice; may he perish, who cares about the morrow."
                              Appendix Vergiliana, The Barmaid 37

"Bacchus was captured and in strong shackles bound;
but the god did not will to be a prisoner of a dungeon's bars.
And so in his cage he broke the chains with his might,
burst through the gates, and emerged from the bolted cage."

CCII. *Immodice Bibite!*

O potores exquisiti,
licet sitis sine siti,
en bibatis expediti
et scyphorum inobliti!
scyphi crebro repetiti
non dormiant,
et sermones inauditi
prosiliant.

Qui potare non potestis,
ite procul ab his festis!
procul ite! quid hic estis?
non est locus hic modestis.
inter letos mos agrestis
modestie
index est et certus testis
ignavie.

Si quis latitat hic forte,
qui recusat vinum forte,
ostendantur ei porte!
exeat hac de cohorte!
plus est nobis gravis morte,
si maneat;
sic recedat a consorte,
ne redeat.

Vina qui non gustat pura,
miser vivat et in cura!
vino sors lenitur dura,
procul ergo sit mixtura!
multum enim contra iura
delinquitur,
cum hec dei creatura
corrumpitur.

Dea deo ne iungatur!
deam deus aspernatur;
nam qui Liber appellatur,
libertate gloriatur.
virtus eius adnullatur

202. *Imbibe Without Bound!*

O exquisite boozehounds,
thirsting, when slaked, is allowed,
so, ho!, you should unrestrainedly drink
and ne'er be unmindful of your mugs!
The goblets repeatedly brimmed
should never come to rest,
and strange new speeches
should rear up their heads!

Ye, who cannot imbibe,
be far off from these fetes!
Get you hence! Why are you here?
This is no place for holding back!
Among exuberant revelers
the savage custom of moderation
is indolence's indicator
and incontrovertible evidence.

If anyone by chance lurks among us,
who hazards to refuse our wine,
let the doors be shown to him!
Let him depart from this company!
To us it would be more disagreeable
than death, if he remain!
Thus he should divorce his wife,
so that he does not ever return.

Who enjoys not unmixed wines
should live wretchedly and in distress.
A harsh lot in life is by true wine assuaged;
thus may the mixed cocktail be far from hence!
For it is a great transgression
against nature's laws,
when this creation of a god
is tainted and marred.

Let not the goddess be joined to the god![20]
Let the god spurn her advance!
For he who is hight "Free"
glories in his liberty.
His virtue is annulled

ad pocula,
et ad mortem infirmatur
ex copula.

Cum regina sit in mari,
dea potest appellari,
sed indigna tanto pari,
quem presumat osculari.
numquam Bacchus adaquari
se voluit,
neque libens baptizari
sustinuit.

Pure sequor tam purarum
puritatem personarum,
quia constat omne rarum
raritate magis carum.
ut in vino vis aquarum
non proficit,
sic in aqua vini parum
non sufficit.

Cura Bacchus et sopore
corda pio solvit more.
sumpto Baccho meliore
dulcis sapor est in ore;
vini constat ex sapore
letitia,
recalescit in amore
mens saucia.

CCIII. *Ludi Hiemales*

Hiemali tempore,
dum prata marcent frigore
et aque congelescunt,
concurrunt in estuario,
qui regnant cum Decio
et postquam concalescunt,
socius a socio   ludens irretitur.
qui vestitus venerat,   nudus reperitur.
hei, trepidant divitie,
cum paupertas   semper servit libere.

in the chalice and is enfeebled
to the point of death
through their copulation.

Since she is a queen in the sea,
a goddess can she be called;
still is she unworthy of so mighty a spouse,
on whom she would presume to plant her lips.
Never did Bacchus want to be
brought to drink on water,
nor was he willing to uphold
the very christening.

I purely pursue the purity
of creations so very pure,
because it is certain that every rarity
is more precious than rareness itself.
As the power of water
is of no use in wine,
so, too, is a little wine
in water of no avail.

Bacchus in benignant custom releases hearts
from their apprehension of death.
When a rather good wine is quaffed,
a sweet flavor sits in the mouth;
gaiety firmly stands
atop the taste of wine,
and with love grows warm
the once distempered mind.

203. *Winter Games*

In the time of winter,
when the meadows droop with frost
and the waters congeal,
around the hearth huddle they,
who with King Dice rule;
afterwards they warm themselves
and each companion ensnares another in a game.
Who came dressed is later found nude.
Alas, riches shake in consternation,
when poverty ever freely serves.

Salutamus, socii,
nos, qui sumus bibuli,
tabernam sicco ore.
potemus alacriter!
scyphi impleantur iugiter!
ludamus solito more!
plana detur tabula!   sortes concedantur!
pro nummis et pro poculis   vestes mutuantur.
hei, nunc appareat,
cui sors magis   aut Fortuna faveat!

† Mox stupam egreditur,
a Chaldeo recipitur,
eius commilitone.
quassantur mandibole,
nudus clamat: «ve ve ve!»
currunt dentes in agone.
«o infelix nimium!   cur venis de calore
decantans regem martyrum   deferens in ore?»
hei, hec est regula,
per quam nobis   cutis erit morbida.

CCIIIa. *Carmen Echei*

Vns seit uon Lutringen Helfrich,
wie zwene rechen lobelich
ze saemine bechomen:
Erekke unde ovch her Dieterich;
si waren beide uraislich,
da uon sie schaden namen.
als uinster was der tan,   da sie an ander funden.
her Dietrich rait mit mannes chraft   den walt also unchunden.
Ereke der chom dar gegan;
er lie da heime rosse uil;   daz was niht wolgetan.

CCIV. *O Augusta Treverorum*

Urbs salve regia,
Trevir, urbs urbium,
per quam lascivia
redit ac gaudium!
florescis, patria,
flore sodalium.

We, comrades, all drinkers,
pay the tavern a visit
when our mouths are dry.
Let us drink with alacrity!
Let the mugs be perpetually filled!
Let us in our custom gamble!
Clear the table! Out with the dice!
For coins and cups, clothes are exchanged.
Alas that now one should appear,
whom dice or Fortune favors more!

Soon he leaves the heated room,
he is received by a Chaldean,[21]
a comrade of his.
His jaws begin to chatter,
and, nude, he exclaims, "Woe, woe, woe!"
His teeth clatter in the wager.
"O child so unlucky, why come you from the warmth,
singing 'The King the Martyr' with a reverent mouth?"
Alas, this is the rule of our order whereby
our skin will assume a sickly hue and cast.

203a. *The Song of Ecke*

Helfrich of Lotharingia sings to us
how two praiseworthy heroes
came to blows with each other:
Ecke and Lord Dietrich.
They both were terribly strong;
therefore they both came to damage.
Quite dark was the forest where they met.
Through the unknown wood Lord Dietrich rode
with undaunted virility to him. Ecke came thither on foot.
He left at home his many steeds; this was not prudent deed.

204. *O Trier*

Greetings, royal city,
Trier, city of cities,[22]
through which cheer
and joy return!
You blossom, fatherland,
through the flower of your burghers.

per dulzor!

Refl.   Her wirt, tragent her nu win,
         vrolich suln wir bi dem sin.

Trevir metropolis,
urbs amenissima,
que Bacchum recolis,
Baccho gratissima,
da tuis incolis
vina fortissima!
per dulzor!

Refl.   Her wirt, tragent her nu win,
         vrolich suln wir bi dem sin.

Ars dialectica
nil probat verius:
gens Teutonica
nil potat melius;
† et plus munifica
sua dans largius.
per dulzor!

Refl.   Her wirt, tragent her nu win,
         vrolich suln wir bi dem sin.

Iovis in solio
coramque superis
fuit iudicio
conclusum Veneris
rosam rosario
dari pre ceteris.
per dulzor!

Refl.   Her wirt, tragent her nu win,
         vrolich suln wir bi dem sin.

Quid est iocundius
presigni facie:
rosam rosarius
decorat hodie,
unde vox letius

Blessings to you!

Refr.   Now, lord host, bring hither the wine;
            we desire to sit among it happy and blithe!

Trier, metropolis,
city of loveliest grace,
honorer of Bacchus the Great,
burg most grateful unto him,
give to thy inhabitants
the most puissant wines!
To your health!

Refr.   Now, lord host, bring hither the wine;
            we desire to sit among it happy and blithe!

The art of dialectics proves
nothing to be truer than this:
the Teutonic nation
drinks nothing better
and there is no city more generous
that more bountifully pours forth its gifts.
Cheers to you!

Refr.   Now, lord host, bring hither the wine;
            we desire to sit among it happy and blithe!

Before the throne of Jupiter
and the eyes of the gods,
it was concluded
by Venus' judgment
that the rose should be given
to the rose gardener before all others.
Prosit for all eternity!

Refr.   Now, lord host, bring hither the wine;
            we desire to sit among it happy and blithe!

What is more delightful
than an extraordinary face?
The rose gardener today
honors the rose,
wherefor rings more joyfully

sonat letitie!
per dulzor!

Refl.   Her wirt, tragent her nu win,
         vrolich suln wir bi dem sin.

CCV. *Domicilium Domo*

Hospes laudatur,
si habunde datur,
ut bene bibatur,
et hoc propere.

Refl.   Deu sal sit vobiscum, o pecharie!
         modo bibite,
         sortes apponite!

Iocus est generalis,
ubi potus est venalis,
quem vendit socialis
. . . femina.

Refl.   Deu sal sit vobiscum, o pecharie!
         modo bibite,
         sortes apponite!

Pincerna tunc letatur.
habunde propinatur
de vino meliori
atque leniori
et hoc propere.

Refl.   Deu sal sit vobiscum, o pecharie!
         modo bibite,
         sortes apponite!

Bacchus ad amorem
instigat iuniorem,
mente rigidiorem
et hoc propere.

Refl.   Deu sal sit vobiscum, o pecharie!
         modo bibite,

the clarion voice of bliss!
May you forever be blessed!

Refr.   Now, lord host, bring hither the wine;
           we desire to sit among it happy and blithe!

205. *A Home Away from Home*

The host is praised
if it is generously poured,
so that one may drink substantially—
and swiftly, too.

Refr.   God's grace, O goblet, be with ye!
           Drink now, brothers,
           and serve up the dice!

General amusement
abounds where
a draft is for sale,
which an affable lady vends.

Refr.   God's grace, O goblet, be with ye!
           Drink now, brothers,
           and serve up the dice!

The wine-waiter then takes joy.
Plentifully decanted
are drafts of the best
and the mildest wine—
and swiftly poured at that.

Refr.   God's grace, O goblet, be with ye!
           Drink now, brothers,
           and serve up the dice!

Bacchus spurs on to love
the young lad, who
is steadier in mind—
and swiftly spurs, too.

Refr.   God's grace, O goblet, be with ye!
           Drink now, brothers,

sortes apponite!

Hic est locus annalis
festumque natalis,
ubi liberalis
est ista regula.

Refl.   Deu sal sit vobiscum, o pecharie!
modo bibite,
sortes apponite!

Cum ergo salutamus
vinum, tunc cantamus:
«te deum laudamus»
et hoc propere.

Refl.   Deu sal sit vobiscum, o pecharie!
modo bibite,
sortes apponite!

Nos, qui propinamus
et vina portamus,
prius non bibamus,
donec dicamus:

Refl.   Deu sal sit vobiscum, o pecharie!
modo bibite,
sortes apponite!

«Bacchus est suavis,
fit tamen sepe gravis
bibentibus incaute
ac immoderate.

Refl.   Deu sal sit vobiscum, o pecharie!
modo bibite,
sortes apponite!

Proinde non omittatur,
sed lautius bibatur!
dignus iam mittatur
et hoc propere!»

and serve up the dice!

Here is the location
of the funfair and Christmas,
where this liberal statue[23]
actually applies.

Refr.   God's grace, O goblet, be with ye!
Drink now, brothers,
and serve up the dice!

Thus when we greet
the wine, we then sing,
"Mighty God, you we praise!"
and swiftly do we ring.

Refr.   God's grace, O goblet, be with ye!
Drink now, brothers,
and serve up the dice!

We, who pour
and provide the wine,
should not drink sooner
before we exclaim:

Refr.   God's grace, O goblet, be with ye!
Drink now, brothers,
and serve up the dice!

"Bacchus is sweet,
but still often severe
to those who imbibe rashly
and without bound.

Refr.   God's grace, O goblet, be with ye!
Drink now, brothers,
and serve up the dice!

"Therefore it should not be forborne,
but should more amply be drunk!
Now a worthy opponent should be produced—
and swiftly should he come!"

Refl.   Deu sal sit vobiscum, o pecharie!
         modo bibite,
         sortes apponite!

Ergo nos ludamus,
sortes proiciamus.
letanter bibamus
et hoc propere!

Refl.   Deu sal sit vobiscum, o pecharie!
         modo bibite,
         sortes apponite!

CCVI. *Effectus Vini*

Hircus quando bibit,   que non sunt debita dicit,
Cum bene potatur,   que non sunt debita fatur

Cum bene sum potus,   tunc versibus effluo totus.
Cum sitio, siccor,   nec in hoc, nec in hec, nec in hic cor.

CCVII. *Maledicatur Tessera!*

Tessera, blandita fueras michi, quando tenebam,
Tessera perfida, concava, res mala, tessera grandis

Tessera materies est omnis perditionis,
Tessera deponit hominem summe rationis.

Sunt comites ludi   mendacia, iurgia, nudi,
Parva fides, furta,   macies, substantia curta.

Hi tres ecce canes   segnes, celeres et inanes
Sunt mea spes,   quia dant michi res   et multiplicant es.
Pignora cum nummis,   cum castris predia summis
Venantur; te predantur,   michi sic famulantur.

CCVIII. *Aenigma Aleae*

Littera bis bina   me dat vel syllaba trina.
Si michi dematur   caput, ex reliquo generatur
Bestia; si venter,   pennis ero tecta decenter.
Nil, si vertor, ero,   nil sum laico neque clero.

Refr.   God's grace, O goblet, be with ye!
         Drink now, brothers,
         and serve up the dice!

Then let us play,
let us cast the dice!
Merrily let us drink—
and swiftly swallow down!

Refr.   God's grace, O goblet, be with ye!
         Drink now, brothers,
         and serve up the dice!

206. *The Effects of Wine*

When a buck drinks, it says things unmeet; when with drafts
it is generously supplied, it says things that none beseem.

When I brim with booze, then with verse I totally overflow.
When I thirst, I am dry and have no heart for this, these or that.

207. *Cursed Be the Die!*

O casting cube, you coaxed me, when I had property to vend;
O perfidious, hollow die, wicked thing, gargantuan block!

The die is the substance whence every kind of perdition springs;
the die deposes the man of the highest reason.

The players of the game are mendacities, quarrels, naked sots,
breaches of faith, larcenies, hunger, and mutilated stocks.

Behold these three dogs—slow, swift, and of emptiness full—
are my hope, for they make me a profit and multiply my dough.
Pledges and coins, spoils and castles supreme they hunt down.
They pillage you, but me they serve in this way.

208. *Alea's Riddle*

Two times two letters or three syllables shape me.
If my head were subtracted, of the rest is born a beast.
If my abdomen were removed, I will be gracefully with wings decked.
If inverted, I will be nil to the layman or the priest.

CCIX. *Ad Tabulam!*

Roch, pedites, regina, senex, eques, insuper et rex,
Conflictus   vocat edictus   vos Martis ad ictus!
Vox sonat in Rama: «Trahe tost, capra, concine, clama!»
Victus ab hoste gemat, qui dum fit «Schach roch † et hie mat.»

CCX. *Regulae Ludi Schachorum*

Qui cupit egregium   scachorum noscere ludum,
Audiat; ut potui,   carmine composui.
Versibus in paucis   dicam sibi prelia litis:
Quattuor in tabula   bis loca sunt varia.
Albescit primus,   rubet atque colore secundus,
Aut niger aut glaucus   pingitur aut rubeus.
In primo rochus committere bella minatur
Statque secundus eques ludicra iura tenens.
Tertius alficus custos regalis habetur;
Quartus rex re*tine*t;   femina quinta sedet.
Post illos procerum   revocabitur ordo priorum;
Procedit peditum   turba velox nimium.
Stat pedes, et dextra   rapit et de parte sinistra,
Quem sibi diversum   cernit et oppositum.
Et si quando datur tabule sibi tangere summa,
Regine solitum   preripit officium.
Vir factus mulier regi ferus arbiter heret,
Imperat et regnat,   hinc capit, inde labat.
Bella movent primi   pedites, labuntur et ipsi,
Et reliquis timidam   dant moriendo viam.
Per spatium tabule   rocho conceditur ire
In qua parte velit,   si nichil obstiterit.
Maior maiores   rapit et fallendo minores,
Sepius et minimis   fallitur a sociis.
Belliger insignis,   prudens, celer, aptus et armis
Currit eques rapidus,   qua patet arte locus.
Decipit insontes   socios et fraude carentes
Terret et insequitur,   hinc capit, hinc capitur.
Alficus trivius,   cornuta fronte timendus,
Ante, retro comites   decipit invigiles.
A dominis minimi, domini capiuntur ab imis
Sic mixti procerum;   turba perit peditum.
Rex manet incaptus   subtracta coniuge solus;
Coniuge subtracta   rex manet in tabula.

209. *To the Board!*

Rook, pawns, queen, bishop, knight, and above all ye, king: a scheduled
conflict calls ye to the buffets of war! A voice in Rama cries, "Move fast,
goat, blare into battle, and raise a war cry!" Defeated by his opponent, one
may sigh, when the call is made, "Check with the rook and with it mate!"

210. *The Rules of Chess*

Who desires to acquaint himself with the noble game of chess
should give ear to what I have collected in this song at my best.
In a few verses I shall explain to him the rules of the strife.
Eight times the color on the board changes and shifts.
The first field is white, and red is the color of the second—
it can also be painted black or dark blue or simply red.
In the first field the rook threatens to storm into the fray.
In the second stands the knight—amusing is his moving way!
Third in line, the bishop is considered the king's bodyguard.
The king poises in the fourth; in the fifth, a queen is enthroned.
After them the row of officers repeats itself again.
Afore advances a horde of very fleet foot-soldiers.
The pawn stands and captures from the right and left side,
when he spots an opponent diagonally opposed to himself.
And if ever he reaches the summit of the gameboard,
he snatches up the queen's customary functions.
Rendered into a dame, he as a fierce avenger sticks to the king,
commands and rules, spoils here and gives way over there.
The foot-soldiers are first to initiate the battle and first to fall;
by their capture, they leave to the others a precarious path.
The rook may move about the entire playing field
whithersoever it wants, if nothing stands in its way.
Mightier, it seizes the greater and, ere they slip, the lesser men.
Occasionally, it is lured by its lowest compeers into a trap.
Remarkably valiant, prudent, swift, and suited to arms,
the knight briskly dashes whither a narrow opening sits.
He chicanes his harmless mates, and the guileless he terrorizes
and pursues—he captures here and is captured over there.
The bishop sits at the crossroads, inspires awe with his miter,
and snatches frontwards and backwards the unwatchful suite.
The serfs are captured by their lords, the lords by their serfs.
So the noble cortege and hoard of pawns indiscriminately fall.
The king remains when his queen is wrested from him and he
alone is uncaptured. When she is lost, on the board he tarries.

Sepius est mattus   servorum turbine septus
Et mattum suffert, si via nulla patet.

CCXI. *Deus Novus*

Alte clamat Epicurus:
«venter satur est securus.
venter deus meus erit.
talem deum gula querit,
cuius templum est coquina,
in qua redolent divina.»

Ecce deus opportunus,
nullo tempore ieiunus,
ante cibum matutinum
ebrius eructat vinum,
cuius mensa et cratera
sunt beatitudo vera.

Cutis eius semper plena
velut uter et lagena;
iungit prandium cum cena,
unde pinguis rubet gena,
et, si quando surgit vena,
fortior est quam catena.

Sic religionis cultus
in ventre movet tumultus,
rugit venter in agone,
vinum pugnat cum medone;
vita felix otiosa,
circa ventrem operosa.

Venter inquit: «nichil curo
preter me. sic me procuro,
ut in pace in id ipsum
molliter gerens me ipsum
super potum, super escam
dormiam et requiescam.»

CXIa. Palästinalied
Walther von der Vogelweide (ca. 1170 - ca. 1230)

Quite often is he in check, when he is by a swarm of servants
hedged in, and suffers checkmate, if no path for him is clear.

211. *A New God*

Epicurus loudly shouts to all who hear:
"A well-filled belly is free from care.
My stomach will be my god.
Such a god the weasand seeks,
whose temple is the kitchen,
wherein divine scents circulate."

Behold! An advantageous god:
never is he hungry or wasting away;
before his breakfast, he, already intoxicated,
belches up his wine;
his altar and his chalice
betoken true beatitude.

His skin is always taut,
like a hose and a flask;
he combines a late breakfast with lunch,
whereby his cheeks are rosy and fat,
and if ever swells his vein,
it is stronger than a chain.

And so the cult of this religion
stirs up tumults in the paunch:
the belly rumbles in contest;
wine contends with mead.
O blessed life of leisure,
active only around the maw!

The stomach says, "I care
for nothing except myself;
thus I ensure that I,
pleasantly treating myself
to food and drink,
may sleep and repose in holy peace."

211a. The Song of Palestine
by Walther von der Vogelweide (ca. 1170 – ca. 1230)

Nu lebe ich mir alrest werde,
sit min sundeg ovge sihet
daz schone lant unde ovch div erde,
der man uil der eren gihet.
nu ist geschehen, des ih da bat,
ich pin chomen an die stat,
da got mennischlichen trat.

CXII. *Verba de Modo*

Non iubeo quemquam sic perdere gaudia vite,
† Ut nimioque cibo debeat ipse mori.

Sume cibum modice;   modico natura tenetur.
Sic corpus refice,   ne mens ieiuna gravetur.

CXIII. *Mandata Lusorum*

I. Sperne lucrum, versat mentes insana cupido.
II. Fraude carete graves, ignari cedite doctis.
III. Lusuri nummos animos quoque ponere debent.
IV. Irasci victos minime placet, optime frater.
V. Ludite securi, quibus es est semper in arca.
VI. Si quis habens nummos venies, exibis inanis.
VII. Lusori cupido semper gravis exitus instat.
VIII. Sancta probis pax est; irasci desine victus.
IX. Nullus ubique potest felici ludere dextra.
X. Inicio furias; ego sum tribus addita quarta.
XI. Flecte truces animos, ut vere ludere possis.
XII. Ponite mature bellum, precor, iraque cesset.

CXIV. *Patre Absente*
Marbod Redonensis (ca. 1035 - 1123)

Si preceptorum   superest tibi cura meorum,
Parce, puer, nugis,   dum rus colo tempore frugis.
Prefigam metas,   quales tua postulat etas;
Quas si transgrederis,   male de monitore mereris.
Contempto strato   summo te mane levato,
Facque legendo moram   quartam dumtaxat ad horam.
Quinta sume cibum,   vinum bibe, sed moderatum,
Et pransus breviter   dormi vel lude parumper.
Postquam dormieris,   sit mos tuus, ut mediteris.

Only now in the end do I live a life of worth,
since my sinful eyes do behold
the beautiful land and the earth,
to which one pays high respect.
Now has happened what I had prayed:
I have come to the place trodden
by God in human form.

212. *Words On Moderation*

I do not bid anyone to ruin the joys of life in this way,
such that through gluttony he should pass away.

Take up food in moderation; nature's law is upheld thereby.
Refresh the body thus, lest the fasting soul be distressed.

213. *The Players' Commandments*

1. Eschew profit, for insalubrious avarice twists the mind.
2. Dignified men, avoid deceit; dolts, cede to the wise.
3. Who wish to gamble must pledge both their coins and pluck.
4. Anger at losing pleases not at all, greatest brother mine.
5. Play with insouciance, if ye always have money in the chest.
6. If one comes with coins, he will leave with empty hands.
7. A bitter end always threatens a greedy player.
8. To the virtuous peace is holy; cease your anger in defeat.
9. No one can play everywhere with a lucky hand.
10. I unhand the Furies; I am added to them as the fourth.
11. Tame your wild passions, so that you can sensibly play!
12. Pray, lay aside the strife betimes, and cease your ire anon.

214. *Whilst the Father Is Away*
by Marbodius of Rennes (ca. 1035 – ca. 1123)

If any reverence for my teachings still sits in you, then forbear,
my son, nonsense, whilst I sojourn in the country for the harvest.
I shall set for you the boundary stakes, which your age demands.
If you transgress these, you do not deserve a guide such as me.
When you first awaken in the morning, rise from your bed
and occupy yourself with reading until the fourth hour.
At the fifth, have a meal, drink your wine, but moderately,
and when you have lunched, sleep briefly or play but a little.
After you have slept, make meditation your custom.

Que meditatus eris,   tabulis dare ne pigriteris;
Que dederis cere,   spero quandoque videre.
Miseris huc quedam, –   facies, ut cetera credam.
Post hec i lectum,   cum legeris, ito comestum.
Post sumptas escas,   si iam monet hora, quiescas.
Si tempus superest,   post cenam ludere prodest.
Sub tali meta   constet tibi tota dieta.

CXV. *Missa Lusorum*

Incipit Officium lusorum

\<Introitus:\>

Lugeamus omnes in Decio, diem mestum deplorantes pro dolore omnium
lusorum: de quorum nuditate gaudent Decii et collaudant filium Bacchi.

Versus:

Maledicant Decio in omni tempore; semper fraus eius in ore meo.

Fraus vobis!
Tibi leccatori!

Oratio:

Ornemus! Deus, qui nos concedis trium Deciorum maleficia colere: da
nobis in eterna tristitia de eorum societate lugere. Per

Epistola:

Lectio actuum apopholorum. In diebus illis multitudinis ludentium erat cor
unum et tunica nulla, et hiems erat, et iactabant vestimenta secus pedes
accomodantis, qui vocabatur Landrus. Landrus autem erat plenus pecunia
et fenore et faciebat damna magna in loculis accomodans singulis, prout
cuiusque vestimenta valebant.

Graduale:

Iacta cogitatum tuum in Decio, et ipse te destruet.

Versus:

Dum clamarem ad Decium, exaudivit vocem meam et eripuit vestem meam
a lusoribus iniquis. Alleluia.

Versus:

Mirabilis vita et laudabilis nichil.

Delay not in entrusting the fruits of your reflections to your writing tablets.
I hope to see someday what you have committed to the wax.
Send me certain ones on occasion so that I may believe the rest.
After this, set about to read again; when you have read, then sup.
After your meal, if it is already time, then hie to repose.
If there still be time, it is best to play a game after a meal.
In this order your daily regimen should run its course.

215. *Gamblers' Mass*

Now begins the Gamblers' High Mass.

<Introit:>
Let us all mourn in Decius that we beweep the black day
for the sake of the pain of all players: the dice rejoice
at their nakedness and praise Bacchus' son.[24]

Verse:
May they curse Decius always; his deceit will sit ever on my lips.[25]

Fraud be with you!
And with thee, you lecher![26]

Orison:[27]
Let us spiff up! O god, who let us celebrate the evils of three dice,
let us grieve in the eternal unbliss of their society. By...

Lection:
Lection from the Acts of the Fools. In those days, the players' throng had
one heart and no shirt, and it was winter, and they cast their togs before
the feet of the lender called Landrus. But Landrus was full of pelf and
usury and dealt great damage to each man's purse, whilst he lent to each as
much as his clothes were worth.[28]

Gradual:
Cast your thoughts at Decius, and he will destroy you.[29]

Verse:
When I called for Decius, he heard my voice
and snatched my vest from the cheaters' hands.[30] Hallelujah.

Verse:
Wondrous is his life, and wholly unworthy of praise.[31]

Sequentia:
Victime novali zynke ses immolent Deciani.

Ses zinke abstraxit vestes,
equum, cappam et pelles
abstraxit confestim
a possessore.
Mors et sortita duello
conflixere mirando,
tandem tres Decii
vicerunt illum.

Nunc clamat: «O Fortuna,
quid fecisti pessima?
Vestitum cito nudasti
et divitem egeno coequasti.
Per tres falsos testes
abstraxisti vestes.
Ses zinke surgant, spes mea!
Precedant cito in † tabulea!»

Credendum est magis soli
ses zinke quatter veraci
quam dri tus es ictu fallaci.
Scimus istos abstraxisse
vestes lusoribus vere.
Tu nobis victor ses, miserere!

Evangelium:
Sequentia falsi evangelii secundum marcam argenti. Fraus tibi Decie! Cum
sero esset una gens lusorum, venit Decius in medio eorum et dixit: «Fraus
vobis! Nolite cessare ludere. Pro dolore enim vestro missus sum ad vos.»
Primas autem, qui dicitur Vilissimus, non erat cum eis, quando venit
Decius. Dixerunt autem alii discipuli: «Vidimus Decium.» Qui dixit eis:
«Nisi mittam os meum in locum peccarii, ut bibam, non credam.» Primas
autem, qui dicitur Vilissimus, iactabat decem, alius duodecim, tertius vero
quinque. Et qui quinque proiecerat, exhausit bursam et nudus ab aliis se
abscondit.

Offertorium:
Loculum humilem salvum facies, Decie,
et oculos lusorum erue, Decie.

Sequence:
To the new victim should the Decians consecrate the five-six.[32]

The six-five abstracted the clothes,
the steed, the cape, and the pelt—
the roll speedily snatched them
from their former possessor.
Death and misfortune
fought an outlandish duel;
finally, three dice
conquered the war.

Now it shouts: "O Fortuna,
what have you, wicked girl, done?
You swiftly stripped me of my clothes
and made a mendicant of a wealthy lord.
Through three false witnesses
my raiment you have purloined.
May six and five, my only hope, now rise!
With celerity may they march onto the gaming table!"

More credence should be given
to the veridical six-five-four
than to the three-two-one in one ruinous throw.
We know that they have verily abstracted
from the players their clothes.
You, victor six, have mercy on us!

Gospel:[33]
The sequence of the false gospel according to a mark of silver. Fraud be with you, Decius![34] When in the evening there was a gamblers' flock, Decius came into their midst and said: "Fraud be with you! Do not stop your game. For your sorrow's sake I was sent to ye." But Primas,[35] called Basest, was not among them, when Decius came. And the other disciples said: "We have seen Decius." Primas said to them: "Unless I set my mouth on the glass' rim, to imbibe, I will not believe." But Primas, called Basest, cast a 10, another an 11, and a third a 5. And the roller of the 5 exhausted his purse, and, since he was nude, hid himself from the rest.

Offertory:
Bring salvation, Decius, to an insignificant purse
and gouge out the gamblers' eyes, O Decius our Lord.[36]

Humiliate vos, avari, ad maledictionem!

Oratio:

Ornemus! Effunde, domine, iram tuam super avaros et tenaces, qui iuxta culum ferunt sacculum, et cum habuerint denarium, reponunt eum inclusum, donec vertatur in augmentum et germinet centum. Pereat! Hic est frater pravitatis, filius iniquitatis, † fixura scamni, † genus nescitandi, † visinat amare, quando timet nummum dare. Pereat! Quod ille eis maledictionem prestare dignetur, qui Zacheo benedictionem tribuit et diviti avaro guttam aque denegavit.
Amen.

Et maledictio dei patris omnipotentis descendat super eos!

Communio:

Mirabantur omnes inter se, quod Decius abstraxerat cuilibet vestes.

CCXVa. *Prex Mala*

Omnipotens sempiterne deus, qui inter rusticos et clericos magnam discordiam seminasti, presta, quesumus, de laboribus eorum vivere de mulieribus ipsorum uti et de morte dictorum semper gaudere.

CCXVI. *Felix Festus*

Tempus hoc letitie,
dies festus hodie!
omnes debent psallere
et cantilenas promere
et affectu pectoris
et toto gestu corporis
et scolares maxime,
qui festa colunt optime.

Stilus nam et tabule
sunt feriales epule
et Nasonis carmina
vel aliorum pagina.
quicquid agant alii,   iuvenes amemus
et cum turba plurium   ludum celebremus.

CCXVII. *Ad Salutem Dignorum*

Kneel down, greedy souls, to receive your curse![37]

Orison:
Let us wager! Pour, lord, your fury o'er the niggards and skinflints,
who carry a moneybag on their caboose[38] and lock up their every penny,
so that it may propagate itself and spawn one hundred. To hell with him!
He is the brother of depravity, iniquity's son, the hexer of the stool, of the
ignoramuses' race, who pitifully pules when he fears he must hand over
one coin. To the devil with him! May He deign to send His curse to them,
He, Who blessed Zacchaeus[39] and denied the rich miser a drop of water.
Amen!

And may God the Almighty Father's curse fall upon them![40]

Communion:
All marveled inter se that Decius had reft the togs from every man.[41]

215a. *A Malicious Prayer*

Almighty, Eternal God, Who between the rustics and the clerics sowed
great discord, grant us our prayers to live by their labors,
to serve their wives, and to forever rejoice in their demise.

216. *The Merry Fete*

This is the time of mirth;
today is a festal day!
All should make music
and let their songs ring
from hearts brimming with love
and with a thrilling motion of the form—
young scholars especially,
who know best how to fest.

Since the stylus and blackboards
are festive centerpieces of a feast
along with the poems of Ovid
and the pages of other bards.
Whatever the others may do, we youths should love
and with a massive throng celebrate a merry ball!

217. *Wassail to the Worthy*

Iocundemur, socii,
sectatores otii!
nostra pangant ora
cantica sonora,
ut laudemus dignos laude
virtuosos et carentes fraude!

Refl.   O et o
         cum iubilo
         largos laudet nostra contio!

Ad honorem hospitis,
cuius festum colitis,
canite benigne
carmen laudis digne!
merorem repudiemus
et psallentes omnes intonemus:

Refl.   O et o
         cum iubilo
         largos laudet nostra contio!

«Invidos hypocritas
mortis premat gravitas!
pereant fallaces
et viri mendaces,
munus qui negant promissum,
puniendi ruant in abyssum!»

Refl.   O et o
         cum iubilo
         largos laudet nostra contio!

CCXVIII. *Monitus ad Parcipromos*

Audientes audiant:
diu schande uert al uber daz lant
querens viles et tenaces.
si hat sich uermezzen des,
quod velit assumere
di bosen herren, swie ez erge,
ad perdendum in Dothaim.
nu hin, nu hin, nu hin, nu hin.

Friends, let us make merry,
adherents of leisure we!
Let our mouths raise
sonorous songs, so we
may praise those worthy of laud,
virtuous and void of fraud!

Refr.   O and o with a jubilant song
           our throng should praise
           all munificent souls!

To the glory of the host,
whose festival you celebrate,
generously raise high
notes of praise condign!
Let us repudiate every dole
and, with a loud cheer, all intone:

Refr.   O and o with a jubilant song
           our throng should praise
           all munificent souls!

"May the weight of death
crush jealous hypocrites!
May they all perish,
fraudsters and beliers!
May renegers on promised gifts
fall in punishment into hell!"

Refr.   O and o with a jubilant song
           our throng should praise
           all munificent souls!

218. *A Warning to Penny-Pinchers*

Let them, who can hear, hearken well:
disgrace wafts through all the lands
in search of worthless pinchpennies.
It has boldly decided
to bring under its control
wicked men, as always wonted to do,
in order to destroy them in Dothan.[42]
It should be so, it should be so.

O liberales clerici,
nu merchent rehte, wi deme si:
date, vobis dabitur,
ir sult lan offen iwer tur
vagis et egentibus,
so gewinnet ir daz himel hus
et in perenni gaudio
alsus, also, alsus, also.

Sicut cribratur triticum,
also wil ih die herren tun:
liberales dum cribro,
die bosen risent in daz stro;
viles sunt zizania,
daz si der tieuel alle erslahœ
et ut in evum pereant.
avoy, avoy, alez avanz!

Rusticales clerici
semper sunt famelici.
die geheizent unde lobent vil
unde lovfen hin zer schande zil.
quisque colit et amat,
daz in sin art geleret hat;
natura vim non patitur.
hin vur, hin vur, hin vur, hin vur!

CCXIX. *Ordo Vagorum*

Cum «In orbem universum»   decantatur «ite»,
sacerdotes ambulant,   currunt cenobite
et ab evangelio   iam surgunt levite,
sectam nostram subeunt,   que salus est vite.

In secta nostra scriptum est: «omnia probate!»
vitam nostram optime   vos considerate,
contra pravos clericos   vos perseverate,
qui non large tribuunt   vobis in caritate!

Marchiones, Bawari,   Saxones, Australes,
quotquot estis nobiles,   vos precor sodales,
auribus percipite   novas decretales:
quod avari pereant   et non liberales.

O ye generous clerics,
consider now how things stand:
give, it shall be given you,[43]
let your doors stand open
to vagrants and those in need,
then you gain a house in heaven
and a seat in perennial bliss—
in so doing, in this way.

In the way that wheat is winnowed[44]
I intend to deal with men:
whilst I sift out the munificent,
the wicked fall down into the straw,
and the base are simply darnel—
the Devil fetches them all,
so they may for all eternity be lost.
Fie, fie, avaunt, avaunt!

The churlish village priests
are starvelings for life.
They promise and praise a lot
and yet bump straight into disgrace.
Each one practices and loves
what his nature has taught him;
nature does not force itself.
Hence! Begone! Hence! Begone!

219. *The Order of Vagrants*

When "Go forth unto all the world"[45] is sung,
the priests set out, the monks hurry on,
and the deacons now rise from their gospel,
to join our denomination, which is life's salvation.

In our sect there is a law: "Examine all!"
Look very carefully at our way of life,
persevere against depraved clerics,
who give not generously to you as charity demands!

Margraves, Bavarians, Saxons, Austrians—
all ye who are nobles, I pray ye as friends,
drink in with keen ears the new decrees:
damned be the misers who all liberality lack.

Et nos misericordie   nunc sumus auctores,
quia nos recipimus   magnos et minores;
recipimus et divites   et pauperiores,
quos devoti monachi   dimittunt extra fores.

Nos recipimus monachum   cum rasa corona
et si venerit presbyter   cum sua matrona,
magistrum cum pueris,   virum cum persona,
scolarem libentius   tectum veste bona.

Secta nostra recipit   iustos et iniustos,
† claudos et debiles   senio combustos
bellosos, pacificos,   mites et insanos,
Boemos, Teutonicos,   Sclavos et Romanos,
stature mediocres,   gigantes et nanos,
in personis humiles   et econtra vanos.

Ordo procul dubio   noster secta vocatur,
quam diversi generis   populus sectatur;
ergo «hic» et «hec» et «hoc»   ei preponatur,
quod sit omnis generis,   qui tot hospitatur.

De vagorum ordine   dico vobis iura,
quorum vita nobilis,   dulcis est natura,
quos delectat amplius   pinguis assatura
*r*evera quam faciat   hordei mensura.

Ordo noster prohibet   matutinas plane.
sunt quedam phantasmata,   que vagantur mane,
per que nobis veniunt   visiones vane.
si quis tunc surrexerit,   non est mentis sane.

Ordo noster prohibet   semper matutinas,
sed statim, cum surgimus,   querimus popinas;
illuc ferri facimus   vinum et gallinas.
nil hic expavescimus   preter Hashardi minas.

Ordo noster prohibet   uti dupla veste;
tunicam qui recipit,   ut vadat honeste,
pallium mox reiicit.   Decio conteste
cingulum huic detrahit   ludus manifeste.

Quod de summis dicitur,   in imis teneatur;

We are now the authors of Christian mercy
because we take in both great and lesser men;
we receive both the rich and the poor,
whom the pious monks cast out of their doors.

We take in monks with shorn crowns of hair,
even if a presbyter with his frau should come,
a teacher with his pupils, a man with his girlfriend,
and, most of all, the scholar who is finely dressed.

Our community receives the just and unjust,
the lame, the decrepit, those consumed by old age,
the belligerent, the pacific, the mellow and insane,
Bohemians, Germans, Slavs, and Romans,
those of average stature, giants, and dwarves,
those of humble dispositions and the vain.

Our order is rightly called a community of faith,
because such a variety of peoples come to partake;
thus "Der," "Die," "Das"[46] should be set before our name,
since the many people who lodge here are of every species and race.

I shall explain to you the rules of the Order of Vagrants:
their way of living is noble; their disposition is kind;
a rich roast forsooth delights their palettes
more than a paltry slice of barley bread.

Our order strictly forbids attendance of the matins.
There are wicked spirits that wander about in the morn,
ghosts through which empty visions come unto us.
If anyone rises at that time, he is not of sound mind.

Our order always forbids the attendance of the matins,
but immediately upon rising we seek out the taverns;
thither we have wine and chicken ferried to us;
here we fear nothing save the threats of the hashard.[47]

Our order prohibits the wearing of two sets of clothes;[48]
who receives a tunic, so he may go about respectably,
anon divests himself of his mantle. Under Decius' aegis
the game doubtlessly takes his belt away from him.

What is said of the body's upper half should apply to the lower, too.

camisia qui fruitur,   bracis non utatur.
caliga si sequitur,   calceus non feratur.
nam qui hoc transgreditur,   excommunicatur.

Nemo prorsus exeat   hospitium ieiunus
et, si pauper fuerit,   semper petat munus.
incrementum recipit   sepe nummus unus,
cum ad ludum sederit   lusor opportunus.

Nemo in itinere   contrarius sit ventis
nec a paupertate ferat   vultum condolentis,
sed proponat sibi spem   semper confidentis.
nam post grande malum sors   sequitur gaudentis.

Ad quos perveneritis,   dicatis eis, quare:
singulorum cupitis   mores exprobrare;
«reprobare reprobos   et probos probare
et probos ab improbis   veni segregare!»

CCXX. *Poeta Indiges*
Archipoeta (ca. 1161/67)

Sepe de miseria   mee paupertatis
conqueror in carmine   viris litteratis;
laici non capiunt   ea, que sunt vatis,
et nil michi tribuunt,   quod est notum satis.

Poeta pauperior   omnibus poetis
nichil prorsus habeo   nisi quod videtis,
unde sepe lugeo,   quando vos ridetis;
nec me meo vitio   pauperem putetis.

Fodere non debeo,   quia sum scolaris
ortus ex militibus   preliandi gnaris;
sed quia me terruit   labor militaris,
malui Virgilium   sequi quam te, Paris.

Mendicare pudor est,   mendicare nolo;
fures multa possident,   sed non absque dolo.
quid ergo iam faciam,   qui nec agros colo
nec mendicus fieri   nec fur esse volo?

CCXXa. *Parcipromi Sartores*

Who enjoys a shirt should not trousers wear,
and if a shoe follows, a sock he should not bear.
For whoever transgresses this edict is excommunicated.[49]

Under no circumstances should one leave the lodge hungry,
and he should always ask for a gift, if he is poor.
Often but one coin receives an increase in itself,
when a dexterous player sits at the gaming table.

No one should, whilst on his way, march against the winds
nor, because of his penury, assume a face of dole,
but should always don the hope of a faithful man.
For, after a great misfortune, follows a blessed lot.

You should say to those, to whom you come,
why you desire to reproach the conventions of each:
"I have come to reject the false and exalt the good
and to separate the virtuous from reprobate curs!"

220. *The Pauper-Poet*
The Archpoet (ca. 1161/67)

Often to the erudite I complain in my verses
of the wretchedness of my pauperdom;
the lay cannot fathom what is born of a bard
and give nothing to me—this is very well known.

I, a poet poorer than all other bards,
possess nothing at all except what you see,
which is why I often grieve when you laugh at me;
you wouldn't believe I am poor through the fault of me.

I ought not till fields because a scholar am I,
sprung from knights, who were experts at war;
but because warfare and soldiering terrified me,
I preferred to turn to Vergil rather than, Paris,[50] to thee.

I am ashamed to beg; I am unwilling to entreat.
Brigands possess more than I, but only through deceit.
What then am I to do, who neither cultivate fields
nor am willing to become a mendicant or a thief?

220a. *The Miser Tailors*

Nullus ita parcus est,   qui non ad natale
emat cappam, pallium,   pelles vel quid tale,
sed non statim dissipat   vel custodit male,
induens ad quodlibet   festum, sed annale.

Parcus pelles perticat   et involvit pannis
et indutas rarius   multis servat annis
a lesura, maculis,   notis et a damnis
ignis, fumi, pulveris,   vini, sed et amnis.

Vidi quosdam divites   nuper convenire,
festivarum vestium   gestu superbire,
cum haberent pallia   vetustatis mire,
que Ulixes rediens   posset reperire.

Color sepe palliis   ac forma mutatur:
color, cum pro viridi   rufus comparatur,
vel quod est interius   foras regyratur,
vel cum a tinctoribus   color coloratur, –

Forma, cum in varias   formas sint formata
vestimenta divitum   vice variata.
«in nova fert animus»   dicere mutata
vetera, vel potius: in reveterata.

Vidi quendam clericum   fame satis clare
formas in multiplices   vestes variare:
contra frigus hiemis   pallium cappare,
veris ad introitum   cappam palliare.

Cum hoc tritum sepius   sepius refecit
et refectum sepius   sepius defecit,
noluit abicere   statim, nec abiecit,
sed parcentem tunice   iuppam sibi fecit.

Sic in modum Gorgonis   formam transformavit,
immo mirus artifex   hermaphroditavit;
masculavit feminam,   marem feminavit,
et vincens Tiresiam   sexum tertiavit.

Parum sibi fuerat   pallium cappare,
e converso deinceps   cappam palliare,
recappatum pallium   in iuppam mutare,

No one is so stingy that he does not buy for Christmas
a cap, a mantle, a pelt, or something of the sort,
but he does not circulate it at once or fail to keep it safe:
he wears it on some holiday, but only once a year.

The niggard hangs up his fur and envelopes it in cloths;
by donning it so rarely, he preserves it for many years
from tearing, staining, marking, and damage
by fire, smoke, dust, wine, and even water.

Recently I saw a gathering of wealthy men,
how they gloried in the gestures of their festive vests,
although they had cloaks of wondrous antiquity,
which a returning Odysseus could recognize.

The color and the shape of the mantles often shifted:
it was a color formed when a red is made from a green,
or when what sits within is turned inside-out,
or when a color is by the dyers restored.

It was a shape forged when the raiment of the rich
is fashioned into multicolored forms with alternating hues.
"My mind is bent to tell"[51] of old apparel transformed
into new forms—or, rather, just renewed.

I saw a certain cleric of considerably bright fame
changing shapes into manifold works of cloth,
tailoring, against the chill of winter, a cloak,
draping a capuchin around himself at spring's dawn.

When this used article was repeatedly revamped
and started to tear from being hemmed again and again,
he was unwilling to discard it at once, nor did he toss it at all,
but tailored for himself a heavy coat that spared his tunic.

He transformed its shape in the manner of a Gorgon[52]—
nay, the miraculous artist forged a hermaphroditic frame;
he masculinized a woman, he feminized a man,
and, surpassing Teiresias, executed a threefold sex change.[53]

It would not have seemed enough to him to turn the coat into a capuchin,
and, conversely, to turn the capuchin back into a coat,
and change a rendered coat back again into a jacket,

si non tandem faceret   iuppam caligare.

Primas in Remensibus   iusserat decretis,
ne mantellos veteres   vos refarinetis,
renovari prohibens   calce vel in cretis.
quod decretum viluit,   ut iam vos videtis.

Nos quoque, secundum quid   eius successores,
excommumcamus hos   et recappatores
et omnes huiusmodi   reciprocatores.
omnes anathema sint,   donec mutent mores!

CXXI. *In Eius Nomine Bibite!*

«Cum animadverterem» dicit Cato.
quis me redarguit de peccato?
laudem et honorem canimus
nostro hospiti, cui bonus est animus.

Ergo, fratres carissimi, intelligite
et ad ora pocula porrigite!
et si aliquis inebrietur ex vobis,
declinet seorsum a nobis.

Si aliquis debibat tunicam,
postea deludat camisiam.
et si aliquid plus de re sapitis,
denudetur a planta pedis usque ad verticem capitis.
tunc eritis comites apostolorum,
quia «in omnem terram exivit sonus eorum
et in fines orbis terre verba eorum».

Conventus iste nobilis
letetur his conviviis
et mero mente gaudeat
et dignas laudes referat
summi Patris Filio
et hospiti largissimo
tali dicto nomine,
ut longo vivat tempore!

CCXXII. *Abbas Cucaniensis*

if he could not in the end use the jacket as a shoe.

Primas had enacted the decree in Rheims[54]
that ye should not blanch old gray coats,
and prohibited their restoration with lime or chalk.
That decree has become worthless, as you now see.

We, too, as devout successors of this decree
excommunicate these and coat-to-cowl converters
and all the old-cowl-to-coat alterers of this sort.
May they all be anathema, until they change their ways!

221. *Drink In His Name!*

"Since I am aware," Cato begins,[55]
who could accuse me of committing a sin?[56]
We sing to the glory and praise of our host,
whose heart is good and in the right place.

Therefore, dearest brothers, understand
and direct the goblets to your lips!
And if anyone of you cannot hold his liquor,
let him be sundered from hence and us.

If anyone should spend his coat on booze,
he should afterwards gamble away his shirt.
And if you know anything more about this affair,
he should be stripped from his sole to his crown of hair.
Then you will be companions of the apostles,
because "their sound penetrated every land
and their words the world's every frontier."[57]

That noble fellowship
disported itself with these feasts
and took joy in hearts pure
and should give back condign laud
to the Son of the Highest Father
and to our most munificent host
of such a name hitherto unknown—
may he live long!

222. *The Abbot of Cockaigne*

Ego sum abbas Cucaniensis
et consilium meum est cum bibulis
et in secta Decii voluntas mea est,
et qui mane me quesierit in taberna,
post vesperam nudus egredietur
et sic denudatus veste clamabit:
«wafna, wafna!
quid fecisti, sors turpissima!
nostre vite gaudia
abstulisti omnia.»

CCXXIII. *Verba Sapientium*

Res dare pro rebus,   pro verbis verba solemus.

Pro nudis verbis   montanis utimur herbis,
Pro caris rebus   pigmentis et speciebus.

CCXXIV. *Nolite Pauperes Contemnere*

Artifex, qui condidit   hominem ex luto
et linivit oculos   ceci sacro sputo,
salvet vestras animas   crimine soluto:
«pax vobis omnibus»   ego vos saluto.

O prelati nobiles,   viri litterati,
summi regis legati,
o presbiteri beati,
genus preelectum,
me omnibus abiectum
consolans despectum
virtutis vestre per effectum,
pauperie mea conteste
patet manifeste,
quod eo sine veste
satis inhoneste.
si me vultis audire:
contestor me scire
viros probitatis mire.

Qui virtutes faciunt,   nobiles appello,
qui autem me despiciunt,   avaros evello
de libro viventium,   ad inferos repello,

I am the abbot of Cockaigne
and my counselors are all boozers
and my love belongs to the Order of Decius,
and he, who seeks me in the tavern in the morn,
after the vespers, will leave there naked
and, thus divested of his clothes, will shout:
"To arms, to arms!
Most wicked Luck, what have you done!
All the joys of our life
you have robbed!"

223. *Words of the Wise*

For a gift we are wont to make a return, as we do words for words.

In lieu of sheer words we use mountainous herbs;
in lieu of valuable things, we collect pigments and spices.

224. *Detest Not the Poor*

May the Artist, Who created the human race from loam
and coated the eyes of the blind man with sacred sputum,
efface our sins and save our souls:
"Peace be with you all," is my greeting to you.[58]

O noble prelates, O lettered men,
legates of the highest king,
O blessed priests,
O chosen race
that consoled me,
dejected and repudiated by all,
through your practiced virtue:
it is so very ostensible—
my privation is a testament to that—
that for lack of clothing
I come in rather tattered and torn.
If you wish to lend me your ears:
I testify that I am acquainted
with men of wondrous integrity.

Who practice virtue, noble I call, but who
contemn me, I expurgate for their avarice
from the book of life and thrust back into hell,

ut ibi permaneant   Plutonis in cancello.

CCXXV. De sacerdotibus—*Tamen Alterum Carmen!*

Sacerdotes et levite,
quotquot estis, me audite!
vos debetis sine lite
verba mea intelligere.

Vos doctores consecrati
et virtutibus ornati,
non sint vobis hic cognati
nisi qui sint litterati
et honesti comprobati;
illis simus commendati.

Non sit vobis cor iratum
adversum me sic denudatum
et ab omnibus separatum.

Ergo mites domini,   caritatem diligatis
michi vero egenti   solamen impendatis,
ut particeps efficiar   vestre largitatis,
nam vos esse socios   scio Caritatis.

Non debet homo pius
causa schillink unius
verti, quod sit mentis alius
nisi ut fuit prius.

CCXXVI. De mundi statu

Mundus est in varium   sepe variatus
et a status ordine   sui degradatus:
ordo mundi penitus   est inordinatus,
mundus nomine tenus   stat, sed est prostratus.

Transierunt vetera,   perit mos antiquus;
inolevit nequior   mos et plus iniquus.
nemo meus, quilibet   suus est amicus;
non Saturnus regnat nunc,   immo Ludowicus.

Sperabamus, quod adhuc   quisquam remaneret,

so that they may remain there behind Pluto's bars.

225. On Priests—*Yet Another Song!*

O all ye deacons and priests,
hearken to me now!
You should take in my words
without dispute or quarrelsome remarks.

O ye teachers, who are consecrated
and with virtues adorned,
no one else should be your kin,
except those, who are learned
and morally beyond reproach.
We should be counted among these men.

Your hearts should not be hardened
in wrath against me, who am so
denuded and stripped of all means.

Therefore kind lords, make brotherly love
a matter of the heart and solace my truly needy self,
so that I may be blessed with your liberality,
for I know you are friends of Caritas.

No pious man should
for the sake of one shilling
be altered such that he is of another mind
and becomes different from what he was before.

226. On the State of the World

The world has changed often in various ways
and has been demoted from its olden rank:
the order of the world is completely disturbed;
it still stands in name, but has on its stomach been turned.

The vintage have passed; the old ways are no more;
a more vile and iniquitous consuetude has evolved.
No one is a friend; each loves only himself.
Saturn holds no sway now; nay, Ludwig wields it all.[59]

We once hoped that hitherto someone would remain,

mundum qui precipitem   dando sustineret,
pleno cornu copie   munera preberet,
nomen largi, sed et rem,   quod plus est, haberet.

Avem raram nondum hanc   potui videre,
est Pheinice rarior,   hircocervus vere.
hanc quesivi sepius;   felix, tu iam quere!
ei nomen interim   dabimus Chimere.

Mundus ergo labitur,   nullus hunc sustentat;
currit, cadit, corruit,   quis eum retentat?
largitatis semitas   nemo iam frequentat,
actus largi strenuos   nemo representat.

Unam tamen video   formam largitatis,
quam vos specialiter,   clerici, libatis;
hanc edicam nudius,   si vos sileatis,
si cum patientia   me sustineatis.

Dicet quis: «enuclea!   quid est hoc, quod ais?»
dicam: «larga munera   vestra sentit Thais,
Thais illa celebris   thermis, Cumis, Bais,
illa Troie pestilens   et damnosa Grais.
Hec dum nudo nudam se   propter hoc iniungit,
manu, lingua, labiis   palpat, lingit, ungit;
at Venus medullitus   scalpit, prurit, pungit:
Pamphilum dupliciter   sic Thais emungit.
Tamen est, qui Thaidem   ut cadaver odit,
ab hac ut a bestia   cavens se custodit;
sed dum Ganymedicum   pusionem fodit,
inguen ei loculos   pari dente rodit. »

Nullum hic est medium: quivis clericorum,
si non in Glycerium,   largus est in Sporum.
licet ambidextri sunt   multi modernorum,
*mor*i tamen prefero   ioc*is* geminorum.

Restat adhuc alterum   largitatis genus,
sed hoc totum ventris est,   nil hic capit Venus.

HIC FINIUNTUR CARMINA POTORIA.

who would bear up the world's plunge through magnanimous giving,
furnish gifts from a full horn of plenty, and have a reputation
for generosity and—more importantly—a record thereof.

Not yet have I been able to glimpse this rare bird:
it is rarer than the phoenix, truly a mythical wonder deer.[60]
So often have I sought it; O man of luck, seek it now!
Meanwhile we shall give it the name of Chimera.[61]

Thus the world is sinking, and no one is lifting it up;
it runs, falls, and shatters—who is holding it back?
No one any longer treads generosity's paths;
no one at all performs great feats of munificence.

Nevertheless one form of liberality I behold,
which you especially, O clerics, do pour out:
I shall describe it more unclad, if you remain silent
and if you with patience endure my words.

One then will say, "Explain! What is this of which you speak?"
I then shall respond, "Thais feels your copious flow of gifts,
that Thais who is known in bathhouses, Cumae, and Baiae,
that pestilence of Troy and juggernaut of the Greeks![62]
When she gives her nude body to a naked man, with this end in view,
she, with her hand, tongue, and lips, strokes, licks, and wets his nude form;
but Venus grates, tickles, and stings him to his very core;
thus Thais doubly cheats Pamphilus.[63]
Still there is one, who loathes Thais as one does a corpse,
who guards himself from her as one would against a beast;
but whilst he fornicates with a young Ganymede-like lad,
his lustfulness gnaws with the same teeth at his money bags."[64]

In this case there is no middle: every single cleric,
who is not generous to Glycerium, lavishes gifts on Sporus.[65]
Though there are many contemporaries who are ambidextrous in this way,
I still would rather die than abandon myself to both's drolleries.

Hitherto there remains yet another type of generosity,
but it wholly pertains to the paunch, and in it Venus has no hand.

HERE END THE DRINKING SONGS.

The
Major Plays

CCXXVII. *Natus Christi*

Primo ponatur sedes Augustino in fronte ecclesie, et Augustinus habeat a dextera parte Isaiam et Danielem et alios prophetas, a sinistra autem archisynagogum et suos Iudeos. Postea surgat Isaias cum prophetia sua sic:
Ecce virgo pariet   sine viri semine,
per quod mundum abluet   a peccati crimine.
de venturo gaudeat   . . . Iudea numine
et, nunc ceca, fugiat   ab erroris limine.

Postea:
Ecce virgo concipiet et pariet filium, et vocabitur nomen eius
Emmanuel.

Iterum cantet:
Dabit illi Dominus sedem David patris eius et regnabit in
eternum.

Postea Daniel procedat prophetiam suam exprimens:
O Iudea misera!   tua cadet unctio,
cum rex regum veniet   ab excelso solio,
cum retento floride   castitatis lilio
virgo regem pariet   felix puerperio.

Iudea misera,   sedens in tenebris,
repelle maculam   delicti funebris
et leta gaudio   partus tam celebris
erroris minime   cedas illecebris!

Postea cantet:
Aspiciebam in visu noctis <et ecce in nubibus celi filius hominis venit, et
datum est ei regnum et honor, et omnes populi, tribus et lingue servient ei.

Versus:
Ecce dominator Dominus cum virtute veniet>.

Tertio loco Sibylla gesticulose procedat, que inspiciendo stellam cum gestu mobili cantet:
Hec stelle novitas   fert novum nuntium,
quod virgo nesciens   viri commercium
et virgo permanens   post puerperium

227. The Birth of Christ

First in front of the church a seat for Saint Augustine should be set. On his right should be Isaiah and Daniel and other prophets, and on his left should be the head of the synagogue and his Jews. Afterwards Isaiah should rise and deliver his prophecy:
Behold, a virgin will give birth without the seed of man,
whereby she will cleanse the world of the crime of sin.
Judea should rejoice in the coming of God,
and, hitherto blind, it will the threshold of error shun.

Afterwards:
Behold the virgin will conceive and give birth to a Son,
and His name will be called Emmanuel.

Again he should sing:
The Lord shall give Him the throne of His father David,
and He will forever rule.

Afterwards Daniel should issue his prophecy, expressing:
O hapless Judea! Thy anointing will lose its significance,
when the King of kings comes from His heavenly throne,
when the virgin with the lily flower of chastity still intact
and beatified by such a birth, brings the King into the world.

O hapless Judea, sitting in darkness,
free thyself of the stain of your deadly sins,
rejoice in the joy of this so celebrated a birth
and do not cede to the allure of heretical belief!

Afterwards he should sing:
I beheld in a vision of the night: lo! in the clouds of the firmament
the Son of man came, and He received dominion and glory;
all the people, tribes, and tongues will serve Him.

Verse:
Behold, the ruling Lord with virtue will come.

Third in line, the Sibyl, gesticulating, should come forth and, looking into the stars, with animated gestures, sing:
The uncanny nature of this star brings new tidings,
that a virgin, knowing nothing of a union with a man
and remaining a virgin after the birth,

salutem populo   pariet filium.

E celo labitur   veste sub altera
nova progenies   matris ad ubera
beata faciens   illius viscera,
que nostra meruit   purgare scelera.

Intrare gremium   flos novus veniet,
cum virgo filium   intacta pariet,
qui hosti livido   minas excutiet
et nova secula   rex novus faciet.

E celo veniet   rex magni nominis
coniungens federa   Dei et hominis
et sugens ubera   matris et virginis,
reatum diluens   mundani criminis.

Item cantet hos versus:
Iudicii signum: tellus sudore madescet.
E celo rex adveniet per secla futurus,
Scilicet in carne presens, ut iudicet orbem.
Unde Deum cernent incredulus atque fidelis
Celsum cum sanctis evi iam termino in ipso.

**Deinde procedat Aaron, quartus propheta, portans virgam, que
sumpta super altare inter XII virgas aridas sola floruit. Illam
personam conducat chorus cum hoc responsorio:**
Salve nobilis virga Iesse; salve, flos campi, Maria, unde ortum est lilium
convallium.

Versus:
Odor tuus super cuncta pretiosa uguenta, favus distillans labia tua, mel et
lac sub lingua tua.

Et dicat hanc prophetiam:
Ecce novo more frondens dat amigdala nostra
Virgula: nux Christus, sed virgula virgo beata.

Et dicat:
Ut hec virga floruit   omni carens nutrimento,
sic et virgo pariet   sine carnis detrimento.
Ut hic ramus viruit   non Nature copia,
verum ut in virgine   figuret mysteria,

will beget a Son Who is the Savior of the world.

Dressed in different garb, a new Son
from the empyrean glides down to the mother's breasts
and blesses the body of the woman,
deemed worthy to absterge us of our crimes.

A new Flower is preparing to enter into her lap,
when the virgin, still intact, births a Son,
Who will cast out threats to the hateful enemy
and as the new King usher in a new age.

From the sky will come a King of mighty name
Who will forge a pact between God and man,
and, drinking from the breasts of the mother and virgin,
wash away the sins and guilt of the world.

And she should sing these lines:
A sign of justice: the earth grows moist with sweat.
From the sky the future King will arrive at our age,
presenting Himself incarnate, to judge the world.
Whence the incredulous and the faithful will know
God on high and the saints at the end of time.

**Aaron, the 4th prophet, should emerge with a staff that he took from
the altar and which alone amongst 12 dry staffs bloomed. The chorus
should lead out this actor with this responsorium:**
Health to you, noble staff of Jesse;[1] health to you, Mary,
flower of the field, whence came forth the Lily of the vales.

Verse:
Thy fragrance is more sublime than all precious salves, dripping
honeycomb is thy lips, and honey and milk lie under thy tongue.

Then this prophecy should he pronounce:
Lo! In a new way our leafy almond tree is putting forth its sprays!
The fruit is Christ, but the blessed virgin is the bough.

And he should say:
Just as this spray has flowered without nutriment of any kind,
thus the virgin will give birth without damage to her flesh.
Though this bough has grown verdant not from nature's effect,
but to give form to the mysteries within the virgin,

clausa erunt virginis   sic pudoris ostia,
quando virgo pariet   spiritali gratia.

Quinto loco procedat Balaam sedens in asina et cantans:
Vadam, vadam, ut maledicam populo huic.

Cui occurrat angelus evaginato gladio dicens:
Cave, cave, ne quicquam aliud quam tibi dixero loquaris!

Et asinus, cui insidet Balaam, perterritus retrocedat. Postea recedat angelus, et Balaam cantet hoc responsorium:
Orietur stella ex Iacob, et consurget homo de Israel et confringet omnes duces alienigenarum, et erit omnis terra possessio eius.

Versus:
Et adorabunt eum omnes reges, omnes gentes servient ei. Et erit.

Archisynagogus cum suis Iudeis valde obstrepet auditis prophetiis et dicat trudendo socium suum, movendo caput suum et totum corpus et percutiendo terram pede, baculo etiam imitando gestus Iudei in omnibus, et sociis suis indignando dicat:
Dic michi, quid predicat   dealbatus paries!
dic michi, quid asserat   veritatis caries!
dic michi, quid fuerit,   quod audivi pluries!
vellem esset cognita   rerum michi series.
Illos, reor, audio   in hec verba fluere,
quod sine commercio   virgo debet parere.
o quanta simplicitas   cogit hos desipere,
qui de bove predicant   camelum descendere!

Auditis tumultu et errore Iudeorum, dicat episcopus puerorum:
Horum sermo vacuus   sensus peregrini,
quos et furor agitat   et libertas vini.
sed restat consulere   mentem Augustini,
per quem disputatio   concedatur fini.

Statim prophete vadant ante Augustinum et dicant:
Multum nobis obviat   lingua Iudeorum,
quibus adhuc adiacet   vetus fex errorum.
cum de Christo loquimur,   rident et suorum
argumenta proferunt   nobis animorum.

thus the virgin's gates of modesty will be shut,
when she delivers the Child by the power of the Holy Ghost.

Fifth, Balaam[2] should advance, sitting on an ass, and sing:
I shall go, I shall proceed, to curse the people in this ring.

An angel should rush at him with sword unsheathed and say:
Beware, beware of uttering aught other than what I have said!

And the ass Balaam is riding should retreat in terror. Then the angel should depart and Balaam should sing this responsorium:
A Star shall spring from Jacob's house, and a Man from Israel shall rise
and dash all the foreign rulers and all the world will be His.

Verse:
All kings will adore Him; all nations will serve Him. It shall be.

The synagogue leader, with his Jews, should vehemently cry out against the prophecies they have heard, shove his associate, move his head and entire body, and strike the earth with his foot and mimic in every way the gestures of a Jew with his staff, and, displeased at his associates, say:
Tell me what this whitewashed wall foretells!
Tell me what the decay of truth affirms!
Tell me what it was that oftentimes I heard!
Would that I knew the succession of things!
So much do I hear flowing into these words: that a virgin,
without having lain with a man, should give birth.
O what great naivety besots these men,
who predict that a camel from a cow will descend!

After the Jews have voiced their protest and heresy, the Boy Bishop[3] should say:
Meaningless and devoid of sense are the words of these men,
whom madness agitates and the disinhibiting wonder of wine,
but it remains for us to consult Augustine's judgment,
through whom this discussion may be brought to an end.

Quickly the prophets should go before Augustine and say:
In great opposition to us is the vicious tongue of the Jews,
to whom the dregs of old heresies still adhere.
When we speak of Christ, they laugh and present
to us the arguments of their base of beliefs.

Respondet Augustinus:
Ad nos illa prodeat   tenebris abscondita
et se nobis offerat   gens errori dedita,
ut et error claudicet   re ipsis exposita,
et scripture pateat   ipsis clausa semita.

Veniat archisynagogus cum magno murmure sui et suorum, quibus dicat Augustinus:
Nunc aures aperi,   Iudea misera!
rex regum veniet   veste sub altera,
qui matris virginis   dum sugit ubera,
Dei et hominis   coniunget federa.

Respondet archisynagogus cum nimio cachinno:
O Augustine,
de profundo maxime   portans hec ingenio
dum futurum predicas   id, quod negat ratio!
nam si virgo pariet,   et sine commercio,
id Nature rubor est   et rerum confusio.

Tu quid contra resonas   labe tactus veteri,
qui non illud respicis,   quod est iustum fieri?
nam si virgo pariet,   quod prophetant pueri,
Natura de proprio   iure potest conqueri.

Quando virgo pariet,   Xanthe, retro propera!
lupus agnum fugiet,   plana fient aspera.
si moderna colligis   et attendis vetera,
in adiecto ponitur   «est virgo puerpera.»

Vel si virgo pariet   vel iam forte peperit,
que non carnis copulam   ante partum senserit,
ut propheta garrulus   incessanter asserit, –
quod phantasma fuerit,   lex docet et aperit.

Quod de clausa virgine   sic procedat parvulus,
est erroris credere,   non doctrine cumulus.
vel ergo respondeat   ad obiectum emulus,
vel erroris fugiat   et ruboris baiulus!

Voce sobria et discreta respondeat Augustinus:
In eventu prospero   talis casus unici
argumenta claudicant   moresque sophistici.

Augustine should respond:
Let the benighted people, disposed to folly, step forth
before us from the darkness and offer themselves to us,
so that, by the exposition of the error, it may grow lame
and the closed path of scripture may open itself unto them.

**The leader of the synagogue should come, roaring with his people,
to whom Augustine should say:**
Now open your ears, hapless Judea!
The King of kings will come in different dress;
when He drinks from the virgin mother's breasts,
He will forge a pact between God and man!

The leader of the synagogue should derisively respond:
O Augustine,
from the profoundest depths of your insight do
you proclaim these prophecies that reason denies!
For if a virgin give birth, without commerce with a man,
Nature blushes and chaos ensues.

Why do you, infected with the old plague, object to
and disregard what must forsooth have happened?
For if a virgin give birth, as these boys do foretell,
Nature can bewail an intrusion upon its rights.

When a virgin gives birth, then, Xanthus, thy current reverse![4]
The wolf will flee the lamb; things rough will become smooth.
If you gather things contemporary and attend to relics of old,
then a contradictio in adjecto[5] is set: "A virgin bears a child."

If a virgin give birth or by chance already has, a virgin,
who has not experienced the union of flesh before her throes,
as this garrulous prophet continuously asserts, then the law[6]
teaches and reveals that it will be but a fiendish ghost.

To believe that a child should thus spring from a virgin
of unbroken womb is folly's pinnacle, not wisdom's peak.
Either let my opponent expostulate with me
or let him, the bearer of folly and shame, flee!

Augustine with a sober, deliberate tone should respond:
In this prosperous event of such a singular case,
arguments and sophisticated methods of analysis fail.

docet enim ratio   Naturam non reici,
si quid preter solitum   semel vides obici.

Dicas: «‹homo mortuus›   in adiecto ponitur,
quod in Aristotile   pueris exprimitur»;
sed hec vestra regula   tunc repulsam patitur,
cum de matre virgine   sermo nobis oritur.

Augustinus dicat:
Ne phantasma dixeris,   quod virgo concipiet,
quod pudoris ostio   non aperto pariet, –
de Iudea multiplex   testis nobis veniet,
qui vobis contrarius   et nobiscum faciet.

Ut specular solidum   solis intrat radius
et sincere transitus   servit ei pervius,
sic in aulam virginis   summi patris filius
lapsum quidem faciet,   et tamen innoxius.

Postea incipiat Augustinus cantare:
Letabundus <exultet fidelis chorus, Alleluia!>.

Primum versum, et secundum prophete:
Regem regum intacte profudit thorus,
res miranda!

Dicat archisynagogus cum suis:
Res neganda!

Iterum Augustinus cum suis:
Res miranda!

Iterum archisynagogus cum suis:
Res neganda!

Hoc fiat pluries.
Augustinus incipiat:
Angelus consilii
natus est de virgine,
sol de stella.

Respondeant prophete:
Sol occasum nesciens,

For reason teaches us that Nature is not rejected,
if but once you see something that transcends custom.

You may say, "'A dead man' is a contradiction in adjecto,
which is expressed to youths in Aristotle."[7]
But this your rule then suffers repulse,
when talk of the virgin mother from us doth rise.

Augustine should say:
Call it not a devil's spook that a virgin will conceive,
that she will give birth, without having opened the gate of her shame—
to us a myriad of witnesses from Judea will come,
who will testify against you and with us.

As the sun's beam enters a solid pane of glass
and the unhindered passage devoutly open to it stands,
so the Son of the Highest Father will assuredly glide
into the palace of the virgin and yet harmlessly.

Afterwards Augustine should begin to sing:
Let the chorus of the faithful leap up in joy. Hallelujah!

First a refrain; second, the prophets:
The bridechamber of the intact virgin has birthed the King of kings!
What a wondrous affair!

The leader of the synagogue with his followers should say:
An impossible affair!

Again Augustine with his supporters should say:
A wondrous affair!

The leader of the synagogue with his followers:
An impossible affair!

This exchange should happen several times.
Augustine should begin:
An Angel of wisdom,
of a virgin born,
a Sun sprung forth from a star.

The prophets should respond:
A Sun that knows no decline,

stella semper rutilans,
semper clara.

Dicat Augustinus:
Cedrus alta Libani
conformetur ysopo
valle nostra.

Dicant prophete:
Verbum ens altissimi
corporali passum est
carne sumpta.

Postea dicat Augustinus:
Isaias cecinit,
Synagoga meminit;
nunquam tamen desinit
esse ceca.

Respondeant prophete:
Si non suis vatibus,
credat vel gentilibus,
Sibyllinis versibus
hec predicta.

Postea dicat Augustinus cum prophetis omnibus:
Infelix, propera,
crede vel vetera!
cur damnaberis,   gens misera?
Natum considera,
quem docet littera:
ipsum genuit   puerpera.

Postea Augustinus solus cantet:
Discant nunc Iudei, quomodo de Christo consentientes nobiscum
amplexari debent novi partus novum gaudium, nove spem salutis ipsum
expectantium. Nunc venturum credant et nasciturum expectent nobiscum
dicentes: Rex novus erit salus mundo.

**Inter cantandum omnia ista archisynagogus obstrepet movendo
corpus et caput et deridendo predicta. Hoc completo detur locus
prophetis, vel ut recedant vel sedeant in locis suis propter honorem**

a Star that always redly shines,
a Star that is forever bright.

Augustine should say:
Let the lofty cedar of Lebanon
fashion itself after the hyssop[8]
in our vale.

The prophets should say:
The word, being of the highest,
submitted to bodily pain,
after it took up flesh.

Afterwards Augustine should say:
Isaiah sang the prophecy—
the synagogue remembers it,
but still never ceases
to persevere in its blindness.

The prophets should respond:
If it trust not its own prophets,
it should at least trust
these heathen prophecies
in the Sibylline verses.

Afterwards Augustine with all the prophets should say:
O unhappy race, hasten,
trust at least in the prophecies of eld!
Why do you desire to damn yourselves, wretched clan?
Give the Son your regard,
Whom scripture doth pronounce:
the mother has given birth to Him.

Afterwards Augustine alone should sing:
The Jews should now learn how they, in accord with us concerning Christ,
must embrace this new joy over this miraculous birth, the Hope of a new
salvation for all who are awaiting Him. Now they should believe in His
coming and await His incipient birth and say with us:
the new King will be the salvation to our world.

**Between these prophecies and songs, the synagogue leader will clamor
against it, shake his body and head, and deride the predictions.
Afterwards, the prophets should either withdraw or take their seats,**

ludi.

Deinde angelus appareat Marie operanti muliebriter et dicat:
Ave Maria, gratia plena, Dominus tecum.

Et iterum:
Ecce concipies et paries filium et vocabis nomen eius Iesum.

Illa stupefacta dicat:
Quomodo fiet istud, quia virum non cognosco?

Respondet angelus:
Spiritus sanctus superveniet in te et virtus altissimi obumbrabit
tibi.

Versus:
Ideoque quod nascetur ex te sanctum vocabitur filius Dei.

Respondet Maria:
Ecce ancilla Domini: fiat michi secundum verbum tuum.

**Deinde Maria vadat casualiter nichil cogitans de Elisabeth vetula
Iohanne impregnata et salutet eam et Elisabeth dicat:**
Unde hoc michi, <ut veniat mater Domini mei ad me?>

Et cantabit:
Ex quo facta est vox salutat<ionis tue in auribus meis, exultavit in gaudio
infans in utero meo, alleluia.>

Eadem dicat:
Benedicta tu in mulieribus <et benedictus fructus ventris tui.> Tu que
portabis p<acem> h<ominibus> et an<...> gen<...>.

Respondet Maria:
Magnificat anima mea Dominum.

**Deinde recedat Elisabeth, quia amplius non habebit locum hec
persona. Deinde Maria vadat in lectum suum, que iam de Spiritu
sancto concepit, et pariat filium. Cui assideat Ioseph in habitu honesto
et prolixa barba. Nato puero appareat stella, et incipiat chorus hanc**

so as not to thwart the play.

Then an angel should appear to Mary, as she occupies herself in womanly handiwork, and say:
Hail, Mary, full of grace, the Lord is with thee!

And again:
Lo! Thou wilt conceive and birth a Son and call Him Jesus.

Stupefied, she should say:
How will that be, for I am acquainted with no man?

The angel responds:
The Holy Spirit will come upon thee and virtue of the highest will shade thee.

Verse:
And so a Holy Being born of thee will be called the Son of God.

Mary responds:
Behold the handmaiden of the Lord! May it befall me according to your word.

Then Mary should casually depart and, not knowing that old Elizabeth was pregnant with John,[9] should greet her and Elizabeth should say:
How have I merited a visitation from the mother of my Lord?

And she should sing:
As soon as the voice of your salutation resounded in my ears,
with joy sprang the infant in my womb. Hallelujah!

She then should say:
Blessed are you among women, and blessed is the fruit of your womb.
You will bring peace to men and honor to the angels.[10]

Mary responds:
My soul praises the Lord.

Then Elizabeth should depart, for she has no other part. Then Mary, who has already conceived through the Holy Spirit, should go to her bed and birth her Son. Beside her should sit Joseph in noble dress and with a long beard. When the Boy is born, a star should appear, and

antiphonam:

Hodie Christus natus est, <hodie salvator apparuit; hodie in terra canunt
angeli, letantur archangeli; hodie exultent iusti dicentes: Gloria in excelsis
Deo, alleluia>.

**Qua finita stella appareat. Qua visa tres reges a diversis partibus
mundi veniant et ammirentur de apparitione talis stelle. Quorum
primus dicat:**

Per curarum distrahor   frequenter quadruvium
rationis patiens   et mentis naufragium,
cum hanc stellam video   portantem indicium,
quod ipsius novitas   novum portet nuntium.

Cursus ego didici   et naturas siderum
et ipsorum memini   perscrutari numerum.
sed cum hanc inspicio,   ego miror iterum,
quia non comparuit   apud quemquam veterum.

Quando Luna patitur,   et Sol quando deeris,
quem effectum habeat   Stilbon comes Veneris,
in quo gradu maxime   Mars nocivus diceris,
michi fecit cognitum   lingua secte veteris.

Sed elinguem efficit   hic me stelle radius.
quid portendat, nescio,   sed querens attentius
hoc unum conicio,   quod est natus filius,
cui mundus obediet,   quem timebit amplius.

**Hoc dicat primus semper inspiciendo stellam et disputet de illa. Dicat
secundus:**

Mea iam precordia   dulce vestit gaudium;
michi vie factum est   non parvum compendium:
in eo, quod ambigo,   se monstrantem dubium
et cure participem   iam inveni socium.

Quando mente vigili   planetas inspicio,
mea vim cuiuslibet   deprehendit ratio,
de Marte, de Venere,   de Sole, Mercurio,
de Iovis clementia,   de Saturni senio.

Sed in hac, quam aspicis   et quam monstras digito,
qualitate cognita   de effectu dubito.
sed quid inde sentiam,   tu mecum accipito,

the chorus should sing this antiphon:
Today Christ is born; today the Savior appeared. Today the angels sing
on earth, and the archangels rejoice. Today the just should exult and say:
Glory to God in the highest. Hallelujah.

**Afterwards a star should appear. Three kings see it and from different
parts of the world should come and marvel at the appearance of such a
star. The first should say:**
Often am I dragged through the crossroads of despair,
suffering a shipwreck of my reason and soul,
when I see this star carrying an indication
that novel as itself are the tidings it carries forth.

I have studied the courses and natures of stars,
and their numbers I know I have explored,
but when I look upon this star, I marvel anew,
for it has no reference in any of authors of eld.

When the moon is eclipsed and the sun's light fails,
which effect, Stilbon, the companion of Venus, holds,
at which elevation, you, Mars, are said to be most injurious,
which the teachers of the old school to me made known.

But the radiance of this star makes me speechless.
What it portends I do not know, but through careful examination
this one thing I infer: that a Child has been born,
Whom the world shall obey and for all time awe.

**The first should say this, always looking up at the star, and should
dispute over it. The second should say:**
Sweet joy now clothes my heart;
a considerable shortcut has been forged for my path:
I have found a companion who exhibits uncertainty in that,
which remains unclear to me, and who my questions shares.

When I gaze at the planets with watchful mind,
my reason perceives the power of each one:
of Mars, of Venus, of the Sun and Mercury,
the clemency of Jupiter, and Saturn's old age.

But in this, which you behold and with your finger indicate,
I, though recognizing its nature, waver in mind over its effect.
But what I sense from it, you should experience with me,

ut fruamur pariter   quesiti proposito.

Id iubar, quod inspicis,   quod in tantum radiat
et planetas ceteros   in pallorem variat,
regem natum predicat,   quo maior non veniat,
cuius cedens nutui   totus orbis serviat.

Dicat tertius monstrando et disputando de stella:
Questionum noverat   enodare rete
ille, per quem habeo,   quod, quando comete
se producit radius,   tunc hebent planete
et quorundam principum   se presentant mete.

Quid sit stella, novimus,   et quid sit planeta;
horum hec est neutrum,   sed cum sit cometa,
inungamur gaudio,   sit mens nobis leta,
magni enim principis   verus est propheta.

Vide, stelle claritas   quanta propagatur,
in planeta quolibet   splendor hebetatur!
quod ei, qui natus est,   satis adaptatur;
cuiusvis potentia   per hunc obscuratur.

Ergo cum muneribus   una procedamus,
et quo stella duxerit,   gressus dirigamus,
ut, quando viderimus,   quem natum speramus,
nostra ei munia   reges offeramus!

Modo procedant reges usque in terram Herodis querendo de puero et cantando:
Ubi est, qui natus est <rex Iudeorum? Vidimus enim stellam eius in
oriente, et venimus adorare eum>.

Quibus occurrant nuntii Herodis dicentes:
Vos, qui regum habitus   et insigne geritis,
nobis notum facite,   quare sic inceditis,
vel si mirum aliquid   reserandum noscitis,
quod ad aures . . .   regis ferre queritis.

Nos Herodis vernule   sumus et vicarii,
ad quem sepe transvolant   ex diversis nuntii.
nulla nobis clausa sunt   secreta palatii;
ergo scire poscimus   vestri rem negotii.

so we together may delight in the question that has been posed.

That splendor you behold that emits beams over distances great
and causes the other planets to turn pale proclaims
the birth of a King, mightier than Whom none will come,
yielding to Whose nod, the whole world shall serve.

The third should speak, pointing at and disputing the star:
The whole web of questions that man knew how to untie,
he, from whom I learned that when the ray of the comet
draws itself out, the planets then will grow sluggish
and the end of certain princes will present itself.

We know what a fixed star is and what a planet is.
This is neither of these things, but since it's a comet,
let us join in joy, let our hearts be happy,
for it is the true prophet of a Mighty Prince!

See how greatly the radiance of the star is increased,
whilst the brilliance of each planet is diminished!
It is perfectly fitted to the Being, Who was born!
Through Him every human power is in shadows placed!

Therefore let us proceed together with gifts,
and let us direct our steps whither the star has led,
so that, when we have seen Who we hope has been born,
we kings may offer our gifts unto the Lord!

**Now the kings should proceed into the land of Herod, asking about
the child and singing:**
Where is He Who was born the King of Jews?
For we have seen His star in the east and have come to adore Him.

Messengers of Herod should accost them, saying:
Ye, who wear the habits and insignia of kings,
make known to us, why you thus advance,
or, if you know of some marvel that should be revealed,
speak what you seek to bring to the ears of our king.

We are servants of Herod and are his delegates;
to him messengers from various parts often wend.
No secrets of the palace are closed to us; therefore
we demand information about the nature of your enterprise.

Respondent reges:
Sepelire nolumus,   quod a nobis queritur;
ipsum stella reserat,   que a nobis cernitur.
regem natum querimus,   de quo stella loquitur,
quod eius imperium   nullo fine clauditur.

Respondent nuntii:
Felix istud veniet   Herodi preconium,
et libenter audiet   hoc de rege nuntium.
ut hinc ergo primitus   per nos sumat gaudium,
vos nostrum sequimini   . . . vestigium.

Postea nuntii festinent ad Herodem dicentes:
Rex Herodes, accipe   quiddam ammirandum
iam a tribus regibus   tibi reserandum:
ipsi natum asserunt   regem venerandum,
cui esse non ambigunt   orbem subiugandum.

Respondet Herodes cum magna indignatione:
Cur audetis talia   regi presentare?
nolite vos, consulo,   falsum fabricare!
nam Herodes ego sum   potens subiugare,
quicquid mundus continet,   celum, terram, mare.

**Post hec Herodes maxime indignatus vocari faciat archisynagogum
cum Iudeis suis dicens:**
Huc Iudea veniat   fecunda consilio,
ut nobiscum disserat   super hoc negotio.
ego vos precipiam   exponi supplicio,
si vos esse devios   comprobabit ratio.

**Modo veniat archisynagogus cum magna superbia et Iudeis suis, cui
dicat Herodes:**
Te, magister, alloquor,   et advertant alii!
nostra mordet viscera   duri fama nuntii.
huc tres magi veniunt   non astrorum inscii,
qui ad ortum properant   prepotentis filii.

Respondet archisynagogus cum magna sapientia et eloquentia:
Ne curarum, domine,   verseris in bivio!
tres huc reges veniant   querendo de filio,
quibus te concilies   diligenti studio,
et sic eis loquere   sub amoris pillio:

The kings should respond:
We do not wish to conceal what it is we seek;
the star that we discerned reveals our design.
We seek the newly-born King, Whose dominion
extends without end, as the star in the welkin doth declare.

The messengers should respond:
These tidings will be welcome to Herod,
and he will fain hearken to this news about a king.
So that we may be the first through whom
he takes up joy, in our footsteps follow us.

Afterwards the messengers should hie to Herod, saying:
King Herod, receive a wonderful secret
to be revealed now by three kings to you.
These men aver that a venerable King has been born
to Whom they have no doubt the whole world will bow.

Herod should respond with great indignation:
Why do you dare to present such news to a king?
Do not, I advise, fabricate mendacities!
For I am Herod, with the power to subjugate
anything the world contains: sky, land, and sea.

**After this, Herod, most indignant, should cause the synagogue leader
to be summoned with his Jews, saying:**
Come hither, Judea, fruitful in counsel,
to discuss this affair with us. But I shall order
your punishment, if examination confirms
that you are deviating from the truth!

**Now the synagogue leader should come with great arrogance
and his Jews, and Herod should say to him:**
I turn to you, master, and the others should take heed!
Unfortunate tidings harrow my soul!
Three wise men come hither, authorities on stars,
who hasten to the birth of an Omnipotent Son.

The synagogue leader with great wisdom and rhetoric rejoins:
Do not whirl yourself in the crossroads of solicitude!
Three kings should come here, asking about the child;
you will dispose them to yourself with great zeal,
and speak to them thus under the pretense of love:

«Reges estis, video,   quod prophetat habitus.
vester michi gratus est   factus ad nos transitus.
sed quid vos huc traxerit,   reserate penitus;
nam vobis ad omnia   rex erit expositus.»

Respondent reges:
Stella nova radiat   eius ortus nuntia,
cui mundus obediet,   et qui reget omnia,
et nil stare poterit   absque huius gratia.
nos ad illum tendimus   hec ferentes munia.

Herodes respondet:
Ne sim vos impediens   ad vie propositum,
ite, ad nos postea   maturantes reditum,
ut et ego veniens   munus feram debitum
ei, cui non ambigo   mundum fore subditum!

Ab Herode discedant tres magi paulatim, inspicientes stellam et disputantes de illa. Interim angelus appareat pastoribus et dicat:
Magnum vobis gaudium,   pastores, annuntio:
Deus se circumdedit   carnis vestre pallio,
quem mater non peperit   carnali commercio,
imnio virgo permanens   mater est ex filio.

Pastoribus euntibus dicat diabolus:
Tu ne credas talibus,   pastorum simplicitas!
scias esse frivola,   que non probat veritas.
quod sic in presepio   sit sepulta Deitas,
nimis est ad oculum   reserata falsitas.

Iterum pastoribus ad negotium suum redeuntibus dicat angelus:
Pastores, querite   natum presepio
et votum solvite   matri cum filio!
nec mora veniat   isti consilio,
sed vos huc dirigat   mentis devotio.

Iterum pastoribus abeuntibus dicat diabolus ad aures eorum:
Simplex cetus, aspice,   qualis astutia
eius, qui sic fabricat   vero contraria;
utque sua phaleret   nugis mendacia,
in rhythmis conciliat,   que profert, omnia.

"Kings you are, I see, as your clothing indicates.
To me it is a pleasure that your journey has brought you to us.
But as to what has brought you here, reveal the true reason:
for the king in all things will show himself propitious unto you.

The kings should respond:
A new star radiates as the harbinger of His birth,
Whom all the world will obey, and Who will rule over all,
and nothing without His favor will be able to perdure,
and we, bearing these gifts, are travelling to Him.

Herod should respond:
I will not impede you on the journey you've proposed,
so go, and afterwards hasten your return to us,
so that I, too, may come and bring to Him the gift I owe,
to Whom I have no doubt the whole world will bow.

The three wise men should depart from Herod for a spell, looking at the star and debating about it. Meanwhile an angel should appear to some shepherds and say:
Great joy do I announce to you, O shepherds of the flock.
God in a cloak of flesh has enveloped Himself;
the mother did not birth Him through the union of the flesh,
but remains a virgin through the power of her Son.

The devil should speak to the shepherds on their way:
Do not believe in such nonsense, O foolish-minded shepherds!
You should know that what truth demonstrates not is frivolous.
That a divinity has thus been laid in a crib
is a falsehood laid wide open before your eyes.

The angel again should speak to the shepherds, as they return to their business:
Ye shepherds, seek out the Child in the manger
and present your felicitations to the mother and her Son!
Let no delay infiltrate your resolve,
but let the devoutness of your heart guide you thither.

As they continue, the devil should whisper in their ears:
O foolish company, behold the nature of his cunning,
who thus fashions things that the truth contravene;
see how his mendacity adorns nonsense with trappings
and he sets in harmonic verses everything he affirms.

Mirentur pastores, et unus dicat ad alterum:
Numquid, frater, colligis   ea, que audio?
quedam vox insinuat   de nato filio;
verum in contrarium   ab hoc suscipio,
quod audita resident   iuncta mendacio.

Dicat iterum angelus ad pastores:
Cur non aures vertitis   ad hunc veri nuntium?
quis est iste subdolus   vertens vos in devium?
ne vos error induat   propter adversarium,
ite, nam quod predico,   monstrabit presepium!

Dicat iterum euntibus diabolus:
O gens simplex nimium   et sensu vulnerata!
fer fenum et pabulum,   que bubus non ingrata
in presepi comedat   Deitas reclinata!
debaccharis nimium,   cum putas ista rata.

Iterum pastores ad socios suos:
Audi, frater, iterum,   qualis repugnantia!
inde quedam audio,   hinc quedam contraria.
meus simplex animus,   mea mens non sobria
ignorat, que potior   sit horum sententia.

Postea simul conveniant angeli et simul cantent:
Gloria in excelsis Deo, et in terra pax hominibus bone voluntatis.
Alleluia, alleluia!

Qua voce audita dicat pastor ad socios suos:
Ad hanc vocem animi   produco suspirium,
ex hac intus habeo   citharizans gaudium.
procedamus igitur   simul ad presepium
et curvatis genibus   adoremus filium!

Deinde procedant pastores ad presepe cantando hanc antiphonam:
Facta est cum angelo multitudo celestis <exercitus laudantium et
dicentium: Gloria in excelsis Deo, et in terra pax hominibus bone
voluntatis, alleluia.>

**Quo cantato adorent puerum. Deinde revertantur pastores ad officia
sua. Quibus occurrant tres magi dicentes:**
Pastores, dicite, quidnam vidistis, et annuntiate Christi nativitatem!

The shepherds should marvel and say to one another:
Do you gather, brother, what I am hearing?
A certain voice is telling us of a Son, Who was born,
but I am hearing the opposite,
that what we heard rests on a lie.

Again the angel should say to the shepherds:
Why do you not open your ears to this courier of truth?
Who is that chicaner who is leading you off the road?
Let no error befall you on the adversary's account;
go, for as I do declare, the manger will be shown!

The devil again should say to them on their way:
O thou simple-minded clan, wounded in sense! Bring hay
and fodder, not unwelcome to oxen, so that the Divinity may eat
whilst lying in His crib! Like maenads you rave,
when you think such things are ratified by truth!

Again the pastors should say amongst themselves:
Listen again, brother, to such contradictions!
Thence I hear one thing, hence its opposite!
My simple spirit and bemused mind see not clearly
which of these statements is the better to adopt!

Afterwards angels simultaneously should convene and sing:
Glory in the highest to God, and peace on earth to men of goodwill.
Hallelujah! Hallelujah!

Having heard this, one shepherd says to his confederates:
At the sound of this voice I heave a sigh,
and from it I feel deep within a jubilating joy.
Let us therefore proceed together to the crib
and on bent knees let us adore the Son!

Then the shepherds should proceed to the crib, singing this antiphon:
There entered with the angel a great heavenly throng
singing in praise: glory in the highest to God
and peace on earth to men of goodwill. Hallelujah!

Then they should laud the child and return to their business.
The three magi should run into them on the way and say:
Shepherds, speak of what you have seen and proclaim the nativity
of the Christ!

Respondeant pastores:
Infantem vidimus pannis involutum et choros angelorum laudantes
salvatorem.

**Postea reges vadant ad presepe, et primo adorent puerum et postea
offerant ei munera sua, primo aurum, postea thus, tertio myrrham.
Deinde modicum procedant et tunc dormiant; et angelus appareat eis
in somnis dicens:**
Nolite redire ad Herodem <...>

Postea non revertentibus ad Herodem sic dicat:
Gens Iudea properet,   ut Herodem audiat,
et prestet consilium   de re, que me sauciat.
rex Herodes anxius   ignorat, quid faciat,
cum a tribus regibus   se lusum inspiciat.

Venit archisynagogus cum suis, cui dicat Herodes:
Tu, magister, aperi   prophetarum edita,
si qua sunt de puero   a prophetis tradita!
nam a te fideliter   re michi exposita
se monstrabunt proprii   cordis . . . abscondita.

Respondet archisynagogus:
Tu Bethlehem, terra Iuda, <non eris minima; ex te enim exiet dux, qui
regat populum meum Israel>.

Deinde Herodes iratus dicat ad milites suos:
Ite, ite pariter   manu iuncta gladio,
etas adhuc tenera   nulli parcat filio!
immo mater quelibet   nudo fleat gremio,
ut de nato puero   michi detur ultio!

**Vadant milites et interficiant pueros, quorum matres sic lugeant et
lamententur:**
Heu, heu heu!
Mens Herodis effera
cur in nostra viscera
bella movet aspera?

Heu, heu, heu!
† Que . . . etas tenera
adhuc sugens ubera

The shepherds should respond:
We have seen an Infant wrapped in swaddling-clothes
and choruses of angels exalting the Savior!

**Afterwards the kings should approach the crib, first praise
the Child, and afterwards offer Him their gifts: first gold, then
frankincense, then myrrh. Thence they should walk a small distance
and then sleep. An angel should appear in their dreams and say:**
Do not return to Herod, for he strives after the Child's blood.

Seeing that they are not returning, Herod should say:
The race of Judea should hasten to hearken to Herod's words,
and should offer counsel in this affair, which me deeply wounds.
 King Herod is anxious and knows not what he should do,
since he sees himself by three kings mocked and ridiculed.

**The synagogue leader should come with his men, and Herod should
say to him:**
You, master, open the scriptures of the prophets,
and see if the seers transmitted anything about the boy!
For when you have faithfully explained this event to me,
my heart's cloistered intentions shall evince themselves!

The synagogue leader should respond:
You Bethlehem, land of Judah, will not be the least:
for out of you a Leader will arise, Who will lead My people Israel.[11]

Then a incensed Herod should address his soldiers:
Go, go together with hand joined to sword,
His tender age hitherto must not spare the Boy!
Rather every mother should beweep her empty lap, so that
vengeance may be permitted me through the newborn son!

**The soldiers should depart and kill the boys, whose mothers should
grieve and weep:**
Alas, alas, alas!
Why does Herod's bestial mind
lead against our offspring
so cruel an attack?

Woe, woe, woe!
What crimes has this tender age,
drinking from our breasts,

perpetravit scelera?

Heu, heu, heu!
Iste dolor anxius,
dum transegit impius
innocentes gladius!

Heu, heu! heu!
Proles adhuc tenera,
per te mater misera
descendet ad infera!

Heu, heu, heu!
Michi vite gaudium,
fili, nunc supplicium,
mortis eris ostium!

**Postea Herodes corrodatur a vermibus et excedens de sede sua
mortuus accipiatur a diabolis multum congaudentibus. Et Herodis
corona imponatur Archelao filio suo. Quo regnante appareat in nocte
angelus Ioseph dicens:**
Accipe matrem et filium et vade in Egyptum.

Precedens Maria asinum dicat:
Omnia dura pati   vitando pericula nati
Mater sum presto;   iam vadam, tu comes esto!

CCXXVIII. *Antichristus Babylonis*

**Rex Egypti cum comitatu suo in locum suum producatur cum
conductu:**
Estivali gaudio
<tellus renovatur,
militandi studio
Venus excitatur.
gaudet chorus iuvenum,
dum turba frequens avium
garritu modulatur.

Refl.   Quanta sunt gaudia
         amanti et amato,
         sine fellis macula
         dilecte sociato!

perpetrated as yet?

Alas, alas, alas!
This strangling grief,
when the ruthless sword
pierces innocent pates!

Woe, woe, woe!
Tender offspring until now,
through you your hapless mother
will descend into the netherworld!

Alas, alas, alas!
Joy of life to me, son,
now a punishment,
you will be my gateway to death!

Afterwards Herod should be consumed by worms and, departing his throne, be taken by rejoicing devils. Herod's crown should be placed on Archelaus his son. In his reign, an angel should appear to Joseph in the night and say:
Take the wife and Child and go to Egypt.

Mary leading an ass should say:
To endure all trials, to avoid danger to my Son, I am ready as a mother;
I am already en route; You shall my companion be!

228. *The Antichrist of Babylon*

The King of Egypt with his retinue should be lead to his place with this song:
In estival joy
the earth renews itself;
by the zeal of service to love
is Venus aroused.
A chorus of young lads takes delight,
whilst a populous throng of avians
twitters and chirps.

Refr.   How great are the joys,
when one loves and is loved,
when without the stain of gall
a lad is joined to a beloved girl!

iam revernant omnia
nobis delectabilia,
hiems eradicatur.

Ornantur prata floribus
varii coloris,
quorum delectatio
causa fit amoris.
gaudet chorus iuvenum,
dum turba frequens avium
garritu modulatur.

Refl.   Quanta sunt gaudia
amanti et amato,
sine fellis macula
dilecte sociato!
iam revernant omnia
nobis delectabilia,
hiems eradicatur.

Ab estatis foribus
nos Amor salutat,
humus picta floribus
faciem commutat.
flores amoriferi
iam arrident tempori;
perit absque Venere
flos etatis tenere.

Omnium principium
dies est vernalis,
vere mundus celebrat
diem sui natalis.
omnes huius temporis
dies festi Veneris.
regna Iovis omnia
hec agant sollemnia!

Et tam iste comitatus quam comitatus regis hec sepius cantent:
Ad fontem Philosophie   sitientes currite
et saporis tripertiti   septem rivos bibite,
uno fonte procedentes,   non eodem tramite!

Now spring forth again
all our delights and bliss:
eradicated is the winter's chill.

The meadows are adorned
with flowers of various hues,
the delightfulness of which
becomes an occasion for love's suits.
A chorus of young lads takes delight,
whilst a populous throng of avians
twitters and chirps.

Refr.   How great are the joys,
when one loves and is loved,
when without the stain of gall
a lad is joined to a beloved girl!
Now spring forth again
all our delights and bliss:
eradicated is the winter's chill.[12]

From summer's threshold
Cupid greets us; and earth,
now bloom-spangled,
her visage transmutes.
Flowers, love's awakeners,
now smile upon the season.
Without Venus the blossom
of tender youth fades.

The beginning of all things
is the day of the spring,
when the world celebrates
the day of her birth.
All the days of this season
are the festivals of Venus.
May all the realms of Jove above
observe these celebrations![13]

And so this suite, like that of the king, should repeatedly sing:
Run, thirsty ones, to Philosophy's spring
and drink of the seven rivers of tripartite flavor[14]
that proceed from one font, but run ye not to the same spot!

Quem Pythagoras rimatus   excitavit Physice,
inde Socrates et Plato   honestarunt Ethice,
Aristoteles loquaci   desponsavit Logice.

Ab his secte multiformes   Athenis materiam
nacte hoc liquore totam   irrigarunt Greciam,
que redundans infinite   fluxit in Hesperiam.

Hec nova gaudia
sunt veneranda,
festa presentia
magnificanda.

Refl.   Dulcia flumina
         sunt Babylonis,
         mollia semina
         perditionis.
         concupiscentia
         mixti saporis
         ingerit somnia
         lenis amoris.

Heccine frivola
cupiditatis
tribuunt idola
captivitatis.

Refl.   Dulcia flumina
         sunt Babylonis,
         mollia semina
         perditionis.
         concupiscentia
         mixti saporis
         ingerit somnia
         lenis amoris.

Apta deliciis
caro letatur,
hac . . . vitiis
mens violatur.

Refl.   Dulcia flumina
         sunt Babylonis,

Pythagoras explored it and invoked it for natural philosophy's sake;
thence Socrates and Plato with Ethics adorned it,
and Aristotle betrothed it to loquacious Logic.

From these men different schools in Athens received
their subjects and watered all of Greece with this liquor,
which, superabounding without end, flowed into Hesperia.

These new joys
are to be revered.
These present festive days
are to be glorified.

Refr.   Sweet are the rivers
of Babylon;
enticing are
perdition's seeds.
Concupiscence
of mixed flavor
induces dreams
of gentle love.

These frivolities
of passionate desire
the idols in the land
of captivity give.

Refr.   Sweet are the rivers
of Babylon;
enticing are
perdition's seeds.
Concupiscence
of mixed flavor
induces dreams
of gentle love.

Flesh created
for pleasure rejoices;
hereby the soul
is by debaucheries defiled.

Refr.   Sweet are the rivers
of Babylon;

mollia semina
perditionis.
concupiscentia
mixti saporis
ingerit somnia
lenis amoris.

Affectionibus
motus tumultus
tollit virtutibus
proprios cultus.

Refl.   Dulcia flumina
       sunt Babylonis,
       mollia semina
       perditionis.
       concupiscentia
       mixti saporis
       ingerit somnia
       lenis amoris.

Ista sunt devia
felicitatis,
otia mollia
sunt voluptatis:

Refl.   Dulcia flumina
       sunt Babylonis,
       mollia semina
       perditionis.
       concupiscentia
       mixti saporis
       ingerit somnia
       lenis amoris.

Ista negotia
plena malorum
et desideria
flagitiorum.

Refl.   Dulcia flumina
       sunt Babylonis,
       mollia semina

enticing are
perdition's seeds.
Concupiscence
of mixed flavor
induces dreams
of gentle love.

The tumult aroused
by the passions takes
civilization away
from virtue's pate.

Refr.   Sweet are the rivers
of Babylon;
enticing are
perdition's seeds.
Concupiscence
of mixed flavor
induces dreams
of gentle love.

These are the things that lead
away from felicity's path:
the effeminizing
leisures of lust.

Refr.   Sweet are the rivers
of Babylon;
enticing are
perdition's seeds.
Concupiscence
of mixed flavor
induces dreams
of gentle love.

These activities are
replete with evils
and the hot desire
for opprobrious deeds.

Refr.   Sweet are the rivers
of Babylon;
enticing are

perditionis.
concupiscentia
mixti saporis
ingerit somnia
lenis amoris.

Et sepius repetant:
Deorum immortalitas   <est omnibus colenda,
corum et pluralitas   ubique metuenda.>
Stulti sunt <et vere fatui,   qui deum unum dicunt,
et antiquitatis ritui   proterve contradicunt.>

**In ingressu Marie et Ioseph cum Iesu omnia idola Egyptiorum
corruant. Ministri vero sepius ea restituant et thura incendant
cantantes:**
Hoc est numen salutare,
cuius fundat ad altare
preces omnis populus.
huius nutu reflorescit,
si quandoque commarcescit,
manus, pes vel oculus.

Honor Iovi cum Neptuno!
Pallas, Venus, Vesta, Iuno
mire sunt clementie;
Mars, Apollo, Pluto, Phebus
dant salutem lesis rebus
insite potentie.

Quod quia non proficit, minister precedat regem et cantet:
Audi, rex Egiptiorum,
lapsa virtus idolorum,
destituta vis deorum
iacet cum miseria.
iam delubra ceciderunt,
simulacra corruerunt,
di fugati fugierunt,
heu, cum ignominia.

Quibus rex mirabili gestu respondeat:
Scire volo, que causa rei, vel qualiter ipsa
Numina placentur.   Sapientes ergo vocentur!

perdition's seeds.
Concupiscence
of mixed flavor
induces dreams
of gentle love.

And they should repeat multiple times:
All are obliged to praise the immortal gods
and everywhere their plurality must be feared.
Foolish and truly fatuous are they, who say there is but one god
and who wantonly speak against the cult of antiquity.

**At the entrance of Mary and Joseph with Jesus all the idols of Egypt
should fall to the ground. The ministers should repeatedly raise them
up and burn the incense and sing:**
This is the godhead to salute,
onto whose altar all the people
should pour forth their prayers.
By her nod, spring back to life,
if ever they are languishing away,
the hand, the foot, or the eye.

Honor be to Jove and Neptune!
Pallas, Venus, Vesta, Juno
are of wonderful grace!
Mars, Apollo, Pluto, Phoebus
heal all that are wounded
by their inherent might.

Since this works not, a valet should go to the king and sing:
Hearken, King of the Egyptians,
the strength of the idols has passed away,
the enfeebled power of the gods
lies dead with misery.
The shrines have already fallen;
the images have sunk to the ground;
the routed gods have taken flight,
alas, in ignominy.

The king with a gesture of astonishment should respond:
I wish to know this affair's cause and how the very gods
can be pacified. Wise men therefore should be called!

Tunc armiger vocet sapietiam ad presentiam regis, et cantet:
Regia vos mandata vocant, non segniter ite!

Tunc dicat rex sapientibus:
Scire volo, <que causa rei, vel qualiter ipsa
Numina placentur.> Vos date consilium!

Sapientes respondeant:
Nostrum est consilium   deos honorare,
aras, templa, tripodes,   lucos innovare,
thus, storacem, balsamum,   stacten concremare
et humanum sanguinem   superis libare.
Tali quippe modo virtute ministeriorum
Et prece devota placabitur ira deorum.

Tunc rex preparet se ad immolandum et cantet:
Hoc est numen salutare,
<cuius fundat ad altare
preces omnis populus.
huius nutu reflorescit,
si quandoque commarcescit,
manus, pes vel oculus.

Honor Iovi cum Neptuno!
Pallas, Venus, Vesta, Iuno
mire sunt clementie;
Mars, Apollo, Pluto, Phebus
dant salutem lesis rebus
insite potentie.>

Comitatus respondeat:
Stulti sunt <et vere fatui,   qui deum unum dicunt
et antiquitatis ritui   proterve contradicunt.>

Tunc idolis restitutis rex ad locum suum redeat, et idola iterum corruant. Quo audito iterum vocentur sapientes, quibus rex dicat:
Dicite, quid nobis et quid portendat Egipto
Mira mali species, prodigiosa quidem!

Cui sapientes:
Rex et regum dominus,   Deus Hebreorum,
prepotens in gloria   Deus est deorum,

A shield-bearer should call the sages before the king and sing:
A royal mandate summons you; go to the king in haste!

The king should then say to the sages:
I wish to know this affair's cause and how the gods
themselves can be pacified. Render us your counsel!

The sages should answer:
Our advice is to honor the gods, altars,
temples, tripods; to renew the sacred groves;
to burn the incense, storax,[15] balsam, and myrrh;
and to pour human blood as a libation to the gods.
For in such a wise through the power of the ministers
and pious prayer will the wrath of the gods be allayed.

Then the king should prepare a human sacrifice and sing:
This is the godhead to salute,
onto whose altar all the people
should pour forth their prayers.
By her nod, spring back to life,
if ever they are languishing away,
the hand, the foot, or the eye.

Honor be to Jove and Neptune!
Pallas, Venus, Vesta, Juno
are of wonderful grace!
Mars, Apollo, Pluto, Phoebus
heal all that are wounded
by their inherent might.

The retinue should answer:
Foolish and truly fatuous are they, who say there is but one god,
and who wantonly speak against the cult of antiquity.

**Then, after the idols are raised, the king to his seat should return,
and the idols again should fall. Hearing this, the wise men should be
bidden again, and the king should say:**
Tell me what this astonishing sight of ill portends
for us and Egypt, for a prodigy it assuredly is!

The wise men should say to him:
The King and Lord of kings, the God of the Hebrews,
the God of gods is plenipotentiary in His glory,

cuius in presentia   velut mortuorum
corruit et labitur   virtus idolorum.

Tunc rex cantet:
Ecce novum   cum matre Deum   veneretur Egyptus!

Et omnia idola abiciantur.
Hic est finis regis Egypti.

Tunc assurgat rex Babilonis. Istius comitatus sepius repetat:
Deorum immor<talitas   est omnibus colenda,
eorum et piuralitas   ubique metuenda.>
Stulti sunt <et vere fatui,   qui deum unum dicunt
et antiquitatis ritui proterve contradicunt.>

et hunc versum:
Ille iure cupidus   deus estimatur,
qui spretis ceteris   vult, ut solus colatur.
Stulti sunt <et vere fatui,   qui deum unum dicunt
et antiquitatis ritui   proterve contradicunt.>

In conflictu Gentilitatis, Synagoge et Ecclesie Gentilitas contra eas
cantet:
Deorum immortalitas   est omnibus colenda,
eorum et pluralitas   ubique metuenda.

Comitatus suus respondeat:
Stulti sunt et vere fatui,   qui deum unum dicunt
et antiquitatis ritui   proterve contradicunt.

Gentilitas:
Si enim unum credimus,   qui presit universis,
subiectum hunc concedimus   contrarie diversis.

Comitatus respondeat:
Stulti sunt <et vere fatui,   qui deum unum dicunt
et antiquitatis ritui   proterve contradicunt.>

Gentilitas:
Finxit invidia   hanc singularitatem,
ut homo coleret   unam divinitatem.

Comitatus respondeat:

in Whose presence, like that of the dead,
the power of the idols sinks and perishes.

Then the king should sing:
Behold! Let Egypt venerate the new God and His mother!

And all the idols should be thrown away.
Here ends the role of Egypt's King.

Then Babylon's King should rise. His suite should oft repeat:
All are obliged to praise the immortal gods
and everywhere their plurality must be feared.
Foolish and truly fatuous are they, who say there is but one god,
and who wantonly speak against the cult of antiquity.

and this verse:
Avaricious is the god rightly esteemed, who wishes
the others to be spurned and himself alone to be praised.
Foolish and truly fatuous are they, who say there is but one god,
and who wantonly speak against the cult of antiquity.

In the debate among Paganism, Synagogue and Church, Paganism
should against them sing:
All are obliged to praise the immortal gods
and everywhere their plurality must be feared.

The retinue should answer:
Foolish and truly fatuous are they, who say there is but one god,
and who wantonly speak against the cult of antiquity.

Paganism:
If we in fact believe there is one, who presides over all,
we concede that he is ruled by contradictions of many kinds.

The retinue should answer:
Foolish and truly fatuous are they, who say there is but one god,
and who wantonly speak against the cult of antiquity.

Paganism:
Enviousness fashioned this monism,
so that man might worship one divinity.

The retinue should answer:

Stulti sunt <et vere fatui,   qui deum unum dicunt
et antiquitatis ritui   proterve contradicunt.>

Item rex Babylonis contra hypocritas:
Fraudis versutias   compellor experiri,
per quas nequitia   vestra solet mentiri.
sub forma veritas   virtutis putabatur,
ostendit falsitas,   quod forma mentiatur.

Item devicto rege, cantet in presentia Antichristi:
Tibi profiteor   decus imperiale.
quod tibi serviam,   ius postulo regale.

Comitatus cantet:
Omnium rectorem   te solum profitemur,
tibi tota mente   semper obsequemur.

<. . . . . .:>
Egyptus caput omnium   est et decus regnorum;
calcabit hec imperium   regis Hierosolymorum.

Ve tibi, Hierosolyma,   ve insano tyranno!
deorum vos potentia   subvertet in hoc anno.

Egypti princeps nobilis   ut deus veneretur!
Herodes sed odibilis   ut stultus reprobetur.

Intende, tibi canimus,   quam vilis sis futurus,
cum roderis a vermibus   putre interiturus.

Ingrata gens et perfida,   cum fame laborares,
Egypto eras subdita,   ut ventrem satiares.

HIC FINIUNTUR MAIORES LUDI.

Foolish and truly fatuous are they, who say there is but one god,
and who wantonly speak against the cult of antiquity.

Babylon's King, too, should speak against the hypocrites:
I am compelled to make trial of your cunning deceit
through which your depravity is wont to chicane.
Under virtue's semblance, it was considered truth;
but falsehood makes apparent that the appearance prevaricates.

After he fails, he should sing in the Antichrist's presence:
I solemnly grant to you imperial glory;
for my service to you, I demand regal might.

The retinue should answer:
We confess that you are the sole ruler of all,
you with utmost fealty will we always serve.

<............................:>
Egypt is the capital and ornament of all realms;
the power of Jerusalem's King will trample it underfoot.

Woe to you, Jerusalem, woe to the tyrant insane!
The power of the gods will subvert you this year.

The noble prince of Egypt shall be worshipped as a god!
But odious Herod like a fool will be spurned and condemned.

Hearken, we prophesy to you, how paltry in the future you shall be,
when you, consumed by worms, perish by decay!

Thankless and perfidious race, when you suffered famine,
you were subject to Egypt, that you might fill your maw!

HERE END THE MAJOR PLAYS.

The Supplement

I*/CCXXIX. *Sanctus Erasmus*

Sancte ERASME, martir Domini preciose, qui in die resurreccionis,
quando per martirium oblatus es, et de eo leticiam suscepisti, suscipe hanc
oracionem meam, quam tibi offero pius pro anima mea. Rogo te,
clementissime pater, ut des michi victum et vestitum secundum tuam
voluntatem et meam necessitatem. Memento, quia Deus promisit, ut
quisquis invocaret nomen tuum, exaudiretur. Itcirco conmitto me ad fidem
tuam, quia te Christus conservavit, ut usque in finem vite mee conserves
me, ne incidam in manus inmimicorum meorum visibilium et invisibilium.

II*/CCXXX. *Aliquid Pro Ea*

Ich lob die liben frowen min
vor allen gvten wiben,
mit dienst wil ich ir stete sin
vnd immer stete beliben.
si ist als ein spigel glas
si ist gantzer tvgende ein adamas
vnd schoner zvhte ist si so vol,
von der ich chvmber dol.

Ir roter rosenvarwer mvnt,
der tvt mich senen diche,
ir ovgen brehent ze aller stvnt
sam stern dvrch wolchen blicche.
mins herzen leben ir hant
gebvnden hat an elliv bant.
min ovge sach nie schoner wip.
ein engel ist ir lip.

Min leben stat in ir gewalt,
daz sol si wol bedenchen,
lazze mich mit frovden werden alt,
ich wil ir nimmer wenchen.
wil si, ich lebe wol,
daz diene ich immer swie ich sol.
gebivtet si, ich lige tot.
svs leide ich wernde not.

III*/CCXXXI. *Defessus Bruma*
Marner (ca. 1210 - ca. 1280)

1*/229. *Saint Erasmus*[1]

O Saint ERASMUS, precious martyr of our Lord, who on the Day of
Resurrection, when thou wert presented for martyrdom, sustained thy joy
in the face of it, receive this my prayer, which I piously proffer thee for my
soul. I ask, most merciful father, that thou grant unto me sustenance and
vesture according to thy will and my need. Remember that God promised
that all who invoked thy name would be heard. Thus I commend myself to
thy gracious fidelity, so that, as Christ did thee, thou wilt protect me until
my life's end, lest I fall into the hands of my enemies, visible and unseen.

2*/230. *Anything For Her*

In praise I exalt my beloved mistress
above all other women sublime,
I wish to be her faithful servant
and always her servant remain.
She is like a crystal glass,
a diamond of consummate aptitude,
and so full of beautiful ways—
that maiden, for whose sake I suffer grief.

Her red, rose-colored mouth,
leaves me always pining away;
her eyes shine brightly everyday,
as stars coruscate through the clouds.
Her hand, without cords in its employ,
has wrapped in bonds the life of my heart.
My eyes never beheld a more beautiful maid:
angelic is the sight of her.

My life is subject to her dominion,
a fact she should consider well;
when she lets my spirits soar,
I want never to leave her side.
It's her wish that I be happy,
and for that reason I serve her always, as I should.
If she commands it, dead I lie.
So suffer I always utter privation.

3*/231. *Winter-Worn*
by Marner (ca. 1210 - ca. 1280)

Iam dudum estivalia
pertransiere tempora.
brumalis sevitia
iam venit in tristitia.
grando, nix et pluvia
sic corda reddunt segnia,
ut desolentur omnia.

Nam conticent avicule,
que solebant in nemore
cantica depromere
et voluptates gignere.
tellus caret gramine;
sol lento micat iubare
et dies currunt propere.

Ad obsequendum Veneri
vis tota languet animi.
fervor abest pectori;
iam cedit calor frigori.
maledicant hiemi,
qui veris erant soliti
amenitate perfrui.

In omni loco congruo
sermonis oblectatio
cum sexu femineo
evanuit omnimodo.
tempori preterito
sit decus in perpetuo
et gratiarum actio.

Pro dulcis aure transitu
et tempestatis impetu
tribulato spiritu
in gravi sumus habitu.
ver, nos tuo reditu
refove, quos in gemitu
relinquis aliquandiu.

IV*/CCXXXII. *Per Oculos Mariae*

Flete, fideles anime,

The time of summer
has long since passed.
Winter's ferocity now
in harsh aspect has come.
Hail, snow, and rain
thus render hearts indolent,
so that all is desolate and forsaken.

Verily silent are the little birds
who were wont in the woods
to bring forth songs
and beget delight.
The earth has no grass;
with an idle ray gleams the sun,
and in haste the days rush by.

In submission to Venus
all the strength of my soul wanes;
passion is absent from my chest;
heat now truckles to cold.
Let them curse the winter,
who were wont to enjoy
the loveliness of spring.

In every suitable place
the delight of conversation
with the feminine sex
has wholly evanesced.
May there glory
and gratitude forever be
to the faded time.

For the passing of the sweet breeze
and the onset of the truculent storm
we, with afflicted spirit,
are in a dejected mood.
Spring, refresh us by thy return,
whom thou for a long time
dost leave behind in lament.

4*/232. *Through Mary's Eyes*

Weep, faithful souls,

flete, sorores optime,
ut sint multiplices
doloris indices
planctus et lacrime.
fleant materna viscera
Marie matris vulnera:
materne doleo,
que dici soleo
felix puerpera.

Triste spectaculum
crucis et lancee
clausum signaculum
mentis virginee
profunde vulnerat;
hoc est, quod dixerat,
quod prophetaverat
senex prenuntius,
Hic ille gladius,
qui me transverberat.

Dum caput cernuum,
dum spinas capitis,
dum plagas manuum
cruentis digitis
supplex suspicio,
sub hoc supplicio
tota deficio,
dum vulnus lateris,
dum locus vulneris
est in profluvio.

Ergo quare,   fili care,
pendes ita,   cum sis vita
vivens ante secula?
rex celestis   pro scelestis
alienas   solvis penas,
agnus sine macula.

Munda caro mundo cara,
cur in crucis ares ara,
pro peccatis hostia?
cur in ara crucis ares,

weep, best of sisters,
that so innumerable are
the lamentations and tears:
the proofs of our grief.
Let maternal hearts beweep
Mother Mary's wounds:
then as a mother grieve I,
who am accustomed to be called
happy and blessed in motherhood.

The sad spectacle
of the cross and spear
deeply wounds
the closed seal
of my virgin soul.
This is what
the old soothsayer
had prophesied and told,
this is that sword
that transfixes my soul.[2]

As I on my knees
with bloody fingers
look up at His Head,
stooping towards the earth,
the crown of thorns upon it,
the wounds to His hands—
beneath this humiliation
I lose all sense,
whilst from the wound in His Flank,
from Its site, away drains His Blood.

Why then, Dear Son,
do You hang so, since You are life,
living before all?
O Celestial King, for the wicked
You suffer others' agony,
my Dear, Stainless Lamb.

O sinless Flesh, precious to heaven
and to earth,[3] why are You withering
on the cross' altar as a payment for crime?
Why languish You on the altar of the cross,

caro, que peccato cares,
caro culpe nescia?

O mentes perfidas
et linguas duplices,
o testes subdolos
et falsos iudices,
senes cum iunioribus!
solent maioribus
criminibus
damnati
ferre suspendium
stipendium
peccati.

A damnaticiis
damnatur innocens,
explens, quod expedit,
quod decet, edocens.
fremunt auctores criminum
et viri sanguinum
in dominum
salutis
zelo nequitie
sub specie
virtutis.

Mi Iohannes, planctum move,
plange mecum, fili nove,
fili novo federe
matris et matertere.
tempus est lamenti;
immolemus intimas
lacrimarum victimas
Christo morienti.

Salutaris noster Iesus,
captus, tractus, vinctus, cesus
et illusus alapis
a Gehenne satrapis,
auctor vere lucis,
dies nocte clauditur,
vita mortem patitur,

a body that lacks any trace of guilt,
a body that knows nothing of fault?

O perfidious minds
and duplicitous tongues,
O deceitful witnesses
and judges false,
old and young alike!
Those condemned
of graver offenses
are wont to suffer
the gallows
as payment for
their transgressions.

By the damned
an innocent is condemned,
fulfilling what He foretold,
teaching what is meet.
The authors of crimes
and men of bloody hands
rage against the Lord
of salvation
in the zeal of villainy
under the guise
of virtue.

O my Johannes,[4] grieve,
rue with me, my new son,
son by the new compact
between mother and aunt.
'Tis the time for lamentation;
let us offer up in sacrifice
our inmost griefs and tears
to the dying Christ.

Jesus, our Salvation—captured,
dragged, bound, and slain,
and abused by parasites,
satraps from Hell—
the Progenitor of true light,
Day shut up in night,
life submits to death,

mortem autem crucis.

Hac in vita   sum invita,
hoc in malo   mori malo,
fili mi,   dum reprimi
vel exprimi
nequit estus animi
dolentis,
tantis malis eximi
volentis.

Scelus terre celum terret,
terre motus   terret motus
impios,   nefarios
qui gladios
in sanctorum filios
allidunt
et te, Christe agyos,
occidunt.

V*/CCXXXIII. *Sponsa Christi*

Furibundi
cum aceto mixto felle
temptarunt te, tui velle
contra; quodquod lacte, melle,
de puella maris stella
natus, alvo tamen salvo
matris, pascis tui oris
et amoris.

Letabundi –
nam quos stravit morsus anguis,
hos sanavit tuus sanguis
munda unda et potavit.
recreavit vivus divus
panis iste, o tu Christe,
o benigne, digne odis,
modis.

Sitibundi,
ut pax detur: «osculetur
osculo me oris sui,

death upon the cross.

In this life do I unwillingly remain;
amid this evil I prefer to die,
my Son, since the shock
to my grieving soul
cannot be subdued
or expressed,[5]
amid such great, yet willful, sufferings
of an extraordinary Man.

This crime on earth
terrifies the sky;
an earthquake affrights
their unholy efforts,
who dash execrable swords
against the sons of saints
and slay Your body,
Our Sacred Christ.

5*/233. *The Bride of Christ*

In madness have they tried You,
against Your will,
with a mix of vinegar and gall;
they, whom You nourish with the milk
and honey of Your mouth and love,
as a Child born of a girl,
a star of the sea,
with an unbroken womb.

Joyful are they—whom the snake's bite
threw to the ground,
whom Your blood did heal
and whom You gave to drink
Your clear, clean water.
Your living, divine bread revived them,
O Christ, Benignant One,
and to You hymns are due.

They thirst for peace: "may He
kiss me with the kiss of His mouth,[6]
so that I, His beautiful bride,

que de culpa nigra fui
sponsa pulchra, ut dilecta
et perfecta, simplex, recta
sim de bonis tuis,
que te placent.»

VI*/CCXXXIV. *Prelatus de Solio*
Marner (ca. 1210 - ca. 1280)

Pange, vox adonis,
nobilem   prelatum de Solio,
qui gaudet in donis
et caret   vitiorum lolio.
est iocundus,   letus et affabilis,
in promisso stabilis,
providus,   prudens, honorabilis.

Cum architriclino
dicere   possem eius vultibus:
«tu servasti vino
nobili   finem atque dapibus,
et post primum   non datur deterius:
verum loquor verius:
funditur   bonum atque melius.

Ad gradus virtutum
properas   ut sol ad meridiem.»
paupertatis nutum
sentiens   queres eius faciem.
cur, Fortuna   vitrea, sic deficis,
cur cito non efficis,
quod sit hic   in loco pontificis.

Sed si non est princeps,
cathedre   scilicet officio,
ut clerus deinceps
memoret,   quando fit electio:
est statura   ceteris prestantior,
vultu elegantior,
moribus   cunctis honorantior.

Maior mea laude,
dignior,   forma veri hominis;

who was black with guilt,
may be beloved and perfect,
virtuous and sincere,
through Your gifts,
which please You so."[7]

6*/234. *The Provost of Maria Saal*[8]
by Marner (ca. 1210 – ca. 1280)

Praise, voice of the nightingale,
the noble provost of Maria Saal,
who rejoices in giving
and is free of the weed of vice.
He is pleasant, mirthful, and courteous,
unwavering in his promises,
circumspect, sagacious, and honorable.

With the feastmaster[9]
I could come before him and say:
"You have saved the end
for superior wine and feasts,
and after the first wine, a lesser is not received;
so truly do I speak truth when I say:
'Good,' then one still better is poured!

"To the steps of virtue you hasten,
as the sun does to its midcourse."
Sensing poverty's nod,
you will seek its very face.
Why, glassy Fortune, do you fail so,
why do you not arrange swiftly
that he assume the bishop's throne?

But if he be not prince,
to wit, in the episcopate,
then the clergy in turn should recall
the following, when the election occurs:
in stature, he dwarfs the rest;
in features, he is more fine;
in a habits, he is more honorable.

Greater than my praise is he
and more distinguished, too—

tamen sine fraude
gloriam   cano sui nominis.
verbi Dei   gratia fit ratio,
non est adulatio;
hunc decet   vere collaudatio.

Huic ignoro parem
circiter   per totam Carinthiam.
si perambularem
Saxones,   Francos et Bawariam,
Swevos, Rhenum,   fertilem Alsatiam,
ibi finem faciam, –
non habet   clerus talem gratiam.

VII*/CCXXXV. *Testis Lucis*
Johannes 1:1-14

In anegenge was ein wort, daz wort was mit got, got was daz wort. vnd was
in anegenge mit got, von im sint alliv dinch gemachet an in ist gemacht
nicht, swaz mit im ist gemachet, daz ist daz ewige leben, daz ewige leben
ist ein liecht den livten, daz liecht daz livchtet in der vinster, die vinster
mach sein nicht begreiffen. Ein mennisch wart gesant von gote des name
was Johannes. der chom zvo einer gezivchnvesse daz er gezivch were des
liechtes. er was nicht daz liecht niwer daz er gezivch were des liechtes. daz
ware liecht ist daz, daz ein igesleichen mennisch erlivchtet der in disiv welt
bechumt, er cham in div welt, div welt erchant sein nicht, er chom in sein
aigen lant die seinen enpfiengen sein nicht aver die in da enpfiengen den
gab er den gewalt, daz si gotes chint werden, vnd die an seinen namen
gelavpten die warn nicht geworn von wollveste des plůtes noch von
wollveste des vlaisches wan svnder von gote, daz wort ist ze vlaische
worden, vnd wont in vens wier haben sein ere geschen als eines ainworn
svnes wie den sein vater eret voller genaden vnd voller warheit. durch disiv
rede des hailgen ewangelii vergebe vens venser herre alle venser Missetat.
amen.

VIII*/CCXXXVI. *Repetitio est Mater Memoriae II*

Hoc poema est, verbatim, idem ac poema CXI Codicis Burani.

IX*/CCXXXVII. *Ordo Hypocritarum*
Marner (ca. 1210 - ca. 1280)

Mundus finem properans   vergit ad occasum;

the paragon of an upright man;
nevertheless, without design, I sing the glory of his name.
The justification is furnished by the grace of God's word,
it is not born of canine fawning.
Warm praise truly beseems this man.

I know of no equal to him
in and around all of Carinthia.
If I should walk through Saxony,
Franconia, Bavaria, Swabia,
Rhineland, and fertile Alsace,
there I would my journey end.
The clergy has no such grace as him.

7*/235. *The Witness of the Light*
John 1:1-14

In the beginning was a Word, the Word was with God, God was the Word,
and It was in the beginning with God. By Him all things were created;
without Him, nothing was made. All that was created with Him is eternal
life. Eternal life is a light for mankind. The Light, which glows in the
darkness, the darkness cannot comprehend. By God a man was sent, whose
name was John. He came to attest that he was a witness of the Light. He
was not the Light, but he would offer testimony about the Light. The true
Light is that which illumes every man coming into this world. He came
into the world; but the world did not recognize Him. He came into His own
country; His people did not receive Him. But to those who took Him in, He
gave the power to become the children of God, and they believed in His
name, who were not born of the lust of the blood or of the flesh, but solely
of God. The Word became flesh and lives in us; we have seen His glory,
glory like that of His only-begotten Son, as His Father exalts Him with an
abundance of grace and truth. Through this lesson of the Holy Gospel may
our Lord forgive all our misdeeds.
Amen.

8*/236. *Repetition Is the Mother of Memory II*

This poem is word-for-word the same as CB 111.

9*/237. *The Order of Hypocrites*
by Marner (ca. 1210 – ca. 1280)

The world, hastening to the end, leans towards its decline;

omnis compaternitas   retro vertit nasum.
celeste sacrarium   sic minatur casum,
quasi cum novacula   fundo sit abrasum.

Dolor se multiplicat   ut parturientis;
sevit in ecclesia   pena morientis.
non est, qui respiciat   lacrimas plangentis,
sed manus invaluit   iacula mittentis.

Antichristus nuntios   plurimos premisit,
sed in Christi milites   acies divisit,
quibus arma bellica   plurima commisit
renovare cupiens,   demon quod amisit.

Instituta primitus   patrum floruerunt,
qui carnis et sanguinis   curam non egerunt,
sine mundo vivere   semper studuerunt;
taliter perpetua   regna meruerunt.

Benedicti regula   fuit primitiva,
placuit pre ceteris,   quia fuit diva;
primo constantissima   – sed nunc est procliva –
eminebat ceteris   et compositiva.

Ab hac derivatus est   ordo Griseorum,
qui dat elemosinam   et frequentat chorum;
sudat et inflectitur   studio laborum,
unde sperat fieri   consors angelorum.

Clericorum regulam   pater Augustinus
ornavit sollemniter;   post hec Norperthinus
ordinem instituit.   paulo plus, non minus,
has qui servat regulas,   Deo fit vicinus.

Heu, nostris temporibus   emersit dolosa
novitas, irrutilat   undique famosa.
istam plebem sequitur   turba copiosa
sperans indulgentia   frui spatiosa.

Hi, quos novos nomino,   sunt fratres minores
et maiores sitiunt   nummos et honores.
Deus, qualis novitas   et quales sunt mores!
modo superveniunt   etiam sorores.

all the spiritual fathers turn their faces away.
The heavenly sanctuary threatens its own fall
as if it has been abraded from its base by a razor.[10]

The pain compounds itself like the pangs of birth;
the anguish and agony of death rages in the Church.
There is no one who pays attention to the tears of one in grief,
but the hand of the missile-thrower has grown in strength.

The Antichrist has dispatched myriad harbingers,
but has divided his lines against the warriors of Christ,
lines to which he has commended many weapons of war,
desiring to restore what the demon let go.[11]

The ways of the monastic fathers originally flourished,
who had no care for flesh and blood,
who without the world always strove to live,
and thereby earned their place in the eternal realm.

The Rule of Benedict was the first,
which pleased more than the others, because it breathed a godly air.
At first, most constant—but now in decline—
it stood compositive and above the rest.

From this was derived the Order of the Grey Monks,[12]
which gives alms and brings together the throngs.
It sweats and bends in the zeal of its labors,
whereby it hopes to become the consort of the angels.

Father Augustine[13] accoutered the rule
of the priests with ritual, binding dress;
afterwards, Norbert established his order.[14]
Who follows these rules, comes closer to God, never less.

Alas, in these our times emerges a deceitful innovation:
celebrated, it glimmers ruddily on all sides.
The copious throng follows that ignoble clan,
hoping to enjoy ample indulgence.

These, whom I call the "new ones," are the lesser brothers,[15]
but they are greedy for greater sums of money and office.
God, what a novelty and abomination of morals!
Now even the sisters are coming upon it.[16]

Sorores, sic credite,   sunt Magdalenite,
et fratres ex opere   dicuntur Paulite,
sed, opinor, verius   sunt Ismahelite;
botrus non colligitur   dulcis ab hac vite.

Erant a principio   quasi nil habentes;
modo vivunt omnia   tamquam possidentes.
raro sunt in cellulis,   semper sunt currentes;
quamvis multa habeant,   tamen sunt egentes.

Castra solent querere,   claustra devitare;
domos querunt divitum,   sciunt bene quare:
vesci volunt pinguibus   et vinum potare,
contemnunt cum monachis   olus manducare.

Audite, dilectissimi,   magnum detrimentum:
arbitror, a fratribus   nefas sit inventum;
indulgent pro prandio   dies bene centum,
pro quibus ipsi colligunt   aurum et argentum.

Divites recipiunt   in confessione;
clericis preiudicant   sine ratione;
fremunt et concutiunt   mira torsione.
tua, dum vis, iudica,   Deus, ultione.

Propter laudes hominum   predicant in foro
et cum sacerdotibus   raro sunt in choro,
quosque iunxit Dominus,   contradicunt thoro.
confundantur citius!   illud supplex oro.

X*/CCXXXVIII. *Poena Avaritiae*
Marner (?) (ca. 1210 - ca. 1280)

Deus largus in naturis
cunctis dedit creaturis
sua iura facere.
ignis, aer, terra, mare
consueverunt nobis dare,
largitatem colere.

Sit avari cista fracta,
cuius manus est contracta,
quia dare noluit.

The sisters—trust me, it is so—are Magdalenites;[17]
from their works the brothers are hight Indolentites,[18]
but I believe they are more rightly called the sons of Ishmael.
From this vine no sweet artemisia is ever, ever picked.

In the beginning, they subsisted as if they had nothing;
now they live as if they possess the sum of the world.
Rarely are they in their little cells; always are they on the run.
Though they have a great many things, they are in need still.

Castles are they wont to seek, the cloister wont to shun.
They seek out the homes of the rich, and they know exactly why:
they want to feed on their fats and drink of their wine,
for they contemn eating greens among monastic eyne.

Hearken, most beloved men, to this detriment great—
I believe this sin was wrongly discovered by the Franciscans:
for one lunch they give indulgence for well-nigh one hundred days,
and for each of these they gather the recipient's gold and silver.

They receive the wealthy in confession,
are prejudicial to priests without legal ground,
and rage at and strike one another with eerie contortions.[19]
God, if it is Your will, judge them with Your vengeance!

To woo the praise of the people, they preach
in the forum and are rarely in chorus with priests.
And each marital union sealed by the Lord these men aggress.[20]
Swiftly may they be ruined! That is my solemn prayer.

10*/238. *The Penalty for Greed*
by Marner (?) (ca. 1210 – ca. 1280)

God, munificent in His Nature,
vouchsafed all creatures the right
to forge their own laws:
fire, air, earth, sea were wont
to give us their everlasting gifts
and to practice unceasing liberality.

Let the pinchpenny's coffer be broken,
whose hand was tightly closed,
because he did not wish to give.

eius bursa dirumpatur
et in igne comburatur.
nulli namque profuit.

Parcus dictus a parcendo,
quia parcit, sed arcendo;
sic cum rebus perditur.
parcis rebus, o tu parce,
sed non parcunt tibi Parce;
parcus cito moritur.

Monstruosa res, avare,
scias, quid sit non donare:
dignum anathemate!
monstruosa res es quidem,
iuro tibi per hanc fidem,
quam cepi baptismate.

Sicut Paulus attestatur,
avaritia vocatur
idolorum servitus.
hinc avarus reprobatur
nec in celis collocatur,
quia totus perditus.

XI*/CCXXXIX. *Oda Mariae*

Ave nobilis, venerabilis, Maria,
amicabilis, comes utilis in via,
mentes erige, cursum dirige per hec invia,
mores corrige, tuo remige, lux superna,
nos guberna per hec maria.

Tu post Dominum celi agminum magistra,
virgo virginum, lucis luminum ministra,
cor illuminans et eliminans queque vetera,
fons inebrians, stella radians super astra,
celi castra nobis resera.

Pulchra facie, celi glorie regina,
nobis hodie potum gratie propina,
potens omnium infidelium vim extermina,
Christo credulum munda populum, mundo clara,

May his purse be dashed to pieces
and in fire be consumed,
for he was of service to none.

Declared miserly for his parsimony is he,
because he spares only by warding the needy off;
thus together with his possessions is he lost.
Thou sparest thy possessions, O niggard,
but the Fates do not spare thee!
For the skinflint swiftly dies.

O thou monstrous thing, thou miser man,
thou shouldst know what not giving is:
an execrable thing worthy of a curse!
A hideous thing thou assuredly art;
I do swear this unto thee by this faith,
which I assumed, when I was baptized.

As Paul attested,
avarice is called
service unto idols.
This cupidinous man is condemned
and never in the heavens is placed,
for he is wholly corrupt and stained.[21]

11*/239. *Mary's Ode*

Hail, noble, venerable Mary, affable, suitable
companion on the path of life, raise our minds
and direct our course through these pathless ways;
improve our modes; by thy oarage, light on high,
guide us through these seas.

After the Lord, thou art the mistress of the armies of the sky,
O virgin of virgins, minister of the light of lights,
heart illuminating and turning outdoors all old things,
inebriating fount, celestial body beaming above all the other stars,
open the stronghold of heaven to us.

Queen of beautiful visage and of heaven's glory, vouchsafe
us today the draught of grace! Puissant one, vanquish the force
of all the infidels! Cleanse the people, who believe in Christ,
O light celebrated by our world, treasured by our world,

mundo cara mundi domina.

Mater, assumus et te querimus devote:
ire volumus, sed non possumus sine te.
sola sufficis, si nos respicis. in hoc tramite
nobis clericis, nostris laicis nunc adesto,
custos esto plebis subdite.

Fortis ancora, nostra tempora dispone,
nostra pectora, nostra corpora compone.
nostra omnia sint solatia in te virgine.
plena gratia dele vitia, sis tutamen
nobis, amen, in discrimine.

XII*/CCXL. *Katharina de Alexandria*

Christi sponsa Katharina,
virgo martyr et regina,
rosa florens,   fragrans inter lilia,
te collaudant   angelorum milia.

Refl.   Gaude, virgo,   Costi regis filia,
            per te signa   fiunt mirabilia.

Que convicit oratores
disputantes et rhetores
† obstinatos   plures a Maxentio,
baptizari   suadet cum Porphyrio.

Refl.   Gaude, virgo,   Costi regis filia,
            per te signa   fiunt mirabilia.

Ex ipsius tumba manat
rivus, qui languentes sanat;
oleum resudat   eius tumulo,
per quod salus   datur omni populo.

Refl.   Gaude, virgo,   Costi regis filia,
            per te signa   fiunt mirabilia.

XIII*/CCXLI. *Passio Christi*

Ludus breviter de passione primo inchoatur ita. Quando Dominus

thou commandress of our world!

Mother, here we kneel and in humility pray to thee:
we wish to go, but we cannot go without thee.
Thou alone satifiest us if thou but castest on us thy gaze.
In this crossroads stand now with us, clerics and our lay,
and be the protectress of the mass that is bowed to thee.

O anchor strong, set in harmony our times,
and our hearts and bodies compose.
May all our solace be in thee, O virgin!
O vessel of grace, extirpate our vices,
be our defense in our turning point, amen!

12*/240. *Catherine of Alexandria*[22]

Catherine, bride of Christ,
maiden, martyr, and queen,
blossoming rose, fragrant lily,
thousands of angels together praise thee!

Refr.   Rejoice, maiden, daughter of Costus the King,
              through thee the wondrous standards are made!

She bested orators in debate,
and the many stubborn rhetors,
appointed by Maxentius against her,
she persuaded to be baptized with Porphyrius.[23]

Refr.   Rejoice, maiden, daughter of Costus the King,
              through thee, the wondrous standards are made!

From her very grave a river flows,
which restores the feeble and weary;
olive oil exudes from her tomb,
through which health is granted to all.

Refr.   Rejoice, maiden, daughter of Costus the King,
              through thee, the wondrous standards are made!

13*/241. *The Passion of the Christ*

The brief play about the Passion should thus begin. When the Lord

cum discipulis procedere vult ad locum deputato, ubi mandatum debet esse, et in processu dicant apostoli ad Dominum:
Ubi vis paremus tibi comedere pascha?

Et Dominus respondet:
Ite in civitatem ad quendam et dicite ei: Magister dicit: «Tempus meum prope est; apud te facio pascha cum discipulis meis».

Et in deputato loco faciant mensam parari cum mensale, cum pane et vino. Et Dominus discumbat cum duodecim apostolis suis, et edentibus illis dicat:
Amen dico vobis, quia unus vestrum me traditurus est in hac nocte.

Et unusquisque pro se respondet:
Numquid ego sum, Domine?

Et Dominus respondet:
Qui intinguit mecum manum in parapside, hic me tradet. Filius quidem hominis vadit, sicut scriptum est de illo. Ve autem homini illi, per quem filius hominis tradetur; bonum erat illi, si natus non fuisset homo ille.

Respondet Iudas:
Numquid ego sum, Rabbi?

Et Dominus dicat:
Tu dixisti.

Tunc medio tempore vadat Iudas ad pontifices et ad Iudeos et dicat:
Quid vultis michi dare, et ego vobis eum tradam?

At illi constituant ei:
Triginta argenteos.

Et ista hora accipiat Dominus panem, frangat, benedicat et dicat:
Accipite et comedite, hoc est corpus meum.

Similiter et calicem. Et postquam cenavit, Dominus dicat:
Surgite, eamus hinc; ecce appropinquabit, qui me tradet.

Et Iudas accedens ad Iesum clamando dicat:

wishes to proceed with his disciples to the destined place, whither they were mandated to go, as they wend, the apostles should say to Him:
Where do you wish us to prepare to eat our Passover meal?

And the Lord should respond:
Go to the city, to a certain man and say: "The Master says,
'My time is near; at your house I shall make a meal with my disciples.'"

And at the destined place, they should prepare a table with bread and wine. And the Lord should sit with His ten apostles, and the Lord should say to them as they eat:
Amen I say to you, for one of you will betray me on this night.

Each one should respond in his own defense:
Is it I, Lord?

And the Lord should respond:
He who dips his hand with Mine in the dessert shall betray Me.
The Son of man will in sooth pass, as the writings prophesied; woe,
howbeit, to that man, through whom the Son of man will be betrayed.
A blessing to him it would have been, if he had not been born.

Judas should respond:
Is it I, Rabbi?

And the Lord should say:
Truth thou hast spoken.

Then in the meantime Judas should go to the Jewish high priests and the Jews. And he should say:
What will to give me, when I hand Him over to ye?

And they should propose to him:
Thirty pieces of silver.

And at that hour, the Lord should receive the bread, break it, give the benediction, and say:
Receive this and consume it, for this is My Body.

Likewise the chalice. After they have eaten, He should say:
Rise. Let us hence. Lo! He, My betrayer will approach us now.

And Judas should, as he approaches Jesus, shout:

Ave, Rabbi!

Et osculando irruat in eum. Tunc Dominus dicat:
Amice, ad quid venisti?

Iudei et milites accedant ad Dominum et manus iaciant in eum et teneant eum. Et ita ducant eum ad Pilatum. Tunc discipuli omnes relicto eo fugiant. Et accusent eum coram eo in tribus causis et dicant:
Hic dixit: Possum destruere templum Dei et post triduum reedificare illud.

Secundo:
Hunc invenimus subvertentem gentem nostram et prohibentem tributa dari Cesari et dicentem se Christum regem esse.

Tertio:
Commovit populum docens per universam Iudeam et incipiens a Galilea usque huc.

Tunc Pilatus respondet:
Quid enim mali fecit?

Dicant Iudei:
Si non esset malefactor, non tibi tradidissemus eum.

Respondet Pilatus:
Accipite cum vos et secundum legem vestram iudicate eum. Ego nullam causam invenio in hoc homine. Vultis ergo, dimittam regem Iudeorum?

Iudei clamando dicant:
Non, sed crucifigatur.

Et clamando magis dicant:
Crucifige, crucifige eum!

Et Pilatus respondet:
Accipite eum vos et crucifigite!

Dicant Iudei:
Non, nos legem habemus, et secundum legem debet mori, quia filium Dei se fecit.

Respondet Pilatus:

Hail, Rabbi!

And he should rush at Him with a kiss; then the Lord should say:
Friend, why hast thou come?

The Jews and soldiers should accost the Lord, cast their hands upon Him, take hold of Him, and then lead Him to Pilate. Then all the disciples should abandon Christ and flee. And then they should accuse Him in His presence of three crimes and say:
He said, "I can destroy the temple of God and rebuild it after three days."

The Second Offense:
We found Him subverting our people, debarring the tribute to Caesar, and saying that He is Christ the King.

The Third Offense:
He has disquieted all the people through His teachings throughout all of Judea, from Galilee all the way hither.

Then Pilate should respond:
But what crime has He committed?

The Jews should say:
If He weren't an evildoer, we wouldn't have passed Him to ye.

Pilate says:
Take this Man and judge Him according to your law ! I find no cause in this Man. Do you wish me to send Him to the King of the Jews?

The Jews should say with a shout:
No! He should rather be crucified!

And with a greater shout they should say:
Crucify Him, crucify Him!

Pilate should say:
You take Him and crucify Him!

The Jews should say:
No! We have a law, and according to it, He must die, because He has made Himself the Son of God.

Pilate should respond:

Regem vestrum crucifigam?

Tunc dicant pontifices:
Regem non habemus nisi Cesarem.

Et Pilatus accipiat aquam et dicat:
Mundus sum a sanguine huius iusti; vos videritis.

Et baiulet sibi crucem, et ducant eum, ubi crucifigatur. Tunc unus ex militibus veniat cum lancea, tangat latus eius. Tunc ipse Dominus in cruce alta voce clamet:
Ely, Ely, lema sabactani: Deus meus, Deus meus, ut <quid dereliquisti me?

Tunc Maria mater Domimi veniat et due alie Marie et Iohannes. Et Maria planctum faciat quantum melius potest. Et unus ex Iudeis dicat:
Si filius Dei es, descende nunc de cruce!

Alter Iudeus:
Confidit in Deo; liberet eum nunc si vult.

Item tertius:
Alios salvos fecit, seipsum autem non potest salvum facere.

Et Dominus dicat:
Consummatum est.

Et:
In manus tuas commendo spiritum m<eum>.

Et inclinato capite emittat spiritum. Tunc veniat Ioseph ab Arimathia et petat corpus Iesu. Et permittat Pilatus. Et Ioseph honorifice sepeliat eum.

Et ita inchoatur ludus de resurrectione.

Pontifices:
O domine, recte meminimus.

XIV*/CCXLII. *Lacrimae Virginis*
Gottfridus, Subprior de St. Victor (ca. 1130 - ca. 1194)

Planctus ante nescia,

Am I to crucify your King?

Then the high priests should say:
We have no king except Caesar.

Then Pilate should take up the water and say:
I am innocent of this Just Man's blood—bear you witness to this!

And He should bear His cross and be led unto His crucifixion.
Then one of the soldiers should come and pierce His side with a spear.
Then the Lord on the cross should loudly exclaim:
Ely, Ely, lama sabactani: My God, My God, why have You forsaken Me?

Then Mary, mother of the Lord, should come along with two other
Marys[24] and John. And Mary should raise a lament as best she can.
And one of the Jews should say:
If you be the Son of God, descend now from the cross!

Another Jew:
He confides in God. If He wills, He should free Him now!

Likewise a third:
He has saved others, but cannot save Himself.

And the Lord should say:
It is completed.

And:
Into Your Hands I commend My Spirit.

And with head cast down, He should emit His soul. Joseph of
Arimathea should come and ask for Jesus' body. And Pilate should
permit his request. And Joseph should honorably bury Him.

And with this begins the Play about the Resurrection.

High Priests:
O Lord, we remember well...

14*/242. *Tears of the Virgin*
by Gottfried, Subprior of St. Victor (ca. 1130 – ca. 1194)

I who knew no sorrow before,

planctu lassor anxia,
crucior dolore;
orbat orbem radio,
me Iudea filio,
gaudio, dulcore.

Fili, dulcor unice,
singolare gaudium,
matrem flentem respice
conferens solatium.

Pectus, mentem, lumina
tua torquent vulnera.
que mater, que femina
tam felix, tam misera!

Flos florum,   dux morum,
venie vena,
quam gravis   in clavis
est tibi pena.

Proh dolor,   hinc color
effugit oris,
hinc ruit,   hinc fluit
unda cruoris.

O quam sero deditus,
quam cito me deseris;
o quam digne genitus,
quam abiecte moreris.

O quis amor corporis
tibi fecit spolia;
o quam dulcis pignoris
quam amara premia.

O pia   gratia
sic morientis,
o zelus,   o scelus
invide gentis.

O fera   dextera
crucifigentis,

now am wearied by a troubling grief
and tortured by great dolor.
Judea bereaves the world of its Light
and me of my Son,
my sweetness and delight.

Son, Sweetness unique,
Joy one of a kind,
look back upon Thy weeping mother
and bestow Thy Solace on me.

Thy Wounds do torment
my mind, heart, and eyne.
What mother, what woman
is so blessed and yet so poor?

Flower of flowers, Leader of virtue,
Spring of clemency,
how grave is Thy Pain
in Thy Wounds upon the nails.

O, the grief! All the color
of Thy Mouth flees away.
from Thee rushes and flows
a wave of blood and gore!

O how late wert Thou brought down to me,
O how swiftly dost Thou forsake me.
O how becomingly wert Thou conceived,
O how abjectly dost Thou pass away.

O what love made for Thee
the carnal body's shell;
O how sweet, O how bitter
are the rewards of Thy Pledge.[25]

O the pious grace
in such a death,[26]
O the envy, O the evil
of this jealous clan!

O Propitious Beast of him,
who fixes Thee to the cross,

o lenis   in penis
mens patientis.

O verum eloquium
iusti Simeonis!
quem promisit, gladium
sentio doloris.

Gemitus, suspiria
lacrimeque foris
vulneris indicia
sunt interioris.

Parcito proli,
mors, michi noli,
tunc michi soli
sola mederis.

Morte, beate,
separer a te,
dummodo, nate,
non crucieris.

Quod crimen, que scelera
gens commisit effera,
vincla, virgas, vulnera,
sputa, spinas, cetera
sine culpa patitur.

Nato, queso, parcite,
matrem crucifigite
aut in crucis stipite
nos simul affigite!
male solus moritur.

Reddite mestissime
corpus vel exanime,
ut sic minoratus
crescat cruciatus
osculis, amplexibus!

Utinam sic doleam,
ut dolore peream,

O gentle in Its agony is the Soul
of the suffering Christ.

O! true was the augury
of Simeon the Just![27]
I feel the sword of pain,
which he prophesied.

The groans, the sighs,
and tears without
are proofs
of the wounds within.

Spare posterity, Death,
but do not spare me,
then you alone will be
a cure for lonely me.

Let me by death, beatified one,
be separated from Thee,
so long as Thou, my Son,
art not racked with the cross' pain.

What a crime, what iniquities
hath the truculent tribe committed:
bonds, switches, wounds,
spittle, thorns, and the rest
suffers He, Who no guilt hath.

Spare my Son, I pray:
His mother crucify instead,
or affix us both
to the cross' stake!
Alone He wrongfully dies.

Return His most lugubriously
lifeless Frame, so that it,
diminished and crucified,
may be strengthened again
by our kisses and embrace!

Would that I pained thus,
so that I may perish from the pain,

nam plus est dolori
sine morte mori
quam perire citius.

Quid stupes, gens misera,
terram se movere,
obscurari sidera,
languidos lugere?

Solem privas lumine,
quomodo luceret?
egrum medicamine,
unde convaleret?

Homicidam liberas,
Iesum das supplicio;
male pacem toleras,
veniet seditio.

Famis, cedis, pestium
scies docta pondere
Iesum tibi mortuum
Barrabamque vivere.

Gens ceca, gens flebilis,
age penitentiam,
dum tibi flexibilis
Iesus est ad veniam.

Quos fecisti, fontium
prosint tibi flumina,
sitim sedant omnium,
cuncta lavant crimina.

Flete, Sion filie,
tante grate gratie;
iuvenis angustie
sibi sunt delicie
pro vestris offensis.

In amplexus ruite,
dum pendet in stipite;
mutuis amplexibus

for it is a graver dole to die
without death
than to perish amain.

Why are you stunned, wretched race,
that the earth is quaking now,
that the stars are obscured
and the feeble mourn?

If you deprive the sun of its light,
how would it ever shine?
If you rob a sick man of his medicine,
whereby would he convalesce?

You free a murderer, but subject
Jesus to the agony of death.
Poorly do you sustain peace,
for sedition will arise.

By the weight of famine, slaughter, and pestilence,
you will know the very things
that Jesus taught you in death
and Barabbas in life.

Blind, lamentable race,
repent your sins and crimes,
whilst Jesus is willing to grant
His Mercy and Pardon to you.

May the Streams from the Springs
that you have caused avail you,[28]
for they slake the thirst of all
and wash away all faults.

Weep, daughters of Zion,
for the Son of such dear grace,[29]
the distress of this Youth
becomes a delight to Him
for the sake of your sins.

Rush into His loving clasp,
while He hangs on the stake;
with mutual embraces

se parat amantibus
brachiis protensis.

In hoc solo gaudeo,
quod pro vobis doleo.
vicem, queso, reddite,
matris damnum plangite!

XV*/CCXLIII. *Reventus Christi*

Incipit ludus immo exemplum dominice resurrectionis.

**Cantatis matutinis in die pasche omnes persone ad ludum disposite
sint parate in loco speciali secundum suum modum et procedant ad
locum, ubi sit sepulchrum. Primum veniat Pilatus et uxor sua cum
magnis luminibus, militibus precedentibus, assessoribus sequentibus,
deinde pontificibus et Iudeis; post hec veniant angeli et Marie et
apostoli.**

Ingressus Pilatus <cum Iesu in pretorium; tunc ait illi:
Tu es rex Iudeorum. Respondit: Tu dicis, quia rex sum. Exivit ergo
Iesus de pretorio portans coronam et vestem purpuream; et cum
indutus fuisset, exclamaverunt omnes: Crucifigatur, quia filium Dei se
fecit.

Versus:
Tunc ait illis Pilatus: Regem vestrum crucifigam? Responderunt pontifices:
Regem non habemus nisi Cesarem>.

Primum cantent pontifices:
O domine,   recte meminimus,
quod a turba   sepe audivimus,
seductorem   consuetum dicere:
«post tres dies   volo resurgere.»

Pilatus:
Sicut michi   dictat discretio
† et astuta   vestra cognitio,
michi crimen   vultis imponere
de Iesu, quem   fecistis perdere.

Pontifices:
Vestra virtus   et sapientia

He prepares Himself for
loving, outstretched arms.[30]

On this ground do I rejoice,
for I suffer for the sake of ye.
Now repay me for the pain, I pray,
and lament this mother's loss!

15*/243. *The Return of Christ*

A play, nay, a portrait of the Lord's Resurrection begins.

After the Easter Matins, all the actors should be arranged for the play in a specific place, each according to his role, and should proceed to the tomb's site. First Pilate and his wife should come with many great luminaries—soldiers preceding them and aids following them—then the high priests and the Jews, then the angels, the 2 Marys,[31] and the apostles.

Pilate entered the palace with Jesus, then said to Him, "You are the King of the Jews?" Jesus answered, "You say that I am a king." Jesus then exited the palace, carrying the crown and purple robe, and when He had donned the robe, all cried, "He should be crucified, for He has made Himself the Son of God."

Verse:
Then Pilate said to them, "Am I to crucify your King?" The priests responded, "We have no king except Caesar."

The high priests should sing:
O Lord, we remember well—
we often heard it from the crowd—
what the Seducer was wont to tell:
'after three days I will rise anew.'

Pilatus:
My discernment and empirical knowledge
and your artful inquiry tell me that you wish
me to charge Jesus with a crime, Whose
execution You have already accomplished.

High Priests:
Your virtue and sapience

nobis valde   est necessaria;
seductoris   namque discipuli
machinantur   ruinam populi.

Uxor Pilati:
Versutia   horum non faciat,
ut sepulchrum   preses custodiat;
vestra namque   perpendat gloria,
quanta passa   fui per somnia.

Assessores:
Militibus   ergo precipias
custodire   noctis vigilias,
ne furentur   illum discipuli
et dicant plebi: «surrexit a mortuis».

Iudei stent ante Pilatum et cantent:
Audi, preses,   nostras preces,
ne sis deses;   nobis debes
hos prestare milites
ad sepulchrum, ut defunctus
observetur, ne tollatur
suis a discipulis.

Respondet Pilatus:
En habetis   custodum copiam.
custodite   noctis vigiliam,
ne furentur   illum discipuli
et dicant eum   vivere populi!

Tunc Iudei se vertant ad milites parum:
Militibus   damus pecuniam
ut habeant   semper custodiam
seductoris,   qui dixit temere:
«post tres dies   volo resurgere.»

Milites petant pecuniam:
Quid mercedis   ob hoc habebimus,
si custodes   vestri manserimus,
ne tollant   Iesum discipuli
et credant eum   vivere populi?

Iudei ostendant illis pecuniam:

are very indispensable to our cause;
for the disciples of the Seducer
are machinating the people's harm.

Pilate's Wife:
The cunning of these men should not succeed
in making the governor the guardian of a tomb.
For your glory should consider what portents great
I have suffered in my dreams of late.

Assessors:
You should give orders to the soldiers
to stay vigilant throughout the night,
lest the disciples surreptitiously remove Him
and declare to the rabble, "He is risen from the shades."

The Jews should stand before Pilate and say:
Hearken, governor, to our prayers,
lest you seem lax; you must place
these soldiers in front of the tomb,
so that the dead, if risen,
may by them be espied,
lest He be raised by His disciples' lies.

Pilate should respond:
Lo! You have an abundance of guards.
Maintain your watch of the night,
lest the disciples purloin Him and
the people declare that He is alive.

The Jews should turn themselves slightly to the soldiers:
We give money to the soldiers,
so they may always keep watch
for the Seducer, Who presumptuously said,
"After three days I will rise anew."

The soldiers should ask for money:
What guerdon for this shall we have,
if we remain your guards,
lest the disciples remove Him
and the people believe that He lives?

The Jews should show them the money:

O viri fortes, vobis dabimus pretium. Custodite sepulchrum!

Deinde exhibeant denarios in numero:
Nummos centum   quivis accipiat
vel talentum,   ut non decipiat,
sed custodes   existant tumuli,
ne furentur   illum discipuli.

Demum in toto sine numero:
Pecunia militibus   abunde tradatur,
ne seductor perfidus   furtim auferatur.

Tunc milites accepta pecunia evaginent enses et vadant ad sepulchrum et circumeant illud ordinate cantando simul: Defensores; deinde unusquisque militum suas vigilias solus, si velit.

Defensores   erimus tumuli,
ne furentur   illum discipuli
et fallendo   dicant in populis:
«resurrexit   Christus a mortuis.»

Primus miles:
Non credimus   Iesum resurgere,
sed, ne corpus   quis possit tollere,
providemus   per has vigilias.
Schavwe propter insidias!

Secundus miles:
Non credimus,   ut quicquam conferat,
sed ne corpus   eius quis auferat
custodimus   noctis vigilias.
Schavwe propter insidias!

Tertius miles:
Schavwe alumbe,   ne fures veniant
et corpus Iesu   furtim auferant,
custodimus   noctis vigilias.
Schavwe propter insidias!

Quartus miles:
Non exigit   humana ratio,
ut resurgat   vivus ex mortuo.
seductores   ferunt versutias.

O brave men, we shall give you a reward. Guard His tomb!

Then they should count out denarii to each one:
All should receive one hundred coins or a talent,
so that he will not in skullduggery take part,
but guardians of the tomb remain,
lest the disciples steal His Body in stealth.

At last, they are without money:
Money has abundantly been passed to the soldiers,
lest the perfidious Seducer be furtively stolen away.

**Then the soldiers, now paid, should unsheathe their swords and wend
to the tomb and methodically surround it whilst singing together:
"Defenders"; then each soldier alone takes up his watch, if he wishes.**

Defenders of the tomb we shall be
lest the disciples steal Him away
and through deceit declare among all:
"Christ is risen from the shades."

First Soldier:
We do not believe that Jesus will rise,
but lest someone His Body remove,
maintain we a nocturne, with eyes over tomb.
Be on your guard for tricks and fraud!

Second Soldier:
We do not believe that anything will come to pass,
but lest someone steal His Body away,
we keep our nocturnal watch.
Be on your guard for tricks and fraud!

Third Soldier:
Be on your guard and look around!
Lest thieves come in secret and furtively steal
the Body of Christ, we keep our watch of night.
Be on your guard for tricks and fraud!

Fourth Soldier:
It runs contrary to the reason of men
that a living man can rise from the dead.
O what great cunning seducers possess.

Schavwe propter insidias!

Quintus miles:
Si mortuus   posset resurgere,
potuisset   profecto vivere.
quare tulit   morus angustias?
Schavwe propter insidias!

**Tunc veniant duo angeli, unus ferens ensem flammeum et vestem
rubeam, alter vero vestem albam et crucem in manu. Angelus autem
ferens ensem percutiat unum ex militibus ad galeam, et medio fiant
tonitrua magna, et milites cadant quasi mortui. Et angeli stantes ante
sepulchrum nuntient cantando Christum surrexisse:**

> Alleluia!
> Resurrexit   victor ab inferis,
> pastor ovem   reportans humeris.
> Alleluia!
> Non divina   tamen potentia
> est absorta   carnis substantia.
> Alleluia!
> Reformator   ruine veteris
> causam egit   humani generis.
> Alleluia!

Tunc veniant Marie inquirendo aromata et cantent simul:
Aromata   pretio querimus,
corpus Iesu   ungere volumus.
aromata   sunt odorifera
sepulture   Christi memoria.

Tunc apothecarius audiens eas vocet:
Huc propius   flentes accedite
et unguentum,   si vultis, emite!
† aliter nusquam portabitis.
vere quantus est dolor vester!

Item Marie:
Dic tu nobis,   mercator iuvenis,
hoc unguentum   si tu vendideris,
dic pretium,   pro quanto dederis.
heu, quantus est dolor noster!

Be on your guard for tricks and fraud!

Fifth Soldier:
If a dead man could rise again to life,
he would surely have been able to stay so.
Wherefore did He endure such mortal agony?
Be on your guard for tricks and fraud!

Then two angels should come, one bearing a flaming sword and a red robe and the other a white robe and a cross. The angel with the sword smites one of the soldiers at the helm and in the middle of it all roaring thunders boom, and the soldiers fall as if they are dead. And the angels standing before the tomb announce in song the rising of the Christ:

> Hallelujah!
> Victorious, He is risen from the deep,
> the Shepherd bearing on His Shoulders the sheep.
> Hallelujah!
> Nevertheless His Divine Power is
> not consumed by the substance of flesh.
> Hallelujah!
> He Who turned round the evil of eld
> has championed the cause of mankind.
> Hallelujah!

The two Marys then should come, asking for spice in song:
We seek spices for a price,
to anoint the body of Christ.
The fragrant spices serve
as a memory of Christ's sepulture.

The apothecary, hearing this, should call to them:
Nearer hither approach, weeping ones,
and purchase ointments, if some you want!
Else you will carry off nothing at all.
In sooth, how great is your dole!

Likewise the Marys say:
Speak to us, young merchant,
if you sell this ointment, name the price
for which you will cede it to us.
Alas! how great is our dole!

Apothecarius:
Dabo vobis   unguenta optima,
salvatoris   ungere vulnera
sepulture   eius in memoriam
et nomini   eius ad gloriam.

Uxor apothecarii levet pyxidem et cantet:
Hoc unguentum   si vultis emere,
auri talentum michi tradite,
aliter nusquam portabitis.
vere quantus sit dolor vester!

Et sic ement aromata.
Apothecarius ostendat eis viam ad sepulchrum:
Hec est vera semita,
que recte, non per devia
vos ducet ad hortum.
ibi cum veneritis,
illum, quem vos queritis,
videbitis Iesum,
salvatorem vestrum.

Marie ostensa via vadunt ad sepulchrum et cantant:
Sed eamus et ad eius   properemus tumulum;
si dileximus viventem,   diligamus mortuum.

Marie lamentando cantent et vadant circa sepulchrum:
Heu! nobis internas mentes   quanti pulsant gemitus
pro nostro consolatore,   quo privamur misere,
quem crudelis Iudeorum   morti dedit populus.

Item cantent:
Iam percusso ceu pastore   oves errant misere,
sic magistro discedente   turbantur discipuli,
atque nos absente eo   dolor tenet nimius.

Item cantent:
Iam iam ecce, iam properemus ad tumulum ungentes corpus sanctissimum.

Una sola cantet:
O Deus!

Alia sola cantet:

Apothecary:
I shall give you the best unguents and salves,
so you may anoint the Savior's Wounds
in remembrance of His burial
and to the glory of His Name.

The apothecary's wife should raise a small box and sing:
If you wish to buy this ointment from me,
give me a talent of gold,
otherwise you will have nothing.
In sooth, how great is your dole!

And so they should purchase the spices.
The apothecary should show them the way to the tomb:
This is the true path,
which will lead you
directly to the garden
without a detour.
When you arrive there,
you will see Whom you seek,
Jesus, your Savior.

The Marys take the path to the sepulcher and sing:
Let us go and to His tomb let us hie.
If we loved Him in life, let us love Him in death.

The Marys in grief should sing and go around the tomb:
Alas! How great the sorrows that beat our souls deep within
for Our Consoler, of Whom we wretches are bereft,
Whom the cruel nation of Jews put to death!

Likewise they should sing:
As hapless sheep wander astray when the shepherd is slain,
so the disciples are now confused, when their Master departs,
and pain too strong grips our throng since He now is gone.

Likewise they should sing:
Now, now, lo! Let us hie now to His tomb and His most Holy Body salve!

One Mary should sing alone:
O God!

The other should sing alone:

O Deus!

Tertia sola cantet:
O Deus!

Deinde simul:
Quis revolvet nobis lapidem ab ostio monumenti?

Interea vadant milites ad Pilatum et pontifices et Iudeos et nuntient, quod viderunt et audierunt:
Visionem   gravem sustulimus,
terribiles   iuvenes vidimus,
et in terre   motu, quem sensimus,
crucifixum   surgere novimus.

Item cantent:
Nobis autem   custodientibus
et vigilias   noctis servantibus
supervenit   celestis nuntius,
qui et dixit: surrexit Dominus.»

Tunc pontifices perterriti corrumpunt milites muneribus, ut taceant:
Que refertis,   verba supprimite!
hanc mercedem   ob hoc suscipite!
et ne rumor   in turba prodeat,
<fides vestra   caute provideat.>

Versio K(losterneuburg:)
Morem nobis   in turba gerite,
corpus furtim   sublatum dicite:
«cum nos gravis   somnus oppresserit,
fur de nocte   eum abstulerit.»

Milites accepta pecunia ad populum cantant:
Vigilie   cunctos oppresserant,
iam nos sparsim   dormire noverant.
ad sepulchrum   fures accelerant,
ut magistrum   alias transferant.

In ruinam   igitur populi
furati sunt   Iesum discipuli.
ut valeant   turbam seducere,

O God!

The other should sing alone:
O God!

Then together they should sing:
Who will turn aside for us the stone from the monument's mouth?

Meanwhile the soldiers, high priests, and Jews should return to Pilate, and air what they have seen and heard:
We have witnessed a grievous sight,
formidable youths have we seen,
and by the earthquake, which we felt,
we knew that rising was the Crucified.

Likewise they should sing:
A celestial messenger came to us,
as we were standing guard over the tomb
and maintaining our nocturnal watch,
and said: "Risen is the Lord."

Then the terrified priests should seduce the soldiers with gifts, to buy their silence:
Suppress the words that you report!
Take up this gift in exchange!
And may your fidelity see to it that
rumor among the crowd does not circulate.

(The Klosterneuberg Easter Play):[32]
Maintain the act for us among the crowd;
say that the Body was purloined in stealth:
"When a heavy sleep overcame us,
 a thief stole Him under cover of night."

The soldiers with money in hand, should sing to the crowd:
Our sleeplessness had weighed upon us all,
and they espied us sleeping dispersedly.
To the tomb the thieves did rush,
to carry their Master elsewhere.

Therefore to the ruin of the people,
the disciples have stolen the Christ.
To succeed in the seduction of the mass,

mentiuntur   magistrum vivere.

Tunc Marie redeunt ad discipulos cantando:
En angeli   aspectum vidimus
et responsum   eius audivimus;
nam testatur   Dominum vivere.
sic oportet   te, Simon, credere.

 Apostoli cantant:
Ista sunt similia   deliramentorum
nec persuasibilia   mentibus virorum.

**Tunc Petrus et Iohannes properant ad monumentum, et precurrens
Iohannes et inveniens sudarium cantat:**
Monumentum   inveni vacuum
nec in eo   video mortuum
miror quidem,   si resurrexerit
an aliquis   eum abstulerit.

**Postea venit Petrus tollens linteamina. Revertuntur ad omnes
apostolos cantantes:**
Monumentum   vidimus vacuum
nec in eo   vidimus mortuum;
sed nescimus,   si resurrexerit
an aliquis   eum abstulerit.

**Tunc Maria Magdalena, que fuerat vestigio secuta Petrum et
Iohannem ad monumentum, illis redeuntibus ipsa sola remanet
cantans:**
Cum venissem   ungere mortuum,
monumentum   inveni vacuum.
heu! nescio   recte discernere,
ubi possim   magistrum querere.

En lapis est   vere depositus,
qui fuerat   in signum positus.
munierant   locum militibus;
locus vacat   eis absentibus.

Dolor crescit,   tremunt precordia
de magistri   pii absentia,
qui salvavit   me plenam vitiis
pulsis a me   septem demoniis.

they mendaciously state that the Teacher is alive.

Then the Marys should return to the disciples and sing:
Lo! We have seen the sight of the angel
and we have heard his response:
he attests that the Lord is yet alive;
thus it behooves you, Simon, to believe.

The Apostles should sing:
These rantings are pure absurdities
and are not persuasive to the minds of men.

Then Peter and John should hasten to the monument, and John, running ahead and finding a handkerchief, should sing:
I have discovered a cenotaph,
nor in it do I see a dead man.
I marvel indeed at whether He rose
or someone stole Him away.

Afterwards Peter should come, raising the cloth of linen. They should return to the apostles and sing:
A vacant tomb have we seen
and in it no dead man at all!
But we know not whether He did rise
or someone stole Him off.

Then Mary Magdalene, who had followed Peter and John's footprints to the tomb, there alone, as Peter and John have returned, should sing:
When I had come to anoint the dead Lord,
I came upon an empty tomb.
Alas! I know not how rightly to discern
where I can the Master procure.

Behold! The stone forsooth is displaced,
the stone that had been placed on the seal;
with soldiers they had garrisoned the site,
but all are absent and the place is void of anyone.

The pain increases and my heart quakes
o'er my Pious Teacher's absence,
Who saved me when I was fraught with vice,
by casting seven demons out of me.

Heu! redemptio Israel ut quid mortem sustinuit!

Tunc Iesus quasi ut specie hortulani apparens cantat:
Mulier, quid ploras?

Tunc Maria:
Quia tulerunt Dominum meum, et nescio, ubi posuerunt illum.

Cui iterum Iesus:
Mulier, quid ploras? Quem queris?

Item Maria:
Domine, si tu sustulisti eum, dicito michi, ubi posuisti eum, et ego eum
tollam.

Iesus in specie Christi:
Maria!

Maria respondit:
Rabboni!

Eaque volente iam tangere pedes eius, dicit ei Iesus:
Noli me tangere; nondum enim ascendi ad patrem meum. Vade autem ad
fratres meos et dic eis: «Ascendo ad patrem meum et patrem vestrum,
Deum meum et Deum vestrum.»

Tunc duo angeli precedentes Iesum ad infernum cantant:
[Alleluia! Surrexit Christus et illuxit populo suo, quem redemit sanguine
suo.]

Iesus veniens ad portas inferni et inveniens clausas cantat:
Tollite portas, principes, vestras, et elevamini, porte eternales, et introibit
rex glorie.

Tunc diabolus:
Quis est iste rex glorie?

Iesus:
Dominus fortis et potens, Dominus potens in prelio.

**Hoc ter repetito Iesus magno impetu tandem confringit portas inferni.
Infernales vero intuentes vultum eius cantant:**
Advenisti, desiderabilis, <quem expectabamus in tenebris, ut educeres hac

Alas! For what purpose did Israel's Redemption sustain death?!

Then Jesus, in the guise of a gardener, should sing:
Lady, why do you cry?

And Mary:
Because they have taken my Lord, and I know not where they've Him laid.

To her Jesus again should sing:
Why do you cry, lady? Whom do you seek?

Likewise Mary:
Lord, if you have taken Him, tell me where you have placed Him, and I
shall fetch Him there.

Jesus in the form of Christ:
Mary!

Mary should respond:
Rabbi!

She wishing to grasp his feet now, Jesus should sing:
Don't touch me! For not yet have I ascended to My Father.
Go, howbeit, to My brothers and tell them: "I am ascending
to My Father and your Father, My God and your God."

Two angels, preceding Jesus to the underworld, should sing:
Hallelujah! Christ is risen and has given light
to His people, whom He with His blood redeemed.

Jesus, at and finding the gates of Hell closed, should sing:
Raze your doors, princes, and raise yourself, eternal gates,
and the King of glory shall enter.

Then the devil should say:
 Who is this King of glory?

Jesus:
The brave and mighty Lord; a Lord puissant in war.

Thrice repeated, Jesus amain should break down Hell's doors at last.
And the netherfolk in wonder should sing to his face:
You have come, Desired One, Whom we awaited in the gloom,

nocte vinculatos de claustris. Te nostra vocabant suspiria; te larga requirebant tormenta; tu factus es spes desperatis, magna consolatio in tormentis.>

Postea Maria Magdalena inveniens alias duas Marias cantat:
Vere vidi   Dominum vivere,
nec dimisit   me pedes tangere.
discipulos   oportet credere,
quod ad patrem   velit ascendere.

Tunc ille tres iam certificate de resurrectione Domini nuntiant eam apostolis cantantes:
Galileam   omnes adibitis;
ibi Iesum   vivum videbitis.
quem post mortem   vivum non vidimus,
nos ibidem   visuros credimus.

‹Apostoli sine cessatione murmurant hymnum istum plangentes Dominum:
Iesu, nostra redemptio
amor et desiderium,
Deus, creator omnium,
homo in fine temporum,
que te vicit clementia,
ut ferres nostra crimina,
crudelem mortem patiens,
ut nos a morte tolleres?

Inferni claustra penetrans,
tuos captivos redimens,
victor triumpho nobili
ad dextram Patris residens,
ipsa te cogat pietas,
ut mala nostra superes
parcendo et voti compotes
nos tuo vultu saties.

Tu esto nostrum gaudium,
qui es futurus premium;
sit nostra in te gloria
per cuncta semper secula.

Gloria tibi, Domine,

to lead out on this night the shackled from their bars. Our sighs did call
for You; Your catapults large did we seek; You have become to the hapless
a hope, a great comfort in torments great.

Then Mary Magdalene, finding the other two Marys, should sing:
Verily have I seen the Lord alive;
He forbade me to touch His Feet;
the disciples must trust that He wishes now
to ascend up to His Father in the sky.

**Then the three, now certain of the resurrection of the Lord, should
report it to the apostles in song:**
You all shall go to Galilee;
there you shall see the living Christ,
Whom after death we did not see alive,
though we believe in that place you will Him espy.

**The apostles without pause should murmur a hymn, grieving over
the Lord:**
Jesus, our Redemption,
Love, and Desire,
God, Creator of all,
Man in the end of time,
what clemency conquered You,
that You bore all of our crimes,
suffering cruel, torturous death,
so that You might raise us from it?

Bursting through the gates of hell,
redeeming all of Your captives,
sitting a Victor in noble triumph
at the Right Hand of the Father,
let Compassion itself impel You,
to vanquish our sins by sparing us,
and to satiate us with Your Visage,
all participating in prayer.

Be You our Joy,
Who will be our Reward;
may our glory forever be in You,
throughout all the ages forevermore.

Glory to You, Lord,

qui scandis super sidera,
cum Patre et Sancto Spiritu
in sempiterna secula.

**Item apostoli videntes eam eminus in talem vocem prorumpunt
cantando:**
Dic nobis, Maria,
quid vidisti in via?

Maria respondit:
Sepulchrum Christi viventis
et gloriam vidi resurgentis,
angelicos testes,
sudarium et vestes.
surrexit Christus, spes mea;
precedet suos in Galilea.

Tunc apostoli omnes:
Credendum est magis soli Marie veraci
quam Iudeorum turbe fallaci.
scimus Christum surrexisse a mortuis vere.
tu nobis, victor rex, miserere.

**Deinde omnes apostoli et mulieres veniunt ostendere linteamina
populo. Cantant:**
Cernitis, o socii, ecce linteamina et sudarium, et corpus Iesu in sepulchro
non est inventum.

Illis ostensis chorus totus cantat:
Post pass<ionem> Do<mini factus est conventus, quia non est inventum
corpus in monumento; lapis sustinuit perpetuam vitam, monumentum
reddidit celestem margaritam, Alleluia.> Currebant duo simul, et ille alius
discipulus precucurrit citius Petro et prior venit ad monumentum. Alleluia.

Et populus universus iam certificatus de Domino, cantor sic imponit:
Christ, der ist erstanden
<von der marter alle,
des sull wir alle fro sein,
Christ sol unser trost sein.
Kyrie eleyson.>

XVI*/CCXLIV. *Passio Christi* (*Extensa Editio*)

Who climbs above the stars,
with the Father and Holy Ghost,
in ages everlasting.

Likewise should the apostles, seeing her, break with lighter voices into song:
Tell us, Mary,
what did you see on the road?

Mary should respond:
I saw the tomb of the living Christ
and the glory of the risen Lord,
and angelic witnesses,
handkerchiefs and many robes.
Christ is risen, my Hope; He will lead
His friends' way straight to Galilee.

Then all the apostles should say:
Veracious Mary must be given more
credence than the fallacious Jewish throng.
We know forsooth that Christ has risen from death.
Take pity on us, Victorious King.

Then all the apostles and the women should come to show the handkerchief to the people. They should sing:
See, comrades and behold the linen cloth and handkerchief,
and the Body of Christ was not found in the tomb.

After this display, the entire chorus should sing:
After the passion of the Lord, a covenant was formed that His Body was not found in the tomb; a stone sustained perpetual life, the tomb rendered a supernal pearl. Hallelujah. Two ran together, and that other disciple ran ahead faster than Peter and ere him arrived at the tomb. Hallelujah.

And all the people, certain of the Lord, should lay down this song:
Christ has risen
from all manner of ordeals,
wherefor we all should be happy
and Christ should be our Comfort.
Kyrie eleison.

16*/244. *The Passion of the Christ (Extended Edition)*

Primitus producatur Pilatus et uxor sua cum militibus in locum suum, deinde Herodes cum militibus suis, deinde pontifices, tunc mercator et uxor sua, deinde Maria Magdalena.

Ingressus Pilatus <cum Iesu in pretorium; tunc ait illi: Tu es rex Iudeorum. Respondit: Tu dicis, quia rex sum. Exivit ergo Iesus de pretorio portans coronam et vestem purpuream; et cum indutus fuisset, exclamaverunt omnes: Crucifigatur, quia filium Dei se fecit.

Versus:

Tunc ait illis Pilatus: Regem vestrum crucifigam? Responderunt pontifices: Regem non habemus nisi Cesarem.>

Postea vadat dominica persona sola ad litus maris vocare Petrum et Andream et inveniat eos piscantes, et Dominus dicit ad eos:

Venite post me, faciam vos piscatores hominum.

Illi dicunt:

Domine, quid vis, hec faciemus et ad tuam voluntatem protinus adimplemus.

Postea vadat dominica persona ad Zacheum et obviet ei cecus:

Domine Iesu, fili David, miserere mei.

Iesus respondet:

Quid vis, ut faciam tibi?

Cecus:

Domine, tantum ut videam.

Iesus dicit:

Respice, fides enim tua salvum te fecit.

His factis Iesus procedat ad Zacheum et vocet illum de arbore:

Zachee, festinans descende, quia hodie in domo tua oportet me manere.

Zacheus dicit:

Domine, si quid aliquem defraudavi, reddo quadruplum.

Iesus respondet:

Quia hodie huic domui salus facta est, eo quod et tu sis filius Abrahe.

Iesus venit.

Cum appropinquaret Dominus <Hierosolymam, misit duos ex discipulis

Pilate first and his wife should be brought forth with a coterie of soldiers to their place, then Herod with his soldiers, then the high priests, then the merchant and his wife, then Mary Magdalene.
Pilate entered his palace with Jesus and said to Him: "Are you the King of the Jews?" He responded: "You say that I am a king." Jesus exited the palace with the crown and purple robe, and when He donned them, they all exclaimed: "He should be crucified, for He made Himself the Son of God."

Verse:
Then Pilate said unto them: "Am I to crucify your King?" The high priests responded, "We have no king except Caesar."

Afterwards the actor playing the Lord should go alone to the seashore to call upon Peter and Andrew, find them fishing, and say to them:
Follow after Me; I shall make fishers of men.

They should say:
My Lord, whatever You wish, we shall perform
and we shall forthwith fulfill Your Will.

Jesus should go to Zacchaeus and meet a blind man en route:
Lord Jesus, Son of David, take pity on me.

Jesus should respond:
What do you wish Me to do for thee?

Blind Man:
Lord, so great would it be that I should see.

Jesus should say:
Look about, for thy faith has restored thee.

After this He should go to Zacchaeus and call him from a tree:
Zacchaeus, descend with haste, because today in thy house must I stay.

Zacchaeus should say:
My Lord, if I have cheated anyone, I return it fourfold.

Jesus should respond:
Today salvation shall befall this house, for thou art also Abraham's son.

Jesus comes.
As the Lord approached Jerusalem, He sent ahead two of His disciples

suis, dicens: Ite in castellum, quod est contra vos, et invenietis pullum
asine alligatum, super quem nullus hominum sedit; solvite et adducite
michi. Si quis vos interrogaverit, dicite: Opus Domino est. Solventes
adduxerunt ad Iesum et imposuerunt illi vestimenta sua, et sedit super eum.
Alii expandebant vestimenta sua in via, alii ramos de arboribus
externebant, et qui sequebantur, clamabant: Osanna, benedictus, qui venit
in nomine Domini, benedictum regnum patris nostri David. Osanna in
excelsis. Miserere nobis, fili David.>

Et:
Cum audisset <populus, quia Iesus venit Hierosolymam, acceperunt ramos
palmarum et exierunt ei obviam; et clamabant pueri dicentes: Hic est, qui
venturus est in salutem populi, hic est salus nostra et redemptio Israel;
quantus est iste, cui throni et dominationes occurrunt! Noli timere, filia
Sion, ecce rex tuus venit tibi sedens super pullum asine, sicut scriptum est.
Salve, rex, fabricator mundi, qui venisti redimere nos.>

Et pueri prosternentes frondes et vestes:
Pueri Hebreorum <tollentes ramos olivarum obviaverunt Domino
clamantes et dicentes: Osanna in excelsis.>

Item:
Pueri <Hebreorum vestimenta prosternebant in via, et clamabant dicentes:
Osanna filio David, benedictus, qui venit in nomine Domini.>

Item:
Gloria, laus <et honor tibi sit, rex Christe, redemptor, Cui puerile decus
prompsit Osanna pium.>

Tunc veniat Phariseus et vocet Iesum ad cenam:
Rabbi, quod interpretatur magister, peto, ut mecum hodie velis manducare.

Iesus respondet:
Fiat, ut petisti.

Phariseus dicat ad servum:
Ite citius, preparate sedilia
ad mense convivia,
ut sint placentia.

Maria Magdalena cantet:
Mundi delectatio   dulcis est et grata,
eius conversatio   suavis et ornata.

thus: "Go to the place, which lies before you and you will find an ass' foal bound, upon which no man has sat. Release it and bring it to Me. If anyone questions you, say, 'The Lord has need for it.'" They released it, brought it to Jesus, bedecked it with their clothes, and He sat upon it. Some were spreading out their clothes upon the road and others were strewing boughs from the trees, and those who followed Him, shouted: "Hoshana![33] A blessed man be He, Who came in the Lord's name, blessed be the kingdom of our father David. Hosanna in the loftiest heights! Pity us, Son of David.

And:
When the people heard that Jesus was coming to Jerusalem, they gathered palm branches and went out to meet Him. The boys shouted: "Here He is, Who will come to the people's rescue. He is our Salvation and Israel's Redemption. How strong is He, Whom thrones and dominions serve. Fear not, daughter of Zion, and see! To you your king upon an ass' foal is come, as written. Hail, King, Maker of the world, Who are come to redeem us."

And the boys strewing fronds and vestments before Him:
The children of the Hebrews, raising olive trees' boughs, met
with the Lord, shouted, and said: "Hosanna in the highest!"

Likewise:
The Hebrews' children strewed togs on the road before Him and shouted:
"Hosanna to David's Son. Blessed be He, Who came in the Lord's Name!"

Likewise:
Glory, laud, and honor be to You, Christ the King, Redeemer,
to Whom splendid youths offer holy Hosanna!

Then a Pharisee should come and invite Jesus to a meal:
Rabbi, that is, Teacher, I pray that You be willing to dine with me today.

Jesus should answer:
It shall be done, as thou hast prayed.

The Pharisee should say to his servant:
Go quickly, and prepare our seats
at the meal table and arrange it
such that it will please our Guest.

Mary Magdalene should sing:
The pleasure of the world is sweet and delightful;
its intercourse is alluring and bejeweled.

mundi sunt delicie,   quibus estuare
volo nec lasciviam   eius devitare.

Pro mundano gaudio   vitam terminabo,
bonis temporalibus   ego militabo.
nil curans de ceteris   corpus procurabo,
variis coloribus   illud perornabo.

Modo vadat Maria cum puellis ad mercatorem cantando:
Michi confer, venditor,   species emendas
pro multa pecunia   tibi iam reddenda,
si quid habes insuper   odoramentorum.
nam volo perungere   corpus hoc decorum.

Mercator cantet:
Ecce merces optime!   conspice nitorem!
hec tibi conveniunt   ad vultus decorem.
hec sunt odorifere,   quas si comprobaris,
corporis flagrantiam   omnem superabis.

Maria Magdalena:
Chramer, gip die varwe mier,
div min wengel roete,
da mit ich die iungen man
an ir danch der minnenliebe noete.

Item:
Seht mich an,   iungen man,
lat mich ev gevallen.

Item:
Minnet, tugentliche man,
minnekliche vravwen.
minne tuoet ev hoech gemuet
vnde lat evch in hoehen eren schavuven.

Refl.   Seht mich an,   iunge man,
        <lat mich ev gevallen.>

Item:
Wol dir werlt, daz du bist
also vreudenreiche.
ich wil dir sin vndertan

The world contains joys, for which I lustfully burn,
voluptuousness, which I dare not eschew.

For worldly pleasures, I shall end my life;
I want to serve as soldieress all secular wares.
Caring nothing about the rest, I shall put my body in my care;
with various cosmetics I shall embellish it and bedeck.

Now Mary should come with boys to a merchant and sing:
Merchant, bring to me the spices I wish to buy
for money's high sum—I will pay you now—
and any other perfumes you have in your store,
for I wish to anoint this my glorious form.

The merchant should sing:
Behold my best merchandise! Look at these splendid goods!
These items harmonize with the beauty of your face!
Fragrant are these, and if you test them,
the scent of your body will earn you nonpareil praise.[34]

Mary Magdalene:
Merchant, give me the maquillage.
It should redden my soft cheeks,
so that I may inveigle young men,
whether willing or not, into love.

Likewise:
Look at me, young men,
and take pleasure in my body.

Likewise:
Ye splendid fellows,
give to fair lasses your love!
Love makes you proud and gay
and augments your prestige in the eyes of the world.

Refr.   Look at me, young men,
         and take pleasure in my body.

Likewise:
Praised be you, world, because
you offer a bounty of delights.
I want to serve you always steadfastly,

durch dein liebe immer sicherlichen.

Refl.   Seht mich an,   iunge man,
          <lat mich ev gevallen.>

Postea vadat dormitum, et angelus cantet:
O Maria Magdalena,
nova tibi nuntio:
Simonis hospitio
hic sedens convivatur
Iesus ille Nazarenus
gratia, virtute plenus,
qui relaxat peccata populi;
hunc turbe confitentur
salvatorem seculi.

Recedat angelus. Et surgat Maria cantando:
Mundi delectatio   <dulcis est et grata,
eius conversatio   suavis et ornata.
mundi sunt delicie,   quibus estuare
volo nec lasciviam   eius devitare.

Pro mundano gaudio   vitam terminabo,
bonis temporalibus   ego militabo.
nil curans de ceteris   corpus procurabo,
variis coloribus   illud perornabo.>

Tunc accedat amator, quem Maria salutet, et cum parum loquuntur,
cantet Maria ad puellas:
Wol dan, minneklichev chint,
schavwe wier chrame.
chauf wier di varwe da,
di vns machen schoene vnde wolgetane.
er muez sein sorgen vrie,
der da minnet mier den leip.

Iterum cantet:
Chramer, gip di varwe mir,
<div min wengel roete,
da mit ich die iungen man
an ir danch der minnenliebe noete.

Refl.   Seht mich an,   iunge man,

so I may receive your goodwill.

Refr.   Look at me, young men,
              and take pleasure in my body.

Afterwards she should sleep, and an angel should sing:
O Mary Magdalene,
I report these tidings to thee:
Invited by Simon, that Jesus of Nazareth
sits here feasting
with His Wonderworking Grace,
full of virtue, forgiving
all the people's sins.
The throngs affirm that He
is the Savior of this age.

The angel should withdraw and Mary should rise in song:
The pleasure of the world is sweet and delightful;
its intercourse is alluring and bejeweled.
The world contains joys, for which I lustfully burn,
voluptuousness, which I dare not eschew.

For worldly pleasures, I shall end my life;
I want to serve as soldieress all secular wares.
Caring nothing about the rest, I shall put my body in my care;
with various cosmetics I shall embellish it and bedeck.

**Then a lover should approach, whom Mary should salute, and when
they speak for a bit, she should sing to the girls:**
Up then, ye sweet girls,
we will seek the merchant out.
There we will purchase maquillage,
which will make us lovely and of mien soigné.
Whoever comes to me for love
should lose all his solicitudes.

Again she should sing:
Merchant, give me the maquillage.
It should redden my soft cheeks,
so that I may inveigle young men,
whether willing or not, into love.

Refr.   Look at me, young men,

<lat mich ev gevallen.>

Mercator respondet:
Ich gib ev varwe, deu ist guoet,
dar zuoe lobelich,
dev eu machet reht schoene
vnt dar zuoe uil reht wunecliche.
nempt si hin, hab ir si,
ir ist nihtgeleiche.

Accepto unguento vadat dormitum.
<Angelus:>
O Maria Magdalena,
<nova tibi nuntio:
Simonis hospitio
hic sedens convivatur
Iesus ille Nazarenus
gratia, virtute plenus,
qui relaxat peccata populi;
hunc turbe confitentur
salvatorem seculi.>

Et iterum evanescat. Tunc surgat Maria et cantet:
Mundi delectatio   <dulcis est et grata,
eius conversatio   suavis et ornata
mundi sunt delicie,   quibus estuare
volo nec lasciviam   eius devitare.

Pro mundano gaudio   vitam terminabo,
bonis temporalibus   ego militabo.
nil curans de ceteris   corpus procurato,
variis coloribus   illud perornabo.>

Et iterum postea obdormiat.
Et angelus veniat cantando ut sopra:
<O Maria Magdalena,
nova tibi nuntio:
Simonis hospitio
hic sedens convivatur
Iesus ille Nazarenus
gratia, virtute plenus,
qui relaxat   peccata populi;
hunc turbe confitentur

and take pleasure in my body.

The merchant should answer:
I shall give you an excellent makeup,
which one can really recommend;
it will endow you with a brilliant pulchritude
and will make you simply irresistible.
Accept it and pack it up,
for it is nonpareil.

With the salve received, she should go to sleep.
An angel should sing:
O Mary Magdalene,
I report these tidings to thee:
Invited by Simon, that Jesus of Nazareth
sits here feasting
with His Wonderworking Grace,
full of virtue, forgiving
all the people's sins.
The throngs affirm that He
is the Savior of this age.

Again he should vanish. Then Mary should rise and sing:
The pleasure of the world is sweet and delightful;
its intercourse is alluring and bejeweled.
The world contains joys, for which I lustfully burn,
voluptuousness, which I dare not eschew.

For worldly pleasures, I shall end my life;
I want to serve as soldieress all secular wares.
Caring nothing about the rest, I shall put my body in my care;
with various cosmetics I shall embellish it and bedeck.

And again afterwards she should go to sleep.
Then an angel should come singing to her as she sleeps:
O Mary Magdalene,
I report these tidings to thee:
Invited by Simon, that Jesus of Nazareth
sits here feasting
with His Wonderworking Grace,
full of virtue, forgiving
all the people's sins.
The throngs affirm that He

salvatorem seculi.>

Et iterum evanescat.
<Maria Magdalena:>
Heu, vita preterita,   vita plena malis,
luxus turpitudinis,   fons exitialis,
heu, quid agam misera,   plena peccatorum,
que polluta palleo   sorde vitiorum!

Angelus dicit sibi:
Dico tibi: gaudium est angelis Dei super una peccatrice penitentiam agente.

Maria:
Hinc, ornatus seculi,   vestium candores!
procul a me fugite,   turpes amatores!
ut quid nasci volui,   que sum † defedanda
et ex omni genere   criminum notanda!

**Tunc deponat vestimenta secularia et induat nigrum pallium, et
amator recedat et diabolus. Veniat ad mercatorem:**
Dic tu nobis,   mercator iuvenis,
hoc ungentum   si tu vendideris,
dic pretium,   pro quanto dederis.
heu, quantus est dolor noster!

Mercator respondet:
Hoc ungentum   si multum cupitis,
unum auri   talentum dabitis.
aliter nusquam portabitis.
optimum est.

Et chorus cantet:
Accessit ad pedes <Iesu peccatrix mulier Maria.>

Accepto unguento vadat ad dominicam personam cantando flendo:
Ibo nunc ad medicum   turpiter egrota
medicinam postulans;   lacrimarum vota
huic restat ut offeram   et cordis plangores,
qui cunctos, ut audio,   sanat peccatores.

Item:
Iesus, troest der sele min,

is the Savior of this age.

And again he should vanish.
Mary Magdalene:
Alas my past life, a life replete with sin,
a surfeit of infamy, a fount of destruction, alas!,
what is a wretch like me to do, full of sin,
who, defiled, grows pale from vice's filth!

The angel should say to himself:
I say to thee: a joy it is to the angels of God on high
to see one sinner doing penitence for her crimes.

Mary:
Hence, worldly jewels! Avaunt, brilliant dress!
Fly far from me, base customers!
Did I desire to be born only for this,
to be defiled and be marked with a panoply of sins?!

**She should lay aside her worldly togs and don a black cloak—the lover
and devil should withdraw—and she should go to the merchant:**
Tell us, young merchant,
if you are selling this salve,
name the price and how much in exchange you will give.
Alas, how great is our grief!

The merchant should respond:
If you really desire this unguent,
give me a talent of gold,
otherwise you will leave with nothing at all.
It is the very best.

And the chorus should sing:
The sinner woman approached Jesus' Feet.

Having received the salve, she should go the Lord and sing in tears:
I now shall go to a doctor, to request medicine, sick as I am
from my vile past. What remains is to offer a vow
of my tears and smites to my chest to Him,
Who heals all sinners, as the angels have said.

Likewise:
Jesus, the Solace of my soul,

la mich dir enpfolhen sin,
unde loese mich uon der missetat,
da mich dev werlt zuoe hat braht.

Item:
Ich chume niht uon den fůzzen dein,
du erloesest mich uon den sunden mein
vnde uon der groezzen missetat,
da mich deu werlt zuoe hat braht.

Loquatur Phariseus intra se:
Si hic esset propheta, sciret utique, que et qualis illa esset, que tangit eum,
quia peccatrix est.

Et dicat Iudas:
Ut quid perditio hec? Potuit enim hoc venundari multo et dari pauperibus.

Iesus cantet:
Quid molesti estis huic mulieri? Opus bonum operata est in me.

Item statim:
Simon, habeo tibi aliquid dicere.

Simon Petrus:
Magister, dic.

Dicit Iesus:
Debitores habuit   quidam creditorum
duos, quibus credidit   spe denariorum.
hic quingentos debuit,   alter quinquagenos,
sed eos penuria   fecerat egenos.
cum nequirent reddere,   totum relaxavit,
quis eorum igitur   ipsum plus amavit?

Simon respondet:
Estimo, quod ille plus,   cui plus donavit.

Iesus dicat:
Tua sic sententia   recte iudicavit.

Item Iesus cantet ad Mariam:
Mulier, remittuntur tibi peccata. Fides tua salvam te fecit; vade in pace.

let me be commended to Ye,
and divest me of my malefactions,
in which the world has trammeled me.

Likewise:
I shall soak first Your Feet,
when You rid me of my sins
and free me from my great misdeeds,
in which the world has trammeled me.

The Pharisee should say to himself:
If He were a prophet, He would surely know who
and of what character she was, who touches Him, for she is a sinner.

And Judas should say:
Why this ruin? For it could be sold for much more and given to the poor.

Jesus should sing:
Why harrow ye this woman? A good deed she has done Me.

Forthwith he should continue:
Simon, I have something to tell thee.

Simon Peter:
Master, speak.

Jesus should say:
A certain creditor had two debtors, to whom
he had given credit in the hope for a profit's turn.
One owed five hundred denarii; the other owed fifty.
A crisis had left them both in penury.
When they could not pay back the loan, he released them
from his debt—which of them loved him for it the more?

Simon:
I trow the latter loved him more, to whom he had more lent.

Jesus should say:
Thy opinion has judged correctly.

Then Jesus should sing to Mary:
Woman, thou art forgiven thy sins. Thy faith hath protected thee.
Go in peace.

Tunc Maria surgat et vadat lamentando cantans:
Awve, auvve, daz ich ie wart geborn.
han ich verdient gotes zorn,
der mier hat geben sele vnde leip.
awve, ich uil vnselaeich wiep.
Owve, awve, daz ich ie wart geborn,
swenne mich erwechet gotes zorn.
wol uf, ir gůeten man vnde wip,
got wil rihten sele vnde leip.

Interea cantent discipuli:
Phariseus iste fontem misericordie conabatur obstruere.

**Tunc vadat Iesus ad resuscitandum Lazarum, et ibi occurrant Maria
Magdalena et Martha plorantes pro Lazaro, et Iesus cantet:**
Lazarus, amicus noster, dormit. Eamus et a somno resuscitemus eum.

Tunc Maria Magdalena et Martha flendo cantent:
Domine, si fuisses hic, frater noster non fuisset mortuus.

Et sic tacendo clerus cantet:
Videns Dominus flentes sorores Lazari ad monumentum lacrimatus est
coram Iudeis et clamabat:

Et Iesus cantet:
Lazare, veni foras.

Et clerus cantet:
Et prodiit ligatis m<anibus> et p<edibus>, qui f<uit> q<uadriduum>
m<ortuus.>

**Interim Iudas veniat festinando et querat opportunitatem tradendi
dicens:**
O pontifices, o viri magni consilii, Iesum volo vobis tradere.

Cui pontifices respondeant:
O Iuda,   si nobis Iesum iam tradideris,
triginta   argenteis remuneraberis.

Iudas respondeat:
Iesum tradam, credite;
rem promissam michi solvite;
turbam mecum dirigite;

Then Mary should rise and go off singing in lamentation:
Woe is me, woe is me, that I was born at all!
I have earned the wrath of God,
Who had given me a body and a soul.
Woe to me, ill-fated woman.
Woe is me, woe is me, that I was born at all,
when once the wrath of God calls me to His Court.
Wake up, noble men and women sublime!
God will hold court on your body and soul.

Meanwhile the disciples should sing:
That Pharisee assayed to obstruct the fountain of pity.

Jesus should go to resurrect Lazarus and there Mary Magdalene and Martha, ruing Lazarus, should meet Him there, and Jesus should sing:
Lazarus, our friend, is asleep. Let us go and raise him from his dream.

Then Mary Magdalene and Martha should sing and weep:
Lord, if You had been here, our brother would not have died.

And when they grow silent, the cleric should say:
When the Lord saw the sisters of Lazarus weeping at the tomb,
He wept in the presence of the Jews and shouted:

Jesus should sing:
Lazarus, come forth into the open!

And the cleric should sing:
And he came forth with hands and feet bound, who had died four days before.

Meanwhile Judas should come in haste and seek the opportunity to betray Christ in these words:
O priests, men of wisdom great, I wish to hand Jesus over to you.

The high priests should respond to him:
O Judas, if you hand Jesus over to us now,
we shall give you thirty pieces of silver.

Judas should respond:
I will betray Jesus, believe me;
but keep your promise to me;
send a crowd together with me,

Iesum caute deducite!

Pontifices cantent:
Iesum tradas propere;
hanc turbam tecum accipe
et procede viriliter;
Iesum trade velociter!

Iudas tunc det Iudeis signum cantando:
Quemcumque osculatus fuero, ipse est; tenete eum!

**Tunc turba Iudeorum sequatur Iudam cum gladiis et lucernis donec
ad Iesum. Interea Iesus faciat, ut mos est in cena. Postea assumat
quatuor discipulos et ceteris dicat, quos relinquit:**
Dormite iam et requiescite.

Deinde vadat orare et dicat quatuor discipulis:
Tristis est anima mea usque ad mortem. Sustinete hic et orate, ne intretis in
temptationem.

**Tunc ascendat in montem Oliveti et flexis genibus respiciens celum
petat dicendo:**
Pater, si fieri potest, transeat a me calix iste. Spiritus quidem promptus est,
caro autem infirma. Fiat voluntas tua.

**Hoc facto redeat ad quatuor discipulos et inveniat eos dormientes et
dicat Petro:**
Simon, dormis? Non potuisti una hora vigilare mecum? Manete hic, donec
vadam et orem.

Postea vadat iterum orare ut antea:
<Pater, si fieri potest, transeat a me calix iste. Spiritus quidem promptus
est, caro autem infirma. Fiat voluntas tua.>

**Tunc iterato veniat ad discipulos et inveniat eos dormientes et dicat ad
eos:**
Manete hic!

Et iterum dicit:
Pater, si non potest hic calix transire, nisi bibam illum, fiat voluntas tua.

Tunc redeat ad discipulos et cantet:

and lead Jesus away without a scene.

The high priests should sing:
You should hand over Jesus in haste;
take this throng with you and proceed
with courage and intrepidity.
Hand over Jesus swiftly!

Judas then should signal the Jews, singing:
Whomever I should kiss is He; arrest Him!

Then the throng of Jews should follow Judas with swords and lamps until they reach Jesus. Then Jesus should hold Communion; then He should take four disciples and say to the others He is leaving behind:
Sleep now and rest.

He then begins to pray and should say to the four disciples:
My soul is sad all the way to the point of death.
Stay here and pray that you don't enter into temptation.

He should then ascend the Mount of Olives and, looking up to the sky on bent knees, pray:
Father, if it be possible, let this Chalice pass away from Me.
The spirit is willing, but the flesh is weak. May Your Will be done!

After this, He should return to the four disciples and, finding them asleep, should say to Simon Peter:
Simon, art thou asleep? Wert thou unable to stay awake
for one hour with Me? Stay here, until I come and pray.

Afterwards He should begin to pray again as before:
Father, if it be possible, let this chalice pass away from Me.
The spirit is willing, but the flesh is weak. May Your Will be done!

Then, once again, He should come to the disciples and find them sleeping and should say to them:
Stay here!

And again He should say:
Father, if it be not possible for this chalice to pass away
from Me, unless I drink from it, May Your will be done!

He should then return to the disciples and sing:

Una hora non potestis vigilare mecum, qui exhortabamini mori pro me.
Vel Iudam non videtis, quomodo non dormit, sed festinat tradere me
Iudeis? Surgite eamus. Ecce appropinquat, qui me traditurus est.

Veniat Iudas ad Iesum cum turba Iudeorum.
Quibus Iesus dicat:
Quem queritis?

Qui respondent:
Iesum Nazarenum.

Iesus dicit:
Ego sum.

Et turba retrocedat.
Item Iesus dicit:
Quem queritis?

Iudei:
Iesum Nazarenum.

Iesus respondet:
Dixi vobis, quia ego sum.

Item:
Si ergo me queritis, sinite hos abire.

Tunc apostoli dent fugam excepto Petro.
Et Iudas dicat:
Ave, Rabbi.

Iesus illi respondet:
O Iuda, ad quid venisti?
peccatum magnum tu fecisti.
me Iudeis traditum
ducis ad patibulum
cruciandum.

Et Iesus dicat:
Tamquam ad latronem existis cum gladiis et fustibus comprehendere me;

You were not able to stay awake for but one hour with Me, ye, who urged
Me to die for My own sake? Or see you not Judas, how he does not sleep,
but hies to betray Me to the Jews? Rise, let us go! Lo! He, who is about to
betray Me, approaches.

Judas should come to Jesus with a crowd of Jews.
Jesus should say to them:
Whom do you seek?

They should respond:
Jesus of Nazareth.

Jesus should say:
I am He.

The crowd should recede.
Likewise Jesus should say:
Whom do you seek?

The Jews:
Jesus of Nazareth.

Jesus should respond:
I told you that I am He.

Likewise:
If it is I you seek, allow these men to leave.

The apostles should then take to flight, except Simon Peter.
And Judas should say:
Greetings, Rabbi!

Jesus should respond to him:
O Judas, why hast thou come?
Thou hast committed a great sin.
Thou hast handed Me over to the Jews
and art leading Me to the gibbet
to be crucified.

And Jesus should say:
You emerge with swords and clubs to arrest Me, as if you are after a thief.
Everyday among you have I sat, teaching in the temple, and you did not
arrest Me then.

Et ducatur Iesus ad pontifices.
Et chorus cantet:
Collegerunt pontifices <et Pharisei concilium et dicebant>:

Et pontifices cantent et cogitent, quid faciant:
Quid facimus, quia hic homo multa signa facit? Si dimittimus eum sic,
omnes credent in eum.

Et Caiphas cantet:
Expedit vobis, ut unus moriatur homo pro populo et non tota gens pereat.

Clerus cantet:
Ab ipso ergo die cogitaverunt <interficere eum dicentes: Ne forte veniant
Romani, et tollant nostrum locum et gentem.>

Postea ducitur ad Pilatum Iesus. Et dicunt Iudei:
Hic dixit: Solvite templum hoc, et post triduum reedificabo illud.

Pilatus respondet:
Quam accusationem affertis adversus hominem istum?

Iudei respondent:
Si non fuisset hic malefactor, non tibi tradidissemus eum.

Pilatus:
Accipite eum vos et secundum legem vestram iudicate eum.

Iudei:
Nobis non licet interficere quemquam.

Postea ducatur Iesus ad Herodem, qui dicat ei:
Homo Galileus es?

Iesus vero tacebat. Et Herodes iterum dicit:
Quem te ipsum facis?

**Iesus non respondet ei ad unum verbum. Tunc Iesus induatur veste
alba, et reducunt Iesum ad Pilatum. Tunc conveniunt Pilatus et
Herodes et osculantur invicem. Et Iesus veniat ad Pilatum et ipse dicit:**
Nullam causam mortis invenio in homine isto.

Iudei dicunt:

And Jesus should be brought before the high priests.
And the chorus should sing:
The high priests and the Pharisees held a council and said:

The high priests should sing and ponder what to do:
What should we do with that Man Who works many miracles? If we send
Him off, all will believe in Him.

And Caiphas should sing:
It is better that one man die for the people than for an entire race to perish.

A clergyman should sing:
From that day on they plotted His death, saying: lest the Romans by chance
come and destroy our city and race.

Afterwards Jesus is brought to Pilate. The Jews should say:
He said: "Destroy this temple and after three days I will rebuild it."

Pilate should respond:
What accusation do you bring against this Man?

The Jews should respond:
If He weren't an evildoer, we wouldn't have given Him to ye!

Pilate:
Take Him and judge Him according to your law.

Jews:
We are not permitted to kill anyone.

Afterwards Jesus should be led to Herod, who should say:
Are You a Galilean?

But Jesus remained silent. And Herod again says:
What do You purport to be?

**Jesus should not respond to one word. Then Jesus should be draped in
a robe of white and led back to Pilate. Then Pilate and Herod meet
and kiss each other in turn. And Jesus should come to Pilate,
whereupon Pilate should say:**
I find no cause to put this Man to death.

The Jews should say:

Reus est mortis.

Tunc Pilatus dicat ad Iesum:
Tu es rex Iudeorum?

Iesus respondit:
Tu dicis, quia rex sum.

Pilatus dicit:
Gens tua et pontifices tui tradiderunt te michi.

Iesus paulatim dicat:
Regnum meum non est de hoc mundo.

Pilatus item dicat:
Ergo quem te ipsum facis?

Iesus vero taceat. Et Pilatus dicit ad pontifices:
Quid faciam de Iesu Nazareno?

Iudei:
Crucifigatur.

Pilatus:
Corripiam ergo illum et dimittam.

Tunc ducitur Iesus ad flagellandum. Postea Iesus induatur veste purpurea et spinea corona.

Tunc dicant Iudei blasphemando ad Iesum:
Ave, rex Iudeorum.

Et dent ei alapas:
Prophetiza, quis est, qui te percussit?

Et ducant eum ad Pilatum. Cui Pilatus dicit:
Ecce homo.

Iudei:
Crucifige, crucifige eum.

Pilatus:
Accipite eum vos et crucifigite. Nullam causam invenio in eo.

He is deserving of death.

Then Pilate should say to Jesus:
Are You the King of the Jews?

Jesus should respond:
You say that I am a king.

Pilate should say:
Your people and high priests have handed You over to me.

Jesus should say after a pause:
My Kingdom is not of this world.

Pilate then should say:
Then what do You purport to be?

Jesus should be silent. And Pilate should say to the high priests:
What should I do with Jesus of Nazareth?

The Jews:
He should be crucified.

Pilate:
Then I will punish Him and send Him off!

Jesus is sent off to be flagellated. Afterwards Jesus should be dressed in a purple robe and a crown of thorns.

Then the Jews should say to Jesus blasphemously:
Hail, King of the Jews.

Then they should deal him blows to the cheek:
Prophesy! Who is it who has smitten You?

And they should bring him to Pilate. Pilate should say to them:
Behold the Man!

The Jews should say:
Crucify Him, crucify Him!

Pilate:
You take Him and crucify Him. I find no cause in this Man.

Iudei:
Si hunc dimittis, non es amicus Cesaris.

Item:
Omnis, qui se facit regem, contradicit Cesari.

Pilatus:
Unde es tu?

Iesus tacet. Pilatus:
Michi non loqueris?

Item:
Nescis, quia potestatem habeo crucifigere te et potestatem dimittere te?

Iesus respondet:
Non haberes in me potestatem, nisi desuper tibi datum fuisset.

Pilatus ad Iudeos:
Regem vestrum crucifigam?

Iudei respondent:
Crucifigatur, quia filium Dei se fecit.

Pilatus lavans manus suas cum aqua, et dicat ad Iudeos:
Innocens ego sum a sanguine huius. Vos videritis.

Tunc Iesus ducatur ad crucifigendum. Tunc Iudas ad pontifices vadat cantando et reiectis denariis dicit flendo:
Penitet me graviter, quod istis argenteis Christum vendiderim.

Item:
Resumite vestra, resumite! Mori volo et non vivere. Suspendii supplicio me volo perdere.

Pontifices:
Quid ad nos, Iudas Scariotis? Tu videris.

Statim veniat diabolus et ducat Iudam ad suspendium, et suspenditur. Tunc veniant mulieres a longe plorantes flere Iesum, quibus Iesus dicat:

The Jews:
If you let Him go, you are not a friend to Caesar.

Likewise:
Every man who makes himself king is a foe to Caesar.

Pilate:
Whence come You?

Jesus is silent. Pilate:
Speak You not to me?

Pilate:
Do You not know that I have the power to crucify You and the power
to set You free?

Jesus should respond:
You would not have any power over Me, if it had not been given to you
from above.

Pilate to the Jews:
Am I to crucify your King?

The Jews should respond:
 He should be crucified, for He has made Himself the Son of God.

Pilate, laving his hands with water, should say to the Jews:
I am innocent of this Man's Blood. Bear witness to that!

**Then Jesus should be lead to His crucifixion, and Judas should go
to the high priests and, rejecting their denarii, in tears sing:**
It aggrieves me deeply that I have sold Christ for this silver.

Likewise:
Take back your silver—take it back! I wish to die, not to live. I wish to kill
myself by the noose's agony.

High priests:
What is that to us, Judas Iscariot? See to it yourself!

**Immediately the devil should come and lead Judas to the gallows; he is
hanged. Then the women should come from far off, weeping for Jesus.
Jesus should say to them:**

Filie Ierusalem, nolite flere super me, sed super vos ipsas.

Tunc Iesus suspendatur in cruce. Et titulus fiat:
Iesus Nazarenus rex Iudeorum.

Tunc respondent Iudei Pilato cantando:
Regem non habemus nisi Cesarem.

Pilatus:
Quod scripsi, scripsi.

Tunc veniat mater Domini lamentando cum Iohanne evangelista, et ipsa accedens crucem respicit crucifixum:
Awe, awe, mich hiuet vnde immer we!
awe, wi sihe ich nv an
daz liebiste chint, daz ie gewan
ze dirre werlde ie dehain wip.
awe, mines shoene chindes lip!

Item:
Den sihe ich iemerlichen an.
lat iuch erbarmen, wip vnde man.
lat iwer ovgen sehen dar
vnde nemt der marter rehte war.

Item:
Wart marter ie so iemerlich
vnde also rehte angestlich?
nv merchet marter, not unde tot
vnde al den lip von blute rot.

Item:
Lat leben mir daz chindel min
vnde toetet mich, die muter sin,
Mariam, ich vil armez wip.
zwiv sol mir leben vnde lip?

Item mater Dommi omni ploratu exhibens multos planctus et clamat ad mulieres flentes et conquerendo valde:
Flete, fideles anime,
flete, sorores optime,
ut sint multiplices
doloris indices

Daughters of Jerusalem, weep not for Me, but for yourselves.

Then Jesus should be fixed on the cross; a sign above should be made:
Jesus of Nazareth, King of the Jews.

The Jews should respond to Pilate in song:
We have no king, except Caesar.

Pilate:
What I have written, I have written.

Jesus' mother should come in grief with John the Evangelist and, approaching the cross, look up at her crucified Son:
Woe, woe, woe is me, today and for all eternity!
Alas! How I now behold
the most beloved Child
Whom ever a woman in this world has born.
Alas the beautiful Body of my Son!

Likewise:
I look at Him, full of agony
Have pity for Him, O women and men!
Let your eyes rest on Him
and into His agony plunge.

Likewise:
What place ever would have given a martyrization
so agonizing and heart-rending?
Now look at His suffering, His mortal anguish
and His Body streaming with blood.

Likewise:
Let me live with my darling Child,
and kill me, his mother Mary,
who so hapless and miserable is.
What care have I for my body and life?

Then the Lord's mother raising under tears many plaints should shout to the weeping women and stoutly declaim:
Weep, faithful souls,
weep, best of sisters,
that so innumerable are
the lamentations and tears:

planctus et lacrime!
fleant materna viscera,
Marie matris vulnera.
materne doleo,
que dici soleo
felix puerpera.

Triste spectaculum
crucis et lancee!
clausum signaculum
mentis virginee
profunde vulnerat.
hoc est, quod dixerat,
quod prophetaverat
senex prenuntius,
hic ille gladius,
qui me transverberat.

Dum caput cernu<um,
dum spinas capitis,
dum plagas manuum
cruentis digitis
supplex suspicio,
sub hoc supplicio
tota deficio,
dum vulnus lateris,
dum locus vulneris
est in profluvio.>

Tunc Maria amplexatur Iohannem et cantet eum habens inter bracchia:
Mi Iohannes, planctum move,
plange mecum, fili nove,
fili novo federe
matris et matertere.
tempus est lamenti,
immolemus intimas
lacrimarum victimas
Christo morienti.

Et per horam quiescat sedendo. Et iterum surgat et cantet:
Planctus ante nescia,
planctu lassor anxia,

the proofs of our grief.
Let maternal hearts beweep
Mother Mary's wounds:
then as a mother grieve I,
who am accustomed to be called
happy and blessed in motherhood.

The sad spectacle
of the cross and spear
deeply wounds
the closed seal
of my virgin soul.
This is what
the old soothsayer
had prophesied and told,
this is that sword
that transfixes my soul.

As I on my knees
with bloody fingers
look up at His Head,
stooping towards the earth,
the crown of thorns upon It,
the Wounds to His Hands—
beneath this humiliation
I lose all sense, whilst
from the wound in His Flank,
from Its site, away drains His Blood.

Then Mary should embrace John and, holding him in her arms, sing to him:
O my Johannes, grieve,
rue with me, my new son,
son by the new compact
between mother and aunt.
'Tis the time for lamentation;
Let us offer up in sacrifice
our inmost griefs and tears
to the dying Christ.

For an hour she should sit and rest, and then rise and sing:
I, who knew no sorrow before,
now am wearied by a troubling grief

crucior dolore;
orbat orbem radio,
me Iudea filio,
gaudio, dulcore.

Fili, dulcor unice,
singulare gaudium,
matrem flentem respice
conferens solatium.

Pectus mentem, lumina
tua torquent vulnera.
que mater, que femina
tam felix, tam misera!

Flos florum,   dux morum,
venie vena,
quam gravis   in clavis
est tibi pena.

Proh dolor,   hinc color
effugit oris,
hinc ruit,   hinc fluit
unda cruoris.

O quam sero deditus,
quam cito me deseris;
o quam digne genitus,
quam abiecte moreris.

O quis amor corporis
tibi fecit spolia;
o quam dulcis pignoris
quam amara premia.

O pia   gratia
sic morientis,
o zelus   o scelus
invide gentis.

O fera   dextera
crucifigentis,
o lenis   in penis

and tortured by great dolor.
Judea bereaves the world of its Light
and me of my Son,
my sweetness and delight.

Son, Sweetness unique,
Joy one of a kind,
look back upon Thy weeping mother
and bestow Thy Solace on me.

Thy Wounds do torment
my mind, heart, and eyne.
What mother, what woman
is so blessed and yet so poor?

Flower of flowers, Leader of virtue,
Spring of clemency,
how grave is Thy Pain
in Thy Wounds upon the nails.

O, the grief! All the color
of Thy Mouth flees away.
from Thee rushes and flows
a wave of blood and gore!

O how late wert Thou brought down to me,
O how swiftly dost Thou forsake me.
O how becomingly wert Thou conceived,
O how abjectly dost Thou pass away.

O what love made for Thee
the carnal body's shell;
O how sweet, O how bitter
are the rewards of Thy Pledge.

O the pious grace
in such a death,[26]
O the envy, O the evil
of this jealous clan!

O Propitious Beast of him,
who fixes Thee to the cross,
O gentle in its agony is the Soul

mens patientis.

O verum eloquium
iusti Simeonis!
quem promisit, gladium
sentio doloris.

Gemitus, suspiria
lacrimeque foris
vulneris indicia
sunt interioris.

Parcito proli,
mors, michi noli,
tunc michi soli
sola mederis.

Morte, beate,
separer a te,
dummodo, nate,
non crucieris.

Quod crimen, que scelera
gens commisit effera,
vincla, virgas, vulnera,
sputa, spinas, cetera
sine culpa patitur.

Nato, queso, parcite,
matrem crucifigite
aut in crucis stipite
nos simul affigite!
male solus moritur.

Reddite mestissime
corpus vel exanime,
ut sic minoratus
crescat cruciatus
osculis, amplexibus!

Utinam sic doleam,
ut dolore peream,
nam plus est dolori

of the suffering Christ.

O! true was the augury
of Simeon the Just![27]
I feel the sword of pain,
which he prophesied.

The groans, the sighs,
and tears without
are proofs
of the wounds within.

Spare posterity, Death,
but do not spare me,
then you alone will be
a cure for lonely me.

Let me by death, Beatified One,
be separated from Thee,
so long as Thou, my Son,
art not racked with the cross' pain.

What a crime, what iniquities
hath the truculent tribe committed:
bonds, switches, wounds,
spittle, thorns, and the rest
suffers He, Who no guilt hath.

Spare my Son, I pray:
his mother crucify instead,
or affix us both
to the cross' stake!
Alone He wrongfully dies.

Return His most lugubriously
lifeless Frame, so that it,
diminished and crucified,
may be strengthened again
by our kisses and embrace!

Would that I pained thus,
that I may perish from the pain,
for it is a graver dole to die

sine morte mori
quam perire citius.

Quid stupes, gens misera,
terram se movere,
obscurari sidera,
languidos lugere?

Solem privas lumine,
quomodo luceret?
egrum medicamine,
unde convaleret?

Homicidam liberas,
Iesum das supplicio;
male pacem toleras,
veniet seditio.

Famis, cedis, pestium
scies docta pondere
Iesum tibi mortuum
Barrabamque vivere.

Gens ceca, gens flebilis,
age penitentiam,
dum tibi flexibilis
Iesus est ad veniam.

Quos fecisti, fontium
prosint tibi flumina,
sitim sedant omnium,
Cuncta lavant crimina.

Flete, Sion filie,
tante grate gratie;
iuvenis angustie
sibi sunt delicie
pro vestris offensis.

In amplexus ruite,
dum pendet in stipite;
mutuis amplexibus
se parat amantibus

without death
than to perish amain.

Why are you stunned, wretched race,
that the earth is quaking now,
that the stars are obscured
and the feeble mourn?

If you deprive the sun of its light,
how would it ever shine?
If you rob a sick man of his medicine,
whereby would he convalesce?

You free a murderer, but subject
Jesus to the agony of death.
Poorly do you sustain peace,
for sedition will arise.

By the weight of famine, slaughter, and pestilence,
you will know the very things
that Jesus taught you in death
and Barabbas in life.

Blind, lamentable race,
repent your sins and crimes,
whilst Jesus is willing to grant
His Mercy and Pardon to you.

May the Streams from the Springs
that you have caused avail you,
for they slake the thirst of all
and wash away all faults.

Weep, daughters of Zion,
for the Son of such dear grace,
the distress of this Youth
becomes a delight to Him
for the sake of your sins.

Rush into His loving clasp,
while He hangs upon the stake;
with mutual embraces
He prepares Himself for

brachiis protensis.

In hoc solo gaudeo,
quod pro vobis doleo.
vicem, queso, reddite,
matris damnum plangite!

Tunc iterum amplexetur Iohannem et cantet:
Mi Iohannes, planctum move,
plange mecum, fili nove,
fili novo federe
matris et matertere.
tempus est lamenti,
immolemus intimas
lacrimarum victimas
Christo morienti.

Iohannes ad hanc:
O Maria, tantum noli
lamentare tue proli!
sine me nunc plangere,
que vitam cupis cedere.

Et Iohannes teneat Mariam sub humeris.
Et dicat Iesus ad eam:
Mulier, ecce filius tuus.

Deinde dicit ad Iohannem:
Ecce mater tua.

Postea vadant Maria et Iohannes de cruce.
Et Iesus dicat:
Sitio.

Statim veniant Iudei prebentes spongiam cum aceto.
Et Iesus bibat:
Consummatum est.

Tunc Longinus veniat cum lancea et perforet latus eius et ille dicat
aperte:
Ich wil im stechen ab daz herze sin,
daz sich ende siner marter pin.

loving, outstretched arms.

On this ground do I rejoice,
for I suffer for the sake of ye.
Now repay me for the pain, I pray,
and lament this mother's loss!

Then again she should embrace Johannes and sing:
O my Johannes, grieve,
rue with me, my new son,
son by the new compact
between mother and aunt.
'Tis the time for lamentation;
Let us offer up in sacrifice
our inmost griefs and tears
to the dying Christ.

John to her:
O Mary, grieve not
so boundlessly for thy Son!
Allow me now to weep for thee,
who desirest to leave this life.

And John should hold Mary under his shoulders.
And Jesus should say to her:
Woman, behold your son!

Then he should say to John:
Behold thy mother.

Afterwards Mary and John should go up to the cross.
And Jesus should say:
I thirst.

Forthwith the Jews should come offering a sponge soaked in vinegar.
And Jesus should drink:
It is completed.

Then Longinus should come with a spear and pierce Jesus' side and say openly:
I will pierce His Heart,
to end His agony.

Iesus videns finem dicit clamando:
Ely, Ely, lema sabactany, hoc est: Deus meus, Deus meus, ut quid
dereliquisti me?

Et inclinato capite emittat spiritum.
Longinus:
Vere filius Dei erat iste.

Item:
Dirre ist des waren gotes sůn.

Item:
Er hat zaichen an mir getan,
wan ich min sehen wider han.

Et unus ex Iudeis dicat ad Iudeos:
Eliam vocat iste. Eamus et videamus, si Elias veniens liberet eum an non.

Alter Iudeus:
Si filius Dei es, descende de cruce.

Item alter:
Alios salvos fecit, seipsum non potest salvum facere.

XVII*/CCXLV. *Margaritae Freidanci*
Freidank (ca. 1215/33)

Diu mukke mûz sich sere muen,
wil si den ohsen uber luen.

Gienge ein hunt des tages tausent stunt
ze chirchen, er ist doch ein hunt.

Manich hunt wol gebaret,
der doch der leute varet.

Ez dunchet mich ein tumber sin,
swer waent den ouen obergin.

Swa ich waiz den wolues zant,
da wil ich hueten meiner hant,
daz er mich niht verwnde,
sein beizzen swirt uon grunde.

Jesus, seeing His end, shouts:
Eli, Eli, lama sabactani? That is: My God, My God, why have You
forsaken Me?

And with upturned head, He should send up His soul.
Longinus:
In sooth that Man was the Son of God.

Likewise:
He is the Son of the true God.

Likewise:
He has performed a miracle on me:
through Him I have my sight regained.[35]

And one of the Jews should say to the Jews:
He calls to Elijah. Let's go and see if Elijah is coming to free Him or not.

Another Jew:
If you be the Son of God, come down from the cross!

Likewise another:
Others did He bless; Himself he cannot save.

17*/245. *Freidank's Pearls*
by Freidank (ca. 1215/33)

The gnat must tire itself out greatly,
if it wishes to drown out the ox.

If a dog should go to church one thousand times a day,
it nevertheless a dog doth stay.

Many a dog acts friendly
and still attacks the folk.

I consider him less than wise, who thinks
he can open his gullet wider than an oven's door.

If I know that a wolf's tooth is lurking somewhere nearby,
I will in that place take care of my hands,
so that it won't give me any wounds.
Its bite causes deep ulcers.

Der lewe sol auch nimmer lagen,
wellent in die hasen iagen.

Div fliug ist, wirt der sumer heiz,
der chuenste uogel, den ich waiz.

Der bremen hohgezit zergat,
so der augest ende hat.

Die cheuern uliegen unuerdaht,
des uallet maniger in ein paht.

Die froesche tuent in selben schaden,
wellent si den storchen zu hûse laden;
di wisen chunnen wol uerstan,
waz ich tore gesprochen han.

Der lewe fuerhtet des mannes niht,
wan ob er in hoeret und niht siht.

Der cheuer sich selb betriuget,
swenn er ze hohe fliuget.

Diu nahtegal diche muet,
swenn ein esel oder ein ohse luet.

Der hunt hat leder urezzen,
so man dienstes wil uergezzen.

Der hofwart vnd der wind
selten gûte friunde sind.

Swer schalchait lernt in der iugent,
der hat uil selten staete tugent.

Man siht uil selten richez hûs
ane dieb und ane mûs.

Von reht iz auf in selben gat,
swer dem andern geit valschen rat.

Der esel und di nahtigal
singent ungelichen schal.

The lion surely will not lie in wait anymore,
if already hunting him are the hares.

When high summer has arrived,
the fly is the boldest bird I know.

The high time for the horsefly is over,
when August comes to an end.

The beetles fly wildly with indiscretion,
for which reason many fall into the muck.

The frogs inflict injury on themselves,
when they invite the stork for a meal.
The wise will surely fathom
what I, a fool, have said.

The lion has no fear of a person,
unless it hears him, but sees him not.

The beetle deceives itself,
when it flies too high.

The nightingale oft thinks it bothersome,
when a donkey or an ox bellows.

The dog has gnawed at leather, when one
wants to give nothing for the service it performed.

The watchdog and the greyhound
are seldom good friends.

Who learns in his youth to be a trickster
hardly ever displays steadfast virtue.

A rich house will hardly ever
be exempt from thieves and mice.

It rightly falls back on him, when one
gives another a pernicious bit of advice.

The donkey and the nightingale
do not sing the same tune.

Swa man den esel chroenet,
da ist daz land gehoenet.

Minne, schatz, groz gewin
vercherent gûtes mannes sin.

Man minnet nu schatz mere
danne got, lyb, sel vnd ere.

So staete friundin nieman hat,
er fuerihte doch ir missetat.

Vremede scheidet herzelieb,
stat machet manigen dieb.

Swer lieb hat, der wirt selten urei
vor sorgen, daz ez unstaete sei.

Herzelieb hat manich man,
der doch gar uerniugeret dran.

XVIII*/CCXLVI. *Rota Precum*

I. Magnificat <anima mea Dominum . . .>

II. Ad Dominum, cum tri<bularer, clamavi: et exaudivit me>.

III. Retribue servo <tuo, vivifica me: et custodiam sermones tuos>.

IV. In convertendo <Dominus captivitatem Sion: facti sumus consolati>.

V. Appropinquet <deprecatio mea in conspectu tuo, Domine: iuxta
eloquium tuum da michi intellectum>.

VI. Maria virgo semper <letare, quae meruisti Christum portare, celi et
terre conditorem, quia de tuo utero protulisti mundi salvatorem>.

VII. Ave, spes nostra, Dei <genitrix intacta; ave, illud Ave per angelum
accipiens; ave, concipiens Patris splendorem benedicta;
ave, casta sanctissima virgo, solam innuptam te glorificat omnis creatura
matrem luminis, alleluia, alleluia>.

When an ass is crowned,
it spells disgrace for all the land.

Love, property, and profit change
the mind of a righteous man.

These days one loves property more
than God, life, soul, and honor.

Nobody has a woman so truly beloved
that he does not fear a misdeed on her part.

Separation divorces intimate love;
opportunity creates many thieves.

Who has a sweetheart is hardly ever free
from the dread that she unfaithful be.

Many men have an affair
because they need a diversion again.

18*/246. *The Prayer Wheel*[36]

1. My soul magnifies the Lord...

2. When afflicted, I cried out to the Lord and He heard me.

3. Requite Your servant, restore me, and I will observe Your Words.

4. Because the Lord overturned Zion's captivity, we were all consoled.

5. In Your Sight should come my prayer for pardon, Lord. Give me insight, according to Your Word.

6. Rejoice, Virgin Mary, who were granted the privilege to carry Christ, the Creator of heaven and earth, because from your womb you brought forth the Savior of the world.

7. Hail, our hope, intact mother of God. Hail, you who receive that "hail" from an angel. Hail, Blessed One, Who the Father's Splendor conceived. Hail, chaste, most sacred virgin, every creature exalts you as the sole, unwed mother of the Light. Hallelujah, hallelujah!

VIII. Regali ex progenie Maria <exorta refulget, cuius precibus nos adiuvari mente et spiritu devotissime poscimus>.

IX. In prole mater, <in partu virgo, gaude et letare, virgo, mater Domini>.

X. Ave, domina mundi, ave, regina celorum, ave, virgo virginum, per te venit redemptio nostra; tu inter mulieres speciosissima, inter omnes et super omnes benedicta, iuxta filium tuum super choros angelorum posita, pro nobis, rogamus, rogita, ut valeamus te in eterna requie videre tecumque sine fine gaudere.

XI. Post partum, <virgo, inviolata permansisti; Dei genitrix, intercede pro nobis>.

XII. Ora pro nobis, beata mater.

XIII. Exurge, Domine, a<diuva nos . . . >

XIV. Sanctissima et gloriosissima et piissima virgo Maria! Ego indignus peccator commendo tibi esse, posse, vivere, valere, animam meam.

XIX*/CCXLVII. *Gloria Katherinae*

Katharine collaudemus
virtutum insignia,
cordis ei presentemus
et oris obsequia,
ut ab ipsa reportemus
equa laudis premia.

Fulta fide Katharina
iudicem Maxentium
non formidat; lex divina
sic firmat eloquium,
quod confutat ex doctrina
doctores gentilium.

Victi Christum confitentur
relictis erroribus.
iudex iubet, ut crementur;
nec pilis nec vestibus
nocet ignis, sed torrentur
inustis corporibus.

8. Mary sprung from a royal line shines; by her prayers for us we pray with heart and soul for aid.

9. Mother through your Son, O virgin in birth, rejoice and be mirthful, virgin, mother of the Lord.

10. Hail, mistress of the world, hail, queen of heaven, hail, virgin of virgins, through you came our great Redemption! You, most beauteous of women, blessed among and before all, placed above the angels' choruses next to your Son, we beg you, beseech for us that we may see you in our eternal rest and rejoice with you without end.

11. After birth, you remained inviolate; O mother of God, for us intercede.

12. Pray for us, blessed mother.

13. Rise, Lord, and succor us.

14. Most sacrosanct, glorious, and pious Mother Mary! I, an unworthy sinner, do commend to you my being, power, life, strength, and soul.

19*/247. *Catherine's Glory*

Let us laud the remarkable virtues
of Catherine of Alexandria,
let us present to her the devotion
of our hearts and mouths,
in the hope that we may bring back from her
praise's commensurate rewards.

Catherine, sustained by her faith,
does not fear Maxentius the judge.
Divine law strengthens
her eloquence such
that she silences the teachers of the gentiles
with her erudite words.

Outwitted, they confess to Christ
and leave behind their heretical ways.
The judge bids that they be burned;
neither hair nor clothes the fire harms,
and though they are surrounded by flames,
their bodies catch no fire.

Post hec blandis rex molitur
virginem seducere,
nec promissis emollitur
nec terretur verbere;
compeditur, custoditur
tetro clausa carcere.

Clause lumen ne claudatur,
illucet Porphyrio,
qui regine federatur
fidei collegio;
quorum fidem imitatur
ducentena contio.

Huius ergo contionis
concordes constantia
vim mundane passionis
pari patientia
superemus, ut cum bonis
letemur in gloria.

XX*/CCXLVIII. *Magna Martyr*

Pange, lingua, gloriose
virginis martyrium:
gemme iubar pretiose
descendat in medium,
ut illustret tenebrose
mentis domicilium!

XXI*/CCXLIX. *Femina Amata a Christo*

Presens dies expendatur
in eius preconium,
cuius virtus dilatatur
in ore laudantium,
si gestorum teneatur
finis et initium.

Verbo vite solidatus
prosilit Porphyrius;
cum ducentis decollatus
migrat palme socius.

Following this, the king works
at seducing the virgin with flatteries,
but she is not mollified by promises
nor terrified by the lash.
She is shackled and confined
and locked in a dungeon of dread.

Lest the light of the prisoner remain shut up,
it shines in Porphyrius,
who allies himself with the queen
by the union of faith.
Their example of faith
the throng of two hundred follows.

Let us therefore, in accord
with the steadfastness of this crowd,
defeat the onslaught of earthly suffering
with equal patience,
so that we may rejoice together
in glory with the just and good.

20*/248. *The Great Martyress*

Sing, tongue, of the martyrdom
of the glorious virgin.
Let the splendor of that precious gem
descend into our midst,
to illumine the home
of our caliginous souls!

21*/249. *The Woman Christ Loved*

The present day should be devoted
to the celebration of her,
whose virtue is amplified
in her laudators' mouths,
if the beginning and end
of her deeds are known.

Strengthened by the word of life,
Porphyrius leaps forth;
decapitated with two hundred others,
he dies a companion of her victory's palm.

Katharine cruciatus
maturat Maxentius.

Imminente passione
virgo hec interserit:
«assequatur, Iesu bone,
quod a te petierit,
suo quisquis in agone
mei memor fuerit.»

In hoc caput amputatur,
fluit lac cum sanguine;
angelorum sublevatur
corpus multitudine
et Sinai collocatur
in supremo culmine

Hoc declarat, hoc explanat
meritum virgineum,
quod ex eius tumba manat
incessanter oleum,
cuius virtus omnis sanat
doloris aculeum.

Vim doloris corporalis
ut hec sanat unctio,
sic liquoris spiritalis
mundet nos infusio,
ut eterno temporalis
dolor cedat gaudio.

Gloria et honor Deo
<usquequo altissimo,
una patri filioque,
inclito paraclito,
cuius laus est et potestas
per eterna secula.>

XXII*/CCL. *Femina Quae Rotam Fregit*

Hac in die mentes pie
celi iungant harmonie
plausus et tripudia,

Maxentius then hastens the torture
and execution of Catherine the saint.

With her passion impending,
the virgin sows these words:
"O benignant Jesus, let whoever
in the throes of death bethinks himself
of mine own receive everything
that he besought of You."

With these words,
her head is lopped off,
milk flows together with blood.
Her body by a multitude of angels
is lifted off the ground
and placed on Sinai's highest peak.

This bespeaks, this makes clear
the worth of the virgin dear;
for from her tomb drips
olive oil without end,
all of whose effect
heals the sting of any pain.

Just as this salve diminishes
the force of corporeal pain,
so the infusion of this spiritual liquor
should cleanse us amain,
so temporal dole may truckle
to an eternity of bliss.

Glory and honor be
always to the highest God—
to the Father and Son together
with the illustrious protector—
whose praise and power
are eternal and without end.

22*/250. *The Woman Who Broke The Wheel*

On this day, pious souls should unite
the clapping and dancing
to the harmony of heavenly heights.

qua conscendit ad divina
sponsa Christi Katharina
sublimi victoria.

Virgo dolens Christianos
a profanis ut profanos
subici martyrio
Christum palam confitetur
neque super hoc veretur
opponi Maxentio.

Cuius victus documentis
et conclusus argumentis
querit adiutoria.
Grecos querit oratores
et in Grecis meliores;
hinc surgunt litigia.

Ad certamen provocatur,
datur locus, disputatur,
succumbit rhetorica.
Gaudet virgo, rex inflatur;
credit et martyrizatur
turba philosophica.

«Virgo, decus puellare,
virgo, proles regia,
forma comprovinciales
vincens elegantia,
tua stet in dicione
res imperatoria;
tantum diis ne detrectes
dare sacrificia.»

Ad hec virgo: «quid, Maxenti,
quid dixisti, bestia?
nescit verus declinari
Deus per pluralia.
unde diis plura tuis
dans aticularia
miser a divinitate
transis ad demonia.

On this day, Catherine,
Christ's bride, ascends to heaven
after a magnificent victory.

The virgin, bewailing the subjection
to martyrdom of Christians
as heretics by heretics themselves,
she professes her faith in Jesus openly
nor does she fear that her belief
is by Maxentius opposed.

Defeated by her written testimony
and cornered by her arguments,
he searches for assistance.
He seeks the Greek orators
and the best amongst them;
hence rises the dispute.

Rhetoric is called forth
to the contest, given a place,
disputed, and then finally sinks.
The virgin rejoices; the king is incensed.
The throngs of orators believe her
and for this offense suffer martyrdom.

"Virgin, maidenly glory,
virgin, issue of kings,
conquering in beauty and grace
all sovereign lands,
regal power should stand
beneath your sway—
only do not refuse to give
oblations to the Gods."

In response the virgin says:
"What, Maxentius, what didst thou say,
O beast? The true God cannot
in the plural be declined.
When thou givest
thy Gods plural forms,
thou passest from divine
to demonic norms.

Resipisce, resipisce
protinus a diis hisce,
Christo te concilia;
cecus ceca veneraris,
falsus falsa deprecaris,
similis similia.»

Rex ad ista perturbatur,
furit, frendet, stomachatur,
latrat, exit hominem.
Rota fieri mandatur;
paganorum, dum rotatur,
sternit multitudinem.

«Hinc, hinc maga rapiatur,
hinc venefica trahatur
ad squalorem carceris!»
Assunt mox apparitores,
mox laniste, mox tortores,
iussa complent sceleris.

Luce carcer perlustratur,
angelorum deputatur
virgini solacium.
Visitatur a regina;
Christi datur disciplina,
subitur martyrium.

Virgo caput et mamillas
offert; comitatur illas
insigne prodigium:
iam mamilla dat cruorem,
caput lactis sudat rorem
commutando proprium.

Tibi, Christe, sit perenne
decus et imperium,
tu beate Katharine
nobis da consortium.

XXIII*/CCLI. *Cantus Josephi*

Cantus Ioseph ab Arimathia:

Recover, recover thyself
forthwith from these thy Gods,
and with Christ reconcile thyself!
Blindly dost thou venerate that which is blind,
falsely pray thou for pardon to false things,
from like to like."

The king is confounded at these things:
he rages, he gnashes his teeth, he fumes,
he barks, he is a human being no more.
He orders that a wheel be made;
whilst it is being turned it rolls over
and crushes the heathen throng.

"Hence, hence, the witch should be snatched;
hence should this conjurer be haled
to the squalor of our jail!"
The executioners appear anon,
then the henchmen, then the torturers,
who villainous biddings execute.

The prison is purified by light:
the comfort of the angels
is allotted to the virgin.
She is visited by the queen,
who is given the knowledge of Christ;
then she is subjected to martyrdom.

The virgin offers her head and her breasts;
a remarkable portent
accompanies her torture:
now her breast yields blood
and her head exudes drops of milk,
a reversal of their natural qualities.

Perennial glory and supremacy
be forever to You, Christ;
vouchsafe us a fellowship
with Catherine the Saint!

23*/251. *Joseph's Song*

Joseph of Arimathia sings:

Iesus von gotlicher art
ein mensch an alle sunde,
der an schuld gemartret wart,
ob man den vurbaz vunde
genaglet an dem chrivze stan,
daz wer niht chuneges ere.
darumb solt ihr mich in lan
bestaten, rihter, herre.

Pilatus:
Swer redelicher dinge gert,
daz stet wol an der maze,
daz er ir werde wol gewert.
du bitest, daz ich laze
dich bestaten Iesum Christ.
daz main ich wol in gůte.
seit er dir so ze herzen ist,
num in nach dinem můte.

XXIV*/CCLII. *Domine, Miserere Nostri*

Kyrie. Cum iubilo iubilemus   virgini Marie.
Kyrie. In hac die laudes demus virgini   Marie.
Kyrie. Cum gaudio decantemus   canticum Marie.

Christe. Deus homo \<natus\> sine semine,
Christe. nos tuere interventu Marie,
Christe. natus de Maria virgine.

Kyrie. Exaudi,   preces audi,   Deus optime,
Kyrie. Nos defende precibus Marie.
Kyrie. Precantes salva   semper et tege,   nos guberna,
nos defende,   nos protege, Domine,
Deus trine,   pro Marie meritis eleyson.

XXV*/CCLIII. *Novissimae Horae Christi*

Nota. Tempore completorii traditus est Dominus. Unde:
Educes me de laqueo quem abs\<c\>on\<derunt\> michi.[38]

In matuino captus. Unde:
Quia ecce ceperunt a\<nimam\> meam: irruerunt in me fortes.[39]

Jesus of godly substance,
a Man without any sin,
Who undeservedly suffered torment—
if one should see Him any longer
hanging on nails from the cross,
it would befit not the honor due a king.
Therefore you should allow
me to bury Him, O governor!

Pilatus:
When someone desires a noble thing,
then it is entirely appropriate
that his enterprise find ears.
You ask that I let you
bury Jesus Christ.
I receive this request amicably.
Since He is very much in your heart,
take Him according to your intent.

24*/252. *Lord, Have Mercy On Us*

Kyrie.[37] With a jubilant song, let us call out to Virgin Mary.
Kyrie. On this day let us give praise to the Virgin Mary.
Kyrie. Joyful, let us sing a song for Mary.

Christe. God, born a Man not from seed,
Christe. watch over us by the intercession of Mary,
Christe. Son of the Virgin Mary.

Kyrie. Listen, most benignant God, hear our pleas,
Kyrie. Protect us according to Mary's prayers.
Kyrie. Save and shelter us always, as we pray, guide us,
defend us, protect us, Lord, triune God,
for the sake of Mary's merits, eleison.

25*/253. *The Last Hours of Christ*

Mark. At the time of the compline the Lord was betrayed. Thence:
You will draw Me out of the gin that they have secretly set for Me.

In the morning He was captured. Thence: Behold! They have captured
My Soul; the strong have descended upon Me!

Tempore prime iniuste ac<c>usatus. Unde:
Quoniam alieni insurrex<erunt> in me.[40]

In tertia flagellatus. Unde:
Funes peccatorum <circumplexi sunt me>.[41]

In sexta crucifixus. Unde:
Factus sum sicut uter i<n> pr<uina>.[42]

In nona expiravit. Unde:
Os meum apperui quia m<andata> t<ua> de<siderabam>.[43]

In vespere sepultus est. Unde:
Educ de custodia a<animam> m<eam>.[44]

XXVI*/CCLIV. *Dominus Apparet*

**Incipit exemplum apparitionis Domini discipulis suis iuxta castellum
Emaus, ubi illis apparuit in more peregrini et tacuit videns, quid
loquerentur et tractarent.**

<Discipuli:>
Surrexit Christus et illuxit populo suo, quem redemit sanguine suo.
Alleluia.

Iesus audiens, se fingens peregrinum ad premissa respondet:
Qui sunt hi sermones, quos confertis ad invicem ambulantes, et estis
tristes? Alleluia, alleluia.

Discipuli:
Tu solus peregrinus es in Ierusalem et non cognovisti, que facta sunt in illa
his diebus? Alleluia.

Quibus Iesus respondet:
Que?

Discipuli:
Nos loquimur de Iesu Nazareno, qui fuit vir propheta, potens in opere et
sermone coram Deo et omni populo. Alleluia, alleluia.

Iesus respondet:
O stulti et tardi corde ad credendum in his, que locuti sunt prophete.
Alleluia.

At the time He was charged with the first offense. Thence:
For foes have risen against Me!

At the third hour He was flagellated. Thence:
The cords of sinners have embraced Me.

At the sixth hour He was crucified. Thence:
I have become like a wineskin in the hoarfrost.

At the ninth hour, He passed away. Thence:
I opened My Mouth, because I longed for Your Commandments.

In the evening, He was buried. Thence:
Draw My Soul from the confines of My Body.

26*/254. *The Lord Appears*[45]

Here begins a play about the Lord's coming before His disciples, near the stronghold of Emmaus, where he appeared to them in a pilgrim's form, silently observing their acts and words.

Disciples:
Christ has risen and given light to His people, whom He redeemed with His Blood. Hallelujah.

Jesus, hearing this, molds Himself into a palmer and rejoins:
What are these words that you are exchanging as you walk with sad hearts? Hallelujah. Hallelujah.

Disciples:
Are you but a foreigner in Jerusalem, who knows not what has happened here in these past few days? Hallelujah.

Jesus should respond to them:
What?

Disciples:
We speak of Jesus of Nazareth, Who was a prophet, mighty in His Acts and Words before the eyes of all men and God. Hallelujah. Hallelujah.

Jesus should respond:
Foolish and lazy at heart are ye to believe in the things the prophets have said. Hallelujah.

Item Iesus:
Nonne sic oportuit pati Christum et intrare in gloriam suam? Alleluia.

Clerus:
Et coegerunt eum dicentes:

Et discipuli invitabant eum:
Mane nobiscum, Domine, quoniam advesperascit et inclinata est iam dies.
Alleluia, alleluia.

**Tunc vadat cum discipulis et colloquatur de prophetis et petat
comestionem et in fractione panis cognoscatur ab eis. Tunc evanescat
Iesus ab oculis eorum. Tunc discipuli cantent:**
Nonne cor nostrum ardens erat in nobis de Iesu, dum loqueretur nobis in
via? Alleluia.

Tunc Iesus appareat discipulis cum vexillo et cantet:
Pax vobis, ego sum. Alleluia. Nolite timere. Alleluia.

Clerus cantet:
Thomas, qui dicitur Didymus, non erat cum eis, quando venit Jesus.
Dixerunt alii discipuli: Vidimus Dominum. Alleluia.

Tunc Iesus monstret manus et pedes, et cantet:
Videte manus meas et pedes meos, quoniam ego ipse sum. Alleluia,
alleluia.

Tunc iterum evanescat Iesus, et discipuli cantent:
Christus resurgens a mortuis iam non moritur; mors illi ultra non
dominabitur. Quod enim vivit, vivit Deo. Alleluia, alleluia.

Tunc apostoli conferentes inter se de Iesu et dicunt Thome:
Vidimus Dominum. Alleluia.

Thomas respondet illis:
Nisi mittam digitos meos in fixuras clavorum et manus meas in latus eius,
non credam.

Tunc appareat Iesus secundo et dicat discipulis:
Pax vobis, ego sum. <Alleluia. Nolite timere. Alleluia.>

Et clerus cantet:
Post dies octo ianuis clausis ingressus Dominus et dixit eis:

Jesus likewise:
Was it not ordained that Christ suffer and enter into His Glory? Hallelujah.

Cleric:
And they pressed Him and said:

And the disciples invited him:
Stay with us, Lord, since twilight is coming on and the day has drawn to a close. Hallelujah. Hallelujah.

He should go with the disciples and speak about the prophets, seek a meal, and be agnized by them in the breaking of bread. Jesus should vanish from their sight. The disciples should sing:
Was the heart in us not burning for Jesus, whilst He was speaking to us on the road? Hallelujah.

Then Jesus should appear to them with a banner and sing:
Peace be with you, I am He. Hallelujah. Fear not! Hallelujah.

The cleric should sing:
Thomas, called Didymus, was not with them, when Jesus came. The other disciples said: "We have seen the Lord." Hallelujah.

Then Jesus should show His hands and feet and sing:
Behold My Hands and My Feet, for I am He.
Hallelujah. Hallelujah.

Then again Jesus should disappear and the disciples sing:
Christ, rerisen from the shades, is dead no more. Death has no further power over Him. But He lives His life for God. Hallelujah.

The apostles, talking together on Jesus, should say to Thomas:
We have seen the Lord. Hallelujah.

Thomas responds to them:
Unless I cast my fingers into the pits of the nails
and my hands into His Side, I will not believe.

Then Jesus should appear again and say to the disciples:
Peace be with you, I am here. Hallelujah. Fear not! Hallelujah.

And the cleric should sing:
After eight days the Lord entered through closed doors and said to them:

Tertio apparet:
Pax vobis. <Alleluia, alleluia.>

Tunc dicit ad Thomam:
Mitte manum tuam et cognosce loca clavorum. Alleluia. Et noli esse
incredulus, sed fidelis. Alleluia.

Et Thomas procidendo ad pedes Domini cantet:
Dominus meus et Deus meus. Alleluia.

Iesus dicit:
Quia vidisti me, Thoma, credidisti. Beati, qui non viderunt et crediderunt.
Alleluia.

Tunc apostoli simul cantent hymnum:
Iesu, nostra redemptio
amor et desiderium,
Deus, creator omnium,
homo in fine temporum,

Que te vicit clementia,
ut ferres nostra crimina,
crudelem mortem patiens,
ut nos a morte tolleres?

Inferni claustra penetrans,
tuos captivos redimens,
victor triumpho nobili
ad dextram Patris residens,

Ipsa te cogat pietas,
ut mala nostra superes
parcendo et voti compotes
nos tuo vultu saties.

Tu esto nostrum gaudium,
qui es futurus premium;
sit nostra in te gloria
per cuncta semper secula.

Gloria tibi, Domine,
qui scandis super sidera,
cum Patre et Sancto Spiritu

He should appear a third time:
Peace be with you. Hallelujah. Hallelujah.

Then He should say to Thomas:
Put out your hand and recognize the nails' sites. Hallelujah.
And do not be incredulous, but have faith. Hallelujah.

And Thomas, falling at the feet of the Lord, should sing:
My Lord and my God. Hallelujah.

Jesus should say:
Because thou hast seen Me, Thomas, thou didst believe.
Blessed are those who have not seen, but still believed. Hallelujah.

Then the apostles together should sing a hymn:
Jesus, our Redemption,
Love, and Desire,
God, Creator of all,
Man in the end of time,

what clemency conquered You,
that You bore all of our crimes,
suffering cruel, torturous death,
so that You might raise us from it?

Bursting through the gates of hell,
redeeming all of Your captives,
sitting a Victor in noble triumph
at the Right Hand of the Father,

let Compassion itself impel You,
to vanquish our sins by sparing us,
and to satiate us with Your Visage,
all participating in prayer.

Be You our Joy,
Who will be our Reward;
may our glory forever be in You,
throughout all the ages forevermore.

Glory to You, Lord,
Who climbs above the stars,
with the Father and the Holy Ghost,

in sempiterna secula.

XXVIa*/CCLIVa. *Sponsa Carminis Solomonis*

Hoc finito producatur mater Domini, cum ea duo angeli portantes sceptra, et cum ea Maria Iacobi et Maria Salome.

<. . . . . :>
Egredimini et videte, filie Sion, regem Salomonem in diademate, quo coronavit eum mater sua in die desponsationis sue et in die leticie cordis eius. Alleluia, alleluia.

<Dominus:>
Vox turturis audita est in turribus Ierusalem. Veni, amica mea. Surge, Aquilo, et veni, Auster; perfla hortum meum, et fluent aromata illius.

Respondet Maria:
Veniat dilectus <meus in hortum suum, ut comedat fructus pomorum suorum.>

Dominus:
Comedi <favum cum melle meo, bibi vinum meum cum lacte meo.>

Maria:
Talis est dilectus <meus, et ipse est amicus meus, filie Ierusalem.>

Dominus:
Tota pulchra <es, amica mea, et macula non est in te. Favus distillans labia tua, mel et lac sub lingua tua, odor unguentorum tuorum super omnia aromata. Iam enim hiems transiit, imber abiit et recessit, flores apparuerunt, vinee florentes odorem dederunt, et vox turturis audita est in terra nostra. Surge, propera, amica mea, veni de Libano, veni, coronaberis.>

HIC FINITUR SUPPLEMENTUM.
HIC FINIUNTUR CARMINA BURANA.

in ages everlasting.

26a*/254a. *The Bride of Solomon's Song*

Then the Lord's mother should appear and with her two angels carrying scepters in hand, and Mary Jacobi and Mary Salome.

<.............................:>
Come out and see, daughters of Zion, King Solomon in the crown,
with which his mother crowned him on the day of his marriage
and the joy of his heart. Hallelujah. Hallelujah.

Lord:
The dove's voice has been heard in the towers of Jerusalem.
Come, My friend. Rise, North Wind, and, South Wind, come;
blow through My garden and its pleasant aroma will spring.

Mary should respond:
May my beloved come into His garden, to consume the fruits of His fruit
trees.

Lord:
I have eaten the honeycomb together with My honey; I have drunk My
milk with My wine.

Mary:
Such is my beloved, He is my friend, O ye daughters of Jerusalem.

Lord:
Wholly fair art thou, My friend, and there is no stain upon thee. Honeydew
is thy lips; honey and milk sit under thy tongue; the scent of thy salves
overpowers every spice's perfume. For now the winter has passed, the rain
hath departed and withdrawn, the flowers have appeared, the blossoming
vineyards sweet odors put forth, and the dove's voice has been heard in our
land. Rise, hasten, My friend, come down from Lebanon, come, to receive
thy crown!

HERE ENDS THE SUPPLEMENT.
HERE END THE SONGS FROM BENEDIKTBEUERN.

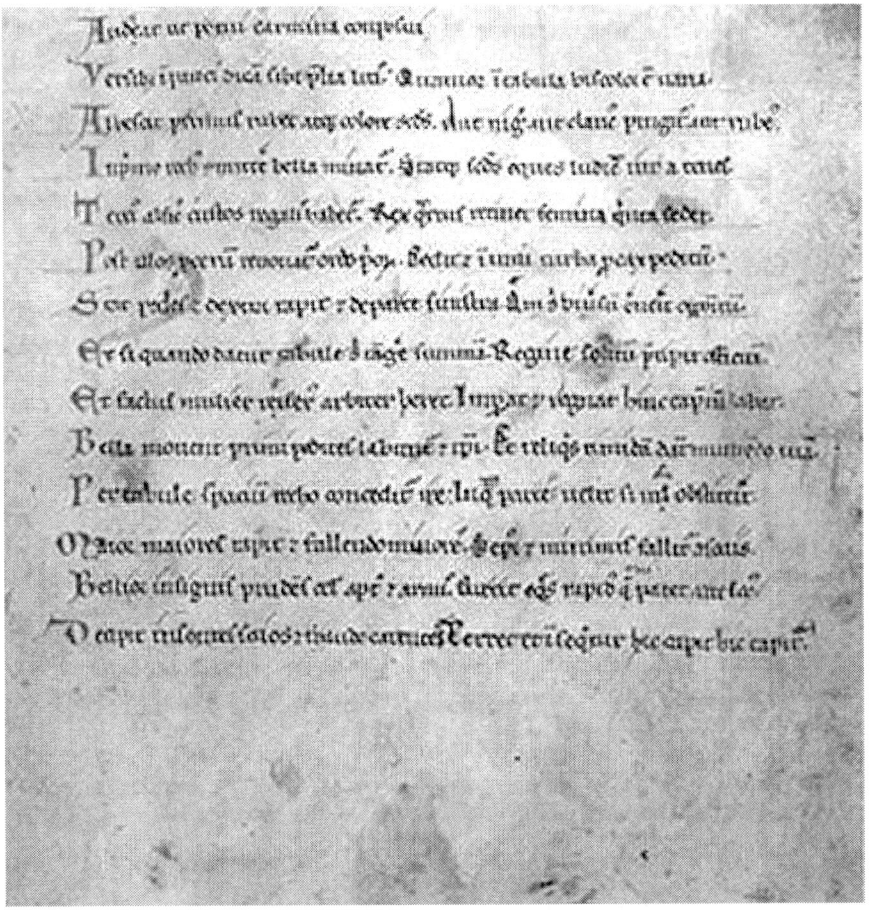

Critical Notes and Commentary on the Carmina Burana

Part I of the *Carmina Burana* (Poems 1 - 55):

1. Cf. *Jeremiah* 31:3, "*ideo adtraxi te miserans*" ("therefore I have drawn thee, taking pity on thee").

2. Cf. *Matthew* 25:12, "*at [Dominus] respondens ait amen dico vobis nescio vos* ("but [the Lord] responding said, 'Amen I say to you, I know you not")

3.An indigent poet in Juvenal's *Satirae* 3.203, Codrus in Medieval Latin became synonymous with the phrase "poor devil."

4. Grammatical terms were often transferred in the Middle Ages to living conditions (viz. J.A. Alford's *The Grammatical Metaphor*, Speculum 57 (1982), pp. 728-760). The ablative is the case of "taking away," the sullying of which the disenfranchisement of the poor effects; the dative is the case of "giving," through which the genitive, the case of "possession"—but an allusion to the tools of generation—is aroused: basically the giving of money arouses the generation of rulings that favor the highest bidder.

5. Cf. *Ezekiel* 26:16, "*principes...adtoniti super repentino casu [Tyri] admirabuntur*" ("and in astonishment shall the princes wonder at [Tyre's] sudden fall").

6. Cf. *Psalm* 136:1 (*Vulgate*), "*super flumina Babylonis ibi sedimus et flevimus cum recordaremur Sion*" ("there upon the rivers of Babylon we sat and wept, when we remembered Zion").

7. Cf. *Matthew* 24:12, "*et quoniam abundabit iniquitas refrigescet caritas multorum*" ("and because iniquity hath abounded, the charity of many shall grow cold.")

8. The false god of avarice and wealth described in *Luke* 16:13 and *Matthew* 6:24.

9. *Scurra* can mean either coxcomb or droll. In light of the context, I have opted for the former.

10. Probably the name of an obscure, though beloved, bishop or abbot (Schumann).

11. Cf. *Regula Benedicti* 58.16 ("Rule of Saint Benedict"), "*collum excutere desub iugo regulae*" ("[it is no longer permitted him] to wrest his neck from the yoke of the Rule").

12. Cf. *Matthew* 15:14, "*sinite illos caeci sunt duces caecorum caecus autem si caeco ducatum praestet ambo in foveam cadunt*" ("Let them alone: they are blind leaders of the blind and if the blind lead the blind both fall into the pit").

13. Burnellus, or Brunellus, is the protagonist of Nigel de Longchamps' 11th century *Speculum Stultorum* (Mirror of Fools), in which the donkey, Brunellus, goes on a quest to lengthen his tail. He is thus the personification of foolishness.

14. Pope Gregory I (540-604 AD), who became the patron saint of musicians, singers, students, and teachers, was widely known for his liturgical reforms, Biblical commentaries and ecclesiastical writings.

15. Saint Jerome (347-420 AD) was the father is the Vulgate, or Latin translation of the Bible.

16. Saint Augustine of Hippo (354-430 AD).

17. Saint Benedict of Nursia (480-547 AD) was the founder of the Order of St Benedict and thus Western Monasticism. This line is an allusion to *Regula Benedicti* 40.6, "*Licet legamus vinum omnino monachorum non esse...saltem vel hoc consentiamus, ut non usque ad satietatem bibamus, sed parcius*" ("Although we read that wine is not proper for all monks...let us at least agree that we drink not to satiety, but sparingly").

18. Saint Mary of Bethany and Saint Martha of Bethany, respectively. They are described in *Luke* 10:39, "*et huic erat soror nomine Maria quae etiam sedens secus pedes Domini audiebat verbum illius. Martha autem satagebat circa frequens ministerium quae stetit et ait Domine non est tibi curae quod soror mea reliquit me solam ministrare dic ergo illi ut me adiuvet*" ("And she had a sister hight Mary, who, even sitting at the Lord's feet, heard His Word. Martha, however, was busy serving. She stood and said, "Lord, carest thou not that my sister hath left me here alone to serve? Tell her therefore to help me"). Their inclinations in this backward age have been reversed.

19. Leah and her sister Rachel were two of the wives of Jacob, one of the Biblical Patriarchs. Leah had weak eyes, and Rachel was infertile (viz. *Genesis* 29).

20. The Roman statesman Cato the Elder, or Cato "the Censor," was widely known for his abstemiousness.

21. Lucretia, a legendary figure in the history of the Roman Republic, was the personification of chastity. Her rape by Sextus Tarquinius, the son of Lucius Tarquinius Superbus, the last king of Rome, and consequent suicide on the altar of her own virtue prompted the establishment of the Roman Republic (viz. Livy *Ab Urbe Condita* ("From the Foundation of the City") Book I, sections 57-60, Dionysius of Halicarnassus Ῥωμαϊκὴ Ἀρχαιολογία ("Roman Antiquities") Book IV, sections 64-85).

22. Cf. *Matthew* 7:21, "*non omnis qui dicit mihi Domine Domine intrabit in regnum caelorum sed qui facit voluntatem Patris mei qui in caelis est ipse*

intrabit in regnum caelorum" ("Not every one who saith to me, 'Lord, Lord,' shall enter the kingdom of heaven, but he who doth the will of my Father who is in heaven shall enter the kingdom of heaven.")

23. Cf. Juvenal, *Satirae* 8.20, *"nobilitas sola est atque unica virtus"* ("the sole, unparalleled nobility is virtue") (Schumann).

24. Cf. Horace, *Ars Poetica* 303, *"ergo fungar vice cotis"* (therefore I shall play the whetstone").

25. Cf. *Luke* 23:28, *"filiae Hierusalem nolite flere super me sed super vos ipsas flete et super filios vestros"* ("weep not for me, daughters of Jerusalem, but weep for yourselves and your children").

26. Simon Magus, or Simon the Sorcerer, was a Samaritan magician, who appears in *Acts of the Apostles* 8:9-24. He seduced with his magic the people into believing he had the power of God. He was converted to Christianity by Philip the Evangelist and witnessed many of his miracles. When he saw Philip give people the Holy Ghost with his hands, he offered to pay him for this power. Philip warned him of the punishment for those who try to purchase the gift of God, whereupon Simon prayed for absolution. In the Medieval mind he was an embodiment of the great seducer.

27. Gehazi, mentioned in *2 Kings* 4:12-36, 5:20-27, and 6:1-8, was the Prophet Elisha's servant, who solicited from Naaman the Syrian a talent of silver and two changes of togs in the prophet's name, whereupon Elisha cursed Gehazi and his descendants with leprosy. He personifies avarice.

28. *Ephesians* 5:23-24 identifies the Church as Christ's bride: *"quoniam vir caput est mulieris sicut Christus caput est ecclesiae ipse salvator corporis sed ut ecclesia subiecta est Christo ita et mulieres viris suis in omnibus"* ("since the husband is the head of the wife, as Christ is the head of the church. He is the savior of the body. So as the church is subject to Christ, let wives be subject to their husbands in all affairs").

29. An allusion to Gehazi. The Syrian is Naaman.

30. Cf. *Ephesians* 5:5, *"avarus quod est idolorum servitus non habet hereditatem in regno Christi et Dei"* ("a man of avarice, which is a service of idols, has no inheritance in the kingdom of Christ and God").

31. Cf. *Proverbs* 30:15, *"sanguisugae duae sunt filiae dicentes adfer adfer tria sunt insaturabilia et quartum quod numquam dicit sufficit"* ("there are two daughters of the horseleech that say, 'Bring, bring!' There are three insatiable things and the fourth never saith, 'It is enough'"). In this poem the first daughter is simony and the second is avarice.

32. Cf. *Ecclesiastes* 12:1, "*memento creatoris tui in diebus iuventutis tuae antequam veniat tempus afflictionis et appropinquent anni de quibus dicas non mihi placent*" ("remember thy Creator in the days of thy youth, before the time of affliction come and the years approach about which thou wilt say, 'They please me not'").

33. The Latin here is unclear. While the heirs of Simon are clearly the corrupt prelates, it is unclear whether *heredes* is the subject or object of *fovent*, and the sentence can thus be rendered in two ways: (1) "But the heirs of Simon caress them with their allurements"; or (2) "But they foster the heirs of Simon with their flatteries." I have opted for the former, since the prelates, though many hate Simon himself, beguile money out of the mass by the threats and enticements they deliver in their sermons.

34. Ephron was a Hittite whom Abraham persuaded to sell land for a tomb for Sarah; Ephron was willing to give him the site for free, but Abraham insisted on paying him (viz. *Genesis* 23:10-16). St. Jerome in *Hebraicae Quaesitiones in Genesim* 23.16 explains the meanings of the two names: Ephron means "perfect, complete" and Ephran means "imperfect, defective." The poet is therefore stating that since he took Abraham's money, Ephron "the Perfect" deserves the name Ephran "the Incomplete" (Bernt).

35. Cf. *Isaiah* 40:3, *Matthew* 3:3, and *John* 1:23, "*vox clamantis in deserto*" ("the voice of one crying in the desert").

36. Cf. *Ephesians* 5:1, "*estote ergo imitatores Dei*" ("be ye therefore followers of God").

37. Cf. *Luke* 14:27, "*et qui non baiulat crucem suam et venit post me non potest esse meus discipulus*" ("and whosoever doth not carry his own cross and come after me cannot be my disciple").

38. Cf. *Romans* 5:14, "*sed regnavit mors ab Adam usque ad Mosen etiam in eos qui non peccaverunt in similitudinem praevaricationis Adae qui est forma futuri*" ("but death reigned from Adam unto Moses and even over those who had not sinned, in the likeness of Adam's transgression, who is a figure of him who was to come").

39. The nard is a wild flowering plant with medicinal and aromatic properties. It is mentioned in *Song of Solomon* 1:12 and 4:13, *John* 12:1-10, *Matthew* 20:2 and 26:6-13, *Mark* 14:3-9).

40. Cf. *Daniel* 11:5, "*et confortabitur rex austri et de principibus eius praevalebit super eum et dominabitur dicione*" ("and the king of the south shall be strengthened and one of his princes shall prevail over him and he shall rule with great might").

41. The black priors refer to the Benedictine and Cluniac Orders (Bernt).

42. This is an example of the rich man's victory in every suit, even when he refuses to distort the facts in his favor (Bernt).

43. Cf. Juvenal, *Satirae* 11.208, "*voluptates commendat rarior usus*" ("rarer use commends pleasures").

44. Cf. Juvenal, *Satirae* 7.197, "*si Fortuna volet, fies de rhetore consul*" ("If Fortune wishes, you will, rhetorician, become a consul").

45. I have taken *opera* as a noun of agent, as do Diemer and Diemer.

46. Probably Darius III (380-330 BC) during whose reign Persia fell under Alexander the Great's control; whilst fleeing Alexander, he was killed by a satrap (Schumann).

47. Pompey was one of the members of the First Triumvirate and Julius Caesar's adversary.

48. Troy had the upper hand until the gods decided to seal its fate.

49. Cf. Horace, *Epistles* 1.11.27, "*caelum, non animum, mutant, qui trans mare currunt*" ("they change their climate, not their minds, who run across the sea"). Horace states that those who are unhappy with their surroundings must change their casts of mind, not their abodes. This passage reverses the sense: those who are constant change indeed their scene but not their dispositions.

50. Cf. *Matthew* 7:26, "*et omnis qui audit verba mea haec et non facit ea similis erit viro stulto qui aedificavit domum suam supra harenam*" ("and every one who heareth these my words and doth not as they say shall be like the foolish man who builds his house upon the sand").

51. Cf. *1 Corinthians* 10:12, "*itaque qui se existimat stare videat ne cadat*" ("and so he who thinketh himself to stand, let him be aware lest he fall").

52. Cf. Horace, *Epistulae* 1.2.40, "*dimidium facti, qui coepit, habet*" ("half the deed he holds, who the enterprise began").

53. Proteus was the son of Poseidon and personifies fickleness.

54. Opportunity, or Occasio, was the Roman equivalent of Caerus, the Greek god of opportunity. This deity differed from Fortuna in that Caerus brought at the right moment what was convenient and fit, the due measure that achieved the aim.

When the god arrived, one could grasp the long tresses over his brows, but once he passed, his departure could not be stopped because the back of his head, or occiput, had no hair to grasp. Since the Latin word occasio is feminine, Caerus becomes a goddess in the Latin mind. In *Disticha Catonis* 2.26, or Dionysius Cato's Distichs, the author writes, "*rem tibi quam scieris aptam dimittere noli: fronte capillata, post haec occasio calva*" ("Don't let pass by what you know to be good for you: Opportunity has over her forehead hair, but behind is completely bald").

55. Queen Hecuba was the ill-fated queen of Troy.

56. This flippant title pays homage to Carl Orff's masterful musical translation of this magnificent poem.

57. Cf. Boethius, *Philosophiae Consolatio* (*The Consolation of Philosophy*) 2.*Metrum* 1.7, "*sic illa ludit*" ("thus she plays her game") (Diemer).

58. Cf. Ovid, *Metamorphoses* 2.137, "*medio tutissimus ibis*" ("in the middle you will course most safely").

59. From *Monosticha Catonis*, Breves sententiae 6 (Bernt).

60. Cf. Juvenal, *Satirae* 3.30, "*donandi gloria*" ("the glory fo giving").

61. Cf. *Monosticha Catonis*, Breves sententiae 17, "*cui des videto*" ("know to whom you should give").

62. In other words, if the reader hearkens to the poet well and thus becomes completely acquainted with his cast of mind he will know how to achieve glory through giving. This is an allusion to Persius, *Satirae* 3.30, "*ego te intus et in cute novi*" ("I know you within and without") (Bernt).

63. Cf. *Isaiah* 49:3, "*servus meus es tu Israhel quia in te gloriabor*" ("thou art my servant, Israel, for in thee will I glory").

64. Poorer than poor. See note 3 above.

65. If *omnibus* is dative, as I have translated it, then the sentence means that the listener's generosity flows in abundance to all and the father takes pride that although he is poorer than his son and can never earn the glory of which he speaks, his son has the wealth to give rightly and thus acquire great renown; if it is ablative, then the line reads, "you abound in all things," which seems less likely because the father is encouraging right giving rather than parsimony.

66. A variation of Horace, *Satirae* 1.1.206, "*est modus in rebus; sunt certi denique fines*" ("there is a right measure in all things; in short, there are fixed bounds") (Färber).

67. Horace is the author of the first half of these lines, "Virtue is...well-nigh good," and Ovid is the author of the other moiety, "Due to...vice's stead."

68. Horace penned the line "When the fool...he runs," and Juvenal authored "for vice...silhouette."

69. A play on *Ecclesiastes* 1:2. "*vanitas vanitatum*" ("vanity of vanities").

70. Cf. *John* 14:6, "*dicit ei Iesus ego sum via veritas et vita*" ("Jesus saith to him, 'I am the path, the truth, and the life'").

71. Cf. *1 Corinthians* 13:13, "*nunc autem manet fides spes caritas tria haec maior autem his est caritas*" ("and now there remain faith, hope, and charity, these three: but charity is the best of these").

72. Cf. *John* 5:8, "*dicit ei Iesus surge tolle grabattum tuum et ambula*" ("Jesus saith to him, 'Arise, take up thy bed and walk'").

73. The bite of the forbidden fruit (viz. *Genesis* 3:6).

74. Viz. *Genesis* 2:17, "*in quocumque enim comederis ex [ligno scientiae bonorum et malorum] morte morieris*" ("on whatsoever day thou shalt eat of [the tree of the knowledge of good and evil] thou shalt die the death"), and *Romans* 5:12, "*propterea sicut per unum hominem in hunc mundum peccatum intravit et per peccatum mors et ita in omnes homines mors pertransiit in quo omnes peccaverunt*" ("wherefore as by one man sin entered into this world and through this sin death, so death passed upon all men in whom all have sinned").

75. Christ. See note 28 above.

76. That is, God waits until the measure of their sins is full.

77. Cf. *Matthew* 7:16, "*a fructibus eorum cognoscetis*" ("by their fruits you shall know them").

78. Cf. *Matthew* 3:12, "*cuius ventilabrum in manu sua et permundabit aream suam et congregabit triticum suum in horreum paleas autem conburet igni inextinguibili*" ("whose fan is in his hand, and he will thoroughly cleanse his threshing floor and gather his wheat into the barn, but he will burn the chaff with an inextinguishable fire").

79. Cf. *Psalms* 15:6 (*Vulgate*), "*Funes ceciderunt mihi in praeclaris: etenim*

hereditas mea praeclara est mihi" ("The lots have fallen upon me with clarity, and forsooth my inheritance is very clear to me"). Basically, a lordly lot, God, has been awarded to mankind.

80. The path of love; cf. *1 Corinthians* 12:31, "*aemulamini autem charismata maiora et adhuc excellentiorem viam vobis demonstro*" ("but be zealous for the better gifts and I shall show you yet a more excellent path").

81.There are two possible translations here. If *ascellas* (shoulders) is a corruption of *cellas* (chambers), then the line is *turturis retorqueas os ad cellas* ("thou shouldst turn the head of the dove to the chambers"). In this case the turtle dove designates the Holy Spirit that should withdraw itself from the hustle and bustle of the world and devote itself to contemplation: viz. *Distinctiones monasticae* (Pitra II 491b), "*turtur, quia strepitum odit, et quietem ac solitudinem diligit, significat Spiritum sanctum*" ("the turtledove, because it hates noise and cherishes rest and solitude, signifies the Holy Ghost") (Diemer). If the line be *turturis retorqueas os ad ascellas* ("thou shouldst twist the dove's beak back unto its shoulders"), then it is a reference to *Leviticus* 1:14 et seq., "*sin autem de avibus holocausti oblatio fuerit Domino de turturibus...offeret eam sacerdos ad altare et retorto ad collum capite ac rupto vulneris loco*" ("but if the offering of the holocaust to the Lord be of birds, or turtledoves...the priest shall present it to the altar, twist back the head to the neck and break the site of the wound") (Schumann). The line then is both a reference to a holocaustal ritual intended to propitiate God and an allegory that exhorts men to accord their deeds (which their shoulders bear, thus *ascellas*) with what they preach (the origin of which is the mouth, thus *os*). Given what follows this line, I have elected the latter as the author's intended meaning.

82. Cf. *Matthew* 18:15, "*si autem peccaverit in te frater tuus vade et corripe eum inter te et ipsum solum si te audierit lucratus es fratrem tuum*" ("but if thy brother shall sin against thee, go to him and rebuke him between him and thee alone; if he shall hear thee, a brother shalt thou gain").

83. The Philistines were the occupants of southern Canaan who were referred to in the Bible as the archenemies of the Israelites.

84. Delilah, a figure from *Judges* 16, was the love of Samson, the secret of whose strength the Philistines wished to learn. They approached her with a handsome offer of silver and she accepted. He told her three riddles, then the true reason revealed: he cut not his hair in fulfillment of a vow to God. The Philistines captured him, shore his hair, gouged out his eyes, and imprisoned him.

85. Cf. *Matthew* 6:28, "*considerate lilia agri quomodo crescunt non laborant nec nent*" ("consider ye the lilies of the field, how they grow: they toil not nor do they spin").

86. Cf. *Hebrews* 7:16, "*qui non secundum legem mandati carnalis factus est sed*

secundum virtutem vitae insolubilis" ("who is made, not in accordance with the law of a carnal commandment, but according to the power of an indissoluble life"); and *Romans* 7:5, "*cum enim essemus in carne passiones peccatorum quae per legem erant operabantur in membris nostris ut fructificarent morti*" ("for when we were in the flesh, the passion of sins, which were by the law, worked in our members to bring forth fruit unto death").

87. Cf. *Job* 14:2, "*quasi flos egreditur et conteritur et fugit velut umbra*" ("who cometh forth like a flower, is destroyed, and fleeteth like a shadow"); and *Wisdom* 5:9, "*transierunt omnia illa tamquam umbra*" ("all those things have passed away as a shadow").

88. Cf. *Isaiah* 1:30, "*cum fueritis velut quercus defluentibus foliis et velut hortus absque aqua*" ("when you shall be like an oak without leaves and as a garden without water").

89. Cf. *Galatians* 5:16, "*spiritu ambulate et desiderium carnis non perficietis*" ("walk ye in spirit and you shall not fulfill the desires of the flesh").

90. The "law" is a reference to the Old Testament.

91. Cf. *Ecclesiasticus* 21:7, "*et qui timet Deum convertet ad cor suum*" ("and he who feareth God shall turn unto his own heart").

92. A reference to the human condition after the Fall.

93. Only the virtuous life is worth living.

94. Cf. *Psalms* 118:133 (*Vulgate*), "*gressus meos firma in sermone tuo*" ("direct my steps according to your word").

95. Cf. *Isaiah* 40:14, "*et docuit eum semitam iustitiae*" ("...and taught him the path of justice").

96. Cf. *Matthew* 3:10 and *Luke* 3:9, "*iam enim securis ad radicem arborum posita est omnis ergo arbor quae non facit fructum bonum exciditur et in ignem mittitur*" ("for now the ax is laid on the root of the trees; therefore every tree which doth yield no good fruit is cut and sent into the fire"). In *Matthew* 21:18-22 a hungry Christ, seeing a fig tree beside the road, came to it (*videns fici arborem unam secus viam venit ad eam* 21:19); finding nothing but leaves on it (*nihil invenit in ea nisi folia tantum* 21:19), he commanded that it never bear fruit again for all eternity (*et ait illi numquam ex te fructus nascatur in sempiternum* 21:19), which caused to the tree to wither away immediately (*et arefacta est continuo ficulnea* 21:19). The lesson he intended to show through this, aside from a display of hypoglycemic spite, was that faith accomplishes any feat, even casting mountains into the sea (*et si monti huic dixeritis tolle et iacta te in mare fiet* 21:21). The idea

of the fig now makes sense: Christ watches all and will strike down those who do not fulfill their creation—to feed a wayfarer in the case of the "foolish" fig and, in the case of man, to lead a virtuous life and thus benefit the world through charity and magnanimity and avoidance of sin. In this context, the tree is also a man who has failed to keep his faith through charity. *Mark* 11:12-14 and 11:19-25 follows up on this as well, adding in 11:13, "*non enim erat tempus ficorum*" ("indeed it was not the season for figs"), which advises, in the context of the poem, that here and now is the time to bear the fruit of faith and through charity benefit the world, for procrastination will only be met with punishment and seasonableness will not be considered a valid pretext. On the next morning the disciples "*viderunt ficum aridam factam a radicibus*" ("saw that the fig tree had been dried up from the roots") (11:20).

97. Cf. *2 Corinthians* 6:6, "*in casitate in scientia in longanimatate in suavitate in Spiritu Sancto in caritate non ficta*" ("in chastity, in knowledge, in long suffering, in sweetness, in the Holy Spirit, in charity unfeigned").

98. The nuptial vest is the vest earned through good works and faith in the Lord.

99. The royal court is the Kingdom of Heaven.

100. The bridegroom is Christ; this scene imports the meeting with Christ in the Last Judgment.

101. Ten virgins were invited to the wedding of Jesus and the Church; five brought oil in their lamps and five did not. Whilst the latter went off to purchase oil, Christ opened the doors to the five who had oil. When the other five returned with oil, Jesus told them that he knew them not (*Matthew* 25). The lamp betokens the soul and the oil is the Holy Spirit that illuminates it (*Proverbs* 20:27).

102. Cf. *Psalms* 117:9 (*Vulgate*), "*melius est sperare in Domino quam sperare in homine*" ("better it is to confide in the Lord than to place thy hope in man").

103. Cf. *Genesis* 3:19, "*in sudore vultus tui vesceris pane donec revertaris in terram de qua sumptus es*" ("and in the sweat of thy face thou shalt eat bread, until thou return to the land whence thou wast taken").

104. Cf. *Matthew* 8:12, "*ibi erit fletus et stridor dentium*" ("there shall be weeping and gnashing of teeth").

105. Cf. *Matthew* 3:12 (*vide supra*).

106. *Matthew* 5:8.

107. Cf. *Matthew* 5:6, "*beati qui esuriunt et sitiunt iustitiam*" ("blessed are they who hunger and thirst for justice").

108. Cf. *Psalms* 2:13 (*Vulgate*), "*cum exarserit post paululum furor eius beati omnes qui sperant in eum*" ("when His wrath shall be kindled in a short while, blessed are all who truth in Him").

109. Cf. *Matthew* 6:34, "*nolite ergo esse solliciti in crastinum crastinus enim dies sollicitus erit sibi*" ("be not then solicitous for the morrow, for it will be solicitous for itself").

110. A standard weight used in the measurement of gold, silver, etc.

111. Cf. *Luke* 12:35, "*sint lumbi vestri praecincti*" ("let your loins be girt").

112. Cf. *Wisdom* 1:11, "*os autem quod mentitur occidit animam*" ("and the mouth that lieth slayeth the soul").

113. Cf. *Psalms* 39:3 (*Vulgate*), "*et eduxit me de lacu famoso de luto caeni*" ("and he lifted me from the pit of misery and the mire of filth").

114. Pamphilus, the Latinized Greek for "friend to all," was an archetypal young lover in Terence's plays *Hekyra* and *Andria*, and personifies the foolish pursuits that lead to self-destruction and shame.

115. The Hydra who regains a head for each one lost, brings to mind both an indomitable battle that cannot be won physically and also the Herculean hero who slew the monster, but was later undone by his wife—a woman, and the ultimate cause of lust—Deianira.

116. Antaeus, who gained more strength each time he was thrown to the earth. Antaeus is the personification of lust in the medieval mind, as attested in Fulgentius' *Mitologiarum* 2.4.

117. Potiphar's wife who failed to seduce Joseph, but later calumniated him anyway (viz. *Genesis* 39:7-20).

118. In the Middle Ages the age of manhood spanned from 35 to 50 (Diemer).

119. The mistakes he made in that age, which he now repents, served as wise counselors of what not to do.

120. This is quite difficult to interpret. Schumann and Bernt liken this to the narration of Hercules, as he stood at the crossroads, though the speaker did not hesitate at all to enter upon the path of vice. The speaker may be stating that of the two possibilities for sexual intercourse he chose not "unnatural" sodomy with men, but a "natural" sexual union with the opposite sex. Along with his mention of his refusal to commit adultery, this stanza seems like both a subtle self-vindication for avoiding sodomy and adultery whilst in the heat of unrestrained desire and a

self-accusation for failing to control his sexual desire in whole.

121. The original Latin text reads *nec fraudavi temere /coniugis amplexus;/ Dalidam persequere, / ne fraudetur sexus!* ("nor did I beguile the embrace of a spouse. Take vengeance upon Delilah, lest the sex be deceived!"). I have, however, chosen the alternate reading adopted by Diemer: *nec fraudavi temere / coniugis amplexus / Dalidam dans, tenere / ut fraudetur sexus* ("nor...by giving them to Delilah, so that the sex be deceived"). The imperative in the former reading is so adventitious that it seems unlikely Peter wrote it in his original work.

122. This is a reference to the prodigal son in *Luke* 15:16 who desired to consume the husks the sows were eating when his father denied him food on account of his impious excesses. The husks can either betoken female flesh, or coitus, which summarizes the author's past exploits, or simply the bland life he sought to pursue to divert himself from his debaucheries.

123. Dinah, a figure in *Genesis* 34, was the daughter of Jacob and Leah. She was abducted and raped by a Canaanite prince, whereupon her brothers Simeon and Levi entered the city in stealth, slew all its male inhabitants, and plundered.

124. Cf. *Proverbs* 26:11, "*sicut canis qui revertitur ad vomitum suum sic imprudens qui iterat stultitiam suam*" ("as a dog that returneth to its vomit, so doth the imprudent man who repeateth his folly").

125. Cf. *Psalms* 90:3 (*Vulgate*), "*quia ipse liberavit me de laqueo venantium et a verbo aspero*" ("for He hath freed me from the hunters' snare and from the harsh word").

126. Belus was a purported Assyrian King, who fathered Ninus, the founder of Nineveh, the capital of Assyria.

127. Sinon was the Greek warrior, who, as a Trojan captive, pretended to be a deserter and persuaded the Trojans to allow the wooden horse to enter, as it would "protect" them from the Achaean invasion.

128. Either Zeno of Elea, a philosopher renowned for his paradoxes, or Zeno of Citium, the founder of the Stoic school of philosophy. Given the context of requisite stoic restraint, it is likely the latter.

129. The Latin in Clm 4660/4660a reads *ni fugando fugiam Dalidam Samsonis* ("unless I flee Samson's Delilah by routing her"), but I have chosen *ni fugiendo fugiam Dalidam Samsonis*, since routing Delilah, as the former reading suggests, entails resistance which is not consonant with the author's previous advice to "escape by fleeing."

130. That is, temporal and eternal punishment, which stands in contrast to the

previous line, which speaks only of punishment on earth.

131. Cf. Horace, *Epistulae* 1.14.36, "*nec lusisse pudet, sed non incidere ludum*" ("I am not ashamed of my former games, but shameful would it be not to bring them to an end").

132. Cf. *Titus* 2:12, "*sobrie, et juste, et pie vivamus in hoc saeculo*" ("so that we may live soberly and justly and piously in this age").

133. See note 96.

134. Cf. *1 Timothy* 3:2, "*oportet ergo episcopum irreprehensibilem esse*" ("therefore it behooves a bishop to be beyond reproach").

135. Literally, "inflicts upon them the cost of infamy."

136. Cf. *Isaiah* 38:1, "*dispone domui tuae quia morieris tu et non vives*" ("put thy home in order, for thou shalt die and shalt not live").

137. Cf. *1 Thessalonians* 5:22, "*ab omni specie mala abstinete vos*" ("abstain from every type of evil").

138. Cf. *Lamentations* 2:18, "*deduc quasi torrentem lacrimas per diem et noctem*" ("let tears like a torrent run down throughout the day and night").

139. Quoted almost verbatim from *Psalm* 44:17 (*Vulgate*).

140. Cf. *Isaiah* 1:23, "*principes tui infideles, socii furum*" ("thy rulers are unfaithful, the fellows of thieves").

141. The head is the holder of a high ecclesiastical office, whose misdeeds infect all under his sway.

142. Cf. *Matthew* 24:12, "*et quoniam abundavit iniquitas refrigescet caritas multorum*" ("and because iniquity hath abounded, the charity of many will grow cold").

143. Cf. *Psalm* 16:13 (*Vulgate*), "*eripe animam meam ab impio*" ("rescue my spirit from the impious one").

144. Cf. *Jeremiah* 7:11, "*numquid ergo spelunca latronum facta est domus ista, in qua invocatum est nomen meum in oculis vestris*" ("has that house then, in which my name is called, become a robbers' cave in your eyes?"); and *Matthew* 20:13, "*vos autem fecistis illam speluncam latronum*" ("but ye have made it a robbers' den").

145. This is a reference to Nebuchadnezzar's capture of Jerusalem and the violation of the Temple of Solomon through the Seleucids (viz. *2 Maccabees* 6:1-5). It likens the heads of the Church to the Antichrist (the King of Babylon is identified as the Antichrist in CB 228) and compares the present state to the desecration of Solomon's Temple (Diemer).

146. In *John* 2:14-16, Jesus overturned the tables of the temple's moneychangers and evicted the men *"qui columbas vendebant"* ("who were selling doves").

147. This use of grammar, specifically, degrees of comparison, to describe the human condition is similar to that found in CB 1.

148. Cf. *Luke* 12:48, *"omni autem cui multum datum est multum quaeretur ab eo"* ("so then of all to whom much hath been given much will be required").

149. Quoted from *Acts of the Apostles* 1:16.

150. A play on *Philippians* 3:17, *"imitatores mei estote fratres"* ("be imitators of me, my brothers").

151. Cf. *Luke* 12:34-35, *"Ubi enim thesaurus vester est, ibi et cor vestrum erit sint lumbi vestri præcincti, et lucernæ ardentes in manibus vestris"* ("for where your treasure is, there your heart will also be; let your waists be girt and let there be lamps burning in your hands").

152. Gideon was the judge of the Hebrews who was appointed by God to free the Israelites from their idolatry (viz. *Judges* 6-8). They had turned away from God after 40 years of peace and were sustaining the attacks of the Midianites. God instructed him to free them. Gideon asked for a sign and pledged to place a fleece on his threshing floor and if he found dew on the fleece and not the floor he would accept that as a sign that by his own hand he would free Israel as God said. Since in this poem moths eat the fleece instead, something is astray.

153. Cf. *Matthew* 6:19, *"nolite thesaurizare vobis thesauros in terra ubi aerugo et tinea demolitur"* ("store not treasures for yourselves on earth where rust and moth consume").

154. The she-ass of Balaam, a diviner found in *Numbers* 22-24 (Bernt). Whilst the Israelites were sojourning in Midian, shortly before Moses' death and after defeating two opposing kings, Balak, King of Moab, sent messengers to Balaam to persuade him to come and curse the Israelites. God in a dream told him not to go, but after pressing God further, Balaam was given permission to go. Incensed, God dispatched an angel to obviate Balaam's approach. Balaam's donkey saw the angel and refused to move; Balaam beat her for halting, whereupon she asked him why he beat her so. He then saw the angel, who told him that if the donkey had not turned aside, he would have slain Balaam.

155. An 11th century monastery in France once admired for its strict austerity by all, including the kings of France and England, who bestowed favors upon it. The system of lay brothers, however—members of an order who were occupied with manual labor and temporalities instead of study and spiritual insight, which the choir monks were wont to adopt, but were not ordained by a cleric and thus were tied to the cloister only by their vows—precipitated its golden age's end, as they outnumbered the choir monks and soon caused the relaxation of the rules, which led to possessions that conflicted with the convent's doctrine and the lay brothers' claims to equality with the choir monks—the cause of scandalous scenes. The lay brothers revolted in 1185 and the continual expulsion of priors and choir monks by them carried on for many years.

156. The order was founded in 1076 and was young in comparison to the Benedictines (Diemer).

157. Literally, "kingly anointing." This is probably a reference to King Henry II of England (1130 – 1189), who favored the laity and sought to have the secular law predominate over ecclesiastical law, as the clergy were not required to obey the state's laws (Bernt).

158. The incomprehensible order established by men and not God.

159. The lay king sticks to the brothers of the convent because the lay are generally foolish.

160. Cf. *John* 10:1, "*qui non intrat per ostium...ille fur est, et latro*" ("who entereth not through the door...he is a thief and a robber"). This is likely another reference to Henry II, who is not a good shepherd of the cloister, but a robber who makes money out of it.

161. A reference to the contemplative life of the choir monks.

162. Cf. *Psalms* 112:7 (*Vulgate*), "*de stercore erigens pauperem*" ("he raiseth the pauper from muck").

163. Cf. *Proverbs* 26:16, "*sapientior sibi piger videtur septem viris loquentibus sententias*" ("the indolent man seemeth to himself wiser than seven men speaking judgments").

164. A reference to Tharsia, the daughter of King Antiochus, from the text *Apollonius*; pirates sold her to a pimp. In like fashion, the cloister is being prostituted to the laity (Bernt).

165. Greed.

166. Cf. *Lamentations* 4:6, "*peccato Sodomorum quae subversa est in momento*"

("...the sin of Sodom, which was overturned in a moment").

167. Rachel, a wife of Jacob, is here a symbol for the Church.

168. Rahab was a prostitute of Jericho in *Joshua* 2 and 6; she assisted the Israelites in capturing the Promised Land. Since, however, she is held in esteem in the Bible, Rahab likely refers not to the biblical figure, but to the Hebrew word that means "noise," "tumult," and "arrogance," which is mentioned throughout the Hebrew Bible, such as *Psalm* 86:4, among many, wherein the name is synonymous with Egypt, the enemy of the Israelites. Due to all the hostility towards this figure or word, I have translated *ancilla* (normally "maid") as harlot, to capture the poem's loathing of her/it.

169. Albinus is here used parodistically as the personification of the light, thus, Saint Silver; Rufinus is a saintly name that personifies redness, thus Saint Gold (Bernt).

170. Cf. *Matthew* 15:14, "*autem si caeco ducatum praestet ambo in foveam cadunt*" ("but if the blind are in charge of the blind, both shall fall into the pit").

171. Cf. *Leviticus* 8:17, "*cremans extra castra*" ("he burned [the offering] outside the camp").

172. In place of tonsures, they wear crowns.

173. Cf. *Matthew* 18:6, "*expedit ei ut suspendatur mola asinaria in collo eius et demergatur in profundum maris*" ("it would be better to have the ass' millstone hung around and be drowned in the deep").

174. The occiput of Fortune is bald, since she cannot be grasped once she passes by; in other words, "this often throws them into calamity."

175. Cf. *2 Samuel* 1:23, "*aquilis velociores, leonibus fortiores*" ("they were swifter than hawks and stronger than lions").

176. Cf. *Psalms* 139:4 (*Vulgate*), "*acuerunt linguas suas sicut serpentis*" ("they have sharpened their tongues like a serpent").

177. Cf. *Ephesians* 5:16, "*redimentes tempus, quoniam dies mali sunt*" ("atoning for this age, since this is an evil time").

178. The secularization of the prelates is connected with their status as princes (The Ottonian Imperial Church). Breaking this dependence of bishops on the emperor was the avowed aim of the Gregorian reformers (south and north of the Alps).

179. This is a reference to the Decree of Gratian, the 12th century jurist, who compiled into a compendious textbook on canon law, *Concordia discordantium canonum*, or the Concord of Discordant Canons, which attempted to resolve seemingly contradictory canons from earlier centuries. He is known as the "Father of the Science of Canon Law."

180. Cf. *Ezekiel* 20:21, "*et exacerbaverunt me filii*" ("but their sons provoked me"); and *Jeremiah* 32:30, "*filii Israel qui usque nunc exacerbant me in opere manuum suarum dicit Dominus*" ("'the sons of Israel, even up to now, provoke me in their hands' work,' says the Lord").

181. Quoted verbatim from *Isaiah* 1:4.

182. The Benedictine (and Clunian) monks wear black (Bernt).

183. The Premonstratensians, or Norbertines, wear white habits (Bernt). The order was founded in 1121. Since their habits are something new, this poem must have been written in the 12th century.

184. The beginning of *Ecclesiastes.*

185. Cf. *1 Corinthians* 2:14, "*animalis autem homo non percipit ea quae sunt Spiritus Dei*" ("but the animal nature of man does not perceive the things that are of the Spirit of God").

186. Cf. *Ecclesiastes* 1:13, "*de omnibus quae fiunt sub sole*" ("concerning all that happens beneath the sun").

187. Cf. *1 Corinthians* 5:7, "*expurgate vetus fermentum*" ("purge the old leaven").

188. *Psalm* 42:1 (*Vulgate*), "*Iudica me Deus*" ("judge me, O God").

189. Judah was the Biblical Kingdom ruled by David and his line. Together with Israel it is a metaphor for the congregation. Perhaps these last four lines are both the poet's instructions to the prelate and the very words the prelate should use when addressing his flock.

190. Cf. *Matthew* 9:37-38, "*messis quidem multa operarii autem pauci rogate ergo Dominum messis ut mittat operarios in messem suam*" ("indeed the harvest is great, but the laborers few; therefore petition the Lord to send out laborers to the harvest"); and *John* 4:35, "*levate oculos vestros et videte regiones quia albae sunt iam ad messem*" ("lift your eyes and see the countryside, for it is already ripe for the harvest").

191. Cf. *John* 4:36, "*ut et qui seminat simul gaudeat et qui metit*" ("so that both he who sows and he who reaps may together rejoice").

192. *Isaiah* 62:1.

193. Cf. *Isaiah* 62:1, *"donec egrediatur ut splendor Iustus eius et Salvator eius ut lampas accendatur"* ("until [Jerusalem's] Just One advances in splendor and her Savior blazes like a lamp").

194. Cf. *Lamentations* 1:11, *"video Domine et considera quoniam facta sum vilis"* ("see and consider, O Lord, for I have become vile").

195. Cf. *Lamentations* 1:1, *"princeps provinciarum facta est sub tributo"* ("The Prince of the provinces hath been placed under tribute").

196. Cf. *Isaiah* 62:4, *"non vocaberis ultra Derelicta et terra tua non vocabitur amplius Desolata"* ("thou wilt no longer be called Forsaken, and thy land will no longer be called Desolate").

197. Marcus Licinius Crassus, the richest man in Roman history and financier of the First Triumvirate.

198. Scylla is a rock between Italy and Sicily opposite Charybdis. Personified as the daughter of Phorcys, she was transformed by Circe through jealousy into a sea monster with dogs about her haunches. Charybdis was the daughter of Poseidon and Gaia; once a beautiful naiad, she assumed the form of a huge bladder whose face was all mouth and whose limbs were flippers and who swallowed up and belched back huge quantities of water thrice a day; in other accounts she was a huge whirlpool. Both Scylla and Charybdis occupied the narrow Strait of Messina.

199. The Syrtes are two shallow, sandy gulfs on Libya's coast that pose a danger to ships.

200. The Sirens were three birds with women's heads, who lured sailors to shipwreck with their beguiling music and voices.

201. Franco was the papal camerlengo between 1174 and 1179 (viz. Walter Holtzmann, *Propter Sion non Tacebo* in Deutsches Archiv 10, 1953, pg. 171 et seq.). This double sea refers to an imagined vortex set in the bottleneck between either the Atlantic and the Mediterranean (Gibraltar), the Black Sea and the Mediterranean (Bosphorus), or the Tyrrhenian Sea and the southern Mediterranean (Messina). The to seas between which the ship of the supplicant is hurled hither and thither, are probably both groups of the Curia: the lower curial officials without whom one does not come to the policymakers, and the cardinals, who demand money for their rulings in favor of the seeker (Diemer).

202. *Psalm* 121:4 (*Vulgate*).

203. Scylla had four to six dog heads ringing her waist.

204. Pope Gelasius I, who held the office from 492-496, supported the Primacy of the Rome over all the Church and papal supremacy.

205. The *finium regundorum actio*, or action for definition of boundaries, derives from ancient Roman Law. If the boundaries of contiguous estates were accidentally confused, each of the parties interested in the re-establishment of the boundaries might have an action against the other for that purpose. In this action each party was bound to account for the fruits and profits which he had received from any part of the land which did not belong to him, and also to account for any injury which it had sustained through his culpa. Each party was also entitled to compensation for improvements made in the portion of land which did not belong to him (viz. *Codex Justianus* 3.39). In this case the third counselor of the court looks not yet into the petitioner's case, but first opens jurisdictional proceedings.

206. The bulla was the seal of a papal document (later the ceremonial enactment itself); the bulla was made out of lead and is worth more than gold and silver.

207. Zacharias was a prophet and the father of St. John the Baptist. In *Zechariah* 5:7 et seq. he wrote of a vision in which he saw a woman sitting on a container, which an angel shut with lead. The woman represents godlessness (*impietas*) and in Jerome's commentary is called injustice (*iniquitas*). In the Curia injustice is not locked up, but runs rampant over the Bulla's lead.

208. According to Fournial's *Histoire monétaire de l'occident médiéval*, silver currency was used throughout the Middle Ages and gold coins were struck only in Byzantium, the Eastern Roman Empire founded by the Emperor Constantine (Diemer).

209. In 1159 Pope Alexander III became the successor of Pope Adrian IV; a minority of cardinals, however, elected the priest Octavian, who became Victor IV, the German emperor Barbarossa's antipope. This schism ended in 1177 with the Treaty of Venice, whereupon Alexander was recognized as the true pope. The French took the side of Alexander III during the schism (Bernt).

210. The Council of Montpelier in 1162 in France, in which Pope Alexander III excommunicated the antipope Victor IV (Schumann).

211. Cf. *Matthew* 16:19, "*et tibi dabo claves regni caelorum*" ("and I shall give thee the keys of the kingdom of heaven").

212. Cf. *Psalms* 149:8 (*Vulgate*), "*ad alligandos reges eorum in compedibus et nobiles eorum in manicis ferreis*" ("to bind their kings with shackles and their nobles with manacles of iron").

213. This is a play of words: *car-di-nales*, or cardinals in Latin, and *di-car-nales*, gods of the flesh (Bernt).

214. That is they present themselves as the Christs (lambs) of Christendom (sheep).

215. *Psalm* 18:13 (*Vulgate*).

216. Cf. *Matthew* 23:24, "*duces caeci excolantes culicem camelum autem glutientes*" ("you blind leaders, straining out a gnat whilst swallowing a camel").

217. This probably means that the Church behaves like a noble, spoiled dame (Diemer).

218. Probably the antipope Calixtus III (viz. Holtzmann, loco citato 173 et seq.).

219. The Latin here literally reads "with thick stomach and broad skin."

220. While elsewhere the ship is the avaricious Church, here the ship is that of the petitioner that capsizes if he offers the counselors of the Curia no money.

221. Cf. Juvenal, *Satirae* 10.22, "*cantabit vacuus coram latrone viator*" ("the wanderer who has nothing shall sing in the robber's sight") (Schumann).

222. The ostiaries, or papal doorkeepers.

223. Pietro da Pavia was a cardinal who was invited by Pope Alexander III in 1175 to claim the bishopric, which he, elected in 1771, had not yet assumed.

224. Pope Alexander III.

225. Literally, "unless Gehazi should corrupt Elisha's body"; my rendering captures this as well, but more vividly, as Gehazi attacks and corrupts Elisha unawares. In other words, Alexander will be a true servant of God, unless the Pope's next neighborhood be wicked and venal."

226. Cf. *Romans* 11:16, "*et si radix sancta et rami*" ("and if the root is holy so too are the boughs").

227. Cf. *Matthew* 6:38, "*date, et dabitur vobis*" ("give and it shall be given you").

228. A bastardization of *Matthew* 6:30, "*omni autem petenti te tribue*" ("but allot to all who ask of thee").

229. Cf. *Galatians* 6:8, "*quae enim seminaverit homo haec et metet*" ("for whatever man hath sown that he shall also reap"); and *2 Corinthians* 9:6, "*qui parce seminat parce et metet*" ("who sows sparingly will also reap sparingly").

230. Justinian as an eastern Roman emperor who codified Roman law.

231. Laws are empty husks and money golden grain.

232. Parca was one of the Parcae, the goddesses of fate.

233. The mark is a weight equivalent to eight ounces.

234. Saint Mark, one of the Evangelists.

235. Cf. Ovid, *Ars Amatoria* 3.505, "*non es mihi, tibia, tanti*" ("flute, you are not of great value to me").

236. French for "Pay! Pay!"

237. Tityos was the son of Zeus and Elara. After a failed rape of Leto at Hera's behest, he was slain by Apollo and Artemis; in Tartarus he was stretched out, and two eagles fed on his liver, which grew back daily.

238. This is a reference to the miters that bishops wear, but the literal translation also intimates the devilish nature of their souls and acts.

239. The god of heaven is banished to the underworld, and the god of riches rules the world above.

240. The model of good works, the center of Christendom has failed in that regard.

241. Some kind of heresy, possibly a sardonic reference to Arnold of Brescia, who called on the Church to renounce all property, stated that the clergy with property had no power to administer the Sacraments, and tried, and failed, to found a Commune of Rome.

242. Possibly Pope Eugene III, the shepherd of greed, who was Arnold's opponent. In 1148, Arnold succeeded in driving him into exile.

243. Possibly Arnold again.

244. Either Satan or Arnold, who curried the favor of the people and led the blossoming republic in Rome despite his excommunication.

245. This stanza refers to the events of 1167. The bad lot may be the epidemic in Barbarossa's army or the deaths of many nobles (Rainald of Dassel, for one). Based on the time of Arnold of Brescia, the evil lot could be seen in the coup d'état of the traditional order. The aristocratic Roman families (Pierleone, Frangipani) who were embroiled in the strife are probably meant (Bernt).

246. Probably the throne mentioned in the previous stanza.

247. Cf. *Luke* 7:9, "*nec in Israel tantam fidem inveni*" ("not even in Israel have I

found such great faith").

248. References too all of the following are made in this poem: *Matthew* 25:31;
Matthew 26:50; *Luke* 11:8; *Matthew* 25:30; *Luke* 8:1; *Matthew* 15:22; *Job* 19:21;
Psalms 69:6 (*Vulgate*); *Zephaniah* 1:15; *Matthew* 20:24; *Acts of the Apostles* 8:20;
Mark 8:33; *Matthew* 5:26, 13:46; *Luke* 22:36; *John* 6:9, 9:34; *Matthew* 26:75;
Lamentations 1:9; *Deuteronomy* 32:15; *Mark* 15:7; *Matthew* 20:10; *Philippians*
2:27; *John* 5:9; *Matthew* 20:25; *Hebrews* 3:12; *Colossians* 2:8; *John* 13:15.

249. Cf. Horace, *Epistulae* 1.14.33, "*quem scis immunem Cinarae placuisse
rapici*" ("he, as you know, without any gifts pleased not mercenary Cinara").

250. Cf. Prudentius, *Psychomachie* 22-26, "*fides, agresti turbida cultu / nuda
umeros... / nec telis meminit nec tegmine cingi, / pectore sed fidens valido*" ("faith,
unclad in a peasant's guise, with shoulders bare, remembers not to arms herself
with weapons and armor, but relies on her own brave heart") (Bernt).

251. Cf. *Psalms* 136:8-9 (*Vulgate*), "*filia Babylonis misera beatus qui retribuet
tibi retributionem tuam quam retribuisti nobis beatus qui tenebit et allidet
parvulos tuos ad petram*" ("O wretched daughter of Babylon, blessed is he who
will repay you with the payment you have paid to us; blessed is he who will take
hold of thy little one and strike them against a rock"). The crushing of children on
the rock was in the Patristics allegorically interpreted, for example to combat
sinful thoughts (Benedict, *Regula*, Prologue 28). Thus it here is a call for the
destruction of the cult of gods rather than the actual daughter of Babylon.

252. Here in the final battle of Fides Babel loses all its followers and repents its
previous crimes: the seduction of souls.

253. Viz. *Revelation* 17:3-5.

254. Cf. *Ezekiel* 23:32-34. This is the decisive blow against Babylon stands in the
conversion of all pagans, which CB 46 sees as incipient.

255. A prophecy addressed to King Louis VII of France, who by it was called to
the Second Crusade (Schumann). The prince of princes, the leader in the crusade
and promised final emperor is named in CB 46, but is not named. It is possibly
Conrad III of Germany as the upcoming *Ludus de Antichristo*(CB 228) this role is
very strongly assigned to the German emperor. The Latin verb *scandat* takes the
subjunctive because it is used in the reported speech of the prophecy.

256. Schumann: the eternally seated rectangle is according to Giesebrecht in
Geschichte der deutschen Kaiserzeit Vol. VI, p. 501, the Greek emperor and the
coast is Constantinople, where the German and French armies intended to meet.

257. The Pillars of Hercules, or Gibraltar. The point is that if the princeps sets off

for the crusade, the Muslim power will end from the Mediterranean all the way up to Spain.

258. The ship is Christianity, the headsail is the "prince of princes," and the Holy Trinity is its mainsail.

259. Vision of Peace is the patristic, medieval translation of Jerusalem.

260. Bedlam, or confusion, is the translation of Babylon.

261. Cf. *Isaiah* 36:6, "*ecce confidis super baculum harundinem confractum istum super Aegyptum cui si innixus fuerit homo intrabit in manum eius et perforabit eam*" ("behold thou art trusting in Egypt, in that broken staff of a reed; if a man were to lean on it, it would enter his hand and pierce it").

262. Cf. *Ecclesiastes* 7:14 (*Vulgate*), "*considera opera Dei*" ("consider the works of God").

263. The Judeo-Chrstian polemic against polytheism, as seen in *Psalm* 113:13-16 (*Vulgate*), "*os habent et non loquentur...manus habent et non palpabunt pedes habent et non ambulabunt non clamabunt in gutture suo similes illis fiant qui faciunt ea et omnes qui confidunt in eis*" ("mouths they have and do not speak... hands they have and do not touch, feet they have and do not walk, nor will they shout from their throat; let their makers become like them, along with those who confide in them"). Erroneously applied to the Islam in the Middle Ages (i.e. in *Roland's Song*) (Diemer).

264. Blessed are the swords because they keep the Muslims from perishable idolatry.

265. Cf. *Luke* 14:23, "*exi in vias et saepes et compelle intrare ut impleatur domus mea*" ("go out to the highways and hedges and compel them to enter that my home may be filled"). After the chosen people of Israel declined the invitation to the feast, the beggar folk, or heathens, were called. The author knows that the Christian Church was largely made up of converts and that is why he can capture both Christians and Muslims in "we are compelled." Only a few have taken up the invitation before, and the Muslims should take this opportunity to "taste and see how sweet that the Lord is sweet," from *Psalm* 33:9 (Vulgate). The Crusade is being likened to a feast whereto Muslims and Christians have been invited by the Lord.

266. The Syrophenician was a Gentile woman who was born in the Phoenician part of Syria. She besought the Lord to exorcise her daughter, who was afflicted by a demon, and her faith was tested by his silence, his refusal, and his affirmation that "the bread of the children should not be cast unto dogs." She passed the tests and the Lord healed her daughter (viz. *Matthew* 15:21-28). Here the daughter is

the Muslim population of Palestine that have responded to the invitation of the heavenly Lord of the home.

267. The Crusaders are likened to overseas tradesmen, as they are in the crusade encyclical of Bernard of Clairvoux (*Opera*, vol. VIII, 1977, pp. 311-317) which was indited in the spring of 1146 (Kahl, ibid., p. 305 et seq. and p. 294) (Diemer).

268. Cf. *Isaiah* 11:10, "*et erit sepulchrum eius gloriosum*" ("and his sepulcher will be glorious").

269. Cf. *Matthew* 7:6, "*nolite dare sanctum canibus neque mittatis margaritas vestras ante porcos*" ("give not what is sacred to dogs, and cast not your pearls before swine").

270. Cf. *John* 14:2, "*in domo Patris mei mansiones multae sunt*" ("in the home of my Father there are many dwelling places").

271. Following the parable of the workers in the vineyard (viz. *Matthew* 20:1-16)

272. Viz. *James* 2:1-6.

273. Cf. *Hebrews* 6:6, "*rursum crucifigentes sibimeitipsis Filium Dei et ostentui habentes*" ("they are crucifying in themselves again the Son of God and are yet maintaining pretenses"). Jerusalem's fall is seen as the 2nd crucifixion of Christ.

274. The Latin literally reads "let it crucify them all."

275. Christ's cross is the healing tree. According to Helena, Constantine's mother, the cross on which Christ was crucified was found and stored in Jerusalem, the present theater of war. In the decisive battle against Saladin, the Christian leaders of the Crusader States took hold of the cross; but the hoped-for benefits it brought them not. In the crushing defeat of the Christians at Hattin on the Sea of Galilee (July 4, 1187), in which almost 18,000 Christian warriors were captured or killed, the cross was lost and it has since never been found (Korth, p. 188).

276. Cf. *Lamentations* 1:1, "*quomodo sedet sola civitas plena populo*" ("O how a city once peopled now sits alone").

277. Viz. *Matthew* 25:32 et seq. The sheep are the good and the rams are the bad.

278. Zion, the Church, is Christ's bride; the gifts are the cross and tomb of Christ.

279. Ananias was a member of the early Christian Church in Jerusalem mentioned in *Acts of the Apostles* 5:1-5; in keeping with the covenant that Jesus' followers possess no property, he sold his land, but kept a portion of the sales; he claimed to Peter that it was the entire amount, whereupon accused him of lying to the Holy

Spirit and Ananias fell dead; here it is probably the direct translation "Yahweh is gracious," or "the grace of God."

280. According to *Luke* 1:69, the horn of David was a symbol of strength that was erected by God upon the birth of Christ; through Jerusalem's fall it is bent.

281. The staff of the cross. Viz. *Psalm* 22:4 (*Vulgate*), "*virga tua et baculus tuus ipsa me consolata sunt*" ("your rod and your staff, they have consoled me").

282. The Latin literally reads "the universal side," or Christianity, "yields to the faction of the gentiles," or heathendom.

283. Viz. *1 Peter* 2:9.

284. Cf. *Exodus* 1:14.

285. In *Exodus* 17:11-13, the Israelites fought the Amalec in Raphidim, who would be overcome so long as Moses atop a hill, with the rod of God in his hand, raised his hands to the sky. In this allegory, the Arab invaders are the Amalec and the destruction of Jerusalem was facilitated by Moses' infirmity.

286. Mankind is a vassal to God (Christ), his Lord, and it is his duty to assist his feudal Lord in His tribulation. The vassal is also a child of God (Christ); from this arises the need to take up arms for the legitimate rights of the father.

287. Eternal bliss is the goal.

288. The mark is the cross with which one is signed at his baptism and the cross Crusaders wear on their tunics.

289. Cf. *Isaiah* 5:29, "*rugitus [gentis] et leonis*" ("the heathen's roaring is like the lion's").

290. Cedar was the son of Ishmael (*Genesis* 25:13). The name means "darkness." The Bedouin tribe Cedar inhabited the Arabian Desert and was Israel's enemy (*Isaiah* 21:16). Here the reference plays on *Psalm* 119:5 (*Vulgate*), "*heu mihi...habitavi cum habitantibus Cedar*" ("Woe is me...I have dwelt with the inhabitants of Cedar").

291. The crusader should desist from worldly cast of mind that is adverse to God.

292. The eternal life.

293. Direct quote from Ovid, *Amores* 3.4.17.

294. Cf. *Luke* 10:37, "*vade et tu fac similiter*" ("go, and act similarly").

295. Cf. *Luke* 5:4, *"duc in altum et laxate retia vestra in capturam"* ("lead us into deep water, and release your nets for a catch").

296. Viz. *John* 4:35-38.

297. Cf. Ovid, *Ars Amatoria* 1.1.1, *"siquis in hoc artem populo non novit amandi"* ("if anyone in this nation knows not the art of loving") (Burger).

298. A play on *"vivit Deo"* ("he lives for God), viz. *Romans* 6:10.

299. Cf. *Luke* 10:42, *"Maria optimam partem elegit"* ("Maria has chosen the best portion").

300. A celebrated hetaera during the time of Alexander the Great (356-323 BC).

301. *Psalm* 73:7 (*Vulgate*), *"incenderunt igni Sanctuarium tuum in teera polluerunt tabernaculum nominis tui"* ("they have to Your Sanctuary set fire; they have defiled the tabernacle of Your name on earth").

302. In this case the Seljuks.

303. *Psalm* 67:2 (*Vulgate*).

304. The prophet Elijah had asked the widow of Zarephath for something to eat; she wanted to cook something for him on two logs, which she had picked up as a precious find. The food she cooked for the prophet brought her the blessing of heaven (viz. *1 Kings* 17:7 et seq.). The two logs are the cross of Christ.

305. A woman at whose house Elisha stopped (viz. *2 Kings* 4:8). When her son died, she called on him for aid.

306. Elisha's servant who was sent out in his place.

307. The widow is the Church, the dead son is the throng of sinful believers, Gehazi is the flock of Simon Magus-like priests, and Elisha is Christ. Only when he comes in compassion (through the forgiveness of their sins) can the cross be recovered by the resurrected son (the sinless faithful).

308. Not even Saladin can withstand Christ's might.

309. Cf. *Ephesians* 5:14, *"surge qui dormis et exsurge a mortuis et illuminabit te Christus"* ("rise, thou who art asleep; awaken from the dead and Christ shall illuminate thee").

310. Cf. *Ecclesiastes* 12:1, *"memento Creatoris tui in diebus iuventutis tuae"* ("remember thy Creator in the days of thy youth").

311. Cf. *Matthew* 3:10, "*iam enim securis ad radicem arborum posita est*" ("for even now the axe hath been placed at the trees' root").

312. Cf. *Galatians* 5:24, "*qui autem sunt Christi carnem suam crucifixerunt cum vitiis et concupiscentiis*" ("for those who are Christ's have crucified their flesh, together with vices and desires").

313. Viz. *Genesis* 28:12-18. In a dream Jacob saw a ladder that reached from earth to heaven with angels going up and down it. In this case the "other" ladder is the cross of Christ.

314. Cf. *Ezekiel* 28:11, "*fili hominis leva planctum super regem Tyri*" ("son of man, take up a lamentation for the king of Tyre").

315. Cf. *Psalms* 129:1 (*Vulgate*), "*de profundis clamavi ad te Domine*" ("from the depths I have cried out to You, O Lord").

316. Cf. *Matthew* 24:29, "*statim autem post tribulationem dierum illorum sol obscurabitur et luna non dabit lumen suum et stellae cadent de caelo et virtutes caelorum commovebuntur*" ("and forthwith after the tribulation of those days, the sun will be darkened, the moon will not give its light, and the stars will fall from heaven and the powers of the heavens will be shaken").

317. Cf. *Revelations* 1:5, "*lavit nos a peccatis nostris in sanguine suo*" ("he has washed us of our sins with his blood").

318. Lazarus was dead for four days and was resurrected by Jesus (viz. *John* 11:39). Like Lazarus the sinner smells foul, but through Jesus can be revived.

319. Cf. *1 Corinthians* 3:16, "*nescitis quia templum Dei estis et Spiritus Dei habitat in vobis*" ("do you not know that you are the temple of God and the spirit of God liveth in you?").

320. The sultan of Egypt and Syria, who defeated the French at Hattin in 1187.

321. Cf. *Psalms* 112:7 (*Vulgate*), "*de stercore erigens pauperem*" ("he raises the poor from the filth").

322. Count Raymond III of Tripoli was enemies with King Guido of Jerusalem and called on Saladin as aid against him. (Bernt).

323. At the end of April 1187, 7,000 men from Saladin's army advanced over the upper Jordan (Schumann).

324. Hagar was the second wife of Abraham, who begot Ishmael (viz. *Genesis* 16), the patriarch of the Ishmaelites.

325. An unidentified tribe that is possibly the "Turcmeni," to wit, the Turkmen.

326. Cf. *2 Kings* 8:12, "*et parvulos eorum elides et praegnantes divides*" ("and you will destroy their little ones and eviscerate pregnant women").

327. King Guido of Jerusalem.

328. The Templar Knights were an order of knights, founded in about 1118, with monastic vows and a commitment to war against heathendom.

329. Cf. *Psalms* 111:10 (*Vulgate*), "*dentibus suis fremet et tabescet*" ("he will gnash his teeth and waste away").

330. Acre was surrendered without a fight on July 10, 1187.

331. Marquis Conrad of Montferrat, the de fact King of Jerusalem by marriage from 1190. He successfully defended Tyre from August 8-16, 1187 and from November 25, 1887 to January 1188.

332. Paladins were the foremost warriors of Charlemagne's court.

333. Cf. *Luke* 2:7, "*et pannis eum involvit et reclinavit eum in praesepio*" ("and she wrapped him in swaddling clothes and laid him in a crib").

334. Viz. *John* 1:29-34.

335. Cf. *John* 19:34, "*sed unus militum lancea latus eius aperuit et continuo exivit sanguis et aqua*" ("instead one of the soldiers opened his flank with a spear and forthwith blood and water went out").

336. Cf. *Matthew* 15:26, "*non est bonum sumere panem filiorum et mittere canibus*" ("it is not good to take the children's bread and cast it to the dogs").

337. Cf. *Luke* 1:52, "*deposuit potentes de sede et exaltavit humiles*" ("He hath deposed the powerful from their seat, and exalted the humble").

338. Viz. *1 Samuel* 4-6. The Ark of the Covenant was stolen by the Philistines. God then crushed the Philistines with the bubonic plague, and they returned it.

339. Viz. *Genesis* 3:23 et seq.

340. Gihon was one of the rivers of Eden and the place of Solomon's coronation (viz. *1 Kings* 1:33).

341. In *Genesis* 2:7, mankind was crafted from *limus terrae*, or the loam of earth, which is worth little in the household of the great lords compared with dishes of

gold and silver. The lords above are not identified with God or gods, but an earthenware stein.

342. This refers to the devil's sway under which mankind has been since the Fall.

343. Manuel I Komnenos, who with Amalrich I, the King of Jerusalem, entered into an alliance to conquer Jerusalem.

344. This passage in the Greek is an interpolation of the Roman Good Friday liturgy: *Agios o Theos, agios ischyros, agios athanatos, eleison imas* ("Holy God, Holy Strength, Holy Immortal, have pity on ours!)

345. Amalric I (1136-1174), whose name comes from the Old German words "amal" (work) and "ric" (power), was the son of King Fulk of Jerusalem.

346. Solignac is a commune in France.

347. A not very widely known monk, probably from Solignac (Bernt). In *Matthew* 19:12, castration is seen as a route to heaven, "*et sunt eunuchi qui seipsos castraverunt propter regnum caelorum*" ("and there are chaste men who have emasculated themselves for the kingdom of heaven").

348. Aeacus was one of the three judges of Hades in Greek mythology.

349. Christ.

350. Dagon was the sea god of the Philistines. His effigy fell and shattered, when the Philistines installed in his shrine the Ark of the Covenant they had purloined from the Israelites (viz. *1 Samuel* 4 et seq.).

351. The Amalek were a tribe on the Sinai Peninsula that sought to hinder the Israelites' migration. The Israelites were victorious, so long as Moses raised his hands (viz. *Exodus* 17:8 et seq.). Thus medieval interpreters saw a type of cross.

352. Ishmael (viz. *Genesis* 21:9 et seq.).

353. Christ.

354. Cf. *Acts of the Apostles* 2:2, "*et factus est repente de caelo sonus tamquam advenientis spiritus vehementis et replevit totam domum ubi erant sedentes*" ("and suddenly there came from heaven a sound like that of an approaching violent wind, and it fill us the entire home where they were sitting").

355. The fire is the Holy Ghost (Schumann).

356. Arunah, whose threshing floor became the site for the Temple of Solomon

(viz. *2 Samuel* 24 and *1 Chronicles* 21).

357. Christ.

358. The double election of Pope Alexander III and antipope Victor IV.

359. The ship of Peter: the Church.

360. In reality 18 years from 1159 to 1177.

361. Viz. *Matthew* 24:12.

362. Wichmann von Seeburg (1115-1192), Archbishop of Magdeburg, who was a staunch supporter of Frederick Barbarossa against Pope Alexander III and a valiant military leader.

363. This plays on the parable of two swords: in the pre-Gregorian version, Christ gives the secular sword unto the emperor and the spiritual sword unto the pope; in the Gregorian version, Christ gives both swords to the pope, who then gives the secular sword unto the king, who serves as the pope's representative (Diemer).

364. The two swords work jointly to crush the tribulations that threaten the Church and State.

365. The pope.

366. This praise is applied to Wichmann his negotiating skills, and his conciliatory character.

367. Cf. *Psalm* 101:14 (*Vulgate*), "*tu exurgens misereberis Sion quia tempus miserendi eius quia venit tempus*" ("you will rise up and take pity on Zion, for it is a time for its mercy, for the time has come").

368. The year of jubilee is a special year of remission of sins and universal pardon (viz. *Leviticus* 25:10).

369. This is actually Alexander IV (1254-1261); in the Buranus tradition, the ordinal number was shown probably with Roman numerals and thus IV was probably mistaken for III (Schumann).

370. Cf. *Revelation* 12:3, "*et visum est aliud signum in caelo et ecce draco magnus rufus habens capita septem et cornua decem et in capitibus eius diademata septem et cauda eius trahebat tertiam partem stellarum caeli et misit eas in terram*" ("and another sign in the heavens was seen; and behold, a great red dragon, with seven heads and ten horns, and on his heads were seven diadems; and his tail drew out a third part of heaven's stars and cast them to the earth"). It is unclear what the

meaning of Gordan, Ingordin, and Ingordan is. They are part of a magical formula. Gordan may be Jordan. Ingordan may fall on a German rendering of "in the Jordan." Ingordin may simply complete the tripartite formula of incantations (Diemer).

371. The Seal of Solomon was a five-pointed star of lines that served as a magical symbol. It has also been presented as a hexagram similar to the Star of David.

372. Viz. *Matthew* 2:1-12. The three wise men who attended Jesus' birth.

373. Cf. *1 Samuel* 16:23, "*igitur quandocumque spiritus Domini malus arripiebat Saul David tollebat citharam et percutiebat manu sua et refocillabatur Saul et levius habebat recedebat enim ab eo spiritus malus*" ("and so whenever the wicked spirit of the Lord assailed Saul, David lifted up his lyre, and struck it with his hand, and Saul was refreshed and uplifted. For the baleful spirit withdrew from him"). Saul was the first King of Israel.

374. Y-HW-H, or YAHWEH, the ineffable name of God.

375. The well-known demons of the ancient gods, here of the lower gods.

376. This is reminiscent of the *vas electionis* (the vessel of election) from the *Acts of the Apostles* 9:15, which is meant to be the Apostle Paul, and *vas suum* (his vessel) in 1 *Thessalonians* 4:4, which is meant to be his wife. In this case the vessel of Christianity is the Christian man.

377. Amara tanta tyri is the essential part of a devil's maxim which has been recorded in many versions. The words were probably meaningless from the outset, as they are demonspeak, such as Dante's Pape satan, aleppe (*Divina Commedia [Inferno]* 7.1). Three longer versions of the spell were published in the middle ages. Amaratunta (-tonta), as an adverb of time composed from Syrian or Arabic—"finally" or "in the end." Amaratunta = upon the arrival or return of our Lord. There is an anecdote about amaratunta. A young scholar who succeeded not in composing verse was harrowed by the studies for his master's degree, so he committed to the Devil, who helped him compose and gave him the longer line (Bernt).

Part II of the *Carmina Burana* (Poems 56-186):

1. This verse makes use of the time used in the Middle Ages. The new year, Janus, begins in the spring, when Phoebus, the sun, leaves the constellation Aries on April 21 and moves into Taurus, the Bull.

2. Cf. Vergil, *Eclogae* 10.69, "*omnia vincit Amor et nos cedamus Amori*" ("love conquers all; let us, too, submit to love").

3. Dione was the mother of Venus; the name is often Venus herself as well.

4. Pallas is another name for Athena, the Greek goddess of wisdom.

5. Cupid.

6. A nymph who eschewed Apollo's suit and was turned into a laurel tree (viz. Ovid, *Metamorphoses* 1.452).

7. Hymenaeus was the god of weddings.

8. Thetis, a goddess of the ocean and mother of Achilles, wishes for the end of love's hostile storm.

9. Ceres is the mother of Proserpine, who was raped by Pluto and taken to the underworld.

10. The elements above, air and fire, betoken masculinity, and the elements below, water and earth, represent femininity. Their union in this poem is a metaphor for copulation.

11. From February 21st until March 20th the sun is in the constellation Pisces.
12 In Fulgentius' *Mitologiarum* I.3, Juno is the personification of the wind, and in the *Aeneid* she raises a storm. But she allows herself to be calmed by Jupiter, the sun, and thus wins back her beauty.

13. An allusion to an unknown tale (a *frizon* is a form of the courtly love poetry by Guiraut de Cabreira, viz. H. Patzig, *Romanische Forschungen* 4, 1891, p. 549 et seq.). Raby in *Secular Poetry* 2.270, footnote 1 reads: Phrison accompanies the king's daughter to an unwelcome bridegroom. The song is a spell, which should overpower her resistance. The dwarf falsely accuses him, Phrison must suffer an injustice, but he brings the bride to the groom. Probably also Phrison sings it to court her, the daughter feigns sickness to break off the journey to her betrothed, the dwarf mentions this, is chastised as a slanderer and yet can finally get through with the news.

14. Tereus, a Thracian king, was the husband of Procne, who together had Itys. But he desired Philomela, Procne's sister. He forced himself upon her and excised her tongue and told his wife that her sister had died. But Philomela wove in a tapestry Tereus' crime and sent it to Procne. In revenge Procne killed her son Itys and served him to the father. When Tereus discovered this, he tried to kill the sisters, but the gods transformed all three into birds: Tereus became a hoopoe, Procne a nightingale, and Philomela a swallow.

15. These figures of mythology should be allegorically viewed as the sum of cosmic forces: Hera and Zeus are heaven (sun, light, warmth) and earth, Venus

and Cupid love and reproduction, Argus the stars, Narcissus the flora, and Faunus/Pan the fauna. They are held together by musical harmony forged by the divine singer Orpheus and the birds. Viz. *De Planctu Naturae* 4.30-32 (Häring p. 822).

16. I've read *nubilo*, which literally means "I become clouded," as "I am turbid," in that the speaker, when he sits beneath the lime tree, is muddled with lascivious thoughts. I have also read *semoto* as *in semoto* ("in a secluded place, or retreat). The putative ablative absolute *nubilo semoto* ("when the clouds have been parted") makes little sense in context as the main clause then has no finite verb.

17. The Latin literally reads, "the linden's foliage being a pause in the longing for Cypris," but I have rendered it in the first person. Cypris is another name for Venus, or venery.

18. Dido was the mythical queen of Carthage in Vergil's *Aeneid*, who committed suicide out of love for Aeneas.

19. See CB 92.

20. Literally "worn out by their deeds."

21. This corrupt line is somewhat unclear. I have read the line "*spes adulta caris*" as "*[eorum] spes adulta sit [et] caris*" ("let their hope [for a lover] and grace [that attracts a lover] be consumed"). I believe that the writer employed asyndeton and omitted *sit* from a jussive/optative clause and that *caris* is a variant spelling of *charis*, grace.

22. The ranunculus species, which includes the buttercup.

23. A female character in Terence's *Andria*.

24. Atropos was one of the three Moirae, or goddesses of fate.

25. Cf. Horace, *Epistulae* 1.18.103, "*fallentis semita vitae*" ("the path of a life of lies").

26. Bacchantes were female followers of Bacchus.

27. In the *Vulgate* Lamia is the name of the female night demon Lilith (viz. *Isaiah* 34:14; the lamia also appears in ancient mythology (i.e. Horace's *Ars poetica* 340) as a witch who sucks children's blood.

28. Most likely Pan; cf. Vergil, *Aeneid* 7.81 "*At rex...oracula Fauni, fatidici genitoris*" ("but the king [sought] the oracles of Faunus, his mantic sire").

29. Anacreontic verse, a seven syllable meter created by the Greek poet Anacreon.

30. In *2 Samuel* 14:25, Absalom is described as the most handsome man in Israel.

31. The Latin literally reads "not of such character that you are of mortal nature."

32. Priam's son here must be Paris.

33. The smile of Jove is good weather, a clear, sunny day.

34. Diana is the goddess of the moon and the glassy lamp is the moon.

35. The sun. Apollo, the sun god, is Diana's twin. Also cf. Lucretius, *De Rerum Natura* 5.610, "*rosea sol alte lampade lucens*" ("the sun with a rosy light beams high atop the firmament").

36. Morpheus is the son of Sleep and the god of dreams.

37. Viz. William of St Thierry, *De natura corporis et animae* I (Migne, PL, 180.698 CD), "*De digestione etiam ista fumus ascendens lenis et suavis, molliter tangit cerebrum, et ventriculos ejus opprimit, in tantum ut omnes ejus actiones sopiat: hic est somnus. □...□Anima vero interius requiescens, exclusis omnibus sensuum officiis, revolvit penes se praeterita, praesentia et futura: et haec sunt somnia*" ("from the digestion this gentle, sweet steam ascends, gently touches the brain, and presses upon its hollows, to completely put to sleep all its actions. This is sleep ... but the soul resting deep within, when all the senses' functions have ceased, is busy with the past, present, and future. These are dreams"). The three chambers of the head are the subdivisions of the brain in medieval physiology. They are called cells or hollows, but often likened with the divisions of a ship: the bow, the stern, and the body of the ship. In the foremost part is the imagination, in the middle part the understanding, and in the hindmost the memory (Diemer).

38. The bodily/animal powers are the autonomic functions such as ingestion, digestion, and procreation.

39. Cf. Ovid, *Amores* 3.5.8, "*fronde sub arboris.*"

40. When Hercules conquered Oechalia, he took Iole as a prize. Deianira, his wife, feared she would lose his love and applied to a chiton the blood of Nessus, who claimed it would end any infidelity. The blood poisoned Hercules, and he died.

41. Lerna's Hydra was one of the beasts Hercules defeated during his 12 Labors.

42. Cacus, Nessus, Garyon, and the Stygian gate-hound (Cerberus) are more references to Hercules' Twelve Labors.

43. Additional references to his Twelve Labors.

44. Earth's son, whose strength grew every time he was thrust to the ground.

45. *Casus sophisticus* is a play on the ambiguity inherent in the Latin, as it can mean both a "sophistic fall," that is, the cunning falls Antaeus suffered, which were not indicative of true defeat, and a "sophistic matter," a problem that is seemingly resolved with a fallacy. In this case it is the former.

46. Lycoris was a poetical name for Volumnia, aka Cytheris, a notorius actress and mistress of Cornelius Gallus, a Roman poet and statesman (viz. "Cornelius Gallus" in *Encyclopedia Britanica*).

47. These labors are actually out of order. The traditional order found in Apollodorus, *Bibliotheke* 2.5.1-2.5.12 is: (1) slay the Nemean Lion; (2) slay the nine-headed Lernean Hydra; (3) capture the Golden Hind of Artemis; (4) capture the Erymanthean Boar; (5) clean the Augean stables in a single day; (6) slay the Stymphalian Birds; (7) capture the Cretan Bull; (8) steal the Mares of Diomedes; (9) obtain the girdle of Hippolyta, Queen of the Amazons; (10) obtain the cattle of the onster Geryon; (11) steal the apples of the Hesperides; and (12) capture and bring back Cerberus.

48. Though the Latin reads "the lion of Cleonae," the mythological record recognizes him as the Nemean lion. It was at Cleonae, however, that Hercules was challenged to defeat it.

49. Eucrasis is a Latinization of the Greek ευκρασια, which literally means a "perfect mixing of the humors."

50. Philogeus, which translates as "loving the Earth" in Greek, is one of the four steeds of the chariot of the sun, mentioned in Fulgentius' *Mitologiarum* I.12. Since the four horses' names are based on the sun's positions throughout each season, Philogeus is the evening or winter sun.

51. Erythreus is yet another of the four steeds and means "the red," or the morning/spring sun.

52. Acteon is the midmorning or summer sun and yet another steed.

53. Lampas means "glowing" as the midday or autumnal sun.

54. Venus and with her his maiden.

55. Basythea, which translates from Greek as "the winsome girl," is the *virgo* in the glimpse. After but one, the author wishes she were his love.

56. Euryale was one of the immortal Gorgons.

57. Euphrosyne was one of the Charites, or Three Graces

58. Allotheta is a Latinized form of the Greek αλλος (another) + θετης (one who places [text]).

59. Macrobius writes in his *Saturnalia* 3.8.2, "*Signum etiam eius est Cypri barbatum corpore, sed veste muliebri, cum sceptro ac natura virili: et putant eandem marem ac feminam esse. Aristophanes eam Ἀφρόδιτον appellat. Laevinusetiam sic ait: Venerem igitur almumadorans, sive femina sive mas est, ita uti alma Noctiluca est. Philochorus quoque in Atthide eandem adfirmat esse lunam, et ei sacrificium facere viros cum veste muliebri, mulieres cum virili, quod eadem et mas aestimatur et femina*" ("there is also a statue of Venus in Cyprus that is bearded, but shaped and dressed like a woman, with a scepter and male genitals: they think that she is both male and female. Aristophanes calls her "Aphroditus." Laevius also says this: "adoring then the nourishing god Venus, whether she be female or male, just as the Moon is a nurturing goddess. Philochorus also states that in Athens she is the same as the moon and that men sacrifice to her in women's dress, women in men's dress, because she is considered both male and female"). The duplicity of her sexuality captures the duplicity of the lass: a *virgo* in society, a *femina* for the singer.

60. Nature here means both "nature" and "sex organ."

61. In this case, Venus is the maiden and Adonis is the singer.

62. Cithaeron is a mountain range in central Greece.

63. It was the custom of freedman to hang as thanks to a deity his shackles on a shrine.

64. Minerva in this context represents his poetic art.

65. The former refers to mythological scholarship, the latter barefaced eroticism.

66. The prose refers to the free rhythm of the classical sequence (stanzas 1-3 and all of 7). Verse references the metrically quantized verse (6-7). *Satira* refers to the mixture of both prose and verse following the model of the Menippean satire that attacked mental attitudes in prose and verse. The *rhythmachia* is a reference to the accented, rhythmic verse (4-5, 8-11) (Diemer).

67. According to *Leviticus* 25:10-13, the year of jubilee was celebrated every fifty years.

68. Coronis is the name of the maiden and is derived from Greek mythology.

Coronis was one of Apollo's lovers, who fell in love with Ischys. Apollo sent Artemis to slay her and Hermes cut Asclepius from her dead womb and gave him to the centaur Chiron.

69. Cf. Ovid, *Heroides* 20.45 er seq., "*retia...quae...tetendit Amor*" ("nets that Cupid has laid").

70. In *Mythographi* 3.1.4 we read "*huius stella fridissima existimatur ... quum in signis remotissimis ... aquario videlicet et capricorno, domicilia sua habeat*" ("[Saturn's] star is considered the coldest, for it keeps its home in the remotest constellations, to wit, Aquarius and Capricorn.") (Bernt).

71. Apollo is likened to the sun and Jove is the cloudless sky.

72. This references Erythreus, the solar chariots' fiery red steed of spring.

73. The ruler of the winds (viz. Vergil, *Aeneis* 1.71-75; Homer, *Odyssey* 10.2).

74. April 21 to May 21.

75. Thisbe is yet another maidenly name derived from mythology (viz. Ovid, *Metamorphoses* 4.55-166).

76. Cf. Terence, *Phormio* 203, "*fortes fortuna adiuvat*" ("Fortune succors the brave").

77. Cf. Vergil, *Aeneis* 4.2, "*caeco carpitur igni*" ("an invisible fire rankles her").

78. Vulcan. The Latin literally reads "sophistic chains/bars" which I read as "delicate steel nets," as their slenderness is deceptive in its imperceptibility.

79. Greek for "the gleaming" and a name for the planet Mercury or the god.

80. This line does not appear in the Latin, but must be added to disambiguate the English translation of the last two lines that are otherwise clear in the Latin. *Dulcissime* is the masculine vocative singular ("sweetest man") and *totam...me* means "my whole [female] self" and serves as the maiden's response that the poet hoped to elicit through his song.

81. Cybele was the Phrygian deification of the Earth Mother and here is the Earth.

82. Dionysus was Semele's son.

83. The five steps of love are sight, conversation, touch, kiss, and union. Myrrha in Ovid's *Metamorphoses* relates them thus "*retinet malus ardor amantem, / ut praesens spectem Cinyram tangamque loquarque / osculaque admoveam, si nil*

conceditur ultra" (unhappy passion keeps a lover here, that I may see Cinyras in person, touch him, speak to him, and kiss him, if nothing further be granted" 10.342-344). These steps are also mentioned in Terence's *Eunuchus*: *si non tangendi copiast, / eho ne videndi quidem erit? si illud non licet, / saltem hoc licebit. certe extrema linea / amare haud nil est*" ("if there be no opportunity for touch, alas, will not even a chance for sight remain? If the former be not permitted, at least will the latter be. Forsooth the final step is to make love" 638-641).
The strict establishment and order seem to arise first in the late antique classical commentaries of Porphyrio and Donat.

84. The white raven sent to spy on Coronis, whom Apollo loved, failed to prevent her affair with Ischys and was scorched by a curse that turned it black. Apollo sent Diana to kill her and regained his presence of mind when he saw her on the funeral pyre. *Singultus* can mean "the death rattle of a person" or the "croaking of a crow" and captures both Coronis' assassination and the crow's third degree pain.
85. Mount Cynthus sits on the island of Delos, Apollo's birthplace; therefore one of his epithets is the Cynthian.

86. Rhea is another name for Cybele, or Earth.

87. *Philomena* can mean both swallow and nightingale. Since *luscinia* translates only as nightingale, I translated *philomena* as swallow.

88. The Dryads were the nymphs of oak trees and were often represented as tree nymphs in general.

89. This contrast of Venus and Dione marks the distinction between love's grief and love's bliss, respectively. Remigius Autissiodorensis, a 9th century Benedictine monk and commentator on various Greek and Latin texts, wrote in his *Commentum in Martianum Capellam*: "*Dione dicitur quasi dianoia, id est sensus delectatio, ideoque mater Veneris fingitur quia omnis libido ex delectatione carnalium sensuum nascitur*" ("Dione means 'dianoia,' that is, the delight of the senses, and so is considered the mother of Venus, because all sexual pleasure is born of the delight of the bodily senses" 479.22).

90. The Oreads were mountain nymphs.

91. Vale of Tempe is a gorge in Thessaly, Greece that is situated between Olympus to the north and Ossa to the south. The ancient poets hailed it as the favorite haunt of Apollo and the Muses.

92. The Latin literally reads "who has mastery over his wish."

93. In the Latin this is a relative clause, but the English favors its conflation with the main clause. *Fit* here is taken as the middle voice.

94. Literally, "there shines the moving frolicsomeness of their limbs."

95. *Sedens invitatus* literally means "while sitting, I was invited," but logic tells us that *sedens* is meant to mean *ut sederem* "to sit."

96. *Vos/vester* can be addressed to a single person who represents more than one (viz. *tu* L&S IIB). The line, which is most likely in the genitive singular, literally reads "of your retinue" with an implied *gratia* (for the sake of) and is therefore translated as the final clause "to be among your retinue."

97. Venus was the goddess Paris chose in the contest of Venus, Juno, & Minerva.

98. *Genus* is a variant of *genu*, knee. Literally, "I shall forever venerate your knee," I have rendered it "I will forever bow before you and kiss your feet."

99. *In loco munito* literally means "in a secured place."

100. Cf. *1 Corinthians* 13:1, "*si linguis hominum loquar et Angelorum*" ("if I should speak in the language of men of Angels").

101. Cf. Ovid *Heroides* 5.115, "*quid harenae semina mandas?*" ("Why do you commit seeds to the sand?").

102. Cf. Luke 1:47, "*exultavit spiritus meus*" ("my spirit rejoiced").

103. Cf. Luke 1:39, "*exsurgens autem Maria...cum festinatione*" ("But Mary rose up and hurried away").

104. This entire scene is taken from the Annunciation, in the pictorial representations of which the angel is always on bended knee.

105. Cf. Luke 1:28, "*Have, gratia plena*" ("hail, maiden full of grace").

106. Blanscheflur was a heroine of a love story in many folktales, *Flore und Blanscheflur* (viz. E. Frenzel, *Stoffe der Weltliteratur*, 1970, p. 214 et seq.). The poet addresses her in a triad of praise: as a domestic heroine (Blanscheflur), a Grecian heroine (Helen of Troy), and a Roman goddess (Venus).

107. *Song of Solomon* 4:10 "*super omnia aromata*" ("above all aromatic spices").

108. In *Pamphilus, seu de Amore* 1 (Pamphilus, or, Concerning Love), a twelfth-century apocryphal poem, we find: *Vulneror et clausum porto sub pectore telum* ("I am wounded and carry a latent missile in my breast").

109. Cf. *Luke* 15:21, "*Pater, peccavi in caelum et coram te*" ("Father, I have sinned against heaven and in your sight").

110. *Psalm* 91:13 (*Vulgate*), "*iustus ut palma florebit, ut cedrus Libani multiplicabitur*" ("the just man will flourish like the palm: he will be propagated like the cedar of Lebanon").

111. *Secuntur* is a variant of *sequuntur* ("they follow"), not the present indicative passive of *seco*. Also similar line is found in Ovid's *Amores* 1.5.25, "*cetera quis nescit?*" ("Who knows not the rest?").

112. *Psalm* 148:13 (*Vulgate*), "*exaltatum est nomen eius solius*" ("his name alone is exalted").

113. *Amaretur* is from *amareo/amaro*, a coinage that means "to make bitter."

114. Cf. Sallust, *Bellum Catilinae* 20.4, "*idem velle atque idem nolle, ea demum firma amicitia est*" ("wanting the same and not wanting the same, that forsooth is solid friendship").

115. *Estu...sudore* translates as "by passion and sweat"—that is the heat inside the poet and the atmosphere.

116. The Naiads were river nymphs.

117. Here, the goddess of flowers.

118. Literally, "a more pleasant heat."

119. I translated *adest* as "at bay" because the coming of the flowers is inexorable and has no way to flee.

120. These seven vowels correspond to the base rhythm of the stanza. Diemer believes this may have read *Oro, cor iam aspice, | amor, insolabile!* ("prithee, look back now upon my disconsalte heart, my love!").

121. These are the *colores rhetorici* (the jewel of speech), a technical term for rhetoric and poetics in the Middle Ages (viz. *Lexikon des Mittelalters*).

122. Probably a derivative of the female names Phyllis ("green leaf" in the Greek) and Flora ("flower child" in the Latin). This is likely an argument over the virtues of the cleric and knight, respectively, put into the mouths of two maidens. The dialogue renounces narrative sections, so the speaker must always be inferred from the content of the assertion (Phyllis is in favor the cleric, Flora the knight).

123. This does not appear in the Latin, but is added for sense. The literal translation is "Anon the peroration of Love on every cleric is made." The peroration can be taken as a final judgment on the two arguments presented.

124. I have taken *blando...lenimine* as an ablative of specification or cause that modifies *vota*: (desires for/caused by the alluring, soothing remedy," which is likely her vaginal tract.

125. The Latin reads literally "in a maiden of tender down" (ablative of quality). The tender down to which he is referring are the soft vellus hairs (or "peach fuzz") that appear around the pubic area, among other places, before the thicker androgenic hairs sprout after puberty. His maiden is so developed that she already has androgenic hairs (*pubes*) that inspire in him cravings for the elixir atop which they sit: her vaginal tract.

126. *Radians candore* modifies *crus* and *levigatur* is its verb; the sentence literally reads "her leg, radiating with fairness/whiteness and bedecked with a tempered fatness, is illuminated by the junction of her nerves (her vagina or possibly clitoris)." Though *levigatur* suggests no heat, I translated it as "brightened to incandescence" (rather than luminescence) to capture her legs' intense light and the scene hot passion.

127. All throughout the mythological course, Jupiter, whenever he was enamored of a girl, takes pains to hide his concubine from Hera, usually through his mistress' bodily transformation (viz. Ovid *Metamorphoses*).

128. Clm 4660/4660a reads "*aurum*," which makes no sense in context with the genitive *Danes*. The best translation of this would be "he, raining down, would bewitch Danaë's gold with sweet dew." *Antrum* is a better fit because Danaë was shut up in a cave when Jove came down upon her as golden rain; cave is also suggestive of the female sex organ (viz. Ovid, *Metamorphoses* 6.113 et seq.).

129. Jupiter abducted Europa in the guise of a bull and seduced Sparta's queen Leda in the form of a swan.

130. Literally, "with a well ordered brow." *Frons* can also mean the mirror of the feelings (L&S I, A, 2) and is translated as "mien."

131. This is a lost line that simply reads "*sed...........-ias*"; I have taken it as "*sed propter delicias*" ("but on account of these delights").

132. Her responding to him will mean the loss of her modesty.

133. Tantalus offered his son Pelops to the gods in sacrifice. His punishment was to stand in a pool of water beneath a fruit tree with low branches. When he reached for the fruit, the branches were raised; when he bent down for a drink, the water did recede.

134. Literally, "to enclose within boundaries the hinge of the gate/chief point."

135. The word rhyme does not appear in the Latin, but is added for sense. Though

my translation does not preserve the rhyme scheme, for reasons noted in the preface, the poet retold this duel in rhyme to claim his conquest over virgin frontiers and forever preserve his victory in indelible meter.

136. This is yet another lost line that reads "*sed..........-ito*" which I have taken as "*sed cum placito.*"

137. The highest god is probably Cupid.

138. *Caecilia* (for the blind) makes no sense in context. *Sessilia* better fits the tone (Diemer).

139. Bernt: "A sentence from a much used grammar textbook (Donat, *De partibus orationis ars minor*, De interiectione, last sentence; B. Bischoff viva voce)."

140. This is a corrupt line with a false syllable count and rhyme. Diemer believes that it served as the gloss for the original line: *Amor cecus, nudus, durus, lepidus* (Cupid is blind, naked, dismissive, and loveable").

141. Cf. Horace, *Ars Poetica* 169, "*multa senem circumveniunt incommoda*" ("many afflictions besiege the old man") (Schumann).

142. *Va t'an oy* is Old French for "begone!" Since the French is antiquated, I translated it into archaic English.

143. Cf. Horace, *Odes* I.33.13 et seq., "*me □...□ grata detinuit compede Myrtale*" ("with welcome shackles Myrtale has bound me fast").

144. The original line read *frigidus et calidus*, but the context compels us to change *et* to *nec*, otherwise, since Cupid is both hot and cold, the poet's ode to love becomes a diatribe. It is also interesting to note the following: *Mythographi* III.1.4, "*Senem eum depingunt, quia sicut senex est a calore iuventutis destitutus et frigiditate laborat* [*minuitur enim in iis sanguis, unde et tremunt*]" ("they depict Saturn as an old man, because like an old man he is devoid of the heat of youth and toils in the cold [for old men's blood has been diminished, wherefore they also tremble"); Tibull, *Carmina* I.8.29 et seq., "*munera ne poscas: det munera canus amator,* | *ut foveat molli frigida membra sinu*" ("demand no gifts: a lover with a grey head should give them, so that he may warm his cold limbs in a tender breast") (Willige).

145. In Medieval Latin *natura* can mean sex organ.

146. Cf. Tibull, *Carmina* I.8.50 et seq., "*in veteres esto dura, puella, senes,* | *parce, precor, tenero: non illi sontica causa est*" (Against old men be hard, O girl! But spare, I pray, a young lad: no serious suffering belongs to his lot") (Willige).

147. *Cardo* can mean "that on which everything else depends" (L&S II) and is therefore the girl's quintessence, her base nature, her core in which she houses the darkest of creatures.

148. Though *motus* usually means earthquake, in this context it is best translated as storm, or violent winds since by suppressing the storms—Neptune's domain—Cupid proves his rule over him.

149. *Virgino* is a variant of the deponent verb *virginor* and does not appear in classical Latin.

150. According a medieval notion, a unicorn could be captured with a maiden's help (viz. CB 93a)

151. Literally, "And yet I do not grow lukewarm."

152. Literally, "the sport/play/jest of the girl."

153. This is the horoscope of the singer's girl, born around the end of May.

154. Cf. Virgil, *Eclogae* 5.1, "*boni quoniam convenimus ambo*" (Bernt).

155. Cf. Horace, *Odes* I.16.24, "*celeres iambos*" ("swift iambs"); and Ovid, *Remedia* 377, "*liber in adversos hostes stringatur iambus /seu celer*" ("the free or swift iamb should attack an enemy").

156. In Vergil, *Eclogae* VII.9-11, when all the other shepherds have taken refuge from the heat, Meliboeus is approached by his flock's dominant he-goat, who says, "*huc ades, o Meliboee: caper tibi salvus et haedi; / et si quid cessare potes, requiesce sub umbra. / huc ipsi potum venient per prata iuvenci...*" ("come hither, Meliboeus, your goat and kids are safe, and if you can cease your labor, rest under the shade. Hither will your bullocks come through the meadows to drink").

157. The girl is a nun.

158. The hardship is her asceticism.

159. Cf. *John* 10:11-13, "*bonus pastor animam suam dat pro ovibus suis mercenarius autem...cuius non sunt oves propriae videt lupum venientem et dimittit oves et fugit et lupus rapit et dispergit oves mercenarius autem fugit...et non pertinet ad eum de ovibus*" ("the good shepherd gives his life for his sheep; but the hired hand...to whom the sheep do not belong, sees the wolf approaching, abandons the sheep, and flees; and the wolf snatches and scatters the sheep; and the hired hand flees...and has no concern for them").

160. These mute watchdogs appear in *Isaiah* 56:10 and represent the priests and bishops, who don't fight against evil.

161. This line is missing and *sic...cura / opus femine* has been added as a likely candidate for what would have been there, as it fits the meter and rhyme scheme and turns the previous two lines into an imperative.

162. *Parvula fides* means "very little confidence (in oneself) and thus is translated as "faintheartedness."

163. *Subdolus* means "sly, deceitful," which often involves doing something behind another's back.

164. Cf. *1 Peter* 1:16, "*sancti eritis quoniam ego sanctus sum*" ("you shall be holy, for I am holy").

165. Cf. *John* 15:1, "*ego sum vitis vera et pater meus agricola est*" ("I am the true vine, and my Father is the vinedresser").

166. Cf. *Song of Solomon* 4:4, "*omnis armatura fortium*" ("all the armor of the strong"); and *Ephesians* 6:14, "*propterea accipite armaturam Dei*" ("therefore receive ye the armor of God").

167. Cf. *Isaiah* 1:13-15, "*incensum abominatio est mihi...manus vestrae sanguine plenae sunt*" ("your incense is an abomination to me...for your hands are full of blood").

168. In other words, the kisses he gives Christ are disingenuous.

169. The Morningstar Venus.

170. This image is a hybrid of Vergil, *Aeneis* 6.282, "*ramos annosaque bracchia pandit ulmus*" ("the elm spread out its aged branches and boughs") and Juvenal, *Satirae* 1.149, "*utere velis, totos pande sinus*" ("let fly the sails, let them blow themselves full") (Diemer).

171. The Trojan king's son whom Venus favored.

172. A student of Socrates, a spiritual man who was also was a bon vivant (Schumann).

173. Not in the Latin, but added to balance the line and still true to the original, as Flora states that not any voice can describe the cleric's possessions.

174. Bucephala was Alexander the Great's steed and conjures up the image of a hand-to-hand battle with a fearsome warrior.

175. Cf. *Matthew* 19:24.

176. Cf. Plautus, *Cistellaria* 69, "*amor et melle et felle est fecundissimus*" ("love brings forth both honey and gall in profusion").

177. In the Middle Ages the bishops had knightly vassals in their service.

178. Adonis was a beautiful hunter whom Venus loved. Finally, he was slain by a boar that was sent by either Artemis, jealous of his hunting skills, or Ares, jealous of Venus' love, or Apollo, to punishment Venus for blinding Erymanthus his son.

179. Nereus was a Titan who with Doris sired the Nereids.

180. This is an allusion to Martianus Capella's *De Nuptiis Philologiae et Mercurii* ("On the Marriage of Philology and Mercury," viz. CB 182). Mercury (intelligent or profitable pursuit), who has been refused by Wisdom, Divination, and the Soul, is wed to Philologia ("love of words"), who is immortalized by the gods. It is an allegorical union that references the union of the intellectually profitable pursuit of learning through the art of letters. The gifts they receive are the seven liberal arts: Grammar, Dialectic, Geometry, Musical Harmony, Astronomy, Arithmetic, and Rhetoric. Architecture and Medicine were also at the wedding, but were kept silent for they cared for earthly things.

181. The shield of Achilles was the shield Achilles used to fight Hector, when the gods ordained that it was Troy's time to fall (viz. Homer, *Iliad* 18.478-608).

182. Venus.

183. Byssus was an ancient cloth, thought to be made of linen, cotton, or silk.

184. Both plants appear in Vergil's *Georgics* 4.123 (Walsh).

185. Cf. Ovid, *Metamorphoses* 11.90, "*at Silenus abest. titubantem annisque meroque / ruricolae cepere Phryges*" ("but Silenus is absent. The rubes of Phrygia caught him, reeling from his age and wine").

186. Cf. Ovid *Ars Amatoria* 1.543, "*ebrius ecce senex pando Silenus asello | vix sedet*" ("the drunken old man Silenus with difficulty upon a crooked ass").

187. Cf. Maximianus, *Elegiae* I.9, "*dum iuvenile decus, dum mens sensusque maneret, | orator toto clarus in orbe fui*" ("so long as I had youthful beauty, heart, and sense, I was in all the world a famous orator").

188. Cf. *ibid.* I.71, "*sic cunctis formosus ego gratusque videbar*" ("so I seemed handsome and pleasant to all").

189. Viz. *Physiologus* 3 *De Unicorni* (F. Wilhelm, *Denkmäler deutscher Prosa des 11. und 12. Jahrhunderts*, 1960, B: Kommentar, p. 22) □...□ *atque nullus*

uenator eure capere potest. Sed hoc argumento capiunt illum: ducunt puellam uirginem in illum locum, ubi moratur, et dimittunt eam ibidem solam. Ille autem ut uiderit eam, salit in sinum virginis et complectitur eam sicque comprehendituret perducitur ad palacium regis" ("and no hunter can catch it. But men catch it in the following way: they lead a virgin into a place, where it dwells, and leave her there alone. And as soon as it sees her, it jumps into the virgin's lap and embraces her and so it is captured and brought to the king's palace").

190. *bela mia* and *da zevaleria* are Northern Italian.

191. *Tort a vers mei ma dama* is Old French for *Tort a ma dame a mon avis*.

192. The denizens, according to *Genesis* 19:1-11, were devoted to sodomy.

193.This entire poem is based on a late antique novel entitled *Historia Apolonii Regis Tyri* ("History of Apollonius the King of Tyre"). Antiochus, King of Antioch, lived with his daughter in an incestuous relationship. To prolong the incest, he sets a riddle whose solver could marry his daughter and whose inaccurate guesser is beheaded; both types are in reality put to death. Then comes Apollonius, the Prince of Tyre, to whom the king reads the riddle: *by crime I am carried away, on maternal flesh I feed, I seek my father, my mother's consort, my wife's daughter and I find not*; Apollonius then correctly solves it: the king's incest with his daughter. Antiochus denies it and sends Apollonius back to Tyre. Antiochus then sends his steward Thaliarchus after him with the promise of freedom for Apollonius' death by his hand; he fails and Antiochus puts a bounty on Apollonius' head, of which Apollonius is informed by Hellanicus at Tharsus. Apollonius then meets Stranguilio (Strangolio), who informs him of the country's desperation; Apollonius offers him and his citizens a bounty of wheat if they conceal his flight, to which he agrees. Months later, Stranguilio and his wife Dionysias instruct him to go to Pentapolis. A storm hits the ship, everyone but Apollonius perishes, and he is left naked on the strand. He goes to a bagnio where he meets Arcestrates the king, who takes him up into his court; Apollonius wins the affection of the king's daughter Astrages and marries her. Upon the beach they meet a man from Tyre who tells Apollonius that the Antiochus and his daughter were struck by lightning and the kingdom has fallen to Apollonius. Apollonius and Astrages set out to claim the throne, but during a sea storm Astrages purportedly dies on the ship in childbirth. He buries her at sea, but her coffin reaches the physician Cerimon on the shores of Ephesus. About to bury her, he notices her heartbeat, for she is indeed alive. Apollonius with his daughter Tharsia reaches Tharsus, and at Strangulio's mansion he entrusts her to the lord, who commends her education to Ligoridis the nurse. When Tharsia is fourteen, a dying Ligoridis tells her of her true heritage. Later in the forum a crowd praises Tharsia's daughter and vilifies Philothemia, Dionysias' daughter and Tharsia's stepsister. Dionysias enlists her steward Theophilus to kill Tharsia. He approaches Tharsia at the nurse's monument, which she visits after school, asks her forgiveness for the murder he is about to commit, but is interrupted by pirates who steal Tharsia away.

The pirates take her to Machilena, where she is put up for sale. Athanagoras (Arfaxus), the prince, and Leno bid for her; Leno wins. Around the city Leno puts up a price for Tharsia's dishonor. Athanagoras comes first, but she dissuades him by telling him her woeful tale; instead he gives her twenty gold pieces. Another, Aporiatus, comes; after hearing her jeremiad he gives her a pound of gold. Many more come and leave in tears. Tharsia then brings Leno the price for her dishonor. Learning that her shame is still intact, he is enraged, but she persuades him to take her to the forum where she will earn him money through her music. Meanwhile Apollonius returns to Tharsus, where Dionysias informs him of his daughter's demise. He sails back to Tyre but winds carry his ship to Machilena. Athanagoras meets Apollonius and calls for Tharsia. Tharsia sings to Apollonius and reads him a riddle, which he solves. He, angered, pushes her from him; she then discloses her griefs, by which he identifies her. Athanagoras begs Apollonius for his daughter's hand and he it grants. But he seeks vengeance against Leno. Athanagoras urges the people to capture Leno and present him to Apollonius, which they do. They condemn him to be burnt alive. Apollonius intends to return to his kingdom by way of Tharsus, but an angel urges him in a dream to visit Ephesus. Apollonius enters a temple of Diana devoted to Astrages and, seeing her, thinks she is the goddess herself; they are reunited and sail to Tyre and establish Athanagoras as king; then they go to Tharsus to seize Stranguilio and Dionysias. Both are by the townspeople stoned to death, but Theophilus by Tharsia is saved. They then return to Pentapolis to visit the king; after a year, Arcestrates dies and leaves half his kingdom to Apollonius and the other moiety to Astrages. The fisherman, who first rescued him, Apollonius brings to the court as a companion and gives him two hundred pence. Hellanicus, too, is invited and made rich. Finally Apollonius begets a son.

194. Ephesus is called the Island of John because his Gospel is reported to have been written there.

195. The following poems are adapted from Vergil's *Aeneid*, the tale of Aeneas, a survivor of the Fall of Troy, who on a fated quest journeys to Italy. Along the way he lands in North Africa, where Dido, the Queen of Carthage, receives him as a guest. But the gods are unhappy at their marital bliss, for Aeneas must complete his fated odyssey and found the Roman colony on Italy's shores. Dido, when he leaves, commits suicide.

196. Vergil never supplied a complete physical description of Aeneas. His hair color, however, was described in Dares Phrygius' *Daretis Phrygii de excidio Troiae historia* as auburn, a text that was available to writers of the Middle Ages and possibly this poet.

197. Elissa is the Latin name for Dido.

198. Juno, Athena, and Venus all vied for Paris' favor. Paris chose Venus and incurred the others' wrath; the two spurned goddesses crafted the Fall of Troy.

199. Literally, "O fraternal treasures about to be mangled." This references Dido's brother, Pygmalion, who killed her husband Sychaeus and whose hidden treasure she used to found Carthage.

200. Aeneas and his men.

201. Celaeno was one of the Harpies.

202. Cf. Ovid, *Heroides* 7.17, "*altera Dido.*"

203. Aeneas' pilot.

204. Two rivers of the Underworld.

205. Pyrois was one of the horses of the sun (viz. Ovid, *Metamorphoses* 2.153).

206. An invocation of the Muses on Mount Helicon.

207. One of the Achaeans' mightiest warriors, second only to Achilles.

208. Helen, the daughter of Leda and Tyndareus.

209. Menelaus.

210. Achilles.

211. A reference to Agamemnon's daughter, Iphigenia/Iphianassa, who at Aulis was sacrificed to Diana to propitiate the wind.

212. Hector was the mightiest Trojan warrior.

213. Turnus was the King of the Rutilians, who waged war against the Trojan when they landed in Italy.

214. Lavinia, the daughter of King Latinus.

215. Venus is known as the Cyprian.

216. According to William of St. Thierry's *De natura corporis et animae* I (Migne, *PL* 180.700-704), there are three forces in the human body: *virtus naturalis, virtus spiritalis,* and *animalis.* The *virtus naturalis* is localized in the liver and is associated with vegetative functions (reproduction, diet, growth); the *virtus spiritalis*, located in the heart, handles breathings; and the *virtus animalis* in the brain is associated with sensory perception and spontaneous movement. The *virtus naturalis* is the lowest in rank, common to plants, animals, and people. The *virtus spiritalis* comes to animals and people, but the *virtus animalis* is not equally

shared (Diemer).

217. The golden arrow arouses love, the lead arrow an aversion to it (viz. Ovid, *Metamorphoses* 1.468 et seq.).

218. The breaking wheel was a method of torture and execution in which the condemned's' limbs were stretched out on the spokes of a wheel. A large hammer was then applied to the limb over the gap between the beams, breaking the bones.

219. The west wind.

220. An abbreviation for *Salva Navem Nostram*, the Latin equivalent of SOS.

221. A member of an Iranian people who were well-versed in archery.

222. Hybla was a Sicilian town renowned for its honey. Dodona was an oracle in Epirus devoted to a Mother Goddess.

223. The English king lamented is possibly Richard the Lionheart.

224. The dative case is the "case of giving" as it indicates an indirect object, that is, to whom something goes.

225. The vocative case is the "case of calling, summoning, addressing."

226. Cf. *Job* 30:31 (*Vulgate*), "*versa est in luctum cithara mea*" ("my cithara has turned to grief").

227. The Mount of Olives, the site of Christ's death and ascension and also, in the medieval mind, the place where the Antichrist will show himself (Diemer).

228. King Philip of Swabia (1998-1208), who was murdered by the count Palatine Otto of Wttelsbach in Bamberg.

229. Cf. *Job* 5:7 (*Vulgate*), "*homo ad laborem nascitur*" ("the man is born to tribulation").

230. A valley near Jerusalem found in *Isaiah* 22:1 and 22:5.

231. Pope Theonas of Alexandria, head of the Coptic Church and the Greek Church of Alexandria. The cave points to a hermit, who represents the ideal counter-image to the secularized ecclesiastical office of the 12th and 13th century (Diemer).

232. Viz. *Exodus* 2:1-10.

233. The papal bull: the round seal with cords attached to a document issued by the Papal Chancery.

234. Viz. *Luke* 10:30-37, the parable of the kindhearted samaritan.

235. A prophet during the reigns of Solomon and David (viz. *2 Samuel* 11 et seq.), who rebuked David for Uriah the Hittite's murder.

236. Uriah the Hittite was King David's field commander after whose wife Bathsheba David lusted and for this was murdered by David who gave the soldiers the order to retreat from him in battle.

237. At baptism one is anointed. The basic meaning of this is that the Church is at strife, which is conveyed through the imagery of the rent state of its king's robe and a Christian's ("an anointed one," probably an ecclesiastical official) defiling the sacred laws of the Church and thus acting as a witness against Christ by polluting his bride, the Church (Bernt).

238. Viz. *Matthew* 23:24.

239. Viz. *Matthew* 22:21.

240. Proteus was the herdsman of Poseidon's seals and had the ability to foretell the future and often changed his shape to avoid having to do so.

241. The constellation of the Seven Stars.

242. These last three names reference the western border of Germany. Isabel and Gaudile are Romanesque; Baldine is the Flemish equivalent of Baldwin (Diemer).

243. Quoted from *Matthew* 26:66.

244. A jubilant shout or possibly *lo dir cuideie* ("I wanted to say") (Bernt).

245. The oblique case is a noun case used when a noun is the object of a preposition or a verb. The nominative (straight) case is the nominative case. This is an instance of erotic grammar: the oblique case probably references a flaccid (not straight) penis and the rectus case (straight) an erect member.

246. To wit, there is no opportunity for a clever plan along the path of love.

247. An enhanced adaption of Terence, *Eunuchus* 732, "*sine Cerere et libero friget Venus*" ("without bread and wine love grows cold") (Bernt). The poet has enjoyed Ceres' gifts, grain, but knows it is better to sip the Gods' nectar than wine.

248. An untranslatable "tra-la-la."

249. The son of Theseus who is the paragon of chastity.

250. Cf. *Luke* 10:40, *"Martha autem satagebat circa frequens ministerium"* ("But Martha was sedulously busying herself serving"). A frivolous parody of the Gospel text because the "treatment" rests in the alleviation of Venus's torment (Bernt).

251. A reference to *De Nuptiis Mercurii et Philologiae* (vide note 180). Another possible translation is "O, if I were Mercury, eager for Philology, I would join as a cleric myself to her, even if she be in chains" (thus a criminal).

252. That is, "enliven me."

Part III of the *Carmina Burana* (Poems 187-226):

1. Pylades and Orestes are the paragon of true, unwavering friendship.

2. Viz. Ovid, *Metamorphoses* 8.405 et seq. (Theseus to Pirithous), *"o me mihi carior...pars animae...meae"* ("O dearer to me than my own self, the other half of my soul") (Bernt).

3. Cf. *Matthew* 13:12, *"qui enim habet dabitur ei"* ("for to him who has it shall be given").

4. A student of Socrates who founded the Cyrenaic school of Philosophy and taught that life's goal was to seek pleasure by adapting all circumstances to oneself and by maintaining proper control over both adversity and prosperity.

5. Gaius Verres was the corrupt praetor of Sicily whom Cicero prosecuted (viz. Cicero, *In Verrem*).

6. Diogenes the Cynic.

7. Cf. *Sirach* 2:14, *"vae duplici code"* ("woe to the duplicitous heart").

8. Probably meant is that they are lords of seductive words and song.

9. Cf. *Job* 10:1, *"loquar in amaritudine animae meae"* ("I shall speak in bitterness to my soul").

10. Pavia had a name as a place of an enjoyable modus vivendi (Bernt).

11. The son of Theseus and the epitome of a chaste youth.

12. The names of slaves in Terence's *Andria, Adelphoe*, and again *Andria*, respectively.

13. Viz. Ovid, *Metamorphoses* 3.511 et seq.

14. Thomas the Apostle (viz. *John* 20:24).

15. Another name for Bacchus, which here means wine. Thetis represents water.

16. In Saint Jerome's *Liber interpretationis Hebraicorum nominum* (de Lagarde p. 136) we find that *phariseus* comes from *prš* "to divorce." (Diemer).

17. Late Latin for "die," here it represents the players' God of Dice.

18. A dice roll.

19. Clotho was one of the goddesses of fate.

20. The goddess of water Thetis and Bacchus the god of wine.

21. The Chaldeans/Babylonians in the time of Jeremiah led the chosen people into captivity, the Chaldean mentioned is an enemy to the boozers. It is probably also a wordplay on "Kälte," "coldness."

22. A city in Germany and the oldest seat of a Christian bishop north of the Alps.

23. The statue of Bacchus.

24. This is a play on the Feast of All Saints: *"Gaudeamus omnes in Domino, diem festum celebrantes sub honore sanctorum omnium: de quorum sollemnitate gaudent angeli, et collaudant filium Dei"* ("let us rejoice in the Lord, celebrating the festal day in honor of all saints, at whose festival the angels take delight and together praise the Son of God") (Bischoff).

25. A play on *Psalm* 33:2 (*Vulgate*), *"Benedicam Dominum in omni tempore semper laus eius in ore meo"* ("I shall bless the Lord at all times; his praise will forever be in my mouth.

26. A play on the blessing of bishops of the offertory: *"pax vobis"* ("peace be with you"); in response, the congregation says, *"et cum spiritu tuo"* ("and with you").

27. A play on *"oremus"* ("let us pray!"). The remainder is a travesty of *Commune plurimorum II*, *"deus, qui nos concedis sanctorum matyrum tuorum...natalitia colere: da nobis in aeterna beatitudine de eorum societate gaudere"* ("God, who let us celebrate the festive birthday of your holy martyrs, give us leave to rejoice in the eternal bliss of their society") (Diemer).

28. A play on *Acts of the Apostles* 4:32-35. *Apopholorum* ("of the vain, of the fools") takes the place of *apostolorum* ("of the Apostles"). Landrus is the name of

a moneylender probably in Paris (Bernt).

29. A play on *Psalm* 54:23 (*Vulgate*), "*iacta super Dominum curam tuam et ipse te enutriet*" ("cast thy cares upon the Lord, and he will nurture thee").

30. A play on *Psalm* 54:17 (*Vulgate*), "*ego autem ad Deum clamavi et Dominus salvabit me*" ("but I have cried out to God and the Lord will save me").

31. This closely follows the Hallelujah verse of the 8th Sunday after Pentecost: "*magnus Dominus et laudabilis valde*" ("great is the Lord and most worthy of praise"). It also parallels *Psalm* 47:2 (*Vulgate*), "*Magnus Dominus et laudabilis nimis*" ("Great is the Lord and exceedingly worthy of praise") (Bernt).

32. Similar to a sequence prescribed by the Roman Catholic Mass of Easter Sunday, *Victimae Paschali Laudes*, "*victimae paschali laudes immolent Christiani*" ("may Christians offers songs of praise to the Paschal victim"). The five-six is roll in a game of dice; the names zynke ses are derived from the Latin cardinal numbers *quinque* (five) and *sex* (six) (Bernt).

33. The name of the Gospel is a play on "The Holy Gospel according to Mark." The content is a parody of *John* 20:19-25.

34. Cp. "*Laus tibi, Christe!*" ("praise to you, Christ!").

35. The illustrious poet Hugo Primas of Orleans (the author of CB 194).

36. Similar to *Psalm* 17:28 (*Vulgate*), "*quoniam tu populum humilem salvum facies et oculos superborum humiliabis*" ("for you will save the humble folk and the eyes of the arrogant cast down").

37. Cp. "*Humiliate vos ad benedictionem*" ("kneel to receive your blessing!").

38. The money bag was hung on a belt from behind (Bernt).

39. Zacchaeus was a Jewish tax collector for the Romans (viz. *Luke* 19), whose home Jesus visited as a guest.

40. Cp. "*et benedictio dei omnipotentis patris...descendat super vos et maneat semper*" ("may the blessing of God the Almighty Father come upon you and always remain") (Bernt).

41. Cf. *Luke* 4:22, "*et mirabantur in verbis gratiae quae procedebant de ore ipsius*" ("and they marveled at the words of grace that issued from his mouth").

42. Dothan was the city where Jacob's sons sold Joseph to the Ishmaelites (viz. *Genesis* 37:17).

43. Cf. *Luke* 6:38, "*date et dabitur vobis*" ("give and it shall be given you").

44. Cf. *Luke* 22:31, "*satanas expetivit vos ut cribraret sicut triticum*" ("Satan has called for you so he may sift you like the wheat").

45. From *Mark* 16:15.

46. The German masculine, feminine, and neuter definite articles, respectively. The idea present in the Latin (that we take in every king of "the") cannot be expressed in the English, since the English definite article has but one form. I therefore elected to use the articles of the language from whose fatherland the *Carmina Burana* sprouted.

47. A borrowing from the Arabic. The corresponding word is "die" (as in the numbered block); this evidences cultural contact with the Arab world (Bernt).

48. Cf. *Regula* 55.10, "*sufficit enim monacho duas tunicas et duas cucullas habere*" ("it is sufficient for a monk to have two tunics and hoods") (Diemer).

49. Cf. *Regula* 51.3, "*quod si aliter fecerit, excommunicetur*" ("if he does otherwise, he should be excluded") (Diemer).

50. In some writings Paris is portrayed as a valiant fighter rather than a cowardly connoisseur.

51. A play on the beginning line of Ovid's *Metamorphoses*, "*in nova fert animus mutatas dicere formas corpora*" ("my mind is bent to tell of forms into new bodies changed").

52. The Gorgon was a winged demon with snake hair and huge teeth. The most famous of the sisters was Medusa, whom Perseus slew (viz. Ovid, *Metamorphoses* 4.777 et seq.). Here the poet alludes to Medusa's ability to turn things to stone.

53. Tiresias was a blind prophet famous for being transformed into a woman for seven years (viz. Ovid, *Metamorphoses* 3.316 et seq.). The sex change mentioned in this poem refers to the conversion from a *pallium* (neuter) to a *cappa* (feminine) to a *pallium* (neuter) again .

54. Bernt: "The Dress Satire of Primas [*Zeitschr. f. deutsches Altertum* 49, 1908, p. 185] determined at the end: '*do decretum ad extreme | quod sit dives anathema | qui has vestes induit*' ("I finally adopt the decree that every rich man be proscribed, who dons these [fashioned] clothes").

55. The beginning of Cato's *Monostichae*, "*cum animadverterem quam plurimos graviterin via morum errare*" ("since I am aware of how many stray along the path of morals").

56. Cf. *John* 8:46, "*quis ex vobis arguet me de peccato?*" ("which of you shall accuse me of sin?").

57. Cf. *Romans* 10:18.

58. A parody of the Episcopalian formula for a benediction with a preliminary forgiveness of sins (Bischoff). Also cf. *John* 9:6, "*expuit in terram lutum ex sputo et linivit lutum super oculos eius*" ("he spat upon the earth and made clay from the spittle and smeared clay over his eyes").

59. Saturn was the father of Jupiter and the reigned during the Golden Age (*Mythographi* 1.105; 2.16; 3.1.9). Bischoff believes that Ludwig here is Louis VII of France (1120-1180).

60. A mythical creature that is a hybrid of a ram and a deer (Bernt).

61. Yet another mythical beast that is of lion body with a snake's head at the tip of the tail and a goat's head that rises from the center of its spine.

62. Thais was a famous Greek hetaera during the time of Alexander the Great who accompanied him on various campaigns. Cumae was an ancient Greek settlement northwest of Naples. Baiae was a hedonistic resort that sported many bathhouses towards the end of the Roman Republic; it was mentioned in Ovid's *Ars Amatoria* 1.253 et seq.). The pestilence of Troy and juggernaut of the Greeks is Helen of Troy, because of whom the Greeks were spurred to war and Troy fell.

63. The name of a young lover in Terence's *Andria* and *Hekyra*.

64. Ganymede was the cupbearer and male lover of Zeus.

65. Glycerium was an unseen character in Terence's *Andria*, who was beloved of Pamphilus. Sporus was a boy the Emperor Nero castrated and tried to turn into a woman. He married him and treated him as a wife (viz. Suetonius, *De Vita Caesarum* 28).

Part IV of the *Carmina Burana* (Poems 227-228):

1. Cf. *Isaiah* 11:1, "*et egredietur virga de radice Iesse et flos de radice eius ascendet*" ("and from the root of Jesse a rod will grow forth and a flower will rise from his root").

2. Viz. *Numbers* 22-24. See note 154 of Part I.

3. On the day of the innocent little children, December 28, the choristers of the cathedrals enjoyed special freedoms. They chose a boy bishop to whom a bishop's staff or rod of the praecentor, or cantor, was given as a sign of his worth. The

presence of this boy bishop suggests that the play was performed on December 28th (Bernt).

4. Cf. Ovid, *Heroides* 5.31 (Bischoff). Xanthus was a great river of Troy.

5. Latin for "a contradiction in itself."

6. The Torah.

7. Aristotle here means "logic," not the man.

8. The hyssop bush is a low plant, thus: cedar:hyssop = God:man (Bernt).

9. Elizabeth was Mary's cousin and wife of Zacharias; the couple were blameless in God's eyes but childless. Gabriel visited and informed him of his future son.

10. This scene appears in *Luke* 10:42 et seq. I speculate that an<...> gen<...> perhaps was *angelis generositatem* (honor to the angels).

11. From *Matthew* 2:6.

12. From CB 80.

13. From CB 161.

14. The seven free arts: grammar, rhetoric, dialectic, arithmetic, geometry, music, and astronomy. The tripartite flavor is physics, ethics, and logic (cf. Isidor, *Etymologiae* 2.24.3 et seq.) (Bernt).

15. A pleasant-smelling resin.

Part V of the *Carmina Burana* (Poems 229-26*/254):

1. Saint Erasmus, or Saint Elmo, was supposedly martyred twice. Under Diocletian's rule he was beaten , spat on, thrown into a pit of worms and snakes, and boiling oil and sulfur were poured on him, as he lay there thanking and loving God. But thunder and lightning came and electrocuted everyone, whereupon Diocletian threw him into another pit, but an angel appeared and slew all the snakes. Under Maximian he was placed in a pan with rosin, pitch, and brimstone lead, and oil—all of which were poured into his mouth. Then a hot cloak and metal coat were placed on him to no effect, and an angel carried him away to safety. He was recaptured, eviscerated, and his intestines were tied around a windlass in Illyricum.

2. Cf. *Luke* 2:35, "*et tuam ipsius animam pertransibit gladius ut revelentur ex multis cordibus cogitationes*" ("and a falchion shall pass through your very soul,

so that the thoughts of many hearts may be revealed").

3. Mundus can mean universe, heaven, or earth.

4. John the Apostle, Mary's nephew.

5. Exprimere can mean to "force out" or to "express." I chose the latter to convey the inveterate dismay of Mary who is so shocked that she can neither overcome her pain nor express it in words or gestures.

6. Quoted from *Song of Solomon* 1:1.

7. The bride of Christ is the Church.

8. Provost Heinrich of Maria Saal, the second bishop of Seckau (Bernt).

9. From the parable of the marriage in Cana (viz. *John* 2:1-11).

10. Cf. *Isaiah* 7:20.

11. The souls hell lost when Christ freed them.

12. The Cistercian Monks (Bernt), who sought to return to a strict observance of the Rule of Benedict.

13. Augustine, Bishop of Hippo, who led an exemplary spiritual community.

14. The Norbertine, or Premonstratensian, order, founded by Norbert of Magdeburg, that followed closely Augustine's rule.

15. The order founded by Saint Francis of Assisi in 1209, the Franciscans (Bernt).

16. The Poor Clares, the second (female) order of Saint Francis of Assisi, who together with Saint Clara founded in 1212 (Bernt).

17. The followers of Mary Magdalene, one of Jesus' disciples, whom he cleansed of seven demons; according to the poet they fashion themselves in the image of Mary before her exorcism.

18. So called because they do so little (*paulum*) (Bernt). Since they serve indolence, I call them "Indolentites," or "the Indolent Ones"

19. This verse describes the Franciscans as epileptic or mentally ill or possessed by the devil (Diemer).

20. A good hint advocating the stricter observance of Canon Law.

21. Viz. *Ephesians* 5:5 and *Colossians* 5:5.

22. Catherine was the daughter of Costus, a pagan governor of Alexandria. A great scholar of her time, she converted to Christianity Emperor Maximinus Daia's wife and the many pagan philosophers the Emperor sent to dispute her. She was condemned to the breaking wheel, but it broke when she touched it, so she was beheaded instead.

23. Porphyry of Tyre, who died the same year as Catherine (AD 305) and was a Neo-Platonist philosopher.

24. Mary Magdalene and Mary of Clopas (?).

25. This stanza is quite difficult to translate. I have taken *spolia* as "mortal shell" and *corporis* as its genitive object. Though *dulcis* appears to qualify *pignoris*, it probably was meant to qualify *premia* as *dulcia*, but for the meter was changed. Thus we end up with "how sweet, how bitter are the rewards of your pledge," where the reward (human salvation) is sweet because of its object, but bitter and painful for Mother Mary and Christ himself.

26. Literally, "of one dying thus."

27. Simon the Just prophesied Jesus' death in *Luke* 2:25-35.

28. The streams are the jets of Christ's blood that shoot from the sites of his wounds, the springs.

29. I read the lines as *flete...[filium] tante grate gratie"* ("weep for the son of such thankworthy grace").

30. Probably the arms of the Father.

31. Mary Magdalene and Mary the mother of James (?).

32. A Roman Catholic monastery in Leopoldsberg, Austria.

33. Hebrew for "please save," a cry for salvation or of praise.

34. Literally, "you will surpass every scent of a body."

35. In *Aurea Legenda*, or the *Golden Legend*, by Jacobus de Voragine (ca. 1260), Longinus' blindness is cured by Christ's blood.

36. Items 1-9 reference, respectively and consecutively, *Luke* 1:46-55, *Psalm* 119:1 (*Vulgate*), *Psalm* 118:17 (*Vulgate*), *Psalm* 125:1 (*Vulgate*), *Psalm* 118:169 (*Vulgate*), Antiphon (Hesbert, III, Nr. 3708), Antiphon (Hesbert, III, Nr. 1546),

Antiphon (Hesbert, III, Nr. 4591), and Antiphon (Hesbert, III, Nr. 3274). Item 11 references Antiphon (Hesbert, III, Nr. 4332). Item 13 references *Psalm* 43:26 (*Vulgate*) (Diemer).

37. Short for "Kyrie eleison," Greek for "Lord have mercy upon us."

38. *Psalm* 30:5 (*Vulgate*).

39. *Psalm* 58:4 (*Vulgate*).

40. *Psalm* 53:5 (*Vulgate*).

41. *Psalm* 118:61 (*Vulgate*).

42. *Psalm* 118:83 (*Vulgate*).

43. *Psalm* 118:131 (*Vulgate*).

44. *Psalm* 141:8 (*Vulgate*).

45. For the appearance of Jesus before the children of Emmaus, see *Luke* 24:13-32; for the appearance of Jesus before the apostles in Jerusalem, see *John* 20:19-29.

HERE END THE CRITICAL NOTES AND COMMENTARY ON THE CARMINA BURANA.

ALPHABETICAL INDEX OF THE FIRST LINE OF THE LATIN POEMS

Mundus est in varium 226
Mundus est properans 9*/237
Musa venit carmine 145

Nobilis, mei miserere 115
Nomen a solemnibus 52
Nomina paucarum sunt hic 134
Non contracto quam affecto 86
Non est crimen amor 121a
Non honor est, sed 104a
Non te lusisse pudeat 33
Nos duo boni 89
Nulli beneficium iuste 36
Nullus ita parcus est 220a

O Antioche, cur 97
O comes amoris, dolor 111; 8*/236
O conscii, quid vobis videtur 162
O curas hominum 187
O decus, o Libye regnum 100
O fortuna, velut luna 17
O mi dilectissima! vultu 180
O potores exquisiti 202
O varium Fortune lubricum 14
Ob amoris pressuram 164
Olim lacus colueram 130
Olim sudor Herculis 63
Omittamus studia dulce 75
Omne genus demoniorum 54
Omnia sol temperat 136
Omnipotens sempiterne deus, qui inter 215a

Pange, lingua, gloriose 20*/248
Pange, vox adonis 6*/234
Passeres illos, qui 53a
Pergama flere volo 101
Planctus ante nescia 14*/242
Pre amoris tedio vulneror 175
Prebuit Eneas et causam 99b
Presens dies expendatur 21*/249
Prima Cleonei 64
Procurans odium effectu 12
Propter Sion non tacebo 41
Puri Bacchi meritum 199

Quelibet succenditur 170
Quam Natura ceteris 181

ALPHABETICAL INDEX OF THE FIRST LINE OF THE M.H.G. POEMS

BIBLIOGRAPHY

Alanus de Insulis. *De Planctu Naturae.* Ed. N.M. Häring. Spoleto: Centro Italiano di Studi Sullálto Medioevo, 1978.

Alford, J.A. *The Grammatical Metaphor: A Survey of Its Use in the Middle Ages.* 1982. Speculum 57 pp. 728-760.

Becker, Franz, ed. *Pamphilus.* Düsseldorf: Henn Verlag, 1972. Beihefte zum Mittellateinischen Jahrbuch volume 9.

Benedict. *Regula Benedicti des Cod. 915 der Stiftsbibliothek von St Gallen: die Korrekturvorlage der lateinisch-althochdeutschen Benediktinerregel.* Ed. Achim Masser. Göttingen: Vandenhoeck & Ruprecht, 2000.

Bischoff, Bernhard et al., ed. *Carmina Burana Mit Benutzung der Vorarbeiten W. Meyers kritisch hg. v. A. Hilka und O. Schumann. I. Band: Text. I. Die moralisch-satirischen dichtungen. 2. Dies liebeslieder. 3. Die Trink- und Spielerlieder—Die geistlichen Dramen. Nachträge. Hg. v. O. Schumann und B. Bischoff –II. Band: Kommentar. I. Einleitung (Die Handschrift der Carmina Burana). Die moralisch-satirischen Dichtungen.* Heidelberg: C. Winter Verlag: 1930 (2 vols.).

Bischoff, Bernhard, ed. *Faksimile-Ausgabe der Handschrift Clm 4660 und Clm 4660a.* München: Prestel Verlag, 1967.

Bode, G.H., ed. *Scriptores Rerum Mythicarem Latini Tres Romae Nuper Reperti (Mythographi Vaticani).* Hildesheim: 1968 (2 vols.).

Boethius. *Consolatio Philosophiae.* Ed. Ludwig Bieler. Turnholti: Brepols, 1984. Corpus Christianorum, Series Latina 94.

Carmina Burana. <http://www.hs augsburg.de/~harsch/Chronologia/Lspost13/ CarminaBurana/bur_car0.html>.

Cato, Dionysius. *Catonis Disticha.* Ed. Marcus Boas. Amsterdam: North Holland Publishing Company, 1952.

de Longchamps, Nigel. *Speculum Stultorum.* Ed. J.H. Mozley et al. Berkeley: University of California Press, 1960.

de Voragine, Jacobus. *Legenda Aurea.* Ed. Giovanni Maggioni. Tavarnuzze-Firenze: SISMEL, Edizioni del Galluzzo, 1998 (2 vols.).

Diemer, Peter and Dorothea Diemer, trans. *Carmina Burana: Texte und Übersetzungen.* Ed. Benedikt Konrad Vollmann. Frankfurt:

Deutscher Klassiker Verlag, 1987.

Dionysius of Halicarnassus. *The Roman Antiquities: Vol. II: Books III-IV.* Cambridge: Harvard University Press, 1993.

Dronke, Peter. *Medieval Latin and the Rise of European Love-Lyric.* Oxford: Clarendon Press, 1968.

Dronke, Peter. *The Medieval Poet and His World.* Rome: Edizioni di Sotria e Letteratura, 1984.

Encyclopedia Britannica. New York: Encyclopedia Britannica, Inc., 1911.

Fischer, Carl and Hugo Kuhn, trans. *Carmina Burana: Die Gedichte des Codex Buranus Lateinisch und Deutsch.* Ed. Günter Bernt. Zürich/München: Artemis Verlag, 1974.

Fournial, Etienne. *Histoire Monétaire de l'Occident Médiéval.* Paris: F. Nathan, 1970.

Frenzel, Elisabeth. *Stoffe der Weltliteratur.* Stuttgart: A. Kröner, 1963.

Friedrich, W., ed. *Denkmäler deutscher Prosa des 11. und 12. Jahrhunderts.* München: M. Hueber, 1960.

Fulgentius, Fabius Planciades. *Mitologiarum.* <http://www.thelatinlibrary.com/fulgentius.html>.

Hesbert, René-Jean, ed. *Corpus Antiphonalium Officii.* Rome: Herder, 1970.

Hieronymus. *Liber interpretationis Hebraicorum nominum.* Ed. P. de Lagarde. Turnholti: Brepols, 1959. Corpus Christianorum, Series Latina 72.

Holtzmann, Walther. *Propter Sion non tacebo zur Erklärung von Carmina Burana 41.* Münster: Böhlau, 1953. Deutsches Archiv 10, p. 71 et seq.

Horatius Flaccus, Quintus. *Opera.* Ed. E.C. Wickham. Oxford: Oxford University Press, 1975.

Josephus. *Antiquitates Iudicae Books XIV-XVII.* Ralph Marcus, trans. Cambridge: Harvard University Press, 2001.

Justinianus. *Codex Justinianus 1-3.* Ed. Johannes Spruit. Amsterdam: Koninklijke Nederlandse Akademie van Wetenschappen, 2005.

Juvenalis, Decimus Iunius. *Satirae.* Ed. W.V. Clausen. Oxford: Oxford University Press, 1992.

Koller, Erwin, Werner Wegstein, and Norbert Richard Wolf. *Neuhochdeutscher Index Zum Mittelhochdeutschen Wortschatz.* Stuttgart: S. Hirzel, 1990.

Korth, Michael, ed. *Carmina Burana: lateinisch-deutsch: Gesamtausgabe der mittelalterlichen Melodien.* München: Heimeran, 1979.

Kulcsár, Péter, ed. *Mythographi vaticani I et II.* Turnholti: Brepols, 1987. Corpus Christianiorum, Series Latina, 91c.

Lexer, Matthias. *Matthias Lexers Mittelhochdeutsches Taschenwörterbuch.* Stuttgart: S. Hirzel Verlag, 1981.

Lexikon des Mittelalters. Ed. Robert Auty et al. Zürich: Artemis-Verlag, 1999.

Livius, Titus. *Ab Urbe Condita Tomus I Libri I-V.* Ed. Robert Ogilvy. Oxford: Oxford University Press, 1974.

Lucretius Carus, Titus. *De Rerum Natura Libri Sex..* Ed. C. Bailey. Oxford: Oxford University Press, 1922.

Macrobius. *Ambrosii Theodosii Macrobii Saturnalia.* Ed. James Willis. Leipzig: Teubner, 1994. Bibliotheca Teubneriana.

Maigne D'Arnis, W. H. *Lexicon Manuale Ad Scriptores Mediae Et Infimae Latinitatis.* Paris: Garnier Fratres, 1890.

Martianus Capella. *De nuptiis Philologiae et Mercurii.* Ed. James Willis. Leipzig: Teubner, 1983. Bibliotheca Teubneriana.

Maximianus. *Elegies.* Ed. Richard Webster. Princeton: Princeton Press, 1900. Migne, J.P. *Patrologiae cursus completus. Patrologiae latinae.* Turnhout: Brepols, 1981.

Missale Romanum ex decreto Sacrosancti Concilii Tridentini restitutum. New York: Catholic Book Pub. Co., 1964.

Niermeyer, J.F. *Mediae Latinitatis Lexicon Minus.* Leiden: E.J. Brill, 1976.

Offermanns, W. *Die Wirkung Ovids auf die literarische Sprache der lateinischen Liebesdichtung des 11. und 12. Jahrhunderts.* Düsseldorf: A. Henn, 1970.

Ovidius Naso, Publius. *Amores...Ars Amatoria, Remedia Amoris.* Ed. E. Kenney. Oxford: Oxford University Press, 1994.

Ovidius Naso, Publius. *Heroides; Amores.* Grant Showerman, trans. Cambridge: Harvard University Press, 1996.

Ovidius Naso, Publius. *P. Ovidi Nasonis Metamorphoses.* Ed. R.J. Tarrant. Clarendon: Oxford University Press: 2004.

Ovidius Naso, Publius. *Tristia; Ex Ponto.* Arthur Leslie Wheeler, trans. Cambridge: Harvard University Press, 1975.

Patzig, H. *Zur Handschrift und zum Text der Carmina Burana.* Berlin: 1892.

Phrygius, Dares. *Daretis Phrygii de Excidio Troiae Historia.* <http://www.thelatinlibrary.com/dares.html>

Pitra, J.B., ed. *Spicilegium Solesmense.* Graz: Akad. Dr. – und Verl.-Anst., 1963 (*Distinctiones monasticae*).

Plautus, Titus Maccius. *Comoediae.* Ed. Wallace M. Lindsay. Oxford: Oxford University Press, 1922 (2 vols.).

Prudentius. *Aurelii Prudentii Clementis Carmina.* Ed. M. Cunningham. Turnholti: Brepols, 1966. Corpus Christ., Series Latina, 126.

Raby, F.J.E. *A History of Secular Latin Poetry in the Middle Ages.* Oxford: Clarendon Press, 1957.

Remegius of Auxerre. *Commentum in Martianum Capellam.* Ed. Cora E. Lutz. Leiden: E.J. Brill, 1965.

Sallustius Crispus, Gaius. *Sallust's Bellum Catilinae.* Ed. J.T. Ramsey. Oxford: Oxford University Press, 1984.

Schmeling, Gareth, ed. *Historia Apollonii Regis Tyri.* Leipzig: Teubner, 1988. Bibliotheca Teubneriana.

Souter, A., et al. *Oxford Latin Dictionary.* Oxford: Clarendon Press, 1968.

Suetonius, Gaius. *Nero.* Ed. Brian Warmington. London: Duckworth Publishers, 1999.

Terentius Afer, Publius. *Comoediae.* Ed. Wallace M. Lindsay. Oxford: Oxford University Press, 1926.

Tibullus. *Liebeselegien: lateinisch und deutsch.* Zürich: Artemis, 1964. Bibliothek der älten Welt, Römische Reihe.

Touber, A.H. *Rhetorik und Form im deutschen Minnesang*. Groningen: J.G. Woters, 1964.

Vergilius Maro, Publius. *Opera*. Ed. Roger A.B. Mynors. Oxford: Oxford University Press, 1969.

Walsh, P.G. *Love Lyrics from the Carmina Burana*. Chapel Hill: University of North Carolina Press, 1993.

Weber, Robert, ed. *Biblia Sacra iuxta vulgatam versionem*. Stuttgart: Würtembergische Bibelanstalt, 1975.

William of St. Thierry. *Opera Didactica et Spiritualia*. Ed. Stanislaus Ceglar et al. Turnhout: Brepols, 2003.

ABOUT THE TRANSLATOR

Tariq Marshall was born in Studio City, CA, and began his study of Latin and Greek at the age of 15. He formally studied and completed his degree in Latin at the University of California, Berkeley, where he first became aware of the Carmina Burana while taking a Medieval Latin literature course. Observing that it had never been translated into English in its entirety, Tariq resolved to undertake the arduous, yet fulfilling, year-long labor of rendering the work into English and thoroughly annotating a text replete with a plenitude of obscure allusions.

CPSIA information can be obtained at www.ICGtesting.com
Printed in the USA
LVOW010304141111

254838LV00006B/84/P